D1256208

Mental Logic

List of Contributors

Luca Bonatti, Laboratoire des Science Cognitives et Psycholinguistique, Paris France

Martin D. S. Braine, Department of Psychology, New York University

Shalom M. Fisch, Department of Psychology, New York University

Joshua B. Cantor, Long Island University

Maria G. Dias, Department of Psychology, Federal University of Pernambuco, Recife, Brazil

Joseph R. Hosie, Department of Psychology, Baruch College of the City University of New York

R. Brooke Lea, Department of Psychology, Bowdoin College, Brunswick, Maine

Ira A. Noveck, Centre de Recherche en Epistmologie Appliquée, Paris, France

David P. O'Brien, Department of Psychology, Baruch College and the Graduate School of the City University of New York

Guy Politzer, Centre National de la Recherche Scientifique, Saint Denis, France

Brian J. Reiser, Department of Psychology, New York University

Antonio Roazzi, Department of Psychology, Federal University of Pernambuco, Recife, Brazil

Barbara Rumain, Department of Psychology, New York University

Mark C. Samuels, Department of Psychology, New York University

Yingrui Yang, Department of Psychology, New York University, and Department of Psychology, Princeton University, Princeton, New Jersey

Mental Logic

Edited by

Martin D. S. Braine
New York University

and

David P. O'Brien
Baruch College and the Graduate School
of the City University of New York

LEA LAWRENCE ERLBAUM ASSOCIATES, PUBLISHERS
1998 Mahwah, New Jersey   London

Lawrence Erlbaum Associates, Inc., Publishers
10 Industrial Avenue
Mahwah, New Jersey 07430

Cover Design by Kathryn Houghtaling Lacey

Library of Congress Cataloging-in-Publication Data

Mental logic / edited by Martin D. S. Braine and David P.
O'Brien
     p. cm
    Includes bibliographical references and index
    ISBN 0-8058-2388-3 (alk paper).
    1. Logic. 2. Reasoning. I. Braine, Martin D. S. II.
O'Brien, David P.
    BF442.M45 1998   98–24744
    160—dc21   CIP

Books published by Lawrence Erlbaum Associates are
printed on acid-free paper, and their bindings are chosen
for strength and durability.

Printed in the United States of America
10 9 8 7 6 5 4 3 2 1

Contents

Introduction: Some Background to the Mental-Logic Theory and to the Book

David P. O'Brien
Baruch College and the Graduate School of the City University of New York

I entered graduate school with the conviction that a mental logic is a basic part of what allows humans to have coherent experiences, although exposure to modern logic had led me to believe that this mental logic is not the classical logic that Kant had included among the a priori categories. I had thus started looking through the literature to find a reasonable theoretical account of this mental logic. The most prominent mental-logic theory at that time was Piaget's, but his logic seemed confused and did not bear any obvious relation to the sorts of reasoning tasks he presented.[1] The most promising approach that I found was the "natural logic" of the logician Gentzen (1935/1964), but the attempts at a psychological realization of this approach (Johnson-Laird, 1975; Osherson, 1975a, 1976) were clearly initial steps. In 1978, Braine published his *Psychological Review* article, "On the Relation Between Standard Logic and the Natural Logic of Thought." After reading the article I called Marty and arranged to meet him. Our meetings continued until his death in April 1996, and during these years we worked together to develop the mental-logic theory presented in this volume.

Marty's article, as well as my first meetings with him, convinced me that he was bringing something to this search that I was not finding

---

[1]Piaget asserted, for example, that formal-operational structure is equivalent to the 16 propositional operators of normal-disjunctive form (e.g., Inhelder & Piaget, 1958). The formal-operational tasks, however, present objects and their attributes that require quantification that cannot be captured by a logic at the propositional level.

elsewhere. Marty already was established as a leading investigator of language acquisition. As Melissa Bowerman (personal communication) said to me, Marty approached children's speech like a linguist studying an unknown language—he identified regularities in collocation and proposed accounting for these in terms of a simple set of grammatical rules (including his influential *pivot grammar*). He brought the same inclinations and talents to the issues of reasoning, and he conveyed to me two basic insights that seemed to be obviously right. First, although logicians have provided myriad systems, their interests have not been psychological. Indeed, the sorts of things logicians provide, such as metalogical proofs of completeness, or construction of a parsimonious set of operators, are often of little benefit to someone investigating mental logic. Although a theory of mental logic will bear an interesting relation to standard logic, for example, including sound schemas, it need not be the same as any particular system presented in the logic literature, and its basic parts need not have the power to derive all the theorems of some standard system. Thus, although one needs to attend to what logicians have discovered about logic, the psychological researcher should begin by observing the ways people use natural-language particles, such as *if, and, not, or, some, all, none, any,* and so forth, in natural speech. Second, we should not be seduced by our training in experimental methods, which can lead us to look for differences and deflect us from looking for universals. Linguistics, for example, would not have made progress if it had focused on differences; it was in looking for universals that it found its way. The mental-logic theory presented in this volume reflects these two concerns: We have sought to discover what is basic about the ways these logic particles are used in speech and in reasoning.

Across the past 10 years, the question of whether there is a mental logic has become subject to considerable debate. There have been attacks by critics who believe that all reasoning uses mental models (e.g., Johnson-Laird & Byrne, 1991, 1993; Johnson-Laird, Byrne, & Schaeken, 1992, 1994) and return attacks on mental-models theory (e.g., Braine, 1995; O'Brien, Braine, & Yang, 1994). This controversy prominently invaded journals such as *Psychological Review, Behavioral and Brain Sciences, Cognition,* and the *Journal of Experimental Psychology: General*. There have also been issues between mental logic and the biases-and-heuristics approach to reasoning (as represented, e.g., by Evans, 1989), and the content-dependent theorists (e.g., Cheng & Holyoak, 1985; Holyoak & Cheng, 1995). However, despite its pertinence to current issues in cognition, few cognitive scientists really know what the mental-logic theory is, and misapprehensions are rife. Actually, there have been two mental-logic theories, ours and another developed by Rips (1994). The two mental-logic theories are similar to one another in some respects but are significantly different in others. The question of whether there is a mental logic thus is different from the question of what that mental logic is, although this distinction often has been lost in much of the debate.

The theory of mental logic presented here has three parts. One part is the mental logic per se, and it consists of a set of inference schemas of the sort first proposed by Gentzen. For example, when one knows that two propositions of the form *p or q* and *not p* are true, one can assert *q*. We take the issue of which schemas to include to be empirical; for example, the schema that derives *p or q* from the premise *p*, which is found in most logic textbooks, is not among our proposed schemas because the evidence does not support its inclusion (see chap. 7). The set of basic schemas that are included is not intended to be an exhaustive inventory of all of the sorts of inferences people make, but to be an inventory of those logic inferences that are made routinely.

The second part of the theory is a reasoning program that applies the schemas in lines of reasoning, and it includes both a direct-reasoning routine and some more sophisticated indirect-reasoning strategies. The direct-reasoning routine is claimed to be universally available and applied with minimal effort both in reasoning and in comprehension. The most basic prediction of the theory thus is that inferences that are made by the application of basic schemas with the direct-reasoning routine (the basic part of the theory) will be made routinely. Although there is evidence for availability of the more sophisticated reasoning strategies among college students, and presumably they often are available in other populations (see chap. 7), reasoning that requires such strategies is proposed as neither universal nor effortless, and inferences that require this part of the reasoning routine should be made far less often than those that are available on the basic part of the theory.

The third part of the theory is pragmatic. Our theory proposes that the basic meaning of each logic particle is in the inferences that are sanctioned by its inference schemas. How any particular proposition is construed, however, may go beyond what is sanctioned by the schemas. We discuss several pragmatic principles that account for some of the judgments that are beyond the basic mental logic (e.g., chap. 9), although these principles are not intended to provide a complete inventory of what would be required to account for all of the extralogical processes involved in comprehension and reasoning. A complete account would go well beyond the scope of our theory, and indeed would require not only a complete theory of pragmatics but would constitute a large part of a general theory of cognition. For example, it would need to include the processes by which information is stored in, and retrieved from, long-term memory.

Several criticisms of our approach have stemmed from misunderstandings about its pragmatic part. Some commentators have held, for example,

4

O'BRIEN

that a mental logic does not account for the influences on reasoning of various sorts of content (e.g., Holyoak & Cheng, 1995); such criticisms ignore the fact that our theory includes a pragmatic aspect. Others have claimed that the pragmatic part of our theory has been added on merely as an afterthought (e.g., Evans & Over, 1996); this criticism overlooks our argument that because logic refers to propositions rather than to sentences, the mental logic is embedded in a profoundly pragmatic architecture (see, in particular, chaps. 3 and 9 for discussions).

This volume was planned as a comprehensive presentation of the theory of mental logic we have worked on over the past 20 years and the evidence for it, together with its implications for cognition and development, including the acquisition of language. It includes both revisions of articles that were published previously, as well as chapters containing unpublished material. Its unity and focus come from the comprehensive presentation of the theory. Other theories are, of course, discussed. Rips is discussed in chapters 8 and 11, and chapters 13, 14, and 15 address nonlogical theories, especially the mental-models theory.

The first section presents four introductory chapters on mental logic. Chapter 2 is written by the philosopher Luca Bonatti, who has written on mental logic in *Psychological Review* (1994) and *Cognition* (1994). Bonatti discusses the development of mental logic as a scientific theory and addresses why an idea that has been available for 2,000 years is only recently becoming scientifically fruitful. Chapter 3 is a revision of an article by David O'Brien that addresses many misunderstandings of our mental-logic theory. Originally published as part of a volume about human rationality, this chapter addresses how a person with a mental logic often makes irrational judgments. This chapter also addresses some of the implications of the propositional nature of a mental logic.

Chapter 4, by Braine and O'Brien, is a revision of an article published previously that further discusses the relevance of pragmatics to mental logic and shows how mental logic is related to the notion of a syntax or language of thought, and via the syntax of thought, to language acquisition. Chapter 5 is by R. Brooke Lea, an assistant professor at Bowdoin College and a former member of the Braine laboratory. This chapter describes Lea's work on how people spontaneously make logical inferences as they read text, and by implication, discourse; that mental logic plays an important role in discourse is a central claim of Sperber and Wilson (1986) in their relevance theory. Lea also addresses the mutual needs of mental logic and comprehension researchers to attend to one another's findings, particularly if one wants to make online predictions.

The next five chapters deal with the most developed part of the theory—mental propositional logic—the part on which most empirical work has been done and the part for which there is the most supporting evidence. Chapter 6 presents the most recent version of the mental propositional logic with considerable illustration. Chapters 7 and 8 are reprints (with considerable revision) of the major evidence supporting the theory at the propositional level, and they discuss other theories in relation to the data; in particular, chapter 8 discusses how Rips's logic and Johnson-Laird's mental-models theories fare in relation to the evidence from the experiments. Chapter 9, reprinted from *Psychological Review*, presents our theory of *if* and compares it with other theories, from both the psychological and philosophical literatures. Chapter 10, written with Maria Dias and Antonio Roazzi of the Federal University of Pernambuco in Brazil, presents a mental-logic view of children's conditional reasoning, including how they reason towards an *if* statement and how they work out the consequences of suppositions made in the course of pretend play. We expect this work will be of interest to developmentalists concerned with theory of mind or with pretend play, as well as to reasoning researchers.

Chapter 11, by Marty Braine, presents a theory for a mental predicate logic and compares its predictions with those of Rips's logic. Chapter 12, by Yang, Braine, and O'Brien, presents an initial empirical test of the theory, using methods similar to those presented in the empirical test of the propositional-logic theory in chapter 7.

The last section of the book presents comparisons of our mental-logic theory with the mental-models theory of Johnson-Laird. Chapter 13, by Ira Noveck and Guy Politzer, presents some experiments comparing the mental-models with the mental-logic treatment of *or*, and Chapter 14, by O'Brien, Maria Dias, and Antonio Roazzi, presents a comparison between the mental-logic and mental-models treatment of *if*, using conditional syllogisms to illustrate the difference. Chapter 15, by O'Brien, Maria Dias, and Joseph Hosie, the latter a colleague of O'Brien's at Baruch College, addresses a controversy about the suppressibility of modus ponens, begun by Ruth Byrne (1989) in an article in *Cognition*, to which Politzer and Braine (1991) responded. In addition to discussing the issue, it presents some new data that reveal that Byrne's methods can suppress premises when no inference at all is made, bringing into doubt whether inferences are suppressed at all, or whether the premises are. Chapter 16, by Bonatti, addresses some further issues raised in the mental-models versus mental-logic debate. Finally, chapter 17, by O'Brien, Dias, Roazzi, and Joshua Cantor, presents some new data to answer the claim made in criticism of mental logic that the mind uses some content-specific reasoning processes.

Marty Braine died shortly before the book was completed, and I have finished those parts of the book on which he was working that were unfinished at that time. In doing so, I made as few changes as possible in the material on which Marty was working. When Marty realized that his illness was terminal, he expressed to me his frustration with spending his remaining time and energy debating our critics—he preferred to spend his energies developing the mental-logic approach. I made him the following offer: I would write all of the sections that responded to the critics so that he could spend his time working on the material presented in chapter 11, which presents the extension of the theory to a mental-predicate logic. Chapter 11 thus is authored only by Marty and the chapters primarily concerned with debate were authored primarily by me. This does not reflect a lack of participation on my part in developing the ideas in chapter 11, nor a lack of participation on Marty's part in developing the approaches taken in the other chapters—we consulted one another constantly as we worked on our respective parts of the work. It does reflect, however, the division of work on which we had agreed.

At the time of Marty's death, chapters 4 and 6 were almost completed and required only minor additional work. Chapter 11—the new mental-predicate-logic theory—was largely complete, although parts of the manuscript consisted of handwritten notes, some of which were quite difficult to read. I have included these notes in the published version without alteration, although an occasional word could be worked out only from its context. I am indebted to Lila Braine for her assistance in deciphering Marty's handwriting in these few instances, although any errors that may have been made are completely my responsibility. In addition, some small amount of material that Marty and I had been discussing that was not in the manuscript has been added to chapter 11. Chapter 12, which reports an initial empirical test of the mental-predicate-logic theory, was completed by Yingrui Yang and myself, although the data collection had been completed when Marty was alive.

I am grateful to several people for their help in completing this volume. In addition to Lila Braine, I would like to thank Ira Noveck for help in translating computer files, Luca Bonatti and Gennaro Chierchia for their helpful comments about the material in chapter 11, Brooke Lea and Patty Brooks in preparing the revisions of articles that had been published previously, and Doris Aaronson, Mark Balton, Murray Glanzer, and Gay Snodgrass for a variety of helpful comments on the work in chapter 12. Finally, I would like to thank Marty Braine for his friendship and inspiration.

Why It Took So Long to Bake the Mental-Logic Cake: Historical Analysis of the Recipe and Its Ingredients

Luca Bonatti
Laboratoire des Science Cognitives et Psycholinguistique

> *. . . at least to me, the use of technically advanced machinery in analyzing reasoning is encouraging; after all, Aristotle thought about reasoning; one would like to see clearly what one has that he did not have! (It is no comfort to know that over 2000 years have passed since his time unless one sees just how one has used the experience of these 2000 years.)*
> —Kreisel (1967, p. 271)

"Enough with mental logic! It has been around for three millennia, and no theory came out of it. It's a dead research program!" You certainly must have happened to overhear speech streams very much like this. (They generally continue with the utterer praising the virtues of sexier alternatives, such as models, interconnected networks, space phases, or what have you.) In case you wanted to know what to respond, I can help you. The right response is, "Yes and no."

However, "yes and no" is a contradiction and you will not be happy with it, because you, like me and everybody else, possess a natural logic and natural logic abhors contradictions. The *real* right answer is, "In one sense yes, and in another sense, no." The "In one sense, yes" part is easy: It is a fact that the idea that we have a logic in our mind goes back 3,000 years or so. The "in another sense, no" part is a bit more complicated. I tell a long story about how certain ideas have to be blended with the right ingredients, how the ingredients have to be carefully mixed together, and how the mixture must be stored in a warm place far from drafts in

7

order for the yeast to grow. This paper is a memo to recall the basic steps for the recipe in order to be successful.

BLEND LOGIC WITH PSYCHOLOGY, BUT NOT TOO MUCH: WHEN LOGIC AND PSYCHOLOGY WERE ONE

Yes, something like the idea that there is a logic in our mind has been floating around for millennia. But could it actually develop into a real psychological thesis? Have the cake ingredients been available all along? Consider a step as trivial as this: If you want to claim that there is a relation between logic and our psychology, first, you had better be clear about the difference between logic and psychology, and, second, you had better get it right.

Yet this has not been a step easy to achieve, because the mental logic thesis was almost always meant in a very strong sense—as the thesis that logic *is* the science of the laws of thought. As a consequence, logic was considered *part of* psychology. This inclusive thesis remained surprisingly stable across the centuries, although it was clearly stunting its development by cutting its ties with the rest of mathematics.[1]

To a certain extent, however, this stability should not be a surprise. As Kant noticed (1781/1966, pp. 17–18), logic also remained substantially unchanged for centuries, as if all possible forms of reasoning had been laid down once and for all by Aristotle and his medieval commentators. So, for a long time there was no reason to change the doctrine of the psychological nature of logic, because logic was stable because considered complete and psychology was stable because non-existent.

What begins to be surprising is that this thesis resisted even when the horizons of logic broadened, for the first time with the work of Boole. Boole first distinguished propositional and predicative logics, and first noticed a central element for all future developments, namely, the formal nature of logic.[2] Yet, even if he dared to unrest its millennial stability,

---

[1]The fact that logic developed so late if compared with the rest of mathematics is indeed a puzzle. The puzzle is even deeper if one think that little or no mathematics was necessary to develop it, and that the necessary mathematics existed centuries before logic started its own solid development. I am suggesting that part of the explanation has to be found in the fact that the pie was cut in the wrong way. Logic was just not considered a discipline of the same nature as mathematics. The strong inclusive version of the mental-logic hypothesis bears part of responsibility for the anomalous development of logic.

[2]So also in Mangione (1993): "What does the revolutionary nature of Boolean logic consist in? . . . Boole clearly and definitely states the *formal* nature of the calculus in general, in the sense that also the formulation of a logical calculus is a formal construction to which interpretation is added from outside and does not constitute any longer the exclusive and primary basis from which the formal structure is abstracted" (pp. 106–107).

Boole did not abandon the idea that an investigation of logic is at the same time an investigation of "the fundamental laws of those operation of the mind by which reasoning is performed" (1854, p. 1). Moreover, Boole also made free use of another traditional ingredient that gives scarce results when added to the mental-logic cake. He considered logic as a discipline *sui generis* whose laws are not to be discovered by empirical inspection, like all other sciences require, but can be known entirely by introspection. This conception may be perfectly adequate for logic—after all, this is what intuitionism claims—but obviously cannot work for psychology. Yet, because for Boole logical laws are laws of thinking, a consequence of the mixture of the two traditional ingredients was that for him the "science of the mind"—what we would today call the *psychology of reasoning*—need not be grounded in experience:

> The general laws of nature are not, for the most part, immediate objects of perception.... On the other hand, the knowledge of the laws of the mind does not require as its basis any extensive collection of observations. The general truth is seen in the particular instance, and it is not confirmed by the repetition of instances. (1854, p. 4)

Let me stress that for centuries this view, according to which in order to achieve "knowledge of the mind" you need only to introspect your own mind, was never seriously questioned. Yet, it is as plausible as the view that you can discover the laws of your natural language parser by introspection; psycholinguistics would not go that far with the latter, nor the psychology of reasoning with the former.

Even if his view of mental logic was so much indebted to the past, Boole's (1854) analysis did break with tradition in an important point: He introduced the idea that the "laws of thought" have a mathematical character, more precisely algebraical. And this agreement between algebra and logic of thought, he conceded, must be found a posteriori:

> There is not only a close analogy between the operations of the mind in general reasoning and its operations in the particular science of algebra, but there is to a considerable extent an exact agreement.... Of course the laws must in both cases be determined independently; any formal agreement between them can only be established a posteriori by actual comparison. (p. 6)

Boole also speculated that because the *content* of number theory and logic are different, the "agreement" between operations of the mind and algebra must concern only the *processes* involved. Mental processes and algebraic processes have something in common. What, though, and why?

He did not give a full answer. Perhaps an answer cannot be given, he suggested, because it lays beyond our intellectual capabilities:

> Whence it is that the ultimate laws of logic are mathematical in their form, ... are questions upon which it might not be very remote from presumption to endeavor to pronounce a positive judgment. Probably they lie beyond the reach of our limited faculties. (1854, p. 11)

This profession of necessary ignorance was too pessimistic. There was a possible explanation of what unifies mathematics and thinking. Boole himself had remarked insightfully that reasoning is a process of compositions of symbols according to laws, that symbols are arbitrary signs, and that their rules of composition are common to both logic and the science of numbers. In order to see the full answer, however, he needed some other ingredients. The missing parts of the recipe were a foundational theory of mathematics that would stress the centrality of signs and combinations of signs, and a psychologically plausible theory that would assign to signs a key role in our thought processes. Both were to be provided in our century, but only, paradoxically, when philosophers and logicians had already abandoned the program of mental logic.

BUT NOT TOO LITTLE EITHER: LOGICIANS ABANDON PSYCHOLOGY . . .[3]

The first dissonant tune was sung by Frege and Russell. With their works, for the first time logic became theoretically separated from psychology. This is indeed good news, if I am right in thinking that confusion about the boundaries between the two disciplines was slowing the development of both. The trouble is, they got separated too much. Logic divorced psychology only to find itself married with metaphysics, and, in order to be accepted in the new family logicians, gave up any ties with the investigation of thinking processes.

Frege (1979) argued forcefully not only that logic—the science of thought, in the special sense he was conceiving it—is separated from psychology—for him, the science of thinking—but also that the latter is the mortal enemy of the former. In his colorful terms:

> [I]t is the business of the logician to conduct an unceasing struggle against psychology and those parts of language and grammar which fail to give untrammeled expression to what is logical. (p. 6)

---

[3]Macnamara (1986, pp. 12–20), to which the reader is also referred, makes much the same point I am arguing in this section.

> Since thoughts are not mental in nature, it follows that every psychological treatment of logic can only do harm. It is rather the task of this science to purify logic of all that is alien and hence of all that is psychological. (pp. 148–149)

The reasons motivating his calls for purification are interesting for us because they show that Frege was moved by his deep anti-idealism[4] rather than by an opposition to the mental logic hypothesis *qua* psychological hypothesis. If we fail to separate logical and psychological content, Frege argued, we obliterate the difference between the strictly subjective and noncommunicable ideas and the universal logical principles, so nothing would guarantee that two persons can entertain *the same* content, asserting it or denying it. As a consequence, a contradiction between two persons would be impossible, and with it communication as well as science. There would be no way to explain the notion of truth, idealism could not be refuted, solipsism would be inescapable, everyone would forever be condemned to live in his or her own private world.[5]

Even for Russell (1919)—and even more directly—logic became an instrument for the discovery of the correct ontology, a position pushed to its extreme consequences by his claim that logic should not include unicorns any more than zoology does (see 1919, pp. 169–170). As Di Francesco (1991) commented, "for Russell 'Logic' does not mean anything linguistic or formal in nature, in our sense. Quite the contrary, what he was looking for was not a set of syntactic rules, but rather the correct description of the objective relations between entia or propositions, considered as complex groups of entia" (p. 87).

Russell and Frege were not alone. For different reasons the logical neopositivists also accepted the new dogma. They saw in the novel developments of logic an occasion to explain at the same time the necessity of mathematical truth—a real mystery for traditional empiricism—and the construction of complex experiences: Mathematics is necessary because it is as empty as logic, and experience is structured in public objects because objects are a logical composition of sense data. Notice that in both roles logic takes over functions that have no connection whatsoever with psychology or the mind. This was somewhat a forced choice for the neopositivists. They were trying to play cards on two separate tables. They wanted both to hold that the origin of meaning is entirely grounded in experience, and to free experience from any connotation of privacy. As

---

[4]"Idealism" here does not include transcendental idealism, but the mixture of psychologism and post-Hegelianism that was current in Germany and England at the end of the century.

[5]See Frege (1979); for example, in "Logic," and "The Thought." See also Macnamara (1986), pp. 14–16.

a result, to their ears any talk of inner rules of thought or of mental entities appeared suspect, and behaviorist or reductionist conceptions of the mind sounded more appealing. In America, where the neopositivists migrated to escape Nazi fascism, the climate was perfect for these ideas to flourish. So even Quine, the philosopher who killed the neopositivist program with his criticisms of the analytic–synthetic distinction, still maintained their radical skepticism about the mind and their wary attitude towards any use of logic for psychological purposes.

In short, among the large majority of philosophically minded logicians, showing interest in psychological processes became a sort of behavior that well-mannered people should avoid. Logic and reasoning took different routes precisely when logic was undergoing an impressive development, and precisely under the influence of the pivotal figures of this development.

However, this turn was motivated less by any substantial arguments, or by any problems with the psychological feasibility of mental logic, than by a change in the general cultural climate. This is clear especially in Frege and Russell, whose statements about the separation between logic and psychology can be seen as an epiphenomenon of the general rebellion against German and English idealism from which 20th-century analytic philosophy stemmed,[6] but it is worth recalling that in the first decades of the century many other philosophers of different orientations, such as Moore, Meinong, and Husserl, attacked idealism in one way or another.[7]

So the antipsychological shift really was radical. However, it is important to realize that even conceding to Frege and the anti-idealists that the logic of thought is not the logic of thinking, there still is the possibility of having *both*: a metaphysical theory of thought *and* a theory of logical thinking, in which some of the logical rules discovered in the investigation of thought have a causal role in our thinking processes. For some reason, Frege and the post-Fregeans never conceived of this intermediate possibility.

So, although of extreme historical importance, the rejection of the mental-logic hypothesis by the new logicians was not really motivated. In the past, logicians had made the mistake of including logic within psychology and had made the further mistake of assuming the mental-logic point of view without giving any substantial argument for it. The new logicians corrected the first mistake by sharply separating logic from psychology. However, in one sense they made the same basic second mistake already made by their predecessors: They took a stand towards

---

[6]See Dummett (1981) for Frege, and Di Francesco (1991) for Russell.

[7]Macnamara (1986) makes this point especially with respect to Husserl's view of logic, which drastically changed under the influence of Frege. But Husserl was no special case: A plethora of authors was coming to the same conclusions in the same years.

the mental-logic program—a negative one in this case—without advancing any real argument.

... AND PSYCHOLOGISTS ABANDON LOGIC

Nevertheless, for independent reasons the same ideas were gaining the favor of experimental psychologists and became the standard view at least until the early 1960s. Many factors would probably need to be analyzed to explain the success of this attitude, but a major one is to be found in an unusual alliance of interests between otherwise opposite approaches. Notwithstanding the gulf separating behaviorism and cognitive psychology, at least for a certain period both schools held the same critical position about mental logic. Behaviorists were led to it by their general skepticism about talk of inner mental processes, including inner mechanisms of reasoning. In the limited interest shown for the problem, behaviorism seemed to have its own way to explain the "logical" appearance of people's responses. Problem solution was considered a learned drive, a kind of associative behavior. To the objection that thinking did not really look like a type of behavior, the answer was that it is in effect an evolutionary sophistication of action, a sort of delayed action that does leave silent behavioral traces in the form of implicit responses whose behavioral realization is only more difficult to be detected, such as subvocal talk or other muscular movements that repeat the full normal behavioral response at a smaller scale.

The underlying idea was that a "central controller" (of which mental logic is a partial description) is not needed for mental tasks: Ultimately, those can be traced back to peripheral muscular activities. So Watson (1924) wrote:

> The behaviorist advances the view that *what the psychologists have hitherto called thought is in short nothing but talking to ourselves....* My theory does hold that the muscular habits learned in overt speech are responsible for implicit or internal speech (thought). (pp. 14–15, italics added)[8]

Skinner later rejected the subvocal theory of thought, but not the idea that thinking and reasoning can be reduced to behavior. If it was impossible to explain it away by means of a single correlated behavior, for him thinking could be seen as an emergent property of complex behaviors. The basic point remained the same: Thinking is not a succes-

---

[8]See also Humphrey (1963), pp. 185–216.

sion of internal states, but a far consequence of environmental variables on the organism.[9]

The need to dispose of mental vocabulary—and with it, by instantiation, mental logic—looks like a necessary corner into which the behaviorists had to paint themselves. Well, one can say, too bad for the behaviorists. However, paradoxically, even the newborn cognitive psychology, which had no need to put itself in such an uncomfortable position, assumed roughly the same attitude toward mental logic. Although the "New Look" psychology rehabilitated a vocabulary of inner mental processes and flows of information, initially it focused research on the plasticity of mental processes, on the interaction and the mutual influence of reasoning and perception, and on the strong effect of context on both. To this general picture of the functioning of mind the "rigidity" of logical rules was unappealing, whereas a more pragmatic view of reasoning was better suited. Thus we find what is considered the first bible of cognitive science stating that "much of human reasoning is supported by a kind of thematic process rather than by an abstract logic. The principal feature of this thematic process is its pragmatic rather than its logical structure" (Bruner, Goodnow, & Austin, 1956, p. 104). Once again, the intuition was correct but not its implicit conclusion. That pragmatics influences reasoning (as well as other mental processes) is obviously true. However, it is one thing is to say that a theory of reasoning has to take into account pragmatic factors, and another to say that *because* reasoning is influenced by pragmatic factors, it has no *formal* components and no mental logic rules. Compare the following: It is one thing is to say that language interactions among humans are heavily influenced by semantics, and another to say that *because* semantics has a great influence in language, there is no syntax. In both cases the former thesis does not imply the latter. New Look psychologists missed this difference and thus, even if they had no a priori reasons to reject mental logic, they treated it almost as badly as their behaviorist adversaries did.

ADD A GOOD MEASURE OF FORMALISM: HILBERT AND THINKING AS A SYMBOLIC PROCESS

Ideologically, it was again an impulse coming from logicians—not from psychologists—that put logic back in the psychological ballpark. In the rich intellectual debate generated by the problem of the foundations of mathematics, the formalist school has a special role for our story.

---

[9]See Skinner (1957), pp. 437 ff.

Let us distinguish Hilbert's specific program for the foundation of mathematics from the general formalist approach. The former required that a consistency proof for arithmetic be obtained with finitary means, and Gödel's second theorem killed it by showing that this cannot be done. The latter more general framework, however, according to which logic was conceived as the science of signs and their transformations, is not necessarily tied to Hilbert's foundational program. Although this conception falls short of explaining mathematics, it might well be sufficient to explain thinking. It is interesting, and often overlooked, that Hilbert had already realized that his conception would open important new perspectives not only for mathematics, but also (and especially) for the relation between logic and reasoning. Thus when rejecting Brouwer's scorn at this "material" aspect of logic, so cherished by formalists, Hilbert (1927) wrote:

> The formula game that Brouwer so deprecates has, besides its mathematical value, an important general philosophical significance. For this formula game is carried out according to certain definite rules, in which the *technique of our thinking* [his italics] is expressed. These rules form a closed system that can be discovered and definitively stated. *The fundamental idea of my proof theory is none other than to describe the activity of our understanding to make a protocol of the rules according to which our thinking actually proceeds* [italics added]. Thinking, it so happens, parallels speaking and writing: we form statements and place them one behind another. (p. 475)

To this idea of proof theory as a description of the activity of the understanding, Hilbert added a particular interpretation of Kant's thesis that something must be presented in intuition in order for thought to produce knowledge. In the case of mathematics, the extralogical intuitive necessary element is *the symbol itself*, a concrete object which, just by virtue of its *shape*, can trigger elementary processes of recognition, matching, concatenation, and deletion and allow a rule to be applied:

> Kant already taught ... that mathematics has at its disposal a content secured independently of all logic and hence can never be provided with a foundation by means of logic alone; ... Rather, as a condition for the use of logical inferences and the performance of logical operations, something must already be given to our faculty of representation, certain extralogical concrete objects that are intuitively present as immediate experience prior to all thought. If logical inference is to be reliable, it must be possible to survey these objects completely in all their parts, and the fact that they occur, that they differ from one another, and that they follow each other, or are concatenated, is immediately given intuitively, together with the objects, as something that neither can be reduced to anything else nor requires reduction. This is the basic philosophical position that I consider requisite for mathematics and, in general, for all scientific thinking, understanding, and communication. And in mathematics, in particular, what we

consider is the concrete signs themselves, whose shape, according to the
conception we have adopted, is immediately clear and recognizable. (Hilbert, 1925/1967, p. 376)

Liberated from its interpretive parts, the passage contains the clear suggestion that logical rules of thought can be seen as procedures activated
only in virtue of the *form* of the signs with which they are formulated. In
our terms, we may say that a thinking process can be seen as a set of
transformations on symbols according to rules exploiting a high-level
concrete property of the symbols—their shape.

Hilbert's two great intuitions—that a thought process is a kind of proof,
and that a proof is a transformation of symbols according to rules acting
on their form—gave formalism a completely different turn. The syntactic
nature of logical rules, together with the statement that our thinking is
nothing but the application of rules in a certain order, was opening again
the way for undertaking an investigation of the logic of thinking, but this
time with a clearer understanding of the nature of the rules and of how
properties of their forms could be used to generate deductions.

Thus formalism provided two essential ingredients for the mental-logic
cake. Others, however, were still missing. What logic needed to be ready
for psychological investigation was, on the one hand, a more intuitive
presentation of formal systems and, on the other hand, a model of how
a physical structure could use a formal system to carry out derivations.
Gentzen provided the first ingredient, and the second one emerges from
Turing's work.

KNEAD FORMS UNTIL THEY FEEL NATURAL TO
THE TOUCH: GENTZEN AND NATURAL LOGIC

Hilbert's axiomatization of logic was meant to capture the set of theorems
by using few initial sentences and the smallest possible number of inference rules. This system, however useful for handling many domains of
logic and mathematics, fails to be appealing even to represent the particular kind of reasoning it aimed to represent, namely, logical and mathematical reasoning. Far less could it be proposed as a model of how human
reasoning generally proceeds. Gentzen's natural deduction took care of
this problem. An alternative treatment was developed for some parts of
logic, in which axioms disappeared, leaving many inference rules in their
places. Gentzen (1964) consciously intended to provide a system of deduction "as close as possible to actual reasoning":

The formalization of logical deduction, especially as it has been developed
by Frege, Russell, and Hilbert, is rather far removed from the forms of
deduction used in practice in mathematical proofs. Considerable formal

advantages are achieved in return. In contrast, I intended first to set up a formal system which comes as close as possible to actual reasoning. The result was a "calculus of natural deduction." (p. 68)

He noticed that in actual mathematical reasoning, appeal to formal axioms is rare, whereas many—but not too many—forms of inferences are used. He set himself the task of specifying those inferences. To this purpose, he introduced different kinds of calculi in which each logical symbol occurred in two rules specifying when a formula containing it could be introduced and when it could be eliminated in favor of other formulas not containing that symbol.[10] This central difference from axiomatic systems makes proving a theorem a completely different, more natural activity than proving it starting from axioms. Yet, nothing is lost in natural deduction: The crucial metatheoretical properties of axiomatic systems are all preserved.

Another difference with Hilbert-style logics is worth noticing. Ideally, an axiomatic system aims at maximal economy, both in axioms as well as in rules. Gentzen, instead, provided rules for all the logical connectives, even if they were logically redundant. There are technical reasons for it, but there is also an important philosophical motivation. Gentzen intended to provide a system as close as possible to actual mathematical reasoning, and from this point of view economy in rules could not be a value in itself. If mathematical natural reasoning seems to require even redundant rules, so be it. A related point has to do with the interdefinability of connectives. In classical logic equivalence laws, such as, for example, (A → B) ↔ (¬A v B), render connectives interdefinable and thereby dispensable in principle. However, this goes flat in the face of another natural intuition, the feeling that each connective has a separate meaning. Natural deduction also provided a way to account also for this intuition. Even if one adopts classical rules for connectives, and thus the equivalence laws are still theorems, from Gentzen's point of view such extensional equivalences do not show that one can dispense with the rule. If we use them when following a path of thought, if they appear to govern the functioning of certain special words lexicalized even in normal natural language, such as *and*, *or*, *if*, or *all*, then they are likely to correspond to separate units of meaning and they deserve a place in a system of mathematical reasoning.

---

[10]With the exception of classical negation. In the intuitionistic case, negation is governed by the elimination rule $\frac{A, \neg A}{\bot}$ and by the introduction rule $\frac{\begin{array}{c} A \\ \bot \end{array}}{\neg A}$, whereas to get classical logic a special extra elimination rule expressing double-negation redundancy is needed: $\frac{\neg\neg A}{A}$. This rule for Gentzen spurs the "harmony" of a system in which to each connective just one elimination and one introduction rule correspond.

In short, Gentzen's natural deduction achieved for mathematics what Gentzen wanted to achieve: It showed how a proof can be at the same time formal and natural. The route from formal logic to natural reasoning was opened. Gentzen did not provide a *psychological* system of rules for reasoning—he could not, because the psychology to go any further was not yet available—but because *mutatis mutandis* his arguments hold for reasoning in general, he contributed another basic ingredient to its development. He shaped the form of the rules and showed how formal logic (this time, a real discipline separated from psychology) and intuitive logic may be not so distant from each other, after all.

WHIP COMPUTATIONS UNTIL THEY ACQUIRE THE RIGHT CONSISTENCY: THE COMPUTER METAPHOR AND FUNCTIONALISM

The other necessary step for transforming mental logic into a psychological thesis was to develop fully Hilbert's intuitions about how rules exploit the "concrete" aspects of signs. Notoriously, it was Turing who offered the abstract model of a shape-driven machine, which showed how a physical mechanism could perform operations once considered to be typically mental. Turing's intuitions on the role and possibilities of his new machines were of exceptional importance. They finally led to the thesis that the mind can be seen as an information processor, which in turn gave substance to the idea of a mental logic. However, in the development of this view two stages should be distinguished. The first stage, explicitly endorsed by Turing, is expressed by the thesis that *a computer can be a mind*, namely, that certain kinds of properties once attributable only to humans can also be appropriately predicated of other physical configurations. This thesis, however revolutionary, leaves completely undetermined the nature of the operations of the mind. It may imply that mental processes can be *simulated* by a machine but leaves it open the possibility that the mechanisms and procedures intervening in the two physical beings—the *simulandum* and the *simulans*—are totally different. All that the thesis requires is that the input/output relations typical of mental processes are preserved by the simulation device, and simulation only establishes an extensional identity between two physical configurations, but leaves it undetermined whether these share the same *psychology*.

Turing's well-known test for intelligence, entirely based on the control of input/output relations (at least prima facie), uses only dispositional language and is thus compatible with conceptions that do without mental vocabulary, such as behaviorism or logical behaviorism. It does not *require* laws mentioning internal states, and if it does, it doesn't require that they apply to *both* minds *and* computers. To see this, imagine that a computer passes Turing's test; it may still be the case that when we reason we exploit lawfully connected inner states, but the computer does not. Suppose, for example, that *we* parse the computer's responses to our questions by using a grammar for a language. Then, a part of our psychology would be described by linguistic theory. But when the computer "reads" our questions, it consults a huge database of predefined forms and outputs answers to each question that we plausibly may ask by mere physical shape-matching, without really parsing our input.[11] In this case, although the computer may happen to pass Turing's test, we and it would not fall under the same psychological laws: Linguistics would be true for us, and false for the computer.

Turing did intend to go beyond this minimal claim; witness the fact that he proposed tests for machine intelligence couched in more "cognitive" vocabulary.[12] However, his main concern was not to dispel the prejudice that *we* cannot be like machines, but rather to reject the reverse thesis that *machines* cannot be like us. For him, the question of whether the inner structure of mental processes and the computational states of machines are captured by a common set of laws was not at the forefront. He did use analogies to mental processes for finding algorithms, but this was meant to be a heuristic strategy based on introspection rather than a research program.[13] His caution also is shown by his willingness to explore all possible sorts of machines, whether "classical," as we would call them, or "connectionist," with the main task of finding agreement in behavior between minds and machines, rather than agreement in laws.

Turing's ideas were of exceptional value, but for various reasons— mostly due to the widespread behaviorist attitude in psychology and philosophy—further time had to pass before they could be elaborated into a fully coherent program. As Hegel wanted it, philosophy always comes at dawn. The new paradigm had to wait for the development of the theory of computable functions and for the first successes of artificial intelligence before being taken seriously by philosophers. The big further step—the reverse thesis that *we* are like computers—came with function-

---

[11]The computer could not answer *all* questions we may possibly ask, because it wouldn't include a productive language, but lack of productivity would not forbid it to pass Turing's test. The test only requires that we could not *plausibly* tell a computer from a human, not that we could not *possibly* do it.

[12]Specifically, he proposed that a machine that learns (i.e., that modifies its instruction) should be considered intelligent; see Turing (1947b, pp. 122–123).

[13]For example, when outlining a program for playing chess, he wrote, "If I were to sum up the weakness of the above system in a few words, I would describe it as a caricature of my own play. It was in fact based on an introspective analysis of my thought processes when playing, with considerable simplifications. It makes oversights which are very similar to those which I make myself" (Turing, 1947b, p. 294).

alism. Functionalism explicitly defended the thesis that the psychological vocabulary *is* computational vocabulary, and that the natural kinds described by psychology are not organisms but computational devices. Fodor (1981) presented it as a *fairly recent* contender in the arena of the theories of mind:

> The real point is that, if we want a science of mental phenomena at all, we are required to so identify mental properties that the kinds they subsume are natural from the point of view of psychological theory construction. . . . Now, there is a level of abstraction at which the generalizations of psychology are most naturally pitched and, *as things appear to be turning out*, that level of abstraction collapses across the differences between physically quite different kinds of systems. . . . [I]f we wanted to restrict the domains of our psychological theories to just us, we would have to do so by ad hoc conditions upon their generalizations. Whereas, what does seem to provide a natural domain for psychological theorizing, at least in cognitive psychology, is something like the set of (real and possible) information processing systems. (pp. 8–9, italics added)

We are now well beyond the 1960s. Only then were logic and philosophy ready to nurture the development of mental logic as a serious psychological hypothesis. Everything was there, except the psychology.

MIX WITH EMPIRICAL PSYCHOLOGY: ALMOST GETTING THERE

Ideas must be ripe before becoming productive. I argued that the although the idea of a mental logic has been around for centuries, it could not develop because the ingredients necessary to give substance to it either were not available or were seen from a wrong perspective. When, finally, all the conceptual ingredients did become available, the psychology for testing mental-logic theories was still missing. Another 20 years or so had to pass before experimental techniques were sufficiently developed to begin asking nature the right questions in the right way. It is true that Piaget and his school (e.g., Piaget, 1953) spoke a language externally akin to mental logic, but in their hands the thesis was never even spelled out clearly enough to see what it said or how it differed from other alternatives (see Bonatti, 1994; Braine & Rumain, 1983). If one eliminates Piagetianism, which did more harm than good to the mental-logic hypothesis, only a handful of articles and proposals remain that can be considered real attempts to transform it into a testable psychological theory, and until very recent years most of them fell short of being satisfactory, for one reason or another.

Henle (1962) was probably the first attempt to test experimentally a mental-logic hypothesis, but the limits of her work were important. She took natural logic to be classical logic—not even in natural deduction form—but she gave no argument for this assumption. Her method was entirely based on direct analysis of subjects' explicit conscious justifications, but those may not be a good indicator of the real processes involved in reasoning. She assumed that the syllogism has a special role in reasoning, but this too was an unjustified assumption. In short, the merit of Henle's study was less in her arguments and methodologies than in the theses she presented.

It was only in the 1970s that the mental-logic hypothesis marked significant improvement towards its transformation into a psychological theory. In those years natural deduction became the standard form of the theory, and purely qualitative analysis was abandoned in favor of more quantitative methods often accompanied by computational implementations. Nevertheless, the proposed theories still lacked a sufficient psychological motivation. Osherson (1975a) and Johnson-Laird (1975) proposed models of rules that shared many common points and diverged for computational options. Whereas Osherson's model was conclusion sensitive and applied its rules in strict order trying to minimize the difference between premises and conclusions, Johnson-Laird's (1975) program blindly generated consequences of the premises, regardless of the form of the conclusion. Both systems included good and new ideas, but, interestingly for us, both were clearly more concerned with the algorithmic implementation of rules than with their psychological plausibility. For example, in both systems the basic rules were selected somewhat arbitrarily. Both systems took a one-way approach to the role of a conclusion in a problem, one being conclusion sensitive and the other conclusion blind, but neither provided evidence that subjects exclusively or preferentially follow one of those strategies. Likewise, although Johnson-Laird's system introduced the distinction between primary and secondary inferences that remains central also in the system presented in this book, his way to sort the rules in the two classes was not psychologically motivated. It is revealing that at the end of his 1975 article, Johnson-Laird admitted to not being sure of how to test his model empirically, and he concluded that this was a really difficult, almost impossible, task. Clearly, psychological reality was not at the forefront.

In fact, both Osherson and Johnson-Laird could hardly have done any better. They had run into another tricky problem. They lacked another crucial ingredient for a mental logic, a really difficult one to find and to calibrate: the right balance between algorithmic implementation and psychological justification for a mental logic system. Only recently (e.g., Braine, 1978; Rips, 1983) did some researchers start tinkering with it, to find out the right proportions between the two ingredients. This work is still at its beginnings, and much is still needed to nail down the rules for reasoning, their implementations, and the flow of information involved in a reasoning process.

HAVE A TASTE OF THE CAKE: GETTING THERE

So developing a mental-logic theory was not so easy after all. Many ingredients needed to be found and their proportions carefully weighed before a good mixture could be formed. Logic had to be separated from psychology, but this only happened after Boole, with the development of modern logic. Its formal nature had to be put in focus, and the logical properties of forms had to be discovered, but this only happened when logicians started working on the foundations of mathematics, at the beginning of this century and well into the 1930s. The connection between forms and machines acting on forms had to be seen, but this was clear only with Turing and his notion of computability. The philosophical consequences of the new view about mental processes implicit in Turing's ideas had to be drawn, but this only happened some decades later, when philosophical functionalism ripened. Only then could psychology revive the mental-logic hypothesis and look at it with a clearer vision of the claims being made. Psychology too had to make progress. It had to abandon the ancient commonplace that the laws of reasoning can be discovered by immediate introspection. Also, this step was slow to come. It had to devise experimental techniques to investigate the rules, and to test the psychological reality of the proposed algorithms by implementing them in the conditions in which they can be deployed. All of it is very recent development, and much of it has yet to be written.

It should no longer be a surprise that mental logic started developing fairly recently. In fact, it has a development as recent as that of its supposed sexier alternatives, such as models, interconnected networks, space phases, or what have you. The reason is simple: They all require pretty much the same conceptual ingredients to be developed, and they all require a well-developed empirical psychology. There is no dead research program in the area of reasoning; there are only theories in better or worse shape.

"OK, fine. But even if the long history of mental logic does not count against it, its *present state* does! Even now, with all the ingredients available, the mental-logic dough has not leavened. Compare with X [substitute X for models, interconnected networks, space phases, or what have you]: X has gone so much further!" Again, there is an answer. This time, the answer is "No and No." No, it is false that there are better alternatives to mental logic, and, No, it is false that mental logic has not begun to be productive. Have a taste of the cake by reading the rest of this book.

3

Mental Logic and Irrationality: We Can Put a Man on the Moon, So Why Can't We Solve Those Logical Reasoning Problems?*

David P. O'Brien
*Baruch College and the Graduate School
of the City University of New York*

Are people rational or are they irrational? Before starting to write this chapter I posed this question to an undergraduate class in cognitive psychology. No shortage of evidence was offered for either alternative. On the one hand, it was pointed out that people do many things that most of us would judge irrational: We fail to wear seat belts while knowing that this decreases our safety, we smoke cigarettes while knowing that this may lead to a frightful disease, we spend the weekend drinking at parties while knowing that an exam is being given on Monday, we continue to use our credit cards while knowing that we are unable to repay the debts already accumulated. On the other hand, people do many things that reflect a rational nature: We plan for the future, anticipating the effects of our actions; we have created mathematics, formal logic, complex engineering and computing systems, high technology, science, and philosophy. Ironically, our apparently most rational accomplishments can lead to the most irrational results; for example, modern physics has provided for the development of weapons that threaten to bring about our extinction. For me, the tenor of the discussion was captured when one student posed the popular rhetorical protasis, "If we can put a man on the moon," and another student provided the apodosis, "why can't we solve the THOG problem or the selection task?"

*Originally published in Manktelow, K. I., & Over, D. E. (Eds.). (1993). *Rationality: Psychological and Philosophical Perspectives* (pp. 110–135). London: Routledge. Reprinted by permission of Routledge.

The consensus of my class was that as humans we have it in our nature to be both rational and irrational, a conclusion with which I expect most readers will agree. Differences among us are apt to concern which aspects of human nature we propose are rational and which ones we propose are irrational. Evans (1993), for example, proposed that people possess a kind of rationality that enables us to make decisions so as to maximize the prospects of benefit to ourselves, but we do not possess a rationality of inherently logical thought processes. I disagree. People may be motivated to seek benefits for themselves and their families, clans, tribes, nations, and so forth, but my undergraduate students provided many examples of the ways in which people are not adept at maximizing such benefits. Furthermore, I argue, people's thought processes are, in many ways, profoundly logical. I also believe that the empirical evidence per se does not settle the issue: In the practical realm we successfully do some things that appear to be in our self-interest and some that appear to be irrational, and in the realm of laboratory logical-reasoning tasks we do some things that appear to be logical and some that appear to be irrational.

The classical Greek view of human nature included a rationality that allows for logical reasoning. My colleagues and I argued elsewhere (Noveck, Lea, Davidson, & O'Brien, 1991) that we have no adequate reason to abandon this view and that this rationality includes a mental logic that accounts for our basic logical intuitions. In recent years the claim that human reasoning includes a mental logic has met considerable resistance, and the death of mental logic is proclaimed with some regularity (e.g., Cheng & Holyoak, 1985; Cosmides, 1989; Johnson-Laird, 1983; Johnson-Laird & Byrne, 1991; Legrenzi & Legrenzi, 1991). To paraphrase Mark Twain, news of this death is premature; theories of mental logic are alive and well, though often misunderstood. Indeed, I believe that most criticisms of the mental-logic approach stem from a misunderstanding of what it is.

The first section of this chapter describes the mental-logic approach. Theories of mental logic are not monolithic, and what counts as evidence against a particular theory does not necessarily count as evidence against all mental-logic theories. I first discuss the mental-logic approach generally, noting that a mental logic consists of propositional activities, then focus on the three-part theory presented in this volume. The second section addresses some principal criticisms of mental logic. In particular, I argue that (a) failure to solve complex reasoning problems does not count as evidence against mental logic, and (b) we should not interpret evidence of the effects of content on logical reasoning as counting against mental logic. The third section addresses why I do not find the competing nonlogical theories compelling, and focuses on the content-bound theories proposed by Cosmides (1989) and Cheng and Holyoak (1985) and the mental-models theory proposed by Johnson-Laird and his associates (e.g., Johnson-Laird, 1983; Johnson-Laird & Byrne, 1991). Finally, I address irrationality from the perspective of the mental-logic approach.

THE MENTAL-LOGIC APPROACH

An adequate theory of human logical reasoning needs to account for both logically correct and erroneous judgments. We thus are faced with an apparent dilemma. On the one hand, we can assume that the human reasoning repertory includes a mental logic, in which case we have an explanation for those valid logical judgments that people make, but we still require an explanation for reasoning errors. On the other hand, we can assume that there is no mental logic, which provides an explanation for errors in reasoning but leaves the valid judgments unexplained. The proposal that there is no mental logic, though, is based on a misunderstanding of the nature of logic, and adoption of the first horn of this apparent dilemma—that there is a mental logic—is the rational choice.

Kant (1781/1966) proposed that human understanding is made possible in part by a mental logic, and that in the 2,000 years since Aristotle nothing had been added to this logic and nothing altered, so logic could be considered completed and perfect. As Macnamara (1986) noted, this view of logic reflects a Platonic heritage, and encourages the view of a mental logic as the manipulation of symbolic forms. This logic of forms is the sort of logic, I believe, that is being decried by opponents of the mental-logic approach. Since Frege at the end of the 19th century, however, logic has undergone a revolution, and logicians have come to view logic as propositional and intentional (Kneale & Kneale, 1962).

Propositions take truth values, that is, a proposition is either true or false. Note that sentences per se are not propositions. The sentence "I am traveling with an American passport" is neither true nor false, but is true when asserted by myself outside America and false if asserted by Margaret Thatcher. Were logic concerned with sentences, it would be concerned merely with the manipulation of symbolic forms. However, the assumptions and conclusions of logical arguments are propositions.[1]

Logical reasoning consists of propositional activities. Propositions are proposed, supposed, assumed, considered, claimed, believed, disbelieved, doubted, asserted, denied, inferred, and so forth. All of these propositional

---

[1]Images are not propositional; although an image might be an accurate or an inaccurate representation, it can be neither true nor false. Propositions that refer to images, though, are true or false. Probabilistic propositions, however, take truth values. (The claim that "there is an 80% probability of showers next Tuesday" is either true or false; it is not 80% true and 20% false.)

activities concern judgments about truth and falsity, for example, to believe x is to believe that x is true, to doubt x is to doubt that x is true, to
deny x is to claim that x is false. Such propositional activities concern
intentional states of affairs. When I assert that "Napoleon was in Egypt,"
I refer to an historical person and his relation to a country, not to a
symbolic idea in my mind that I can manipulate. This intentionality does
not presuppose any claim to realism—it would be no less propositional
were Napoleon merely the figment of historical imagination. Note that I
also could assert that "Ahab was obsessed with a white whale," which
we also would judge true even though its intentional state of affairs is
fictional. The reason that the sentence "I am traveling with an American
passport" is neither true nor false until its utterer and circumstances are
known is that sentences per se, unlike propositions, do not concern intentional states of affairs.

Because propositional activities refer to intentional states of affairs,
they coexist with pragmatic activities, having to do with the practical
consequences of propositions for their referred states of affairs (James,
1885/1978; Peirce, 1931/1958). These pragmatic activities include setting
goals and understanding goals set by others. The logical processes that
infer propositions and make inferences from them cohabit easily with
other processes that are pragmatic and rely on knowledge of intentional
states of affairs.

Propositions can be atomic or compound, that is, atomic propositions
can be negated, or joined in conjunction, disjunction, conditionality, and
so forth. For example, "If I am traveling with an American passport, then
I must be an American citizen" supposes the proposition described earlier,
and joins it with a conclusion drawn from that supposition together with
other assumed propositional information. We need an account of how
we reason to and from such compound propositions, that is, how we
form and use them.

Forming a compound proposition requires an inference—one does not
observe a disjunction or a conditional. Such connections are inferred, as
both Hume and Kant noted in their different ways, in the understanding.
It would be both a cruel hoax and evolutionarily disadvantageous for
nature to provide us with propositional representations if our ways of
connecting them and reasoning with them failed to preserve their propositional status. Because propositions are profoundly truth functional, their
inference procedures ought to be truth preserving, that is, given a set of
propositions assumed true, further propositions drawn from them by
logical procedures also would be true. Logicians refer to this property as
logical soundness, and a set of inference procedures is sound if, and only
if, given a set of true propositions, the inference procedures will provide
true conclusions only.

Soundness is distinct from validity; an argument is valid unless there is a possible assignment of truth values such that its premises taken conjunctively are true while its conclusion is false. Thus, in standard logic any argument with necessarily false premises is valid. This property is not part of our ordinary logical intuitions, with which we proceed from propositions assumed true. (See chap. 9 for a discussion of deliberately counterfactual suppositions.) Indeed, it is not uncommon for people to reject an argument because they do not accept its premises. Thus, ordinary reasoning proceeds not from premises, but from assumptions, that is, from premises that are assumed true (see Leblanc & Wisdom, 1976; Politzer & Braine, 1991; chaps. 7 and 9). Unlike the standard logic of textbooks, people draw no conclusions from contradictory premises— such premise sets cannot qualify as assumptions. No one ordinarily would assume a contradictory set of premises, but would see such as absurd.

To summarize, logical reasoning is profoundly propositional, and propositional activities, such as asserting, denying, believing, doubting, and so forth, require intentional states of affairs; logical inference procedures cohabit with pragmatic inference procedures that concern the practical consequences of propositions for intentional states of affairs. A mental logic is not, therefore, a matter of mere symbol manipulation but is about making propositional inferences, and ordinary reasoning applies sound inference procedures to propositions assumed true to infer propositions that inherit that truth.

Inference-Schema Models

Piaget (e.g., Inhelder & Piaget, 1958, 1964) proposed that the structure of concrete-operational thought corresponds to a logic of classes, and formal-operational thought is equivalent to the 16 truth-functional operators of normal-disjunctive form processed by the mathematical INRC group. This proposal, however, has been criticized on logical grounds (e.g., Braine & Rumain, 1983; Ennis, 1975; O'Brien, 1987; Parsons, 1959), and in recent years a consensus has developed among mental-logic adherents that reasoning proceeds through the application of sound inference schemas (e.g., Braine, 1990; Braine & O'Brien, 1991; Braine, Reiser, & Rumain, 1984; Johnson-Laird, 1975; Macnamara, 1986; O'Brien, 1987, 1991; Osherson, 1975a, 1975b; Rips, 1983; Sperber & Wilson, 1986). Inference schemas are procedures that specify which propositions can be derived from assumed propositions of a particular form, and sound inference schemas assure that propositions derived from true assumptions inherit that truth. Thus far, psychological models proposing inference schemas have been developed only for sentential connectives and have not yet addressed the role of quantifiers (see, however, chap. 11; Rips, 1994). People make many sentential inferences that are sanctioned by standard systems of sentential logic, but routinely fail to make others. The primary task of a psychological inference-schema model is to describe those inferences that are made regularly and routinely. A secondary task is to describe those logical inferences that people make only sometimes.

Following Gentzen (1935/1964) logicians described two sorts of inference schemas: those used to introduce a propositional connective in a line of reasoning, for example, a schema for conditional proof to introduce propositions of the form *if p then q*, and those used to eliminate a propositional connective in a line of reasoning, for example, a schema for disjunction elimination (*p or q*, *not-p*; therefore *q*), modus ponens (*if p then q*, *p*; therefore *q*). Note that inference schemas address the forms of propositions, but this syntactic nature of the inference procedure does not diminish the propositional nature of either the atomic or compound propositions that are inferred. Sound inference procedures ensure that the drawn inferences will be truth preserving, that is, that only true propositions will be drawn from true assumptions.

The several varied inference-schema models that have been proposed do not make identical claims about the role of the schemas. For example, Macnamara (1986) proposed that inference schemas are used as logical checking devices, checking the soundness of inferences made by other, nonlogical, devices. Sperber and Wilson (1986) proposed that only elimination schemas are used. The models proposed by Rips (1983), Osherson (1975a, 1975b), Johnson-Laird (1975), and in this volume all use both introduction and elimination schemas to make inferences in lines of reasoning. Differences exist among these theories, however, concerning the particular schemas that are proposed. For example, the model described in chapter 6 does not include the disjunction-introduction schema, which draws propositions of the form *p or q* from *p*, although the models of Rips (1983) and Johnson-Laird (1975) do include such a schema.

The approach that I advocate proposes a three-part model (hereafter referred to as *The Model*), which includes (a) a set of inference schemas, (b) a reasoning program that implements the schemas in a line of reasoning, and (c) a set of independently motivated pragmatic principles that influence interpretation of surface-structure propositions and can suggest or inhibit certain inferences and reasoning strategies. The description of The Model in the next few pages is intended to describe the present state of work—both what has been accomplished and what has yet to be done.

The Inference Schemas and the Reasoning Program

The inference schemas of The Model have been presented in detail elsewhere (chap. 6) so I do not do so here. The Model includes both introduction and elimination schemas, with a set of core schemas and some feeder schemas, both of which are implemented through a direct-reasoning routine, and a set of complex schemas that require coordination through an indirect-reasoning routine. The core schemas describe a set of inferences that people make routinely and without apparent effort.

The Model holds that the core schemas are applied automatically through a direct-reasoning routine whenever the appropriate propositions are considered together, for example, when both *p or q* and *not-p* are jointly considered, *q* will be inferred automatically. The feeder schemas, however, are not applied unless their propositional output feeds into a subsequent inference (see also Johnson-Laird, 1975, on auxiliary schemas), in which case they are applied automatically by the direct-reasoning routine. Lea et al. (1990) presented two reasons for this differentiation of the feeder schemas from the core schemas. One is theoretical: The feeder schemas can lead to infinite loops, for example, from *p and q* to *p*, to *p and (p and q)*, and so forth. People exhibit no tendency to make such inference strings. The second reason to designate these as feeder schemas is empirical; when subjects are asked to write down every inference they can from a set of assumptions, subjects usually omit the output of the feeder schemas while writing down the output of the core schemas, even when the output of feeder schemas is required to make the core-schema inferences.

The complex schemas require use of an indirect-reasoning routine. For example, in order to falsify a proposition *p*, one can suppose *p* and seek to find a contradiction under this supposition. When this indirect-reasoning strategy does lead to a contradiction, a negation-introduction schema allows assertion of *not-p*. Unlike the core and feeder schemas, which are applied effortlessly and routinely, the complex schemas are in nowise claimed to be universally available, and their application depends on the effortful use of an indirect-reasoning routine.

Acquisition of the indirect-reasoning routine requires some tuition or reflection, and its use may be either encouraged or discouraged by knowledge of the referred intentional state of affairs. The direct-reasoning routine, however, is considered basic to logical reasoning. The Model thus predicts that problems requiring sophisticated reasoning strategies will not be solved readily by most people, whereas problems that can be solved through the direct-reasoning routine will be solved most of the time.

Differences exist among the inference-schema models concerning the nature of the reasoning program. Rips (1983, 1994) proposed an approach in which the line of reasoning proceeds towards a goal, either a conclusion to be evaluated or a lemma required to evaluate a conclusion. Hence, if subjects are presented a set of assumptions with no conclusion to judge, the model generally would draw no inferences. However, several investigations have reported a wide variety of problems without any conclusions to be evaluated on which subjects have demonstrated no difficulty in drawing logically appropriate inferences (e.g., Lea et al., 1990; O'Brien & Lee, 1992).

As described earlier, The Model proposes that both the core and feeder inference schemas are applied automatically both in processing discourse and in reasoning. This claim of automaticity is problematic, though, when one considers that the inferences of the feeder schemas are drawn only when they provide the input for drawing further inferences. This seems to indicate that people look ahead to see what inferences are needed before they make these inferences—hardly what one expects of an automatic process.

An additional, empirical reason to think that people look forward when drawing inferences is found in comparison of problems with and without conclusions to be judged. Consider the following two problems that I gave to some undergraduates recently (about toy animals and fruits in a box). The first problem presents assumptions of the form *p or q, if p then r*, and *if q then r*. This problem presents no conclusion to be evaluated but requires subjects to write down everything that can be inferred. Most subjects write down only *r*, which follows directly through one of the core inference schemas. On the second problem subjects are given the same set of assumptions, but are asked to evaluate as a conclusion *if not-p then r*. On this problem subjects usually write down first *q*, and then *r*, before judging the conclusion as true—a line of reasoning that follows from The Model's schema for conditional proof. Clearly, were subjects not looking forward to consider the conclusion, the line of reasoning on the second problem should be the same as on the first problem. At least some of the time, people seem to look forward when they are applying the basic schemas of The Model.

As yet, the reasoning program of The Model does not capture adequately when subjects look ahead and when they do not, but then, neither does the reasoning program proposed by Rips (1983), with its focus on goal-attaining inferences. Relative to the schemas, little empirical work has been done on the reasoning program, but the need for further investigation of how the inference schemas are implemented becomes apparent a fortiori with the realization that lack of sophistication in using the reasoning program is a principal source of reasoning errors. Clearly, future developments in describing a reasoning program must include some forward-looking as well as some automatic processes.

Several possible solutions could be suggested. One possibility is that the feeder schemas are applied automatically but are under processing constraints and subject to a response filter. The processing constraint might limit each feeder schema to a single application for a set of assumptions, and as a function of a filter its output would not be noticed unless it feeds a subsequent inference. A second possibility is that the reasoning program always looks ahead to seek potential goals—either logical or pragmatic. When a clear goal is discovered, reasoning proceeds towards that goal; when no goal is presented, the core schemas are applied automatically.

As the investigation proceeds, the description of the reasoning routines, as well as of the schemas, will rely on empirical investigation. The basic part of The Model is intended to describe real-time processes, and these should be open to real-time measurement. Brooke Lea, as part of a doctoral dissertation with Martin Braine, investigated the core and feeder schemas, both in logical-reasoning problems and in text comprehension, measuring reaction times to investigate when subjects make these inferences, and I believe that this sort of investigation, among others, is needed to address the matter (see chap. 5).

Pragmatic Principles

That propositions are not identical to their surface-structure expressions is well known among memory and text-comprehension researchers (e.g., Bransford & Franks, 1971; Bransford, Barclay, & Franks, 1972). Likewise, the logical connectives in a mental logic are not identical to the natural-language particles used to express them, although the two should be in close correspondence, so that certain words in a natural language would provide regular ways of expressing certain sorts of propositional connectives, such as the English-language words *and* for conjunction, *or* for disjunction, *not* for negation, and *if* for conditionality.

Natural-language logic particles have meanings that allow people to solve problems and draw inferences. Suppose we are given a problem providing assumptions of the form *if p or q then r* and *p*; we would conclude *r*. Given instead *if p and q then r* and *p*, we would conclude that nothing follows. The two problems differ only in the use of *or* in one problem and *and* in the other, so the difference in responses must be based only on the meanings of these words. Braine and O'Brien (chap. 9) proposed that the basic meaning of a logic particle—its lexical entry—is provided by its basic inference schemas. For example, the basic meaning of *if* is provided by modus ponens and a schema for conditional proof.

The basic meaning of a logic particle, given by the basic schemas, can be extended by *invited inferences*. Geis and Zwicky (1971) provided an example of an invited inference that derives *if not-p then not-q* from *if p then q*. Another example of an invited inference for *if* is found in the pragmatic-reasoning schemas of Cheng and Holyoak (1985), who claimed that modus-tollens inferences are provided by conditionals that express permissions and obligations.

Invited inferences can be encouraged or discouraged by knowledge of the referred intentional state of affairs. For example, the Geis and Zwicky invited inference is encouraged by promissory content, for example, "If you mow the lawn, I'll give you five dollars" invites the listener to infer that "If I don't mow the lawn, I'll not receive the 5 dollars." O'Brien, Costa, and Overton (1986) found that the Geis and Zwicky inference is more likely on problems within a mechanical domain than within a biological domain, where knowledge of spontaneous remissions discourages the invited inference. Staudenmayer (1975) reported that this inference is encouraged when the problems express a causal connection.

Such invited inferences, as supplements to the basic inferences, extend rather than restrict the available inferences. Unlike the basic inferences, invited inferences may or may not be sound. Invited inferences can lead to appropriate responses, as with the pragmatic-reasoning schemas of Cheng and Holyoak (1985), or to logically inappropriate responses, such as those that follow from the invited inference of Geis and Zwicky (1971), and lead to the fallacies of the conditional syllogisms.

An invited inference that is not logically sound, however, is not necessarily irrational. The inference that one will not receive the 5 dollars if the lawn is not mowed is not sanctioned by logic, but is sanctioned by knowledge of the intentional state. Invited inferences are inherently pragmatic because they concern the practical consequences of the considered proposition for its referred intentional state of affairs.

Knowledge of an intentional state of affairs also can suggest alternatives or suppositions to be considered. For example, a mechanic faced with a motor that fails to start might draw on intentional knowledge and infer that the problem is either in the electrical system or the fuel system. If testing the electrical system reveals no problem, the mechanic would conclude that the problem must be with the fuel system. Logical inference schemas and pragmatic sorts of inference-making processes cohabit easily within a single line of reasoning, with the output of one sort of process feeding into the inferences made by the other. Generally, it seems unlikely that an inference is marked for its source—whether the inference stems from a logical inference schema or from intentional knowledge. Although the source of the inference is of interest to a cognitive investigator, there is no reason to think it is important to the mind engaged in the line of reasoning.

Some Evidence for The Model

Direct Evidence. Several studies have provided direct tests of The Model's claim that the core and feeder schemas together with the direct-reasoning routine are readily available. On one type of problem subjects were provided propositions that refer to letters written on an imaginary blackboard, for example, "On the blackboard there is either a T or an X." On another type of problem the propositions refer to boxes containing toy animals and fruits, for example, "In this box there is either a lion or an elephant." Note that these blackboard and box problems present materials that allow subjects to refer the propositions to an intentional state of affairs, although not to one that would provide the necessary inferences for solution on a basis other than the meanings of the logic particles.

The problems in chapter 7 presented assumptions together with conclusions to be evaluated, and The Model predicted successfully which problems were solved correctly, response times on simple problems, and subjects' judgments about relative problem difficulty. Lea et al. (1990), Fisch (1991), O'Brien and Lee (1992), O'Brien, Braine, and Yang (1994), and chapter 8 presented problems with conclusions to be evaluated on which subjects were asked to write down every intermediate inference they drew on the way to evaluating the conclusion, and problems that presented assumptions without any conclusions, on which subjects were asked to write down everything they could infer from the assumptions. On both sorts of problems, The Model predicted successfully which inferences subjects wrote down, and the order in which they were written down. Subjects almost always wrote down the output of the core schemas in the order predicted by the model, but they almost never wrote down the output of the feeder schemas, even though the output of the core schemas often depended on the previous output of the feeder schemas. A few subjects, perhaps responding to the instructions to write down *everything*, wrote down the output of the feeder schemas, and when they did, this output was in the order predicted by The Model.

The inferences that The Model predicts should be made effortlessly and routinely were made routinely and with little apparent effort. These findings are not limited to American undergraduate students. Fisch (1991) found that 9- and 10-year-olds make the basic Model inferences as easily as do adults, and O'Brien and Lee (1992) found the same results when American college students were presented problems in English and Hong Kong college students were presented the same problems in Chinese. Although there may be other inferences also made routinely, those included in The Model appear secure.

In an investigation of The Model's predicted inferences in text comprehension, Lea et al. (1990) and Fisch (1991) presented story vignettes of four or five sentences each, and required subjects to judge whether or not a final sentence makes sense in the context of the story. These judgments required integration of logical information in reading the stories— corresponding to the introduction and elimination inferences of the core and feeder schemas of The Model. The stories were isomorphic in logical form to a parallel set of box and blackboard problems, on which subjects made the inferences predicted by The Model. Almost all subjects made the appropriate judgments on the story vignettes, demonstrating that they must have made the basic logical inferences described by The Model.

Following this, on each story subjects were asked to judge each of three different sorts of statements. One was a paraphrase of information in the story, one was the output of a core inference of The Model, and a third was the output of a valid inference of standard logic but was not predicted by The Model. Subjects were asked whether the information in each of the test sentences was presented in the story or had to be inferred from other information in the story. Whereas the non-Model logical inferences were judged as requiring an inference, both the paraphrase items and the items predicted by the core schemas of The Model were judged as having been presented in the story. Fisch (1991) found that subjects, including 9- and 10-year-olds, judged Model-predicted core items as having been presented in the stories even when these inferences were not required to comprehend the story. Thus, the inferences predicted by The Model are made in text comprehension so effortlessly that neither school children nor adults were aware that they made the inferences.

In sum, people seem to behave in the ways that The Model predicts both on logical-reasoning problems and in text comprehension. The Model successfully predicts which problems subjects solve, the relative perceived difficulty of the solved problems, response times on simple problems, and the order in which inferences are written down. I know of no competing model that has had this sort of empirical success.

Indirect Evidence. The basic schemas should be available across languages and cultures. All natural languages should have regular ways of expressing conjunction, disjunction, conditionality, and negation, corresponding to such English language words as *and, or, if,* and *not.* These words should enter early in language acquisition, and the early usage should be like that of adults. Although no exhaustive search has been made of which I am aware, all of those languages that have been surveyed do have such expressions. Across the half-dozen languages surveyed, *and* and *not* appear in speech in the second year, and *or* and *if* appear in the third year (Bates, 1974; Bloom, Lahey, Hood, Lifter, & Feiss, 1980; Bowerman, 1986; Kuczaj & Daly, 1979; Lust & Mervis, 1980; Pea, 1980; Reilly, 1986). These studies show that early use of these particles is like that of adults, these particles are applied across a wide variety or situations and content from the beginning of their use, and the particles are used in ways that are consistent with the basic schemas of The Model.

A REPLY TO SOME ARGUMENTS AGAINST MENTAL LOGIC

No shortage of reasons have been put forth to deny the existence of a mental logic, and those discussed here are not intended to be exhaustive, but rather to be instructive. One argument against mental logic stems from the failure of most people to solve a variety of laboratory logical-reasoning tasks. Most notable are the algebraic-content versions (i.e., about arbitrary letters, numbers, shapes, colors, etc.) of Wason's selection task and the THOG task, a failure that has been interpreted as an impeachment of mental logic, particularly when compared with successful solution on some meaningful-content versions (e.g., Cheng & Holyoak, 1985; Cosmides, 1989; Griggs & Cox, 1982; Johnson-Laird, Legrenzi, & Legrenzi, 1972).

On Wason's selection task (Wason, 1968) subjects are presented four cards showing, for example, A, D, 4, and 7, respectively. They are told that each card has a letter on one side and a number on the other, and are presented with a conditional rule for the four cards, such as, "If a card has a vowel, then it also has an even number." Finally, they are told that the rule may be true, but could be false, and are asked to select those cards, and only those cards, one would need to turn over for inspection to test the truth status of the rule. Typically, few people are able to select correctly only the cards showing A and 7 (see Evans, 1982, for a review).

Cheng and Holyoak (1985) noted that in some studies up to 20% of subjects can fail to select the card showing A, which they interpret as evidence against the ubiquitous availability of modus ponens. However, consider the line of reasoning that is required to select this card. To solve the problem one begins by supposing that the rule is true. The card showing an A provides a satisfying instance of a vowel, and taken together with the supposition of the rule, by modus ponens it follows that the other side of the card must show an even number. At this point there is still no reason to turn over the card; this realization requires the reasoner now to consider the possibility of there being instead an odd number, in which case the supposition that the rule is true could be falsified by reductio ad absurdum, because there might be an odd number where there has to be an even number. Note, then, that selection of the card showing an A goes well beyond making a modus-ponens inference. Indeed, it exceeds the basic skills of The Model. The other potentially falsifying card, showing the number 7, requires an even more complex line of reasoning, with an additional reductio embedded under the original supposition of the rule.

With the exception of Piaget (see Beth & Piaget, 1966, p. 181, which seems to indicate that the selection task should be solvable), none of the theories of mental logic predicts that such problems will be solved, and the basic parts of The Model, including the core and feeder schemas together with the direct-reasoning routine, are nowhere near being sufficient to solve such problems. Thus, failure to solve these complex problems does not count as evidence against The Model.

The literature now includes an algebraic-content version of the selection task that many subjects solve (Griggs, 1989). This problem presents four cards drawn from two decks of ordinary playing cards, one deck with red backs and the other with blue backs. The rule states that "If a card has a value greater than 6, then it must have a blue back." Perhaps subjects perform better on this task version because they can anticipate more easily what might be on the other side of the card. Whatever the reason, these correct responses are difficult to explain unless one assumes some logical reasoning.

Another complex logical reasoning problem that few people are able to solve is the THOG task (Wason & Brooks, 1979), and its solution also requires a reasoning strategy that goes will beyond the basic parts of The Model. Recently, several versions of the THOG task have been reported that many people solve (Girotto & Legrenzi, 1989; O'Brien, Noveck, et al., 1990). None of these task versions seem solvable by nonlogical means, and the finding that some algebraic-content versions of the selection and THOG tasks can be solved indicates that many adults have developed considerable logical-reasoning skills that go well beyond the core and feeder schemas and the direct reasoning program of The Model.

I discuss the claim that some realistic-content versions of the selection task have led to successful solution later in this chapter. For now I limit my comments to how we should interpret the effects of content on reasoning. Cheng and Holyoak (1989) stated that "content effects cannot be explained by theories based solely on formal rules" (p. 286), and I agree. Likewise, theories based entirely on content-bound processes cannot explain success on algebraic-content problems, such as the box and blackboard problems discussed earlier. This is why I advocate the three-part theory. A finding of a content effect presents no problem for The Model, because it does not claim exclusivity for the logical inference schemas. The reason that some algebraic-content problems are more difficult than their realistic-content isomorphs is that the algebraic-content versions are intentionally impoverished—they do not readily evoke an understandable state of affairs and are disconnected from the ordinary concerns of propositional activities.

Not all errors on laboratory logical-reasoning tasks are made on complex problems. For example, on the same problem sets on which subjects (both adults and children) routinely make modus-ponens inferences, they also often commit the denial-of-the-antecedent fallacy. For example, Rumain, Connell, and Braine (1983) reported that given the assumptions "If there is a dog in the box, then there is an apple" and "There is a dog in the box," people almost always conclude "There is an apple," an inference that follows straightforwardly by modus ponens. When given the same first assumption, but with "There is not a dog in the box" as a second premise, many people erroneously accept "There is not an apple." This fallacy disappears, however, when (a) the asymmetry of the conditional is made explicit, for example, "If there is a dog in the box then there is an apple, but if there is not a dog, there may or may not be an apple," and (b) when an additional conditional assumption is provided, for example, "If there is a lion in the box, there is an apple" (see also Markovits, 1984, 1985). Inference-schema theorists, such as Rumain and colleagues, have interpreted the finding that such fallacies can be suppressed as indicating that the fallacies are invited rather than basic inferences.[2]

An additional empirical argument against mental logic concerns the demonstrated effects of a variety of nonlogical heuristics, most notably the use of matching (e.g., Evans, 1982; Evans & Lynch, 1973). The matching hypothesis holds that many responses on a variety of logical-reasoning tasks are merely matches to the values named in the task's rule, for example, selecting the cards showing a vowel and an even number in the original selection task. Some empirical evidence has been reported that supports the claim, particularly the manipulation of negatives with the selection task. However, the matching hypothesis has not yet been worked out in sufficient detail so that its predictions are always apparent. Although there is agreement concerning the matching-hypothesis predictions for the selection task, this is not so for the THOG task. The problem presents four designs—a black triangle, a white triangle, a black circle, and a white circle. Subjects are told that the experimenter has written down one of the shapes and one of the colors, and that any design is a THOG if, and only if, it has either the shape or the color written down, but not both. Told that the black triangle is a THOG, subjects are asked to classify each of the remaining designs as (a) definitely a THOG, (b) insufficient information to decide, or (c) definitely not a THOG. Responses predominantly fall into two erroneous response patterns: Pattern A, in which the white triangle and the black circle are judged as possible THOGs and the white circle is judged as definitely not a THOG; and Pattern B, in which the white triangle and the black circle are judged THOGs and the white circle is judged as definitely not a THOG. Evans (1982) used the matching hypothesis to account for Pattern A, whereas Griggs and Newstead (1983) and Girotto and Legrenzi (1989) claimed that the matching hypothesis predicts Pattern B. To date, then, the matching hypothesis has not been described in sufficient detail to know what its predictions are. Griggs and Newstead, and Girotto and Legrenzi took a strong view of matching, and assume that subjects are matching without using any logical resources. Evans, though, described a situation in which subjects use both the matching heuristic and some logical processes.

Evans and I are in agreement on an essential point—human reasoning consists both of logical and nonlogical processes. We differ, though, in

---

[2]The original version of this chapter included at this point a discussion of the claim made by Byrne (1989) that modus-ponens inferences can be suppressed. This discussion now is presented in an expanded form in chapter 15.

emphasis. In Evans's view, problems are first processed by nonlogical heuristics, which are sufficiently primitive that our fairly weak logical resources are rarely of much use. Indeed, Evans sees such little use for a mental logic that he has not described what he thinks it includes. From the perspective of mental logic, I see people using logic frequently, both in ordinary tasks and in laboratory-reasoning tasks. When mental logic can be applied straightforwardly, it will be. When the reasoner has available the strategic skills required to solve a complex problem, and grasps the problem's requirements, mental logic will allow solution. Otherwise, the problem solver has no other recourse but to nonlogical heuristics or to pragmatic inferences.

Finally, I consider the conceptual question raised by Johnson-Laird (1983): Which logic do we propose is the appropriate model for a mental logic? After all, infinitely many possible logic systems for quantifiers and modal operators could be constructed. Part of the answer is intuitive. I assume a two-valued logic of truth and falsity rather than a three-valued logic. Esoteric logical systems are just that: esoteric. As to which schemas for a two-valued logic should be included, I think this an empirical question—those that are easily expressible across languages, that people make readily, and that appear early in language acquisition should be included. Unlike some theories, the inference-schema models make a wide variety of specific empirical predictions that can be tested and compared, and the appropriate specific features will emerge from experimental investigations motivated by the existing models.

COMPETING NONLOGICAL THEORIES HAVE THEIR OWN PROBLEMS

This section is not meant to provide an exhaustive review of the competing nonlogical theories. First I address the content-bound theories proposed by Cosmides (1989) and by Cheng and Holyoak (1985), and then the mental-models approach of Johnson-Laird (1983) and Johnson-Laird and Byrne (1991).

Content-Bound Theories

Cheng and Holyoak (1985, 1989), Cheng, Holyoak, Nisbett, and Oliver (1986), and Holland, Holyoak, Nisbett, and Thagard (1986) proposed that people reason typically not using logical inference schemas, but using inductively learned rules defined in terms of classes of goals, such as taking desirable actions or predicting future events. Thus far, their theory has described only two rules, one for permission and one for obligation.

The permission rule holds that: If the action is to be taken, then the prerequisite must be fulfilled.

Cosmides (1989) also argued that people rarely reason "according to the canons of logic" (p. 191), and proposed that because 99% of human bioevolutionary history has consisted of hunter/gatherer activities, our biological endowment includes special abilities to reason about social contracts and their associated costs and benefits. These social contracts have a conditional form: If one takes a benefit then one must pay the cost. Social-contract rules appear to be a subset of permission/obligation rules (paying a cost is a special case of fulfilling a prerequisite, and taking a benefit is a special case of taking an action). Thus, supporting evidence for the social-contract theory would also be supporting evidence for the pragmatic-schemas theory. Cosmides would need to show that only problems presenting social-contract rules are solved, and the larger class of other permission/obligation problems are not. This does not seem to be the case. Pollard (1990), Cheng and Holyoak (1989), and Manktelow and Over (1990) showed that subjects are not influenced by the degree of costs or benefits, and that subjects can solve some permission task versions that have neither perceivable costs nor benefits.

The empirical evidence both for the social-contract and for the pragmatic-reasoning-schemas theories thus far has been limited to performance on some quasi selection-task versions, such as the "Drinking-Age Problem" introduced by Griggs and Cox (1982). The subject is told to imagine being a policeman enforcing the rule that "If a person is drinking alcohol, that person must be at least 21 years old." Four cards are presented, each with a person's age on one side, and their beverage on the other. Subjects are instructed to turn over those cards, and only those cards, that might lead to the discovery of a rule violator. Most people are able to select the logically appropriate cards (the card showing someone who is underage and the card showing an alcoholic beverage).

Note that the realistic-content versions of the selection task that have led to solution, such as the "Drinking-Age Problem," are structurally distinct from the selection task. On the pragmatic-schemas problems, the rule is assumed true and can be used directly to draw a conclusion. This is not a trivial difference, because the original selection task is a meta-logical rather than a logical reasoning problem. After all, the title of Wason's (1968) seminal paper was "Reasoning About a Rule," not "Reasoning From a Rule." On these quasi-selection tasks, the need to turn over the card corresponding to A in the original task follows straightforwardly by modus ponens. The problem is inherently easier.

The most impressive evidence for the pragmatic-reasoning-schemas theory has been Cheng and Holyoak's (1985) abstract permission problem. On this problem subjects are told to imagine that they are working in a company enforcing the rule, "If a person takes Action A, then that person must first fulfill Prerequisite P." The four cards show: "has taken Action A," "has not taken Action A," "has fulfilled Prerequisite P," and "has not fulfilled Prerequisite P." This problem differs from the original selection task in three crucial ways: First, it requires a search for a rule violator rather than a test of the rule's truth status. Second, it presents what Jackson and Griggs (1990) referred to as *a checking context*, that is, subjects are asked to assume the role of a rule enforcer. Third, the cards present explicit rather than implicit negatives—"has not taken Action A," rather than the card showing D. Jackson and Griggs found that when any of these three task features are changed to parallel the original task, subjects fail to solve the abstract-permission problem. Recently, in work with Ira Noveck and with two undergraduate students at Baruch College, I have found non-pragmatic algebraic versions that include these three crucial features and that many people are able to solve. It may be that solution of the abstract-permission problem has nothing to do with the permissionary nature of the rules but stems from these other extraneous task features.

I agree with Cosmides that our reasoning skills are the result of our bioevolutionary history, but this history has provided us with some basic logical intuitions that make propositional language and reasoning possible. I see no a priori reason that evolution should provide domain-specific processes but not general processes. Species with overly specified behavioral traits are at an evolutionary disadvantage when their environmental situation changes. A set of content-free inference procedures would be of evolutionary benefit, providing a basis for logic particles that allow communication in a wide variety of situations. To the extent that people have some content-bound inference procedures, they coexist with a set of more general logical inference procedures.

Mental Models

Johnson-Laird (1983) and Johnson-Laird and Byrne (1991) proposed that when people process discourse, they construct internal representations, called *mental models*. Inferences are drawn from models by describing information explicitly represented in them. Reasoning consists of searching for alternative models that could falsify a tentative conclusion. Whereas the mental-logic approach does not claim exclusivity, the mental-models approach claims that it can account for all reasoning, and that people never use inference schemas of the sort in The Model.

Johnson-Laird and his colleagues have not provided a clear description of what a mental model is. Mental models can be images but clearly are intended to go beyond images. As was discussed earlier, images are not propositional, and unlike propositions, mental models do not include variables. The elements of a mental model always refer to specific instances.

This absence of variables in mental models leads to a representational confusion.

Early versions of the theory represented the universally quantified *all p are q* as:

(1) $p = q$
     $p = q$
       (q),

where each line in the model represents an individual case. The parenthetical term in line 3 represents an optional instance of q without p. The problem with the representation in this model is that it fails to capture the universality of *all p are q*. How does one know that other possible instances that could be added to the model fit this pattern? Johnson-Laird and Byrne (1991) seem to have recognized this problem, and proposed the following model instead:

(2) $[p]$ q
     $[p]$ q
      $\cdots$,

where the square bracket notation is an exhaustivity tag. The third line is an ellipsis that functions as a reminder that there might be other model interpretations that have not been considered, but the exhaustivity of p in lines 1 and 2 means that any "fleshing out" of the ellipsis cannot include a p. A fully explicit model can be fleshed out as follows:

(3) $[p]$ $[q]$
     $[p]$ $[q]$
     $[\sim p]$ $[q]$
     $[\sim p]$ $[\sim q]$,

which includes a "propositional-like tag representing negation" (Johnson-Laird & Byrne, 1991, p. 44). So, mental-model representations are not propositional but contain propositional-like tags; they do not contain variables but can attach individual cases with an exhaustivity tag to constrain all other possible cases.[3]

---

[3]The model in (3) is identical to the fully "fleshed out" representation for the simple conditional (*if p then q*), except for the redundancy of lines 1 and 2. Thus, the representation of *if p then q* is equivalent to (3) without line 1. However, Johnson-Laird and Byrne (1991) referred to the representation of *if p then q* as containing three models instead of one model, as with the representation for *all p are q*. At the least this seems notationally weak. How does the mind holding (3) know that it is universal solely because of the redundancy of lines 1 and 2, and how does the mind holding the fully "fleshed out" counterpart for *if p then q* know that it contains three models, whereas (3) contains only one?

This attempt at solving the problem of variables has not been successful. Suppose we ask someone to judge the truth or falsity of "All natural
numbers that end in zero are divisible by five." What would the representation of [p] in (3) become? It could not be [a natural number that ends
in zero], because this expresses a variable, and the elements in a mental
model must refer to individual cases. So suppose [p] in line 1 is represented as [20] and in line 2 as [5970]; in other words, we choose some
positive exemplars randomly. The representation of [q] in lines 1, 2, and
3 presumably would be [divisible by 5]. How, then, does one know that
all natural numbers ending in 0 are divisible by 5? To know that 5970 is
divisible by 5 requires more than reading the model—it requires a computation (unless, of course, the proposition is more primitive than the
model). A rigorous proof that all such numbers have this property requires
a complex line of propositional reasoning that refers to variables.

The propositional-like tag for negation also strikes me as problematic;
representation of negative instances has been a well-known difficulty since
the concept-attainment work of Bruner, Goodnow, and Austin (1956). My
intuition is that negations are represented propositionally, and the propositional activities associated with them are consistent with the inference
schemas for *not*.

In sum, there are many sorts of propositions that are difficult, if not
impossible, to represent with a mental model. Thus, there is a clear need
for some representational and inference processes other than those provided by mental models. I make no claim that people never use mental
models—only that inferences from mental models would cohabit with
inferences from other sources, including those of a mental logic. I do not
think, though, that Johnson-Laird and his associates provided an adequate
account of what such mental models would be, and their introduction of
propositional-like tags suggests that part of a mental-models theory
should be a propositional mental logic.[4]

IRRATIONALITY AND THE MODEL

Both the content-bound theories of Cosmides (1989) and Cheng and
Holyoak (1985) and the mental-models theory of Johnson-Laird and his
colleagues have framed the debate in terms of an exclusive disjunction:
People use only social-contract rules or only the canons of logic; they use
only pragmatic-reasoning schemas or only content-free formal rules; they
use only mental models or only formal rules. Thus, when these theorists

---

[4]Additional criticisms of the theory of mental models are provided in Ford (1985), Rips
(1986), and several other chapters in this volume.

find support for their accounts, they conclude that people do not use logical inference schemas. Such arguments against theories that rely only on formal content-free inference rules are straw-man arguments. Mental-logic theorists have never claimed exclusivity. Even Piaget thought that formal-operational skills are constrained by real-world knowledge. The mental-logic approach does not claim that all of human reasoning is described by some content-free formal rules. To the contrary, a mental logic is what makes reasoning propositional, and propositions refer to intentional states of affairs. Thus, the inference schemas of a mental logic cohabit easily with pragmatic reasoning processes having to do with the practical consequences of propositions for their referred states of affairs. Evidence for some effects of extralogical processes is not inconsistent with the claims of the mental-logic approach.

That people make errors on some reasoning tasks is not a sufficient reason to proclaim the absence of any mental logic. Given the explanatory value of a mental logic, particularly a model that has generated a variety of empirical support, the obituaries are hasty and ill advised. Just as the grammatically untutored might be surprised to learn that they had been using nouns and verbs all of their lives, the nonlogical theorists will be surprised to discover that they have been using a mental logic all along.

A mental logic provides the basis for rational judgments but does not ensure them. Mental logic provides the experience of deductive certainty that often accompanies a logical inference, and leads people to seek consistency among the propositions they assume. Even rationalization is rational in its intent, which is to maintain a consistent set of propositions. When people are irrational, it is not because they lack a mental logic but because the demands of the situation exceed their logic skills, because inferences from nonlogical sources are made, or because they are reasoning from irrational assumptions.

Consistent failure of someone to accept such basic inferences as modus ponens, disjunction elimination, and cancellation of a double negative would make that person irrational. Without such inferences, a person could not maintain the soundness of a line of thought. Accepting a modus ponens inference, however, is not enough to make one rational; many deluded residents of mental hospitals make such inferences routinely. When one applies sound inference procedures to an irrational set of assumptions, one is apt to draw irrational conclusions.

Reasoning can be done skillfully or clumsily, and, as with any skill, practice, coaching, and a joy for the activity can improve the level of skill. A mental logic provides the basis for sound logical reasoning, but does not guarantee skilled play.

How to Investigate Mental Logic and the Syntax of Thought*

Martin D. S. Braine
New York University

David P. O'Brien
Baruch College and the Graduate School
of the City University of New York

Before considering ways of empirically investigating what is in the mental logic, it seems a necessary preliminary, in order to avoid seeming to presuppose what should be argued, that we discuss reasons why it is plausible to expect there to be a mental logic in the first place, and what sort of mental logic those reasons should lead one to expect. So we begin with these sorts of preliminaries, and they will, we hope, situate the concept of a mental logic in a theoretical framework within which it makes sense—one that includes the notion of an innate syntax of thought.

In the second section of the chapter we turn to the main questions of the chapter: How could one determine empirically of what the mental logic consists, and what does the available evidence have to say about it? How could one investigate the syntax of thought? The latter question takes us, in the final section of the chapter, into a discussion of the view of language acquisition as including the learning of a mapping of the grammar of a language onto the syntax of thought.

PRELIMINARIES

We begin by making three points about mental logic:

*This chapter is a revision and expansion of M. D. S. Braine (1994). Mental logic and how to discover it. In J. Macnamara and G. E. Reyes (Eds.), *The Logical Foundations of Cognition*. New York: Oxford University Press. Reprinted with permission of Oxford University Press.

(1) Why should a mental logic exist? Why should it have evolved? One answer is that it is needed to serve pragmatic goals. That is, we propose that one reason the human species evolved a mental logic was to serve purely practical purposes, to make inferences about things and events of immediate concern. Let us illustrate this interdigitation of logic and pragmatics in the service of practical goals.

Table 4.1 shows two story vignettes from among some that we have considered using in experiments on reasoning in text comprehension. Consider the first test question on the first story—did John get a free cola? Evidently, the answer is "no," but why? Knowledge of restaurant menus tells you that the *or* in *free cola or coffee* should be taken to imply "not both"—you get only one free drink, and if you want the other you have to pay for it. Later, the story says that John chose coffee. Given the premises *not both free cola and free coffee* and *free coffee, not free cola* follows by logical inference. Thus the answer to the question is given by a pragmatic inference (that one does not get both a free cola and a free coffee) feeding a strictly logical one (*not both free cola and free coffee, coffee, ∴ not cola*). To Question (b) the answer is evidently "no." Presumably, based on pragmatic knowledge that food and beverage items are not free in restaurants unless explicitly offered as such by the menu or waiter, the reader constructs a conditional *free red wine only if minute steak*; because we are told that John chose soup and salad, which pragmatically entails that he did not choose minute steak, we conclude by logical inference that he did not get a free glass of red wine. Again, the answer comes from an interdigitation of logical inference and pragmatic knowledge.

The second story provides another illustration of the same theme. In response to (a), obviously, Alice did sit down at a table; we know that because we know that coffee shops typically offer only two places to sit

TABLE 4.1
Integrating Logic and Pragmatics:
Sample Texts and Comprehension Questions

John went in for lunch. The menu showed a soup'n salad special, with free cola or coffee. Also, with the minute steak you got a free glass of red wine. John chose the soup'n salad special with coffee, along with something else to drink. . . .
   (a) John got a free cola? (Yes, No, Can't tell)
   (b) John got a free glass of red wine? (Yes, No, Can't tell)

There had been a light drizzle all day Saturday. Alice had spent the afternoon shopping and was feeling rather hungry, tired, and irritable. She went into a coffee shop for some sustenance, including, particularly, some coffee. The counter was full. She sat down and ordered. Later, feeling rejuvenated, she sallied forth into the street with determination. . . .
   (a) Alice sat down at a table? (Yes, No, Can't tell)
   (b) Alice ordered tea? (Yes, No, Can't tell)

---

down—counter and table; because the counter was full, it is a logical inference that she sat down at a table (*counter or table, not counter, ∴ table*). In response to (b), we can infer that she did not have tea because we know that people essentially never order *both* tea and coffee (*not both tea and coffee, coffee, ∴ not tea*). In both cases there is a smooth combination of logical and pragmatic inferences.

We have argued that one reason the mental logic evolved was to serve the practical goal of integrating information coming in at different times, or from different sources, drawing inferences that go beyond the information as given (Braine, 1990; O'Brien, 1993). For instance, one learns *P or Q* from one source and *not Q* from another; an intelligent being needs some mental mechanism that will integrate these pieces of information by inferring *P*; the mental logic satisfies the need. The mental logic is also involved in the comprehension of discourse and text. Some recent work (see chap. 5) suggests that it provides a set of inferences that are routinely made to integrate information from different propositions of a text. The routine role of the mental logic in comprehension has been independently argued by Sperber and Wilson (1986), who propose a psychological and pragmatic framework within which it operates in comprehension. Because it serves practical goals, the mental logic is deeply embedded within a pragmatically motivated architecture, and inferences are regularly drawn from information that includes knowledge retrieved from long-term memory, beliefs, opinions, guesses, and various kinds of implicatures. Logical inferences reside comfortably in a line of reasoning with analogical, causal, pragmatic, and probabilistic ones.

(2) The second point to be made about a mental logic is that among people who have considered the idea of it (e.g., Braine, 1978, 1990; Johnson-Laird, 1975; O'Brien, 1981; Osherson, 1975a, 1975b; Rips, 1983; Sperber & Wilson, 1986), there is a consensus that the mental logic must consist of a set of inference schemas together with some sort of basic program for applying them, that is, some sort of natural deduction system. The basic program would operate routinely in practical reasoning and discourse comprehension and be the first stage of processing in reasoning of a more formal sort.

(3) The concept of a mental logic is intimately connected to the concept of a language of thought. There are two reasons for this. First, to represent inference schemas, some system of representation is needed. It is then natural to assume that the reasoner translates from natural language statements into this representational system, and then reasons in this syntax or language of thought. The second and ultimately more important reason is that some sort of innate format for representing knowledge would seem to be a precondition for memory, at least for declarative (propositional) memory: For a child to be able to record knowledge about

the world in memory, there must be some format available for representing that knowledge—if there is no format for recording something, there is no way to record it. Now, to be adequate to the task of recording information in memory, the format would need some logical structure. For example, it would need some kind of predicate-argument structure in order to distinguish properties from the entities remembered to have the properties, and relations from the objects noticed to be related. Presumably, too, it would have to be able to represent conjunction, negation, and disjunction, because memory will sometimes need to record that two properties are present, or that an expected property is absent, or that two things are alternatives. One can think of other logical structures that would be needed also, for example, quantifying and referring devices.

These arguments are some of those that Fodor (1975) presented for an innate language of thought and are similar to some of Macnamara's (1986). Because the format is innate, the essential parts of the representational system for inferences would be universal, and so there is every reason to expect that an inference form that is easy in one language will be available and easy in another language. The inevitability of the existence of an innate information format with some logical structure provides an important additional reason, over and above the one given earlier, for expecting there to be a mental logic. Because of the fundamental nature of this mental logic, we have elsewhere referred to it as "natural" logic (e.g., Braine, 1978, 1990; chap. 7).[1]

In speaking of a *language of thought*, we do not intend commitment to all Fodor's ideas on the subject—in particular, not to his claim that the content predicates of the language of thought are innate. For an answer to Fodor's arguments for the innateness of most content predicates, and for a promising solution to the difficulties of a compositional approach to lexical meaning, see Jackendoff (1989, 1990). Actually, Fodor had very little to say about the syntax of the language of thought, although it is its syntax that defines it as a system of representation and in which its logical properties are embodied. For our purposes, we can usefully distinguish *syntax of thought* from *language of thought*.

Indeed, one can contrast two language-of-thought concepts. One is Fodor's, in which essentially everything is innate. In the other, the language of thought would be partially innate and partially acquired. The syntax would be innate; this is the innate format for representing knowledge referred to earlier, and the mental logic would be implicit in it; we may refer to this as the *syntax of thought*. The content predicates would be the acquired part. Thus, the partially acquired language of thought would comprise the

---

[1]Thus it is, of course, to be distinguished from logic learned in logic courses, or from logic textbooks, or from other such sources.

innate syntax with the acquired content predicates. This language of thought would be language specific in part, and would correspond to the level of semantic representation in studies of semantic structure like those of Jackendoff (1983, 1990). One additional complexity has to be noted, however: Content predicates can have complex internal structure, and the possible formats for constructing complex predicates would be universal and innate, and are best regarded as part of the syntax of thought. (An example of complex-predicate syntax is given later.) The language-of-thought concept presumed in this book is not Fodor's, but rather this second one, in which the language of thought is partially acquired.

DISCOVERING THE MENTAL LOGIC
AND THE SYNTAX OF THOUGHT

To turn to the main issue, the nature of the mental logic and the syntax of thought, we can see three empirical routes that could contribute information about them. The first route is through reasoning, and it focuses most directly on the basic inference forms and representational system of the mental logic. The second is through universals of language, and the third is through what is semantically and syntactically most primitive in language acquisition; both of the latter two focus on the syntax of thought, that is, on the nature of the representational system, more directly than on inference. We discuss each in turn, the first two in this section and the third, at greater length, in the last main section of the chapter.

The Approach Through Reasoning

Traditionally, most work on logical reasoning has focused on reasoning error, as if it were error rather than correct reasoning that required study and explanation. The notion of a mental logic involves a reversal of focus—towards identifying the forms of inference that people make easily and correctly. The approach through the study of reasoning has developed a general methodology, although the empirical work has until now focused almost exclusively on the mental propositional logic (however, see chap. 12). Methodologically, the concept of a mental logic prescribes that the basic inference schemas of the logic should have certain properties. Empirical work can then proceed to identify the inferences that have these properties. A natural logic based on inference schemas entails that there is a set of logically sound schemas, each of which has the following properties:

   1. Each schema is psychologically valid: Subjects use it essentially errorlessly on maximally simple problems that could be solved using it.

2. Each schema is psychologically elementary: The inference it defines is made in a single step, not as the end product of a chain of inferences. (See chaps. 7, 8, and 12 for illustration of methods of obtaining evidence relevant to elementariness.)

3. Each schema is psychologically primitive—available early to children.

4. Each schema is universal: It has Properties 1 to 3 in all cultures and languages. In addition, the set of schemas as a whole should have properties that warrant it being called a *logic* (e.g., an interesting relation to some standard system). Finally, there should be a simple routine for applying the schemas that is an integral part of ordinary text and discourse comprehension, and the first step in reasoning.

Let us consider whether there is evidence for each of these properties. The evidence is most ample for propositional logic, which we consider first, though incomplete even for that. For the propositional logic, there is a set of schemas for which Property 1 has been demonstrated and for which Property 2 is arguable on the basis of a mixture of experimental evidence and commonsensical argument (see chaps. 7, 8, and 12). With respect to Property 3, there is a substantial amount of evidence, but with lacunae (see chap. 10); and Property 4 has not been directly investigated. We return to Properties 3 and 4 shortly. Also, we think it will be clear to anyone who inspects it that the propositional model as a whole (see chap. 6) warrants being called a *logic*, as is the case for the predicate logic in chapter 11. Finally, for evidence and argument that subjects have a simple routine for applying the schemas, used both in reasoning problems and in text comprehension, see chapters 5, 7, 8, and 12, and Fisch (1991).

We will say a little more about Properties 3 and 4. English *or* and *if*, and their translation equivalents in the approximately half-dozen other languages investigated, appear fairly early in development, typically during the third year; *and* and negation appear even earlier (e.g., Bates, 1974; Bloom, Lahey, Hood, Lifter, & Fiess, 1980; Bowerman, 1986; Kuczaj & Daly, 1979; Lust & Mervis, 1980; Pea, 1980). When they appear they are almost always used in a semantically appropriate way, suggesting that children have an early grasp of their meaning. What is the nature of the meaning grasped? There are two potential ways in which the meaning of a connective might be specified: One is by the inferences that it sanctions; the other is by truth conditions. There are several reasons for thinking that the meaning is more likely to be given by inferences than by truth conditions. First, there is little evidence for the use of truth conditions in studies of deductive reasoning (e.g., Braine & Rumain, 1983; Osherson, 1975a) but plenty of evidence for inference schemas (e.g., chaps. 7 and 8; Braine & Rumain, 1983; Osherson, 1974, 1975b, 1976; Rips, 1983,

1994). Fisch (1991), using problems of the type used in the work with adults, found that the basic model accounted well for the responses generated by 10-year-olds; however, he did not test younger children. The testing methods he used with adults and older children are not appropriate for preschool children. Using methods like those used with adults (but with modifications to assist retention of premises), Braine and Rumain (1981) tested for Schemas 3, 4, 6, 7, and 9 in children as young as 5 to 6 years and found evidence for them. Second, there is an intuitively clearer relation of connective meaning to inference. Thus, there are intuitively tight correspondences between the meanings of particular connectives and particular inference schemas; these are such that if someone were not able to make the inferences, one would be inclined to say that they did not understand the connective. For instance, consider *if* and modus ponens.[2] If someone did not understand that the consequent of an *if-then* statement has to be true if the *if*-clause is fulfilled, one would judge that he or she did not understand *if*. *Or* is similarly related to certain inference schemas, the most obvious being the schema: p or q; not-p / $\therefore$ q. Here again, one would be much inclined to say that someone did not understand *or* if he or she did not understand that when there are only two alternatives and one of them is found not to hold, then the other must hold. The relation of meaning to truth conditions is more opaque. For *if*, people notoriously do not make truth judgments that conform to the standard truth table of the conditional; moreover, those judgments that they do make easily are just the ones that are easy to make by short chains of inference (chaps. 7 and 8).[3] In the case of *or*, children show competence at making standard inferences before they are able to make sensible truth judgments (Braine & Rumain, 1981). Finally, there is direct evidence for spontaneous conditional inference in the conversations of preschool children (Scholnick & Wing, 1991). See chapter 10 for extensive further evidence on development.

On Property 4, we know of no specific survey of languages, but the well-known languages of Europe and Asia appear to have connectives that are at least approximately equivalent to *and*, *or*, and *if*. Negation can be presumed to be universal, even if only because work on universals (e.g., Comrie, 1989) would have found room for comment if someone had found a language without it (which is hard to imagine). Comrie (1986) discussed the typology of conditionals across languages; he presumed that all languages have them but finds variation in the formal devices used to signal conditionality. As noted earlier, the connectives translating

---

[2]Modus ponens is the inference form: *If p then q; p $\therefore$ q.*

[3]For example, the judgment that an *if*-statement (*if A then B*) is false, given that the antecedent is true and the consequent false, is easy to make because applying modus ponens (from *if A then B* and *A*, one deduces *B*) leads immediately to a contradiction (*B & not-B*).

or and *if* appear early in the development of children in the languages investigated, just as they do in English, and conjunction and negation also appear early. In sum, although much investigation remains to be done, the existence of similar early-developing connectives in unrelated languages, taken with the great frequency of such connectives across languages, is certainly consistent with the notion of a universal mental propositional logic and may be hard to explain otherwise.

In addition to mental propositional logic, there must be other mental logics, for example, predicate and modal logics. Chapter 11 presents a hypothesis for a tentative mental predicate logic. Rips (1994) also presented a mental predicate logic. Progress has been more difficult here, in part because to state inference schemas for a predicate logic requires a complex representational system, whereas stating schemas for a propositional logic makes few demands on a representational system. For a propositional logic all one needs are connectives and variables for propositions, whereas a mental predicate logic requires one to make difficult assumptions about the internal structure of propositions in the syntax of the language of thought. For precisely this reason, developing a mental predicate logic that fits reasoning data well provides a way of empirically investigating important aspects of the syntax of thought, especially the issue of how quantifiers and quantifier scope differences are represented. See chapter 11 for further discussion, and chapter 12 for some preliminary evidence on fit to reasoning data.

There is evidence that important aspects of the mental-predicate logic are developmentally very primitive. First, grammatical devices that are the natural language analogs of existential instantiation are available quite early in children. We have in mind the use of pronouns and definite NPs that have indefinite NPs as their antecedents ("I saw a man yesterday. HE/THE MAN . . ."). Such pronouns and definite NPs are in effect discourse names for existentially instantiated objects, and they are present in the speech of most 3-year-olds (e.g., Maratsos, 1974).

Second, there are reasons for thinking that the concept "all" is available early to children. For instance, it is one of the very few logical notions that Piaget (Inhelder & Piaget, 1964) accepts as available preoperationally. Also, reasoning of the form "All A are F, *x* is an A, so *x* is an F" can be elicited easily in 5-year-olds (Harris, 1975; Smith, 1979). The use of *all*, on the one hand, and *each* or *every* on the other, often indicates quantifier scope; for instance, the following sentences (due to Ioup, 1975) are ambiguous but the preferred readings in each pair differ in the scope of the universal quantifier:

1. (a) I saw a picture of each child versus (b) I saw a picture of all the children.

2. (a) Ethel has a dress for every occasion versus (b) Ethel has a dress for all occasions.

Ioup found that the 14 languages she examined all had expressions corresponding to the English *all* and *each/every* and that they differentiated the scope of the universal quantifier in the same way as these. She proposed that this property is universal. Surprisingly, she found no basis for a universal tendency for the left-most quantifier to have outside scope. Recently, Kurtzman and MacDonald (1993) found that even for English, the surface order of quantifiers has no consistent effect on scope. Such findings suggest that the syntax of thought does not indicate scope by ordering quantifiers in positions outside the sentence nucleus in the way that standard logic does. Note that the differences between the preferred readings of the (a) and (b) sentences in 1 and 2 have to do with inference as well as syntax, that is, with permissible instantiations. In 1b (but not 1a) we can allow *a picture* to be the antecedent of the pronoun *it* used in a subsequent sentence, and similarly for *a dress* in 2b (but not for the same expression in 2a): Otherwise said, the (b) sentences permit immediate existential instantiations on their indefinite noun phrases, whereas the (a) sentences do not. In contrast, the (a) sentences allow immediate instantiation on the phrase containing *each/every*: If George is one of the children and the mayor's garden party one of the occasions, then we can immediately infer *I saw a picture of George* from 1a and *Ethel has a dress for the mayor's garden party* from 2a. For the (b) sentences, the same inference is either dubious (1b) or liable to mislead unless qualified (2b); for example, for 2b, one might countermand the misleading implicature (that Ethel has a dress special to the garden party) by expressing the inference in some form like *Ethel has a dress for the mayor's garden party—her usual all-purpose one*.

In recent work, Brooks (1993; Brooks & Braine, 1996) investigated children's understanding of the difference between *all* and *each*. On each trial of one experiment, subjects were presented with three pictures and a sentence, and they had to say which picture went best with the sentence. One picture was always a "group" picture, for example, three men carrying a box between them with two other boxes lying on the ground; another was a "distributed" picture, for example, three men each carrying a box, with two boxes again lying on the ground; the third was a "global" picture, for example, two men each carrying two boxes, a third man carrying one box, and no boxes left over. The sentence presented was either of the form *All the X's are verb-ing a Y* (e.g., *All the men are carrying a box*), or of the form *Each X is verb-ing a Y*, or *The X's are verb-ing the Y's*. (The same three pictures were never used with more than one sentence.) Children 6 years and older reliably chose distributed pictures for *each*-sentences, and the global picture for the sentence with two definite plural noun phrases; they were more catholic for *all*-sentences but preferred the group picture. In two other languages investigated (Portuguese and Chinese), the nearest translation equivalents of *all* and *each* were found to be similarly associated with group and distributed representations, respectively, usually beginning at a younger age than in the English data, and with a stronger association of *all* with the group representation than in the English data (Brooks, Braine, Jia, & Dias, in press). Thus, from at least 6 years of age and onwards, children have some grasp of the semantic distinction between *all* and *each*, and can differentiate their canonical semantic representations from the global representation. It was hypothesized that the innate syntax of thought makes the distinction between canonical group and distributed representations available early; what a child has to learn is to associate them preferentially with the words *all* and *each* (or whatever the equivalent expressions are in the child's own language).

In sum, a number of phenomena corresponding to existential quantification and instantiation, universal quantification and instantiation, and quantifier scope are very widespread in natural languages and may well be universal, and these same phenomena are demonstrable early in child development. By the same token, epistemic and modal notions are certainly also very widespread and probably universal, and where they have been investigated they appear early in children's language (see contributions to Slobin, 1985, 1992). We take these facts as evidence that there are predicate and modal logics for which Properties (c) and (d)—and therefore, a fortiori, Properties (a) and (b)—will ultimately be validated.

In addition to defining a canonical set of primitive inferences, the approach through reasoning can provide an important constraint on hypotheses about the representational system: It must be able to represent inference schemas perspicuously, as well as the train of thought that people go through in solving the deductive problems that they are able to solve.

The Approach Through Language Universals

By any theory, the syntax of the language of thought must constrain the syntax of natural languages and would be expected often to be directly reflected in the syntax of natural languages. Working backwards, universals of syntax are excellent candidates for being properties of the syntax of the language of thought. In reading recent work on language universals (e.g., Comrie, 1989) and on linguistic work oriented towards language-of-thought issues and semantic structure (e.g., Jackendoff, 1983, 1987, 1990; Pinker, 1989; Rappaport & Levin, 1988), tentative conclusions about a number of features of the syntax of the language of thought came to mind.

No originality for the observations is claimed, and the following list borrows extensively from Jackendoff; it is intended as purely suggestive and is far from exhausting what work on language universals has to tell us about the syntax of thought.

1. There is a categorization of entities by ontological category, for example, Material entities, Locations, Times, Actions, Events, Propositions. Moreover, there appear to be subcategories of these, for example, Material entities divide into Objects (individuated) and Substances; Locations comprise Places, Paths, etc.

2. The language of thought has a predicate-argument structure. In addition, there are functions that build reference to arguments compositionally—the functions map one ontological kind of argument into another, for example, locative prepositions like *in* and *on* map object arguments (e.g., *the chest, the bed*) into place arguments (e.g., *in the chest, on the bed*, as in *put the shirt in the chest/on the bed*). There are also functions that build predicates out of predicates, often adding or subtracting an argument, for example, "make + NP + VP" = MAKE-VP (NP), with NP as the non-Agent argument of the complex predicate MAKE-VP. Much the same functions appear over and over again in different languages, without actually being universal.

3. Predicates easily tend to become arguments. For instance, in "Somebody erased the master tape—Well, George didn't do it," *it* refers to the action of erasing the master tape; thus, this action is predicate of the first proposition, but argument in the second. Similarly, in "George is in jail—the police put him there," *there* refers to a place (in jail) that is an argument of *put*; the place is predicate in the first proposition and argument in the second. It seems that there must be an abstraction operator that, given an action- or place-predicate, automatically conceives of an entity that is the action or place, and that can serve as an argument referred to by a subsequent referring expression.

4. There are some primitive relational predicates, which repeatedly occur in the meanings of words (though they do not exhaust their meanings) and which are drawn on to mark (i.e., distinguish) arguments. Examples are *cause, act, go, to,* and these seem to provide the basis of so-called thematic categories (Jackendoff, 1987); for instance, the NP argument of *cause* is an Agent, and having an Agent subject is part of the semantic representation of all causative verbs.

5. Two identifiable and different devices—(a) relative clauses and (b) embedded (genitive) arguments—are used to delineate arguments or argument sets. Thus, (a) there is an analog of relative clauses ("The Xs such that ..."); (b) the predicates used to identify arguments may themselves have arguments (e.g., "The mayor OF NEW YORK" as in *The*

mayor of New York lives in Gracie Mansion—thus, *mayor* is a predicate with two arguments, a person and a city; because the person argument remains undefined if the city is unknown, when *mayor* is used to identify an argument of some other predicate (e.g., the argument of the predicate "lives in Gracie Mansion"), the city is embedded as part of the argument NP, its function signaled by the genitive marker *of* (see chap. 11 for further discussion and illustration).

6. In chapter 11, it is claimed that in the syntax of thought, as in the surface structure of human languages, quantifiers differ in two important ways from those of standard logic: (a) They are inside the host proposition, in the NPs or argument phrases in which they are found in the surface structure (i.e., they are not a separate constituent preceding the host proposition); (b) as advocated by Gupta (1980) and McCawley (1981/1993), they are domain specific (the noun they modify specifying the domain of entities quantified over) rather than domain general.

As we said earlier, the list is intended to be merely suggestive. However, we believe that a lot of progress could be made fairly quickly towards forming a well-developed hypothesis about the syntax of the language of thought. We are impressed that the linguistic literature contains a great deal of relevant work and theorizing that has been done with various goals, but which could be harnessed to the task of formulating such a hypothesis.

The Approach Through Language Acquisition

Fodor (1975), following the computer metaphor, argues that in learning their native language, children learn a compiler between the language of thought and their language. As noted earlier, the notion of a "language of thought" adopted here is not quite as nativist as Fodor's. However, a claim essentially similar to his is still appropriate—that children learn a mapping between the syntax of the language of thought and the grammar of their language. If this claim is correct, it would follow that there is a third empirical route into the syntax of thought—by examining what is developmentally most primitive in grammar. In this scheme, the child's syntactic primitives are the primitives of the syntax of the language of thought. These would include the predicate/argument distinction, connectives, and ontological categories, along, no doubt, with many other notions too. It is worth noting, incidentally, that although ontological categories played no role in the earlier discussion of reasoning, they are strongly implicated in analyses of semantic structure (e.g., Jackendoff, 1990), as noted in the preceding section, and there is evidence for their primitiveness in recent work with young children (e.g., Keil, 1989;

McPherson, 1991; Soja, Carey, & Spelke, 1991; Spelke, 1990; however, most of the work has focused on the object/substance distinction).

There is, of course, a very strong counterclaim to this neo-Fodorian conception in the literature: Chomsky has vigorously argued for innate natural language syntactic primitives—primitives such as NP, VP, N, V, A, P, Subject of, etc., of a universal natural language grammar. However, it is not possible to account for language acquisition with just Chomsky's primitives, because, as various people have noted, beginning with Fodor (1966), in order for such primitives to be useful to a child, he or she must have a means of recognizing instances of them in the input. We are thus led to the *bootstrapping* proposal (Grimshaw, 1981; Pinker, 1984) that the child has innate semantic flags for each of the innate Chomskyan categories: On their first encounter with language, children assign words for objects to the noun class, object arguments to NP, words for actions to Verb, agents to Subject, etc., and their initial rules are based on this assignment. In sum, the Chomskyan theory has to assume two kinds of primitives—the natural-language syntactic categories and a parallel set of semantic categories that are quite similar to the neo-Fodorian syntax-of-thought categories.

From the perspective that we have been taking, the positing of these natural language syntactic primitives seems curiously gratuitous—why would nature have bothered to give us two such similar sets of primitives? Of course, in adult languages—and, indeed, quite early in development—the syntax-of-thought categories and the natural language syntactic categories do not match perfectly (e.g., nouns often do not represent concrete objects nor verbs actions), and the mismatch has to be explained. Nevertheless, the semantic (syntax of thought) categories could be the child's starting point for the natural language syntactic categories, as Macnamara (1972) suggested. The mismatch need not mean that two independent sets of syntactic categories are present innately; it could emerge as a consequence of the mapping (learning) process. Parsimony demands that this possibility be thoroughly investigated before it is assumed that an innate set of natural language syntactic categories exists in addition to the categories of the syntax of thought. What is at issue, therefore, is whether a learning theory can be constructed that accounts for the emergence of the natural language syntactic categories, given just the syntax-of-thought categories as primitives.

Braine (1992) showed elsewhere that such a learning theory can be obtained by a rather straightforward modification of Pinker's (1984, chap. 3) bootstrapping theory, which is the best specified current theory of the acquisition of phrase structure. Pinker's theory posits both types of primitives. However, it can be reformulated, without loss of precision or scope, with only syntax-of-thought categories as primitives. The reformulated theory posits a tendency on the child's part to categorize words and phrases according to their category in the syntax of thought. Because of this tendency, the initial word and phrase categories of the natural language correspond to categories of the syntax of thought. Then, over time, the learning procedures already formulated in Pinker's theory adjust the extensions of these initial natural language categories so that they come to match those of the standard adult grammatical categories of the language the child is learning.

A simple example may serve to illustrate how the reformulated theory works. We suppose, with Pinker, that in the absence of applicable grammatical rules the child uses semantic and pragmatic information from the context to construct a parse-tree for an input sentence, and then derives rules from the tree. Assume that a child has no grammatical rules of English yet, but knows the words *man* and *jump*; the child sees a man jump and hears the sentence, *The man jumped*. Understanding and parsing the sentence involves assimilating the scene into the innate information format, that is, coding its elements by ontological category and predicate/argument status, and labeling the words and phrases accordingly. Thus, because the child knows that a man is an object and jump an action, and that *the man* is argument to predicate *jump*, the child can construct the top tree of Fig. 4.1, and then read off the rules shown. The expressions "construct the tree" and "read off the rules" are partly metaphoric. By "construct the tree," what is meant is that the child perceives the sentence as having two parts, an Object-Argument Phrase *the man* and an Action-Predicate Phrase *jumped*, and also perceives the first component as having two parts, *the* and an Object-Word *man*. "Reading off the rules" means that the child registers that a sentence can consist of an Object-Argument Phrase followed by an Action-Predicate Phrase (the order being part of the regularity registered), and that an Object-Argument Phrase can consist of *the* and an Object-Word (again, in that order). We may assume that rule registration is initially weak but solidifies as similar sentences and scenes are encountered.

Now let us move forward in time, past a number of such sentences and scenes, to the point at which the rules of Fig. 4.1 are solidly learned. Our child now hears the sentence *The wind stopped*. Assume, again with Pinker (and also with Schlesinger, 1982),[4] that where there are known rules that are applicable, the child always uses them first when trying to understand a novel sentence. Applying the rules involves using phrase position and function words like *the* to construct the tree. After constructing the tree, the child puts the category information of the tree into the

---

[4]As noted in Braine (1992), there is much formal similarity between Pinker's bootstrapping theory and Schlesinger's semantic assimilation theory.

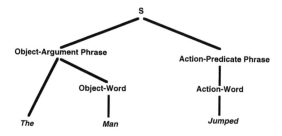

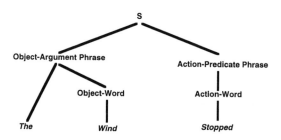

FIG. 4.1. On top is a parse tree for "The man jumped," which a child might construct given the sentence, the scene, knowledge of the words "mind" and "jump," and innate syntax-of-thought categories. Below is a parse tree for "The wind stopped," which a child might construct after having learned the rules of the parse tree for "The man jumped."

lexical entries for the words (Pinker, 1984). According to these assumptions the child constructs the bottom tree of Fig. 4.1. Annotating the lexical entries entails that *wind* becomes marked in the lexicon as an Object-Word, and *stop* as an Action-Word. Note that this means that the category Object-Word, which initially contained just *man* and other names of objects, has now come to include a word that does not designate an object, namely, *wind*; likewise, the non-action word *stop* has come to be included in the category Action-Word, which previously contained only words for actions like *jump*. Similarly, Object-Argument-Phrase has come to include phrases like *the wind*. As this kind of learning procedure operates over time, assimilating many input sentences, the extension of the category Object-Word converges on the extension of Noun; similarly, the extension of Action-Word converges on that of Verb, and the extension of Object-Argument-Phrase on that of NP. Thus, de facto, the child comes to have Nouns, Verbs, and NPs—what one calls the categories is of no importance. In short, given a learning procedure of this sort, word- and phrase-categories that begin as reflexes of categories of the syntax of thought grow into the syntactic categories of the language being learned. The lack of a good one-to-one match in the adult language between the syntax-of-thought categories and the natural-language syntactic categories is a consequence of the nature of the learning process. For detailed presentation of the argument and theory just summarized, see Braine (1992); for additional elaboration and discussion of evidence, see Braine (1994).

In sum, there is a third method of investigating the syntax of thought empirically—by discovering what is developmentally most primitive in grammar. The effort to improve and perfect the learning theory referred to earlier will necessarily force the construction of precise hypotheses about the semantic structures (i.e., the categories and form of the syntax of thought) that provide the point of departure for learning. Given that the same learning theory should be applicable to any language, there is no reason to doubt that there are enough empirical constraints that particular hypotheses can be confirmed or invalidated.

SUMMARY AND CONCLUSIONS

We began by arguing that an intelligent species would need a mental logic to integrate information arriving from different sources or at different times, and that there is indeed evidence for a stock of elementary logical inference forms that people use for such practical purposes. A consensus exists that the core of such a mental logic would be a set of easy inferences defined by schemas. These would be represented in a system of semantic representation akin to Fodor's language of thought: We argued, like Fodor, that there must be an innate proposition-like format—a syntax of thought—to provide a basis for semantic representation and for a child's initial encoding of knowledge in memory. Such a format would necessarily embody a good deal of logical structure, and the inference schemas of the mental logic would use it.

The chapter discussed three complementary ways in which the mental logic and the syntax of thought can be investigated empirically—through reasoning, through linguistic universals, and by discovering what is semantically and syntactically primitive in language acquisition. The reasoning route searches for types of logical inferences that are closely tied to the meanings of natural language logical particles, that are made easily and develop early, and that conserve these properties across languages. There is strong suggestive evidence for such a set of propositional inferences that would indeed form a mental propositional logic. Facts like the apparent primitiveness of quantifying and instantiating devices in language provide reason to believe that the mental logic extends well beyond a propositional logic, and we offer a hypothesis for a mental predicate logic in chapter 11.

The other two empirical routes focus on the structure of the representational system rather than on inference. We enumerated some probable features of the syntax of the language of thought to exemplify what can be culled from linguistic work on links between semantic and syntactic representation in languages. The approach through language acquisition depends on the idea that children learn a mapping between the syntax of the language of thought and the grammar of their language. We show how this idea is viable in that it can, in principle, account for acquisition of phrase structure without requiring innate natural-language syntactic primitives. Thus, because the child begins with just the syntax of thought, it is potentially reconstructible from study of the beginnings of grammar.

In sum, there are means to investigate empirically the specific nature of a mental logic and of the basic syntax of semantic representation; and there is enough evidence to indicate that the investigative enterprise will be productive.

Logical Inferences and Comprehension: How Mental-Logic and Text-Processing Theories Need Each Other

R. Brooke Lea
Bowdoin College

Inferences are a major source of coherence in reading. For more than 20 years considerable research has been devoted to understanding what sorts of inferences contribute to coherence during reading, and the fecund collection of results issued from this research has lead to several recent attempts to produce a large-scale account of text comprehension (e.g., Graesser & Bower, 1990; Graesser, Singer, & Trabasso, 1994; Kintsch, 1988; McKoon & Ratcliff, 1992). Missing from this work, however, is any account of how propositional-logic inferences are made during reading. In fact, even the most promiscuous (with regard to inference-making) of these theories takes a rather pessimistic view of the ease with which logical inferences can contribute to comprehension; in discussing the sorts of inferences that are made during reading (online), Graesser and his colleagues stated: "some classes of inferences [are] normally difficult to generate and are therefore off-line. First, there are logic-based inferences that are derived from systems of domain-independent formal reasoning, such as propositional calculus, predicate calculus, and theorem proving" (Graesser et al., 1994, p. 376). More minimal hypotheses about inference-making claim that very few inferences are made during reading—only those needed for one sentence to make sense in the context of the previous sentence, and those that can be derived from easily available information (McKoon & Ratcliff, 1992, 1995). Thus, current theories of text processing present a somewhat inhospitable frame from which to consider the potential contribution that logical inferences might make to text comprehension.

A principle claim of the mental-logic theory presented in this book is that there is a core set of logical inferences (presented in chap. 6) that are made routinely both in reasoning and in discourse processing. The claim that logical inferences are made routinely in discourse processing clearly is at odds with current theories of text comprehension. In this chapter, I consider both the issues that the mental-logic model raises for theories of text processing, and also several concerns raised by the comprehension literature to which mental-logic research should attend. I begin by describing the available evidence that the mental-logic model described in this book can be extended effectively from abstract-reasoning problems to text comprehension. I consider aspects of comprehension for which the mental-logic theory needs further specification; for example, although the theory claims that people will make inferences based on premises that are received from different sources or at different times, it says nothing about how these distant premises arrive in working memory. I outline recent work in text processing that describes a memory mechanism—resonance—that can account for the activation of distant premise information from which inferences can be drawn. Finally, I discuss an aspect of language processing—negation—that may impose constraints on the functioning of the model in discourse comprehension.

PROPOSITIONAL-LOGIC INFERENCES IN TEXT

Readers of the present volume will become acquainted with the extent and breadth of available research that demonstrates that adults and children have no trouble making propositional-logic inferences from abstract materials (chaps. 4, 7, 8, 9, and 10). In a typical experiment of this sort, participants are given a set of information (the premises) and asked whether another piece of information (the conclusion) is true or false. Usually the problem is presented in an abstract form. For example, Lea et al. (1990, Experiment 3) asked participants to imagine a hidden blackboard on which letters were written, and then presented them with information about which letters are or are not on the blackboard. For example:

1. If there is an A or an S then there is not an M.
2. If there is an H then there is an A.
3. If there is a G then there is an S.
4. There is either an H or a G.

The task was to determine what letters the participants thought were written on the blackboard, and to write down the steps they took on the way to reaching their conclusions. In this example, participants often wrote down *there is an A or an S* and then *there is not an M*. The first inference is produced by combining the two conditional premises in (2) and (3) with the disjunction in (4) to yield the conclusion that there is an A or an S; this inference form is represented by Schema 6 of Table 6.1. The second inference follows from the integration of the first inference (A or S) with the first premise (*If A or S then not M*) to produce "not M" via modus ponens (Schema 7 in Table 6.1). Several studies (e.g., Braine & Rumain, 1983; Lea et al., 1990; chaps. 7 and 8) have shown that the basic theory very accurately predicts the inferences adults and children draw from abstract premises. Thus, we have good evidence that people have a capacity to draw certain logical inferences accurately from abstract materials.

It has been important to demonstrate that people are competent logicians with abstract content because competing theories have proposed that reasoning performance that appears logical may actually be driven by nonlogical forces (e.g., the pragmatic schemas of Cheng & Holyoak, 1985). One advantage of presenting premises as *A*'s and *B*'s on an imaginary blackboard is that the only information from which participants have to reason is provided by the logical particles *if*, *and*, *or*, and *not*; that participants are able to reason logically from these content-free premises cannot be due to a content-based process, such as pragmatic reasoning schemas (Cheng & Holyoak, 1985). Thus, research using abstract content has provided crucial evidence that we possess a reasoning competence that is independent of pragmatics.

Everyday reasoning, of course, usually does not occur with abstract premises embedded in reasoning puzzles, as in the example mentioned earlier. Therefore, an important goal of the mental-logic approach has been to investigate logical reasoning where it typically occurs—in text comprehension. Consider the following text, which has a logical structure that is parallel to the abstract problem in (1) to (3):

5. The Borofskys were planning a dinner party.
6. "Alice and Sarah are vegetarians," Mrs. Borofsky said, "so if we invite either one of them, we can't serve meat."
7. "Well, if we invite Harry, we have to invite Alice," Mr. Borofsky said.
8. "And if we invite George, we have to invite Sarah."
9. "We already decided to invite either Harry or George, or maybe both of them,"said Mrs. Borofsky.

Lea et al. (1990) presented short texts such as this one to participants and asked them to indicate whether or not a final sentence made sense in the context of the story; this was called the Validity Task. Participants were presented either with (10a) or (10b),

10a. "That's right," Mr. Borofsky replied, "so we can't serve meat."

10b. "That's right," Mr. Borofsky replied, "so we can serve meat."

Over the 12 texts Lea et al. presented, 95% of the responses on the Validity Task were logically valid. In the dinner party text, for example, most participants indicated that (10a) does make sense in the context of the story when they were given that sentence to judge, and most responded that (10b) does not make sense when they were asked to judge that final sentence in the context of the story. Immediately following the Validity Task, participants were shown three sentences and asked to indicate whether the information contained in the sentences had been presented explicitly in the text they had just read, or whether they had to infer that information; this was called the Recognition Task. For each story, the participants were given three types of sentences: (a) a paraphrase of information that was presented explicitly in the text, (b) a logical inference that the model predicts readers would make while reading the story, and (c) a logically valid inference that the model does not predict readers would make. For the dinner party text shown earlier, the recognition items were:

11. The Borofskys had decided to invite Harry or George (or both).

12. In their discussion, the Borofskys concluded that they had to invite Alice or Sarah (or both).

13. If the Borofskys invited either Harry or Sarah, they could not serve meat.

Note that (11) is a paraphrase of (9) of the text; that (12) is a predicted inference derived by combining the information in (7), (8), and (9)—and that this inference corresponds to the "A or S" intermediate conclusion from the blackboard version of this problem presented on page 64; and that (13) is a logically valid inference that the model predicts readers could not make without recourse to the more advanced reasoning strategies described in chapters 6 and 7. Lea et al. (1990) predicted that participants would (correctly) recognize the information in (11) as having been presented in the text they just read, that they often would (incorrectly) recognize the information in (12) as having been presented in the text, and that they would (correctly) reject the information in (13) as having been presented in the text. False alarms were expected for (12) because the model predicts that readers would make those logical inferences and incorporate the resulting information into their mental representation of the texts so easily that only moments later they would have difficulty determining whether they had inferred that information or read it. Lea et al.'s results (Experiments 1 and 2) supported this prediction: Sixty-nine percent of the time participants thought that the model-predicted inferences had been presented explicitly in the texts, whereas only 15% of the time did they think the logically valid nonpredicted inferences had been presented in the stories. Eighty-nine percent of the time participants accurately identified the paraphrases as containing information presented explicitly in the passages. Thus, the results from the validity task and the recognition task provide strong evidence that people are able to make the logical inferences described in the model very accurately and easily enough that they often do not realize they are making inferences. Hence, Lea et al. (1990) provided the first empirical evidence that the model's predictions apply to everyday situations such as text processing, and not just to abstract-content laboratory puzzles.

ONLINE MEASURES OF LOGICAL INFERENCES

The question of when inferences are made during the process of comprehension has prompted a recent vigorous investigation of online processing in reading. Early research using off-line measures (e.g., memory for the text) appeared to show that participants were drawing a large number of inferences during reading. However, some of these off-line measures confounded processes that were occurring at the time of test (after the reading was done) with comprehension processes occurring during reading. Consequently, more recent investigations have emphasized online measures that attempt to capture comprehension processes as they are happening. In addition, a useful distinction has been made between those inferences that are needed to maintain the coherence of a text (often called *bridging inferences*) and those inferences that merely elaborate upon the text but are not required for the coherence of the passage (often referred to as *elaborative* or *forward inferences*). For example, consider the following sentences (from Potts, Keenan, & Golding, 1988):

14. No longer able to control his anger, the husband threw the delicate porcelain vase against the wall.
15a. He had been feeling angry for weeks, but had refused to seek help. (p. 405)

When (14) is followed by (15a), the inference that the vase broke is an elaboration on the text, but is not needed for the two sentences to be coherent. However, when (14) is followed by (15b),

15b. It cost him well over 100 dollars to replace the vase,

the inference is required for textual coherence. That is, the inference that the vase broke is required to connect the information in (14) about the husband throwing it against the wall with the information in (15b) about him replacing it. Thus, (14) followed by (15b) requires a bridging inference to establish coherence between the two sentences, and most researchers agree that when an inference is required for coherence it will be made during comprehension. There is considerably less agreement, however, about when nonbridging inferences are made. Opinions vary considerably, but to the extent that a consensus exists, researchers tend to believe that such inferences are either not made or are only made under specific conditions (Keefe & McDaniel, 1993; McKoon & Ratcliff, 1980, 1986, 1989, 1992; Murray, Klin, & Myers, 1993; Noordman & Vonk, 1992; O'Brien, Shank, Myers, & Rayner, 1988; Potts et al., 1988; Singer & Ferreira, 1983; Swinney & Osterhout, 1990).

The mental logic approach described in this book claims that the basic logical inferences in Table 6.1 are made spontaneously at the moment the required premises are simultaneously available to a reader (e.g., chaps. 3, 4, 6, and 9; Lea et al., 1990). The theory does not stipulate that the inference needs to play any role in the coherence of the text, and the claim, therefore, is in conflict with assumptions often made in the text-processing literature about when nonbridging inferences are made. The question thus arises as to whether propositional-logic inferences are made online when their output is not needed for coherence.

The data presented by Lea et al. (1990) do not address this issue because the inferences tested in the recognition task were forced for the purpose of coherence; that is, if the participants had not make those logical inferences while they were reading, then the passages would have lost coherence. Thus, recognition-task inferences were bridging inferences—they were required for coherence. However, Lea (1995) did directly investigate whether model-predicted inferences are made online when their output is not needed for coherence by using passages such as the following:

Dressing for the Weather

16. Paula was getting dressed for work and asked her roommate, Donna, if she knew what the weather would be.

17. "I heard it on the news last night and it didn't sound good," said Donna, "they said it would either be rainy or they said it would be cold—I can't remember which."

18. "Hmm, those are two very different dressing conditions," Paula thought to herself, "I wish she could remember which it was."

19a. "OK, I just called the weather," shouted Donna, "and it's not going to rain."

Participants read 24 stories like this one on a computer screen one sentence at a time at their own pace and were asked to make lexical decisions on words that were semantically associated with the proposition that logically could be inferred. For the story given here, the reader is presented with two premises: Sentence (17) states that the weather *either will be rainy or cold*, and (19a) eliminates one of the disjuncts by stating that *it's not going to rain*. Thus, the reader can deduce—via *or elimination* (Schema 3 in Table 6.1)—that the forecast calls for cold weather; HOT was the lexical decision target. The logic of the design is that if participants spontaneously make the inference "COLD" when they read that the forecast did not call for rain, then words associated with the inference will be activated and lexical decisions on such words will be faster as compared with a control condition in which the inference cannot be made. Accordingly, control versions of the stories were identical, except that the final sentence did not contain the second logical premise. The control sentence for Dressing for the Weather was:

19b. "Well, whatever happens, I hope I don't get caught in the rain."

Note that (17) and (19a) together provide the requisite information to trigger Schema 3 of Table 6.1, whereas (17) together with (19b) do not. Note also that the inference in question is not needed for coherence of the passage; at the time of test, the inference—if it were made—would provide a forward elaboration on the text, not a bridge required to make sense of it.

The model states that the *or-elimination* inference will be made at the moment both premises are simultaneously available. Therefore, lexical decision targets that follow inference stories should be identified significantly faster than those that follow no-inference stores, and that is exactly what Lea (1995) found; when targets followed inference versions of the passages, the average lexical decision latency was 63 ms faster than when they followed the control versions. This difference (reliable at $p < .01$; see Lea, 1995, Experiment 1a for details) demonstrates that the inference targets were primed and strongly indicates that the participants were making the *or-elimination* inference at the moment both premises were available, as the model predicts.

Lea (1995) replicated this result using a naming task instead of lexical decision. He also conducted an experiment that used the modus ponens inference form instead of *or-elimination*. For example:

Sniffing Out the Goods
20. Special Investigator Evans was trying to crack a Cuban cigar smuggling ring.

21. As he entered the dark warehouse he whispered into his walkie-talkie: "If the dog starts to bark, then we know there's tobacco around."

22. "OK, I'll be listening," replied his partner Newstead, who was monitoring the situation from their unmarked patrol car.

23a. There was quiet for a few minutes, then the silence was broken by the sound of Evans's dog barking.

In this passage, the reader is given the conditional premise *if the dog barks, then tobacco*, and the minor premise *the dog barked*, which together yield, via modus ponens, the inference that there is tobacco around; SMOKE was the lexical decision target. Lea (1995) used 28 such passages and found that the response times to targets was facilitated when the texts contained the second premise, as in (23a), compared with when the second premise was replaced by a very similar final sentence that did not satisfy the antecedent of the conditional, as in (23b):

23b. There was quiet for a few minutes, and Newstead wondered whether he was close enough to hear the sound of the dog barking.

The highly reliable effect reported by Lea (1995; Experiment 3) indicates that readers of these texts were making the modus ponens inference at the moment both premises were simultaneously available to them. This result, together with the parallel finding with *or-elimination*, supports the model's claim that people make certain logical inferences easily and spontaneously—even when the inference is not needed to make sense of the text or to answer a question. The latter point is especially relevant to recent work in text processing that has struggled to identify the conditions in which elaborative, nonbridging inferences are made online. As mentioned earlier, numerous studies have concluded that elaborative or predictive inferences, for example, that the vase in Sentence 14 broke, are not made during comprehension unless the reader has some special purpose to do so (e.g., McKoon & Ratcliff, 1992; Potts et al., 1988).

Evidence that logical inferences are made in elaborative, nonbridging circumstances can be seen as surprising for several reasons. First, until very recently, logical inferences were not thought to be part of the province of everyday comprehension; if people used logic while reading, it was under constrained, demanding, and often unpleasant circumstances. Evidence that readers make logical inferences very accurately (95% correct in the validity task), so easily that they often do not realize that they are making inferences (69% false-alarm rate on the recognition task), and spontaneously even when the inference is not needed for comprehension (priming studies) presents a constellation of results clearly at odds with the view that logical reasoning is absent from everyday cognition. Second, such results might be surprising because it has been relatively difficult to find evidence for forward, elaborative inferences, even of the most predictable sort. For example, a passage about a person falling from the 14th floor of a building does not reliably elicit the inference that the person died (McKoon & Ratcliff, 1986). If such obvious inferences are not made on-line, why should we expect logical inferences to be made so?

Two reasons are often cited as to why forward inferences are not made during reading: First, it is not efficient to infer what will likely be given in the text; and second, there is the risk that one will draw the wrong inference (Murray et al., 1993). Logical inferences are different from most pragmatic inferences in that if the premises are true, then the conclusion (inference) must be true. Thus the second reason cited earlier may not hold—or hold as strongly—for logical inferences such as modus ponens and *or-elimination*; the measure of certainty afforded by logical inference may explain why Lea (1995) found evidence for forward inferences whereas some investigations of pragmatic inferences have not.

Other mental-logic models have been proposed, and the data sets discussed here were not designed to distinguish among them. The results of Lea (1995) are compatible with any mental-logic model that includes modus ponens and *or-elimination* (e.g., Rips, 1994), and predicts that the inferences will be made spontaneously in discourse processing. However, not all of the data from Lea (1995) are compatible with the current mental-models account of propositional reasoning (Johnson-Laird, Byrne, & Schaeken, 1992). Specifically, mental-models theory would make different predictions for the modus ponens stories than would the mental-logic theories proposed in this volume (see chap. 6) and by Rips (1994). According to the psychological algorithm of the mental-models theory, there should be no difference in activation of the inference concept between the control and inference versions of the stories, because both versions produce a model containing the concept at the time of test. Thus, mental-models theory would predict no difference between inference and no-inference stories. As we have seen, however, the reliable difference between inference and control version of the modus ponens stories in Lea (1995; Experiments 3 & 4) is inconsistent with that prediction.

WHAT IS MISSING FROM MENTAL-LOGIC THEORY?

The mental-logic model is adequate to predict the propositional-logic inferences readers make in a way that the major theories of text processing are not. The results of Lea et al. (1990), and especially of Lea (1995), cannot be readily explained within the frameworks of Graesser, Singer, and

Trabasso's (1994) Constructionist theory, McKoon and Ratcliff's (1992) Minimalist Hypothesis, nor Kintsch's (1988) Construction-Integration model (see Lea, 1995, p. 1478 for a description of how these models fail to account for his results). However, the mental-logic theory has made no attempt to explain several other important aspects of logical inference-making in text. For example, one reason for suspecting that a mental logic would have evolved in primitive humans is that it would provide them with a means for integrating information arriving from different sources or at different times (see chap. 4). Accordingly, the theory states that when the premises required to trigger an inference schema are simultaneously available in working memory, the inference will be made. The model, however, is silent about *how* premises received at different times might end up in working memory simultaneously. It may be beyond the scope of a model of mental logic per se to explain the memory mechanisms that allow it to function. In order for the theory to be implemented fully in a discourse-processing environment, however, it will need to be integrated with the other cognitive processes that operate during comprehension. How readers access information that is related to the text from long-term memory is an important issue, and one that has received the attention of several recent investigations. As an example of how mental-logic theory needs to be integrated with other theoretical perspectives, I now describe one of those studies by way of suggesting what the mechanism might be that accesses distant premise information and allows the model to operate on premises that are not explicitly presented to readers.

HOW IS DISTANT PREMISE INFORMATION ACCESSED FROM MEMORY?

Greene, Gerrig, McKoon, and Ratcliff (1994) investigated how the accessibility of discourse entities can wax and wane as characters in a story who share knowledge of those entities part and reunite in the text. The authors were interested in how this kind of flow of information allows people to use "unheralded pronouns"—pronouns for which there is no immediate referent—to refer successfully to distant antecedents. For example, consider the text in Table 5.1. In this story, Gloria's use of "she" in the story's penultimate sentence (the "Pronoun Sentence") is unheralded with respect to the local context; the antecedent (COUSIN) last appeared 10 sentences earlier.

Using recognition probes, Greene et al. found that Jane's return to Gloria made a concept that they both knew about, such as COUSIN, more accessible than it had been just before their reunion; I refer to this as the *reunion effect*. Greene et al. (1994) interpreted this result in the following

TABLE 5.1
A Sample Text from Greene, Gerrig, McKoon,
and Ratcliff (1994, Experiment 3)

Common-Ground Introduction
    Jane was dreading her dinner with her cousin, Marilyn.
    She complained loudly to her roommate Gloria.
    "Every time I go to dinner at my cousin's I get sick."
    Gloria asked, "Why did you agree to go?"
    Jane said, "Because I'm too wimpy to say no."
    Jane went off to have dinner.
Continuation
    Gloria decided to cook something nice for herself for dinner.
    "As long as I'm home alone," she thought, "I'll eat well."
    Gloria searched her refrigerator for ingredients.
    She found enough eggs to make a quiche.
    After dinner, she put the dishes in the dishwasher.

Reunion Sentence:	Gloria was still up when Jane arrived home about midnight.
Pronoun Sentence:	Gloria asked Jane, "Did she play you old disco records?"
Final Sentence:	Jane chuckled and said, "I can't get 'Disco Inferno' out of my mind."
Recognition test word:	COUSIN

---

way: Discourse participants maintain memory structures that are devoted to encoding shared experiences—their common ground. As participants enter or exit a discourse situation, the information that is part of their common ground becomes more or less accessible to the remaining participants. The notion of accessing common ground can be extended to readers, who can be seen as side-participants of the discourse presented in the text. Thus, as the reader encodes a reunion between two protagonists, concepts that are part of the characters' common ground—like COUSIN is for Gloria and Jane—become more accessible to the reader than they had been just before the reunion.

Some colleagues and I wondered whether there might be a simpler explanation for the reunion effect. Specifically, our goal was to flesh out whether common ground between protagonists is a necessary condition to yield the reunion effect reported by Greene et al. Our theoretical perspective was based on work showing that simple overlap between concepts can produce spontaneous reactivation of distant information through a memory process that can be described by the resonance metaphor (e.g., Gillund & Shiffrin, 1984; Hintzman, 1986; Ratcliff, 1978; Ratcliff & McKoon, 1988), and several researchers have proposed resonance models that describe, in effect, how we are reminded of information from long-term memory (e.g., Myers, O'Brien, Albrecht, & Mason, 1994). For example, according to Myers and his colleagues, distant information is accessed in the following way: Concepts and propositions in memory resonate in response to related concepts and propositions derived from the text being read. The resonating memory elements then cause elements related to them to resonate, and the process continues until it stabilizes and the most active elements enter working memory. In the example about Jane and her COUSIN, the resonance model would predict that the reintroduction of Jane in the reunion sentence provides sufficient contextual overlap to reactivate concepts strongly linked to her—such as her COUSIN. Thus, the resonance model would account for the reunion effect (higher activation of COUSIN after the reunion than before) by virtue of a passive resonance process, without recourse to concepts such as "common ground" or "reference diaries."

To test this hypothesis, Lea, Albrecht, Birch, Masson, and Myers (1995) created passages in which the target concept was not part of the characters' common ground. In the passage presented in Table 5.2, for example, Lea et al. (1995) changed the introduction of Greene et al.'s story so that the concept COUSIN is known to Jane but not to Gloria; hence, COUSIN is not part of their common ground. Using recognition probes, Lea et al.

TABLE 5.2
A Sample Text from Lea, Albrecht, Birch,
Masson, and Myers (1995, Experiment 3)

Common-Ground Introduction	No-Common-Ground Introduction
Jane was dreading her dinner with her cousin, Marilyn. She complained loudly to her roommate Gloria. "Every time I go to dinner at my cousin's I get sick." Gloria asked, "Why did you agree to go?" Jane said, "Because I'm too wimpy to say no." Jane went off to have dinner.	Jane and her roommate Gloria were leaving work. "Are you headed home?" asked Gloria. "No, but I'll see you later tonight," replied Jane. Jane drove off to have dinner with her cousin, Marilyn. As she drove, she started to have regrets. She usually got sick when she ate at her cousin's. Jane wondered why she had agreed to go. She decided she was just too wimpy to say no.
Continuation	*Continuation*
Gloria decided to cook something nice for herself for dinner. "As long as I'm home alone," she thought, "I'll eat well." Gloria searched her refrigerator for ingredients. She found enough eggs to make a quiche. After dinner, she put the dishes in the dishwasher.	Meanwhile, Gloria went home and decided to cook something nice for herself. "As long as I'm home alone," she thought "I'll eat well." Gloria searched her refrigerator for ingredients. She found enough eggs to make a quiche. After dinner, she put the dishes in the dishwasher.

Reunion Sentence:	Gloria was still up when Jane arrived home about midnight.
Pronoun Sentence:	Gloria asked Jane, "Did she play you old disco records?"
Final Sentence:	Jane chuckled and said, "I can't get 'Disco Inferno' out of my mind."
Recognition test word:	COUSIN

TABLE 5.3
Recognition Response Times in Milliseconds
from Lea et al. (1995, Experiment 3)

Introduction	*Probe Position*		
	Before Reunion	*After Reunion*	*After Pronoun*
Common ground	961	934	926
No common ground	962	940	931

Note. The *reunion effect* is defined by faster recognition times for targets presented in the After Reunion probe position compared with the Before Reunion probe position. In the data set presented here, that difference was statistically significant for both the Common-Ground and for the No-Common-Ground conditions.

measured the activation of the target just before and just after the reunion of the characters. If common ground is required for reactivation, as Greene et al. claim, then there should not be much change in activation of the targets when the targets are not part of common ground. However, if the reintroduction of Jane in the Reunion Sentence begins a resonance process that activates the cousin, then we should see a reunion effect even without common ground, and that is exactly what Lea et al. (1995) found. As Table 5.3 shows, backgrounded concepts like COUSIN were reactivated whether they were part of the protagonists' common ground or not; the pattern of results for common-ground and no-common-ground introductions was identical.

Other studies have revealed the important role that contextual cues play in the resonance process. For example, Albrecht and Myers (1995) found that including seemingly insignificant details in a story can be critical to reactivating backgrounded information associated with those details (see also Albrecht & Myers, in press; Albrecht & O'Brien, 1993; O'Brien, Plewes, & Albrecht, 1990). These results, and the resonance theory of memory activation that they support, provide a strong foundation on which to build a theory of comprehension. With regard to the mental-logic model, the resonance model offers some independent theoretical support for the assumption that primitive humans had the cognitive apparatus to spontaneously assemble premise information coming in from different places and at different times. More importantly, resonance promises to provide a systematic account for how distant premise information is accessed. The mental-logic approach will only benefit from attempts to specify better the collaboration that must exist between psychological models of deduction and the memory processes that serve them.

Note that in many discourse situations a distant premise is simply a fact stored in long-term memory, not information that was presented earlier in the text or conversation. Consider the following example:

24. Bob was asking Barb about her new personal computer.

25. "What did you decide about which type of computer to get?"

26. "Well," said Barb foolishly, "in the end I decided not to get the Mac because they'll probably be out of business before I fill out the warranty card."

Inference: Barb got an IBM-compatible machine.

In this example, the major premise is world knowledge stored in both Barb's and Bob's long-term memory: Personal computers are either Mac or IBM-compatible machines. Barb can take this mutual knowledge about computers for granted, assume that Bob will retrieve the appropriate premise, and be assured that she has provided sufficient information to answer his question (cf. Sperber & Wilson, 1986). Thus, distant premise information can be retrieved from the participants' world knowledge, as well as from their memory of earlier parts of the discourse. This example also illustrates how inference mechanisms permit some economy in discourse; Barb can disregard two important elements of their exchange (the major premise and conclusion), and is free to make a gratuitous joke at Macintosh's expense, and perhaps move the conversation in a more interesting direction (see Singer & Halldorson, 1996, for work on enthymemes).

THE INFLUENCE OF NEGATION
ON INFERENCE-MAKING

A second discourse-processing issue that arises for the logic model concerns the effect that negation might have on the production of logical inferences. Several recent accounts of sentence comprehension include a mechanism that automatically enhances or suppresses the activation of a concept in the reader's mental representation of the text, and negation has been suggested as one discourse factor that can induce suppression (e.g., Gernsbacher & Faust, 1991; MacDonald and Just, 1989). For example, in a series of experiments, MacDonald and Just (1989) found that participants were slower and less accurate at verifying that the word BREAD had appeared in Sentence (27):

27. *Almost every weekend, Elizabeth bakes no bread but only cookies for the children,*

compared with a control sentence in which COOKIES was negated instead of BREAD:

28. *Almost every weekend, Elizabeth bakes bread but no cookies for the children.*

MacDonald and Just (1989) accounted for their findings by suggesting that negation affects activation levels by way of shifts in discourse focus.

Consider, now, two schemas in the logic model that appear to be quite similar but may not be in a text-processing context:

Or-Elimination	Not-Both Elimination
a or b	not both a and b
not a	a
∴ b	∴ not b

Chapter 7 reported difficulty ratings for these schemas based on participants' performance on abstract problems, and these two schemas yielded very similar weights: 1.38 for *or-elimination* and 1.39 for *not-both elimination*. Note that a basic difference between the two schemas is that one produces an affirmative conclusion (therefore *b*), whereas the other yields a negative conclusion (therefore *not b*). Thus the question arises as to whether the effect that negation has on propositions goes beyond explicit negation; that is, does it inhibit or suppress the production of negative information? If it does, then we might expect participants to more readily draw the inference *b* than the inference *not b*, despite the model's prediction that the two inferences are made equally readily. I am currently conducting a study that investigates this possibility, and I predict that readers will be more likely to make logical inferences that clarify what will happen in a story than they will be to generate information about what will not happen in a story. The point of bringing up this example, and the issue about accessing distant premise information, is to illustrate some of the more general cognitive concerns that the mental-logic theory will need to address to be fully implemented in discourse comprehension, particularly if it is to make predictions about online processing.

SUMMARY AND CONCLUSIONS

Recent theories of text processing have not allowed for the role that logical inferences play in comprehension. Indeed, the two leading approaches either explicitly discount the contribution of logic to comprehension (Graesser et al., 1994) or implicitly deny that such inferences occur during reading (McKoon & Ratcliff, 1992). The data presented in this chapter provide an assortment of convergent evidence that logical inferences of the sort specified in the mental-logic model are a part of routine text processing. We have seen that people are very accurate at making these inferences, that readers make them easily enough that they often do not realize that they are making inferences, and that these inferences are made online even in texts that do not require them for coherence.

We also have seen that a mental logic alone cannot fully account for the inferences it predicts in some discourse-processing situations. Fortunately, research done by text-processing researchers may provide an elegant account for how distant premise information is spontaneously accessed by readers and what role negation might play in the production of logical inferences.

In conclusion, it appears that work from these two areas of cognition—reasoning and text processing—promises to be mutually beneficial. A goal of this chapter has been to outline some of the issues that arise when considering the role that logic plays in everyday cognition, particularly reading. Given the data presented here, it is clear that any complete account of the inferences people make while reading must include some propositional-logic inferences. Although more work is needed to fully implement the mental-logic theory in a discourse-processing framework, the current data and theory offer a precise starting hypothesis about how such inferences are made in discourse comprehension.

6

The Theory of Mental-Propositional Logic: Description and Illustration

Martin D. S. Braine
New York University

David P. O'Brien
*Baruch College and the Graduate School
of the City University of New York*

In this chapter, our sole concern is to present the propositional model and to illustrate how it works. Evidence and justification are left entirely to other chapters. Some theoretical background and motivation has already been presented (chaps. 2 to 4). Chapter 5 summarizes some work on the spontaneous use of the logic in reader's comprehension of text. Chapters 7 and 8 describe major pieces of supporting evidence, both for the general form of the model and many of the details. Chapter 9 analyzes and elaborates special characteristics of *if* that distinguish it from ⊃ of standard logic. Chapter 10 presents evidence and argument on the availability of the logic to children. Here we simply describe the model.

The logic has the character of a natural deduction system. The inference schemas are presented in Table 6.1. Table 6.2 describes the program that adults have for applying the schemas. Notice that Table 6.2 has two parts. One part is the Direct Reasoning Routine (henceforth DRR); the other is entitled Some Indirect Reasoning Strategies. The DRR is the key part; only the DRR belongs to the primary skills (i.e., that part of the model that is claimed to be universal). Thus, the schemas of Table 6.1 taken with the DRR of Table 6.2 constitute the primary skills, and we often refer to this combination as the *basic model*. The indirect reasoning strategies are secondary late-acquired skills, which are subject to individual variation, although common in adult subjects.

Table 6.1 contains four subgroups of schemas. Schemas 1 through 7 are the core set of inference forms; they are used without restriction

TABLE 6.1

Basic Inference Schemas Proposed for the Mental-Propositional Logic

Core Schemas

#	Schema	Rate	Example
1.	$\sim\sim p \equiv p$	$(1.09;\ 1\%)$[a]	E.g., It is false that there is not a W /∴There is a W.[b]
2.	IF p_1 OR . . . OR p_n THEN q; p_i ∴ q	$(.49;\ 0\%)$	E.g., If there is either a C or an H then there is a Q; There is a C /∴There is a Q.
3.	p_1 OR . . . OR p_n; $\sim p_i$ ∴ p_1 OR . . . OR p_{i-1} OR p_{i+1} OR . . . OR p_n	$(1.38;\ 2.5\%)$	E.g., There is a D or a T; There is not a D /∴There is a T.
4.	$\sim(p_1\ \&\ \ldots\ \&\ p_n)$; p_i ∴ $\sim(p_1\ \&\ \ldots\ \&\ p_{i-1}\ \&\ p_{i+1}\ \&\ \ldots\ \&\ p_n)$	$(1.39;\ 4\%)$	E.g., It is false that there is both a G and an I; There is a G /∴There is not an I.
5.	p_1 OR . . . OR p_n; IF p_1 THEN q; . . . ; IF p_n THEN q ∴ q	$(.16;\ 0\%)$	E.g., There is an F or an R; If there is an F then there is an L; If there is an R then there is an L /∴There is an L.
6.	p_1 OR . . . OR p_n; IF p_1 THEN q_1; . . . ; IF p_n THEN q_n ∴ q_1 OR . . . OR q_n	$(.47;\ 0\%)$	E.g., There is an I or a B; If there is an I then there is an N; If there is a B then there is a T /∴There is an N or a T.
7.	IF p THEN q; p ∴ q	$(.47;\ 2\%)$	E.g., If there is a T then there is an L; There is a T /∴There is an L.

Principal Feeder Schemas

#	Schema	Rate	Example
8.	p_1; p_2; . . . p_n ∴ p_1 AND p_2 AND . . . AND p_n	$(.34;\ 1\%)$	E.g., There is a G; There is an S /∴There is a G and an S.
9.	$p_1\ \&\ \ldots\ \&\ p_i\ \&\ \ldots\ \&\ p_n$ ∴ p_i	$(.41;\ 0\%)$	E.g., There is an O and a Z /∴There is an O.

TABLE 6.1

Basic Inference Schemas Proposed for the Mental Propositional Logic

Incompatibility Schemas

10. p; $\sim p$ (.20; 1%)   E.g., There is an M; There is not an M / INCOMPATIBLE.
       ─────────
       INCOMPATIBLE

11. p_1 OR ... OR p_n; $\sim p_1$ AND ... AND $\sim p_n$ (.66; 0%)   E.g., There is an R or a W; There is not an R and there is not a W / $\therefore$INCOMPATIBLE.
       ──────────────
       INCOMPATIBLE

Other Schemas

12. Given a chain of reasoning of the form   (.02)
    Suppose p
    ─────────
    q
    One can conclude: IF p THEN q

13. Given a chain of reasoning of the form
    Suppose p
    ─────────
    INCOMPATIBLE
    One can conclude: $\sim p$

14. p & $(q_1$ OR ... OR $q_n) \equiv (p$ & $q_1)$ OR ... OR $(p$ & $q_n)$ (.16; 4%)   E.g., There is a B and there is an L or an R; There is a B and an L or there is a B and an R.[c]

Note. The order of conjuncts and disjuncts and of the propositions in numerators of schemas is immaterial. Where there are subscripts, i indicates any one of the subscripted propositions. "$\sim$" is commonly realized as negation when the negated proposition is realized as a single clause or sentence in surface structure; otherwise, as "It is false (not the case) that ...." "INCOMPATIBLE" stops a chain of reasoning, except as provided for in Schema 13 and the Evaluation Procedure of the reasoning program. Schema 12 says that if q can be derived with the aid of the supposition p, one can conclude IF p THEN q; see chapter 9 for a restriction on Schema 12 relevant to counterfactual conditionals. Schema 13 says that a supposition leading to an incompatibility is false. The schemas are illustrated (right-hand column) with proposition content (letters written on a hidden blackboard) from one kind of content used in the experiments.

[a]The decimal fraction in parentheses is the difficulty weight that STEPIT estimated for the schema in the study reported in chapter 7. The percentage in the parentheses is the percentage of errors on one-step problems involving the schema in the same study.
[b]This is a feeder schema when applied from right to left.
[c]This is a feeder schema. See the text discussion of this schema.

TABLE 6.2
Outline of a Proposed Reasoning Program
That Applies the Schemas of Table 6.1

The program applies both to problem situations where there is a conclusion given whose truth is to be evaluated and when no such conclusion is given (i.e., when subjects are just making inferences from the information they have). In the latter case, the Preliminary Procedure and the Evaluation Procedure of the Direct Reasoning Routine are inapplicable: Then the routine comprises the Inference Procedure only.

The program begins with the Direct Reasoning Routine. The routine terminates when the conclusion is evaluated, or when no new propositions are generated by the Inference Procedure. If the routine terminates without evaluating the conclusion, then available indirect reasoning strategies are applied.

DIRECT REASONING ROUTINE

PRELIMINARY PROCEDURE. (i) If the given conclusion is an *if-then* statement, add the antecedent to the premise set,[a] and treat the consequent as the conclusion to be tested. (ii) Use the Evaluation Procedure to test the conclusion [the given conclusion or the new one created at Step (i)], against the premise set. If the evaluation is indeterminate, proceed to the Inference Procedure.

INFERENCE PROCEDURE. For each of the Core schemas (Schemas 1 through 7, Schema 1 in the left-to-right direction only), apply it if its conditions of application[b] are satisfied or if its conditions of application can be satisfied by first applying one or a combination of the Feeder schemas (Schemas 8, 9, 14, and 1 in the right-to-left direction). Add the propositions deduced to the premise set. When there is a conclusion to be evaluated, use the Evaluation Procedure to test the conclusion against the augmented premise set; if the outcome of the evaluation is indeterminate, repeat the Inference Procedure. When there is no conclusion to be evaluated, just repeat the Inference Procedure. (In executing the Inference Procedure, no schema is applied whose only effect would be to duplicate a proposition already in the premise set.) In reading out conclusions inferred, one-time use of Feeder schemas is optional.[c]

EVALUATION PROCEDURE. To test a given conclusion against a premise set, respond "true" if the conclusion is in the premise set or can be inferred by applying one or a combination of the Feeder schemas; respond "false" if the conclusion, or an inference from it by Schema 9, is incompatible (by Schemas 10 or 11) with a proposition in the premise set, or with a proposition that can be inferred from the premise set by applying one or a combination of the Feeder schemas.

SOME INDIRECT REASONING STRATEGIES

SUPPOSITION-OF-ALTERNATIVES STRATEGY. If the premise set contains a disjunction (or if one is obtained by applying Schema 9), and if some of the propositions of the disjunction do not occur as antecedents of conditionals in the premise set, then suppose each of these in turn and try to derive a conditional with it as antecedent, using Schema 12. (See chapter 7 for discussion of this strategy and a proposed restriction on it.)

STRATEGIES OF ENUMERATION OF ALTERNATIVES A PRIORI: E.g., if the premise set contains one or more conditionals of the form *If p then . . .* or *If not p then . . .* , add the proposition *p or not p* to the premise set and return to the Inference Procedure.

(Continued)

TABLE 6.2
(Continued)

REDUCTIO AD ABSURDUM STRATEGY. Limited form: If there is a conjunction or disjunction embedded within a premise proposition or within the conclusion, then suppose the conjunction or disjunction as per Schema 13 and use the evaluation procedure to test its compatibility with the premise set; if the evaluation is "false," add the negation of the conjunction or disjunction to the premise set; use the evaluation procedure to test the conclusion against the augmented premise set, and if the evaluation is indeterminate, return to the Inference Procedure.

Stronger form: To test the falsity of a conclusion given, or of any proposition embedded within a premise or the conclusion, add the negation of that proposition to the premise set and try to derive an incompatibility as per Schema 13, using the Inference Procedure, any available other strategies, and the Evaluation Procedure.

---

[a]The *premise set* at any point comprises the original premises together with any propositions that have been added by the Preliminary and Inference Procedures.

[b]The conditions of application of a schema are satisfied when the premise set contains propositions of the form specified in the numerator of the schema; to apply the schema is to deduce (generate) the corresponding proposition of the form specified in the denominator of the schema. Schemas that are equivalences are applicable when part (or all) of a proposition in the premise set matches the form specified on one of the sides of the equivalence; application consists of substituting the proposition of the indicated form for the matching part.

[c]For example, if propositions a and b are inferred independently, it is optional to use Schema 8 and read these out as a & b; if a conjunction is in the premise set, it is optional to use Schema 9 to read out the conjuncts separately.

whenever they are applicable. Schemas 8 and 9 make inferences that are especially obvious, and Schema 8 could lead to an infinite loop if it were allowed to reapply continuously. They, along with Schema 1 in the right-to-left direction, and Schema 14 are called *feeder* schemas because the DRR constrains their application—they are used only when their output feeds another schema or the evaluation of a conclusion (apart from a permitted one-time use in reading out inferences).[1] Schemas 10 and 11 define contradictions; the DRR uses them only in the Evaluation Procedure in bringing about the response of False. Schemas 12 and 13 have to do with suppositional reasoning, and they have very restricted roles in the DRR: Schema 12 is involved only in the Preliminary Procedure, and Schema 13 only in the falsification step of the Evaluation Procedure. However, they have a prominent role in indirect (suppositional) reasoning (see later and chaps. 7 and 8 for examples and discussion of indirect reasoning). Schema 14 (a feeder schema) is placed at the end of the list because it is question-

---

[1]Schema 9 could not lead to infinite loops if it were allowed to reapply, and so classification as a feeder schema is not mandatory for it. The fit of the model to data is better with Schema 9 classified as a feeder schema, but the difference is not great. The fit would still be good if it were taken as a core schema.

TABLE 6.3
Examples of How the Direct Reasoning Routine Solves Problems

Problem	Solution Steps	Relevant Schema
1. If Fox or Cat then not Pear False that not Fox		
? Not Pear ?	Fox Not Pear True	1 2
2. Not both Plum and Banana Not Cow Plum		
? Banana or Cow ?	Not Banana Not Banana and not Cow False	4 8 11
3. Goat or Elephant If Elephant then Lemon Not Goat Not both Lemon and Pineapple		
? What follows ?	Elephant Lemon Not Pineapple That's all	3 7 4

Note. Subjects reason about what is in a closed box that can contain toy animals and fruit. The table presents propositions in schematic form: *If Fox or Cat then not Pear = If there is either a fox or a cat in the box then there is not a pear; Fox = There is a fox in the box,* etc. Under Problem, the premises are given above the line, and below it, between question marks, is the conclusion to be evaluated. The column Solution Steps records the sequence of inferences drawn, in order, culminating in the response to the problem. The column Relevant Schema indicates the inference schema in Table 6.1 that determined the form of the inference made at each solution step. (This table and the associated text closely follow Table 7.3 and its description in Braine, 1990.)

able whether it really belongs to the primary skills: It was taken as part of the primary skills in the work reported in chapter 7 (Braine et al., 1984) and in the design of the work reported in chapter 8; however, some of the data reported in chapter 8 made us question this assignment. The schema is included in Table 6.1 because it plays a role in the experiments and for ease of reference by the reader.

We now provide some examples of how the DRR uses the schemas to find answers to some simple deductive-reasoning problems presented to subjects in the form of puzzles. Subjects reason about what is in a closed box that contains toy animals and fruit. The inferences are made by the Inference Procedure, which applies whichever of the core schemas can be applied; the information inferred is added to the stock of information, and then the Inference Procedure reapplies. The nature of the schemas is such that it is rare that the process can be repeated more than a very few times. For example, consider the following problem:

If there is a fox or a cat, then there is not a pear.
It is false that there is not a fox.

? There is not a pear ?

Schema 1 (which cancels a double negative) is the only schema that applies to the premises; it is applied on the first cycle of the routine and adds the information that there is a fox in the box; Schema 2 is now the only schema that applies, and it leads to the conclusion that there is not a pear in the box. After each inference is made, when there is a conclusion to be evaluated the routine tests it for identity or contradiction with the propositions in the growing stock of information. Thus, on this problem a match is found on the second cycle of the routine between the conclusion and the inference just made, bringing about a response of "true." Here is another problem:

There is not both a plum and a banana.
There is not a cow.
There is a plum.

? There is a banana or a cow ?

On this problem, the first and third premises meet the condition of application of Schema 4, which is the only schema that can apply. It generates the inference that there isn't a banana. Schema 8 conjoins this with the second premise to feed the evaluation of the conclusion: A response of "false" is triggered by the incompatibility of the finding that there is not a banana and not a cow with the conclusion to be evaluated, that there is one or the other. On the next problem there is no conclusion to be evaluated, but the routine operates to make inferences in the same way as in the previous problems:

There is a goat or an elephant.
If there is an elephant, then there is a lemon.
There is not a goat.
There is not both a lemon and a pineapple.

? What follows?

Initially, Schema 3 is the only one applicable, and it generates the inference that there is an elephant. Now Schema 7 becomes applicable, yielding the inference that there is a lemon. The condition of application of Schema 4 is now met and the fact that there isn't a pineapple is inferred. The routine now stops as it can make no further inferences. Thus, the predicted series of responses is "Elephant, Lemon, Not pineapple; that's all."

Now let us consider a problem in which the conclusion to be evaluated is an *if-then* sentence, for instance:

If there is a dog in the box, then there is a grape.
If there is a squirrel, then there is a grape.

? If there is either a dog or a squirrel, then there's not a grape?

The Preliminary Procedure applies first: It adds the antecedent of the conclusion (*There is a dog or a squirrel*) to the premise set, and takes the consequent as the conclusion to be evaluated. The new premise set satisfies the condition of application of Schema 5, and generates the inference *There is a grape*, which is added to the premise set. This directly contradicts the new conclusion (Schema 10), and the Evaluation Procedure specifies a response of "false."

In solving problems, the DRR is always the first resource brought into play. Indirect reasoning strategies become applicable only when the DRR can generate no more inferences. For instance, consider the following problem:

If there is a cat then there is a cherry.
If there isn't a cat then there is a cherry.
If there is a cherry then there is a banana.

? There is a banana ?

The DRR generates no output. Most adult subjects will now pass the problem to the Strategies component. The strategy of enumerating alternatives a priori is applicable; it would add the proposition *There is a cat or there isn't a cat* to the premise set and return the subject to the Inference Procedure. The augmented premise set satisfies the condition of application of Schema 5, yielding the inference that there is a cherry. The condition of application of Schema 7 is now satisfied, yielding the inference that there is a banana. The Evaluation Procedure finds that this matches the given conclusion, leading to a response of "true."

COMMENTS ON SOME CHARACTERISTICS
OF THE LOGIC

One characteristic of the logic that deserves some comment is that the negation in Table 6.1 is classical propositional negation: "~" means "it is not the case that p"—the proposition is negated as a whole. Natural language negation is typically attached to the verb phrase (VP) and is typically understood as denying that the predication is true of the subject. Sentence-external negations (e.g., "it is not the case that . . .") are perfectly grammatical, but stilted for atomic propositions (though often a natural way of negating compound propositions where VP-negation is not possible or would be misleading about what was negated). In practice, sentence-negation and VP-negation are usually semantically equivalent (which is no doubt why natural languages can use a negative element on the VP to realize proposition-negation).[2] In any case, possible differences between propositional and predicate negation cannot be modeled in a propositional logic because that does not analyze the internal structure of propositions; a mental predicate logic would be required. We claim that propositional negation exists and is most often realized in surface structure by a negative element attached to the VP.[3]

There are three salient differences from standard logic that also deserve comment. First, like McCawley (1981/1993), we have chosen to treat & and OR as coordinate (i.e., as able to connect n coordinate propositions, not just two); we do so because there is no evidence for binary constituent structure in the English syntax of coordination and plenty of evidence that more than two propositions can be coordinated (e.g., Gleitman, 1965). Second, standard logic includes the schema p, $\therefore$ p or q, as do some other

---

[2]Consider a standard kind of example of non-equivalence, for example,

(i) John is not bald.
(ii) It is not the case that John is bald.

Even when considered in isolation, the normal understanding for both would be that John exists and is asserted not to be bald. However, it is possible to claim that (i) entails the existence of John, whereas (ii) merely implicates it; in that case there is a semantic difference between the two. But it is also possible to argue that John's existence is merely implicated in both cases, in which case they are equivalent. However, in either case in ordinary discourse circumstances it will be known that John exists, and then the two are semantically equivalent whatever stance one takes on whether (i) entails or implicates John's existence.

[3]There is also a quite different kind of natural language negation, which operates on terms, creating opposites often expressed with the prefixes *un-, in-, im-* in English, of which the former is productive: *happy—unhappy, secure—insecure, moral—immoral*, etc. This kind of "negation" is not modeled in our logic, nor could it be in a propositional logic (see LaPalme Reyes, Macnamara, Reyes, & Zolfaghari, 1991, for discussion and a possible model).

proposed mental logics (e.g., Rips, 1983, 1994). The schema is not included in Table 6.1, and there are several reasons for rejecting it as a schema of mental logic. The evidence and arguments are laid out in chapter 7. Third, unlike standard logic, the logic is subject to a global constraint against making inferences from incompatible assumptions (except to infer that some assumption is wrong). The nature of this constraint is spelled out in chapter 7, where it is shown that the constraint accounts for a number of cases in which inferences valid in standard logic are intuitively invalid in ordinary reasoning, and also for differences between *if* and $\supset$ of standard logic.

COMMENT ON PRAGMATIC INFLUENCES
ON REASONING PERFORMANCE

As stressed in chapter 4, everyday reasoning is deployed within a pragmatically motivated architecture. Pragmatic influences can particularly affect the comprehension process—what is taken as the starting information for reasoning. Everyday reasoning uses all the information available, and knowledge relevant to problem content can enrich the given information by providing additional premises (e.g., in Story 2 of Table 4.1 in chap. 4, knowledge that coffee shops typically offer only two places to sit down—counter and table—provides a premise necessary for the response to the first question). In addition, the wording of sentences often gives rise to conversational implicatures and invited inferences, which then serve as additional premises for reasoning (see chaps. 3, 4, 7, and 8 for examples and further discussion). These implicatures are particularly likely if a problem has not been solved by the DRR plus readily available strategies, and if the subject is seeking a determinate response (which, if one can be found, tends to be preferred to "nothing follows" or "can't tell"; see O'Brien et al., 1989).

Biases and nonlogical heuristics (cf. Evans, 1982) can affect reasoning performance at the stage of response choice or during a line of reasoning, but, we predict, will only do so when a problem requires resources beyond the DRR plus readily available strategies: Then, biases and nonlogical heuristics may yield an alternative to "nothing follows" or "can't tell."

There may also be reasoning processes that tend to be elicited by particular kinds of content (e.g., the pragmatic reasoning schemas of Cheng and Holyoak, 1985, or the procedures for finding cheaters on social contracts of Cosmides, 1989). These processes are not necessarily nonlogical—they are largely equivalent to the claim that modus tollens is available for these kinds of contents.[4] However, there are many controversies about these processes and the evidence for them; see chapter 3 for further discussion.

In the empirical work reported in the next two chapters, we deliberately chose content and wording for problems that would minimize pragmatic influences on performance and allow us to focus investigation on the logical component of the theory, and on how it determines performance.

---

[4]Modus tollens is the argument from premises of the form *If p then q* and *not q* to the conclusion of the form *not p*. A modus tollens problem presents the premises and asks for a judgment of the truth of *p* (or of *not p*).

7

Evidence for the Theory: Predicting the Difficulty of Propositional Logic Inference Problems

Martin D. S. Braine
Brian J. Reiser
Barbara Rumain
New York University

INTRODUCTION

There has long been a controversy about the relation of logic to the ordinary deductive reasoning of subjects untutored in logic. Twentieth century philosophy has generally held that logic has only a normative relation to reasoning (e.g., Cohen, 1944): Logic specifies the correct responses but says nothing about how they are achieved. From a psychological standpoint, however, it is often hard to explain correct responses if one cannot assume that the reasoner is following logical principles.

Within psychology, there have been three approaches to the issue of the relation of logic to reasoning. One approach has emphasized nonlogical processes and biases (e.g., Evans, 1972, 1982), of which the best known example is the atmosphere theory of syllogistic reasoning (Woodworth & Sells, 1935). Historically, however, this approach has usually focused on explaining errors rather than correct responses. No comprehensive theory has ever been presented for any kind of deductive reasoning that purports to explain correct responses as well as errors in terms of entirely nonlogical processes and biases.

The second approach posits that subjects proceed by constructing a mental model of the information given and reason from the model. For instance, given the premises *A is inside B* and *B is inside C*, a subject imagines a state of affairs corresponding to the premises; the conclusion that *A is inside C* can then be read off from the image. According to

Johnson-Laird (1980, 1982), reasoning consists of forming a model, reading off a tentative conclusion, and then testing the conclusion by trying to construct alternative models consistent with the premises. This kind of theory has been extensively developed to account for responses to categorical syllogisms (e.g., Erickson, 1974; Johnson-Laird, 1980, 1982; Johnson-Laird & Steedman, 1978), as well as for inferences about spatial and lexical relations (Johnson-Laird, 1980, 1982). It has been urged that it may suffice for all deductive reasoning (Johnson-Laird, 1982, 1983). However, at the time this work was done, no mental-model theory of propositional reasoning had been proposed (see later chapters for extensive discussion of recent proposals of Johnson-Laird and his colleagues).

The third approach assumes that reasoning includes logical principles and has been the standing point for a substantial body of work in recent years, including that reported here. It follows the lead of Henle (1962), who urged a return to the theoretical position of an earlier generation of logicians (e.g., Boole, 1854; Mill, 1874), that natural reasoning incorporates a mental logic of some sort. Since then, several theories of propositional reasoning have been proposed that include a "natural logic" specifying a repertory of the elementary deductive steps that can take a reasoner from one step to the next in a chain of reasoning (Braine, 1978; Johnson-Laird, 1975; Osherson, 1975a; Rips, 1983). The theory of chapter 6 is of this sort. In these theories, the elementary deductive steps are defined through inference schemas. Because an inference schema specifies a way of moving from one step to another in a chain of reasoning, a logic that consists of a set of schemas can offer an hypothesis about the repertory of deductive steps available to people in a given type of reasoning.

The main purpose of the present work was to obtain empirical evidence on the repertory of the kinds of valid inferences made by subjects in propositional reasoning. The repertory that is taken as the hypothesis to be tested is that of Table 6.1. These schemas are a revision of those of Braine (1978), which in turn attempted to improve on those of Osherson (1975a) and Johnson-Laird (1975). Because the present work was done well before Rips's (1983) article appeared, the choice of schemas could not be influenced by his model. Our primary goal was to obtain systematic data to assess whether the schemas of this set define the kinds of valid inferences made by people in propositional reasoning.

A complete theory of propositional reasoning obviously must include more than a logic of inference schemas. The logic specifies only the repertory of steps available to the reasoner; it does not itself generate a chain of reasoning. A complete theory requires at least two further components. One is a comprehension mechanism that understands natural language in terms of the semantic representations of the schemas. Note that the schemas use a set of semantic elements—AND, OR, NEG, and

IF-THEN—which are distinct from the corresponding English words (*and*, *or*, etc.). Given this distinction between the surface structure in which propositions are expressed and the semantic representations provided in the schemas, it follows that before schemas are used in reasoning, there must be a comprehension step in which the given verbal information is decoded into the representations used in the schemas.

The second component is a reasoning program consisting of routines and strategies that can put together a chain of inferences, selecting the schema that is to be applied at each point in the reasoning (Table 6.2). A possible additional component is a set of nonlogical or quasi-logical fallback procedures that determine a response when the reasoning program fails to deliver a solution to a problem.

Although we believe that it is useful to think of all these components (i.e., the schemas, the comprehension mechanism, the reasoning program, and the fallback procedures) as functionally distinct, we do not mean to imply that they are not interrelated and cannot interdigitate. For instance, a particular reasoning heuristic may be associated with a certain schema; a fallback procedure might lead to a reconstruing of a premise, leading in turn to a new cycle of the reasoning program. Of these components, however, it is the schemas and the nature of the reasoning program that are the concern of the present work. The work is designed to minimize the roles of differential comprehension and of fallback procedures in determining responses in order that the contribution of these components to response variance can be neglected. We hoped thus to permit the components we wished to study to be addressed with as much precision as possible.

We used reasoning problems that consist of one or more premises and a proposed conclusion, and the subject evaluated the truth of the conclusion given the premises. A central part of the methodology consists in testing the prediction that, for a large class of reasoning problems, the difficulty of a problem for subjects can be predicted from the schemas of this repertory that are used in solving the problem, together with certain assumptions about how the subjects' reasoning program selects the schemas used, and some performance assumptions. Before explaining the methodology in more detail, we consider these assumptions, beginning with what the theory has to say about mistakes in reasoning.

The theory allows three sources for reasoning errors. We shall call them *comprehension* errors, *heuristic inadequacy* errors, and *processing* errors, respectively. A comprehension error is an error of construal of the premises or of the conclusion: The starting information used by the subject is not that intended by the problem setter. Heuristic inadequacy errors occur when the subject's reasoning program fails to find a line of reasoning that solves a problem, that is, the problem is too difficult for the subject. Processing errors comprise lapses of attention, errors of execution in the application of schemas, failure to keep track of information in working memory, and the like. We assume that the probability of a processing error increases with problem complexity, but overall tends to be low and essentially vanishes in the simplest problems where processing load must be assumed to be minimal.

The work reported is designed so that the expected sources of error are always known. First, we sought to eliminate comprehension errors entirely, by avoiding problems that are likely to give rise to them. In particular, we did not use problems in which the premises might have "conversational implicatures" (Grice, 1975) that would lead to error. Thus, it is well known that a conditional (*If p then q*) invites the inference *If not p then not q* (Geis & Zwicky, 1971), which leads to the standard fallacies of conditional reasoning. In our problems, understanding a conditional as its invited inference could never lead a subject to an evaluation of the problem conclusion. Similarly, we avoided certain problems in which interpreting *or* inclusively versus exclusively could make a difference. In addition, in premises where the relative scopes of negations and connectives had to be understood, we did pilot work to discover a wording that subjects construed in the intended manner. Thus, all situations that could plausibly lead to comprehension errors were avoided, hopefully eliminating this source of response variance.

Second, we tried to localize processing and heuristic inadequacy errors by dividing the problems into two main types. Most of the problems are of a type that we call *direct reasoning* (defined later): These problems are of low-to-moderate complexity, on which we expect all subjects to find the shortest line of reasoning, probably using much the same reasoning routine to do so. On these problems we expect all errors to be of the processing type. The other type of problem is referred to as *indirect reasoning*. The purpose of these problems is to find out whether subjects are indeed all able to find the solutions, and these problems may give rise to heuristic inadequacy errors.

The distinction between direct and indirect reasoning is important for the work reported. We define *direct reasoning* as follows: The reasoner starts with the premises, makes an inference from the premises, and then successively makes further inferences from the premises together with the propositions already inferred, until the conclusion or a proposition incompatible with it is reached. (We assume that a response of "false" is triggered by the discovery of an incompatibility among the premises, inferred propositions, and conclusion; thus, all responses of "false" involve either Schema 10 or 11 of Table 6.1.) In the special case in which the conclusion to be evaluated is an if-then statement, we also consider the reasoning direct if the reasoner first adds the antecedent of the conclusion to the premises as an additional starting formula, taking the consequent as the conclusion to be reached, and then solves the reformulated problem by successive inferences as described earlier, starting with the premises together with the antecedent. It follows that direct reasoning contains no lemmas (i.e., auxiliary propositions used to prove another proposition), and, with one exception, does not use suppositions. (The exception is the adding of the antecedent of an *if-then* conclusion to the premises, as noted earlier. Technically, the antecedent becomes a supposition; however, because the choice of this supposition is dictated by the conclusion, making it is a routine matter that we count as part of direct reasoning, unlike other uses of supposition as in reductio ad absurdum arguments.) Certain schemas are characteristic of indirect reasoning, notably Schema 13 of Table 6.1, which is involved in reductio ad absurdum arguments. In general, indirect reasoning may require some "intelligent" heuristics to find the successful line of reasoning (e.g., the Indirect Reasoning Strategies of Table 6.2), and the difficulty of the problem will likely reflect the difficulty of finding that line of reasoning. Hence problems that require indirect reasoning may show heuristic inadequacy errors. (Of course, direct reasoning problems could be made very long and complicated and might then also elicit heuristic inadequacy errors. We tried, however, to avoid that level of complexity.)

This distinction between direct and indirect reasoning seemed to us an intuitively useful one to draw. In addition, there is developmental evidence that indirect reasoning is a later-appearing and more sophisticated phenomenon than direct reasoning (see Braine & Rumain, 1983, for a review).

The only assumption about subjects' reasoning programs that is crucial for the present work is that their programs routinely find the shortest line of reasoning that solves our direct reasoning problems using the schemas of Table 6.1. That assumption specifies uniquely the sequence of inferences made in solving each problem, information needed to predict problem difficulty. Table 6.2 outlines the program that we propose that subjects bring to bear on the problems. The program provides an operational definition of direct reasoning (reasoning generated by the *direct reasoning routine*) and solves the direct reasoning problems by the shortest line of reasoning possible with the schemas of Table 6.1. The program is discussed later.

We now outline our methodology. We examined the set of schemas in two principal ways. First, if a schema is one of a universal repertory, and if processing errors are minimal on easy problems, then performance on the simplest reasoning problems demanding a schema should be essentially error free. Therefore, we sought to discover whether this condition was satisfied for the schemas investigated.

Second, we used the set to predict the difficulty of problems requiring short chains of direct reasoning. The methodology was a modified version of that used by Osherson (1974, 1975a, 1976) and Rips (1983). Osherson assumed that when a problem requires a chain of reasoning steps to get from the premises to the conclusion, its difficulty should be predictable from the sum of the difficulties of the component inferences that make up the chain. In our version of Osherson's methodology, many deductive reasoning problems were presented to subjects, and empirical measures of the difficulty of each problem were obtained. We used two prediction schemes. In Scheme 1, one set of data was used to estimate difficulty weights for each schema, the difficulty weight of a schema being an index of the difficulty of adopting and using that schema in solving a problem. We then inquired whether it was possible to predict systematically the empirically measured difficulty of a problem from the sum of the difficulty weights of the component inferences claimed to be used in solving the problem, together with some difficulty contributed only by problem length. The second prediction scheme is simpler. We assigned equal difficulty weights to all the schemas, thus taking the difficulty of an argument as proportional only to the number of reasoning steps, not to their nature. Thus, Scheme 2 examines how well problem difficulty can be predicted just from problem length and the number of steps needed to solve it.

In general in this chapter, we shall use the word *theory* to refer to our claims about the nature of subjects' inference schemas and reasoning program. We shall use the term *model* to refer to the theory taken with a particular prediction scheme. Thus, Model 1 is the theory combined with Scheme 1, and Model 2 is the theory taken with Scheme 2.

To the extent that these models predict successfully, we take it as evidence that the inference schemas of Table 6.1 are psychologically real, that is, actually used by the subjects in solving the problems. The difference between the effectiveness of the models provides information about the relevance of kind of inference to problem difficulty.

Three measures of problem difficulty were used. First, we obtained difficulty ratings: Subjects did each problem and rated its difficulty on a 9-point scale. Two sets of difficulty ratings were obtained, one set being used to estimate difficulty weights for the schemas and the other for crossvalidation. A second measure of problem difficulty was derived from the time taken to solve a problem, as estimated from reaction time measures. Errors provided a third measure of problem difficulty.

In the case of the difficulty ratings, we assume that in doing a problem the subject forms a subjective impression, reflected in the rating, of the amount of processing the problem demanded, and that this processing is, in turn, a function of the number and kind of mental steps required to solve the problem. Although the difficulty rating is the least orthodox of the measures, it is likely that it reflects subjects' inferential operations in solving a problem as well as either the reaction time or error measures. The reaction times are of the order of seconds and tens of seconds, and thus much longer than in most studies in cognitive psychology that use latency measures. Some of the response time is undoubtedly spent not on making inferences but on other things, such as rereading premises after the conclusion to be evaluated has been presented; consequently, the latencies cannot be taken as a good index of the time required to execute a chain of inferences. Thus, there is no principled reason for preferring latency to the difficulty rating as a measure; neither can claim to be more than a reasonable index of the overall difficulty of a problem, or of the gross amount of processing it demanded. Although errors provide a well-motivated index of difficulty, the low error probability overall meant that an unduly large number of subjects would be required for errors to provide a highly reliable index. In general, because no single measure seemed ideal, it seemed preferable to use all three. It turned out, however, that the difficulty ratings had better psychometric properties than the latencies or errors: They were the least skewed, subjects showed relatively more consensus in their ratings than in their latencies or errors, and problems were differentiated the best. So we gave relatively more weight to the ratings and used them to estimate parameters. In his work on reasoning, Osherson (1974, 1975a, 1976) also found difficulty ratings to be preferable to latencies as measures.

Three studies were conducted. In the first study the main measure was solution latency; this is referred to as the *Reaction Time Study*. The second study, referred to as *Rating Study 1*, used a new group of subjects who rated the difficulty of each problem after they had done it. Rating Study I and the Reaction Time Study used essentially the same set of problems. Some afterthoughts about the problem set, as well as the need for cross-validation, suggested a third study, *Rating Study 2*. In this study another group of subjects rated the difficulty of a new set of problems, many of which differed from problems of the previous set. The method of sampling of schemas within the problems made Rating Study 2 the most appropriate study for estimating difficulty weights for the schemas. So, in the Results the schema difficulty weights are obtained from this study and then used to postdict the data from Rating Study 1. After that, they are used in models that seek to account for the reaction time and error data. Thus, the order of presenting results will not correspond exactly to the order of conducting the experiments. The procedures are all described together.

METHOD

Materials

Types of Problems. The problems used were of the following five types. The Appendix to this chapter contains examples illustrating the first four types and includes a nearly complete listing of all problems of the first three types that were used in Rating Study 2. The first three types are referred to collectively as *direct reasoning* problems.

1. One-step problems. These were problems in which the conclusion could be reached from the premises in one step using one of the schemas.

2. One-step + contradiction. In these the negation of the conclusion could be reached from the premises in one step using one of the schemas.

3. Multistep problems in which the usual, or only, solution is by direct reasoning (defined earlier). The multistep problems used involved a chain of two or more inferences; those for which the expected response was "false" also involved finding an incompatibility between the premises and the conclusion. Some indication of the range of difficulty sampled can be obtained from the listing in the Appendix.

4. "Control" problems, true and false. In control problems with answers of "true," the premise and conclusion were identical and merely had to be matched. In control problems with "false" as the answer, either the conclusion directly negated the premise, or vice versa. (Formally, control-false problems are one-step problems involving Schema 10.) In the Reaction Time Study, the control-true problems provided information about how long it took to find a "match" when no reasoning was involved. In the rating studies they served to anchor the low end of the difficulty rating scale.

The above-mentioned four types of problems constituted a large majority of the problems used, and most analyses of the data involved only these.

5. Other problems. One other problem that occurred in both rating studies tested the possibility that subjects might use the standard logic schema, p, $\therefore$ p OR q, which we did not believe was a schema of natural logic. The remaining other problems required indirect reasoning, according to the schemas of Table 6.1 and the program of Table 6.2. There was a lemma, or a suppositional step was involved to set up a reductio ad absurdum, or a starting proposition of the form p OR F (p). Some of these were problems for which the schemas of Table 6.1, and of Braine (1978), made somewhat different predictions—they required indirect reasoning using the schemas of Table 6.1 and the strategies of Table 6.2, but had short direct solutions by the schemas of Braine (1978). These problems are cited later when the results on them are presented.

Content and Wording of Problems. To standardize the problems as much as possible, all problems concerned the presence or absence of letters on an imaginary blackboard, as in Osherson (1975a). This served to minimize differences in length and comprehensibility between sentences of different problems and to reduce the contribution of substantive content to response variance.

The conjunctions and disjunctions used in the problems always contained exactly two coordinate propositions. Thus, although the schemas of Table 6.1 allow for more than two coordinate propositions, the work does not bear on the distinction between binary and n-ary coordination in schemas. The same logical form was always reflected in the same wording. The wording adopted was based on the results of some pilot work in which subjects assessed the clarity and lack of ambiguity of various possible wordings. The wordings we used are illustrated in the Appendix.

The Set of Problems for the Reaction Time Study. There were 121 problems. The set included 10 one-step problems (apart from control-false problems), one for each of Schemas 1 through 6 and 8, 9, 11, and 14. Eleven problems were one-step + contradiction. There were 33 direct reasoning multistep problems, of which 13 combined a single schema with modus ponens (Schema 7), with or without a contradiction; the other 20 involved two or more different schemas other than Schema 7, with or without a contradiction. These types combine to a total of 54 direct reasoning problems that are of primary interest in the data analyses.

There were also 48 control problems. Twelve true and 12 false control problems were created, so that there was a control problem whose conclusion was identical in length and logical form to each different conclusion found among the 54 reasoning problems just specified. Because of their importance, two instances of each control problem were included in the stimulus set.

In addition, there were 19 other problems that involved indirect reasoning. Their form is specified later when the results for them are discussed. The expected answer to exactly half the problems was "true" and to the other half "false."

To order the problems of the stimulus set, the total problem set was first divided into two equal-sized blocks. An instance of each control problem was included in each block, and all other problems were randomly assigned to a block with the constraint that for each type of problem the number of trues and falses within a block was kept as equal as possible. The problems were then placed in random order within each block, with the constraint that only three true or three false problems could occur consecutively. The problems were divided into blocks and ordered twice in this way, to generate two different problem orders. In addition, we also generated the reverse order of each of these orders, yielding four different orderings of the problem set.

Seven true and seven false "practice problems" were also designed. These included a true and a false control problem and several one- and two-step problems. None appeared in the actual stimulus set. The practice set familiarized subjects with the equipment and procedure before the start of the experiment proper. The entire set of problems and practice problems was recorded on magnetic tape for display by a computer.

The Set of Problems for Rating Study 1. The set comprised 99 problems. These included the same 54 problems used in the Reaction Time Study (i.e., one-step, one-step + contradiction, and multistep direct-reasoning problems). They also included the same 24 control problems, now given once each instead of twice. The same 19 indirect reasoning problems were also in the set. There were two new problems. One of these involved the questionable schema p, $\therefore$ p OR q, and would have been a one-step problem if subjects used that schema. The other (identified later) was a new version with changed wording of 1 of the 19 indirect reasoning problems.

The same four orderings of the set of problems were used as in the Reaction Time Study, except that half the control problems were omitted, and the two new problems were inserted at random positions into each of the four orders. The four orders of the problems were assembled into typewritten booklets.

The practice problems for the Reaction Time Study were augmented by two problems to ensure that the range of difficulty of the main problem set should be adequately sampled within the practice problems. Experience with the practice problems could then permit subjects to form a useful rough calibration of their internal difficulty rating scale prior to beginning the main set of problems.

The Set of Problems for Rating Study 2. There were 85 problems. These included 12 one-step problems involving the regular versions of schemas. Another 14 problems involved one step together with a contradiction. Eight of these involved modus ponens; they had the same form but varied in length from 19 to 39 words and were especially designed to explore the relation between problem length and rated difficulty, holding the reasoning process constant (see examples xxi and xxii in the Appendix to this chapter). An additional 39 problems were direct reasoning, multistep problems, involving from two to four steps. Within these 65 problems specified so far, an effort was made to have adequate representation of each of the assumed set of reasoning steps. Thus, each of the schemas occurred at least eight times (except for Schema 13, which cannot occur in direct reasoning problems).

In addition, there were 11 control problems and 9 other problems. Eight of the latter involved indirect reasoning (all cited later), and the ninth tested the potential schema p, $\therefore$ p OR q. Omitting that problem, the expected answer to 42 problems was "true," and to 42 "false." Of the 85 problems, 49 had the same form as problems that occurred in both the Reaction Time Study and Rating Study 1; 36 of these were direct reasoning problems, 9 were controls, and 4 were indirect reasoning problems. Four orders of the problems were created as before and assembled into typewritten booklets preceded by the practice problems, as in Rating Study 1.

Procedure

Reaction Time Study. The basic task was to read a reasoning problem, including a premise or premises and a tentative conclusion, one sentence at a time, and then to evaluate the conclusion as true or false on the basis of the premises. The task was implemented as follows. Subjects were seated before a 15-inch TV screen and a three-button response box. The buttons formed an inverted triangle, with the bottom button labeled *move*, and the top vertices labeled *true* and *false*. The subject's preferred thumb rested on the move button, and the index fingers of either hand rested on the true and false buttons. For half of the subjects, the button pressed by the dominant hand was used to respond "true," and the other to respond "false." For the other half of the subjects, this was reversed. The screen and response box were connected to a PDP-8/I minicomputer, located in an adjacent room.

It was explained that each problem would concern the presence or absence of letters on an imaginary blackboard. The problem would contain some facts, followed by a final statement about the blackboard, the tentative "conclusion." The facts or premises contained the information that was known about the blackboard and were to be accepted at face value. Each problem would begin with the word *ready* displayed on the screen. When the subject was ready to begin, a press of the move button would clear this ready signal and bring the first premise to the screen. He or she was then to read that premise as quickly and accurately as possible, and then to press the move button, repeating the same process for succeeding premises. (These latencies to push the move button provided reading times for the premises.) The last premise was underlined and, after the button press, was followed by the proposed conclusion. The conclusion was marked by a question mark. Upon reading the conclusion, subjects were to decide if that sentence were definitely true or definitely false, given the premises for that problem, and to respond by pressing the appropriate button. The screen then cleared, and 1.5 seconds later a new ready signal was displayed, indicating the start of a new problem. If the subject could not solve the problem, or thought it impossible to solve, he or she was to press move in response to the conclusion and proceed with the next problem.

Because each sentence was displayed beneath its predecessor without clearing the screen, subjects were reading for comprehension rather than memorization. The subjects were instructed that they should respond as quickly as possible, trying to commit as few errors as possible. All reaction times, including those to read the premises and those to respond true or false, were recorded by the computer. The subjects first responded to the practice trials. After the practice problems, any difficulties were discussed, and any further questions about the procedure answered. The subjects then received the first block of problems, and after a brief intermission, received the second block.

Rating Studies 1 and 2. Subjects were told that they were to participate in a reasoning experiment, in which they would answer each problem in the booklet provided and then judge its difficulty. The explanation of the problems was identical to that in the Reaction Time Study. The subject was told to read each problem, accepting the sentences above the line as true, and then to evaluate the proposed conclusion. In addition to true and false, the response alternative of "indeterminate" was available, although its use was not encouraged: Subjects were told that there should be enough information in almost all of the problems to reach a definite conclusion. There were a few problems that were "controversial," however, in which some people thought there was enough information, whereas others thought there was no way to prove or disprove the conclusion. If they were to find such problems, they were to respond "indeterminate," rather than "true" or "false."

After solving each problem, the subject was to rate its difficulty relative to the other problems, using a 9-point scale, with 1 being the easiest and 9 being the most difficult. They were to evaluate how difficult it was to arrive at an answer, and to try not to be unduly influenced by the length of the sentences, or of the problem itself. Subjects were instructed to try to use all the numbers on the scale, although not necessarily equally often.

Besides familiarizing subjects with the procedure, the practice problems gave them an impression of the range of difficulty of the problem set: Because the practice problems included all levels of difficulty, they would permit subjects to establish their mental scale. Difficulties or questions were discussed, and then the subjects were given the experiment proper. Subjects worked alone, undisturbed, and at their own pace. We asked only that they follow the order of the problems in the booklet. For most subjects, after they had finished the written problems, introspections were gathered orally on between 15 and 36 problems, depending on time considerations and the subject's stamina. Each problem was re-presented in written form, and subjects were asked to solve it and then summarize their reasoning as best they could.

Subjects

Reaction Time Study. Twenty-eight undergraduates participated either as paid subjects or to fulfill a course requirement. Data from three other subjects were discarded, because their extremely high error rates relative to the other subjects resulted in too few usable data points and rendered their compliance with the instructions of the task suspect.

Rating Studies 1 and 2. There were again 28 student subjects in each study. Some were paid and some participated to fulfill an Introductory Psychology course requirement. In both studies the difficulty ratings of only 24 subjects were used. The subjects whose ratings were discarded either failed to follow the rating instructions satisfactorily (e.g., rated most problems as "1," the lowest rating, thus providing no information about problem difficulty), or they had high error rates relative to the remaining subjects.

RESULTS

We first analyze the data from the direct reasoning problems of Rating Study 2, using the prediction schemes of Models 1 and 2, described in the Introduction. The reason for beginning with Rating Study 2 is that study was better designed for estimating the schema weights required in Model 1, because the schemas occurred with more nearly equal frequency in its problems than in those of the other studies.

Next, we investigate how far the prediction equations predict the difficulty ratings of the direct reasoning problems of Rating Study 1. Because the subjects and some of the problems used were not the same as those of Rating Study 2, this analysis provides a crossvalidation of the prediction equations. Then we inquire how well the models predict the reaction time data and the error data from all studies combined. The final section of the Results discusses the data on the indirect reasoning problems of the various studies.

Direct Reasoning Problems: Rating Study 2

In Model 1, each of the schemas is associated with a difficulty weight, which is the difficulty (in the subjective units of the rating scale) of adopting and applying that reasoning step in a reasoning problem. The length of a problem (measured here by the total number of words in premises and conclusion) may also contribute to the subjective difficulty independently of the reasoning process (e.g., more or longer sentences may demand more effort to comprehend), the simplest assumption being that the contribution is a linear function of the number of words. (Other measures of length, such as number of embedded simple propositions, number of logical connectives, and the like, were investigated; they were all highly correlated with number of words and did not show closer relations to problem difficulty than did the number of words.) Thus the predicted difficulty of any problem is equal to the sum of the difficulty weights of each reasoning step involved in a problem, plus some constant times the number of words in the problem, plus some other constant that sets the lower end of the rating scale at 1.0.

We posit that the difficulty of a problem should depend on the sum of the difficulty weights of the component reasoning steps (rather than, say, their product, or some other function) because additivity is the simplest assumption to make, and no other assumption appears to have a better rationale. Also, Osherson (1975a) assumed additivity without anomalous results. Model 2 is just like Model 1, except that all the difficulty weights are set equal.

Contribution of Problem Length to Rated Difficulty. It will be recalled that in eight problems, each involving modus ponens and a contradiction, problem length was deliberately varied while holding the reasoning steps constant. (See the Appendix, Problems xxi and xxii, for examples of a short and a long problem.) Problem length varied from 19 to 35 words in this set, and the difficulty ratings from 2.04 to 3.71. On these problems there was a correlation of .93 between the mean rated difficulty and the number of words. (The mean difficulty ratings used are those for correct responses, but there were in fact only four errors among the 192 responses.) The regression equation indicated that each additional word added .0728 to mean rated difficulty. The correlation of .93 was sufficiently high that we decided to adopt .0728 as the multiplying constant for problem length, rather than use the entire set of problems to estimate this parameter.

Fixing the multiplying constant for problem length permits the other constant also to be fixed, by the following line of reasoning. The low end of the rating scale is 1.0. The easiest problem possible is a control-true problem of minimum length, that is, in which both premise and conclusion are the same and are just four words long (see Problem i of the Appendix). Such a problem involves no reasoning, and so reasoning steps make no contribution to its difficulty rating. For such an eight-word problem to have a predicted rating of 1.0, the constant must be .4176. The equation predicting the difficulty of a problem for Model 1 is then:

Predicted difficulty = .4176 + .0728 (number of words)
$$+ \text{E (difficulty weights of reasoning steps)} \quad (1)$$

(When the last term is zero, and number of words = 8, the predicted difficulty is 1.0, as required.) The prediction equation of Model 2 is:

$$\text{Predicted difficulty} = .4176 + .0728 \text{ (number of words)} + nD, \qquad (2)$$

where n is the number of reasoning steps on a problem, and D is the average difficulty of a reasoning step.

Model 1: Estimating Difficulty Weights for the Reasoning Steps. Our "natural logic" provides a set of 14 elementary reasoning steps. Schema 14 occurs only in indirect reasoning problems, and a difficulty weights cannot be estimated for it. Weights were estimated for Schemas 1 to 12 and 14 of Table 6.1.

Data from 60 problems were analyzed; 57 of these were the 65 one- and multistep direct reasoning problems, minus the 8 modus-ponens–plus–contradiction problems used to estimate the problem-length parameter just fixed. In addition, one control-true problem was included, the one of minimum length. The other two problems were constituted as follows: One condensed the 8 modus-ponens–plus–contradiction problems into a single datum: the difficulty (predicted from the equation regressing rated difficulty on problem length for the 8 modus-ponens–plus–contradiction problems—*not* Equation 2) of a modus-ponens–plus–contradiction problem with a length of 19 words. The other condensed the control-false problems into a single datum; these problems involve finding a contradiction only and are one-step problems involving Schema 10 of Table 6.1; two of these had just nine words, and the average of their rated difficulties was used. (The reason for these condensations was to control the sampling of the reasoning steps: It did not seem desirable that the estimate of the difficulty of modus ponens should be heavily determined by the single type of modus ponens problem used to obtain the problem length parameter; nor did we desire that control-false problems should contribute unduly to the estimated weight of Schema 10.)[1] The other control problems and the indirect reasoning problems were not used in this part of the data analysis. Each hypothesized reasoning step was represented either 8 or 9 times in the 60 problems, except for Schema 10, which occurred 23 times. (Either Schema 10 or Schema 11 necessarily occurred in all problems with "false" as the correct response.)

Difficulty weights for the 13 reasoning steps were estimated using the program STEPIT (Chandler, 1969) to obtain the best least-squares fit of

---

[1]In fact, different decisions about how to include control-false and modus-ponens–plus–contradiction problems in the problem set used to estimate difficulty weights would not have affected the weights much.

the predicted problem difficulties (from Equation 2) to the obtained mean difficulty ratings. (The mean difficulty ratings were based on correct responses only.) The difficulty weights yielded by the program are given in parentheses alongside each schema in Table 6.1.

The correlation between the predicted and the obtained mean difficulty ratings for the 60 problems was .92.

Model 2. The same 60 problems and the same analytic procedure were used as for Model 1, except that all the reasoning step difficulty weights were set equal. Thus, only one parameter, D in Equation 3, was estimated from the data. (It turned out to be .51.) The correlation between the predicted and obtained mean difficulty ratings was .79 for Model 2. This correlation is significantly less than that obtained with Model 1 [t (57) = 4.82, $p < .001$—the test is Hotelling's (1940) t test for $\rho_{xy} = \rho_{xz}$ on the same population].

Direct Reasoning Problems

Crossvalidation With Rating Study 1

Because the predicted difficulties for Rating Study 2 were based on parameters estimated from the data of that study, we next investigated how well the model would predict the difficulties obtained in Rating Study 1, without any new estimation of parameters. Fifty-five problems from Rating Study 1 were used. These comprised the control-true problem of minimum length, a control-false problem (as before, this was the average of 2 minimum length control-false problems, treated as a single datum), and 53 of the original 54 one-step and multistep direct reasoning problems. The other problem was omitted because 46% of the subjects made errors on it. (This problem is identified and discussed at the end of this section.)

For these 55 problems, the correlation between the Model 1 predictions and the obtained mean difficulty ratings was .95. The Model 2 predictions correlated .73 with the same ratings. Thus, in neither case was there shrinkage of correlation, despite the fact that the two rating studies used different subjects and a partially different set of problems. The correlation for Model 2 is again significantly less than for Model 1 [t (52) = 7.21, $p < .01$].

A subset of 38 problems had the same form in both rating studies, and this subset permits the strength of the prediction to be compared with the test–retest reliability of the mean ratings. For these 38 problems, the correlation of the mean ratings given by the subjects of Study 2 with the mean ratings of the subjects of Study 1 was .92. For the same subset, the Model 1 predictions (Equation 2) correlated .94 with the mean ratings obtained in each study. Thus, for both studies, Model 1 predicts the data slightly better than the data predict themselves. The comparable Model 2 predictions for these 38 problems correlated .76 and .71 with the ratings for Studies 2 and 1, respectively.

The other 17 problems of Rating Study 1 did not have the same form as problems of Rating Study 2, and they thus permit a test of how well the models predict to new direct reasoning problems, of forms not originally used in the estimation of the schema difficulty weights. For these 17 problems the correlation between the predicted and obtained mean difficulty ratings was .96 for Model 1 and .69 for Model 2, suggesting satisfactory generalization to new problems.

Because the Model 1 predictions are obviously excellent, it is pertinent to inquire how much of the quality of the prediction comes from problem length and how much is due to the difficulty weightings of the reasoning steps. Taken alone, the correlation of problem length (number of words) with the obtained mean difficulty ratings was .71 for the 60 problems of Study 2 and .67 for the 55 problems of Study 1. The sum of the difficulty weights for the reasoning steps involved in a problem (the problem length parameter omitted) correlated .65 and .69 with the obtained mean ratings of problems for Study 2 and Study 1, respectively. Thus, both the sum of the reasoning step weights and problem length contribute heavily and about equally to the quality of the overall model predictions. The correlations of the sum of the reasoning step weights on a problem with the length of the problem were .09 and .03 in Study 2 and 1, respectively, and neither were significant. When length is partialed out, the partial correlations of the sums of the reasoning step weights with the difficulty ratings are .83 and .91 in Studies 2 and 1, respectively. Thus, most of the variance in the subjective difficulty of problems that is not associated with problem length (70% to 80%) is associated with the sum-of-the-reasoning-step-weights parameter of Equation 2.

For Model 2, the comparable correlations are of the number of reasoning steps with the ratings. For Studies 2 and 1, respectively, these were .67 and .66 and shrank to .51 and .52 when length was partialed out. Thus, about a quarter of the variance that is not associated with problem length is associated with number of reasoning steps.

As noted earlier, one problem of Rating Study 1 was omitted from the preceding analyses because 46% of the subjects made errors on it. (No other direct reasoning problems had more than 11% errors in Rating Study 1.) The problem was also rated as very difficult by those who solved it. It was:

There is a G and there's not a P
There is a P or there's not an L
? There is an L   (3)

The difficulty probably comes from the form *p or not q* of the second premise. It is known that disjuncts with one negative proposition are confusing to reason with (Johnson-Laird & Tridgell, 1972; Roberge, 1976), considerably more confusing even than disjuncts in which both propositions are negative. Our model seriously underpredicts the difficulty of this problem and would need some special processing parameter to accommodate it. We might add that, although almost two thirds of the problems used in our studies contain negatives, this problem is the only one that seems to require special treatment.

Significance of the Schema Weights. It would be desirable to be able to demonstrate that each of the weights estimated by STEPIT was significantly greater than zero, but there is no available statistical test. The smallest weight, however, that for Schema 12, is very low, only .02. We therefore did a separate test to see whether there was evidence that this step added significant difficulty to problems. The clearest comparison would involve comparing one-step problems with the same problems with a Schema 12 inference added. There were five such pairs in each of the rating studies, the one-step problems involving Schemas 2 to 6 (Appendix, Problems ix and xxiv, x and xxix, xi and xxxviii, xii and xxvi, xiii and xl). Analyses of variance were conducted for each study, with the differences among Schemas 2 to 6 as one within-subjects variable and the distinction between one-step and one-step + Schema 12 as the other. In both studies, the one-step + Schema 12 problems were rated slightly but significantly more difficult than the one-step problems [$F(1, 23) = 5.39$, $p < .05$ in Study 1, and $F(1, 23) = 13.80$, $p < .01$ in Study 2]. There were also significant differences among the five schemas, but that is not relevant to the question at issue. There was no significant interaction and thus no evidence that the difference made by Schema 12 was greater for one schema than another. Although significant, the average increment in the difficulty rating associated with Schema 12 was quite small (.336). There was also a significant difference between the one step and one-step + Schema 12 problems in errors [$t(4) = 3.01$, $p < .05$, using the *ranked errors* measure that is discussed later], but no significant difference in reaction times. Altogether, the evidence indicates a small but real penalty associated with Schema 12. Presumably, STEPIT's low estimate indicates that in the more complex problems, the contribution to difficulty of Schema 12 was submerged.

Reaction Time Study

Adjustment of Reaction Times. It will be recalled that the premises were presented and read seriatim, and then the conclusion to be evaluated was presented. Times to read each premise and to evaluate the conclusion were obtained. It seemed to us that the raw latencies (i.e., the time to respond "true" or "false" after the presentation of the conclusion) must be inadequate as measures of problem difficulty for two reasons. First, they include the time to read the conclusion and match it against the information obtained from the premises: Because the conclusions varied widely in length (from 4 to 18 words), the raw times would tend to overestimate difficulty for the problems with relatively long conclusions. We therefore adjusted the latencies for conclusion length. Second, in problems with more than one premise, it would usually be possible for subjects to do some reasoning while still reading the premises, before the conclusion had been presented; such reasoning would not be included in the raw times. We attempted to assess whether such anticipatory reasoning was occurring and to add an estimate of it to the latencies.

The conclusion length adjustment was straightforward. The control-true problems provide a baseline time for the operations of reading a conclusion, matching it against known information, and responding. It turned out that in control-true problems, the number of words in the conclusion (identical, of course, to the words in the premise, in control-true problems) correlated .98 with the latencies. A regression equation of mean latency on number of words was computed for these problems. This equation provided an estimate of the time required to read a conclusion of a given length and to match it against given information. For each reasoning problem, the raw latencies were adjusted by subtracting the time required to process the conclusion, as estimated from this equation. This subtraction constituted the conclusion length adjustment.

There was evidence that subjects sometimes did significant reasoning before the conclusion was presented that is concealed in the times taken to read the premises. We compared the mean reading time for each sentence type as a function of its serial position among the premises. For those sentence types that occurred in more than one serial position, the reading time was slower the later the sentence occurred among the premises. There are two conceivable explanations of this result. As the subject is reading through the problem, successively more information must be held in active memory. Rehearsal of the preceding premises could slow the processing of each new premise. Thus, as the number of premises increases, there is more information to rehearse, and reading time for a sentence type would increase as a function of its serial position. Alternatively, the processing of the later premises could be slower because subjects are making inferences; subjects sometimes reported that while not deliberately attempting to anticipate the conclusion, they could not help but "put together" the facts as these appeared.

In an attempt to decide between these explanations, we separated the reading times for each second position premise into those where the sentence provided information about letters in previous premises and those that involved no letter previously mentioned in the problem. We refer to these two types of premises as *integrable* and *nonintegrable*, respectively. For instance, the sentence type *There is an X* would be integrable if it followed *If there is an X then there is a Y*, but would not be integrable when it followed *If there is a Y then there is a Z*. If the increased reading time of the later premises is due merely to rehearsal of an increasing quantity of information, integrable and nonintegrable versions of the same sentence type should not differ. If the increased reading time is due instead to some logical manipulations being performed, this should occur to a greater extent in the integrable versions. In fact, the reading times for the nonintegrable second position premises were generally quite close to the first position times, whereas the times for the integrable second premises were substantially higher. The reading times for third and fourth position premises (always integrable) were also higher than for the same sentence type in the first position. For instance, the sentence type *There is an X* took 1.98 sec to read in the first position; in the second position when not integrable it took 2.01 sec, about the same; but in the second position when integrable it took 3.02 sec, and in third position it took 3.46 sec. Similarly, the sentence type *There's not an X* was read in 2.23 sec as a first premise; as a second premise it required 2.57 sec when not integrable, but 3.44 sec when integrable, and as a third premise 5.18 sec. Again, the form *If there is an X then there is a Y* took 3.92 sec to read in the first position; in the second position it took 3.99 sec when not integrable, but 5.32 sec when integrable; it took 6.84 sec in the third position and 8.55 in the fourth position. It seems fairly certain therefore that some time-occupying integration of information took place during the reading of the later premises. To obtain an estimate of the time spent in this anticipatory reasoning, in problems with more than one premise the observed reading time for each additional premise was compared with the mean reading time for that sentence type when it occurred in the first position (averaged over all problems). If the average reading time was greater than this baseline, the excess time was taken as the anticipatory reasoning time and was added to the solution latency. Thus, the adjusted reaction time on a problem was the raw latency plus the anticipatory reasoning time, less the conclusion length adjustment.

Prediction of the Adjusted Latencies. Fifty-five problems were analyzed, the same 55 direct reasoning problems that were analyzed for Rating Study 1. For these problems, the adjusted latencies correlated .77 with the mean difficulty ratings assigned to the same problems by the subjects of Rating Study 1. Thirty-eight of the problems had the same form as problems of Rating Study 2: For this set, the adjusted latencies correlated .73 with the mean ratings assigned by the Study 2 subjects. Thus, these two measures of difficulty, adjusted latency and subjective rating, correlate fairly highly with each other.

Equations 1 and 2, used to predict difficulties in the rating studies, both have problem length as a predictor variable. The length measure most relevant for predicting latency is not the total length of a problem (premises plus conclusion), however, but the length of the premises only, because an adjustment for the length of the conclusion has already been subtracted in adjusting the latencies. The length of the premises (total number of words in the premises combined) correlated .74 with the mean adjusted reaction times of the 55 problems, using latencies for correct responses only.

From Model 1, the correlation of the sum of the difficulty weights of the reasoning steps with the adjusted latencies was .37 ($p < .01$). The correlation of this predictor with the number of words in the premises was low (.13, not significant). Using both the sum of the reasoning step difficulty weights and the length of the premises as predictor variables yielded a multiple correlation with adjusted latency of .79. From Model 2, the correlation of the number of reasoning steps with the adjusted latencies was .49 ($p < .001$). This predictor, however, correlated significantly with problem length ($r = .41$, $p < .01$). Using both number of reasoning steps and premise length as predictors yielded a multiple correlation of .77. With the length of the premises partialled out, the adjusted latencies correlate .41 ($p < .01$) with the sum of the reasoning step difficulty weights, but only .24 (not significant) with the number of reasoning steps. The difference itself is not statistically significant, however.

In general, it appears that solution latency is primarily associated with problem length. Neither of the measures of reasoning complexity in the two models predicts much independent variance, but one (the sum of the reasoning step difficulty weights) is significantly associated with latency independently of length.

Errors on the Direct Reasoning Problems

Our third measure of problem difficulty used errors. To obtain a measure based on as much data as possible, we considered the 38 problems that had been used in all studies. On these problems, errors range from 0 to 11% on Rating Study 1, from 0 to 13% on Rating Study 2, and from 0 to 25% on the Reaction Time Study. The greater frequency of error on the latter study is no doubt due to subjects' attempting to work fast. To obtain an error measure to which each study would contribute equally, we ranked the 38 problems for error proneness independently for each study (the three rankings correlated well with each other); we then summed each problem's three ranks and then reranked the problems. The result was a ranking of the problems from easy to hard, according to their mean relative tendency to cause the subjects of the three studies to err. We refer to this measure as *ranked errors*. (The use of ranks also eliminated the problem that the distribution of errors is heavily skewed.)

For the 38 problems, ranked errors correlated .59 with the mean ratings of Rating Study 2, .68 with those of Rating Study 1, and .57 with the adjusted latencies.

The correlation of ranked errors with problem length is only .13, not statistically significant. Thus, among the measures of problem difficulty, errors apparently have the interesting property of being essentially uncorrelated with problem length. This lack of shared covariation with problem length may be the reason why the error measure did not correlate with ratings and latency measures quite as highly as these correlated with each other.

The correlation of ranked errors with the sum of the reasoning step difficulty weights was .73. Thus, the reasoning step weights account for a little over half of the variation in ranked errors. Because errors are not significantly associated with problem length, there is no point in partialing out length, or in using it as a second predictor in a multiple correlation. The number of reasoning steps alone (Model 2) correlated .57 ($p < .01$) with ranked errors. This is not significantly less than the correlation of errors with the summed difficulty weights. Hotelling's (1940) $t(35) = 1.39$. Thus, both theoretical estimates of reasoning complexity predict the error proneness of the problems quite well, with the better one accounting for about half the variance.

Direct Reasoning Problems:
Summary of Results and Comment

Two of the three measures of problem difficulty (subjective difficulty rating and latency) are fairly highly correlated with problem length, and one (error proneness) is not. Table 7.1 summarizes how well the two theory-derived indices of expected problem complexity predict these measures, both in combination with length as a predictor, and with length partialed out.

The index from Model 1, the sum of the difficulty weights of the inferences that the theory provides to solve a problem, predicts both sets of ratings excellently; it also predicts errors well and latencies significantly. Although this index contains 13 parameters estimated from one set of ratings data, it was shown that the quality of prediction was not dependent on possible idiosyncrasies of performance for the particular problems or subjects used to estimate the weights, because excellent predictions

TABLE 7.1
Correlations of Theory-Based Predictors
With Empirical Measures of Problem Difficulty*

Type of Correlation	Sum or Reasoning Step Weights	Number of Reasoning Steps	Difference
Rating Study 2 (n = 60 problems; r rating × length = .71)			
Equation 2 or 3	.92	.79	$p < .001$
Partial	.83	.51	$p < .001$
Rating Study 1 (n = 55 problems; r rating × length = .67)			
Equation 2 or 3	.95	.73	$p < .001$
Partial	.91	.52	$p < .001$
Latency (n = 55 problems; r latency × length = .74)			
Multiple	.79	.77	NS**
Partial	.41	NS	NS
Errors (ranks) (n = 38 problems; r rank × length = .13)			
Simple	.73	.57	NS

*The Equation 2 or 3 correlations are of the difficulty rating with the prediction from Equation 2 (sum of weights) or 3 (number of steps). The multiple correlation uses length of the premises as the second predictor and the partials have length partialed out. The difference test is Hotelling's (1940) t test for $Q_{xy} = Q_{xz}$ on the same population.
**NS, Not significant.

were obtained not only for the data set used to estimate the weights but also for ratings of the same problems by fresh subjects, and for new problems with new subjects. The other index, the number of reasoning steps from Model 2, also yields significant predictions, with fairly good correlations with the ratings and error measures. The correlations are lower overall than with the sum-of-the-weights index but are nonetheless high considering the lack of parameters estimated from the data.

One might wonder whether the sum-of-the-reasoning-step-weights index showed so much higher independent correlations with the ratings than the latencies because of our use of ratings rather than latencies to estimate parameters. It is possible that this decision played a role, but it seems unlikely that it played a large role. First, the index correlated well with the error measure, which was also not used to estimate parameters; it is only for the latency measure that the correlations are not high. Second, the Model 2 index of complexity, the number of reasoning steps, contains no parameters estimated from data, but, although the correlations are lower overall for it, it shows the same pattern of correlations with the measures as the sum-of-the-weights index—higher with the ratings and errors than with the latencies. We are inclined to think that on these problems, the length of the premises may have tended to submerge other factors contributing to latency. It seems intuitively plausible that subjects might spend much time rereading premises on the longer problems—we invite the reader to examine the longer problems in the Appendix from this point of view. Unfortunately, it is hard to find or construct nontrivial problems that are short enough that all the premise information is within most subjects' span of short-term memory.

The Indirect and Other Reasoning Problems: All Studies

The remaining reasoning problems fall into four groups. One group was designed to elicit the strategy of enumeration of alternatives a priori (see Table 6.2), the second explored some simple arguments containing lemmas, the third was concerned with reductio ad absurdum arguments, and the fourth concerned the putative schema $p, \therefore p$ OR q. We consider these in turn.

Strategy of Enumeration of Alternatives a Priori. This consisted of the following three problems used in all studies:

> If there is an M then there is a Y
> If there's not an M then there is a Y
> ? There is a Y   (4)

> If there is an R then there's not a C
> If there's not an R then there's not a C
> ? There is a C   (5)

> If there is an F then there is an L
> If there's not an F then there is a V
> ? There is an L or a V   (6)

In Problem 4, the strategy of enumeration of alternatives a priori feeds Schema 5, Problem 5 involves Schema 10 as well, and in Problem 6 the strategy of enumeration of alternatives a priori feeds Schema 6. Responses were 88% correct on these problems across the three studies; incorrect responses most often fell into the undecidable category. The average difficulty rating given to these problems in the rating studies was 4.33 and indicates that they were considered moderately hard[2]; the error rates are consistent with this rating. There was no tendency for subjects who made errors on one of these problems to make errors on the others, that is, no subjects responded consistently as if they failed to use the strategy

---

[2]For purposes of comparison: The mean difficulty rating for all the direct reasoning problems of Rating Study 2 was 3.38, range 1.06 to 6.00. See the Appendix for the problems with their rated difficulties.

of enumeration of alternatives a priori. The data indicate, not surprisingly, that elementary deductions involving the strategy of enumeration of alternatives a priori are well within the competence of undergraduates, although not without a scattering of errors.

Lemmas. The simplest kind of lemma was contained in the following problem:

> *If there is an I then there is an X*
> *There is an I or an L*
> *? There is an X or an L* (7)

One subject verbalized the solution "If there's an *I* there's an *X*; if there's *L* then there's *L*; both possibilities result in there being an *X* or an *L*." This solution uses Schema 6. To use this schema, however, the subject has to construct the proposition *If there's an L then there's an L*. Because this proposition is not given in the premises, it has to be formed as a lemma, albeit a trivially simple one. (In our system, a proposition of the form *If p then p* is formed with schemas 12 and 9.) Another line of reasoning is also possible on this problem and was verbalized by one subject as "If there's an *I* there's an *X*; if there's not an *I* there's an *L*, so there's an *X* or an *L*." In this line the strategy of enumeration of alternatives a priori feeds Schema 6, using the lemma *If there's not an I there's an L* formed with Schemas 12 and 3, and the second premise. We think, however, that the first line of reasoning was the more usual one.

The reasoning of Problem 7 was embedded in three other problems. In Problems 8 and 9 it fed a contradiction (Schemas 9 or 10), and in Problem 10 it was combined with Schema 12:

> *If there is an F then there is an X*
> *There's an F or an H?* (8)
> *? It's not true that there is either an X or an H*

> *There is an H or a C*
> *If there is an H then there is a P*
> *? There's not a C and there's not a P* (9)

> *If there is a C then there is a Y*
> *? If there is either a C or a D, then there is either a Y or a D* (10)

All of these problems were comparatively hard. Problem 7 was easiest, with 6% errors and a rating of 4.15; the others had ratings of 4.95, 5.50, and 5.14, respectively, and averaged 16% errors, a very high error rate for our problems. It is possible to use Equation 2 to predict a difficulty rating for these problems based on their length and the schemas needed to solve them (e.g., Problem 7 has 24 words and taking it as using Schemas 6, 12, and 9, Equation 2 predicts a difficulty of 3.07 units). Each problem was rated very significantly more difficult by the subjects than the prediction for it from Equation 2 ($p < .01$ by t test in all cases). This fact, together with the high error rate, suggests that the need to construct the lemma is itself a source of difficulty over and above the particular schemas used.[3]

A different lemma was involved in Problem 11:

There is a P or an S
If there is either a P or a K then there is a D
If there is an S then there is an N
? There is a D or an N   (11)

In order for Schema 6 to be used, the lemma *If there is a P then there is a D* has to be formed, using Schemas 12 and 2. A similar lemma was also needed in two other problems. The three problems were all fairly difficult, with 5% errors and difficulty ratings from 3.96 to 5.96. Another problem required two lemmas, one like Problems 7 to 10 and the other like Problem 11. It has 21% errors and a rating of 6.10, harder on both indices than any direct reasoning problem used. In general, these arguments involving lemmas were within the reach of most subjects, although they generally found them harder and made more errors on them than on direct reasoning problems involving the same schemas.

Reductio ad Absurdum Arguments. Our reductio problems fell into two groups. One was specially designed to explore the use of such arguments. The other group involved deriving a statement that a conjunction or disjunction was false; with the schemas of Table 6.1 they require reductio arguments, but would not necessarily do so in other systems. We begin with the first group, which more certainly demand reductio solutions.

---

[3]Braine (1978) had a schema (p_1, OR ... OR p_1, OR ... p_n; IF p_1, THEN q; ... p_1 OR ... OR q OR ... OR p_n), which would solve Problem 7 in a single step. This schema is not in our present set (Table 7.1) for several reasons. First, the evidence summarized of a relatively high failure rate on these problems suggested that the argument is not universally immediate among our subjects. Second, self-reports of methods of solution (e.g., the two cited in the text) indicate that problems of the form of Problem 7 need not be solved in a single step but may involve a chain of inferences (as Table 7.1 assumes). Finally, the high subjective difficulty (e.g., Problem 7 is rated much more difficult than other one-step problems—see Appendix, Problems iii to xiv) also suggests that the solution is not immediate for subjects but involves a chain of inferences.

In the reaction time and first rating study, we sought to investigate the use of the reductio ad absurdum with the two following problems, which we thought might exemplify Schema 13 straightforwardly:

> If there is a C then there is an N
> If there is a C then there's not an N
> ? There's not a C   (12)

> If there is an E then there is a G
> If there is an E then there's not a G
> ? There is an E   (13)

In the Reaction Time Study, responses of "true" to Problem 12 and of "false" to 13 occurred in only about half the subjects, and in the first rating study a majority of subjects voted both problems undecidable. The problems were given average difficulty ratings of 7 and 7.5, respectively, the highest ratings of the entire set of problems. Thus, most subjects did not see, or did not accept, the reductio solution to these problems.

In the second rating study, we discarded this pair of problems and substituted a pair of modified modus tollens problems:

> If there is a G then there is a P
> If there's not a G then there may or may not be a P; you can't tell
> There's not a P
> ? There's not a G
>
>   (14)

> If there is an A then there is a D
> If there's not an A then there may or may not be a D; you can't tell
> There's not a D
> ? There is an A
>
>   (15)

A normal modus tollens problem consists of the first and third premises together. The purpose of the second premise was to block the inference invited by the first premise (i.e., for Problem 14, *If there's not a G then there's not a P*; Geis & Zwicky, 1971). A normal modus tollens problem has two solutions, one primitive and the other involving a reductio (Wason & Johnson-Laird, 1972). The primitive solution consists of accepting the invited inference and concluding, for Problem 14, that G and P are either both present or both absent (which is tantamount to taking *if* as the biconditional); thus, the primitive solution has the same basis as the standard fallacies (i.e., *If p then q, not p, ∴ not q* and *If p then q, q, ∴ p*).

Our extra premise blocks this solution and forces the reductio solution. (The reductio solution of 14 might be verbalized as "Suppose G were present, then P would have to be, but P isn't, so G must be absent.")

Problem 14 was solved by 71% and 15 by 67% of the subjects. All but one of the other responses was "indeterminate." Subjects who solved the problems gave them average difficulty ratings of 6.94 and 7.38, respectively, again the highest ratings of the set. Thus, reductio solutions did not come easily to subjects in any of Problems 12 to 15.

Turning now to the second group of reductio problems, those that required deriving the falsity of a conjunction or disjunction, we consider first the following pair:

There's not an R
? It is not true that there is both an R and a U   (16)

There's not a J
? There's not both a J and a Q   (17)

These are both solved without a reductio in some systems, for example, Osherson (1975a), and Braine (1978) has a schema that would solve them in one step.[4] They proved surprisingly difficult, however, with 27% and 21% errors and ratings of 4.76 and 4.38, respectively, suggesting that not all subjects have a schema that carries from premise to conclusion in a single step.

The relative difficulty of these problems makes an interesting contrast with the simplicity of a formally related problem:

There's not a C
? There is a C and an H   (18)

Subjects made no errors at all in saying the conclusion was false, and they rated the problem easy [1.96, very significantly easier than both of Problems 16 and 17: $t(20) = 9.02$, $p < .001$, and $t(21) = 7.34$, $p < .001$, respectively]. The greater simplicity of Problem 18 cannot be accounted for merely in terms of the greater ease of falsifying affirmative over verifying negative propositions (e.g., Carpenter & Just, 1975; Clark & Chase, 1972) because the difference is too large. Thus Problem 16 had an adjusted reaction time of 5.81 sec as opposed to 1.25 sec for 18 [$t(17) = 5.57$, $p < .001$], a difference of over 4.5 sec and an order of magnitude greater than the usual difference between falsifying affirmative and veri-

---

[4]The schema of Braine (1978) is: $F(p_1)$, $\therefore$ $F(p_1$ AND p_2 AND . . . AND $p_n)$, $1 < i < n$, with notation as in Table 7.1. Osherson (1975a) has the similar schema: $\sim$A v $\sim$B, $\therefore$ $\sim$(A and B).

fying negative sentences, which is less than half a second (Carpenter & Just, 1975).

In the present theory, subjects solve Problem 18 by inferring the presence of *C* from the conclusion and noting its incompatibility with the premise. Problems 16 and 17 involve a suppositional process: In 16 the subject has to suppose the proposition embedded in the conclusion (that there is both an *R* and a *U*), carry out the reasoning of Problem 18, conclude that the supposition is false (by Schema 13), and then conclude that the conclusion given is true. Thus, Problems 16 and 17 involve a supposition leading to a reductio, whereas 18 does not.

The reasoning of Problems 16 and 17 was combined with another schema in two other problems and occurred as a lemma in two further ones. Problems 19 illustrates the latter:

If there is not both a B and a C, then there's not a W
There's not a B
? There is a W (19)

The proposition *There's not both a B and a C* has to be derived as a lemma. All these problems were rather difficult, with error rates from 9% to 23% and ratings from 4.05 to 6.50.

Problems 20 and 21 required deriving the falsity of a disjunction, and another problem combined that with another schema. This set raised issues similar to 16 to 19.

There's not an M and there's not a Q
? It is not true that there is either an M or a Q (20)

There's not an S
There's not a P
? It's not true that there is either an S or a P (21)

Braine (1978) had a schema that would solve these problems directly.[5] Like Problems 17 and 18, however, they proved quite difficult, with a mean error rate of 17% and a mean rating of 4.93, suggesting that they were not solved in one step by a universally available schema. On the other hand, the formally similar direct reasoning Problems 22 and 23 proved fairly easy:

---

[5]The schema was: $F(p_1)$ AND ... AND $F(p_n)$, $\therefore$ $F(p_1$ OR ... OR $p_n)$, with notation as in Table 7.1.

There's not an A and there's not a V
? There is an A or a V   (22)

There's not a T
There's not a U
? There is a T or a U   (23)

There were only 2% errors and the difficulty ratings (2.79 and 2.38) were each very significantly less than both of 20 and 21 (all comparisons, $p < .001$). The reaction time differences (5.70 and 5.31 sec for 20 and 21, respectively, against 1.10 and 1.01 sec for 22 and 23, respectively, were significant [$t(18) = 4.55$, $p < .001$ for 20 vs. 22, and $t(17) = 3.76$, $p < .01$ for 21 vs. 23]; as in the similar case of Problems 16 and 17, these differences are too large to be accounted for simply as the difference between falsifying affirmative and verifying negative sentences.

In the present theory, Problems 22 and 23 are easy because they feed directly into Schema 11, which declares premises and conclusion incompatible. Problems 20 and 21 are a good deal harder because they involve a suppositional step (supposing the proposition embedded in the conclusion), proving it false (by Schemas 11 and 13), and concluding that the given conclusion is true.

Although these problems that involve deriving the falsity of a conjunction or disjunction require a reductio in our system, and were hard relative to the direct reasoning problems, they were nevertheless considerably easier than the first set of reductio problems discussed (Problems 12 to 15); there is no overlap between the two sets, in either error rates or difficulty ratings. In the Discussion, we consider a possible reason for this difference in difficulty in terms of subjects' reasoning strategies.

p, ∴ p OR q? The final problem to be discussed was:

There is an H
? There is an H or an M   (24)

If the schema *p, ∴ p OR q* was a natural one for subjects, then Problem 24 would be a one-step problem; it is of the simplest type that could be designed to elicit this schema. In the two rating studies, 52% of the subjects responded "true," 25% "false," and 23% "indeterminate." Those who responded "true" gave the problem an average difficulty rating of 4.30, harder than most problems and substantially harder than all the one-step problems. Thus, about half the subjects thought that the conclusion does not follow from the premise, and those who thought that it does follow found the inference to be relatively difficult. We argue later that p, $\therefore$ p OR q is not a natural schema for subjects.

DISCUSSION

We use two theory-based indices of expected problem complexity—the number of reasoning steps needed to solve a problem in our system and the sum of the difficulty weights of these steps. The results indicate that these indices were highly predictive of empirical measures of the difficulty of direct reasoning problems. Correlations ranged up to .95, for the joint prediction of rated difficulty from the weighted-sum index combined with problem length. There were high correlations with both errors and rated difficulty that were independent of problem length. These relationships make a case that in solving these problems, subjects do in fact go through the mental steps that the theory claims that they do, and thus that the schemas of Table 6.1 are a psychological reality. This claim, however, is affected by a number of topics that require discussion. In what follows, we first consider whether nonlogical processes or response biases could account for subjects' responses. Second, we discuss the variable of problem length—how it is measured and how it relates to problem difficulty. Third, we consider the processing assumptions of our prediction models and, particularly, the kind of reasoning program that subjects may bring to the task. Fourth, we discuss whether there are alternative logical models that could predict difficulty equally well. Fifth, we consider how far the postulated mental processes may generalize to propositional problems using other kinds of content. Finally, we present the claims we wish to make about natural propositional logic and consider how far these data support them.

Can Nonlogical Models Explain the Results?

Evans (1972, 1982) has claimed that subjects' responses on reasoning problems are often determined by various responses or matching biases, not by reasoning. Although this kind of explanation has been contested for some of his type cases (van Duyne, 1973, 1974; Evans, 1975), let us consider whether such processes could explain the present results. We consider first whether biases could have determined subjects' responses of "true" or "false," and then whether they could have affected reaction times or ratings.

Because half the problems have "true" and half "false" as the correct response, simple yea- and nay-saying biases are controlled for. Many matching or "atmosphere"-type biases are conceivable. For example, subjects could have tended to say "true" to affirmatively phrased conclusions and "false" to negative ones, or they might have had the opposite bias; they might have tended to say "true" if all proposition were affirmative and "false" if any of the premises or conclusion were negative; or perhaps they tended to say "false" if the problem contained an odd number of negatives and "true" if an even number. For each of these biases there were a substantial number of problems on which the bias would lead to error, and any considerable prevalence of the bias among subjects would lead to large error percentages for these problems. Because errors were few on all the direct reasoning problems (the median percentage of error on the Appendix problems was 3%, range 0 to 13%), it follows that subjects' responses could not have been controlled by these response biases. The same argument would presumably apply against other response biases.

Latencies and ratings could be affected by biases that do not determine the choice of response because a subject might take longer or consider a problem more difficult when a bias has to be overcome. We have no evidence that biases did not affect the latencies. On the ratings, however, the excellent crossvalidated prediction of rated difficulty from the sum of reasoning step weights together with problem length suggests that response or matching bias was not a factor with which one should be concerned.

Length as a Factor Affecting Difficulty

There are two kinds of questions to be discussed about length, one, as it were, tactical, and the other strategic. The tactical question has to do with the choice of a length measure to use in computing correlations with indices of problem difficulty, the strategic with whether length does affect the real difficulty of problems, how it does so, and how it should be brought into a prediction model.

The tactical question can be dealt with briefly. Number of words proved to be an effective measure of problem length in this work; however, one would certainly not expect it always to be so. For example, Osherson (1975a) used content very similar to ours; in one experiment (see chap. 8) he included some "wordy" problems in which proposition length was increased without effectively changing content (e.g., *There is a C* became *A C has been written down on the paper* in one of the wordy problems, an immaterial change that more than doubles the number of words). He found that such changes had no effect on problem difficulty. Obviously, number of words was a good measure of length in our work only because the content was highly stereotyped, and we adopted a constant format for expressing it in English. In any work with different content, the appropriate measure of problem length would have to be determined for that content.

On the more theoretical issues, we should first note that our results do not prove that length affects the real difficulty of problems. Length was not significantly related to errors. The relationship to the difficulty ratings shows that longer problems are perceived as more difficult; it does not prove that they actually are more difficult. The relationship of length to adjusted latency could plausibly be because the longer the premises, the more difficult they are to hold in mind, and so the more likely it is that subjects will need to spend time rereading them. Thus, it is clear that length is not related to all indices of difficulty and may be related to different indices for different reasons.

What is it about length that affects difficulty ratings? A problem can be made long in several ways. One way is by increasing the number of words used to express an idea. Osherson's (1975a) result on his wordy problems, cited earlier, indicates that merely padding propositions does not affect perceived difficulty. A second way of varying length occurs in the problems of Rating Study 2, in which length was manipulated while holding the reasoning steps constant: We varied the length and compositeness of the propositions that had to be substituted for the ps and qs in the schemas (cf. Problems xxi and xxii of the Appendix). Let us call this variable *substitution complexity*. The results for these problems demonstrate that this substitution complexity does affect perceived difficulty. A third way in which a problem can be long is by involving a large number of propositions or connectives or both (without complex substitutions): This was the most frequent way in which our longer and shorter problems differed. Length brought about in this way is inevitably confounded with reasoning complexity: Most problems that involve a chain of reasoning of several steps have to contain a fairly large number of propositions and connectives, and certain schemas (e.g., Schemas 14, 5, and 6) necessarily involve fairly long problems just in order to present the information used in the schema.

Our method of analysis has tacitly assumed that length affects perceived difficulty to the same degree regardless of whether it is caused by substitution complexity or by the number of propositions and connectives used in a problem. This assumption has worked in the sense that it proved consistent with good predictions of problem difficulty ratings. But other assumptions were possible, and they might have "worked" too. For instance, we could have assumed that length only affects difficulty ratings when it is brought about by substitution complexity. The prediction equation would then have had a parameter for substitution complexity but none for length per se. Any effect of length (other than substitution complexity) on difficulty ratings would then be absorbed into the difficulty weights for the schemas: The weights of schemas that necessarily involve many or long propositions (e.g., Schemas 14, 5, and 6) would be relatively greater than with our present procedure. These are essentially the assumptions and prediction strategy used by Osherson (1975a).

We chose not to follow Osherson's predictive strategy for two reasons. First, with this strategy, the sum of the difficulty weights of the reasoning steps on a problem would be highly correlated with the length of the problem (as it is in Osherson's, 1975a, studies), and it would be hard to be sure how much of the observed difficulty of problems could be due to length and how much *had* to be due to the difficulty of the reasoning steps. We viewed this uncertainty as a troublesome feature of Osherson's studies. Our prediction strategy is conservative in that it results in reasoning step difficulty estimates that are not significantly influenced by problem length. Hence, the correlation of a difficulty measure with the sum of the reasoning step weights cannot be due to length under any assumptions about how length really affects difficulty; it represents a minimum estimate of the covariation of the difficulty measure with reasoning complexity. It may underestimate this covariation, because if the assumption is correct that length only affects difficulty through substitution, then some possibly large fraction of the covariance of difficulty measures with length that we found is really caused by aspects of reasoning complexity that are inextricably confounded with length.

A second reason for preferring our prediction strategy was that it seemed to offer some hope of obtaining weight estimates for the schemas that would be independent of subject matter. If length is not factored out, then the schema difficulty weights that result from STEPIT's procedure must depend on the particular way that the propositions are expressed in English (because that affects length): Any change in subject matter will change length measures and require new schema weight estimates. By eliminating the influence of length, however, we can hope to have obtained weights for schemas that apply to propositions as they are understood, independently of the precise expression in English. That is, they may exclude any difficulty contributed by encoding factors. Our prediction scheme would then apply to new direct reasoning problems with a different subject matter, using just the same set of weights; it would require only that a suitable length-cum-complexity parameter be estimated from the data to take account of difficulty contributed by length and encoding factors connected with the content, but not with the form of the reasoning. But of course we cannot tell from the present work how far this hope has been realized.

That the error measure is correlated with the reasoning step weights but not with length provides, we think, some after-the-fact support for a prediction strategy that ensures weight estimates that are substantially independent of length.

Processing Implications and Subjects' Reasoning Program

The results imply a substantial uniformity among subjects in the way their comprehension and reasoning programs apply to the direct reasoning problems we used. Moreover, the subjects' program finds the shortest solutions (for our problems) without getting lost in blind alleys. Wide variation in how premises were understood, or in how a line of reasoning was selected, would make it unlikely that our methodology could be used to predict problem difficulty successfully. Uniformity in comprehension is plausible because, as noted in the Introduction, we did not use problems that contained propositions that could easily be misconstrued because of conversational implicatures (Grice, 1975) or for other reasons.

We suggested in the Introduction that subjects might have a direct reasoning routine that matches premises (plus the antecedent of the conclusion, when that is an *if-then* statement) with the numerators of schemas and applies any of the direct reasoning schemas that fit. If the conclusion or some proposition incompatible with it is not reached, the process is repeated on the newly created problem that consists of the original premises plus the new proposition produced by applying the schema. The program outlined in Table 6.2 contains a direct reasoning routine that works in this way. The program uses the schemas of Table 6.1 and consists of a direct reasoning routine supplemented by strategies for use when the routine fails[6]; it provides a concrete hypothesis about subjects' reasoning procedures. The direct reasoning routine solves all the Appendix problems using the line of reasoning given there.

For the reductio ad absurdum strategy, Table 6.2 proposes both a *limited form* and a *stronger form*; the limited form is assumed to be more widely available to subjects than the stronger form. In particular, the limited form would solve our easier reductio problems (e.g., Problems 16 to 17 and 19 to 21—see Table 6.2, reductio strategy), whereas a stronger strategy is needed to solve the more difficult reductio problems (12 to 15). We do not have the data to formulate the stronger form more precisely. In general, a skilled reasoner would have a more elaborate and powerful set of strategies than those proposed, but we estimate that the program (without the stronger form of the reductio) comes close to representing the skill of our average subject as we have seen it.

---

[6]The routine goes beyond the intuitive conception of direct reasoning in containing processes that prevent useless operations, such as the duplication of propositions in the premise set or the pointless iteration of Schema 8 (cf. Rips, 1983). Thus, the use of Schema 8 is confined to positions where it would be useful and cannot iterate. In addition, Schema 9 is made available in Part B of the evaluation procedure to account for the simplicity of the solution of Problem 18 (cited in The Indirect and Other Reasoning Problems: All Studies), in which subjects clearly must use Schema 9 to make an inference from the problem conclusion.

We should point out that there is one situation in which the theory as a whole (i.e., the schemas of Table 6.1, taken in conjunction with the program of Table 6.2) predicts responses that are at variance with those dictated by standard logic. When a problem has a conditional as a conclusion, the program categorizes that conclusion as "false" when the assumption of the antecedent leads to denial of the consequent. That is, a conclusion *If p then q* will be identified as "false" when *not q* is derivable from the problem premises together with *p*. According to standard logic, *If p then q* is not decidable under these circumstances (because *p* might be false). Appendix problems xxx, xxxvi, and xxxix illustrate the situation. The program predicts a response of "false," although standard logic demands "indeterminate." The subjects agree with the program (95% of responses were "false" and hardly any were "indeterminate"). It is Step 2 of the program taken with the evaluation procedure that is responsible for the prediction, not the schemas.

It may be noted that the program will draw inferences when there is no conclusion to be tested (i.e., when only a set of premises is given and the task is to say what follows from them). Steps 1 and 2, and the evaluation procedure, are then inoperative. The inferences drawn are just the succession of propositions added to the premise set at successive cycles of Step 3.

Table 6.2 may not be the only program consistent with our results. There is developmental evidence (Braine & Rumain, 1983), however, that the schemas involved in direct reasoning tend to be available to children at least by the early school years, considerably before the strategy of enumeration of alternatives a priori or the reductio ad absurdum (see also chaps. 6 and 10). Thus, a direct reasoning routine may be developmentally earlier than other reasoning strategies. Moreover, our adult subjects made few errors on the direct reasoning problems, fewer than on the indirect reasoning ones. These considerations suggest that subjects' reasoning problems have a two-part structure, as in Table 6.2. The direct reasoning routine would be largely shared among subjects; individual differences in the strategies available would account for variation in reasoning skill.

In addition to having a two-part structure that seems well motivated, the program in Table 6.2 (without the stronger reductio strategy) meets the following conditions: (1) It uses the schemas of Table 6.1; (2) it solves all the problems that the great majority of subjects solve; (3) it predicts that the direct reasoning problems will be easier than the indirect ones; and (4) it predicts that the difficulty of a direct reasoning problem will be a function of the length of the chain of inferences of Table 6.1 needed to solve it. To apply to the ratings, predictions (3) and (4) require the assumption that subjects have some gross awareness of the amount of processing a problem has demanded. The direct reasoning problems usually demand more processing than the indirect ones (because the program runs through the direct reasoning routine before initiating strategies), and the amount of processing on direct reasoning problems depends mostly on the number of cycles of Step 3, which is a function of the length of the chain of inferences. Our program-writing efforts have convinced us that any program meeting conditions (1) to (4) would be quite similar to that of Table 6.2.

The primary research goal was to discover subjects' repertory of schemas. The support that the results provide for the schemas of Table 6.1 does not depend on the program in Table 6.2. So far as support for Table 6.1 is concerned, the only crucial processing assumption is that subjects' programs, whatever they are, routinely find the shortest line of reasoning with these schemas that solves the direct reasoning problems—this is the only assumption needed to specify the sequence of inferences for each problem. On the other hand, support for the program of Table 6.2 does depend on the accuracy of Table 6.1—different schemas might require a different kind of program.

Alternative Logical Theories

Johnson-Laird (1975), Osherson (1975a), and Rips (1983) all present theories that include sets of propositional schemas for which psychological reality is claimed. We first discuss one putative schema that is common to all three theories as well as to standard logic, but missing in our system, and then we consider the theories in turn.

The Schema p, ∴ p OR q. As we have seen, one-step inferences based on this schema were often rejected by subjects as invalid. The schema is, of course, not valid for exclusive *or*. One cannot, however, explain subjects' rejection on the simple grounds that they interpret *or* exclusively or are uncertain whether to take or inclusively or exclusively, because Schema 2 is also valid for inclusive *or* only; yet subjects make no errors on simple problems involving this schema (e.g., Problems ix, xvii, xxiv in the Appendix). It seems that the inferences that are valid only for inclusive or that subjects regularly make (e.g., the Appendix problems cited) are well captured by Schema 2. It would be a theoretical nuisance to assume that *p*, ∴ *p* OR *q* was in the subjects' repertory because that assumption predicts responses whose failure to occur would need to be explained away.

The inconsistency of subjects' responses to problems of the form *p*/ ? *p or q*, concords with the fact that the program in Table 6.2 would not deliver a solution to such problems. (*p* OR *q* can be derived from *p* using the schemas of Table 6.1, but the program in Table 6.2 is not adequate to finding a derivation.)

Let us consider what information might be contained in subjects' lexical entry for *or*. There are two theories of the meanings of the connectives that are formally adequate to explain inferences: truth tables and schemas. Recent years have seen a consensus against the truth-table theory (e.g., Braine & Rumain, 1983; Osherson, 1975b; Wason & Johnson-Laird, 1972). In the case of *or*, the idea that the basic meaning relevant for reasoning is given by schemas is consistent with the fact that many simple inferences sanctioned by schemas (e.g., Schemas 2, 3, and 5) occur developmentally earlier than truth judgments and are made much more consistently than truth judgments by adults (Braine & Rumain, 1981). If the schema p, $\therefore$ p OR q were part of the essential meaning of *or* for subjects, then it should not be possible for them to reject the inference on simple problems.

Johnson-Laird's Model.   Johnson-Laird's (1975) set of schemas is fairly similar to ours but lacks schemas equivalent to Schemas 5, 10, 11, and 14, and the strategy of enumeration of alternatives a priori. The inferences defined by these schemas can be achieved in his system, but only by relatively long chains of reasoning. For example, the effect of Schema 11 can be achieved by a line of reasoning involving Schema 3 and a reductio, and with further reasoning and another reductio the strategy of enumeration of alternatives a priori can be derived; the effect of Schemas 14 and 5 can be achieved by lines of reasoning involving Schema 6. If one-step problems that involve Schemas 11, 14, and 5 were solved with Johnson-Laird's schemas, then one would have to predict several errors and high subjective difficulties for them. But the data indicate that they are very simple, about as easy as problems solved in one step in both systems. In addition, problems involving Schemas 14 and 5 are not more difficult than comparable problems involving Schema 6, as his derivations would have to predict. In general, it is not surprising that our system fits the evidence better than Johnson-Laird's because the present system was arrived at by starting with a set like his and successively altering the system where indicated by introspective reports or data on relative difficulties of problems.[7]

Osherson's Model.   This model (Osherson, 1975a) contains 22 schemas listed in the Appendix to Osherson (1975a), apart from modus ponens. The set includes schemas similar to only Schemas 1, 2, 3, 9, and 14 of Table 6.1. None of the 22 schemas contains more than one formula in the numerator, so that many very simple lines of reasoning (e.g., those that

---

[7]Johnson-Laird (1983) does not now agree with his 1975 model, but not for our reasons.

use Schema 5) are not covered. Osherson stresses that his system is both logically and psychologically incomplete. In fact, only a few of our problems can be solved with his system.[8] Some of these are solved in quite counterintuitive ways. For example, consider:

It is not true that there is both an L and an S
? If there is an L, then there's not an S

His system would first infer *Either there's not an L or there's not an S*; it would then convert this into *If it is not true that there's not an L, then there's not an S*, and thence into the conclusion. Such roundabout derivations would force his model to predict unduly high difficulties for some problems that subjects do not rate particularly hard.

Of Osherson's schemas that are not in our set, some (e.g, the schema *p*, ∴ *p* OR *q* and some derivatives of it) are omitted for reasons discussed. Other schemas are omitted because we do not believe the inferences are performed in one step by subjects. For instance, the effects of Osherson's schema IF *p* THEN *q* AND *r*, ∴ IF *p* THEN *q* are obtained by applying Schemas 12, 7, and 9 (i.e., by positing *p*, inferring *q* and *r*, and then *q*). Some of his schemas involve indirect reasoning in our system, using either the strategy of enumerating alternatives a priori or Schema 13. For example, the effects of IF NOT *p* THEN *q*, ∴ *p* OR *q* are obtained by the strategy of enumerating alternatives a priori feeding Schema 6.

Osherson presented subjects with one-step and multistep problems, and also some problems using invalid arguments. Subjects decided which conclusions were valid and then rated the difficulty of the problem. Correlations were computed between the average difficulties of the multistep arguments and the sum of the average difficulties of the one-step arguments required to solve them. The correlations were generally fairly high, ranging from .54 to .89, over eight experiments. These correlations are consistent with our theory. Although the line of reasoning to solve a problem in our theory is usually not the same as it is in his, it is often the case that the operations our theory provides to solve an Osherson multistep problem are the sum of the operations used to solve his component one-step arguments. Thus, if his subjects consistently solve his problems our way, one would still expect the difficulties of his multistep

---

[8]Of the 59 noncontrol, direct reasoning problems in the Appendix, only 8 are solvable in Osherson's system. This is in part because his system lacks a mechanism, like Schema 10, for generating a response of "false." If one granted such a mechanism, seven additional problems would be solved. The poor coverage is also in part because Osherson associates his schemas with "helping conditions" (i.e., constraints on the problem context in which the schema is permitted to apply). Eliminating these constraints would permit another 12 problems to be solved.

problems to correlate with the sum of the difficulties of the supposed component one-step inferences.

In assessing our model against Osherson's data, Experiments 4 and 5 of Osherson (1975a) were used. These experiments used a wider range of schemas than his earlier experiments and employed the same kind of wording and subject matter (letters on an imaginary blackboard) as our studies. The experiments included 38 different problems (14 one-step and 24 multistep in Osherson's system, all but 1 multistep in ours). Five problems were omitted that involve modus tollens (or contraposition) because such problems invite an easy solution based on misinterpretation of the intent of the premises (see the earlier discussion of modus tollens). That left 33 problems. Where the same problem occurred in both experiments, the percentages of errors and the difficulty ratings were each averaged over the two experiments; for problems occurring in one experiment we used the data from that experiment.[9]

The direct reasoning routine of Table 6.2 solves 13 of the 33 problems; the full program including the strategies (without the stronger reductio strategy because of its imprecise formulation and doubtful use by many subjects) solves a further 8; the program fails to solve 12 problems. Osherson's subjects' error rates for these sets of problems were 21%, 34%, and 51%, respectively. To obtain a rough measure of the program's ability to predict problem difficulty, an ordinal index of predicted difficulty was created by assigning the values of 0, 1, and 2 to these three categories of problems, respectively. This index correlated .66 with errors and .32 with the difficulty ratings. The index has a nonsignificant negative correlation with problem length. Length correlated only .19 with errors, but .78 with ratings. (The low correlation of errors with length is an interesting replication of our finding that error probability is largely independent of problem length.) With length partialled out, the index correlated .71 with errors and .69 with the ratings ($p < .001$ in both cases). We conclude that Osherson's data do not conflict with our theory.

Rips's Model. A natural deduction system (ANDS; Rips, 1983) is based on 11 inference schemas. In ANDS, however, the application of a schema can be made conditional on a subgoal as well as on the propositions whose form is specified in the schema. Similarly, the action taken in applying a schema can include the setting of subgoals in addition to making an inference. For example, the schema of ANDS that corresponds to our Schema 5 (Rips, 1983, p. 46) is:

---

[9]Treating each experiment separately, at the cost of a smaller n, does not change the import of the analysis.

R11. Conditions: (1) Current subgoal = r.
(2) Assertion tree (i.e., premises + inferred propositions) contains p OR q.

Actions: (1) Add new subordinate node to assertion tree with assumption p.
(2) Set up corresponding subgoal node to deduce r.
(3) If Subgoal 2 is achieved, add new subordinate node to assertion tree with assumption q.
(4) Set up corresponding subgoal node to deduce r.
(5) If Subgoal 4 is achieved, add r to assertion tree.

Thus, R11 cannot come into action without a current subgoal, and the subgoals set by Actions 2 and 4 have to be identical to that in Condition 1. ANDS also contains backward and forward versions of certain schemas. The backward version sets a new subgoal and incorporates an element of planning, for example, given IF p then q and a current subgoal q, the backward version of modus ponens sets a new subgoal, p. (The forward version is just like Schema 7 of Table 6.1.)

This conditionality of inferences on subgoals places ANDS on a very short leash that has counterintuitive consequences. For example, consider the following premises:

There is an F or an R
If there is an F then there is an L
If there is an R then there is an L

It seems intuitively obvious that there has to be an L. If ANDS is given the conclusion *There is an L*, then ANDS makes the deduction. But if the conclusion given is anything else (e.g., *There is an X*, or *There is not an L*), ANDS will not notice that there has to be an L. The direct reasoning routine of Table 6.2 makes such deductions in any environment, and subgoals appear only in the strategies component.

Nine of ANDS's schemas correspond to schemas of Table 6 (Schemas 2, 3, 5, 7, 8, 9, 12, 13, and the strategy of enumeration of alternatives a priori). Our schemas 1, 4, 6, 10, 11, and 14 are without analogs in ANDS. ANDS has two schemas not in Table 6 [p, $\therefore$ p OR q, already discussed, and De Morgan's ~(p AND q), $\therefore$ ~p OR ~q, discussed later].

Schemas like 10 and 11 are needed by ANDS. As described by Rips, ANDS cannot prove a conclusion false. One could easily add this capability without Schemas 10 and 11 by allowing ANDS two attempts at a problem, first trying to derive the given conclusion, then its negation; ANDS would then respond "false" if the negation of the conclusion was derived. (We assume this procedure later, in discussing how ANDS fares with our problems.) Rips himself notes, however, that subjects respond "invalid" immediately on detecting a contradiction among the premises and conclusion (1983, p. 67), and schemas like 10 and 11 are needed to define "contradiction."[10]

ANDS fails to solve one-step problems involving Schemas 1 and 4 (Problems vii and xi of the Appendix). ANDS would solve them if the conditions of application of certain of Rips's schemas were loosened, but even then, the derivations would be quite roundabout and would thus predict that these problems should be more difficult than they are. In part because ANDS fails problems involving Schemas 1 and 4, it solves only 42 of the 61 problems of the Appendix.

Although ANDS can solve problems involving Schemas 14 and 6 (e.g., viii and xiii of the Appendix), for both problems the solution has several steps and includes use of the schema $p, \therefore p$ OR q. These problems would therefore be predicted to be more difficult than they are. In particular, because Rips's own data indicate a low availability of $p, \therefore p$ OR q (a probability of usage of only .197 in problems involving it—an implicit confirmation of our critique of this schema), his system would have to predict huge numbers of errors on these problems, on which there were hardly any. In sum, ANDS would need to incorporate our schemas to account for the simplicity of many problems, as well as responses of "false."

In Rips's main supporting experiment,[11] adult subjects received 32 problems soluble by ANDS with all its schemas available, together with 32 in valid problems (and some filler problems). Subjects judged whether the conclusion had to be true when the premises were true. Subjects judged valid problems to be valid 51% of the time, and Rips attempted to predict the proportion of valid responses to each such problem, using a prediction model with 11 parameters. The model assumed that each schema has a certain probability of being "available" to subjects on any trial, and 10 such probabilities were estimated from the data. (One schema was not used.) An additional parameter was the probability of guessing; this was obtained from the proportion of valid responses to invalid problems and turned out to be quite high (.46). With 10 parameters

---

[10]Schema 11 is logically redundant in that its effects could be obtained just with 10 and the other schemas. One-step problems involving 11 are sufficiently simple, however, to indicate that the contradiction is immediately apparent to subjects. Much greater difficulty would be predicted if subjects used the roundabout reasoning that would be needed if 11 were not in their repertory.

[11]A second experiment analyzed introspective data and showed that subjects' lines of argument on some of Osherson's problems resembled ANDS's somewhat more than Osherson's models. A third experiment on memory for arguments was consistent with ANDS but also does not uniquely support it.

estimated from 32 data points, predicted and obtained proportions correlated .93.

The direct reasoning routine of Table 6.2 solves 9 of Rips's problems; the routine together with the strategies (omitting the stronger reductio strategy) solves a further 6; the program fails to solve 17. On these three sets, respectively, 73.2%, 44.4%, and 40.8% of responses were that the conclusions followed from the premises. The ordinal index of predicted difficulty used with Osherson's problems (values of 0, 1, and 2 assigned to the three problem categories, respectively) correlated −.61 with the proportion of judgments of valid. The correlation is considerably less than Rips's .93, but has no parameters estimated from the data. The main reason the correlation is not higher is that the program fails to solve three problems that use Rips's schema from De Morgan, $\sim(p \text{ AND } q)$, $\therefore \sim p$ OR $\sim q$; these were solved by most subjects. This inference can be made with our schemas, but it requires several steps and needs more clever strategies than those in Table 6.2. Rips's data suggest that the De Morgan inference is simpler for subjects than our theory predicts, and that provision should be made for it. We return to this issue later.

If the n-ary version of De Morgan's schema [i.e., $F(p_1 \text{ AND } \dots \text{ AND } p_n)$, $\therefore F(p_1)$ OR $\dots$ OR $F(p_n)$] were added to Table 6.1, then the correlation of −.61 would jump to −.81. Also, the proportion of conclusions rejected for problems soluble by the direct reasoning routine (26%) and the proportion accepted on problems not soluble by the program at all (34%) would both be close to the proportion expected from Rips's estimate of guessing (23%).[12] Thus, amended to provide for the De Morgan inference discussed, our theory concords well with Rips's subjects' judgments, without estimating parameters.

Generalization Across Propositional Content

Merely changing the subject matter of propositions does not seem to change subjects' reasoning. For example, Rips (1983) used two kinds of content and found no difference; Osherson's books (1974, 1975a, 1976) replicated several experiments changing the subject matter of propositions without finding evidence for changes in reasoning. Thus, there is good reason to believe that the theory proposed is general across subject matter.

---

[12]Surprisingly, many of Rips's subjects rejected conclusions on problems where the conclusion seems to follow transparently from the premises, for example, p; q or r/ ? If not q then p and r. (With one type of content used, this could have read: *Mary is in New York; Jane is in Detroit or Barbara is in Washington/ ? If Jane is not in Detroit, then Barbara is in Washington and Mary is in New York.*) One third of the subjects responded "not necessarily true." So a high failure rate on transparent problems suggests that the experiment often failed to engage the reasoning procedures of subjects.

The theory does not include a comprehension mechanism, however. It describes subjects' reasoning from the information given, as it is understood; but what a subject understands may not always be identical with what the problem-setter intended that he or she understand. Thus, if the information given is presented in a verbal form that has conversational implicatures (Grice, 1975), some subjects will reason from an expanded premise set that includes the conversational implicature. Similarly, if the subject matter concerns factual knowledge, some subjects may expand the premise set from which they reason to include relevant information they know. The theory only accounts for reasoning from the premise set used, and to predict behavior in such cases it would need parameters estimating the effective premise set.

Implications for "Natural" Propositional Logic

We now conclude by trying to make precise what we are claiming about schemas of natural propositional logic and the ground for the claims. A set of schemas for a natural propositional logic should satisfy three conditions, we believe. Let us consider each condition in turn and assess how far it is satisfied by the schemas of Table 6.1.

First, the schemas should be logically and psychologically valid. That is, for the inferences the schemas define, the conclusions should follow from the premises, and essentially all adult subjects should reason as if they did on straightforward problems. Note that our notion of psychological validity implies some degree of universality. Obviously, a claim of universality becomes more interesting the broader it is, but the present data limit us to discussing it with respect to our subject population. Questions of logical validity can be raised about five of the schemas of Table 6.1: Schemas 1, 2, 12, 13, and the strategy of enumeration of alternatives a priori. For the others, we do not see how any question could be raised about their logical validity, and the low error rates reported, especially for the one-step problems, confirm their psychological validity. Let us consider the debatable schemas. The validity of Schema 12 has been questioned in some philosophical work on the meaning of *if* (Lewis, 1973; Stalnaker, 1968), which we will not discuss here, having done so elsewhere (Braine, 1979a, 1979b; Braine & Rumain, 1983; see chap. 8). Suffice it to say now that Schema 12, as used in Step 2 of the program, appears to have been an easy schema for our subjects. Schema 2 is valid for inclusive but not for exclusive *or*. Although our subjects did not consistently take *or* inclusively—witness their performance on problems involving the rejected schema p, $\therefore$ p OR q—they did all use Schema 2 in their reasoning, making no errors at all on one-step problems involving this schema. As discussed in Braine (1978), the logic, through Schema 2, contains a concealed commitment to inclusive *or*. The validity of Schemas 1 and 13, and the strategy for enumeration of alternatives a priori, depends on the number of truth values of natural logic: They must be logically valid for two truth values only. The data show that Schema 1 and the strategy of enumeration of alternatives a priori were in the subjects' repertories, indicating that they reasoned as if there were just two truth values. The availability of Schema 1 is also indicated in work on comprehension models for negations (e.g., Carpenter & Just, 1975). On the other hand, the general availability of Schema 13 could be questioned on the basis of these data. It could reasonably be argued, however, that Schema 13 can enter into subjects' reasoning at two levels. The most primitive and routine level occurs at Part B of the evaluation procedure in Table 6.2, when encountering an incompatibility triggers a response of "false." That use is universal among subjects. What is not universal is the strategic use in reductio ad absurdum strategies. Schema 12 also has a routine use at Step 2 and a strategic use in the lemma-producing strategy.[13] In sum, all the schemas meet the first condition, although Schemas 12 and 13 can claim universality only in their routine use at Step 2 and in Part B of the evaluation procedure, respectively.

Second, the schemas should be psychologically elementary as well as valid. That is, each reasoning step defined should be carried out as a single inferential step by subjects, not as a chain of inferences. For many of our schemas, it is hard to see how they could be other than elementary because of the difficulty of imagining a chain of more elementary schemas that achieve the same effect. Where competing hypotheses about what is elementary are imaginable, we conclude that a schema is elementary if (a) it is psychologically valid (i.e., one-step problems involving it are solved essentially without error) and (b) its difficulty is substantially less than the sum of the difficulties of any chain of putative more elementary schemas that could conceivably be used to solve one-step problems involving it. Examples of how the kind of data collected bear on elementariness are provided in various parts of the article (e.g., the arguments in Footnote 3 and in the discussion of other logical theories). In general, evidence on difficulty cannot directly prove the elementariness of a schema, but can lead it to be questioned and should permit a decision between rival hypotheses. The schemas of Table 6.1 are those that have survived this sifting process of comparison with rival hypotheses. The

---

[13]For both of these schemas, the distinction between supposition and premise is much clearer for the strategic use than for the routine one. From a strict logical point of view, the response of "false" to a conditional conclusion when the antecedent taken with the premises is found to be incompatible with the consequent—a response universally made by subjects—implies a failure to mark the suppositional status of the antecedent that was posited at Step 2.

work shows that good predictions of behavioral data on difficulty can be obtained from the schemas proposed, especially when taken with the difficulty weights associated with them.

The third condition is that the set of schemas should be psychologically complete: It should contain all the psychologically valid elementary schemas that there are. One candidate schema missing from Table 6.1 is De Morgan's schema from the model of Rips (1983). That schema was clearly available to most of Rips's subjects. In one-step problems involving it, however, surprisingly many of Osherson's (1975a) subjects rejected the conclusion (41% in one experiment and 34% in another). It may be a common derived schema rather than elementary, as we discuss shortly. The transitivity of *if* (IF p THEN q, IF q THEN r; $\therefore$ IF p THEN r) is another possible elementary schema. Apart from these possibilities, the argument that the set is psychologically complete is indirect. First, we may note that the set is *logically* complete, in the sense that all the schemas of propositional logic found in standard works in logic are either contained in this set or derivable from it. So the question of psychological completeness reduces to the following: Are there any schemas logically derivable from this set, but not included in it, that are in the repertoires of our subjects and elementary by our criterion? In the course of this chapter we have examined a number of candidate schemas; for example, some of our former schemas (cf. Footnotes 4, 5, and 6) and some of Osherson's, and found them not to be elementary by our criterion. We do not know of other plausible candidates and tentatively conclude that the set is probably complete (apart from the question of De Morgan's schema and the transitivity of *if*). It may be noted that our set of schemas is not logically a minimum set; that is, there are several cases, as we have noted, where one schema could be logically derived from others. As exemplified in our discussion of other theories, however, in these cases of potential redundancy, the schemas meet the criterion of elementariness: One-step problems involving them are solved without error, and their subjective difficulty is much smaller than would be anticipated if they were actually carried out as chains of inferences, not as a single step.

It is possible that there are individual differences among subjects with respect to derived schemas. Some subjects may be more practiced in propositional reasoning than others and, after going through the same sequence of steps many times, might become able to treat the chain as a single step. Common observation suggests that this conflation of multiple steps into one often occurs in mathematical reasoning with increasing practice. The difficulty of the conflated sequence might then become less than the sum of the difficulties of its components. It is doubtful, however, that this sort of conflation has occurred to any great extent among our subjects; if it had, subjective difficulty would presumably have been less predictable than it was. Nevertheless, the sampling of potential schemas in our problems has no claim to completeness, and there may well be some derived schemas not sampled in our problems, which have become unitary steps for many subjects. The De Morgan schema discussed and the transitivity of *if* are obvious candidates.[14]

We conclude that there are residual questions about the status of certain schemas, notably the De Morgan schema discussed, but that otherwise the data reported provide support for the schemas proposed here as constituting Natural Propositional Logic. Of course, true universality— cross cultural—remains to be investigated. In addition, questions remain about the nature and organization of subjects' reasoning strategies.

Finally, we would recall that it was a central point of Braine (1978) that people do not have direct introspective access to their schemas as such. They have introspective access to the products of reasoning, the propositions that are the output of a reasoning step and may be the input for another, for example, a subject can often report the succession of propositions derived in a chain of reasoning. Subjects do not have access to the schemas by which the propositions are derived, however. They never see them neatly arrayed as in Table 6.1. Thus, they cannot access the information that would permit them to play metalogician to their own logic. Consequently, it is consistent with our theory that subjects should be ignorant of, and their behavior and judgments uninfluenced by, very many facts, for example, certain truth tables, that a logician could prove from or about Table 6.1.

SUMMARY

We have provided evidence supporting a particular repertory as the repertory of the kinds of inferences basic to the propositional reasoning of adults untutored in logic. It was found that measures of the difficulty of direct reasoning problems can be predicted from the number of inferences of this repertory needed to solve a problem, and very well predicted

---

[14]It is also likely that, to serve elaborated strategies of enumerating alternatives a priori, most undergraduates have, alongside the strategy of enumerating alternatives a priori, a schema:

$$\frac{*}{(p \text{ and } q) \text{ OR } [p \text{ AND } F(q)] \text{ OR } [F(p) \text{ AND } q] \text{ or } [F(p) \text{ and } F(q)]}$$

Such a schema would provide a theoretical link to the "formal operations" (Inhelder & Piaget, 1958; see Braine & Rumain, 1983, however, for a review of problems with Piaget's logic). The derived status of this schema is suggested by the fact that studies of the formal operations imply that this schema, and elaborated alternative-enumerating strategies associated with it, are a product of development in adolescence, whereas there is evidence for most of the schemas in Table 7.1 well before that age (Braine & Rumain, 1983).

if one also takes into account problem length and the kind of inference. Correlations with difficulty measures ranged up to .95, and up to .91 with problem length partialled out. The repertory was incorporated into a reasoning program that consists of a direct reasoning routine, coupled with some strategies to be used when the routine fails to solve a problem. The routine is largely shared among subjects; intersubject variation in the strategies component would account for differences in reasoning skill. Problematical features of other models and the logical, psychological, and universalistic claims of the present model were discussed.

APPENDIX: THE PROBLEMS OF RATING STUDY 2

The list is complete, except that it includes only one example each of the control-true and control-false problems, two examples of the modus ponens + contradiction problems (one short and one long—numbers xxi and xxii) used to obtain the relation between problem length and rated difficulty, and none of the indirect reasoning problems. After each problem, we list the schemas from Table 7.1 that it was anticipated the subjects would use and then the mean of the difficulty ratings given by all subjects who solved the problem correctly.

Control-true

i.   *There is a W*
        ? There is a W? (—) (1.06)

Control-false

ii.   *There's not an M*
        ? There is an M ? (10) (1.18)

One step

iii.   *There is a G*
        There is an S
        ? There is a G and an S? (8) (1.57)

iv.   *There is an O and a Z*
        ? There is an O? (9) (1.42)

v.   *There's not an R, and there's not a W*
        ? There is an R or a W? (11) (2.79)

vi.   *There is a J or a Q*
        ? There's not a J and there's not a Q? (11) (2.71)

vii.   *It is false that there's not a W*
         ? There is a W? (1) (2.37)

viii.   *There is a B, and there is an L or an R*
         ? There is a B and an L, or there is a B and an R? (14) (2.81)

ix.   *If there is either a C or an H, then there is a P*
         There is a C
         ? There is a P? (2) (2.50)

x.   *There is a D or a T*
         There's not a D
         ? There is a T? (3) (2.35)

xi.   *It is not true that there is both a G and an I*
         There is a G
         ? There's not an I? (4) (3.10)

xii.   *If there is an F, then there is an L*
         If there is an R, then there is an L
         There is an F or an R
         ? There is an L? (5) (2.61)

xiii.   *If there is an I, then there is an N*
         If there is a B, then there is a T
         There is an I or a B
         ? There is an N or a T? (6) (2.98)

xiv.   *If there is a T, then there is an L*
         There is a T
         ? There is an L? (7) (1.71)

One step + contradiction

xv.   *There is an F, and there's not an L*
         ? There is an L? (9, 10) (2.15)

xvi.   *It is false that there's not an M*
         ? There's not an M? (1, 10) (2.64)

xvii.   *If there is either a D or a J, then there's not a Q*
         There is a D
         ? There is a Q? (2, 10) (2.88)

xviii.   *There is a Q or an N*
         There's not a Q
         ? There's not an N? (3, 10) (2.96)

xix.   *It is not true that there is both a V and an H*
        There is a V
        ? There is an H? (4, 10) (3.25)

xx.   *If there is an E, then there's not a V*
        If there is an O, then there's not a V
        There is an E or an O
        ? There is a V? (5, 10) (3.17)

xxi.   *If there is an E, then there's not a K*
        There is an E
        ? There is a K? (7, 10, short) (2.04)

xxii.   *If there is either an E and a K, or an O and a V, then there is a Y*
        There is either an E and a K, or an O and a V
        ? There is not a Y? (7, 10, long) (3.46)

Multistep (direct reasoning)

xxiii. *There's not an R*
        There's not a W
        ? There is an R or a W? (8, 11) (2.38)

xxiv.   *If there is either an E or an O, then there is a K*
        ? If there is an E, then there is a K? (**P13**, 2) (2.52)

xxv.   *There is a D*
        There is a J and an X
        ? There is a D and a J? (9, 8) (2.71)

xxvi.   *If there is an A, then there is a G*
        If there is an S, then there is a G
        ? If there is either an A or an S, then there is a G? (12, 5) (2.71)

xxvii. *If there is either a B or an R, then there is a Z*
        There is a B
        ? There is a B and a Z? (2, 8) (2.71)

xxviii. *If there is both an A and an M, then there's not an S*
        There is an A
        There is an M
        ? There is an S? (8, 7, 10) (2.79)

xxix.   *There is an F or a C*
        ? If there's not an F, then there is a C? (12, 3) (2.86)

xxx.   *If there is a C, then there is an H*
        If there is a P, then there is an H

*? If there is either a C or a P, then there's not an H? (12, 5, 10)
(3.00)*

xxxi. *It is false that there's not a C
There is an H
? There is a C and an H? (1, 8) (3.04)*

xxxii. *If there is a C, then there is either a P or an H
There is a C
? There's not a P, and there's not an H? (7, 11) (3.13)*

xxxiii. *There is a J
There is a Q or an X
? There is a J and a Q, or there is a J and an X? (8, 14) (3.17)*

xxxiv. *There is a B
If there is a T, then there is an N
There is a T
? There is a B and an N? (7, 8) (3.17)*

xxxv. *If there is either an E or a K, then there is an O
There is an E and a V
? There's not an O? (9, 2, 10) (3.43)*

xxxvi. *It is not true that there is both a U and a D
? If there is a U, then there is a D? (12, 4, 10) (3.46)*

xxxvii. *There is an E
? If there is a K, then there is an E and a K? (12, 8) (3.50)*

xxxviii. *It is not true that there is both an L and an S
? If there is an L, then there's not an S? (12, 4) (3.50)*

xxxix. *There is an N or a P
? If there's not an N, then there's not a P? (12, 3, 10) (3.60)*

xl. *If there is a D, then there is a J
If there is a Q, then there is an X
? If there is either a D or a Q, then there is either a J or an X?
(12, 6) (3.63)*

xli. *There is a B, and there is an I or an N
If there is both a B and an I, then there is an X
If there is both a B and an N, then there is a Z
? There is an X or a Z? (14, 6) (3.65)*

xlii. *It is not true that there is both a J and a Q
There is an X and a J
? There is a Q? (9, 4, 10) (3.74)*

xliii.   *There is an L, and there is an R or a W*
          If there is both an L and an R, then there is a Z
          If there is both an L and a W, then there is a Z
          ? There is a Z? (14, 5) (3.86)

xliv.   *There is a B, and there is a T or a Z*
          If there is both a B and a T, then there is an N
          If there is both a B and a Z, then there is an N
          ? There's not an N? (14, 5, 10) (3.91)

xlv.   *If there is a B, then there is a T*
          It is false that there's not a B
          ? There is a T? (1, 7) (3.96)

xlvi.   *There is an H, and there is an R or an S*
          If there is an R, then there's not a Z
          If there is an S, then there's not a Z
          ? There is a Z? (9, 5, 10) (4.06)

xlvii.   *It is false that there's not a J*
          There is a D or an X
          ? There is a J and a D, or there is a J and an X? (1, 8, 14) (4.08)

xlvii.   *If there is either a K or an O, then there is an N*
          It is false that there's not a K
          ? There's not an N? (1, 2, 10) (4.48)

xlix.   *If there is an R, then there's not an X*
          It is false that there's not an R
          ? There is an X? (1, 7, 10) (4.50)

l.   *There is a G or an S*
          If there is a G, then there is a Z
          If there is an S, then there is a Y
          ? There's not a Z, and there's not a Y? (6, 11) (4.57)

li.   *If there is both an N and an I, then there's not a B*
          It is false that there's not an N
          There is an I
          ? There is a B? (1, 8, 7, 10) (4.73)

lii.   *If there is a P, then there is a C*
          There is a P
          It is not true that there is both a C and an M
          ? There's not an M? (7, 4) (4.78)

liii.   *If there is an A, then there is a G and there is an M or an S*
          There is an A
          ? There is a G and an M, or there is a G and an S? (7, 14) (4.83)

liv.   *There is a Y or an L*
          There's not a Y
          If there is either an L or on R, then there's not a W
          ? There is a W? (3, 2, 10) (5.00)

lv.   *If there is an R, then there is an F*
          If there is a W, then there is an L
          There is an R or a W
          If there is either an F or an L, then there's not a Z
          ? There is a Z? (6, 7, 10) (5.11)

lvi.   *It is not true that there is both a C and an H*
          There is a C
          There's not a P
          ? There is an H or a P? (4, 8, 11) (5.13)

lvii.   *There is a P, and there is a Q or an R*
          If there is both a P and a Q, then there is an S
          If there is both a P and an R, then there is a T
          ? There's not an S, and there's not a T? (14, 6, 11) (5.27)

lviii.   *There is a B or a Z*
          There's not a Z
          It is not true that there is both a B and an R
          ? There's not an R? (3, 4) (5.33)

lix.   *It is not true that there is both a K and an L*
          It is false that there's not a K
          ? There is an L? (1, 4, 10) (5.76)

lx.   *There is an L or a W*
          If there is an L, then there's not an E
          If there is a W, then there's not an E
          There is an E or an O
          ? There is an O? (5, 3) (5.80)

lxi.   *There is an E or an X*
          If there is an E, then there's not an H
          If there is an X, then there's not an H
          There is an H or a T
          ? There's not a T? (5, 3, 10) (6.00)

ACKNOWLEDGMENTS

This chapter is essentially a reprint of M. D. S. Braine, B. J. Reiser, and
B. Rumain (1984). Some empirical justification for a theory of natural
propositional logic. In G. H. Bower (Ed.), *The Psychology of Learning and
Motivation: Advances in Research and Theory*. Vol. 18. New York: Academic
Press (© 1984, by Academic Press; reprinted by permission of the pub-
lisher). We have made some changes in the introduction, brought notation
into line with that of the rest of the volume, and made some other changes
we thought appropriate. However, no literature subsequent to the publication date of the original article is discussed. (Relevant recent literature
is discussed in detail in chap. 8.) The original research was partially
supported by a grant (MH30162) from the National Institute of Mental
Health (Martin Braine, Principal Investigator).

8

Further Evidence for the Theory: Predicting Intermediate and Multiple Conclusions in Propositional Logic Inference Problems

Martin D. S. Braine
New York University

David P. O'Brien
*Baruch College and the Graduate School
of the City University of New York*

Ira A. Noveck
Centre de Recherche en Épistémologie Appliquée

Mark C. Samuels
New York University

R. Brooke Lea
Bowdoin College

Shalom M. Fisch
New York University

Yingrui Yang
New York University and Princeton University

Chapter 7 used reasoning problems that had neutral content (so that preexisting knowledge or domain-specific skills could not provide a basis for inferences). It found that adults performed almost errorlessly on maximally simple problems embodying the model's inferences (i.e., on problems that can be solved in one step with one of the inference forms of the repertory, without any other complexity). Furthermore, the difficulty of a problem was highly correlated with the number and kind of the inferential steps in the line of reasoning used by the model to solve the problem.

However, these kinds of evidence are not as direct as one would like. Although it is useful evidence that problem difficulty is highly predictable from the number and kind of the inferences used by the model to solve a problem, that kind of evidence does not show directly that participants are solving the problems by going through the model's line of reasoning. Empirical estimates of problem difficulty are rather gross measures. Because, over a broad range of problems, the model predicts the exact line of reasoning that will be used by people on a problem, a finer and more direct test of the model could be obtained from data that inform directly about participants' actual line of reasoning. We report that kind of test here.

In the experiments discussed later, participants were given problems that presented a set of premises concerning the presence or absence of an item (e.g., letters written on an imaginary blackboard or toys hidden in a box). The problems were presented either as premises alone or as premises with a conclusion to be evaluated. Participants were asked to write down all the inferences that followed from the premises. When there was a conclusion to evaluate, participants also had to determine whether the conclusion was true or false. The following Example Problem 1, using toy fruits and animals in a box, illustrates the nature of the task:

It is false that there is not a Strawberry.
There is not both a Cat and a Lemon.
If there is a Strawberry or a Peach, then there is a Cat.

? There is a Lemon ? (for problems presented with a conclusion).

When no conclusion was presented, participants were asked to write down everything that they inferred from the premises provided in the order in which they made the inferences. When a conclusion was given, they were asked to write down everything they inferred on the way to evaluating the conclusion. In Example Problem 1, it was predicted that they would write down:

There is a Strawberry.
There is a Cat.
There is not a Lemon.

and, when the conclusion *There is a Lemon* was provided, they would mark it "false."

The inferences participants made were compared with those predicted by the mental logic model specified in Tables 6.1 and 6.2 in chapter 6. Participants' lines of reasoning on problems are predicted from the schemas taken with the Direct Reasoning Routine of Table 6.2. We remind the reader of the way the model predicts participants' responses with some examples. Consider first the earlier Example Problem 1, as presented without a conclusion to be evaluated. The Preliminary Procedure does not apply and the inferences are all made by the Inference Procedure of the reasoning routine. On the first cycle of the Inference Procedure only one schema applies to the premises, Schema 1; this leads to the inference *There is a Strawberry* because Schema 1 transforms a doubly negated proposition into an affirmative one. This proposition is added to the premise set. On the second cycle of the Inference Procedure, again only one schema applies, Schema 2; this takes the third premise and the proposition just inferred as input and makes the deduction *There is a Cat*, and this proposition is added to the premise set. At the third cycle, this proposition and the second premise together satisfy the condition of application of Schema 4; this leads to the inference *There is not a Lemon*, which is added to the premise set. At this point, no further schemas can be applied so no more inferences are made.

Now suppose that the same problem is presented with the conclusion *There is a Lemon* to be evaluated. The Preliminary Procedure yields no output. The Inference Procedure operates in the same way as before to make the same three inferences. However, now the Evaluation Procedure applies; it finds that the last inference (*There is not a lemon*) contradicts the provided conclusion (*There is a lemon*), as Schema 10 specifies, and the response "False" is generated.

As a second example, we take a Example Problem 2 with a conditional conclusion:

If there is a pineapple then there is an orange
If there is a horse then there is a rabbit.

? If there is either a pineapple or a horse then there is not an orange and not a rabbit?

On this problem, Clause (i) of the Preliminary Procedure applies: It adds the antecedent of the conclusion (*There is a pineapple or a horse*) to the premise set and sets up the consequent (*There is not an orange and not a rabbit*) as the conclusion to be tested. Clause (ii) of the Preliminary Procedure yields no output and the Inference Procedure is engaged. The three propositions of the premise set jointly satisfy the condition of application of Schema 6; this yields the inference *There is an orange or a rabbit*, which is added to the premise set. The Evaluation Procedure then finds that this proposition and the conclusion set up by the Preliminary Procedure are incompatible (by Schema 11), triggering a response of "False."

To illustrate how the feeder status of schemas constrains the choice of inference, consider the following Example Problem 3, which we cite using the content in which participants reason from information about the presence or absence of letters written on an imaginary blackboard. The problem has three premises with no conclusion to evaluate:

> There is an S, and there is a K or an R
> If there is a K then there is a V
> If there is an R then there is an A.

Two schemas (9 and 14 of Table 6.1) could apply to the first premise. If both applied freely three inferences would be drawn—*There is an S, There is a K or an R* (Schema 9), and *There is an S and a K, or an S and an R* (Schema 14). However, the Inference Procedure seeks to apply core schemas; because neither Schemas 9 nor Schema 14 are core schemas, the Inference Procedure can apply them only to feed a core schema.[1] In this problem, only Schema 9 can feed a core schema, and only by generating *There is a K or an R*; this, taken with the other two premises, feeds Schema 6, which generates *There is a V or an A*. Thus, the reasoning routine predicts the two inferences—*There is a K or an R*, and *There is a V or an A*.

Compare this problem with Example Problem 4, with the following premises:

> There is an E, and there is a K or an S
> If there is an E and a K, then there is a J
> If there is an E and an S, then there is an N

Note that the first premise of this problem has the same form as the first premise of Example Problem 3. Schema 6 is again the only core schema that can apply, but now its conditions of application can only be satisfied by applying Schema 14 to the first premise, to yield *There is an E and a K, or an E and an S*. Hence the predicted inferences are this proposition and the output of Schema 6, *There is a J or an N*.

The distinction between *feeder* and *core* schemas is important for the present experiments not only because it constrains inferences, but also because one might expect participants to be more aware of the outputs of the core schemas than those of the feeder ones. According to the

---

[1]Free application of feeder schemas could generate infinite loops. For example, given a conjunction of two propositions, *p and q*, one could deduce *p* by Schema 9, and *p and q and p* by Schema 8, and continue reapplying these schemas. Similarly, given two premises, *p or q* and *r*, Schemas 8 and 14 could alternate indefinitely; again, by repeated application of both directions of Schema 1, from a proposition, *p* one could deduce *not not-p*, and then *p* again, and so forth.

Inference Procedure, people attempt to apply core schemas; they primarily use the feeder schemas in checking whether the conditions of application of core schemas can be satisfied. Thus, the feeder schemas are primarily used as part of the application of a core schema. We therefore expected that the outputs of core schemas would be written down more often than those of feeder schemas. There are other reasons, too, why participants might not write down the outputs of the feeder schemas, which have to do with their conception of what constitutes an "inference." Fillenbaum (1977) reported that participants considered inferences of the form defined by the conjunction schemas (8 and 9) to be too trivially simple to be called *inferences*; many participants seem to consider the outputs of Schemas 8 and 14 to be paraphrases of their inputs rather than "inferences" from the inputs, and, similarly, the output of Schema 9 seems to many people to have already been stated in its input, rather than be an "inference" from it. Thus, asked to write down "inferences," or what they "work out" from the information given, such participants may omit these outputs because they do not think of them as inferences. Lea et al. (1990, Experiment 3) presented a few problems in which participants had to write down everything they inferred from a set of premises, and they found, as expected, that participants usually wrote down the output of core schemas, and did so much more often than the output of feeder schemas.

Note that the schemas and the direct reasoning routine often predict the order in which inferences are made. Thus, on Example Problem 1 discussed earlier, the model does not allow the inference *There is not a lemon* prior to the inferences *There is a strawberry* and *There is a cat* because the condition of application of the requisite schema cannot be satisfied until these inferences have been made. This fact provides an additional way to test the theory: Finding on such problems that participants do not make the inferences in the order predicted would falsify an essential prediction of the model. Finding that they do make the inferences in the predicted order would favor the model, and competing theories that argue against a mental logic would need to provide their own alternative accounts.[2]

---

[2]However, our direct reasoning routine does not make unambiguous predictions about inference order on all possible problems. One could easily construct problems in which more than one core schema could be applied, and in such problems the routine would not decide the order. For example, consider a problem with three premises of the form *If not p then q, p or r,* and *not p.* Two schemas are available: Schema 7 can combine the first and third premises to derive *q,* and Schema 3 can combine the last two to derive *r.* The reasoning routine makes no prediction about inference order in this sort of situation; O'Brien has unpublished data on some problems like this, and he found that most participants make both inferences but that the order in which they write them down varies. We do not present such problems here because a finding that the order varied would not falsify the model.

When a problem asks what follows from a set of premises, it may be that the direct reasoning routine fails to make any inferences at all. When that happens, participants may say "nothing follows" (which we list as the model's prediction in later tables), or they may seek a response outside the direct reasoning routine, for instance, from strategies they have available, or from pragmatic implicatures of the premises (Geis & Zwicky, 1971; Grice, 1975; Politzer, 1986). Several strategies are discussed in chapter 6, but the only one that plays a role in interpreting any of the data reported here is what we have called the *supposition-of-alternatives* strategy (see Table 6.2). We illustrate and discuss this strategy later on.

The schemas of Table 6.1 taken with the direct reasoning routine of Table 6.2 define only a minimum level of logical competence, although we claim it is the one that is typically first brought to bear on a problem. Many college students, and presumably other populations, show evidence of strategic skills that go beyond—sometimes well beyond—those available on the direct reasoning routine alone. Schemas in addition to those of Table 6.1 may also be available to some participants. Thus, our theory does not exclude the possibility of some logically valid inferences beyond those predicted on the schemas taken with the direct reasoning routine; its principal prediction is that the predicted inferences will greatly outnumber all others. Further, as already noted, people also have pragmatically motivated resources for reasoning that are not strictly logical that they may sometimes bring to our problems; in particular, certain invited inferences or conversational implicatures can lead to inferences that do not follow on the mental logic schemas, for example, an *if*-statement, *If p then q*, can invite the inference *If not p then not q*, and a statement of alternatives, *p or q*, can invite *not both p and q* (see Braine, 1990, and Braine & O'Brien, 1991, chap. 9, for discussion of pragmatic principles relevant to the model). Although such invited inferences can be encouraged or discouraged by the content or context of a problem, they are associated with particular logic particles, and can extend their meanings beyond those available on the logic alone. Although we can say some things about when such invited inferences may be made (e.g., especially on problems where nothing follows on the direct reasoning routine and participants take the problems as requiring their finding something that follows), the principal prediction that is relevant in the work reported is that such inferences will occur with far less frequency than those that follow on the direct reasoning routine.

Note that the lines of reasoning on problems are carried out free of any context other than imagining letters written down on a blackboard, or boxes filled with toy fruit and animals. This kind of content is sufficiently abstract that it would not engage pragmatic (domain-specific) reasoning schemas, such as the permission schema of Cheng and Holyoak

(1985) or the social bargaining procedures of Cosmides (1989). Hence participants' inference making on such problems could not be accounted for by such proposals.

We report three experiments. The first reports data on two sets of 13 problems each, each problem presented with a conclusion to evaluate to half the participants, and without a conclusion to the other half. This experiment began with a moderately elaborate training procedure to encourage participants to write down intermediate as well as final conclusions. To allay concerns that the feedback in the training could have affected participants' lines of reasoning, we conducted a second experiment without any feedback in the training: Most of the same problems were presented again without a conclusion to evaluate. Experiments 1 and 2 are presented and discussed together. These two experiments were conducted before a mental-models theory of propositional reasoning had appeared (Johnson-Laird & Byrne, 1991; Johnson-Laird, Byrne, & Schaeken, 1992). They could not be designed to contrast the mental-models and mental-logic theories, although it turns out that many of the problems are revealing about the differences. Experiment 3 was designed to test some contrasting predictions from the two theories.

EXPERIMENTS 1 AND 2

Experiment 1: Method

Participants. Thirty-two native English-speaking introductory psychology students at New York University participated in partial fulfillment of a course. None had any prior tuition in formal logic.

Materials. Participants received two sets of the 13 problems on which we report. The two sets were similar in that each was designed to elicit the model's schemas an approximately equal number of times. The logical forms of the 26 problems along with the lines of reasoning predicted by the model are shown later (see Table 8.2). Each set of problems was prepared with two parallel types of content—letters written on an imaginary blackboard, and toy fruits and animals hidden in a box, as illustrated earlier. (These kinds of content will be called *Blackboard* and *Box* content, respectively.) Eight booklets were prepared (2 sets × 2 types of content × 2 formats), and each participant received two of them. Participants received both problem sets with the same type of content; one was presented with a conclusion to be evaluated and the other with premises only. Each problem set was presented in one of two randomized orders. The order of problems, the presentation order of the two problem sets, and the type of content were balanced across participants.

Procedure. Participants met individually with the experimenter over 2 days. They were told, "The basic task of the experiment is to solve reasoning puzzles." On the first day, they received 15 practice problems and one set of 13 experimental problems. As a means of orienting the participants to the experimental task, the first seven practice problems asked participants simply to evaluate a provided conclusion as either true or false based on the propositions in the premises. There was no feedback on correctness of responses. The next eight practice problems were similar in format to the experimental problems the participants were to receive that day.

The instructions stated that the task was to write down "everything that you work out about what is or is not on the blackboard (in the box)." If the problems contained conclusions to be evaluated, the phrase "on the way to evaluating the conclusion" was added. Participants were asked to write their inferences down "in the order in which they occur to you." Some tuition was used to get participants to write responses in a stand-ardized way (to eliminate coding problems), and participants were given a set of guidelines to follow. These included directions to write down inferences without recopying the premises and to use the following forms: *There is a ___; There is a ___ and a ___; There is a ___ or a ___; If there is a ___, then there is a ___; There is not a ___;* and *Nothing follows* (if nothing seemed to follow from the premises). Participants were allowed to put complex propositions (e.g., conjuncts and disjuncts) in the blanks. If the problem format was one that included a conclusion to be evaluated, participants were directed to circle one of three choices upon concluding the problem (True, False, or Can't tell).

After completion, each practice problem was reviewed with the participant. In the review, participants were not told that there was a right answer; their attention was drawn to intermediate inferences omitted in order to encourage them to be as explicit as possible. For example, in Example Problem 1, if a participant omitted the second inference *There is a Cat*, they were asked "was there any step you made after concluding that there was a strawberry on the way to concluding that there was not a lemon?" If this did not elicit the intermediate inference, as a last resort the participant was told, "Some people might have written down *There is a Cat* after concluding that *There is a Strawberry* and before concluding that *There is not a Lemon*. If you made the same inference regarding the cat you should have written it down too. Try to write down everything you infer." However, such extensive prompting was rarely required. Experiment 2 replicates the results of Experiment 1 without feedback ever being used.

Participants were given special instructions regarding intermediate conclusions that involved the conditional form. They were reminded of the possibility of using a conditional statement as an intermediate conclusion prior to the third to last practice problem, when they were told: "Sometimes the intermediate conclusions to be drawn include statements of possibility such as *If there is a T, then there is a B*. This is often the case when the final conclusion is an 'if-then' statement, as in two of the three following practice puzzles." This instruction was motivated by the fact that in problems where the conclusion to be evaluated is a conditional, the model predicts that the first step will be to add the antecedent of the conditional to the premises as a supposition and treat the consequent as the conditional to be evaluated. Pilot data indicated that participants' usual way of expressing the supposition is by an *if* clause, so we wished to include this situation in the practice problems. After completion and review of the practice problems, participants were left alone to complete the experimental problems.

On the second day of the experiment, participants were reintroduced to the task and given eight practice problems of the same format as the experimental problems to be done that day (e.g., containing only premises when the experimental problems presented no conclusions). These problems were completed individually and reviewed with the experimenter. Participants then received the complementary set of experimental problems. Again, no two problems from either of the problem sets were identical, and none were identical to any practice problems.

Experiment 2: Method

Participants. Thirty-two introductory psychology enrollees participated as partial fulfillment of a course requirement. Data from an additional participant were not used because he failed to follow the experimental instructions. No participants had any prior tuition in formal logic.

Materials. The same seven initial practice problems used in Experiment 1 were used to orient participants to the type of problem they were to complete; participants merely had to circle whether inferences based on the premises were true or false. No feedback of any kind was given, and there were no other practice problems. None of the practice problems were identical in form to any of the problems in the experimental set.

Of the original 26 problems, 21 were used in this experiment. The five omitted problems comprised four that had contained conditional conclusions and another for which the model predicted that no inferences would be made when the problem was presented without a conclusion to be

evaluated. The problems used are indicated in Table 8.2. All were presented with premises only and used blackboard content. Booklets of
problems were prepared in four arbitrary orders and counterbalanced
across participants.

   Procedure.   The only change from Experiment 1 was that no feedback
was given on the practice problems, and participants were not specifically
told that they could use *Nothing follows* as a response.

Results

We consider first the solution rate on the problems presented in Experiment 1 with a conclusion to be evaluated. Across the 26 problems, 95%
of the *True* and *False* responses were correct, indicating that these problems
were simple for participants. All 32 participants solved at least 10 of the
13 with conclusions problems presented to them. Similarly, every problem
was solved by at least 13 of 16 participants. The possibility of accounting
for the correct responses in terms of response biases, matching biases,
and so on can be set aside because of the additional data on intermediate
conclusions to be discussed shortly.
   We now turn to the protocol data on participants' responses. (The term
responses refers to inferences that participants wrote down, and for Tables
8.1 and 8.2, "predicted by the model" means predicted by the schemas
of Table 6.1 taken with the direct reasoning routine of Table 6.2.) In coding
responses into the categories used in the tables, the following guidelines
were used. First, our injunction not to write down premises was
occasionally ignored. Such responses did not seem to be triggered by any
particular circumstances and constituted only 2.4% of all responses;
because they are not inferences and cannot properly be counted for or
against our model or others, they were omitted from all tallies. Second,
repetitions of previously made responses (less than 1% of all responses)
were ignored. Third, an *if-then* statement that had one of the premises or
a previously concluded statement as antecedent was treated as an
assertion of its consequent. For instance, consider the problem *If there is
a fox or a cat then there is not a pear, It is false that there is not a fox / ? There
is not a pear ?;* any participant who wrote *There is a fox, If there is a fox
there is not a pear, True* was treated as if they had written down *There is
a fox, There is not a pear, True.* Similarly, on the problem—*There is an apple
or a cherry, If there is an apple then there is a monkey, If there is a cherry then
there is a monkey ? There is not a monkey ?*—a response of *If there is an apple
or a cherry then there is a monkey, False* was treated as equivalent to *There
is a monkey, False.* In such cases the antecedent is redundant and the *if-then*
statement appears to have been used to assert or justify its consequent
(e.g., in the second example just cited, it is as though the participant was

TABLE 8.1
Overall Frequency With Which the Participants' Responses Were
Predicted and the Inferences Generated by the Model Were Produced

| | Experiment 1 | | Experiment 2 |
| | With Conclusions | Without Conclusions | (Without Conclusions) |
Item			
Total no. of inferences made	694	737	1,329
Percentage of these inferences that were			
predicted	76.4	72.0	78.9
No. of inferences generated by model	688	784	1,408
Using core schemas	480	560	1,088
Percentage of core outputs produced	86.0	87.3	88.4
Using feeder schemas	208	160	320
Percentage of feeder outputs produced	30.3	13.1	27.5
Using *nothing follows*	0	64	0
Percentage produced		37.5	

saying—as some participants indeed said—that because there is an apple
or a cherry there is a monkey). Such *if-then* statements were less than 7%
of all responses, and altogether these three types of omitted or recoded
responses were a small minority (less than 10%) of all responses. Fourth,
in a few cases the response that a participant wrote down deviated from
that listed in the table merely by the inclusion or omission of *and*. That
is, a predicted inference was occasionally written down conjoined with a
premise or the output of another inference; also, in instances in which
the model predicted a conjunction, participants sometimes wrote down
the components of the conjunction on separate lines. Such responses reflect
the optional one-time use of feeder schemas at the read-out stage (see the
last sentence of the inference procedure of Table 6.2) and are not listed
separately.[3]

Table 8.1 presents an overall summary of results collapsed over problems and participants. Table 8.2 identifies the inferences predicted by the
model on each problem and the percentage of participants who wrote down
each predicted inference. We discuss Table 8.1 first. In counting responses

---

[3]It was hard to know how best to treat such responses: To list every response on every
problem would clutter the table inordinately. We adopted the following rule for responses
in which a predicted response was conjoined with something else: When one of the
components of the conjunction was the output of a core schema and the other component
was a premise or the predicted output of another core schema, the response was listed for
the output of the relevant core schema(s). Not to list such responses this way would imply
lack of evidence for the output of the core schema. (Responses so listed amounted to less
than 1% of all responses.) Otherwise, the response was counted as "other" in Table 8.3 and
as "other" in Table 8.4.

for the problems given with a conclusion to evaluate for this table, we excluded the evaluative responses of true and false, and in the case of true problems we also excluded the participant's final conclusion because of its identity with the conclusion to be evaluated. (Inclusion of these responses might be deemed to improperly inflate the hit rate of the model.) In problems with no conclusion to evaluate, *Nothing follows* sometimes occurred as a response and was so counted. We consider, first, the proportion of responses made that were predicted by the model and, second, the proportion of responses predicted by the model that were made. Table 8.1 indicates that, of all the responses produced by participants over the set of problems, about three quarters were predicted by the model and a quarter fell in the category "other"; the proportion predicted was about the same in all three data sets. Of the inferences predicted by the model, it can be seen that those that were the output of the model's core schemas were almost always written down (about 87% of the time, with little variation between data sets); as expected, the outputs of feeder schemas were much less often produced (about 25% of the time). In the without-conclusions condition of Experiment 1, there were four problems on which *Nothing follows* was the predicted response (because when the inference procedure of the direct reasoning routine failed to generate a response to a problem, *Nothing follows* was taken as the response predicted by the model); participants made this response 37.5% of the time, although they almost never made it in other circumstances.

Responses were overwhelmingly made in the order predicted by the model: On the six problems in which an ordered sequence of two core schema responses was predicted,[4] participants wrote down the output of both schemas 82% of the time, and on 94% of those occasions the outputs were written down in the predicted sequence; on the three problems on which a sequence of three core schema responses was predicted,[5] participants wrote down all three outputs 76% of the time, and on 92% of those occasions they wrote the outputs in that sequence. Overall, including feeder schema responses when they were made, when two or more predicted responses were made they were produced in the order predicted over 90% of the time.

Overall, the results from Experiment 2 closely matched those from Experiment 1. To examine the match in detail, the proportion of participants who wrote down all the inferences generated by the core schemas was computed for each problem for each experiment; we then compared the proportions in the two experiments problem by problem. Of the 21 chi-squares obtained, only 2 were significant at $\alpha = .05$ and none at $\alpha =$

---

[4]These were Problems 1, 7, 11, 14, 16, and 23 in Table 8.4.
[5]These were Problems 8, 17, and 18 in Table 8.4.

.01. In one of these two problems participants matched the model better in Experiment 2, and in the other better in Experiment 1. Thus, in only one problem was there a difference consistent with the possibility that the training of Experiment 1 influenced participants' responses to fit the model better. However, in 21 chi-square analyses one would expect at least one to be significant at $\alpha = 0.05$. Thus, the two experiments yielded essentially similar results, indicating that the quality of the fit between the model and the data was not due to feedback to participants on practice problems in Experiment 1.

In general, in all three data sets the great majority of responses were predicted by the model, and most responses predicted by the model were made; in particular, inferences that were the output of the model's core schemas were almost always written down. However, nearly 25% of the responses fell into the other category, and it remains to consider the quality of the fit between model and data for individual problems. We now consider the nature of the other responses and then discuss the evidence of Table 8.2 on how well the theory accounts for participants' reasoning across individual problems.

Nature of the Unpredicted Responses. One major category of other responses consisted of inferences consistent with the one-time use of feeder schemas when reading out conclusions. The great majority of these were uses of Schema 9: When the premise set contained a conjunction partici-pants sometimes wrote down the conjuncts separately, even though only one of them led to further reasoning (e.g., on Problem 3 of Table 8.2, *There is a B* was written down by some participants; and similarly, on Problem 16 several wrote down *There is an H*). The Inference Procedure of the model makes such inferences optional, and thus, though not specifically predicted by the model, all these responses are consistent with it. This category of responses comprised 19.2% of all the other responses across all the prob-lems. We will refer to this category as *feeder-schema responses.*

A second major category of other responses can be interpreted as conversational implicatures or invited inferences (Geis & Zwicky, 1971; Grice, 1975; Politzer, 1986; Sperber & Wilson, 1986).[6] Under this head we included inferences of the following forms: *If not p then not q* and *If q then*

---

[6]Grice distinguished between particularized and generalized conversational implicatures. The generalized implicatures are the ones relevant here; they arise when "one can say that the use of a certain form of words ... would normally (in the absence of special circumstances) carry such-and-such an implicature" (Grice, 1975, p. 56). (Particularized implicatures arise from factors specific to the particular context of an utterance.) Grice used the generalized implicatures to account for extralogical meanings and implications that are commonly read into the use of natural language logical particles (Grice, 1989), and they can apply to the abstract content of our problems.

TABLE 8.2
Percentage of Participants Writing Down Each
Model-Predicted Inference on Each Problem
and the Percentage Writing Down Other Inferences

	Experiment 1		Experiment 2
	With	Without	(Without
Problem and Response	Conclusions	Conclusions	Conclusions)
1. *If V or A then not P; not not V [not P?]*			
V (1)	100	94	94
Not P [True] (2)	94	100	97
Other	13	19	38
2. *If X then not M and not H; X [M or H?]*			
Not M and not H (7)	100	100	100
[False] (11)	100	NP	NP
Other	13	31	0
3. *Not both L and T; L and B; [not T]*			
L (9)	38	6	28
Not T [True] (4)	100	94	97
Other	25	25	22
4. *F or V; if F then W; if V then W [not W?]*			
W (5)	94	100	97
[False] (10)	100	NP	NP
Other	6	0	13
5. *G or R; not G; Q [R and Q?]*			
R (3)	94	100	97
[R & Q/True] (8)	100	NP	NP
Other	0	0	3
6. *Not both G and S; G; not M [S or M]*			
Not S (4)	94	94	91
[Not S and not M] (8)	81	NP	NP
[False] (11)	94	NP	NP
Other	0	0	13
7. *D or S; I or U;*			
if R then not D; R [S and I, or S and U?]			
Not D (7)	75	63	88
S (3)	69	81	91
[S, and I or U] (8)	19	NP	NP
[S and I, or S and U/True] (14)	94	NP	NP
Other	13	19	9
8. *Not not Y; not both E and H;*			
if Y or R the E [H?]			
Y (1)	100	100	94
E (2)	94	94	97
Not H (4)	100	94	81
[False] (10)	100	NP	NP
Other	19	31	19

(Continued)

TABLE 8.2
(Continued)

	Experiment 1		Experiment 2
Problem and Response	With Conclusions	Without Conclusions	(Without Conclusions)
9. *D or K;*			
if K then not not R [if not D then R?]			
If K then R (1)	88	81	NA
[If not D then K] (3[a])	31	NP	NA
[If not D then R/True] (7)	100	NP	NA
Other	31	38	NA
10. *T and I, or T and B;*			
if T or F then not H [not H?]			
T, and I or B (14)	6	25	28
T (9)	81	50	69
Not H [True] (2)	81	81	97
Other	19	44	25
11. *Not both N and D; not not N [not D?]*			
N (1)	94	88	94
Not D [True] (4)	94	69	94
Other	19	31	13
12. *If P or H then E; P [P and E?]*			
E (2)	88	100	100
[E & P/True] (8)	100	NP	NP
Other	19	31	41
13. *B or Z; not B [not Z?]*			
Z (3)	100	100	100
[False] (10)	100	NP	NP
Other	0	0	0
14. *X or M; if X then L; if M then L;*			
if L then not C [not C?]			
L (5)	88	100	97
Not C [True] (7)	94	94	97
Other	6	19	19
15. *If W then O; if H then R;*			
[if W or H then not O and not R?]			
[If W or H then O or R] (6[a])	88	NP	NA
[False] (11)	94	NP	NA
Nothing follows	NP	69	NA
Other	25	31	NA
16. *If S then C; S and H;*			
not both C and Z [not Z?]			
S (9)	25	13	50
C (7)	94	100	94
Not Z [True] (5)	100	100	97
Other	13	31	56

(Continued)

TABLE 8.2
(Continued)

Problem and Response	Experiment 1		Experiment 2
	With Conclusions	Without Conclusions	(Without Conclusions)
17. *X or E; not X; if E then L;*			
not both L and P [P?]			
E (3)	100	100	97
L (7)	88	100	97
Not P (4)	100	88	91
[False] (10)	100	NP	NP
Other	6	13	3
18. *If V or M the J or D; not not V;*			
if J then not A and not N;			
if D then not A and not N [A or N?]			
V (1)	81	88	81
J or D (2)	100	75	81
Not A and not N (5)	88	88	88
[False] (11)	94	NP	NP
Other	19	38	38
19. *K or V; if K the F; if V then F;*			
not not Q [F and Q?]			
F (5)	94	94	94
Q (1)	81	81	97
[F and Q/True] (8)	94	NP	NP
Other	19	19	19
20. *J and T or F [not both (J and T)*			
and not both (J and F)?]			
[J and T or J and F] (14)	44	NP	NA
[False] (11)	88	NP	NA
Nothing Follows	NP	6	NA
Other	81	50	NA
21. *If X then N;*			
if J then N [if X of J then not N?]			
[If X or J then N] (5[a])	100	NP	NA
[False]	100	NP	NA
Nothing follows	NP	6	NA
Other	6	94	NA
22. *T or V; if V or J then E [if not T then E?]*			
[If not T then V] (3[a])	44	NP	NA
[If not T then E] (2)	88	NP	NA
Nothing follows	NP	31	NA
Other	63	69	NA
23. *P, and C of F; if C then M or V;*			
if F then M or V; If M then A;			
If V then L [not A and not L?]			
C or F (9)	19	6	25
M or V (5)	63	88	88
A or L (6)	56	81	44
[False] (11)	100	NP	NP
Other	75	63	53

(Continued)

TABLE 8.2
(Continued)

Problem and Response	Experiment 1		Experiment 2
	With Conclusions	Without Conclusions	(Without Conclusions)
24. S, and K or R; if K then V; if R then A [V or A?]			
K or R (9)	56	0	34
V or A [True] (6)	94	43	59
Other	38	56	88
25. E, and K or S; if E and K then J; if E and S then N [J or N?]			
E & K, or E & S (14)	0	13	13
J or N [True] (6)	100	63	56
Other	63	69	63
26. B and S; G or U; if B and G then K; if B and U then T [K or T?]			
B (9)	6	6	22
B, & G or U (8)	13	0	0
B & G, or B & U (14)	6	6	0
K or T [True] (6)	88	25	47
Other	63	100	75

Note. Problems are defined with the letters-on-an-imaginary-blackboard content. However, the results presented include the problems of Experiment 1 that used box content; the results for each box problem are aggregated with those of the formally equivalent blackboard problem. For each problem, the premises of the problem are given first in italics, with brackets around the conclusion to be tested in the with-conclusion format of Experiment 1. Below the problem form, each model-predicted inference is given together with a number in parentheses that identifies the schema in Table 6.1 that generates the inference. Material in brackets is predicted for the with-conclusion format of Experiment 1 only. NA = not applicable (because the problems were not given in Experiment 2); NP = not predicted.

[a]The preliminary procedure of the reasoning routine is also involved in generating this inference.

p from *If p then q*, inferences of *Not both p and q* and *If p then not q* from *p or q*, and inferences of *p or q* and *If not p then q* from *Not both p and q*. All of these were fairly common. We also included two other kinds of inferences. One of these was the inference of the form *not q* from two premises of the form *If p or q then r* and *p*; this occurred quite often in these problems (e.g., in 25% of the participants on Problems 1 and 12 of Table 8.4 in the "without-conclusions" condition). The other comprised inferences of *p or q* and of *r* from two premises of the form *If p then r*, *If q then r*; these inferences occurred several times on Problem 21 (i.e., *There is an X or a J, There is an N*—these follow, given the pragmatic principle of relevance, because if the premises are to be relevant to the task of drawing inferences, one of X and J has to be present). These conversational implicatures were 23.0% of the other responses across all the problems (i.e., 5.4% of all responses).

Invalid responses that were not conversational implicatures of the preceding types constituted 22.7% of all other responses (i.e., 5.3% of all responses). These responses appeared to be a heterogeneous collection of mistakes (e.g., apparently a result of disregarding negations, misreading *or* as *and*, and the like), thinly spread across problems and participants. The remaining 35.1% of other responses (8.3% of all responses) were valid inferences by standard logic that could not be generated by the direct reasoning routine of the model. Two thirds of these responses fell into one or other of two types that are easily explicable in terms of the model and that we discuss later; the sources for the remaining third were usually obscure and, like the invalid responses, were thinly spread across problems and participants.

Of the two types of valid responses just referred to, one appeared to be generated from conditional variants of schemas in Table 6.1. Some of the schemas have such variants (e.g., *p or q* ∴ *if not p then q* is a conditional variant of Schema 3; *If p then r, if q then r* ∴ *if p or q then r* is a conditional variant of Schema 5). Several of the valid other responses would be generated by such variants (e.g., *If X or J then R*, which sometimes occurred on Problem 21 of Table 8.2 in the "without conclusions" condition). The other response type is interpretable as resulting from a reasoning strategy: the supposition-of-alternatives strategy described in Table 6.2. In chapter 7 evidence for the supposition-of-alternatives strategy was replicated in many student participants, and Fisch (1991) found that many problems that could be solved using Schema 14 were often solved instead with this strategy. We illustrate this strategy using Problems 25 and 26 of Table 8.2. The predicted way of solving Problem 25 uses Schema 14 and is the one shown in Table 8.2. However, if the supposition-of-alternatives strategy is more available to the participants than Schema 14, they will reach the same endpoint by a different line of reasoning. To feed the strategy, they will first generate *There is a K or an S* from the first premise by Schema 9; they will then suppose each of the alternatives in turn and reach the two conditionals *If there is a K then there is a J* and *If there is an S then there is an N* (by reasoning: *If there is a K then there is an E and a K* [Schema 8], *and then there is a J* [second premise], hence *If there is a K then there is a J* [Schema 12]; similarly, *If there is an S then there is an E and an S*, and *then there is an N*, hence *If there is an S then there is an N*). The disjunction *There is a K or a J*, taken with the two deduced conditionals, feeds Schema 6 to again yield *There is a J or an N*. If participants write down the two conditionals as intermediate inferences, it is likely that they have used the supposition-of-alternatives strategy (because the line of reasoning using Schema 14 would not yield *If there is a K then there is a J* and *If there is an S then there is an N* as intermediate inferences). On Problem 26, a participant using the supposition-of-alternatives strategy would start from the disjunction *There is a G or a U* and reason *Suppose there is a G; then there is a B and a G, and so there is a K, hence if G then K,* and *Suppose there is a U, then there is a B and a U, and so there is a T, hence if U then T;* having thus derived the two conditionals *if G then K* and *if U then T,* Schema 6 is applied to derive *There is a K or a T.* The main trace of this strategy in a participant's protocol is the writing down of the conditionals *if G then K* and *if U then T* (which several participants did on this problem). The expected method of solving this problem used Schema 14, but one may note from Table 8.2 that only a few participants wrote any of the outputs specifically predicted for this method.

Survey of Individual Problems. We now consider the results for individual problems, as listed in Table 8.2. Table 8.2 defines problems using the blackboard content; however, the results presented there include the problems that used box content (the results for each box problem are aggregated with those of the formally equivalent blackboard problem). In this table, responses predicted only in the with-conclusions format are enclosed in brackets. (Responses predicted in the without-conclusions format are always a subset of those predicted for the with-conclusions format.) The category other presents the number of participants who wrote down any other response (whether instead of, or in addition to, predicted responses).

The problems fall naturally into two groups. The first group consists of Problems 1 to 19 of Table 8.2: On these problems the Table 8.2 shows that participants rather consistently wrote down the output of the relevant core schemas and only a few participants made other responses (never more than 35% of participants overall, usually fewer), and the table presents no evidence for any logical reasoning routine other than that of the model, which accounts for the huge majority of responses on these problems.

On the remaining seven problems, majorities of participants wrote down unpredicted responses (usually in addition to rather than instead of the model's line of reasoning). These problems fall into two distinct subgroups. One subgroup comprises Problems 20 to 22, characterized by the fact that the direct reasoning routine generates no output in the without-conclusions condition, so that *Nothing follows* is the predicted response. (These problems were not used in Experiment 2.) On these, the responses suggest that participants made the predicted line of reasoning when the problem was presented with a conclusion to evaluate. However, in the without-conclusions condition, although participants were instructed that *Nothing follows* was an admissible response, they were not expecting problems that required this response (in particular, there were no practice problems of this sort), and they made many "other" responses.

There is abundant evidence that participants are biased against "can't tell" responses (see Braine & Rumain, 1983, for a review); they usually need specific training that such responses are acceptable if such responses are to be easily accessible to them (Rumain, Connell, & Braine, 1983; O'Brien et al., 1989). Hence it is a reasonable assumption that on encountering a problem where nothing apparently followed, they might try to think of some inference they could write down. Conversational implicatures were the most common response, with responses seemingly resulting from conditional variants of schemas next most common; altogether, conversational implicatures, conditional variants, and feeder-schema responses constituted 70% of "other" responses on these problems. However, no single response occurred in more than half the participants on any of these problems. Thus, although these problems show that some adults have ready access to conditional variants of some of the model's schemas, they provide no evidence for any shared reasoning routine other than that of the model, whereas the model accounts satisfactorily for the responses in the with-conclusions condition, and also for the fairly common occurrence of *Nothing follows* where it was predicted.

Problems 23 to 26 compose the last subgroup of problems, in which the fit between the model and the data is somewhat more problematic: The responses predicted by the model occurred somewhat less consistently than in the other problems, especially in the without-conclusions conditions, and there were many "other" responses. These were the only problems in which the final response predicted by the model was a disjunction. This should not affect participants' responses in the with-conclusions condition (in which participants' judgments were almost always correct); however, in the without-conclusions condition, some participants may have considered a disjunction too indeterminate to satisfy the instruction to "write down what you work out about what is or is not on the blackboard." This sentiment would discourage writing down the disjunction and encourage other responses; even so, the disjunctive conclusions were usually written down by half or more of the participants on these problems. Of the other responses, 30% are accounted for by the supposition-of-alternatives strategy, which was especially common on Problems 25 and 26. On Problems 23 and 24, there was no evidence for widespread use of any logical reasoning process other than that of the model, and there was good evidence for the latter. However, on Problems 25 and 26 participants' protocols suggest that more of them used the supposition-of-alternatives strategy than the line of reasoning of Table 8.2 in both the with-conclusions and without-conclusions conditions. On both these problems, several participants wrote down the conditionals generated by the strategy as intermediate inferences (*If K then J* and *If S then N* for Problem 25, and *If G then K* and *If U then T* for Problem 26). The direct reasoning routine calls on Schema 14 in these two problems, and it appears that for several participants the supposition-of-alternatives strategy was more accessible to them than this schema. We discuss subsequently the implications of the failure to use Schema 14 consistently, and note that the supposition-of-alternatives strategy could have played some role in a few other problems in which Schema 14 is implicated.

Discussion

Consider again the claims about the model that are under examination. It is claimed that the schemas of Table 6.1 and the direct reasoning routine of Table 6.2 specify a routine part of mental logic that is shared among participants. It is therefore predicted that on every problem the huge majority of participants will go through the line of reasoning generated by the direct reasoning routine. However, the theory expects that some college students have resources for propositional reasoning that go beyond the schemas of Table 6.1 and the direct reasoning routine (e.g., additional schemas or strategies); thus, the model is consistent with the appearance of valid inferences that are not predicted by the model, provided that there is evidence for the predicted line of reasoning and provided also that the unpredicted valid responses are not so consistently given as to suggest a routine shared by many participants. As noted earlier, the theory also accepts that people have nonlogical processes that they may bring to these problems, especially of the kind known collectively as *conversational implicatures* (Grice, 1975); thus, some responses based on implicatures are consistent with the model if they do not replace the predicted line of reasoning.

To evaluate the model against these protocol data, one must consider, first, the extent to which participants made the inferences that the model predicts, and second, the extent to which they confined their responses to those that the model predicts. On the first question, participants rather consistently generated the output of the core schemas: Of the responses predicted from these schemas, 86% and 87% were made in the two conditions of Experiment 1 and 88% in Experiment 2. Participants wrote down the output of the feeder schemas less consistently; however, as discussed earlier, the frequent failure to make feeder inferences explicit was expected and is easily accounted for as resulting from their auxiliary nature and the fact that participants tend not to regard them as inferences (Fillenbaum, 1977). Thus, this failure should not count against the model. With one exception (the line of reasoning involving Schema 14 in some problems), the evidence is consistent with the claim that participants performed the reasoning steps prescribed by the model.

Participants by no means wholly confined themselves to responses predicted by the schemas taken with the direct reasoning routine: Nearly a quarter of all responses were not so predicted. A large group of these responses (23%) comprised inferences that were interpretable as resulting from conversational implicatures. These reflect discourse processes that would be adaptive and useful when reasoning takes place in a discourse context. Although such responses point to a need to define the interdigitation of logical reasoning and discourse processes, as discussed elsewhere (e.g., chaps. 3, 5, and 9), they should not impugn our model as a model of the routine part of mental logic. They are entirely consistent with the pragmatic processes postulated by the model.

The unpredicted responses that reflect the supposition-of-alternatives strategy constituted the only unpredicted valid inferences that were made regularly enough to suggest the existence of reasoning routines common to many participants but not called by the direct reasoning routine. This strategy appeared to be the most common method of approaching Problems 25 and 26, and it provided the only case of a common line of logical reasoning not captured by the schemas taken with the direct reasoning routine. By the same token, the evidence for Schema 14 as routinely available to the participants is poor, inasmuch as problems that could easily be solved through the use of that schema often appeared to be solved by other means. These results corroborate those of Fisch (1991). He, too, found that many adults used the supposition-of-alternatives strategy to solve problems he had expected would be solved with Schema 14. He also found that although fourth graders solved simple problems involving other schemas, they failed problems involving Schema 14 that were formally equally simple (i.e., that contained no more inferential steps): They accessed neither Schema 14 nor the supposition-of-alternatives strategy, although they accessed the rest of the model.

As developed in chapter 6, the complete model of propositional reasoning contained two parts: A routine part claimed to be universal, consisting of basic schemas (putatively those of Table 6.1) and the direct reasoning routine, and a nonroutine part that contained acquired schemas and reasoning strategies for which individual differences were expected. The present data, taken with those of Fisch (1991), indicate that Schema 14 belongs in the nonroutine part, and future versions of the model will so place it (i.e., the basic schemas comprise 1 to 13 of Table 6.1). (Although the use of Schema 14 is not routine, its output was sometimes written down, suggesting that it is often accessed, at least by some participants.) Chapter 7 assigned the supposition-of-alternatives strategy to the nonroutine part, although, as here, there was evidence for it in many college-student participants. This assignment is consistent with the evidence of Fisch (1991) that the strategy becomes easily accessed some time around adolescence. However, that assignment creates a problem: According to the model, responses in the without-conclusions condition are generated from the direct reasoning routine only; yet in Problems 10, 25, and 26, the responses of *There is not an H, There is a J or an N,* and *There is a K or a T,* respectively, require the strategy if Schema 14 is not available.[7] About 90%, 60%, and 40% of the time, respectively, participants wrote these responses down in the without-conclusions condition on these problems, and, as noted earlier, there is further evidence for the strategy in the fact that some participants wrote down the conditionals produced by the strategy. It follows that the strategy must be available in the without-conclusions condition under some circumstances, which raises the question "Under what circumstances?" The strategy does not appear to be elicited whenever the premises contain a disjunction and the model therefore needs to restrict its operation. One solution, which uses the feeder-core distinction and would work well for this problem set, is to require that any feeder schemas used in constructing the conditionals generated by the strategy feed core schemas or else that the output of the strategy (when the conditionals feed Schema 5 or 6) feed some core schema or the evaluation of a conclusion.[8] (In other words, some nontrivial inference—something other than the two AND-schemas—must be involved in the argument, either in constructing the conditionals or in what the strategy enables.) In sum, omitting Schema 14, and with the supposition-of-alternatives strategy used as just described, our protocol data indicate that the model of Tables 6.1 and 6.2 does a good job of capturing participants' reasoning routines on all these problems.

---

[7]In Problem 10, without Schema 14, the conditionals *if T and I then T* and *if T and B then T* are needed to feed Schema 5 in order to deduce *There is a T,* whence *There is not an H* follows by Schema 2. There are also two other problems in which the supposition-of-alternatives strategy is needed, but only in the with-conclusions condition, if Schema 14 is not available to the solver (Problems 7 and 20).

[8]An alternative (or supplementary) possibility would be to posit pragmatic constraints that would operate across the board in reasoning. Two suggest themselves. One is a "specific conclusion" bias. Atomic propositions (not already in the database) and conjunctions of atomic propositions are preferred as inferences to negated atomic propositions, which are preferred to disjunctions of atomic propositions, which are preferred to more complex forms. Such a bias could explain why more participants write down the conclusion *not H* of Problem 10 than the final disjunctions of Problems 25 and 26. The other constraint might be called a *no undue effort* bias; it would posit that there is a cost in effort associated with iterating the inference procedure so that considerable motivation is required to keep the process going over more than a few cycles. It would be consistent with such a bias that in casual reading of text only the most immediate of inferences may be drawn (e.g., those inferred on the first cycle); also that occasional unwilling subject-pool participants may give a perfunctory performance by exiting the inference procedure early. Such constraints are attractive because of their commonsense plausibility. If a mental-logic model threatens to become complex because of restrictions placed on schemas or strategies, such constraints offer a means of keeping the inference engine simple because they would operate together to cause any recursions generating complex or already familiar material to grind quickly to a halt. However, we prefer not to rely on such constraints until obliged to.

Now consider whether the participants' responses could be explained in terms of other theories. We first address other mental-logic theories; we then turn to mental-models theory (the subject of the next main section and Experiment 3). Pragmatic reasoning schemas (Cheng & Holyoak, 1985; Cheng et al., 1986) will be considered in the General Discussion. Early mental-logic theories (Johnson-Laird, 1975; Osherson, 1975; Rips, 1983) were discussed in detail in chapter 7 in relation to performance on propositional reasoning problems reported there, and that discussion will not be repeated here. Recently, Rips (1994) revised and extended his earlier model (ANDS, a natural deduction system), and, in so doing, responded to some criticisms made in chapter 7. The new model, PSYCOP, is able to handle quantifiers as well as propositional reasoning—a considerable advance and accomplishment—but it is PSYCOP's ability to capture participants' propositional reasoning that is our sole concern here.

PSYCOP has two classes of schemas: forward and backward. Forward schemas are just like our core schemas in that their operation is unrestricted. The use of backward schemas is restricted by goals to deduce certain propositions and by other features of the problem environment specified in the schema, and part of the operation of the schema is to set subgoals (e.g., backward modus ponens is restricted to the conditions that a conditional *If p then q* is in the database and that q is the current goal; it sets up a subgoal to deduce p). Some of the backward schemas set up suppositions associated with a subgoal to be derived. In without-conclusions problems, only the forward schemas are used; every such schema that can apply does so, and PSYCOP recycles until no further inferences can be drawn. This is similar to our model, except for some differences in the schemas included and for the absence of the distinction between feeder and core schemas; infinite loops are avoided by omitting schemas that could give rise to them (like AND-introduction [our Schema 8]) from the forward list. When a problem presents a conclusion to be evaluated, the forward schemas apply first until no further inferences can be drawn; then, if the conclusion has not already been deduced, it is set as goal and backward schemas that can apply do so (with certain priorities as to order of application) in a depth-first search until a derivation is found or PSYCOP runs out of search paths.

We hand simulated PSYCOP on our problems. On just half of the "without-conclusions" problems, Rips's (1994) model gives essentially the same responses as our model and, with two exceptions, the same responses as the participants[9]; on the other half, PSYCOP's inferences are

---

[9]The problems are 1, 2, 4, 5, 7, 12 to 15, 18, 19, 21, and 22 of Table 8.4; on the last two, both models predict nothing follows, which is not a good match with how most participants responded.

not the same as those of our model or participants. (In assessing the similarity of PSYCOP's predictions, our predictions, and participants' responses, differences resulting only from generating propositions separately vs. conjoining them were ignored.) On the with-conclusions problems PSYCOP solves all of the problems with an answer of "True," but does so with essentially the same intermediate conclusions as our model and the participants on only 53% of them[10]; on the others there are ways in which PSYCOP's responses differ both from our model and from participants.

Problems answered as "False" are poorly handled by PSYCOP: Rips (1994, p. 412) noted that to handle them PSYCOP would need a process that recognizes when a conclusion is inconsistent with premises (i.e., something that does the work of our Schemas 10 and 11 and the evaluation procedure). In principle, after failing to derive a conclusion, PSYCOP could determine that the conclusion is false by taking its negation as goal and deriving that; however, that method would not simulate what participants do. Even when a proposition contradicting the conclusion can be derived by the forward rules alone (as in most of our problems), PSYCOP would need a way of recognizing what contradicts a complex proposition (e.g., that ~p & ~q contradicts a conclusion p or q, and vice versa). In hand simulating PSYCOP on our problems with answer *False*, we have taken it as using the forward rules alone and as being able to recognize straightforward contradictions (between a proposition and its negation) but not contradictions between complex propositions (e.g., between p or q and ~p & ~q). (Recognizing the first type would be a trivial addition to Rips's program, whereas recognizing contradictions between compound propositions would require decisions as to what contradictions to recognize and how to implement recognition, decisions that should be taken by Rips, not us.) Assuming this procedure, PSYCOP gives the same responses as our model and participants on 27.3% of the problems with the answer as *False*; it solves another 18.2% with a line of reasoning different from our model and participants, and it fails to solve 55.5%.[11] For just half of the latter group, the difficulty is due only to inability to recognize that p or q and not p & not q are contradictory.

Table 8.3 picks out problems from Table 8.2 that illustrate the nature of the discrepancies between PSYCOP's inferences and those of our model. The first problem cited (Problem 2 from Table 8.2) is one where PSYCOP needs to know that the propositional forms p or q and not-p and not-q are contradictory to make the final judgment of *False*; otherwise, its reasoning

---

[10]These are Problems 1, 5, 9, 10, 12, 14, 19, and 22 of Table 8.4.

[11]The problems in these three classes are Problems 4, 13, and 21, Problems 8 and 17, and Problems 2, 6, 15, 18, 20, and 23, respectively, of Table 8.4.

TABLE 8.3

Problems Exemplifying the Discrepancies Between the
Predictions of Rips's Model and Ours, Together With the
Frequencies of Relevant Responses of Participants

Problem and Relevant Response	Participants (%)[a]	Prediction	
		Our Model	Rips's Model
2. *If X then not-M and not-H;* *X/?M or H?*			
Not-M & not-H	100[b]	Not-M & not-H	Not-M & not-H
Not-M; not-H		(Not-M; not-H)[c]	Not-M; not-H
False	100	False	
8. *Not not-Y; not both E & H;* *if Y or R then E*			
Y	100; 94	Y	Y
Not-E or not H	0; 0		Not-E or not-H
E	94; 97	E	E
Not-H	94; 81	Not-H	Not-H
9. *D or K; if K then not not-R*			
If K then R	81	If K then R	No inference
24. *S, & K or R; if K then V;* *if R then A*			
S	0; 41	(S)[c]	S
K or R	0; 34	K or R	K or R
V or A	43; 59	V or A	
10. *T & I, or T & B;* *if T or F then not-H*			
T, & I or B	25; 28	T, & I or B[d]	
T	50; 69	T[e]	
Not-H	81; 97	Not-H[e]	

[a]When two frequencies appear in this column, they represent the percentage of participants in Experiment 1 and the percentage in Experiment 2, respectively.

[b]Percentage of participants making one or the other of these responses.

[c]This response is optional in our model.

[d]This response uses our Schema 14.

[e]This response could be part of the line of reasoning involving Schema 14 or could stem from the use of the supposition-of-alternatives strategy.

is similar to our model's.[12] Many of the other discrepancies between PSYCOP's inferences and the participants' are due to specific schemas. The second problem in Table 8.3 (Problem 8 from Table 8.2) illustrates the consequence for our problems of the fact that PSYCOP has a forward schema $\sim(p \ \& \ q) \ \therefore \sim p \ or \ \sim q$; that predicts a response of the form $\sim p \ or \ \sim q$ whenever there is a premise of the form $\sim(p \ \& \ q)$; participants did not make these responses, and the schema, therefore, needs to be omitted or

---

[12]Problems 6 and 18 of Table 8.4 are two other problems for which these statements hold.

restricted. PSYCOP has our Schema 1 as a one-way rule, not as a paraphrase rule; it therefore cannot apply to subformulae and cancel the double negative in the without-conclusions version of Problem 9 as participants do (see Table 8.3).

Problem 24 illustrates the consequences of the fact that our Schema 6 is not represented in PSYCOP at all: Predictably, PSYCOP has difficulty with problems that call for that inference. On the without-conclusions form of the problem (shown in Table 8.3) it cannot deliver the final disjunction; on the with-conclusions form of the same problem with the answer *True* (not shown in Table 8.5), although PSYCOP finds a derivation, the line of reasoning is quite different from that of our model and much more complex: After inferring *There is a K or an R* as in the without-conclusions version, it takes the given conclusion, *There is a V or an A*, as the goal and tries to reach this goal by means of its analog of our supposition-of-alternatives strategy (backward OR-elimination [Rips, 1994; Table 4.2]). It first supposes there is a K, infers the presence of V by modus ponens, and then infers that there is a V or an A by OR-introduction ($p \therefore p$ or q, not in our model). It then supposes that there is an R, infers the presence of A by modus ponens, and then again that there is a V or an A by OR-introduction; this permits it to conclude that there has to be a V or an A and respond *True*. However, there is no trace of such a line of reasoning in the protocols; also, because OR-introduction is a schema whose probability of use is very low (around .2) in Rips's (1994, p. 156) estimate, such a derivation would predict many errors, whereas participants are accurate (e.g., 94% correct on Problem 22).[13] Despite PSYCOP's difficulty in the preceding examples, in all such cases it would not be difficult to amend PSYCOP to eliminate the problems.

Finally, PSYCOP has a more fundamental difficulty, illustrated by Problem 10 in the without-conclusion condition. The difficulty is that, to capture participants' performance, a backward schema is needed that is not available because there is no conclusion to serve as the goal: Backward OR-elimination—the analog of our supposition-of-alternatives strategy—is needed but cannot be used because it is a backward schema; hence, PSYCOP produces no output at all. Although the difficulty resembles the one our model had with this problem, in PSYCOP the difficulty arises in a broader variety of cases. For instance, consider a hypothetical without-conclusions problem with four premises of the following forms: p, q, r, and *If p & q & r then s*. It is intuitively clear that s follows; however, that inference requires AND-introduction (to feed modus ponens). But AND-

---

[13]Problems 7, 25, and 26 of Table 8.4 are other with-conclusions problems in which PSYCOP uses this line of reasoning. Problem 23 is another problem in which the absence of Schema 6 prevents a disjunction (*A or L*) from being inferred.

introduction is a backward schema restricted to operating with a goal that the problem does not present; hence, PSYCOP cannot infer s. It seems to us that this sort of difficulty can be met only by a kind of restriction not now used in PSYCOP (e.g., something like our feeder-core distinction that would allow certain schemas [like AND-introduction and supposing alternatives] to operate when they enable certain other inferences).

The general lesson to be learned from this discussion is not, we believe, that PSYCOP is a poor model. PSYCOP has virtues (on which we have not dwelt) as well as problems. Most models are found to have problems when investigated deeply enough, and no doubt our model will be no exception. What we hope the discussion has demonstrated is that it is possible to bring data to bear in a fine-grained way on details of models of participants' mental logic so that one can hope, with some confidence, that further work will bring convergence on the proper model. In the meantime, our model works well with these problems, and to do equally well Rips's (1994) model would need to adopt some of its features.

CAN PARTICIPANTS' RESPONSES BE EXPLAINED BY MENTAL-MODELS THEORY?

The mental-models theory (Johnson-Laird, 1983) is the only serious candidate as a theory that might account for our data without postulating a mental logic. Johnson-Laird et al. (1992) extended the theory to propositional reasoning and claim that it accounts for reasoning on precisely the kind of problem that we have used. We therefore devote this section of the chapter to evaluating the models theory with respect to these problems and some new ones. Unfortunately, in some important respects it is not clear exactly what the current models theory holds: Subsequent to this chapter being submitted for publication in its original form as an article, Johnson-Laird, Byrne, and Schaeken (1994), responding to criticism (Bonatti, 1994; O'Brien, Braine, & Yang, 1994), proposed some modifications and additions to the 1992 theory (i.e., the theory of Johnson-Laird et al., 1992); however, the modifications had not yet been spelled out in sufficient detail to provide a firm basis for prediction, and claims for the 1992 theory had not been explicitly altered. Our discussion focuses predominantly on the 1992 theory, which Experiment 3 was designed to examine, but we bring in the more recent proposals where it seems appropriate.

According to the models theory, reasoning involves the construction of a set of mental models to represent a problem's premises. Each premise is processed in turn: A set of models is constructed for it and then combined with the set of models resulting from previously processed premises. The reasoner formulates a conclusion or evaluates a given conclusion on the basis of the final model set obtained.

The theory presents various levels of expertise. The lowest level is represented by the psychological algorithm, which claims to model real reasoning processes and has been implemented in a computer program. An artificial intelligence (AI) algorithm models the kind of perfect performance possible in an organism with unlimited working memory, and no claim of psychological reality is made for it. There are intermediate levels of expertise (Johnson-Laird et al., 1994) that have not yet been fully specified. However, Johnson-Laird et al. (1992) claim that the lowest level accounts for evaluations of conclusions on problems essentially similar to those used here (the problems presented in chapter 7), making it appropriate for making predictions to our problems; we refer to other aspects of the theory in appropriate instances.

There are standard sets of models for each of the truth functions, as shown in Table 8.4. Each model set consists of one or more lines, each line representing a separate model (or state of affairs). For example, the initial model set for *p or q* contains two models, one with a token for *p* and one with a token for *q*. The initial model set of *If p then q* also contains two models. The first contains tokens for *p* and *q*, indicating a state of affairs in which both *p* and *q* are true; the second is an implicit model (the ellipsis is a placeholder that indicates the possibility of there being some other state of affairs than that indicated by the first model).

The models used to represent a premise depend on the level of expertise captured. The two computer implementations do not use the exhaustivity symbol; only intermediate levels do that. The psychological algorithm only uses initial models, and the AI algorithm only fully "fleshed-out" (i.e., complete) model sets. (Note that the initial model of a disjunction is vague as to whether the disjunction is to be taken exclusively or inclusively, and, similarly, the initial model for an *if*-statement is vague in distinguishing between conditional and biconditional.) The main purpose of the exhaustivity symbol (the square brackets) is to constrain how an initial model set can be fleshed out once the reasoner decides to construct a representation more complex than that provided by the initial model set. Thus, the brackets around *p* in the representation for *if* mean that any added models cannot contain *p*; they must contain ~*p*.[14] Once there is some fleshing out, the reasoner is operating above the level of expertise

---

[14]Actually, the meaning of the exhaustivity symbol is much more complicated than this. Tokens in models are not just "exhausted" or "not exhausted," but exhausted in relation to some particular other token. When model sets are combined, complicated situations can easily arise in which a token is exhausted with respect to certain other tokens in the same model and not exhausted with respect to others. Model sets then become very hard to process, and the theory contains no algorithm for doing so (see O'Brien, Braine, & Yang, 1994, for discussion). An additional complexity is that exhaustivity brackets can be embedded within exhaustivity brackets (cf. Johnson-Laird & Byrne, 1991, pp. 121–124).

TABLE 8.4
The Various Mental Models for *if*, *or*, *not both*, and
and Presented in Johnson-Laird et al. (1992)

		Fleshed-Out Model	
Proposition	Initial Model	Conditional	Biconditional
If p then q			
Without exhaustivity	p q	p q	p q
	. . .	~p q	~p ~q
		~p ~q	
With exhaustivity	[p] q	[p] [q]	[p] [q]
	. . .	[q]	. . .
		. . .	
p or q		Inclusive	Exclusive
Without exhaustivity	p	p q	p ~q
	q	p ~q	~p q
		~p q	
With exhaustivity		[p] [q]	[p]
		[p]	[q]
		[q]	
Not both p and q			
Without exhaustivity	~p ~q		
	p ~q		
	~p q		
p and q			
Without exhaustivity	p q		

Note. The psychological algorithm uses only the initial models without exhaustivity. The AI algorithm uses the fleshed-out models without exhaustivity. Intermediate levels of expertise use the models with exhaustivity. Exhaustivity is symbolized with brackets; [p] q means that p is exhausted in relation to q. Any additional models containing a token for q cannot contain one for p.

of the psychological algorithm. However, Johnson-Laird et al. impose two requirements for any fleshing out to occur: "(a) the premises must be simple, for example, a conditional interrelating two or three atomic propositions; and (b) nothing follows from the initial models" (1992, p. 424). It follows that much of the time the reasoner uses the initial models only. Fleshing out is also inhibited by the fact that models are processed in working memory, and the number of models that can be held simultaneously in working memory is limited. Indeed, the models theory holds that these working memory limitations are the major constraint on reasoning effectiveness.

The psychological algorithm specifies how model sets from different premises are combined (Johnson-Laird et al., 1992, p. 425). Each model in the first set is compared, one after the other, with each model in the second set. When both models are elliptical, the result is an elliptical model; when one model is elliptical and the other contains items, no new model results; when two models are inconsistent (i.e., one contains an item and the other contains its negation), no new model results; when two models each contain items that are consistent, the new model conjoins the items. When the combination process results in two models that are the same, one of them is eliminated.

As an example of how the theory works, consider the first problem of Table 8.4. According to the theory, a participant begins by constructing model sets for each premise. The models for the first premise can be represented as follows:

V   ~P
   A   ~P
   . . .

The first line (i.e., model) represents a possible blackboard with a V and without a P, and the second model represents one with an A and without a P; the implicit model indicates that there are other possibilities. The model set for the second premise turns out to consist of a single model—one with a V—after the negations have been processed (the model set for a negation is the complement of the negated element, and the complement of ~p is p). The model sets for the two premises are then combined. Combining them by the psychological algorithm leads to a final set of just two models, a V without a P, and a V and an A without a P, represented as follows:

V   ~P
V   A   ~P

According to Johnson-Laird et al. (1992), conclusions are read out, and given conclusions evaluated, on the basis of the final model set. In reading out conclusions, the theory has two principles: not to repeat premises and not to discard information. Because the presence of V and the absence of P are common to both final models, the conclusion must assert both these properties. The principle not to discard information in reading out conclusions could well be construed as also requiring mention of the possibility of there being an A.

This point illustrates a problem of the current theory: The principles do not fully specify the conclusions to be drawn from final model sets. If we neglect this point, the predicted response would be *There is a V and there is not a P*. Because we largely ignored the difference between conjoining and separate statement in evaluating the other theories, we also accept a separate statement of the model components (*There is a V. There is not a P*) as fulfilling the predictions of the theory.

Thus, as Table 8.4 shows, if we neglect the question of mentioning the possibility of A, the models theory predicts well for this problem. The observed output order, *V* before *not-P*, could be accounted for either as resulting from the processing of the negations in the second premise leading to V being stated first or as resulting from a figural effect (Johnson-Laird & Bara, 1984) causing a left-to-right readout from the final model set. When the problem is given with the conclusion *There is not a P* to be evaluated, comparison with the final model set delivers a match, leading to the answer true.

In the Appendix to this chapter, we list all the problems in the same order as they are listed in Table 8.4, giving the final model set (as determined by the psychological algorithm) and specifying what we take as the predicted response in the without-conclusions condition, and, if different, the predicted response for the with-conclusions condition together with the evaluation. In predicting responses, we assumed that multiple conclusions reflect separate readout of elements of the final model set and that the sequence of statement is determined by the order of elements in the final model set, in accordance with the theory of figural effects (Johnson-Laird & Bara, 1984; Johnson-Laird & Byrne, 1991); the order of elements in the final model is determined by order in the premises.

Overall, in the without-conclusions condition the models theory yields responses similar to those of our theory and (with one exception) to those of participants on half of the 26 problems.[15] On the others there are ways in which the models-theory predictions differ both from our model's and from participants' responses (as discussed later). Ten of the with-conclusions problems are solved with responses and evaluations similar to those of our theory and participants, and a further 12 are evaluated correctly, but the basis of the evaluation does not match that of our theory.[16] The remaining four problems have conditional conclusions, and it does not seem to us that the current models theory gives a determinate response. Johnson-Laird et al. (1992) did not provide rules for assessing a given conclusion against a final model set. Usually, the assessment is transparent; however, we have not known how to evaluate conditional conclusions.

On instances in which the models theory predicts imperfectly, three kinds of difficulty are indicated: (a) It often fails to predict the order in which participants make responses, (b) the psychological algorithm

---

[15]These are Problems 1 to 3, 5, 6, 8, 11 to 13, 15 to 17, and 21. The exception is Problem 21, on which we take the models-theory prediction to be nothing follows, like our theory's.

[16]We have judged with-conclusions Problems 1 to 3, 8, 10, 11, 13, 16, 17, and 20 as solved with predicted responses similar to those predicted by our theory and Problems 4 to 7, 12, 14, 18, 19, and 23 to 26 as evaluated correctly.

wrongly predicts certain fallacies that participants do not make, and (c) the theory lacks sufficient principles to determine what conclusions participants will draw from some final model sets. We illustrate and discuss these concerns in turn.

In terms of the first difficulty, consider first Problem 5 of Table 8.2 and the Appendix, in the with-conclusions condition. The final model set consists of just R and Q. Because the conclusion to be evaluated is *There is an R and a Q*, one would predict an immediate response of *True*; 94% of participants, however, infer *There is an R* before making this response, although this initial inference is unmotivated by the final model. A similar argument applies in the with-conclusions conditions of Problems 6 and 12. On Problem 6, the final model consists of G, ~S, and ~M, and the conclusion to be evaluated is *There is an S or an M*. The response of *False* should be immediate; there is no reason for the initial response of *not S* made by 94% of participants. On Problem 12, the final model set has two models, both of which contain P and E. A response of true to the conclusion *There is a P and an E* should be immediate; the final model set provides no reason why participants should precede this with the response *There is an E*, as 88% do. In each case, the mental-logic theory predicts the obtained response sequence exactly. Problems in predicting inference order can also arise in the without-conclusions condition. Consider Problem 7 in this condition. The final model set consists of two models:

```
S   I     R   ~D
S       U  R   ~D
```

The principle not to repeat premises says that the presence of R, and of I or U, being given as premise, will not be restated as inference. Omitting these, the set predicts the responses that there is an S and that there is not a D. In the 1992 theory, the order of the elements in the final model provides the only basis for predicting response order; if order of mention in the premises is the basis for order in the models—as it evidently is in the practice of Johnson-Laird et al. (1992) and Johnson-Laird and Byrne (1991) and in the theory of figural effects of Johnson-Laird and Bara (1984)—then the absence of D should be asserted after asserting the presence of S, whereas participants overwhelmingly state *not D* before S. In the next experiment, we take up the issue of predicting inference order more systematically.

In regard to the second difficulty, the issue of predicting fallacies that participants do not make, consider first Problem 4. According to the psychological algorithm, the model set obtained by combining the first two premises contains two models:

```
F    W
F  V  W
```

W is common to both and is, therefore, a fallacious inference that could be made on the basis of the first two premises alone. Problem 9 (without-conclusions condition) provides evidence that participants do not make this fallacy; it contains premises analogous to the first two premises of Problem 4 (the double negative in the consequent of the conditional is irrelevant), yielding a final set of two models

```
D  K  R
   K  R
```

K and R are common to both these models; thus, although both are fallacious, *There is an R* and *There is a K and an R* are predicted as possible inferences, and both are predicted to be thought valid by participants. No participant made either of these responses. Returning to Problem 4, the final model set obtained from combining all three premises consists of a single model, containing F, V, and W. This model would naturally lead to, and justify, the inference *There is an F, a V, and a W*, again a fallacious inference; in the without-conclusions condition, in which participants were free to make whatever inferences they wished, no participant made this inference. O'Brien et al. (1994) showed that the psychological algorithm predicts other fallacies that participants do not make. Other problems in which the final model set is fallacious are 14, 18, 19, and 22 to 26 (see the Appendix). Note that the fact that the final model set is fallacious does not mean that the evaluation in the with-conclusions condition must be wrong; in fact, in all these problems it would be correct, though not for the right reasons.

In regard to the third difficulty—predicting from the final model set to the participant's response—the current theory has the two principles mentioned earlier: not to repeat premises and not to discard information in the final model set. These principles are not sufficient. Consider first Problem 20 in the without-conclusions condition. The final model set is:

```
J  T
J     F
```

That there is a J, and a T or an F, cannot be the conclusion because these constitute the premise. What is the response to be? *J & T, or J & F?* Nothing follows? In Problem 10 (without-conclusions condition) the final model set is:

```
T   I           ~H
T       B       ~H
T   I       F   ~H
T       B   F   ~H
```

Because T and not-H figure in all the models, these must be inferences to be read out, and indeed participants are nearly unanimous in making these inferences. But what about I, B, and F, which each appear in two models? The principle not to discard information would dictate some additional conclusion (e.g., asserting the presence of I, or B, or F). In addition, as we noted earlier, there is an issue for Problem 1 as to whether the possibility of an A should be part of the response, and a similar issue arises for Problem 12. In general, the principles fail to specify when mention of possibilities and alternatives should figure in responses.

For several problems, the models theory evinces more than one of the above-mentioned deficiencies (e.g., Problems 14, 19, 23, and 25). In each of these problems the final model set specified by the psychological algorithm consists of a single model containing all the elements mentioned in the premises, and this model would be perfectly consistent with the fallacious response consisting of the conjunction of these elements (the response that is dictated by the principle not to discard information). This response is never made; in particular, it is not made in the without-conclusions condition where participants' inferences are not constrained.

In the examples discussed, the predicted fallacious final models could be avoided if one assumed higher levels of expertise than the psychological algorithm. One possibility might be that participants used fleshed-out rather than initial models. However, to avoid fallacy Problem 9 would require at least four models to be held at once in working memory, Problem 23 at least five, and the other problems mentioned, six or more. All these requirements exceed what the theory expects people to tolerate. Moreover, Johnson-Laird et al. stated that fleshing out occurs only when "nothing follows from the initial models" (1992, p. 424), and something always does follow in the cases cited. Johnson-Laird et al. (1994) opted for another possibility: that participants use an intermediate level of expertise that employs unfleshed-out models. That would involve abandoning the 1992 claim that the psychological algorithm suffices to account for performance on problems like the ones used here. We return to the possibility of an intermediate level of expertise in the discussion of Experiment 3 (see also chap. 14).

In Experiment 3, we explore more systematically the predictability of the order in which inferences are made. We report on two types of test problems concerned with inference order. The issue in the first set may be illustrated with the following problem (which is Problem 1 of Set 1 in Table 8.5):

TABLE 8.5
Problem Set 1 of Experiment 3: Problems, Theory Predictions,
and Percentage of Participants Making Various Responses

Problem	Theory Predictions	Responses	%
1. W → K	Mental logic:		
W	K	K	80.0[a]
————	W & K/False	(W & K)/False[a]	
?~(W & K)?	Mental models:		
	W K; W; WK.	(W & K)/False[b]	12.5[b]
	. . .		
2. E or B	Mental logic:		
~B	E	E	85.0
————	E & ~B/True	(E & ~B)/True	
?E & ~B?	Mental models:		
	E; ~B; E ~B	(E & ~B)/True	12.5
	B		
3. ~(A & F)	Mental logic:		
A	~F	~F	80.0
————	A & ~F/True	(A & ~F)/True	
?A & ~F?	Mental models:		
	~A F; A; A ~F.	(A & ~F)/True	15.0
	A ~F		
	~A ~F		
4. (O or N) → P	Mental logic:		
O	P	P	75.0
————	O & P/False	(O & P)/False	
?~(O & P)?	Mental models:		
	O P; O; O P.	(O & P)/False	7.5
	N P O N P		

[a]The response consisted of writing down K, followed by False, with the conjunction (W & K) possibly written down in between.
[b]The response consisted just of False, possibly preceded by the conjunction.

If there is a W, then there is a K
There is a W

? It is not true that there is both a W and a K ?

The mental-logic theory predicts that participants will first infer K, and then, on consideration of the conclusion to be evaluated, conjoin it with the second premise to form W & K, and then respond False. For this problem, the series of mental models constructed is as follows (in representing models, we follow the notation of Johnson-Laird et al. [1992, 1994] and show the models for the first premise first, followed by the models for the second premise, and, finally, the models resulting from the combination [with model sets separated by semicolons]; when there is a third premise, its models are then shown followed by the models resulting from combining this with the model set for the combination of the first two premises; and so forth):

[W]   K;   W;   W   K
    . . .

The final model corresponds to the conjunction of W and K. Therefore participants should compare this model with the conclusion given and respond *False* directly, without K as a prior inference. For all the problems of Set 1, the two theories make different predictions for reasons parallel to the problem just illustrated.

The second set of test problems concern the fact that when two or more schemas are necessarily applied in a certain order, the mental-logic theory predicts that changing the order of the premises will have no effect on the order in which inferences are made. However, in the same cases, premise order does change the sequence of processing predicted by the 1992 models theory, and hence the theories often make different predictions. The predictions from the models theory depend on the assumptions (Johnson-Laird et al., 1992) that the premises are processed in the order presented and that conclusions are read out from the final model set. Johnson-Laird et al. (1994) proposed changes in these assumptions, which we consider in the discussion of Experiment 3.

Problems 1a and 1b of Set 2 (see Table 8.6) present typical cases. Note that the order of the first two premises is changed, as are the positions of the letters B and N in the premise. For both problems, mental-logic theory predicts that participants will infer—and write down—first B, and after that ~N. For these two problems, respectively, the series of mental models constructed are as follows:

[E]   B;   ~B N;   E B ~N;   E;   E B ~N
  . . .   B ~N
          ~B ~N

and

~N   B;   [E]   B;   ~N E B;   E;   ~N E B
 N   ~B   . . .
~N   ~B

From the final model set, it follows that participants will write down B & ~N for the first problem and ~N & B for the second problem, assuming

TABLE 8.6
Problem Set 2 of Experiment 3: Problems, Theory Predictions,
and Percentage of Participants Making Various Responses

Problem	Theory Predictions	Responses	%
1a. E → B	ML inferences:	B	
~(B & E)	B	~N	55
E	~N	~N	
_____	Final model set:	B	5
What follows?	E B ~N	~N & B/B & ~N	5
1b. ~(N & B)	ML inferences:	B	
E → B	B	~N	75
E	~N	~N	
_____	Final model set:	B	10
What follows?	~N B E	B & ~N/~N &B	0
2a. C → ~M	ML inferences:	~M	
M or J	~M	J	60
C	J	J	
_____	Final model set:	~M	0
What follows?	C ~M J	J & ~M/~M & J	0
2b. J or M	ML inferences:	~M	
C → ~M	~M	J	75
C	J	J	
_____	Final model set:	~M	0
What follows?	J C ~M	~M & J/ J & ~M	0
3a. ~(F & B)	ML inferences:	~B	
B or Z	~B	Z	55
F	Z	Z	
_____	Final model set:	~B	15
What follows?	F ~B Z	~B & Z/Z & ~B	0
3b. Z or B	ML inferences:	~B	
~(F & B)	~B	Z	80
F	Z	Z	
_____	Final model set:	~B	0
What follows?	Z F ~B	Z & ~B/~B & Z	0
4a. A → (D or P)	ML inferences:	D or P	
D → S	D or P	S	40
P → S	S	S	
A	Final model set:	D or P	5
	A D P S	D or P	5
_____		S	40
What follows?		NF	10
4b. P → S	ML inferences:	P or D	
D → S	P or D	S	45
A → (P of D)	S	(P or D) → S	
A	Final model set:	S	25
	P S D A	(P or D) & S	5
_____		S	25
What follows?			

Note. ML = mental-logic theory.

that what they write down replicates the left–right order in the final model. (E is omitted because it is one of the premises.[17]) If we do not assume that participants conserve the left–right order of the final model, then the order in which B and $\sim N$ are written down should be random. In either case the two theories make different predictions. The other problems of Set 2 address the order-of-inference issue in a parallel way.

EXPERIMENT 3

Method

Participants. Forty native English speakers enrolled in an introductory psychology course participated to fulfill a course requirement. The data from three additional participants were excluded because one failed to follow instructions and two made errors on most of the practice problems.

Materials and Procedure. Materials comprised 11 practice problems and 12 test problems (4 in Set 1, and 8 in Set 2). (Some additional problems, not reported here, are discussed in O'Brien et al., 1994.) Throughout the task, each problem was presented on a separate sheet of paper, and participants specified their inferences or answers in writing on lines provided beneath the problem. The 11 practice problems required participants simply to evaluate the truth of a conclusion provided. Four problems presented conclusions that follow from the premises (true), four presented conclusions that must be false given the premises, and the remaining three presented indeterminate conclusions (the appropriate response was *Nothing follows*). None of the practice problems was formally similar to any test problems. As in the prior experiments and as just illustrated, the content and wording of the problems referred to letters written on an imaginary blackboard. The problems are shown in symbolic form in Table 8.5 (Set 1) and Table 8.6 (Set 2).

The task was administered individually. Each participant received three booklets sequentially. Each booklet provided instructions, followed by a set of problems. Within each booklet, problem order was counterbalanced by using two random orders and their reverse orders, with an equal number of participants receiving each of the four orders. The experimenter read the instructions out loud while the participant followed them in the booklet. Once the instructions appeared to be understood, the experi-

---

[17]For the second of these problems, it is not clear whether E should be the second or the third item in the final model. Order of mention in the premises could justify either position depending on how it is interpreted. However, that is immaterial to our argument, which only concerns the order of $\sim N$ and B.

menter sat off to the side reading a book while the participant worked on the problems.

The first booklet presented the practice problems. The second presented problems with conclusions to be judged and included Set 1. Participants were asked to write down everything that they worked out from the premises on the way to evaluating the conclusion, to write their inferences down one below the other in the order the inferences occurred to them, and to evaluate the conclusion. As in Experiments 1 and 2, they were instructed about the kinds of statement forms to use in stating inferences (see Procedure section of Experiment 1). The third booklet presented problems without conclusions to be judged and included Set 2: Participants were asked to write down, one below the other, everything that they thought followed from the premises, or to write *Nothing follows*. For Set 2, half the participants received the "a" problems (i.e., 1a, 2a, 3a, and 4a), and the other half the "b" problems (1b, 2b, 3b, and 4b).

Results

The guidelines used in coding the data were as for Experiments 1 and 2. We discuss the problems of Set 1 first (see Table 8.5). In each case the mental-logic theory predicted that the participants' first step in solving the problem would be to infer the presence or absence of a certain letter (K, E, ~F, and P, in the four problems, respectively); they would then conjoin this with the minor premise and compare the result with the conclusion. The participants' protocols should therefore contain the inferred letter, which should precede the final conclusion of *True* or *False* (with the conjunction possibly written down in between). The models theory predicts that participants should compare the conclusion with the final model and directly respond *True* or *False* depending on whether there is match or contradiction; participants might perhaps also write down the conjunction corresponding to the final model, but there is no reason why they should write down the first inference predicted by the mental-logic theory. In the third and fourth columns of Table 8.5, we show for each problem the percentage of participants who included the first inference predicted by mental-logic theory and the percentage who omitted it, as predicted by the models theory. (The few other kinds of responses are omitted from the table as irrelevant.) The table shows that 75% to 85% of the 40 participants satisfied the predictions of mental-logic theory; only 7.5% to 15% satisfied the predictions of the models theory. Note, incidentally, that a hasty participant, or one who wrongly assumed that we were primarily interested in the final evaluation as true or false, could easily fulfill the prediction of the models theory, even though they had not used mental models but made the inference predicted by mental logic theory.

On the problems of Set 2 (see Table 8.6), for each of the first three pairs (Problems 1a and b, 2a and b, 3a and b), the mental-logic theory predicted that participants would make inferences in a particular order, the same in the a and b versions of each pair: B followed by ~N for 1a and b, ~M followed by J for 2a and b, ~B followed by Z for 3a and b. A clear majority of the participants wrote these inferences down in the predicted order on every one of these problems, and hardly any used the opposite order. For the first pair of problems, 1a and b, the most obvious expectation from the 1992 models theory would be that participants would construct a conjunction, B & ~N, from the final model of Problem 1a (omitting the letter E because it is one of the premises) and ~N & B from the final model of Problem 1b. The data show that only one participant wrote down a conjunction for either problem. Similar expectations would hold for Problems 2a and 2b, and 3a and 3b, but none of the participants wrote any conjunctive form down for any of these problems. However, participants might read out the components of the final model separately. In that case, the two possibilities—readout in a random order and readout in a left-to-right order—are both disproved by the fact that participants consistently order their inferences, the order being the opposite of that predicted by left-to-right readout in Problems 1b, 2b, and 3b.

For the last pair (Problems 4a and b), the mental-logic theory again predicts that participants would make the same inferences in the a and b versions: D or P (or P or D) followed by S. However, on both these problems the final mental model constructed by the psychological algorithm corresponds to a conjunction that is fallacious, thus addressing our earlier objection that this algorithm predicts fallacies that participants do not make. On Problem 4a, the order of elements in the final model is A D P S; because A is a premise, it is protected from readout so participants should choose what to read out from D P S. On Problem 4b, the final model has the order P S D A, and participants should choose what to read out from P S D. In both cases, the obvious choice would be a conjunction—D & P & S for 4a, and P & S & D for 4b—or separate readout of the components of the conjunction. There is absolutely no suggestion of the fallacy in the participants' responses: No participant responded with a conjunction of the three elements on either problem, and every participant who mentioned P and D joined them with *or*, rather than with *and* or asserting them independently. More generally, Table 8.6 provides a complete listing of all the responses on these problems, and there does not appear to be a single response that could be argued to be predictable from the final models. The data fit the mental logic prediction much better, although not perfectly: The most common response across the two problems is exactly the mental logic prediction, and most of the other responses can be understood in its terms. Thus, the second most common response, *S*, reflects, we believe, a preference on the part of participants for writing down simple affirmative propositions as inferences (i.e., they neglect to write down *P or D* because it is a disjunction and therefore does not say anything certain about particular items that are on the blackboard). (This tendency would represent an instance the specific-conclusion bias suggested in Footnote 8 of this chapter. The bias may be manifest on other problems, too; across the first six problems listed in Table 8.6, an average of three participants on each problem wrote down just the simple affirmative proposition but neglected to write down the negation. Perhaps because they think that a negation is not an inference that says anything about what is actually on the blackboard.) The neglecting to write down the disjunction also throws light, we think, on the response made by five participants on Problem 4b. They wrote down *If P or D then S*, followed by *S*. Note that the conclusion *S* follows only if the participants had, in fact, inferred *P or D*; we suggest that their statement *If P or D then S* had, for them, the force *S because P or D* and that these participants have made exactly the mental-logic–predicted inferences but failed to write them down straightforwardly. (We noted earlier, in Experiments 1 and 2, other occasions on which participants used *if* when they seemed to mean *because*; Lea et al. [1990] also reported the same phenomenon.)

Discussion

The results of Experiment 3 confirm the difficulties in the present models theory that were indicated by the protocols from Experiments 1 and 2. In the problems of Set 1, in which the final model can be directly compared with a conclusion given, the models theory provides no basis for anything other than a direct comparison issuing in a response of *True* or *False*. However, most participants do not write down only *True* or *False*; they first write down an intermediate inference that is without motivation in the models theory but predicted by the mental-logic theory. On the problems of Set 2, in which participants are asked to say what follows from a set of premises (with no conclusion to be evaluated), the series of inferences that participants make is shown to be insensitive to the order in which the premises are stated and also insensitive to the order of the elements of a disjunction or conjunction in the premises. This result conflicts with the 1992 models theory, in which changing the order of premises and the order of elements within premise conjunctions and disjunctions changes the order of elements in the final model, which is the device available in the 1992 theory for predicting response order. On all the problems, the order in which inferences are stated is predicted by the order of application of the inference schemas of the mental-logic theory and not by the final model of the models theory.

The last two problems of Set 2 confirm the seriousness of the additional issues raised in the discussion of the protocols of Experiments 1 and 2: that the psychological algorithm can generate fallacious final models that predict logical errors that participants do not make, and that the only principles provided to select a response from a final model set (not to repeat premises and not to discard information) are insufficient to predict participants' actual inferences. On both these problems, participants' responses accorded much better with the mental-logic theory. O'Brien et al. (1994) provide further evidence that the psychological algorithm predicts fallacies that participants do not make.

Can the deficiencies of the 1992 theory readily be removed? Consider first the generation of the fallacious final models. The culprit here is the way model sets for different premises are combined in the psychological algorithm. Within the problems of our experiments, the simplest case of a fallacious final model is to be found in Problem 4 of Table 8.2. (The other cases in our problems embed this fallacy in more complicated problem environments.) The succession of model sets is as follows:

$$F \quad ; \quad [F] \quad W; \quad F \quad W; \quad [V] \quad W; \quad F \quad V \quad W$$
$$V \quad \ldots \quad F \quad V \quad W \quad \ldots$$

The third set is the result of using the algorithm to combine the first two; it fallaciously puts W into both models, thus claiming that W follows from the first two premises alone. Intuitively, the third model set should be:

$$F \quad W$$
$$V$$

This corresponds to the proposition F & W, or V. The fallacy has disappeared. When this model set is combined with the third premise, the fifth model set should be:

$$F \quad W$$
$$V \quad W$$

This set corresponds to F & W, or V & W, with W common to both models and thus a possible (and valid) response; F & V & W would no longer be predicted. Johnson-Laird (personal communication, April 19, 1994) suggests that the intermediate level of expertise of Johnson-Laird et al. (1994) combines model sets (without fleshing out) to yield essentially the just-described Model Sets 5 and 6. Although no set of principles yet described would yield this final model set for these premises, such a level would greatly improve the models theory. One may note, however, that if even the simplest problems (like Problem 4 of Table 8.4) involve a level of expertise above that of the psychological algorithm, then this algorithm (currently the well-defined part of the theory) is accounting for hardly any data at all. In particular, the claim that it explains participants' performance on the problems used by Braine et al. (1984), which are like those used here, is no longer tenable. Notice, too, that the new procedure appears to be tantamount to using a mental logic to update models: The initial disjunction sets up two possibilities (models), one with F and the other with V. Given the second premise, *If F then W*, modus ponens applies to add W to the possibility that contains F; given the second premise, *If V then W*, modus ponens again applies to add W to the possibility containing V. That is standard suppositional reasoning in logical inference. Claims by models theory to account for inference without mental logic become hard to understand.

Now consider the prediction of inference order. Predictions of the models theory would greatly improve if heuristics were found that had the effect that the premises were combined in the same order as they are taken in the logic theory and if conclusions were read out after such combination and not just from the final model set. Johnson-Laird et al. (1994) propose that the reasoner (a) starts with the most informative premise (e.g., a simple affirmative assertion) and (b) combines premises that include the same proposition. That would be very helpful on Problems 1 to 3 of Table 8.6 (e.g., it would cause the first and third premises to be combined first on Problem 2a and the second and third on Problem 2b, to yield a model from which ~M could be read out as the first inference in both problems). However, it would not affect predictions for the problems of Table 8.5. Also, the need would remain for adequate principles defining what is read out from a model set, and many details would need to be spelled out. In addition, there would be a potential new problem, illustrated in Problem 4 of Table 8.2 and Problems 4a and 4b of Table 8.6. On Problem 4 of Table 8.2, the logic model takes all three premises together to yield the conclusion that there is a W by Schema 5. If the new heuristics combine premises by pairs, then, when taken with the new intermediate level of expertise, the result of the first combination of models will be Model Set 5, described earlier, and that should lead to the intermediate inference *F & W, or V*, which never occurred. (On Problem 4a of Table 8.6, the corresponding intermediate inference would be *D & S, or P*, which no one gave.) It is not clear how a heuristic could be designed that would take premises three at a time when our Schemas 5 and 6 would apply and take them in pairs otherwise.

Changes along the lines suggested by Johnson-Laird et al. (1994) would clearly improve the models theory. But notice that they all bring it much closer to mimicking the operations of a mental logic: Processing the premises in the same order and, if the changes are successful, with the same results as the logic theory. Johnson-Laird et al.'s model sets are essentially parts of truth tables; it is possible that procedures might be developed for operating on such truth tables in a way that mimics in detail the operations of a natural deduction system. But if that is done, it is not clear that there would then be any point to denying that participants have a mental logic.

GENERAL DISCUSSION

In Experiments 1 and 2, we presented propositional logic problems under two conditions: premises alone and with a conclusion to evaluate. Participants were asked to write down, in sequence, everything they inferred, ending with an evaluation of the conclusion if one had been given. We assessed the extent to which the mental logic model of chapter 6 (including the schemas of Table 6.1 taken with the direct reasoning routine of Table 6.2) accounted for the inferences and evaluations that participants made. On most problems and in both conditions, there was a very high consensus among participants about the inferences to be drawn. Three quarters of the inferences drawn were predicted by the model, and of the inferences that could be made with the model's core schemas, seven eighths were in fact written down by participants. Of the quarter of responses that were not predicted, many were consistent with logical and pragmatic processes postulated by the theory. With one exception, the model captured all the inferences that were made regularly enough to indicate logical reasoning routines common to many participants. The exception involved a few problems in which one of the schemas (Schema 14) was apparently not accessed as predicted, whereas a strategy that we called *supposition of alternatives* was. We proposed modifying the model to drop Schema 14 from the set of routinely available schemas and to posit that most adults have access to the supposition-of-alternatives strategy under certain restrictions. With that modification, the model captured all the valid inferences (which constituted about 90% of all responses) that were made with more than marginal frequency by participants.

We compared the performance of our model with that of two others, the model PSYCOP of Rips (1994) and the mental-models theory of Johnson-Laird et al. (1992). Rips's PSYCOP is a model of the same general type as ours, a mental-logic model consisting of inference schemas embedded in a reasoning program. It is not surprising, therefore, that there should be a great deal of overlap in the processes postulated, and indeed the predictions made are essentially identical for about half of the problems used. On problems in which there are differences in prediction, the participants' responses show a better match with our model. However, the differences mostly involved easily modifiable features of PSYCOP. One salient difference is that PSYCOP lacks a mechanism that detects a contradiction between a premise set (premises plus inferences drawn) and a conclusion, and uses the contradiction to determine that the conclusion is false. In addition, PSYCOP has a schema that our model lacks that causes it to predict certain inferences that participants did not make. PSYCOP also lacks a schema that our model has, and has a second schema in a different form from our model. The differences cause PSYCOP to have difficulty with problems in which those schemas would be useful. It either fails to make the inferences at all or, in some cases, evaluates a conclusion by a circuitous and rather counterintuitive line of reasoning for which there is no evidence in participants' responses. Possibly the most far-reaching difference between the models has to do with the kinds of restrictions placed on schemas (such as AND-introduction) or strategies (such as supposing alternatives) that could lead to many useless inferences unless restricted. In PSYCOP, such schemas can operate only when there is a particular proposition as the goal, this goal being either the conclusion to be evaluated or a subgoal in a goal stack headed by the conclusion to be evaluated. This kind of restriction hamstrings PSYCOP when there is no conclusion to evaluate or when the conclusion to be evaluated is false. Our model uses a different kind of restriction: It labels certain classes of inference as significant (core) inferences and allows noncore inferences to operate (apart from optional one-time use of the schemas in reading out conclusions) only if they enable a significant inference or the evaluation of a conclusion. The evidence favors this sort of restriction.

Having made these criticisms of PSYCOP, we should note that PSYCOP has merits that are not manifest in this problem set (notably an ability to handle quantifiers, which our model does not yet have). Also, a significant outcome of the comparison of these mental-logic models is, we believe, the demonstration that it is possible to bring data to bear in a fairly fine-grained way on issues of detail between mental-logic models.

The mental-models theory of Johnson-Laird et al. (1992) claims to model how problems like the ones we used are solved without a mental logic: People construct mental models for each premise, combine them, and then read out or evaluate conclusions on the basis of the final model set reached. The 1992 theory claims to account for performance on the problems using its psychological algorithm for combining models. We assumed that single or multiple conclusions are read out from the final model set and that the sequence in the case of multiple conclusions is determined by the order of elements in the final model set (in accordance with the figural effects of

Johnson-Laird & Bara, 1984, and Johnson-Laird & Byrne, 1991). The theory gave a satisfactory prediction of participants' responses on not quite half of the problems of Experiments 1 and 2. Three defects were indicated. First, the psychological algorithm often generates final model sets that are fallacious, whereas there were no traces of the fallacies in participants' protocols. Second, the theory's principles for predicting from the final model set to the reasoner's response—not to repeat premises and not to discard information—are often insufficient to determine a prediction; in particular, they do not say when possibilities and alternatives will figure in the response and when they will not. Third, the theory sometimes failed to predict the order in which participants made responses.

The issue of predicting inference order was taken up in more detail in Experiment 3, in which two kinds of new problems were used. One kind offered a conclusion to evaluate; the final model set was always well described by a conjunction of two elements and the conclusion to be evaluated either was that conjunction or denied that conjunction. Because conclusions are evaluated on the basis of the final model set, the evaluation should be immediate—beyond the response of *True* or *False*, there is no basis for any response other than a statement of the conjunction itself. Yet participants overwhelmingly made an intermediate inference pre-dicted by the logic theory. The other kind of problem varied the order of premises and the position of propositions in the conjunctions and dis-junctions in the premises (with no conclusion to evaluate). This manipu-lation changes the order of elements in the final model set. The results demonstrated conclusively that inference order is not determined by the order of elements in the final model set. In sum, the results of Experiments 1 to 3 indicate serious deficiencies in the 1992 mental-models theory.

Responding to some of these criticisms, Johnson-Laird et al. (1994) propose that reasoners use an intermediate level of expertise at which fallacious final models are not generated. They also propose to account for inference order by positing that people combine premises according to rules that would usually cause premises to be combined in the same order as in our theory. Changes along these lines promise greatly to improve predictions from the models theory. However, the details have not yet been spelled out, and significant difficulties would remain. For instance, the new level of expertise uses an exhaustivity symbol that has serious complexities (see Footnote 14, and O'Brien et al., 1994, for discussion). Also, as discussed earlier, premises sometimes need to be combined two at a time and sometimes three at a time to predict inference order well, and it is hard to see how the procedures could achieve that. Furthermore, the need would remain for adequate principles to specify what is read out from a final model set. Finally, every proposed change would bring the models theory closer to the logic theory in the processes it posits.

The results of the present experiments extend and strengthen those of prior work. Braine et al. (1984) asked participants to evaluate conclusions on problems similar but not identical to those used in this study; they found that the difficulty of a problem for participants (as indexed by ratings of difficulty and error rates) was highly predictable from the number and type of schemas in our model used to solve the problem, thus indirectly confirming the model. Experiment 3 of Lea et al. (1990) was similar to the present study but used only a small number of problems. The model accounted for the protocol data reasonably well in both studies. Fisch (1991) tested 9 year olds and 12 year olds, as well as adults, using one-step and two-step inference problems of the same sort, and found evidence for competence in the youngest participant group both with the schemas (except for Schema 14, as noted earlier) and with the direct reasoning routine as applied to short chains of inferences. Collectively, these studies provide clear evidence that there is a substantial realm of problems, the responses to which our model predicts well. Further support comes from recent studies of propositional-logic inferences made in text comprehension. Lea et al. (1990) found that participants regularly made the basic inferences of the model that were necessary to judge the sensibleness of the final sentences of stories and also that, in a memory task, they often thought that inferences predicted by our model had actually been presented in the stories, although they rarely thought the same of other kinds of logically valid inferences. Lea (1995) reports further evidence that some logical inferences tend to be made by readers as soon as both premises are available.

We have already concluded that the mental-models theory of Johnson-Laird et al. (1992) and Johnson-Laird and Byrne (1991) accounts poorly for the protocol data reported. The suggestions for improving that theory, if successful, could yield a theory that would be hard to distinguish from a mental logic. Pragmatic schema theory (Cheng & Holyoak, 1985) also cannot account for participants' inferences because of the arbitrary nature of the problem content (as Cheng et al., 1986, wrote "arbitrary problems do not evoke any pragmatic schema"; p. 303). In the absence of other kinds of theories that can account for participants' responses, it seems to us that our work provides strong support for the existence of a mental logic. Our model is an advance over the prior mental-logic models of Braine (1978), Osherson (1975), and Rips (1983) in that it accounts better than they do for participants' performance on problems (see chap. 7 for detailed comparisons and discussion). We have shown that our model has advantages over that of Rips (1994) in accounting for the present protocol data; there is no reason to doubt that further work will bring convergence on an optimal mental-logic model.

We turn now to the various arguments against a mental logic, beginning with those of Cheng and Holyoak (1985), Cheng et al. (1986), and

Holland et al. (1986). Although they accept that some people may sometimes use context-free inference schemas like those of our logic, they repeatedly claim that people typically make inferences based on pragmatic reasoning schemas. The most they allow is that some context-free inference schemas *may* be available to some participants as default strategies in the event that pragmatic reasoning schemas are not engaged. We take issue with the claim of Cheng and her colleagues. First, to determine the kinds of reasoning that are typical, one would have to carry out an ecological study or otherwise obtain a sample of real-life inferences that are representative of everyday reasoning, which has not been done. Second, the reasoning scenarios on which they base their claim are variations on the Wason Selection task (Wason, 1966), which has little intuitive face validity as a typical everyday reasoning task. On the face of it, many kinds of strictly logical inferences seem to have at least as good a claim to typicality (e.g., the inference that when one of two alternatives turns out wrong, the other must be right; or that when both horns of a dilemma lead to the same result, one should expect that result no matter what Schemas 3 and 5 of Table 6.1). Thus, there is no reason to suppose that mental-logic–based inferences are any less typical than those that Cheng and her colleagues have studied.

Although Cheng and Holland and their associates allow for some coexistence of context-free and domain-specific schemas in populations, and even in individuals, they believe (e.g., Holland et al., 1986) that context-free schemas of a logical sort are rather rare and subject to individual differences. Thus, they posit no logic that is shared among participants. A set of schemas, some of which may be present in some participants, would account neither for the data reported here nor for those of chapters 7 and 12 and other work cited earlier. Hence, it is extremely doubtful that the pragmatic approach could be viable without being founded on a mental logic; to provide a sufficient theory by itself, pragmatic theory would need to define pragmatic schemas that cover all possible contents with which people are able to reason and their various possible forms. That is not a satisfiable goal, given the principle that arbitrary content does not invoke pragmatic schemas. Thus, we see the pragmatic approach and ours as complementary rather than competitive. There is no impediment to adding pragmatic schemas to our logic, thus providing domain-specific enrichments of its power to make inferences. Indeed, such a pragmatically extended mental logic that contained both context-free and domain-specific schemas would account for a great many reasoning phenomena, including content effects and the kind of data described here.

We have no doubt that mental models in some form also provide a tool available to the human reasoner. Constructing models seems an intuitively natural way of solving the kinds of spatial problems discussed by Johnson-Laird and Byrne (1991, chap. 5). Also, models are particularly effective ways of reaching secure judgments of "undecidable": One need only imagine two models in which the premises are satisfied (in one of which the putative conclusion is true, and in the other, false). (The natural deductive processes of our mental logic are not useful for establishing undecidability.) However, although a complete account of reasoning could well include a subtheory of mental models, the present evidence makes it doubtful that the kinds of processes proposed in the current models theory of propositional reasoning bear any close relation to the way participants actually reason on propositional reasoning problems. We worry that the effort to account for *all* reasoning with mental models has led in directions ultimately inimical to understanding how people reason with models.

These observations are relevant to an argument against a mental logic based on parsimony (e.g., Johnson-Laird, 1986b; Johnson-Laird et al., 1992): that it does not provide an economical account of reasoning because it allows for the existence of other reasoning mechanisms (mental models, pragmatic processes). How could such a combined theory be refuted (Johnson-Laird & Byrne, 1991)? Although the general claim that reasoning contains all these processes might be hard to refute, that is not the case for specific models for any of the processes. Our mental logic model is certainly quite specific enough to be refuted, and chapter 7 contains extensive discussion in which aspects of several mental-logic models are assessed against reasoning data, parts of them being accepted and parts rejected. The earlier comparison of our model with Rips's (1994) also indicates that it is perfectly possible to bring data to bear on details of a mental-logic model. The way to test the general claim that there is a mental logic is to try to construct that logic by testing specific models against data. Such work either converges on a satisfactory model (sustaining the claim), or else it reaches an impasse in which any attempt to improve the fit of the model to one data set worsens it in relation to another (tantamount in practice to refuting the claim).

It is true that our approach assumes that humans have a rich set of devices for accomplishing various kinds of reasoning, a claim that is perhaps more plausible than it is parsimonious. However, the mental-logic theory has a special interest and potential parsimony that derive from its universalistic claims that extend beyond the domain of reasoning. A mental-logic theory is a specific elaboration of the "language of thought" hypothesis (Fodor, 1975) in that its representations would be representations in the language of thought and their syntax a proposal about an aspect of the language of thought. The universality would derive from innate aspects of the language of thought. A mental-logic theory aims to define a set of resources for reasoning that are the common property of humankind (cf. Macnamara, 1986). Thus, our theory leads to the expectation of specific intercultural and interlinguistic similarities in reasoning processes and would provide a parsimonious account of them. It follows that it can be refuted not only by failures of predictions with English-speaking participants but also by a failure to find evidence for similar lines of reasoning in other languages and cultures.

In sum, we conclude that there is now much evidence for a mental logic that is very widely shared among people. The data suggest that the logic we propose is a suitable starting approximation to the required logic for propositional reasoning. It would provide a useful and probably necessary foundation for theories that propose other reasoning processes. It provides a basic repertory of inferential skills that could be enriched by domain-specific processes, and, for theories that invoke mental models, it could provide some basic rules for updating and selecting among models. A complete inventory of inferences must include those of a mental logic.

APPENDIX

All the problems used in Experiments 1 and 2 are listed in the same order as in Table 8.7. In the table, semicolons separate the premises; the conclusion given in the with-conclusions condition is enclosed in brackets with a question mark. The first column gives the final model as predicted by the models theory of Johnson-Laird, Byrne, and Schaeken (1992; and determined by the psychological algorithm). The middle column specifies what are taken as the predicted inferences in the without-conclusions condition (multiple conclusions come about by separate statements of conjoined propositions). When there is a good fit with participants' responses in this condition, the annotation [good] is appended; when the final model set is fallacious, the annotation (*) is appended. Problems involving neither of these annotations are individually discussed in the text. The final column specifies the inferences predicted for the with-conclusions condition (where they are different from those for the same problem without conclusions), together with the evaluation of the conclusion.

ACKNOWLEDGMENTS

This chapter is essentially a reprint from "Predicting intermediate and multiple conclusions in propositional logic inference problems: Further evidence for a mental logic," by Braine et al. *Journal of Experimental Psychology*, 124, 263–292. Copyright © 1995 by the American Psychological Association. Reprinted with permission.

TABLE 8.7
Mental Models for the Problems Used in Experiments 1 and 2

Final Model Set	Without Conclusions: Predictions	With Conclusions: Predictions[a]
1. *If there is a V or an A, then there is not a P; it is false that there is not a V. [There is not a P?]*		
V not-P V A not-P	V & not-P [good]	Same / True
2. *If there is an X then there is not an M and not an H; there is an X. [There is an M or an H?]*		
X not-M not-H	Not-M & not-H [good]	Same / False
3. *There is not both an L and an R; there is a T and a B. [There is not a T?]*		
L not-T B	Not-T [good]	Same / True
4. *There is an F or a V; if there is an F then there is a W; if there is a V then there is a W. [There is not a W?]*		
F V W	F & V & W (*)	Same / False
5. *There is a G or an R; there is not a G; there is a Q. [There is an R and a Q?]*		
R Q	R [good]	R & Q / True
6. *There is not both a G and an S; there is a G; there is not an M. [There is an S or an R?]*		
G not-S not-M	Not-S [good]	Not-S & not-M / False
7. *There is a D or an S; there is an I or a U; if there is an R then there is not a D; there is an R. [There is an S and an I, or there is an S and a U?]*		
S I R not-D S U R not-D	S & not-D & (I or U)	Same / True
8. *It is false that there is not a Y; there is not both an E and an H; if there is a Y or an R then there is an E. [There is an H?]*		
Y E not-H Y E not-H R	Y & E & not-H [good]	Same / False
9. *There is a D or a K; if there is a K then it is false that there is not an R. [If there is not a D then there is an R?]*		
D K R K R	K & R (*)	Same / ?
10. *There is a T and an I, or there is a T and a B; if there is a T or an F then there is not an H. [There is not an H?]*		
T I not-H T B not-H T I F not-H T B F not-H	T & not-H & ?	Same / True
11. *There is not both an N and a D; it is false that there is not an N. [There is not a D?]*		
N not-D	N & not-D [good]	Same / True
12. *If there is a P or an H then there is an E; there is a P. [There is a P and an E?]*		
P E P H E	E [good]	P & E / True
13. *There is a B or a Z; there is not a B. [There is not a Z?]*		
Not-B Z	Z [good]	Same / False
14. *There is an X or there is an M; if there is an X then there is an L; if there is an M then there is an L; if there is an L then there is not a C. [There is not a C?]*		
X M L not-C	X & M & L & not-C (*)	Same / True

(Continued)

196

TABLE 8.7
(Continued)

Final Model Set	Without Conclusions: Predictions	With Conclusions: Predictions[a]
15. *If there is a W then there is an O; if there is an H then there is an R. [If there is a W or an H then there is not an O and there is not an R?]*		
W O H R	? Nothing follows ?	? / ?
. . .		
16. *If there is an S then there is a C; there is an S and an H; there is not both a C and a Z. [There is not a Z?]*		
S C H not-Z	C & not-Z [good]	Same / True
17. *There is an X or an E; there is not an X; if there is an E then there is an L; there is not both an L and a P. [There is a P?]*		
E L not-P	E & L & not-P [good]	Same / False
18. *If there is a Y or an M then there is a J or a D; it is false that there is not a Y; if there is a J then there is not an A and not an N; if there is a D then there is not an A and not an N. [There is an A or an N?]*		
Y J D not-A not-N	Y & J & D & not-A & not-N (*)	Same / False
Y M J D not-A not-N		
19. *There is a K or a V; if there is a K then there is an F; if there is a V then there is an F; it is false that there is not a Q. [There is an F and a Q?]*		
K V F Q	K & V & F & Q (*)	Same / True
20. *There is a J, and there is a T or an F. [There is not both a J and a T and there is not both a J and an F?]*		
J T	?	? / False
J F		
21. *If there is an X then there is an N; if there is a J then there is an N. [If there is an X or a J then there is not an N?]*		
X J N	? Nothing follows ?	? / ?
. . .		
22. *There is a T or a V; if there is a V or a J then there is an E. [If there is not a T then there is an E?]*		
T V E	E & ? (*)	Same / True ?
T J E		
V E		
V J E		
23. *There is a P, and there is a C or an F; if there is a C then there is an M or a V; if there is an F then there is an M or a V; if there is an M then there is an A; if there is a V then there is an L. [There is not an A and there is not an L?]*		
P C F M V A L	P & C & F & M & V & A & L (*)	Same / False
24. *There is an S, and there is a K or an R; if there is a K then there is a V; if there is an R then there is an A. [There is a V or an A?]*		
S K R V A	S & K & R & V & A (*)	Same / True
25. *There is an E, and there is a K or an S; if there is an E and a K then there is a J; if there is an E and an S then there is an N. [There is a J or an N?]*		
E K S J N	E & K & S & J & N (*)	Same / True
26. *There is a B and an S; there is a G or a U; if there is a B and a G then there is a K; if there is a B and a V then there is a T. [There is a K or a T?]*		
B S G V K T	G & U & K & T (*)	Same / True

[a]*Same* in this column means that the predictions are the same as those in the without-conclusions condition.

9

A Theory of If: A Lexical Entry, Reasoning Program, and Pragmatic Principles

Martin D. S. Braine
New York University

David P. O'Brien
Baruch College and the Graduate School of the City University of New York

Making inferences to integrate information coming from different sources or from different events is a basic part of human cognition. A complete inventory of the sorts of inferences people make obviously would include those that involve conditionals, conjunctions, disjunctions, and negations—information often conveyed by the English words *if*, *and*, *or*, and *not*, respectively. Just as obviously, people do not make all of the inferences sanctioned in standard systems of propositional logic (nor could they, because the number is infinite). The present proposal comes from a research program that seeks to describe the logical inferences that are made regularly and routinely in a variety of tasks, including reasoning, conversational discourse, and text processing (e.g., Braine, 1978, 1990; Braine, Reiser, & Rumain, 1984; Lea, O'Brien, Fisch, Noveck, & Braine, 1990; O'Brien, 1987, 1993; O'Brien & Braine, 1990). Our approach proposes that these inferences depend on a mental logic that defines a set of highly accessible inference forms.

We present a theory of *if* from this perspective, and show how it can account for available data in children and adults on understanding and evaluating conditionals, and reasoning with them. *If* has been called "the heart of logic" (Anderson & Belnap, 1975, p. 1), and the conditional is the sole logical connective that is parallel to the metalogical concept of inference (Hunter, 1973). Universally quantified conditionals constitute the core form of scientific principles (e.g., Hempel, 1965; Popper, 1959). In artificial intelligence, both procedural knowledge and declarative knowledge are represented by *if*-statements (e.g., Cummins, 1986). In addition, *if* is psychologically richer than the other connectives, *and* and *or*, because the process of supposition is crucial to its meaning. For this reason, *if* has important relations to pretense and fantasy as well as to hypothesis-making and logical deduction. Thus, an account of how people understand *if* is central to an adequate description of human cognition.

We consider, first, what a theory of a logical particle of a natural language (like *if*, *or*, and *and*) should be and do, that is, what form the theory should take and the kinds of facts it should explain. Then we present our theory of *if*. After that, we review research findings relevant to the behavior of *if*, and show how the theory explains them. In the last part of the chapter we consider whether there are possible alternative theories in the psychological literature that could account equally well for the available data. We also discuss the relation of the theory to several philosophical issues relevant to reasoning—the paradoxes of implication, the work on conditional logic based on "possible worlds" semantics, and the problem of accounting both for sound logical intuition and reasoning error.

WHAT A PSYCHOLOGICAL THEORY
OF A LOGICAL PARTICLE SHOULD BE AND DO

Suppose we are given a problem with premises of the form *p if q* and *not p*. We are then likely to infer *not q*. Now, if the form of the first premise is changed to *p or q* while the second premise remains *not p*, we infer something different—*q*. If the form of the premises were again changed, to *p and q* and *not p*, we would find the given information contradictory—if we inferred anything it might be that whoever constructed the premises made a mistake, or was trying to catch us. These three problems differ only in whether *if*, *or*, or *and* occurs as the middle word of the first premise; otherwise, context, content, and problem form are the same across the three problems. It follows that the difference in response must be due to information about the meanings of the words *if*, *or*, and *and*, carried in semantic memory and brought to the problems. Let us call that information—whatever its form—the *lexical entry*. Note that the conclusion that there must be some knowledge of the logical particles stored in semantic memory implies that there are necessarily lexical entries for them, given our definition of *lexical entry*. Thus, one major component of a theory of a logical particle will be a theory of the lexical entry for it.

It is important to distinguish the lexical entry for a word from the construal-in-context of the same word. There is a pernicious ambiguity to the expression *the meaning of the word* x. It could refer to the meaning stored in semantic memory, that is, the lexical entry; or it could refer to the way the word is understood on some occasion of usage, that is, its construal. It is axiomatic that the way that a word is construed in context depends on many factors other than the lexical entry, for example, knowledge of the subject matter talked about, conversational comprehension processes, plausibility of particular construals, etc. It follows that a second component of a theory of a logical particle will be a theory of the pragmatic comprehension processes that, taken with the lexical entry, lead to construal in context.

However, the lexical entry, even taken with subject-matter knowledge and pragmatic comprehension processes, will rarely suffice to predict the responses of subjects in experiments. In order to get from a subject's construal of the information given in an experimental problem to the judgment or inference the subject makes, some specification of a subject's typical mode of reasoning will be needed, for example, a model reasoning program. For instance, if the lexical entry were taken to be a truth table, then the truth judgments corresponding to those specified in the table would be directly predicted, but other kinds of responses (e.g., inferences on reasoning problems) could not be predicted without a theory of the mode of reasoning that generates the inferences from the truth table. Similarly, if the lexical entry consisted of some prototypical inference forms, then the responses on simple problems involving just these inferences would be directly predicted, but to predict responses on other problems (e.g., more complex problems involving a chain of reasoning, or requests to evaluate the truth of given sentences against evidence), one would need to know how the subject orchestrates the prototypical inferences into a more or less complex line of reasoning that bears on the problem posed. Thus, the third component of a theory of a logical particle is a description of a reasoning program that specifies the subjects' typical mode of reasoning on the kinds of stimulus materials used in the literature. Note that only the first component, the lexical entry, is specific to the logical particle treated. The pragmatic comprehension processes and the reasoning program should be independently motivated components of a more general psychological theory covering discourse processes and reasoning.

Now let us consider what data a theory of a logical particle of a natural language should account for. It seems to us that it should explicate the following kinds of phenomena. First, concerning inferences, the theory should predict which inferences involving a particle will be made consistently and considered valid by subjects. Along with that it should account for any responses involving the particle that have been traditionally regarded as fallacies. In addition, where there are differences in the degree of difficulty of different inferences involving a particle, or in the consistency with which they are made, the theory should account for the differences. Second, the theory should explain how subjects judge the truth of sentences containing the particle against evidence. Third, the theory should take a stand on any wellknown logical issues involving the particle (e.g., the inclusive-exclusive issue for *or*; the so-called paradoxes of implication for *if*), and provide a sound reason for the stand. Finally, the theory should account for any other data available that bear on errors of comprehension or reasoning that can be laid to the particle.

THE PROPOSED THEORY OF *IF*

We discuss the lexical entry and reasoning program first, and then turn to pragmatic comprehension processes. There are various views about the meaning of *if* that can be regarded as hypotheses about the lexical entry. Standard logic provides two main conceptions. One is in terms of truth tables. However, there are serious difficulties with the truth table approach to the meaning of *if*—see Braine (1978) for a discussion of these—and there is general agreement that ordinary reasoning does not use truth tables (e.g., Osherson, 1975a; Wason & Johnson-Laird, 1972).

The other conception from standard logic uses inference schemas and offers a much more promising approach. Several authors have proposed to describe reasoning with propositions as using inference schemas (e.g., Braine, 1978, 1990; Braine & Rumain, 1983; Braine et al., 1984; Johnson-Laird, 1975; O'Brien, 1981, 1987; Osherson, 1975b, 1976; Rips, 1983). Each inference schema defines a particular kind of inference, by specifying the conclusion that can be inferred given information of a particular form (e.g., from premises of the form *p or q* and *not p*, one can infer the conclusion *q*). A set of such schemas defines a repertory of kinds of inferences, that is, of the types of valid deductive steps possible in propositional reasoning.

The inference schema models proposed by logicians such as Gentzen (1935/1964), Fitch (1952), and Leblanc and Wisdom (1976) generally have had two inference schemas for each logical connective: One is used to make derivations from a previously given statement containing that connective and the other to derive statements with that connective. For the conditional connective, the two schemas are known as modus ponens and the Schema for Conditional Proof. These may be stated informally as follows (taking *p* and *q* as arbitrary propositions):

1. Given *If p then q* and *p*, one can infer *q*. (modus ponens)

Thus, when both a conditional proposition and its antecedent are known to be true, one can immediately assert the truth of the consequent.

2. To derive or evaluate *If p then* ... , first suppose *p*; for any proposition, *q*, that follows from the supposition of *p* taken together with other information assumed, one may assert *If p then q*. (Schema for Conditional Proof)

This schema states that when one can derive the consequent of a conditional from a set of premises taken together with the antecedent of the conditional as a hypothetical assumption, then one can assert the conditional on the premises alone.

The theory that we propose derives from a model of propositional reasoning (chap. 6).[1] This model consists of a set of inference schemas and a reasoning program for using them. The inference schemas specify how *and, or, if*, and negation may be used in reasoning; they define a repertory of the elementary deductive steps available to subjects in going from one step to another in a chain of propositional reasoning. Although many of the schemas are similar to those of standard systems of propositional logic, there are a number of differences in detail. (Those relevant to *if* are described later.) The reasoning program models how subjects construct a chain of reasoning using the schemas. It describes how a schema to be applied at a point in a chain of reasoning is selected, and it includes some routines that are claimed to be universal among adult subjects. Note that in an inventory of all the sorts of inferences that subjects make in reasoning, propositional-logic inferences would only be a subset; it is this subset that the schemas and program of our model address. A reasoning model that accounted for all inferences would be a general theory of reasoning and is well beyond the scope of our model. The repertory of inference schemas and the reasoning program are presented in chapter 6 with supporting experiments in chapters 7 and 8; however, the application of the model to *if* is not discussed there.

It is basic to a sound inference-schema model that whenever a schema is applied to true premises it leads to true conclusions. Our model thus presupposes some general notion of truth and falsity. To assert a proposition is to assert its truth; hence, all propositional assertions are grounded in semantics. However, it does not follow that truth judgments require a semantics for connectives that is separate from the inference schemas: The model does not posit that lexical entries for connectives record truth tables or truth conditions. Nevertheless, it allows predictions about truth judgments: The inference rules provide instructions about how truth may be inherited from premises to conclusions. For instance, if one knows that

---

[1]This model is a significant revision of an earlier model based on similar principles (Braine, 1978). Similarly, the theory of *if* developed here supersedes the earlier proposal (Braine, 1978), as well as an earlier discussion of inferences where intuitive validity is at variance with standard logic (Braine, 1979b).

two propositions, p, q, are true either because one has been told or because one can see that they are true, then the inference rule—p, q ∴ p & q—tells one that the proposition p & q is true. No separate "semantics" for *and* is needed. Thus, truth judgments can be made for simple sentences when direct comparisons with reality are possible; but they can also be made in other circumstances by inference—when information about the truth of other sentences is available from which the truth of a target sentence can be inferred. How our inference schemas for *if* predict subjects' truth judgments is described in detail later.

Our proposed lexical entry for *if* comprises the schemas involving *if* in the model of Braine et al. (1984) and O'Brien (1987). This kind of lexical entry is consistent with the "procedural" approach to semantics, in which meaning is given by procedures for operating on information (Johnson-Laird, 1977; Winograd, 1972, 1975). The two most important schemas involving *if*, and the only ones that involve *if* alone, are modus ponens (i.e., Schema 1, earlier) and the Schema for Conditional Proof (i.e., Schema 2, earlier). However, there is a special constraint on the mode of operation of Conditional Proof that is not to be found in standard systems of propositional logic. The arguments allowable in the system are restricted by this constraint and by some other features of the system that are not shared with standard systems. We now survey these features, beginning with the constraint.

The Constraint on the Schema for Conditional Proof

The constraint reflects a general property of ordinary reasoning that is shared by the model of chapter 6 but not by standard logic. In standard logic anything follows from a contradiction, whereas in our model—and we believe in ordinary reasoning—nothing follows, except that some initial assumption is wrong. It follows that for a supposition to lead to a conditional conclusion via Schema 2, the supposition must be consistent with prior assumptions. It is easy to see that this must be so: Suppose a set of premise assumptions, Σ, which we may take as equivalent to the conjunction of the individual assumptions (α_1 & . . . & α_2 & . . . & α_n), and suppose that a supposition, p, is made (see Argument I of Table 9.1); by Schema 2, q follows from p conjoined with Σ; now, given the principle that nothing follows from a contradiction, q cannot be inferred if p is inconsistent with Σ; hence, for q to be validly inferred, the supposition p must be consistent with the assumptions Σ (which themselves must be consistent).

Note that this requirement, that a supposition be consistent with prior assumptions in order to lead to a conditional, does not bar counterfactual suppositions; it only requires that the premise assumptions be made consistent with the supposition. We discuss counterfactual conditionals in some detail later, and merely note for now that in the case of a deliberate counterfactual supposition the premise assumptions can never be a record of an actual state of affairs. For instance, if we wished to argue from the supposition *If Dukakis had won the 1988 election*, our premise assumptions could not be a record of the actual events of 1988, for example, they could not include the fact that Bush won.

An important corollary of our requirement that the supposition be consistent with prior assumptions is that a premise proposition introduced (reiterated) into a conditional argument cannot contradict the supposition. Consider again Argument I of Table 9.1, and let α_i be a premise proposition that is reiterated into the suppositional argument. Manifestly, if α_i contradicts p, then Σ contradicts p, that is, p is inconsistent with Σ, thus offending our requirement.

Most of the force of our requirement of consistency of the supposition with prior assumptions is contained in this corollary. Consider the following: The only prior assumptions on which a conditional argument is dependent are those that are reiterated into the suppositional argument; the others are superfluous. In almost all cases, when a supposition is inconsistent with a superfluous premise, the premise could in principle be dropped. (We say "almost all cases" because there is an interesting class of exceptions that we illustrate later.) Thus, the only consistency with which the reasoner need usually be concerned is that between the supposition and the premise assumptions that are reiterated into the suppositional argument.

A reasoner may not always know ahead of time that a supposition is consistent with the prior assumptions; nor, indeed, that the prior assumptions themselves form a consistent set. Determining consistency of sets of statements is computationally difficult (and may be formally undecidable where quantifiers are involved). However, meeting the consistency requirement is greatly facilitated in practice by several factors. First, as just noted, in most cases the only consistency that matters is that between the supposition and the individual premises introduced into the suppositional argument. Second, there is a corrective mechanism in the argument process itself that signals inconsistency: If a contradiction develops in the suppositional argument, then one knows that the supposition is inconsistent with the prior assumptions (assuming these to be consistent). (Of course, this is the logic of a reductio ad absurdum—given that the suppositional argument leads to a contradiction, and that the premises are true, then the supposition is false.) In that case, no conditional conclusion can be drawn that has the supposition as antecedent. Third, in practice, people rarely reason from large, unorganized collections of propositions; premise assumptions usually represent some state of affairs. Here we see some potential for the mental-models approach (Johnson-Laird, 1983), in that a useful encapsulation of premise assumptions could be obtained with a mental model of the state of affairs—it could be argued that the coherence of the model would provide a rough check on the consistency of the assumptions, although the approach is short on specifics on how models are constructed. Finally, human processing limitations curtail people's ability to reason from long and complex premise sets (unencapsulated in a model), so that the kind of complexity where consistency checking would be intractable probably rarely arises in practice. However, in any case, our principles are offered as norms that human beings know, not as descriptions of behavior—people often make mistakes that offend against norms that they know; no psychological theory should predict perfect accuracy under conditions of complexity.

In sum, the constraint on Conditional Proof consists of three principles:

3a. Nothing follows from a contradiction except that some assumption is wrong.

3b. A supposition can be the antecedent of a conditional conclusion reached via Schema 2 only if it is consistent with prior assumptions (i.e., premise assumptions plus any previously made suppositions).

3c. An assumption reiterated into a conditional argument cannot contradict the supposition that is to be the antecedent of the conditional.

Principle 3a entails Principle 3b, which entails Principle 3c. The domain of the first principle extends beyond conditionals, and its application to them is spelled out by the other two. Note that Principles 3b and 3c reflect the ordinary meaning of the term *suppose*—that one cannot suppose something and simultaneously hold to information incompatible with one's supposition.

To illustrate the constraint, consider Arguments II to VI in Table 9.1. All are allowed in standard systems, but some are excluded in ours. In Argument II, the contradiction between the two premises is reproduced at Lines 4 to 5 within the subordinate argument headed by the supposition *not B*, leading to the conclusion that *B* is true. Although valid in standard logic, this seems not to be a valid argument in ordinary reasoning, and it is ruled out by Principle 3a in our system. Argument III derives one of the so-called "paradoxes" of implication. It is parallel to Argument II, except that the second premise has become a supposition. In standard logic, this allows an additional reasoning step in which the Conditional Proof schema is used at Line 9 to derive the conditional *If A then B* from the premise *not A*. Our principles make this argument multiply anomalous. If Line 2 is not construed as a deliberately counterfactual supposition,

TABLE 9.1
Some Sample Arguments

I. Argument form	IV. Paradox again
1. $\Sigma(=\alpha_1, \ldots \alpha_i, \ldots \alpha_n)$	1. Not *A* (premise)
2. Suppose *p*	2. Suppose *A* and *B*
3. . . .	3. *A* (2, & elimination)
4. α_i (reiteration)	4. Not *A* (1, reiteration)
5. . . .	5. Incompatible
6. *q*	6. ∴ Not (*A* & *B*) (6, reductio)
7. ∴ If *p* then *q*	7. Suppose *A*
	8. Not (*A* & *B*) (6, reiteration)
II. Anomalous	9. Not *B* [7,8, by schema *not*(*p* & *q*) ∴ vot θ]
1. Not *A* (premise)	10. ∴ If *A* then not *B* (Conditional Proof)
2. *A* (premise)	
3. Suppose not *B*	V. Contraposition
4. *A* (2, reiteration)	1. If *A* then *B* (premise)
5. Not *A* (2, reiteration)	2. Suppose not *B*
6. Incompatible	3. Suppose *A*
7. ∴ Not not *B* (reductio)	4. If *A* then *B* (1, reiteration)
8. ∴ *B* (double-negation elimination)	5. *B* (3, 4, modus ponens)
	6. Not *B* (2, reiteration)
III. Paradox	7. Incompatible
1. Not *A* (premise)	8. ∴Not *A* (reductio)
2. Suppose *A*	9. ∴ If not *B* then not *A* (Conditional Proof)
3. Suppose not *B*	
4. *A* (2, reiteration)	VI. Anomalous contraposition
5. Not *A* (2, reiteration)	1. If you want some water, there is a fountain in
6. Incompatible	the hall (premise)
7. ∴ Not not *B* (reductio)	2. Suppose there is no fountain in the hall
8. ∴ *B* (double-negative cancellation)	3. Suppose you want some water
9. ∴ If *A*, then *B* (Conditional Proof)	4. If you want some water, there is a
	fountain in the hall (1, reiteration)
	5. There is a fountain in the hall (3, 4,
	modus ponens)
	6. There is no fountain in the hall (2,
	reiteration)
	7. Incompatible
	8. ∴ You do not want any water (reductio)
	9. ∴ If there is no fountain in the hall then you
	do not want any water (Conditional Proof)

then the contradiction between Lines 1 and 2 renders further reasoning
pointless; in addition, Principle 3b blocks the transition from Line 8 to
Line 9, and Principle 3c bans the reiteration of *Not A* at Line 5. If the
supposition at Line 2 is deliberately counterfactual, then the argument
becomes anomalous at Line 5.

Argument IV is another anomalous argument that a conditional is true
when its antecedent is false. It illustrates another facet of our system that
is shared (we believe) with ordinary reasoning but not with standard

logic. At first sight the argument is seductive: Lines 1 to 6 show that *Not A* entails *Not (A & B)*, Lines 6 to 10 seem to show that *Not (A & B)* entails *If A then not B*. In anyone's system, entailment is transitive, hence *Not A* appears to entail *If A then not B*. Yet to ordinary intuition the argument is clearly absurd: If *Not A* is the only reason for believing *Not (A & B)*, then we know nothing specific about *B*—certainly not that it would be false if *A* were true, as Line 10 asserts. Where lies the fallacy? Formally, from the standpoint of our system, although the supposition of the second part (Line 7) does not contradict Line 6 (which is the only proposition reiterated into the second suppositional argument [Lines 7 to 10]), it does contradict the initial premise on Line 1 (which is the only reason for believing Line 6). Thus, by our Principle 3b, either the supposition on Line 7 cannot be made, or, if it is to be made, the premise on Line 1 must be dropped. But if Line 1 is dropped, then Line 6 cannot be asserted; the premise for the second half is lost and the second argument collapses.

In general, a derivation of a conditional *if p then q* must begin by supposing *p*. Principle 3b bans this supposition from issuing in a conditional whenever the premise assumptions contain or entail *not p* (and this premise is not set aside, as in a counterfactual). Thus, in our model a conditional cannot be true merely because its antecedent is false.

As Stalnaker (1968) and Lewis (1973) have pointed out, there are a number of inferences involving conditionals that are valid in standard logic but that fail in particular circumstances. Most of their examples involve counterfactuals, which we consider in detail later. However, examples involving ordinary conditionals are not hard to find. Consider first contraposition. The form of the argument from a conditional to its contrapositive is shown in Argument V of Table 9.1, and is valid in standard logic as it normally is in our model. Unlike Argument III, Lines 1 and 2 are not contradictory; they are allowed into the subordinate argument beginning at Line 3 to feed the reductio, and the Conditional Proof schema can then be used to derive the conditional (Line 9) with the first supposition (Line 2) as antecedent. However, contraposition arguments are not valid in our system under certain circumstances; one circumstance, illustrated in Argument VI ("anomalous contraposition"), is that the consequent of the conditional is true regardless of the antecedent (in the example, the fountain in the hall exists whether or not the interlocutor wants some water). Note that in this case the supposition (*There is no fountain in the hall,*) falsifies the original conditional (Line 1), which can be true only if there is a fountain in the hall. As in Argument III, Principle 3b renders further reasoning pointless unless the supposition on Line 2 is deliberately counterfactual, but even then Principle 3c would ban the original premise from the subordinate argument at Line 4—which is to say that the argument could not proceed beyond Line 3. In the usual contraposition argument (V), the supposition is compatible with the conditional premise and Lines 4 to 5 go through without barrier; then the argument is valid given our constraint.

Another inference that is valid in standard logic and to unguarded intuition is that *If q then r* follows from *If p or q then r*. Yet there are counterexamples. Consider the following maxim that a former boss once gave one of us for the situation when one's car breaks down and one is debating whether the problem lies in the fuel delivery or in the electrical system (it is assumed that both will not be at fault): *If the trouble is in either the electrical system or the carburetor, then it's in the electrical system*. The maxim has proved valuable on several occasions. But, obviously, one cannot infer from it that *If the trouble is in the carburetor then it's in the electrical system*. Our constraint explains why not: The supposition (*the trouble is in the carburetor*) is a counterexample to the maxim itself—hence, the maxim cannot be appealed to in considering what follows from the supposition.

A final example concerns the transitivity of *if*. For instance, consider the following conditional propositions:

4. If Kennedy is alive then Oswald did not kill him.
5. If Oswald did not kill Kennedy, then someone other than Oswald killed him.

From these it might appear to follow, by the transitivity of *if*, that:

6. If Kennedy is alive, then someone other than Oswald killed him.[2]

In the model proposed, an attempt to derive Proposition 6 would start by supposing that Kennedy is alive. On this supposition, Proposition 5 is inadmissible: On the assumption that Kennedy is alive, Proposition 5 cannot be true, and conversely. Because Proposition 5 cannot be taken as a premise if the supposition is to be made, the consequent clause of 6 is not derivable from the supposition that Kennedy is alive, and thus 6 itself does not follow. Arguments like 4, 5, therefore 6, tend to prove *if* intransitive by reducing the idea that it is transitive to an absurdity. In our system, *if* is transitive in the particular sense that, given *If p then q* and *If q then r*, the line of reasoning—suppose *p*, whence it follows first that *q* and then that *r*, therefore *If p then r*—is a valid line of reasoning, except where it is blocked by our constraint. Similarly, Argument V of Table 9.1 is a valid argument form in our system—cases of failure are blocked by our constraint. Thus, our proposal accounts both for the unguarded intuitions of validity as well as for the specific failures in exceptional cases.

---

[2]This example is due to Jack Barense of Sakonnet, R.I., to whom we are indebted.

Our constraint allows for deliberately counterfactual suppositions. However, counterfactual suppositions are not always deliberate; they can be made inadvertently, and then a reasoner could find himself or herself inferring two opposite conditionals (*if p then q, if p then not q*). We comment briefly on this case now. Inadvertently counterfactual suppositions could well arise when a supposition is incompatible with the totality of a reasoner's beliefs without directly contradicting any single component belief.[3] Consider the following possible scenario: You have been trying to get in touch early one morning with an acquaintance named Joseph. You've just telephoned him and there was no answer. You conclude:

7. Either Joseph is asleep or Joseph is not home.

You then wander off to the fountain down the hall to get some water and on your return a colleague tells you that Joseph just called. You conclude:

8. Joseph is not asleep.

Under normal circumstances you would put these two propositions together and directly conclude *Joseph is not home*, and leave it at that. However, on this occasion, instead of reasoning straightforwardly, you contemplate Proposition 7 and the lack of answer to your call and infer *If Joseph is home he is asleep*; then you contemplate your colleague's information and Proposition 8 and infer *If Joseph is home he is not asleep*. That is, the supposition *Joseph is home*, taken with your unintegrated beliefs (Propositions 7 and 8), has led to a contradiction (*Joseph is asleep* and *he is not asleep*). The reductio exposes the supposition as counterfactual and leads you to the same conclusion, that Joseph is not home, that you could have reached directly. As noted earlier, a reductio is a means for uncovering the fact that a supposition is inconsistent with a total set of premises, even though consistent with each individually.

People often may be unaware of relevant logical consequences of their beliefs pertinent to a given topic. They may sometimes make suppositions inadvertently that are not compatible with those beliefs. They may never discover the reductio that would expose a supposition as incompatible with the full set of relevant beliefs. They may even accept a conditional based only on a subset of the beliefs relevant for reasoning from the supposition. The conditional will be validly asserted with respect to the beliefs used in deriving it but not with respect to the full relevant set,

---

[3]We are indebted to an anonymous reviewer both for drawing our attention to this situation, and for the example that follows.

and they will not know that. Such frailties reflect limitations of human information processing but do not impugn our proposed logic for *if*.

If viewed as a logical calculus (instead of as a theory of norms and processes governing everyday reasoning), our theory would have the defect that only to a limited extent is it possible to establish derived inference schemas as theorems. Thus, although in familiar cases like Contraposition and Transitivity, the argument forms are valid lines of reasoning (except for the contrary cases filtered out by our constraint), they cannot be formulated as derived schemas. For example, contraposition as a schema (*If p then q* ∴ *If not q then not p*) is not valid for all *p, q*—Argument VI provides a counterexample. Similarly, transitivity (*If p then q, If q then r* ∴ *If p then r*) is not valid as a general schema for all *p, q, r* whatever—Propositions 4 to 6 are a counterexample. (On this point, our conclusion is the same as that of Stalnaker, 1968, and Lewis, 1973.) Thus, in our model, the convenient shortcuts provided by derived schemas in long chains of reasoning are available to only a limited extent. This consequence may explain in part why previous work (Braine et al., 1984) found little evidence for the use of derived schemas by adult subjects.

How *If*-Statements Are Refuted

Another important difference of our model from standard logic accounts for how conditionals are refuted. The Conditional Proof schema (Schema 2, described earlier) only tells how to establish an *if*-statement, not how to refute one, and thus fails to account for one aspect of subjects' responses. Consider the following two problems used by Braine et al. (1984), in which subjects reason about letters on an imaginary blackboard:

9. There is an F or a C. (premise)
   If there is not an F then there is a C? (conclusion to be evaluated)
10. There is an N or a P. (premise)
   If there is not an N then there is not a P? (conclusion to be evaluated)

Adult subjects unanimously say that the conclusion has to be true for Problem 9 and has to be false for Problem 10. Schema 2 accounts well for the response of *True* to Problem 9. However, on Problem 10, although the schema permits deducing *If there is not an N then there is a P*, in standard logic that is not equivalent to proving that the conclusion given on Problem 10 is false, because there might be an N. (According to standard logic, $p \supset q$ is not decidable when *not-q* is derivable from the problem premises taken with the supposition *p*, because the supposition itself might be false; on such a problem one can conclude only $\sim[p \supset q] \ v \sim p$.) The model of Braine et al. (1984) accounts for judgments on both problems by means of the reasoning program that governs the usage of the schemas in reasoning. One of the ways in which Schema 2 is realized in the program is through a procedure that reads:

> 11. If the conclusion given is an *if-then* statement, add the antecedent to the premise set and treat the consequent as the conclusion to be tested (from Table 6.2).

The program triggers the response of *False* when the premise set together with any inferred propositions is found to be incompatible with a given conclusion (see Table 9.2, Problem 2, for an illustration).

This way of refuting a conditional follows from our constraint on the schema for Conditional Proof. Because of the constraint, no evaluation of *If p then q* is possible when *p* is false (and its falsity is not set aside, as with a deliberately counterfactual supposition). With the case of *p* being false excluded, a finding of *If p then not q* must mean that *If p then q* is false. Note that this means only that *If p then q* and *If p then not q* cannot both be true together; it does not formally exclude the possibility of them both being false.[4]

How Subjects Access Their Inference Schemas

A general property of the system that is not specific to *if* has to do with subjects' access to their inference schemas. People do not have direct introspective access to their schemas as such. They cannot therefore array them neatly into a list and contemplate what might be provable from them. That is, they are not in a position to play meta-logician to their own logic, and it cannot be assumed that they know things that a logician would be able to prove in or about their system. What subjects know is determined by how they reason. In the model of Braine et al. (1984), subjects' use of their schemas is controlled by a reasoning program, whose routines and strategies are very considerably less rich than those available to a professional logician. The program in Table 6.2 is based on data from the propositional reasoning of adult subjects. It models how subjects draw inferences from given information in this kind of reasoning. The program has two parts, a routine part and a strategic part.

---

[4]The question of whether the possibility should be formally excluded is a difficult one on which intuition provides no clear message. Consider the case where *q* is provably undecidable on the basis of *p*. That eliminates any reason for believing either *If p then q* or *If p then not q*, but does not clearly dictate whether they should both be considered false, or merely undecidable. This is the substantive point on which the theories of Stalnaker (1968) and Lewis (1973) disagree. (For Stalnaker, one or the other of *If p then q* and *If p then not q* must be true; for Lewis, they can both be false.)

The routine part is a direct reasoning routine that is claimed to be common to essentially all adult subjects. Its operation is illustrated in Table 9.2. The routine proceeds by matching schemas against the form of propositions in the premise set, applying any that can be applied (excluding schemas that introduce suppositions and with restrictions to prevent infinite loops); each inference drawn is added back into the premise set. For example, in Problem 1 in the table, the schema, p or q; *not* p, $\therefore$ q, is the only schema that applies to the premise propositions; it is applied on the first cycle of the routine and adds the proposition E to the premise set, as shown in the second column; the schema modus ponens then

TABLE 9.2
Illustrations of How the Direct Reasoning Routine Solves Problems

Problem[a]	Solution Steps[b]	Relevant Schemas
1. X or E Not X If E then L Not both L and P		
? Not P?		
	E L Not P	p or q; $F(p)/q$ If p then q; p/q $F(p$ & $q)$; $p/F(q)$
2. If N & I then not B False that not N		
? If I then B?		
	$\{I\}$	
	$\overline{}$	
	?B?	
	N	$F[F(p)]/p$ p; q/p&q If p then q; p/q p; $F(p)$/incompatible

Note. Subjects reason about letters on an imaginary blackboard. Propositions are represented in schematic form: *If E,* then *not H* reads "If there is an *E* (on the blackboard), then there is an *H*," *T* reads "There is a *T*," and so on.

[a]The premises are given above the line, and below it, between quotation marks, is the conclusion to be evaluated.

[b]Entries indicate the sequence of inference drawn, in order, culminating in the response to the problem. In Problem 2, the first solution step is to reformulate the problem—add *I* to the premises as a supposition and treat *B* as the conclusion to be evaluated (see Procedure 11 in the text).

[c]Indicates the inference schema that determined the form of the inference made at each solution step. $F(p)$ means p is false. To increase readability, the schema treat & and *or* as binary connectives (i.e., as joining just two propositions), whereas they are treated as *n*-ary in chapter 6.

applies to E taken with the third premise to yield L; another schema now applies to L and *Not both L & P* to yield *not P*. When the problem provides a conclusion to be evaluated, as do both the problems in Table 9.2, then as each inference is drawn, the conclusion is tested for identity or contradiction with propositions in the premise set. For example, on Problem 1 a match is found when the proposition *Not P* is inferred on the third cycle of the routine. On Problem 2, the response of *False* is triggered by the incompatibility between the last inferred proposition *not-B* and the conclusion B that is being evaluated.

It has been found (chaps. 7 and 8) that adult subjects make very few errors on problems like those of Table 9.2, which can be solved by the direct reasoning routine. However, this routine fails to solve many problems. The strategic part of the program consists of reasoning strategies and comes into operation when the direct reasoning routine fails to solve a problem. However, the strategies are by no means universal, and there are large individual differences among adult subjects. The variability among subjects in the strategies they have available contributes to individual variation in reasoning skill.

Pragmatic Principles

We have now discussed the lexical entry and the relevant aspects of the reasoning program. We now turn to the third component of the theory—pragmatic influences on comprehension. The inference schemas act on the semantic representations that are the output of comprehension processes. Thus, the information from which inferences are made is affected by all the pragmatic factors that influence comprehension. These can be formulated in terms of three general principles.

1. The first principle concerns how the content of propositions affects the way they are construed: An interpretation that is plausible given a subject's specific knowledge of the situation and general knowledge of the world is more likely to be assigned than one that is implausible. This principle is manifest in the "plausibility strategy" of sentence interpretation (Bever, 1970), and is a well-known source of errors of comprehension, particularly prevalent in children and known to affect sentences containing logical particles (e.g., Bucci, 1978; Braine & Rumain, 1983). The principle explains cases where subjects apparently reject modus ponens. Thus, Byrne (1989) reports that when a conditional premise such as *If she meets her friend then she will go to a play* is accompanied by a second conditional like *If she has enough money then she will go to a play*, subjects often fail to make the modus ponens inference from *She meets her friend* to the conclusion *She will go to a play*. Presumably, the second conditional leads subjects to infer that they are not to take for granted that she has

enough money to go to a play; based on this inference they construct a representation like that for *If she meets her friend and she has enough money then she will go to a play,* and they use that as their premise (Politzer & Braine, 1991; see chap. 15). Such results indicate that modus ponens is applied to the conditional understood by the subject.

This first principle would include as important special cases the "pragmatic reasoning schemas" proposed by Cheng and Holyoak (1985). A pragmatic schema defines a class of plausible interpretations into which appropriate content can be assimilated. For example, the "permission" schema defines rules of the form "If Action *x* is to be done, then Condition *y* must be satisfied": The condition gives permission for the action. An example would be *If printed matter is to go first class, it must carry a 32 cent stamp.* Modus ponens is valid for anything assimilated into the permission schema, but the schema also dictates other relationships not directly specified in our lexical entry; for instance, if the particular content of an *if*-statement elicits the permission schema then the contrapositive ("If the condition is not satisfied then the action cannot be done") becomes more accessible to the subject than if the permission schema is not elicited. Using Wason's selection task with adult subjects, Cheng and Holyoak show that if a particular rule (e.g., *If an envelope is sealed, then it has a threepenny stamp*) can be made to elicit the permission schema, then there is a significant increase in the number of subjects responding correctly.

In general, a sentence with content that falls in the domain of the schema will be construed with a semantic representation that includes, but is richer than, the representation that could be gotten from the lexical entry alone. Subjects reason with information as they construe it, and if the permission schema is elicited, the information used is very likely to include the contrapositive. As we discuss later, the existence of pragmatic schemas could pose a challenge to our theory only if it were shown that subjects cannot understand an *if*-sentence without having a content-bound pragmatic schema to cover it.

2. The second principle is the *cooperative principle* (Grice, 1975, 1978): Speakers try to be as informative, truthful, relevant, and clear as they can, and listeners interpret what speakers say under the assumption that they are trying to be informative, truthful, etc. The cooperative principle allows many non-necessary inferences (*conversational implicatures*) to be made, for example, (in most contexts) that the speaker of an *if*- or an *or*-statement does not know the truth value of the component propositions. The cooperative principle is a potent source of error on logical tasks because these may be presented to subjects in ways that flout the principle (Braine & Rumain, 1983; Politzer, 1986).

3. The third principle is that logical particles often carry *invited inferences* (Geis & Zwicky, 1971). For instance, a conditional *If p then q*

invites the inference *if not p then not q,* an *or*-statement invites the inference "not both," and a statement of the form *Some F are G* invites *Some F are not G.* According to Geis and Zwicky (1971), and Fillenbaum (1977), people make such pragmatically invited inferences unless they have reason to believe them inappropriate, that is, unless they are countermanded. The countermanding may be explicit, or it may be implicit in some property of the discourse content or context.

These principles are not necessarily independent of each other. In particular, it may well be possible to regard invited inferences as special cases of conversational implicature.[5] The principles are all consistent with Sperber and Wilson's (1986) concept of *relevance,* which lays out a useful framework for analyzing inferential processes—logical as well as pragmatic—involved in everyday comprehension.

Applying the Theory to Social Discourse

Although we propose to examine the theory primarily against data obtained from experiments, we intend it to apply to conditionals in ordinary social discourse also. In this application it is relevant to note that there is nothing in the Schema for Conditional Proof that requires that the train of thought that leads from the antecedent to the consequent must consist of a propositional-logic argument; the schema allows any kind of argument—causal, psychological, based on a scenario or model, and so on. Moreover, although the schema prescribes that the argument (of whatever sort it is) be valid, this requirement places little constraint on speakers, because the schema does not require that the argument be explicit, and because the speaker is the judge of validity. Thus, the theory in no wise predicts that everybody's ordinary *if*-statements will be defensible. The requirement of validity only becomes socially relevant when a speaker is challenged to defend an *if*-statement. Then speaker and challenger negotiate standards of validity.

Counterfactuals. Negotiation among participants is a prominent aspect of arguments from counterfactual suppositions. The prime issues are the conditions under which a reasoner is entitled to introduce a factual propo-

---

[5]Consider *If you mow the lawn I'll give you five dollars.* Uttered in an appropriate context, the statement would be offered as an inducement to mow the lawn. However, it could be honestly offered as an inducement only if the invited inference (*If you don't mow the lawn I won't give you five dollars*) is true. If the speaker expects to give the five dollars anyway, regardless of whether or not the lawn is mowed, then he or she is not being straight with the listener. Thus, the cooperative principle here clearly mandates the invited inference. However, further detailed discussion of the relation of Geis–Zwicky invited inference to Gricean conversational implicature is beyond our topic.

sition into an argument based on a counterfactual supposition, and the grounds that an opponent might have for rejecting that introduction. Consider, for example, the following argument, in which the speaker is trying to establish *If Napoleon had attacked earlier at Waterloo, he would have won.*

> Well, suppose Napoleon had attacked earlier. As it was, Blucher only arrived in the nick of time. If Napoleon had attacked earlier, Blucher would still have arrived when he did; that would have been too late to affect the outcome of the battle, and Napoleon would have had only the English to deal with. Besides, only a few days before Waterloo, Wellington was miles away from his troops, and they were unprepared for a fight. The French would have demoralized them completely with an unexpected attack and achieved an easy victory.

The argument is from Thomason (1970, p. 405), with some modifications in wording added by us. The first factual proposition introduced into the argument is Blucher's time of arrival. Note that to introduce this is equivalent to asserting the conditional *If Napoleon had attacked earlier Blucher would still have arrived when he did.* In general, according to our Schema for Conditional Proof, if *p* is a counterfactual supposition and *k* is a true proposition that the reasoner wishes to introduce into the suppositional argument, then to introduce *k* is equivalent to asserting *If p then k would (still) be true.*

Now let us consider what an opponent has to do to oppose the introduction of a proposition into an argument based on a counterfactual supposition. In real-life arguments it will rarely happen that an introduced proposition directly contradicts the supposition (presumably because reasoners do not make such obvious violations of our constraint). The most direct way of opposing the introduction of a proposition *k* is to derive something that directly contradicts *k would be true.* But now note that there are two ways in which *k would be true* can be contradicted. One is by deriving *k would be false.* However, that is not the only way: to deny *k would be true* it suffices to show *k might not be true.*

Let us consider why *k would be true* and *k might not be true* are incompatible. Karttunen (1972) notes that English words like *may, might, perhaps, possibly, must, necessarily,* etc. are used overwhelmingly in an epistemic sense. For instance, *John must have left* means, approximately, "From what I know it follows that John has left"; it is thus a weaker statement than the simple *John has left* because the force of the *must* is to indicate knowledge based on inference, not certainty. By the same token, one cannot simultaneously assert *It isn't raining* and *It may be raining*: The former assertion claims knowledge that the latter denies. Similarly, if one of two arguers claims *k would be true* and the other *k might not be true,* they have made incompatible claims (*that k would be true* is decidable on the supposition *p*, and that it is not decidable), and the argument cannot progress until the incompatibility has been resolved. Thus, to counter a proposition *k* that someone wishes to introduce, one can argue either that it would be false or that its truth is undecidable on the supposition. In real-life arguments people negotiate differences of opinion on such matters. If they cannot agree then a common move is to absorb the doubtful premise into the supposition. Thus, if the opponent of the speaker in the Waterloo argument were able to generate an acceptable reason for believing that if Napoleon had attacked earlier Blucher might have arrived earlier, then a likely move on the speaker's part would be to reformulate his or her claim to *If Napoleon had attacked earlier and Blucher had arrived when he did, then Napoleon would have won.*

Stalnaker (1968) and Lewis (1973) present many examples of inferences involving counterfactual suppositions that are apparently invalid, though valid in standard logic. We consider a representative case from the standpoint of our theory. In standard logic (and to unguarded logical intuition), given *If q then r* it follows that *If p and q then r.* Stalnaker's counterexample is: Given *If this match were struck it would light*, it may not follow that *If this match were soaked overnight and were struck, it would light.* On our theory, the validity of the inference depends on whether the conditional premise remains true on the supposition that the match is soaked overnight before striking. If the premise is still true (the match is of a special kind that lights despite soaking), then it can be reiterated into the suppositional argument and the inference is valid. If the premise may not be true on the supposition (the match is an ordinary one), then it cannot be appealed to, and the inference is not valid. It seems to us that this analysis accords perfectly with intuition.

Our theory does not provide a method that would decide for any particular *k* whether it would be true or might not be true. This lack is shared with other theories (e.g., Stalnaker's [1968], as we note later). It is currently inevitable inasmuch as a suppositional argument can be of a variety of kinds, as noted earlier—causal, based on a scenario, etc. To provide a theory of how such decisions are made would require theories of all these different kinds of reasoning, that is, a complete theory of reasoning. However, the failure to define such a method means that our theory does not solve a regress problem that Goodman (1947, 1983) pointed out with respect to his own theory of counterfactual conditionals: To apply the Schema for Conditional Proof to evaluate *If p then q would be true* assumes an ability to decide for a premise *k* whether, *if p, k would (still) be true or k might not be true* ("to establish any counterfactual, it seems that we first have to determine the truth of another"; Goodman, 1983, p. 16); indeed, in its application to counterfactuals our theory comes out quite similar to Goodman's. (As far as we know, Goodman has not discussed ordinary conditionals.) The problem will gradually shrink as theories are developed for the various kinds of reasoning that can appear in suppositional arguments.

The Waterloo example illustrates an argument that supports a counterfactual conditional: To accept the argument is to accept the conditional as true. However, we have yet to discuss the basis for rejecting a counterfactual. It follows from what we have said that there are two ways: One is by failing to find a satisfying argument from the antecedent to the consequent (or by finding a proffered argument unsatisfactory). That leaves the consequent—and therefore the conditional—in doubt. (A plausible example might be *If Napoleon had acquired a larger army he would have won at Waterloo*.) A stronger rejection can be obtained along the lines described in an earlier section (How *if*-Statements Are Refuted). Consider the following:

12. If Napoleon had had one more button on his greatcoat he would have won at Waterloo.

Unless the reasoner produces a cogent argument that an extra button could have made a difference, the still true fact that Napoleon lost can be introduced into the suppositional argument. Then the antecedent of Proposition 12 leads to the conclusion *he would not have won at Waterloo*, giving rise to a judgment of *False* for the reasons discussed in our earlier section.

Questions and Commands. Of course, not all *if*-sentences are statements; some are questions and some are conditional commands. *If*-questions (i.e., of the form *If p then what?* or *If p, is it the case that q?*) pose no problems. In an *if*-question, the speaker provides the listener with the supposition and requests the listener to provide the conclusion of the suppositional argument, or to evaluate the conclusion that was given as the consequent of the *if*-question. The steps prescribed in the Conditional Proof schema are shared between speaker and listener, instead of all being performed by the speaker, as in a statement.

The theory is easily extended to conditional commands too. We posit that in modus ponens the conclusion has the same illocutionary force as the consequent clause of the conditional. Thus, given *If p then do q*, and the state of affairs indicated by *p* transpires, then the injunction *Do q!* follows. It is also possible to derive conditional commands with the Schema for Conditional Proof. For example, suppose your spouse tells you *When you're at the supermarket, please buy red leaf lettuce or endive*. From this, the conditional request *If the supermarket is out of red leaf lettuce, buy endive* follows transparently. Let us spell out how the Schema for Conditional Proof yields this inference: On the supposition that the supermarket is out of red leaf lettuce, the request *buy red leaf lettuce* cannot be obeyed. Hence (by the schema: *p* OR *q*, NOT-*p*, ∴ *q*, interpreted for imperatives) the injunction *buy endive* follows. That is, *If the supermarket is out of red leaf lettuce* you should *buy endive*. Thus, the Schema for Conditional Proof shows how the original command to buy the lettuce or the endive implies the conditional injunction to buy the endive if the market is out of the lettuce. The example illustrates that the schema specifies an intuitively natural format for reasoning from a command to a derived conditional injunction.

ACCOUNTING FOR RESPONSES TO CONDITIONALS

We consider inferences, then judgments of the truth of conditionals against evidence, and finally responses on comprehension tasks.

Inferences

The theoretically simplest inference problems are those whose solutions follow directly from the lexical entry. A problem that involves just a modus ponens inference is of this type, and, in conformity with prediction, children and adults almost never make errors on problems that require just an inference of this form (Braine & Rumain, 1983; O'Brien, 1987), although they often make errors on other types of problems that involve reasoning from *if*-statements.

A problem that requires use of the Schema for Conditional Proof combined with a minimum of other inferences would also be theoretically simple. (Application of this schema necessarily involves other inferences.) Unfortunately, there are almost no studies of how subjects reason to a conditional conclusion (although there is a large literature on reasoning from conditional premises). However, the inference problems used by Braine et al. (1984) included several that had conditional conclusions, and which, like Problems 9 and 10 described earlier, involved the Schema for Conditional Proof along with a minimum of other inferences. The adult subjects made few errors on such problems, confirming the prediction that they should be simple.

The same study also provided more specific evidence for the mental reality of the Conditional Proof schema. Pairs of problems were compared that were formally equivalent, except that one problem of the pair involved this schema and the other did not. For example, Problem 13, which follows, is formally equivalent to Problem 9, except that Problem 9 involves the Conditional Proof schema whereas 13 does not.

13. There is a D or a T. (premise)
     There's not a D. (premise)
     There is a T? (Conclusion to be evaluated)

Problems 14 and 15 are related in the same way:

14. It is not true that there is both an L and an S. (premise)
     If there is an L then there's not an S? (conclusion to be evaluated)
15. It is not true that there is both a G and an I. (premise)
     There is a G. (premise)
     There's not an I? (conclusion to be evaluated)

For a set of such problem pairs, subjects rated the conditional member of the pair as slightly but significantly more difficult than the other in two studies; and, although errors were few, there was a significant difference in errors also. The difference in difficulty, although quite small, is apparently real, and argues that mentally adding the antecedent of a conditional conclusion to a set of premises is a real cognitive operation.

Because of a lack of studies in which children have been given problems that require them to make inferences to a conditional conclusion, we recently gave a set of such problems to 7 and 10 year olds (see chap. 10). The problems were similar to Problems 9, 10, and 14 in this chapter, except that they were about toy animals in a closed box rather than letters on a hidden blackboard. In both age groups the great majority of both *True* and *False* responses were consistent with our model (although only the *True* responses were correct by standard logic). Note that other psychological models would also have to account for *False* responses to problems like Problem 10. In general, these results indicate that young school-age children have some knowledge of how to reason towards an *if*-statement.

There are additional reasons for thinking that the Schema for Conditional Proof should, like modus ponens, be present early in children. The reasons come from children's spontaneous usage of *if*. *If*-statements are present in the speech of many children by 3 years of age (Bloom, Lahey, Hood, Lifter, & Feiss, 1980; Bowerman, 1986; Reilly, 1986). Here are some examples, taken from Bowerman (1986):

16. C (2 years 4 months) (C is getting up on a rainy Sunday): "If we go out there we haf' wear hats."
17. C (same age) (C is wearing a bead crown, which her mother has knocked off once by kissing her): "Don't kiss me 'cause it will fall off if you do that."

18. D (exact age not given) (D is sitting in his bath): "If I get my graham cracker in the water, it'll get all soapy."

Not only is *if* present early, but children's use of it in their spontaneous speech is without apparent anomaly at this age or subsequently (Bloom et al., 1980; Bowerman, 1986). Young children therefore must have a lexical entry for *if* that is capable of supporting non-anomalous production.

Of our proposed lexical entry, modus ponens alone could scarcely explain usage such as in Examples 16 to 18: Intuitively, modus ponens seems most appropriate for understanding *if*-sentences made by others because it would define what follows from an *if*-sentence for a listener. The Conditional Proof schema, on the other hand, could readily explain examples of spontaneous speech such as 16 to 18, because it says that an *if*-sentence is true when the antecedent, taken with other things the speaker knows, leads to the consequent. That seems to capture what the children are asserting in the examples (i.e., that with what the child knows, the antecedent leads to the consequent). Thus, if our theory of the lexical entry for *if* is correct, one should expect the Schema for Conditional Proof to be developmentally fairly primitive.

While supposition in the service of logical argument is not often reported in very young children, supposition in the service of play and fantasy certainly is in pretense and pretend play, which are commonly observed by the third year (e.g., Fein, 1981). Thus, there is no reason to doubt the early availability of an essential intellectual component of the schema—the supposition step. In addition, Leslie (1987) has pointed out that simple inferences can be involved in the elaboration of pretense. For instance, pretending that an empty cup on the table contains water and that it is pushed over leads naturally to imagining the table as wet. It is only a small further step from here to a conditional like *If this cup had water in it and we pushed it over then the table would get wet.* Bowerman (1986) reported just such conditionals by around 3 years of age; she also reported that the children distinguish *if* from *when*, reserving the use of *if* for referring to events whose occurrence is possible but uncertain (i.e., hypothetical), as in all of the above examples. Thus, there is evidence for the availability of the full schema in very young children.

Now let us consider the classical fallacies, which are the best-known and most studied inferential "errors." The *denying-the-antecedent* fallacy consists in reasoning from two premises of the form *If p then q* and *not-p* to the conclusion *not-q*, and the *asserting-the-consequent* fallacy in reasoning from premise forms *If p then q* and *q* to the conclusion *p*. These fallacies are common in adults and are almost always made by children. (See Braine & Rumain, 1983, and O'Brien, 1987, for reviews.) The fallacies would be expected if subjects construed *if* as equivalent to the biconditional *if and only if* (e.g., Matalon, 1962; Peel, 1967; Taplin, Staudenmayer, & Taddonio, 1974). The fallacies and the biconditional construal come from the fact that subjects, especially young subjects, given a conditional *If p then q*, make the pragmatically invited inference *If not p then not q* (Geis & Zwicky, 1971). As noted earlier, Geis and Zwicky argue that people make this pragmatically invited inference unless they have reason to believe it inappropriate. Rumain, Connell, and Braine (1983) showed that the invited inference can readily be countermanded, at least from around age 7 onwards, by changes in the wording or form of the problems, with the result that the fallacies either disappear or change form. Thus, the invited inference and the biconditional construal have to be regarded as due to pragmatic interpretation processes. Performance on these problems can readily be explained on the hypothesis that modus ponens is in the lexical entry, together with the assumptions that interpretation of conditionals is affected by pragmatic comprehension processes and that adults are somewhat better able than children to set aside invited inferences when doing reasoning tasks.

Another much-studied inference problem is modus tollens (i.e., given premises of the form *If p then q* and *not-q*, to evaluate whether *p* must be true or false). On this inference, the theory predicts that the most and the least sophisticated subjects should correctly respond *False* and those of intermediate sophistication respond *Can't tell*. This is exactly what the data indicate, with children making more correct responses than adults (O'Brien & Overton, 1982; O'Brien & Shapiro, 1968; Rumain et al., 1983; Shapiro & O'Brien, 1970; Wildman & Fletcher, 1977). The basis for the prediction is that unsophisticated reasoners (children and many adults) will accept the invited inference and construe *if* as biconditional (as they do on the fallacies), a construal that happens to lead to the correct response for modus tollens. For more sophisticated subjects, usually adults, who do not accept the invited inference, the problem is relatively difficult because the subjects' direct reasoning routine (modeled in the program) does not yield a determinate response; to solve the problem the subject must have sufficient reasoning skill to execute a reductio-ad-absurdum argument ("if p were true then q would have to be true, but it isn't, so p must be false"). Thus, the response of intermediate sophistication is *Can't tell*, given by subjects who resist the biconditional construal but fail to find the reductio argument. The theory also predicts that giving the problem in a form that prevents the subject from making the invited inference should increase the number of *Can't tell* responses, a result that has been found (Rumain et al., 1983).

Chapters 7 and 8 investigated a broad collection of other propositional reasoning problems, many involving reasoning from conditional premises or to a conditional conclusion, and many of other kinds. They found that the overall propositional reasoning model assumed here (i.e., schemas plus reasoning program) allowed excellent predictions of ratings of the subjective difficulties of problems, as well as of error probabilities. The data provide evidence that the model describes reasoning processes over a broad range of propositional reasoning problems in adults. Lea et al. (1990) found that the model can provide an account of propositional inferences routinely made in text comprehension. In general, the work reviewed indicates that both the specific theory of *if* and the more general theory of propositional reasoning of which it is part account well for subjects' responses on the propositional inference tasks sampled in the literature.

Truth Judgments

Let us consider how our theory accounts for judgments of truth for conditionals. According to our schema for Conditional Proof, to evaluate whether a conditional is true in a given state of affairs, one supposes that the antecedent is true in that state of affairs and one tries to derive the consequent given the information known about the state of affairs (i.e., the information known about the state of affairs plays the role of the premises, Σ, in Argument I of Table 9.1). If one succeeds in deriving the consequent, then one judges the conditional as true. If one derives the negation of the consequent, then one judges the conditional as false.

Now consider the situation where the truth values of the antecedent and consequent are known for the state of affairs, as in the work to be reviewed. Consider first the case in which the antecedent is true. The preceding procedure requires one to evaluate the conditional as true if the consequent is true in the state of affairs (because the consequent can be reiterated into the suppositional argument), and as false if the consequent is false (because the negation of the consequent can be reiterated into the suppositional argument). Suppose, however, that the antecedent is false in the state of affairs. Then the schema cannot be applied without changing the state of affairs. If the experimental conditions preclude changing the state of affairs, then the schema cannot be applied and there is no way of evaluating the conditional. Subjects should then resist making a truth judgment.

The literature that addresses evaluations of *if*-statements suggests that children often construe *if* as something other than a conditional. Paris (1973) gave children conditional sentences, each accompanied by a pair of slides. Either both clauses of the sentence were true of the slides, one was true and the other false, or both were false. Subjects judged the sentences as true or false of the slides.

Many young subjects responded as if *If p then q* meant "p & q," a conjunction: The sentence was considered to be true only when both clauses were true of the slides. Note that this response pattern cannot be taken as directly reflecting the young child's lexical entry: On a conjunction interpretation of *if*, in two of the classic inference problems, the premises (*If p then q* and *not p*; *If p then q* and *not q*) would be contradictory, yet no age group responds as though they are.

Many older subjects seemed to take the *if*-sentences as biconditionals; that is, they said that a presented sentence was true when both clauses were true of the slides, and also when both were false, and they judged it false whenever one clause was true and the other false. However, this biconditional response pattern appears only when subjects are limited to the response options of *True* and *False*. Johnson-Laird and Taggart (1969) found that it disappeared in adults when *Irrelevant* was allowed as a response option in addition to *True* and *False*. Under those circumstances, subjects judged a conditional to be true when both clauses were true, false when the antecedent was true and the consequent false, and irrelevant whenever the antecedent was false. Johnson-Laird and Taggart proposed that subjects were judging according to a "defective truth table"— one that assigns no evaluation to *If p then q* when *p* is false.

These judgments are easily explained by our theory, which makes the same predictions as the defective truth table. In the trials in which the slides made the antecedent clause true, a subject who attempted to apply the Schema for Conditional Proof would be led to respond *True* when the consequent clause was also true, and *False* when the consequent was false—and that is how Paris's and Johnson-Laird and Taggart's subjects responded, regardless of age. In the trials where the slides made the antecedent clause false, the schema could not be applied for the reasons noted earlier. Subjects should then prefer not to make a truth judgment, and, indeed, the subjects of Johnson-Laird and Taggart (1969) categorized such sentences as *Irrelevant* in this situation. However, Paris's subjects did not have this response option. Expectably, there was a good deal of noise in the data. The dominant response patterns were to respond *False* (yielding the *conjunction* pattern), or to respond *True* when neither clause was true of the slides and *False* when the antecedent was false and the consequent true (yielding the *biconditional* response pattern). Both of these response patterns represent understandable attempts to cope in a situation where the experimenter is experienced as making an inappropriate demand. The conjunction pattern would come from a pragmatic judgment that when a sentence is irrelevant to a picture, it is more appropriate to consider it false than true if one has to make a choice. The biconditional pattern would come from seeking an interpretation of the test sentence that would make it relevant to the scenes depicted, that is, from assuming that the tester is obeying the Gricean cooperative principle "be relevant," and then seeking a plausible meaning that would be relevant: Any conditional, *If p then q*, has a conversationally invited inference *if not p then not q*, as noted earlier; for the scenes in which the antecedent clause is false, the invited inference is relevant; taking that as the conditional to be tested and applying the schema would lead to the biconditional response pattern.

Evaluating Quantified Conditionals.   In a study involving universally quantified conditionals, Kuhn (1977) found what appears at first sight to be yet another interpretation of *if* in young children. Her scenario presented three kinds of bugs in a garden: big striped, small striped, and small black. Subjects were shown a picture of each kind of bug. All eight possible conditionals of the form *If a bug is ___ then it is . . .* (*If a bug is big then it is striped, If a bug is striped then it is big, If a bug is small then it is striped*, etc.) were presented. Subjects had to judge each conditional as true or false of the bugs in the garden. Eighth graders gave the correct responses, but second and fourth graders responded as though the sentence form meant "There is a bug that is both ___ and . . .".

We have explored an analogous error elsewhere (O'Brien, Braine, Connell, Noveck, Fisch, & Fun, 1989). It appears that the error primarily has to do, not with the conditional form, but with the use of the indefinite article as a reflex of the universal quantifier ("If *a* bug . . ."). Young children's preferred interpretation of *a* is existential: *A bug* is taken as referring to some particular bug—note that, for instance, *There is a bug such that if it is small it is striped* is equivalent (in Kuhn's task, where there are some small bugs) to *There is a bug that is small and striped*. In a task similar to Kuhn's, O'Brien et al. found that using *all* rather than *if a* to express the quantifier greatly reduced the error in young children.

The literature contains many studies with adults and older children in which the truth of universal statements (using *all, if a, if any*, etc.) is assessed against data, using more complicated tasks than those reviewed so far (e.g., Moshman, 1979; O'Brien & Overton, 1980, 1982; Overton, Byrnes, & O'Brien, 1985; Overton, Ward, Noveck, Black, & O'Brien, 1987; and much work using Wason's selection task [Wason, 1968]). Of all problems involving conditionals, it is this type of problem that gives subjects the most trouble. However, the difficulty of the selection task stems not from its conditionality but from its quantification (O'Brien, 1987). The logic and reasoning program of our theory have so far been worked out only for propositional reasoning, and thus do not make precise predictions for tasks where the quantified form critically affects the nature of the problem posed to the subject. Nevertheless, the difficulty of these problems is quite understandable from the standpoint of our theory.

Let us consider the similarities and differences between simple (i.e., unquantified) and quantified conditionals. A similarity is that modus ponens has much the same form for both, that is, *If p then q, p, ∴ q* is similar to *All F are G* (or *If a thing is an F then it is a G*), *x is an F, ∴ x is a G*. This kind of inference appears to be about as easy and as developmentally early for quantified as for simple conditionals (see Braine and Rumain, 1983, for a review). However, the way that a conditional may be derived or evaluated differs considerably for simple and quantified conditionals. In particular, unlike a simple conditional, it is only in one special case that the Conditional Proof schema can be used to derive a quantified conditional. Thus, to derive *All F are G* using the Conditional Proof schema, one must imagine an arbitrarily chosen instance of F (a process that corresponds to the logical schema known as *universal instantiation*), and prove by logical argument that it would be G, whence *All F are G* (by the schema *universal generalization*). Because universal instantiation is not an empirically executable process (i.e., there is no way of selecting an actual instance of F that would be so representative of all Fs that one could conclude *All F are G* if that F was found to be G), there is no way of empirically demonstrating the truth of a quantified conditional.[6] This difference between simple and quantified conditionals obviously derives from the fact of quantification, not from the conditional form, and would be expected to make quantified conditionals more difficult for subjects to evaluate than simple conditionals.

A quantified conditional can be evaluated without using the Conditional Proof schema if it can be falsified. Here we have to distinguish two kinds of competence on the part of subjects. One is knowledge that a case of an F that is not G demonstrates that *All F are G* is false. The other is the use of a search for a falsifying instance as a systematic evaluation strategy. Our theory predicts that the first knowledge should be available to subjects, and in fact the ability to recognize a falsifying instance as falsifying is general among subjects (O'Brien, 1987). However, our theory provides no reason to expect that searching for falsifying instances should be subjects' primary evaluation strategy. There is no point in searching for counterexamples unless there is some prior reason for thinking that a generalization might be true: A generalization must have some empirical support to be worth refuting. Also, refutation of a tentative generalization may be part of a search for a better generalization, a search that involves noting patterns of support for previous generalizations at least as much as counterexamples. (Support for a generalization is often obtained by a procedure analogous to the logical argument using the Conditional Proof schema described earlier: Instead of a logically arbitrary instance of F, one picks random or representative instances, and if they all turn out to

---

[6]We are excepting cases where the class F is so small that all its members can be examined individually.

be G, the generalization *All F are G* achieves some support.) Given the usual purposes of an evaluation, it is not surprising that subjects often show evaluation strategies that give weight to supporting instances and fail to try to falsify (e.g., Moshman, 1979; Wason, 1983). For more detailed consideration of the literature on evaluation of quantified conditionals, see O'Brien (1987).

Comprehension Tasks

An interesting comprehension error occurs in young children and consists in failing to distinguish the form *If p then q* from *p if q*, for example, in confusing *I put up my umbrella if it starts to rain* with *If I put up my umbrella it starts to rain*. The error occurs with decreasing frequency between 5 and 10 years of age in a variety of tasks that involve comprehension or judgments of acceptability (e.g., Emerson, 1980; Emerson & Gekoski, 1980). It has not been found in children's spontaneously produced *if*-sentences at any age (e.g., Bloom et al., 1980; Bowerman, 1986). The source of the error is not established, but we propose that it is due to a widespread tendency in children's language comprehension, namely, that surface-structure neighborhood relations are not preferred cues to semantic subordination. That is, in decoding sentences, hierarchy in the semantic representation is assigned on the basis of semantic plausibility (i.e., in accordance with our first pragmatic comprehension principle), in preference to surface-structure adjacency. Note that if this strategy is applied to *I put up my umbrella if it starts to rain* and *If I put up my umbrella it starts to rain*, both sentences end up with the same interpretation, and so the subject has no basis for finding one more sensible than the other. Thus, in young children's comprehension, the presence of *if* would mark a sentence as a conditional more reliably than the locus of *if* would mark which clause is antecedent. Essentially the same comprehension process was proposed by Bucci (1978) to explain children's errors in interpreting universal affirmatives (i.e., the form *All A are B*), and a similar process has been invoked to explain young children's characteristically wrong interpretations of the questions in Piaget's inclusion problem, e.g., *Are there more flowers or more buttercups?*, given a picture of 15 buttercups and 2 bluebells (e.g., Donaldson, 1976; Hayes, 1972; Kalil, Youssef, & Lerner, 1974). See Braine and Rumain (1983) for a detailed review.

Conclusion

It appears that interpretations and evaluations of conditionals at various ages, early uses of *if*, and both correct responses and errors on reasoning problems involving conditionals, can readily be explained in terms of our hypothesis about the lexical entry for *if*, combined with independently motivated assumptions about subjects' habitual comprehension processes and reasoning strategies.

ALTERNATIVE PSYCHOLOGICAL THEORIES OF *IF*?

Now we consider whether there are other possible psychological theories that could account equally well for responses to conditionals. Until recently the main other kind of theory has been some variant of the truth-table approach: The lexical entry would be taken as the standard truth table, the biconditional truth table, the defective truth table of Wason and Johnson-Laird (1972), or *if* would be ambiguous among these three possibilities. However, this approach has well-known difficulties (e.g., Braine, 1978; Braine & Rumain, 1983; Osherson, 1975a), and no one has seriously advocated it for several years. Because it seems no longer to be an active theory, we shall not discuss it further. More active current theoretical approaches stem from the *pragmatic reasoning schemas* of Cheng and Holyoak (1985) and the *mental models* of Johnson-Laird (1983).

Pragmatic Reasoning Schemas

Although Cheng and Holyoak (1985), Cheng, Holyoak, Nisbett, and Oliver (1986), and Holland, Holyoak, Nisbett, and Thagard (1986) allow for the possibility that some people may sometimes use general inference schemas such as modus ponens and Conditional Proof, they express much skepticism about such schemas, particularly about their universal availability. Thus, they speak of "our negative conclusion about the prevalence of a natural logic based on syntactic rules" (Cheng et al., 1986, p. 318), and they believe "that this level of abstraction in conditional reasoning is seldom attained" (Holland et al., 1986, p. 282). It is pertinent, therefore, to see whether their view can provide a satisfactory theory of *if*.

They propose that reasoning typically uses rules defined in terms of classes of goals and contents. Unlike our inference schemas, these pragmatic schemas are context sensitive in that they apply only when the goals and contents are present. A type case of a pragmatic schema is the permission schema mentioned earlier, in which a condition gives permission for an action as in the example *If printed matter is to go first class it must carry a 32-cent stamp.* The permission schema specifies a pattern of relationships between antecedent and consequent that holds for permissions. The evidence for the permission schema consists in showing that if the schema is elicited, then Wason's selection task becomes relatively easy for adult subjects, thus explaining content effects on this task that had previously resisted explanation. They also propose that there are other pragmatic schemas, for example, for social obligations and cause–effect relations.

We have no quarrel with the concept of a pragmatic reasoning schema, and indeed think that such schemas could nicely explain some effects of content on reasoning. However, there are several reasons why they could not provide a competitive theory of *if*. First, to provide a competitive theory, the lexical entry for *if* would have to consist exclusively of pointers to pragmatic schemas. Thus, subjects should be unable to understand an *if*-sentence if it did not engage such a schema. For these schemas to exhaust the meaning of *if*, there would have to be very many of them. Given that only two such schemas (permission and obligation) appear to have been described in detail so far, a claim that such schemas can provide a competitive theory of *if* would involve a promissory note of rather extraordinary size.

Second, inference difficulty is a function of problem form, not just of problem content. Inferences of certain forms are very easy for adults and are made at a young age by children; they are made even with arbitrary materials, as in deductive puzzles about the content of a closed box (e.g., Braine & Rumain, 1981; O'Brien & Braine, 1990; Rumain et al., 1983) or letters on an imaginary blackboard (chaps. 7 and 8). Other kinds of inferences with arbitrary materials are quite difficult, even for adults (e.g., Wason's, 1968, selection task). These facts raise two kinds of difficulty for any thought that the pragmatic schema approach is sufficient: (a) Letters on an imaginary blackboard and similarly arbitrary content would not elicit a schema for permission, nor for social obligation, nor for cause–effect: Kinds of inferences that are very easy, even with this arbitrary kind of material, are clearly very context broad and have a good prima facie claim to be context free, thus arguing for the existence of context-free schemas. (b) Differences in difficulty that are a function of problem form (with kind of content held constant) themselves require systematic explanation in a theory of reasoning. These are the kinds of facts that the mental-logic approach was designed to explicate. To claim sufficiency, the pragmatic approach would have to show that it can handle them equally well.

Further, according to a thoroughgoing pragmatic approach, the lexical entry for *if* would be highly polysemous—consisting of pointers to a long list of schemas and subschemas, with no claim that these have something in common to tie them together. Thus, the approach can offer no reason why languages typically collect this union of schemas under one word. That fact argues for some unexplained fundamental commonality among the pragmatic schemas. That commonality could well be explained by the modus ponens and Conditional Proof schemas of our theory, and these in turn would permit a default interpretation for *if*-sentences whose content fell outside the domain of any pragmatic schema. Thus, even if the pragmatic approach is fairly successful in fulfilling its program, it will still need something like our theory to complement it.

Probably the most crucial and interesting differences between the expectations associated with the two approaches are developmental, as illustrated in the two following scenarios. On a pragmatic approach, one would expect development to proceed by accretion of pragmatic schemas: The child's first *if*-sentences would have one kind of pragmatic content, then another kind would be added, then a third, and so on, as additional pragmatic schemas were mastered. Abstraction of commonalities among the pragmatic schemas, such as our modus ponens and Conditional Proof schemas, would be a relatively late emergent.

On our approach, the modus ponens and Conditional Proof schemas would be expected to be the core initial entry for *if*. Then, with increasing experience with particular kinds of ideas and relationships, some context-sensitive schemas would be learned; these would retain modus ponens and Conditional Proof, but would specify additional relationships between antecedent and consequent (as the permission schema does).

Our theory has greater interest in the second scenario than the first. Although current evidence is not decisive between these scenarios, it favors the second. Children are able to use modus ponens and several schemas involving *or* with arbitrary content at least by around school-entering age (Braine & Rumain, 1983); we reviewed evidence for the early availability of the Conditional Proof schema. Thus, there is evidence for some major schemas that appear to be essentially context free quite early in development. It also appears to be the case that children's early conditional sentences include a variety of types (Bowerman, 1986), suggesting that they may not emerge by one-by-one accretion of pragmatic types. However, more investigation of the preschool period would be needed to settle the issue.

Mental Models

Johnson-Laird (1983) proposes that people reason by manipulating mental models in working memory. That people often use mental models in reasoning is entirely compatible with our proposal and we believe that a complete account of inference will need a subtheory of mental models. However, Johnson-Laird and his colleagues (e.g., Johnson-Laird, 1986b; Johnson-Laird, Byrne, & Tabossi, 1990) claim that all reasoning is based on mental models, and they specifically exclude any role for inference schemas of the sort we propose.

A mental-model theory has been worked out for several realms (Byrne & Johnson-Laird, 1989; Johnson-Laird & Bara, 1984; Johnson-Laird et al., 1990), but no theory of propositional reasoning has yet been published.

A theory that covers propositional reasoning and conditionals and that would supersede earlier ideas about conditionals (Johnson-Laird, 1986a) has been announced (Johnson-Laird & Byrne, in press); however, the theory was still under revision at the time of writing. The versions we have seen make predictions that differ from those of our theory. However, it would be inappropriate and possibly unfair for us to discuss prefinal drafts. We therefore confine ourselves to two fairly general points that argue against the claim that reasoning is always based on mental models.

First, while it is plausible that a model should be involved in understanding some conditionals, others are more problematic. Nevertheless, it is hard to show that mental models are not crucial because the mental models theory does not define *mental model*. The term includes images but extends beyond them, and mental models may be unconscious. We are told only that mental models are always specific, in the sense that, unlike propositions, they cannot contain variables (Johnson-Laird et al., 1990). Now imagine that a number has been written down and concealed, and consider the conditional *If the number ends in zero then it is divisible by five.* We do not see that a model need be involved in reasoning that this statement must be true, or indeed that a model would be useful even if one were to spring to mind—note that an image/model of some specific (but unknown) number ending in zero could not be the basis for knowing that the conditional cited is true. Surely, there are many conditionals that would be equally hard to capture in a mental model.

Second, the notion of an *unconscious* mental model *in working memory* impresses us as paradoxical. It is precisely the content of working memory that information-processing theories take as accessible to consciousness (Ericsson & Simon, 1984). The unconsciousness postulate appears to be needed only in order to shield the claim of interindividual uniformity in mental models from introspective evidence—some old evidence indicates variability both in the occurrence of mental models and in their nature, even within the same deductive task (Storring, cited in Woodworth, 1938). In any case, the mental-model theory needs to explain the variability in what people are able to report. For other reactions to the general claims for mental models, see Ford (1985), Macnamara (1986), Rips (1986), and chapters 15 and 16.

PHILOSOPHICAL ISSUES AND THEORIES

We discuss the so-called paradoxes of material implication and then we turn to the theories of *if* that are based on "possible worlds" semantics, especially the influential theory of Stalnaker (1968, 1984). Finally, we discuss how we account both for sound logical intuition and reasoning error.

The Paradoxes of Implication

The two most commonly cited paradoxes are the following. For any propositions p and q

19. Given q, one can infer *If p then q*.
20. Given *not-p*, one can infer *If p then q*.

These are sometimes expressed as: A true proposition is implied by anything; a false proposition implies anything. These are both metalogical generalizations, and, as discussed earlier, people do not have the kind of access to their schemas that would enable them to derive metalogical theorems about their own system. It is reasonable to ask, however, how the theory predicts that subjects should react to specific cases of 19 and 20, that is, where p and q are specific concrete propositions. The theory makes different predictions for the two cases. We discuss each in turn.

Instances of 19 are pragmatically strange, because if one already knows that q, what is the point of wondering whether if p then q? However, if one sets aside the strangeness and considers the issue on its merits for some specific p and q (i.e., whether *If p then q* is true, false, or undecidable, given that q is true), the model predicts that the answer has to be "true." Philosophers have differed on the validity of this answer. Stalnaker (1968) and Lewis (1973) agree with it on the ground that if q is true anyway, it must still be true on the supposition that p. In contrast, Anderson and Belnap (1975) argue that it is not sufficient that q should be true on the supposition that p; p should also be *used* in the derivation of q. They modify the Schema for Conditional Proof by adding indices to keep track of the use of suppositions and they require that all suppositions be used. It would be possible to incorporate Anderson and Belnap's modifications into our schema for Conditional Proof; not much of the paper would change significantly. We do not do so for two reasons. First, the change would complicate the theory. The second reason comes from the existence of conditionals in which the consequent is true regardless of the antecedent, for example, *If you're looking for George he's in the mailroom, If you want some water there's a fountain down the hall.* In these the only relevance of the supposition is pragmatic; it does not provide a reason why the consequent is true. Another type is illustrated by *If it rains the rally will still be held.* Such conditionals arise easily on our theory as it stands: For example, given that George is indeed in the mailroom, that fact can be reiterated into an argument headed by the supposition that the addressee is looking for him, justifying *If you're looking for George he's in the mailroom.* The cost of adopting Anderson and Belnap's schema would be to render these common kinds of conditional anomalous.

In such conditionals the truth of q is the justification for asserting *If p then q*. Such conditionals therefore are evidence that 19 is valid for *if*. When instances of 19 are anomalous, it is plausible that the anomaly has a pragmatic basis: Because there is normally no point to a supposition unless it is relevant to drawing consequences, people's default expectation is that the antecedent of a conditional will be logically relevant to the consequent. Evidence that this expectation is pragmatic appears in the fact that English provides a number of ways of warning the listener not to expect logical relevance, without abandoning the conditional form, for example, *even if p ... , if p then still q*. Some experimental evidence that logical relevance is not essential to *if* appears in a reasoning problem presented in chapter 7: The problem presented two premises of the form *If p then q* and *If not p then q*. Here the antecedents could not be logically relevant to the consequent, yet the subjects were not inhibited from concluding *q*.

Now consider instances of 20. We showed earlier (see the discussion of Arguments III and IV in Table 9.1) how the constraint on the Conditional Proof schema blocks the derivation. According to our theory, if subjects are asked to evaluate an instance of *If p then q* given *not-p* as premise, they should either respond "undecidable" or have recourse to nonlogical reasoning strategies or response biases. Hence the theory does not predict that people should think that an *if*-statement is true when its antecedent is false.

Stalnaker's Theory and "Possible Worlds"

Semantic theories that use the notion of possible world are prominent in philosophy and linguistics. Beginning with Stalnaker (1968), several philosophers have proposed to extend the Kripke (1963) possible-worlds semantics for modal logic so as to include conditionals (e.g., Kutschera, 1974; Lewis, 1973; Pollock, 1976; Stalnaker, 1968, 1984). The semantics of *if* is given by defining truth conditions expressed in terms of possible worlds. The work raises both a specific and a more general question. The specific question is whether the philosophical work can be translated into a psychological theory of *if*—it is a rather arcane literature to the uninitiated, and although it has been favorably cited in psychological work (e.g., Johnson-Laird, 1975; Rips & Marcus, 1977), there has been no detailed assessment of its psychological relevance. The more general question is whether the possible worlds construct is useful for cognitive psychology (cf. Hall-Partee, 1979). We shall concentrate on the specific question, but we believe that there is a lesson to be learned on the more general one too.

Although philosophers have not discussed relevance to cognitive psychology, factual psychological considerations play a role in arguments between rival theories (e.g., Lewis, 1973; Stalnaker, 1984), so the theories are intended to have some empirical content. For a theory to explain common intuitions about conditionals, it cannot be sufficient to specify truth conditions; the theory would also have to postulate that people *know* those truth conditions (i.e., postulate that some representation of the truth conditions exists within people, whether or not it is accessible to consciousness). Thus it seems that there is a hidden psychological postulate in the philosophical theories—an implicit claim about what people know. Indeed, one could argue that philosophical theories must lack explanatory value without the claim, inasmuch as it is hard to see how judgments or usage could be explained by a semantics or logic that is unknown to the user. The proper division of labor between cognitive psychology and philosophy with respect to conditionals is therefore problematic. Some philosophical goals have little relevance to psychology (e.g., that the semantics provide a vehicle for assessing completeness for conditional logics), whereas other goals are clearly relevant (e.g., to explain intuitions). The problem of defining the areas of communality and separation in the two disciplines' theoretical interests also arises over a broad range of other topics in semantics, reasoning, and philosophy of mind. The present discussion may provide a case study comparison for one topic.

There is a familial resemblance among the philosophical theories of conditionals. Thus, *If p then q* is true for Stalnaker when (and only when) *q* is true in the world in which *p* is true that is most similar to this one in some selected way; it is true for Lewis (1973) when *q* is true in the worlds most similar to this one in which *p* is true; it is true for Kutschera (1974) when the worlds that are consistent with *p* being true are included in the worlds consistent with the truth of *q*. Lewis proposed his theory only for counterfactuals; unlike Stalnaker, he believes that indicative *if* can be modeled by the material conditional of standard logic. Stalnaker's (1968, 1984) is probably the best known and most influential of the theories, so the discussion will focus on it. However, much of our discussion applies to the other theories as well. The prime issue with which we are concerned is whether the theory can be translated into a psychological theory, which would then compete with ours. From a psychological standpoint, it is important to note that a possible world is not the same thing as a mental model—the former is a complete world, whereas a mental model is only a model (i.e., a representation), and it models only a very small fragment of a world. Models of fragments won't do the philosophical work required of the possible world construct, and possible worlds cannot play the role of representations in cognitive theory that mental models can.

Stalnaker presents his theory as motivated by an intuition about how we evaluate conditionals. According to Stalnaker, one first adds the antecedent (hypothetically) to one's stock of beliefs, adjusting these as necessary to maintain consistency, after which one considers whether or not the consequent is then true. If one considers the consequent true, one considers the *if*-statement true also; and similarly, if one finds the consequent false, then the *if*-statement is also taken as false. The theory is intended to capture this psychological intuition formally.

Note that this intuition contains parallels to the Schema for Conditional Proof, especially as constrained in our theory. Thus, to add the antecedent (hypothetically) to one's beliefs is the same as supposing the antecedent, the first step of the standard Conditional Proof schema. Adjusting one's beliefs to maintain consistency is comparable in its effects with our constraint that a supposition and premise assumptions must be consistent (Principle 3ii). Next, it is part of the standard schema that an *if*-statement is true when the supposition makes the consequent true. Although the standard schema does not say that an *if*-statement is false when the supposition makes the consequent false, that conclusion does follow in our theory, as we discussed earlier. Thus, our theory captures Stalnaker's psychological intuition quite well.

Formally, Stalnaker's theory provides a logic, a semantics, and a completeness proof that relates the two. To turn the theory into a psychological theory, we would have to take either the semantics or the logic (or both together) as defining people's knowledge of *if*, that is, as the lexical entry. We consider first the semantics and then the logic.

The Semantics. This starts with a Kripke (1963) possible-worlds model structure. That is, there is a set of all possible worlds and an accessibility relation, R, among them. (The accessibility relation can be understood as follows: If a and b are possible worlds, then for aRb read "b is possible with respect to a" or "if you are in a then b is imaginable.") R is taken as reflexive. Stalnaker adds to this model structure a selection function, f, given a base world, a, and a proposition, A, the function selects an accessible world—the one that is most similar to a in the way specified by f—in which A is true. Thus, if a is the base world and A is the antecedent of the conditional *If A then B*, then $f(A, a)$ is the selected world, and *if A then B* is true or false in a according as B is true or false in $f(A, a)$.

Presumably, for people the base world is always the actual world. So for a psychological theory we can simplify somewhat by dropping all reference to base worlds in formulae, letting $f(A)$ stand for the world in which A is true that is most similar to this world in the way specified by f. Our putative lexical entry is then:

21. An *if*-statement, *If p then q*, is true iff q is true in some selected world, $f(p)$, in which p is true. The function f selecting the world satisfies the following conditions:

    a. The selected world is this world if p is true in this world.
    b. For any propositions, A, B, that are antecedents of conditionals, if A is true in $f(B)$ and B is true in $f(A)$, then $f(A) = f(B)$.

Conditions 21a and 21b are Stalnaker's; they are designed to ensure that the selected world is maximally similar to this one. Condition 21a merely recognizes that no world is more similar to this world than this world itself. Condition 21b guarantees that, whatever the kind of similarity indicated by f, this function always provides a well-ordering of worlds in terms of their distance from this world. Note that people must be assumed to know these conditions rather precisely—a vague understanding would not suffice because to account for inference the semantics must determine the logic and that requires a precise formulation.

    Aside from a possibly questionable intuitive plausibility, we see two kinds of difficulty with this lexical entry. A technical difficulty is that Condition 21b is problematic, as illustrated in the following pair of conditionals, adapted from Goodman (1947):

22. If Massachusetts were south of Virginia, then Boston would be warmer in winter.
23. If Virginia were north of Massachusetts, then less tobacco would be grown there.

If we set A as the antecedent of 22, then $f(A)$ is roughly the present world modified by moving Massachusetts southward. Setting B as the antecedent of 23, $f(B)$ becomes the present world modified by moving Virginia Mainewards. We have then a case where A is true in $f(B)$ and B is true in $f(A)$, although $f(A) \neq f(B)$, contradicting Condition 21b. Aware of the problem, Stalnaker proposes to regard Condition 21b as an idealization (Stalnaker, 1984, pp. 134–135), a proposal that would take us too far afield to discuss. As psychological theory, a central difficulty with Entry 21 is that it is incomplete without an account of how people work out what is in a possible world. Possible worlds cannot be directly perceived as the actual world can; they are abstract objects that people become partially acquainted with in the course of making and elaborating suppositions. Accordingly, to explicate how possible worlds are known, the lexical entry must contain rules governing the construction of suppositional arguments, that is, a logic. Such rules are given in Stalnaker's logic. Thus, a lexical entry constructed out of Stalnaker's theory should include some of the logic.

The Logic. The original logic (Stalnaker, 1968; Stalnaker & Thomason, 1970) has been reformulated by Thomason (1970) in a natural-deduction format that makes the form of suppositional argument explicit. We therefore discuss only Thomason's formulation. The logic consists of standard propositional logic plus modal operators of necessity and possibility, and a set of rules for the *if*-connective. We review only the part of the logic that has to do with conditionals.

Thomason's logic has two conditionals: the material conditional of standard logic and Stalnaker's *if*-connective. Modus ponens is of course valid for both. Also, both are introduced by suppositional arguments, defined by a Conditional Proof schema. The two schemas have the same generic form, which can be specified as follows:

24. To derive or evaluate a conditional with antecedent *p*, first suppose *p*; for any proposition *q* that follows from the supposition of *p* taken together with "usable" information, it is true that: $p \supset q$ or *If p then q* (as the case may be).

The differences between the two schemas lie in what information is "usable" (i.e., permissible to draw upon to support a suppositional argument).

For the material conditional, all information available is usable—there are no restrictions (other than truth). For Stalnaker's *if*, a proposition *r* is usable in a suppositional argument only if:

25a. *r* is necessarily true, or
25b. The premises contain the proposition *If p then r* (or the proposition *Not-[if p then not-r]*, which is equivalent to *If p then r* for Stalnaker), or
25c. The premises contain the propositions *If p then s*, *If s then p*, and *If s then r*.

Thus, 25a to 25c are Stalnaker's constraints on the Conditional Proof schema.

We see two important psychological problems with the Thomason–Stalnaker logic. One problem is that the logic has two conditional concepts, one corresponding to $\supset$ as well as one corresponding to *if*. As psychological theory, this translates into a claim that people have a concept equivalent to the material conditional that is separate from *if*, a claim for which there is no evidence. A psychological theory that rejects the material conditional as a model for *if* should get rid of the material conditional entirely.

The other problem concerns whether the information that the logic posits to be "usable" in a suppositional argument adequately describes what people do, in fact, feel free to use. The fit is defensible for counterfactuals, but poor for ordinary conditionals.

Consider first the counterfactuals argument from a counterfactual supposition on p. 217 that is mentioned (though not discussed) by Thomason (1970). Note that the argument uses both information about Blucher's time of arrival and the proposition. *Only a few days before Waterloo Wellington was miles away from his troops and they were unprepared for a fight.* To introduce these factual premises into the suppositional argument, the reasoner has to judge that they would still be true if Napoleon had attacked earlier and has to add this information (i.e., that they would be true if Napoleon had attacked earlier [*if p then r*]) to the premise assumptions; then Rule 25b permits their introduction. However, the logic provides no basis on which to make the judgment that they would still be true. To have a basis, the reasoner must have a cognitive representation of the semantics (as well as the logic): The semantics tells the reasoner to make the judgment in terms of the similarities between the world in which Napoleon attacked earlier and the actual world. However, the semantics itself says nothing about how to compute what the world in which Napoleon attacked earlier would be like, nor to what kinds of world similarities the reasoner should attend. So the reasoner is again stymied. On the other hand, as we noted earlier, our own theory does not say how people determine what propositions would remain true given a counterfactual supposition. Ultimately, the same issue arises in both theories.

As indicated earlier, the solution to this issue must wait for a full account of reasoning. That would detail (among other things) a person's resources for working out what remains true and what changes, given a counterfactual supposition. Such an account would have important implications for Stalnaker's theory: It would tell how a person computes how the world in which a counterfactual supposition is true differs from this world. That would circumscribe Stalnaker's *f*-function; with *f* thus circumscribed, a and b of Entry 21 are no longer needed and all the vague talk of world similarities could be dropped. For counterfactuals, the theory would converge toward ours.

Now let us consider ordinary conditionals. Rules 25a to 25c disallow enormously many inferences that are normally taken for granted as logical. For example, according to these rules the conclusion does not follow from the premises in Problems 9 and 14 described earlier. To explain such inferences, Stalnaker (1981) develops the concept of *reasonable inference*—a pragmatic concept for him—which he distinguishes from *semantic entailment*. An inference is reasonable "just in case, in every context in which the premises could appropriately be asserted or supposed, it is impossible for anyone to accept the premises without committing himself to the conclusion" (Stalnaker, 1981, pp. 194–195); whereas a conclusion is entailed "just in case it is impossible for the premises to be true without the conclusion being true as well" (p. 195). The conclusions are "reasonable inferences" from the premises in Problems 9 and 14; for comparison, the conclusions are semantic entailments in Problems 13 and 15. From a psychological standpoint, it is not clear that the distinction between reasonable inference and entailment corresponds to a difference in mental processes. For instance, there is no evidence that people see the inferences in Problems 13 and 15 as qualitatively more compelling than those of Problems 9 and 14. Although on Stalnaker's theory one should presumably expect to find differences in the way problems of the two types are solved, chapter 7 found that the same model of subjects' reasoning steps accounted well for responses to both.

Conclusions on Stalnaker's Theory

There would be a good deal of overlap between predictions made from Stalnaker's theory and from ours. It would be open to Stalnaker to explain the classical fallacies, the subjects' truth judgments, discussed earlier, and the children's comprehension errors along the same lines we did. So far as the paradoxes of implication are concerned, the first one (Problem 19) holds in his logic, that is, given q one can infer *If p then q*. The second (Problem 20) does not hold. Of course, these are the same judgments that our theory made, though not for identical reasons. There is also a lot of overlap between the propositional inferences that our theory predicts that subjects should make and the union of the semantic entailments and reasonable inferences of Stalnaker's system. The overlap is not complete because the reasoning program in our system greatly limits the inferences that subjects are predicted to draw. Stalnaker's system, not having been developed as a psychological theory, is not constrained by the subjects' limited logical skills and does not seek to capture them with a reasoning program. The lack of a reasoning program means that Stalnaker's theory could not predict the relative difficulty of different inferences as our theory does (chaps. 7, 8, and 12).

Our theory is also the simpler of the two. Both the logic and the semantics of Stalnaker's theory are complex, and people's knowledge of *if* must include both. Moreover, additional complexity comes from the fact that in order to predict inferences that subjects routinely make, the rules of the logic have to be supplemented by the new concept of reasonable inference. In sum, in trying to develop Stalnaker's theory as a psychological theory, we find that, although it would probably have a large overlap with ours in data coverage, it would be considerably more complex, without compensating advantages.

Addendum on "Possible Worlds." The preceding discussion of Stalnaker's theory has implications beyond conditionals about whether there is a role in cognitive psychology for the concept of *possible world* and for the semantic theories that exploit it. Possible worlds play a useful role in logic because they provide a basis for completeness proofs. For cognitive psychology, however, use of the concept requires some account of how people intuit possible worlds—presumably, by making and elaborating suppositions. Accordingly, for psychology, *supposition* is a more basic concept than possible world, because the notion of a supposition is needed in order to understand how people work out what is in a possible world. A supposition is, presumably, a premise from which belief is withheld, and is thus also a less mysterious concept than possible world. Hence the move from possible world to supposition is a conceptual gain. It seems to follow that semantic theories that use the possible-world concept have a useful role in cognitive psychology only in so far as they can be reformulated in terms of suppositions and processes of reasoning from suppositions. This conclusion, of course, does not impugn the usefulness of mental models, which may provide a way of representing complex suppositions, as mentioned earlier.

Sound Logical Intuition and Reasoning Error

Macnamara (1986) argued that a theory of logical reasoning must account both for the possibility of sound logical intuition and for logical error. Although detailed discussion is beyond the scope of this chapter, we provide a brief outline of how our approach accomplishes this (for additional discussion, see Braine, 1990; Braine & Rumain, 1983; O'Brien, 1987). We believe that a mental logic evolved in the human species that was concerned about things and events in the real world; it evolved to serve the practical goal of integrating information coming in at different times, or from different sources, going beyond the information as given to draw inferences. For instance, one learns *A or B* from one source and *not B* from another; an intelligent being needs some mental instrument to integrate these items of information and to infer *A*; the mental logic answers the need. Because of the practical goals served, the mental logic is profoundly embedded within a pragmatically motivated architecture, and inferences are routinely made from information that includes world knowledge retrieved from long-term memory, beliefs, guesses, and all sorts of discourse implicatures. Logical, analogical, causal, pragmatic, and narrative inferences cohabit happily in the same line of reasoning.

"Logical" error comes primarily from two sources. The pragmatic architecture is one source. Many pragmatic processes affect comprehension, as we noted earlier. In addition, when the products of reasoning enter awareness, they do not come automatically marked by the nature of the processes—logical or nonlogical—that generated them; consequently, dissociating the logically necessary from the pragmatically plausible is a metacognitive task that requires nonroutine intelligence, and failure to attempt or to succeed at this task easily leads to fallacies. A second source of error is due to characteristics of the usual routines for using the schemas of the logic—ordinarily these are adequate for the rapid execution of short chains of practical reasoning, but they are often not adequate to solve problems set by experimenters, and we suspect that the logic itself includes no routines for making undecidability judgments. When the logic, together with the usual routines, fails, subjects have to respond on the basis of nonlogical heuristics, guesses, and responses biases, or to transfer the problem to other reasoning procedures, for example, probabilistic, narrative, or analogical.

Sound logical intuition is made possible by the existence of the mental logic. However, sound judgments are not necessarily simple because many judgments require metacognitive skills over and above the logic. For example, judgments of logical validity may (implicitly) demand a distinction between inferences that depend only on the form of the information given, and those that owe something to factual knowledge or pragmatic context (cf. Moshman & Franks, 1986). We speculate that the emergence of logic as a discipline required a level of civilization that included a subclass of intellectuals ready to put energy and persistence into the metacognitive (and metalogical) task.

CONCLUSIONS

We have proposed a three-part theory of *if*, consisting of a lexical entry and, independently motivated, a set of pragmatic comprehension processes and a reasoning program. The lexical entry consists of inference schemas, which define the information about *if* in semantic memory that is context free, that is, applicable regardless of context. The pragmatic comprehension processes provide principles that govern how *if* is interpreted in a particular context. The reasoning program specifies a routine available to essentially all subjects for propositional-logic reasoning from information as interpreted to a conclusion.

The two schemas essential to the lexical entry are modus ponens and the Schema for Conditional Proof. However, there is an important difference from standard logic in that a supposition must be consistent with prior assumptions. This constraint explains why an *if*-statement is not considered true when the antecedent is false and why one of the "paradoxes" of material implication appears so odd—in both cases the natural reasoner refuses to make a supposition and then treat it as false. That the schemas are psychologically primitive is supported by the facts that few subjects at any age ever have difficulty with modus ponens problems, and that even young children seem capable of making suppositions and evaluating conditionals. We take the inference schemas as applied through the reasoning program. This also has consequences not found in standard logic—specifically concerning how *if*-statements are refuted. An additional consequence is that subjects are not expected to be able to derive all logically possible inferences; indeed, severe restrictions on their inferential performance are predicted.

We posit that comprehension of *if*-statements in context is mediated by pragmatic principles. These specify how comprehension is affected by the social frame of discourse (Grice's, 1975, "cooperative principle" and Geis & Zwicky's, 1971, "invited inference"; Sperber & Wilson, 1986), and by knowledge of the subject matter the statements are about ("plausibility"). Knowledge of subject matter is apparently often organized by type— permissions, obligations, cause–effect (Cheng & Holyoak, 1985; Cheng et al., 1986)—and hence content-sensitive "pragmatic" schemas play a role in conditional reasoning. However, they provide far less than a complete theory: Although content-specific schemas nicely explain some differences in reasoning that are a function of problem content, they cannot explain differences that are a function of problem form; moreover, the more theoretical work one required them to do, the more they would have to proliferate unparsimoniously. We believe that content-specific schemas act to enrich the inferences that can be made beyond those enabled by the context-free schemas of the lexical entry; there is no evidence that they ever contradict the latter.

There have always been connections between psychological and philosophical thinking about reasoning. Psychological investigations have consistently relied on logicians to provide a description of what subjects "ought" to do—logic provides criteria for judging the validity of arguments. Many theorists have looked to logic for ideas about the possible form of a mental logic. Even those who would deny a role for mental logic still rely on formal logic to define a domain of competence to be explicated. Conversely, although philosophers have not been consumers of the recent psychological research literature, philosophers as early as Aristotle have made assumptions about how humans solve logical problems (Kneale & Kneale, 1962), and many recent issues in philosophy result from the recognition that standard logic fails to capture people's intuitions about logical connectives. Philosophers such as Goodman (1983), Lewis (1973), and Stalnaker (1984) frequently rely on presumed facts about such intuitions as appropriate evidence bearing on philosophical theories.

In this chapter we have attended to both psychological and philosophical concerns, seeking to address the research literature in a way that is both psychologically plausible and philosophically satisfactory. We have avoided philosophical formalisms that are psychologically implausible or that, on analysis, seem to have little psychological application (e.g., possible-worlds semantics). In addition, our theory can be extended naturally beyond assertions to include questions and commands. By attending to psychological concerns, our theory is able to address the philosophical issues without loss of psychological plausibility. At the same time, the psychological research data are accounted for.

The core of the theory is simple—two inference schemas that were originally proposed by logicians. These schemas are the only part of the theory that is specific to *if*. All the other parts are independently motivated: The reasoning program is needed to account for propositional-logic reasoning generally (not just reasoning with conditionals); the pragmatic principles apply to comprehension quite generally. Thus, in form the theory is quite parsimonious: It consists in adding a lexical entry for *if* to general cognitive psychological theory, and explaining extant data from the combination. We challenge those who prefer alternative approaches to demonstrate their ability to handle the same range of issues and data as simply and parsimoniously.

ACKNOWLEDGMENTS

Preparation of this article was supported by an NSF grant (BNS-8409252), Martin Braine, principal investigator, and a grant to David O'Brien from the PSC-CUNY research award program of the City University of New York. We are deeply indebted to Patricia Cheng, Jennifer Hornsby, Phil Johnson-Laird, Alan Leslie, John Macnamara, David Moshman, and two anonymous reviewers for comments on earlier versions of the manuscript—comments that led to considerable improvements. Requests for reprints should be sent to David O'Brien, Department of Psychology, Baruch College of the City University of New York, Box 512, 17 Lexington Avenue, New York, NY 10010.

10

Conditional Reasoning: The Logic of Supposition and Children's Understanding of Pretense

David P. O'Brien
Baruch College and the Graduate School of the City University of New York

Maria G. Dias
Antonio Roazzi
Federal University of Pernambuco

Martin D. S. Braine
New York University

Investigators of conditional reasoning have come to a widely diverse set of conclusions concerning the extent to which either children or adults have an appropriate understanding of conditionals, that is, propositions of the form *if P then Q*. At one end of the spectrum is a leading researcher of adult reasoning, who said that "performance indicates no more than a superficial understanding of the sentence *if P then Q*, and little evidence of any depth of understanding" (Evans, 1982, p. 231). At the other end of the spectrum are those of us who have concluded that young children show evidence of considerable appreciation of the logic of conditionals (e.g., Dias & Harris, 1988, 1990; O'Brien, Braine, Connell, Noveck, Fisch, & Fun, 1989; see also Brainerd, 1977; Ennis, 1971, 1975, 1976; chap. 9). In between are numerous advocates of a developmental scenario in which adults and adolescents have an appropriate appreciation of conditionals (subject to some performance constraints), although children have an incomplete or insufficient understanding (e.g., Knifong, 1974; Kuhn, 1977; Markovits, 1984, 1985, 1992; Matalon, 1962; Moshman, 1979; Overton, 1990; Paris, 1973; Staudenmayer & Bourne, 1977; Taplin, Staudenmayer, & Taddonio, 1974; Ward & Overton, 1990); from this perspective, how adults understand conditionals is qualitatively different from how children understand them.

We propose that these disparities stem from theoretical differences over what constitutes an appropriate understanding of conditionals, and consequently from differences in the sorts of reasoning tasks that have been presented. Those researchers who have concluded that people (either children or adults) do not have an appropriate understanding of conditionals have been using the truth table for the material conditional shown in Table 10.1 as a normative standard and have compared performance to what would be predicted from the truth table. Inspection of Table 10.1 reveals that the material conditional makes an *if* proposition true unless its antecedent is true and its conclusion false. In particular, this interpretation makes a conditional true whenever its antecedent is false, something that researchers have found that people do not appreciate. (See Evans, Newstead, & Byrne, 1993, for a review of the adult data sets for the principal tasks based on the material conditional.)

The fact that people do not respond in the ways that would be predicted from the truth table for the material conditional has been interpreted by some researchers as evidence of a lack of conditional-reasoning competence. We come to a different conclusion: Such responses show that the truth table does not capture what it is that people understand about conditionals. Indeed, viewing conditionals through the lens of the truth table obscures the role of conditionals in ordinary reasoning: *If* indicates supposition, and a reasoner ordinarily supposes something to discover what would be the case under that supposition. Conditional reasoning thus concerns hypothetical and pretense situations and what follows under them. Whereas the material conditional captures none of this suppositional nature of conditional reasoning, the view of conditionals from the perspective of a mental logic of inference schemas does so.

Chapter 9 provides a detailed description of our theory of *if*. It includes some inference schemas, a reasoning program that applies the schemas in a line of reasoning, and some independently motivated pragmatic

TABLE 10.1
Standard-Logic Truth Table for the Material Conditional

Truth Status of the Component Propositions		Truth Status of the Conditional Proposition
P	Q	$P \supset Q$
T	T	T
F	T	T
T	F	F
F	F	T

principles. The inference schemas and a direct-reasoning routine are the basic mental logic, and those inferences that can be made on the basic part should be made routinely and be available early in development.

The theory includes two schemas that are relevant directly to *if*—a *schema for conditional proof* and *modus ponens*—and a closely related *schema for negation introduction*. These three schemas can be stated informally as follows:

1. (Schema for conditional proof)
   To derive or evaluate *If P then* . . . , first suppose *P*. For any proposition *Q* that follows from the supposition of *P* taken together with other information assumed, one may assert *If P then Q*.
2. (Modus ponens)
   Given *If P then Q* and *P*, one can infer *Q*.
3. (Schema for negation introduction)
   When the supposition of proposition *P* taken together with other information assumed leads to a contradiction, one can assert *not P*.

The meaning of *if* is revealed principally by the schema for conditional proof, which states that when the consequent of a conditional can be derived from a set of premise assumptions taken together with the antecedent of that conditional as a supposition, that is, as a hypothetical assumption, the conditional can be asserted on the premise assumptions alone. To assert an *if* clause thus is to assert a supposition, and to assert a *then* clause is to assert what follows under that supposition. When *if* is understood in this way, it becomes clear why modus-ponens inferences are valid: The assertion of *if P then Q* indicates that *Q* is derivable on the supposition of *P*, so *Q* follows when the subsequent assertion of *P* removes the conditional basis of the proof. A modus-ponens inference thus is sound because it inherits the derivation of the consequent that was made under the schema for conditional proof.

The schema for conditional proof, taken together with the direct-reasoning routine, provides a procedural semantics for *if*, that is, a procedure for judging when conditional propositions are true or false. When a conditional is to be evaluated, the direct-reasoning routine adds its antecedent to the set of premises (i.e., to the set of propositions assumed in the evaluation) and treats the conditional's consequent as a conclusion to be evaluated. Thus, *if P then Q* is judged true when the consequent *Q* is true on the premises together with the supposition of *P*, but *if P then Q* is judged false when the consequent *Q* is false on the premises together with the supposition of *P*. In standard logic this latter judgment would not be made because the antecedent might be false; the mental-logic schema for conditional proof thus leads to a procedural semantics for *if* that differs from the semantics provided by the truth table of standard logic's material conditional.

The mental-logic schema for conditional proof differs from standard logic in an additional way. This difference follows from a general constraint in mental logic that is not found in standard logic: In standard logic, anything can be derived when the premises are necessarily false, that is, anything follows from a contradiction. In mental logic, however, nothing follows in such a situation, except perhaps that some mistake has been made, for example, that some proposition is being treated as a premise that should not be. A consequence of this general proscription against reasoning from false premises is a constraint on what propositions can be used in a derivation leading to a conditional conclusion under a supposition: Any proposition used under a supposition leading to a conditional conclusion must be consistent with that supposition (see chap. 9 for a detailed discussion). This constraint has implications for counterfactual conditionals, that is, for conditionals with consequents that follow from supposition of a false proposition: Any proposition that would not be true under a counterfactual supposition cannot be used in an argument leading to a conditional conclusion under that supposition; even a true proposition thus is excluded under a counterfactual supposition unless it would still be true given that supposition.

The final schema that is relevant to our discussion of supposition concerns negation introduction. Not all suppositions are discharged by using the schema for conditional proof to infer a conditional conclusion. (Sometime a supposition simply is abandoned as a reasoner turns attention to some other matter.) The schema for negation introduction provides another way in which a supposition can be discharged: When a supposition leads to a contradiction, that supposition can be judged false.

As we discussed in chapter 4, the basic part of the mental logic—the inference schemas and the direct-reasoning routine—should be psychologically valid, that is, should be applied essentially errorlessly on maximally simple problems that can be solved using it and should be available early in childhood. Furthermore, given our proposal that the basic meaning of *if* is provided by its inference schemas (and is revealed particularly by the schema for conditional proof) together with the direct-reasoning routine, we would expect early use in speech of *if* to conform to the core theory (i.e., that a conditional is judged true when its consequent follows from its antecedent together with other known information). Several basic predictions thus can be made; considerable evidence exists to support these predictions, although there are some notable lacunae.

Modus ponens inferences should be made routinely by children as well as by adults, and the data show that both adults and school children do so, as reviewed in chapter 9 (see also Braine & Rumain, 1983; O'Brien,

1987). There is also reason to think that preschool children make modus ponens inferences; Scholnick and Wing (1991) reported spontaneous modus ponens inferences in the conversations of 4-year-olds.

Both children and adults should make the basic judgments about when *If P then Q* is true and when it is false that follow from our procedural semantics, that is, that when the antecedent of a conditional, taken together with other premise assumptions, entails the consequent of that conditional, the conditional is evaluated true, and when antecedent taken with other assumptions entails the negation of the consequent, the conditional is evaluated false. Chapter 7 presents several problems with *if* conclusions that were given to adult subjects. The problems referred to letters on an imaginary blackboard. Given, for example, a premise of the form *There is either a P or a Q on the blackboard* and asked to judge the conditional conclusion *If there is not a P on the blackboard then there is a Q*, adult subjects universally responded that the conditional is true, and when asked to judge *If there is not a P on the blackboard then there is not a Q*, they responded that the conditional is false. These responses are consistent with the predictions of the procedural semantics of mental logic but are inconsistent with what would be predicted on the truth table of the material conditional. To date the literature provides no data on such problems with children, and we provide such problems in Experiments 1 and 2.

The basic suppositional step should be available to young children, and children's utterances using *if* should be consistent with the schema for conditional proof. As discussed in chapter 9, reasons for thinking that the schema for conditional proof is available early come from the use of supposition in children's pretend play and from their spontaneous usages of *if*. Supposition in the service of play and fantasy is usual by the third year (Fein, 1981). There is thus good evidence for the early availability of an essential intellectual component of the schema—the supposition step. Leslie (1987) noted that simple inferences can occur in the elaboration of pretense. For example, pretending that an empty cup on a table contains water and that it is pushed over leads naturally to imagining the table as wet. It is only a small additional step from this to a conditional, such as *If this cup had water in it and we pushed it over then the table would get wet*. Bowerman (1986) and Reilly (1986) reported just such conditionals by around 3 years of age. Other spontaneous conditionals of the third year also suggest command of the schema of conditional proof. Here are two examples cited by Bowerman (1986):

4. C is wearing a bead crown which her mother has knocked off once by kissing her. She says: "Don't kiss me 'cause it will fall off if you do that."

5. D is sitting in his bath. He says: "If I get my graham cracker in the water, it'll get all soapy."

The schema for conditional proof (i.e., that an *if*-sentence is true when its antecedent taken with other things the speaker knows lead to the consequent) appears to capture what the children are asserting in the examples (i.e., that with what the child knows, the antecedent leads to the consequent).

There also is evidence for use of the schema for negation introduction. Scholnick and Wing (1991), for example, reported what they called *refutations*, and among these are cases in which a child refutes an adult conditional by citing a counterexample: The logical structure of such a refutation is that the adult conditional is taken as a supposition that leads to an entailment that is contradicted by a counterexample (or that supposing the antecedent of the conditional entails a conclusion that is incompatible with the counterexample). The fact that children evidently understand that this falsifies the conditional implies that 4-year-old children have access to negation introduction in their suppositional reasoning.

Additional evidence for early availability of the schema for negation introduction can be seen in the reasoning implicit in 4; the argument form can be spelled out as follows:

6. The supposition of the possibility that mother will kiss her leads C (on the basis on her prior experience) to the inference that the bead crown will fall off.

   C does not want the crown to fall off (an implicit premise).

   The contradiction between the implicit premise and the inference that the crown will fall off that was made on the supposition leads C to request that her mother not kiss her (which applies the schema for negation introduction).

The fact that the implicit premise and the conclusion of 6 are embedded in expressions of desire in no way negates the fact that the argument form of the negation-introduction schema is being used.

The schema for negation introduction, and arguments like that in 6, are found in older subjects in the service of a reductio ad absurdum argument. Modus-tollens problems, for example, with premises of the form *If P then Q* and *not Q*, can be solved with a reductio argument (see chap. 14); a subject first supposes that *P* is the case, which leads by modus ponens to *Q*. This contradicts the minor premise, *not Q*, which on the negation-introduction schema allows the subject to conclude *not P*. Such reductio argument are far from common, however, and given that children in Scholnick and Wing (1991) and Bowerman (1986) reveal an understanding of the schema for negation introduction, why is it that reductio ad absurdum arguments are not more common? Supposition in the service of constructing a proof goes well beyond the core part of mental logic; such skills are not widely available even among adults. Thus, although even preschool children have access to the negation-introduction schema, integration of the schema into complex lines of reasoning is far from available, even for older reasoners.

There is one prediction for which no empirical evidence has been reported: The literature as yet provides no evidence that children appreciate that reasoning under a counterfactual supposition disallows using information that would not still be true under that supposition (even though it otherwise would be true). The fact that children engage in pretense reasoning provides evidence that children make suppositions (including those that are counter to fact) but does not ensure that they do so in a way that is consistent with our proposed constraint. Our claim that the core part of mental logic is available early in development leads us to expect that children's pretense reasoning is governed by the constraint and that children understand that propositions that are inconsistent with a counterfactual supposition in a pretense situation should be excluded under that supposition, even when those propositions would otherwise be true. Experiments 3 to 6 provide investigations of children's appreciation of this constraint on suppositional reasoning.

EXPERIMENT 1

This experiment was designed simply to investigate whether school children would follow the procedural semantics of mental logic and judge as true a conditional in which its antecedent taken together with other premises entails its consequent and judge false a conditional in which its antecedent taken together with other premises entails the negation of its consequent.[1]

Method

Subjects. Forty children from a predominantly White middle-class public school in upstate New York participated. Included were 20 second graders (range = 6 years 11 months to 8 years 2 months) and 20 fifth graders (range = 10 years 1 month to 11 years 2 months). Another 40 children who

---

[1]A difference between our treatment of conditionals and that of standard logic is that there is no need on the mental-logic schema for a derivation leading to a consequent under a supposition to be made on logical grounds—the inference processes under the supposition might be pragmatically based; the only judge of the adequacy of a derivation under a supposition is the reasoner (or any interlocutor).

participated were drawn from a racially mixed middle-class private school in Recife, Brazil. Included were 20 second graders (range = 6 years 8 months to 8 years 6 months) and 20 fifth graders (range = 10 years 5 months to 11 years 7 months).

Tasks and Procedures. Sixteen problems were constructed, each referring to the contents of a small cardboard box. Subjects were told that each box contained some toy animals and fruits, and were shown some examples of the content items. Each problem presented a closed box with a card on its cover. The card showed either one or two premises giving information about the content of the box, and an *if*-statement to be evaluated given the premises. The children were required to judge whether it is right or wrong to claim the conclusion from the premises.

On some problems the premises, taken together with the supposition of the antecedent of the conditional as an additional premise, entail the consequent, and these problems are referred to as the *true problems*, because on mental-logic theory they should be judged true. On other problems the premises, taken together with the supposition of the antecedent as an additional premise, entail the denial of the consequent, and these problems are referred to as *false problems*, because on mental-logic theory they should be judged false. The 16 problems were constructed so that there were eight pairs of problems, with the two problems in each pair providing the same premise forms. In one problem of a pair, the conclusion had an affirmative consequent and in the other a negative consequent. Also, one problem of each pair was a true problem and the other false. Furthermore, half the problems with affirmative consequents were true, and likewise for the problems with negative consequents. Similarly, half of the antecedent clauses were affirmative and half negative, and in each case half were true problems and half false. In addition, occurrences of negatives in the premises were equally balanced across the problems. This balancing of the distribution of affirmatives and negatives in true and false problems controls for possible response biases involving negations, preferences for "right" or "wrong" responses, and any possible strategies or biases in which responses of "right" or "wrong" are contingent on the occurrence or absence of negatives in problems.

The forms of the eight problem pairs and their true and false conclusions are presented in Table 10.2. In the actual problems *P*, *Q*, and *R* were realized as statements about the presence of animals or fruits in the box presented, for example, one of the English-language problems presented the premises *There is either an apple or a banana in the box*, and the conclusion to be evaluated was *If there is not an apple then there is not a banana*. The comparable Portuguese-language problems presented fruits and animals that are familiar to children in Brazil.

TABLE 10.2

Problem Forms, their Predicted Responses, and the Proportion of such Responses for the Problems in Experiment 1

Premises	Conclusions	Predicted Response	Americans		Brazilians	
			7 Years	10 Years	7 Years	10 Years
a. P or Q	If not P then Q	True	.80	.85	1.00	1.00
	If not P then not Q	False	.65	.80	1.00	1.00
b. Not both P and Q	If P then not Q	True	.65	.85	.95	1.00
	If P then Q	False	.65	.95	.95	1.00
c. If P or Q then R	If P then R	True	.75	.90	.95	.90
	If P then not R	False	.80	.75	1.00	.90
d. If not P or not Q then not R	If not P then not R	True	.75	.85	.95	.95
	If not P then R	False	.80	.75	.90	.95
e. P or Q; If Q then R	If not P then R	True	.80	.80	.45	.65
	If not P then not R	False	.65	.95	.70	.75
f. Not both P and Q; If not Q then not R	If P then not R	True	.70	.80	.60	.65
	If P then R	False	.85	.95	.70	.70
g. Not both P and Q; If not Q then R	If P then R	True	.70	.80	.60	.70
	If P then not R	False	.80	.90	.60	.75
h. P or Q; If Q then not R	If not P then not R	True	.65	.95	.65	.75
	If not P then R	False	.60	.90	.75	.70
Totals		True	.73	.87	.77	.84
		False	.73	.86	.80	.83

Subjects were tested individually. They were informed that first they would be told something about what is in a box, and that they were to figure out the answers to a question about what was in the box. Each box had a card providing typewritten sentences with the premise information and the tentative conclusion to be evaluated. On each problem the experimenter read aloud the premise information and the *if* conclusion, and had the child then read the information aloud. Any erroneous reading by the child was corrected and the procedure repeated. (Such reading errors rarely occurred.) For each problem the child was required to state whether the conclusion is right or wrong based on the premise information. (Mental-logic theory predicts a "right" response on true problems, and a "wrong" response on false problems.) Following each judgment, to discourage guessing, subjects were required to provide an explanation of why their response was considered correct. Each subject first was given a practice problem with the premises *If there is a tiger in the box, then there is a lemon the the box* and *There is a tiger in the box,* and the conclusion *There is both a tiger and a lemon in the box.* All subjects gave the appropriate "right" response. The order of presentation of the 16 problems was random, with half of the subjects at each age in each country receiving the problems in the reverse order.

Results and Discussion

Table 10.2 shows the proportions of predicted responses, that is, "right" on the true problems, and "wrong" on the false problems, for each age, problem type, and nationality. In order to assess the overall performance, a 2 (Age) × 2 (True vs. False) × 8 (Problem Pair) × 2 (American vs. Brazilian) ANOVA was computed, with repeated measures for True versus False and for problem pair. Each subject was given a score of one point for each predicted response, that is, "right" on a true problem and "wrong" on a false problem, and zero otherwise. Thus, the score entered into each cell in the analysis was either a zero or a one. (The highest order interaction was used as the error term in computing F values.) None of the main effects were statistically significant, but there was a Grade × Nationality interaction, $F(1, 76) = 7.51$, $p < .01$, and a Grade × Problem Type × Nationality interaction, $F(1, 76) = 4.96$, $p < .05$. The Grade × Nationality interaction was attributable to the American 7 year olds, who were less likely than were the other three groups to make the predicted responses. Preplanned comparisons (one tailed) for all four groups, however, showed that each group mean was significantly greater than chance (= .50), $t(19) = 3.24$, $p < .01$ for the 7-year-old Americans, $t(19) = 5.48$, $p < .001$ for the 10-year-old Americans, $t(19) = 5.09$, $p < .001$ for the 7-year-old Brazilians, and $t(19) = 5.24$, $p < .001$ for the 10-year-old Brazilians. The overall response tendencies for all four groups thus were consistent with the predictions of mental-logic theory.

The Grade × Problem Pair × Nationality interaction was attributable to the 7-year-old Brazilians, whose responses to problem pairs (e) and (g) were less likely to be those predicted than were responses to problem pairs (a) to (d). The true problem of problem pair (e) was the only problem for any group that did not elicit the predicted response by at least 60% of the subjects; inspection of the children's explanations revealed that they resisted the predicted true response on this problem because it involved putting a bird and a fish together, and many children said that a bird cannot live with a fish because fish cannot fly and birds cannot live underwater. When the data for the American and for the Brazilian 7 year olds were combined, on 15 of 16 problems the predicted response was made at an above-chance frequency (for 40 subjects, chance is below 65% on a one-tail binomial test); the sole exception was the true problem (e) for the 7-year-old Brazilians.[2] When the data for the American and for the Brazilian 10 year olds were combined, the predicted response was made at an above-chance frequency on all problems. The absence of any significant effect for true versus false problems indicates that the children were not responding on the basis of simple response preferences, and the incidence of "right" or "wrong" responses was influenced neither by the absence nor number of negations in a problem. The response tendencies thus are consistently those predicted by our theory.

Because their explanations of their responses often were incomplete and difficult to interpret, they were not treated statistically. They generally were consistent, however, with the line of reasoning expected. For example, in explaining a "false" response to the conditional conclusion *If there is not an apple, then there is not a banana* from the premise *There is either an apple or a banana*, one 7-year-old child said "because there would be a banana." Such explanations were typical at both ages in both nationalities. In sum, the children in this experiment were able to give the predicted responses to these problems with conditional conclusions most of the time, and their response tendencies were the same as those reported previously for adults.

EXPERIMENT 2

The results in Experiment 1 showed that school-age children judge as true those conditionals in which a supposition taken together with other premise information leads to the consequent and judge as false those in

---

[2]An additional 20 Brazilian children were presented the same problem, but with different animals so that the epistemic incompatibility was eliminated, and 80% of the children gave the predicted *True* response on this new problem version.

which a supposition taken together with other premise information leads to the denial of the consequent, and in this they responded in the same way as the adults in Braine et al. (chap. 7) and as our mental-logic theory predicts. The results, however, leave a question in that the "false" responses in Experiment 1 were not clearly separated from "can't tell" responses; a subject might use the "false" response option because no clear indeterminate option was provided. (We, of course, would have recorded any such responses if they had been given, but none were.) This matter requires investigation because the predictions of mental logic differ from what subjects would be expected to do on these "false" problems in standard logic, where a "can't tell" response should be forthcoming. Furthermore, in the absence of a clear "can't tell" response option, the "false" option invites being used to indicate that the conclusion does not follow on the premises rather than that its denial follows on the premises. In the problems presented here, subjects were provided a clear "can't tell" response option and some training in its use.

Method

Subjects. Sixty Americans and 60 Brazilians participated. The Americans included 20 second graders (range = 6 years 9 months to 7 years 7 months), 20 fifth graders (range = 9 years 8 months to 11 years 1 month), and 20 college students from the Introductory Psychology subject pool at New York University. Four other second graders were omitted because they failed to reach a criterion on a training task described later. The children were drawn from two racially mixed middle-class schools in New York City, one public and one parochial. The Brazilians included 20 second graders (range = 6 years 4 months to 7 years 11 months), 20 fifth graders (range = 9 years 6 months to 10 years 10 months), and 20 college students from the Federal University of Pernambuco. Two other Brazilian second graders were omitted because they failed to reach criterion on the training task. The Brazilian second and fifth graders were drawn from two racially mixed middle-class private schools in Recife, Brazil.

Tasks and Procedure. Four problems were presented and, as in Experiment 1, they referred to the contents of a closed box that contained toy animals and fruits. All four problems had the same pair of premises: *In this box there is a cow or a horse, but not both. There is also a fruit.* The four conclusions to be evaluated were: (a) *If there is a cow then there isn't a horse* (True); (b) *If there is a cow then there is a banana* (Can't tell); (c) *If there is a horse then there is a cow* (False); and (d) *If there is a horse then there isn't an orange* (Can't tell). For half the subjects in each group, these four problems were presented in the above-mentioned order, and for the other half they were presented in the reverse order.

The format and procedure were the same as for Experiment 1, except for two changes. One was that the conclusions to be evaluated were attributed to a hand puppet named Kermit. Subjects had to say "whether Kermit is right or wrong, or that you can't tell whether he's right or wrong because you don't know enough about what's in the box." The other change was that a training task was given in place of the practice problem. There were 12 training problems, four determinate (two True and two False) and eight indeterminate. These problems also referred to the content (toy animals and fruits) of a closed box. The indeterminate problems illustrate their general nature. The first problem provides the premise *There is a cat or a dog*, and the conclusion to be evaluated is *There is a cat* (Can't tell). None of the training problems had conditional conclusions. Subjects were admitted into the study only if they got four consecutive responses correct (in which case the training was discontinued) or if they got four of the last six problems correct. Four American and two Brazilian second graders failed to meet these criteria and were excluded from the study. No feedback on any problems was given. More details concerning this training procedure are provided in O'Brien et al. (1989, Experiment 2).

Results and Discussion

Proportions of *True, False*, and *Can't tell* responses for the True, False, and Can't Tell problems are shown in Table 10.3. On the four problems, both the American and the Brazilian 7 year olds gave the predicted responses 78% of the time, a proportion that exceeded what would be expected by

TABLE 10.3
Proportions of *True, False*, and *Can't Tell* Responses to the True,
False, and Can't Tell Problems at Each Age Level in Experiment 2

		Response					
		Americans			Brazilians		
Age	Problem Type	True	False	Can't Tell	True	False	Can't Tell
7 years	True	.65	.05	.30	.85	.00	.15
	False	.00	.80	.20	.00	1.00	.00
	Can't tell	.03	.08	.90	.00	.50	.50
10 years	True	.95	.00	.05	.90	.00	.10
	False	.00	1.00	.00	.00	1.00	.00
	Can't tell	.03	.18	.80	.00	.50	.50
Adults	True	1.00	.00	.00	1.00	.00	.00
	False	.00	1.00	.00	.00	1.00	.00
	Can't tell	.05	.18	.78	.00	.44	.56

chance alone (= .33), $z = 4.28$, $p < .001$, and in both groups the proportion of subjects making the predicted responses to all four problems (= .45) was greater than would be expected by chance alone (= .012), $z = 17.99$, $p < .001$. For the 10-year-old and adult Americans, even more subjects made the predicted responses (92% and 93%, respectively), as was also the case for the 10-year-old and adult Brazilians (80% and 85%, respectively). Both nationality groups at all three ages thus made the predicted responses far more often than would be expected by chance.

One feature of the data in Table 10.2 that was not predicted is that the Brazilians showed less use of the *Can't tell* response option on the Can't Tell problems than did the Americans. Of greater interest here, however, is the fact that no group used the *Can't tell* response on false problems, which is consistent with our prediction that the false problems would elicit *False* responses rather than the *Can't tell* responses that would be predicted on standard logic. Taken together with the results of Experiment 1, the data reveal that schoolchildren as well as adults give responses to problems with conditional conclusions that correspond to the mental-logic predictions based on the schema for conditional proof taken together with the direct-reasoning routine.

EXPERIMENT 3

We turn now to the constraint on reasoning under a counterfactual supposition, that is, that propositions are excluded under a counterfactual supposition unless they would still be true on that supposition. The subjects were preschool children; if mental-logic theory is correct that the schema for conditional proof is available early to children, then even preschool children should appreciate that when a counter-to-fact supposition is made, propositions that would not still be true under that supposition should be excluded under that supposition.

Method

Subjects. Forty 4-year-old American children from two middle-class racially mixed preschools in New York City participated (range = 3 years 6 months to 4 years 10 months). Thirty-two 4-year-old Brazilian children from a middle-class racially mixed private preschool in Recife, Brazil participated (range = 3 years 8 months to 5 years 0 months).

Tasks and Procedures. Two sets of cards each were constructed, each set containing six cards. Each card showed a single cartoon drawing. One set of pictures concerned pretense actions, and the other set concerned the use of an object in pretense. The pictures in Set 1 were about Bobby and

Alex, 4-year-old boys. Bobby has a dog named Rex. Picture 1 showed Bobby kicking a football with his friend Alex; Picture 2 showed Bobby on his hands and knees barking like a dog (balloon from his mouth saying "arf, arf"); Picture 3 showed Bobby curled up in Rex's doggy bed; Picture 4 shows Bobby eating from Rex's doggie bowl; Picture 5 showed Bobby talking on a telephone; Picture 6 showed Bobby chewing Rex's rubber doggie bone.

The experimenter showed Picture 1, introducing Bobby and Alex. The experimenter explained that Bobby has a dog named Rex, and that the boys have decided to play a game of "let's pretend," or "make believe," and that the pictures tell a story about Bobby pretending to be a dog like Rex. Picture 1 was placed on the left. The experimenter showed Picture 2, explaining that it shows Bobby pretending to be a dog and barking like a dog; Picture 2 was placed to the right of Picture 1. The experimenter then showed Picture 3, explaining that Bobby now is sleeping like a dog in Rex's doggie bed; Picture 3 was placed to the right of Picture 2. The experimenter then showed Picture 4, explaining that Bobby now is eating from Rex's doggie bowl; Picture 4 was placed to the right of Picture 3. The experimenter now placed Pictures 5 and 6, one above the other, to the right of Picture 4. (For half of the children Picture 5 was placed above Picture 6, and for the other half Picture 6 was placed above Picture 5.) The experimenter explained that Picture 5 shows Bobby talking on the telephone and that Picture 6 shows Bobby chewing on Rex's doggie bone. The child was asked to decide which of the two pictures belongs in the story at this point. This is referred to as the *Picture-Choice Task*, Card 5 is referred to as the *Suppositionally Inconsistent Picture*, and Card 6 as the *Suppositionally Consistent Picture*. The child was encouraged to explain the choice.

An additional procedure, referred to as the *Checking Procedure*, was motivated to ensure that the children understood which pictures are consistent with Bobby's pretending to be a dog and which pictures are consistent with what Bobby could do ordinarily. The same six pictures as were presented in the Picture-Choice Task were presented in random order, and the child was asked for each picture whether it shows something that Bobby can do, and whether it is something he can do when he is pretending to be a dog. For half of the children these questions were asked before the Picture-Choice task, and for the other half these questions were asked after the Picture-Choice task.

Picture Set 2 was about Annie and Carol, 4-year-old girls. Picture 1 showed Annie and Carol playing catch with a ball. Picture 2 showed Annie holding a banana to her ear and mouth like a telephone. Picture 3 showed Annie handing a banana to Carol, telling her that her mother wants to talk to her (a balloon from Annie's mouth says "Your mother wants to talk to you"). Picture 4 showed Carol holding a banana to her mouth and ear like a telephone. Picture 5 shows Carol eating a banana.

Picture 6 shows Carol talking into a banana. The procedures were the same as for Picture Set 1, except that the experimenter explained that the two girls are going to play a game of "let's pretend that the banana is a telephone." Problem Set was a between-subjects variable, and subjects were assigned to problem sets randomly; 21 American children received Set 1, and 19 received Set 2; 16 Brazilian children received Set 1, and the other 16 received Set 2.

Results and Discussion

Only one child (an American) failed to assess the pictures appropriately on the Checking Procedure (this child chose the Suppositionally Inconsistent Picture on the Picture-Choice Task). The children from both countries thus showed that they understood which pictures are consistent with the supposition of the pretense scenario and which would otherwise be appropriate.

On the Picture-Choice Task, of the 21 American children who received Picture Set 1, 18 chose the Suppositionally Consistent Picture as belonging in the story (86%), and only three chose the Suppositionally Inconsistent Picture, $z = 3.30$, $p < .001$; on Picture Set 2, 17 of the American children chose the Suppositionally Consistent Picture (89%), and only two chose the Suppositionally Inconsistent Picture, $z = 3.40$, $p < .001$. Of the 16 Brazilian children who received Picture Set 1, 14 chose the Suppositionally Consistent Picture, and only two the Suppositionally Inconsistent Picture (88%), $z = 3.04$, $p < .005$. On Picture Set 2, all 16 Brazilian children chose the Suppositionally Consistent Picture. The children thus consistently excluded the cards showing a situation that ordinarily would be appropriate, but would not still be true under the counterfactual pretense supposition.

The verbal justifications for the response selections often were incomplete and difficult to interpret, and thus were not analyzed statistically; they did, however, tend to refer to reasons to exclude the Suppositionally Inconsistent Picture. For example, one subject said that "He can't talk on a telephone when he's a dog," and another said that, "Dogs don't use the phone." Some subjects referred to a reason to include the Suppositionally Consistent Picture, for example, "It's OK to eat the bone when you're a dog." The verbal justifications thus support interpretation of the quantitative data as revealing an exclusion of propositions under a supposition that would not still be true under that supposition.

EXPERIMENT 4

The Story Completion Task here is an extension of the Picture Choice Task of Experiment 3; children were required to use the cards one-at-a-time to complete a story. We predicted that the Suppositionally Inconsistent Picture would be withheld from the story, at least until all of the other pictures had been used.

Methods

Subjects. Forty-two American 4 year olds from a racially mixed middle-class preschool in New York City participated (range = 3 years 7 months to 4 years 10 months). Thirty-two Brazilian 4 year olds from a racially mixed middle-class private preschool in Recife, Brazil participated (range = 3 years 10 months to 5 years 1 month).

Tasks and Procedure. The Story Completion Task used the same two picture sets as in Experiment 3. Half of the subjects in each nationality group were presented Picture Set 1, and the other half Picture Set 2. The experimenter place Picture 1 on the left and explained the pretense situation. Picture 2 was placed by the experimenter to the right of Picture 1, and the experimenter explained that it is Bobby pretending to be a dog and barking like a dog (or that Annie is pretending that a banana is a telephone). The experimenter explained that the child was to use the remaining pictures to continue the story about Bobby pretending to be a dog (or about the girls pretending that the banana is a telephone). The remaining four cards were then shuffled and placed in a pile in front of the child (with the proviso that the Suppositionally Inconsistent Card not be placed on the bottom of the pile), who was encouraged to place the cards so that they would continue the story until all the pictures were used (although they were not told in advance that they must use all the cards). As in Experiment 1, half of the children were presented the Checking Procedure (described in Experiment 3) prior to receiving the Story Completion Task, and half after receiving the Story Completion Task.

Results and Discussion

Only one children (an American) failed on the Checking Procedure, and this child subsequently excluded the Suppositionally Inconsistent Card until all other cards had been used on the Story Completion Task. Eighteen of the 21 (86%) American children who were presented Picture Set 1 held the suppositionally inconsistent card until after all other cards had been used, a proportion that exceeded what would be expected by chance alone (= .25 because there were four cards), $z = 6.46$, $p < .001$. An additional two subjects did not place the Suppositionally Inconsistent Card last, but did express that the pretense had been suspended when the suppositionally inconsistent card was encountered, for example, "This picture doesn't go with this story, but they start playing again in the next one." Altogether,

20 of the 21 American subjects showed evidence of understanding that the Suppositionally Inconsistent Card does not belong under the supposition. Of the 21 Americans who received Picture Set 2, 17 (81%) held the Suppositionally Inconsistent Card until all of the other cards had been used, again a proportion that exceeded what would be expected by chance alone, $z = 5.92$, $p < .001$. An additional two subjects did not use the Suppositionally Inconsistent Card at all, and simply put it aside when it was encountered, expressing that it did not go with the story. Thus, 19 of 21 American children who received Picture Set 2 excluded the Suppositionally Inconsistent Card.

All 32 of the Brazilian children excluded the Suppositionally Inconsistent Card from use under the pretense supposition. How they did so, however, differed somewhat from the American children in that for both picture sets the majority did not use the Suppositionally Inconsistent Card at the end of the story, but, rather, simply expressed that the card did not belong in the story when it was encountered (9 of 16 children for Picture Set 1 and 11 of 16 for Picture Set 2). Apart from this difference in how the Suppositionally Inconsistent Card was excluded, both the American and the Brazilian data sets are clear in showing that the 4 year olds excluded the Suppositionally Inconsistent Cards and thus responded in accordance with the mental-logic constraint.

EXPERIMENT 5

The results of Experiments 3 and 4 showed that 4 year olds exclude suppositionally inconsistent propositions from pretense narratives, but, because the children were not asked to produce or evaluate *if* propositions, they bear only indirectly on the schema for conditional proof. In the present experiment, 4 year olds were presented the same picture sets as in Experiments 3 and 4, and were asked to tell a story; the instruction was to begin the story with *If Bobby pretends to be a dog* (Problem Set 1) or *If Carol pretends that the banana is a telephone*. Thus, in the tasks presented here the only cue to the pretense situation is given in the *if* clause used to begin the stories.

Methods

Subjects. Thirty-two Brazilian 4 year olds from a racially mixed middle-class private preschool in Recife, Brazil, participated (range = 3 years 8 months to 4 years 8 months).

Tasks and Procedures. The Story Construction Task used the same two picture sets as Experiments 3 and 4, with half of the subjects presented Picture Set 1 and the other half Picture Set 2. Picture 1 was used by the experimenter to introduce the protagonists of the stories (e.g., Bobby, Alex, and Rex). Children then were instructed to use the other five cards to tell a story beginning with *If Bobby pretends to be a dog* (or *If Carol pretends the banana is a telephone*). The five remaining cards were shuffled and placed in a pile in front of the child (with the proviso that the Suppositionally Inconsistent Picture was not placed on the bottom of the pile).

Results and Discussion

On Problem Set 1, all 16 children excluded the target card when it was encountered. This was done in two different ways. In one sort of response, made by 14 of the children, the Suppositionally Inconsistent Picture, when encountered, was identified as not belonging in the story and the child stated that the supposition was suspended temporarily, for example, "He gave up the make-believe play here," and then continued the story with the next picture. The other two children responded by removing the card until all of the others had been used, then using the Suppositionally Inconsistent Picture to end the story.

On Picture Set 2, 15 of the 16 children responded to the Suppositionally Inconsistent Picture by excluding it from the story when it was encountered. How they did so, however, differed somewhat from how the children did so with Picture Set 1. Only 4 of the 16 children temporarily suspended the pretense, although this was the modal response tendency to Set 1. Instead, the modal response to Set 2, exhibited by 11 children, was to hold the picture until all of the others had been used, or to use the picture to end the story, for example, "Carol is eating because she got hungry, so the make-believe story is over," and "If she is eating the banana here, the banana isn't a telephone anymore, so they stopped the game."

This difference between Problem Set 1 and Problem Set 2 in the suppositionally inconsistent card seems quite sensible and shows some epistemic sophistication—once a banana has been eaten it cannot be used as a pretend telephone (or for anything else), whereas a child can talk on a telephone and then go back to pretending to be a dog. The difference between Picture Sets 1 and 2 in how the Suppositionally Inconsistent Cards were excluded from the stories is not explained by the core part of mental-logic theory (which makes no attempt to do so), but the fact that 31 of 32 children across the two picture sets successfully excluded the suppositionally inconsistent information is explained by the constraint against using information under a supposition that would not still be true given that supposition.

EXPERIMENT 6

The motivation for this experiment was to provide direct evidence that preschool children appreciate that a conditional with a counterfactual antecedent requires a consequent that would still be true given the antecedent. Children thus should perceive a difference between a conditional with a counterfactual antecedent and a consequent that would be true given that antecedent, and a conditional with a counterfactual antecedent and a consequent that might not still be true given that antecedent (although the consequent would be true without the counterfactual antecedent). It was predicted that children would prefer the former and eschew the latter.

Methods

Subjects. Fifty-four Brazilian children from a middle-class private preschool in Recife, Brazil participated. The children ranged in age from 4 years 9 months to 7 years 0 months.

Tasks and Procedure. Ten problems and two practice problems were constructed. Each problem presented a story, followed by two conditional sentences. As described shortly, children were required to decide which conditional sentence was sensible and which was not. Presentation of the stories was preceded by the following instructions (although the problems were presented in Portuguese, they are presented here in English):

> Sam and Paul are brothers, but they are very different from one other. Sam is like a saint; he always is sensible and everything he says is true; he never tells a lie. Paul, however, is more like Pinocchio; he always is foolish, and everything he says is a lie or is silly; he never tells the truth. The two brothers enjoy reading stories together, and after reading a story, each brother says something about the story. Remember, Sam always is sensible and tells the truth, and Paul always says something foolish or tells a lie.

Before receiving the 10 problems, the subjects were presented two practice problems. The practice problems and the other 10 problems are shown in the Appendix to this chapter. For each problem, the child was read a story, followed by two conditionals, one of which is labeled in the Appendix as "appropriate" and the other as "inappropriate." The child then was told:

> After reading this story, Sam and Paul each said something about the story. Remember, Sam always is sensible and always tells the truth, and Paul always says something foolish or tells a lie. Which brother, Sam or Paul,

said which thing about the story? Remember, Sam always is sensible and always tells the truth, and Paul always says something foolish or tells a lie.

Each child received all 10 problems, with order of presentation and order of conditional sentence varied randomly. For half of the children, the even-numbered problems presented the inappropriate conditional with the word *still* added, for example, "If Maria had been feeling well, she still would have stayed in bed reading a book," and the odd-numbered problems presented the inappropriate conditional without the word *still*, for example, "If Silvia had stayed at home on Saturday, she would have eaten the cake at her grandmother's house." For the other half of the children, the odd- and even-numbered problems reverse the presence and absence of the word *still*. This condition was introduced because we thought that the addition of the word *still* might cue the children to understand that the counterfactual conditional requires something that would not ordinarily be the case.

Results and Discussion

The proportions for each problem with which the appropriate conditional was attributed to Sam (i.e., judged as appropriate) and the inappropriate conditional was attributed to Paul (i.e., judged as inappropriate) are shown in Table 10.4. Inspection of Table 10.4 reveals that relatively few choices were made that were not those predicted. On a binomial expansion, all 10 problems led to the predicted responses more often than would be expected by chance alone (the prior probability = .50; any proportion greater than .69 differs from chance with $p < .01$). Indeed, performance was almost errorless, with 93% of the responses overall being those predicted. Because of this ceiling effect, there were no differences associated with the ages of the children, and the 4-year-olds were as accurate as the 7-year-olds; also, given the ceiling effect, the addition of the word *still* did not increase the likelihood of children making the appropriate choices. Clearly, the children were able to chose counterfactual conditionals in which the consequent would be true given the supposition as appropriate, and to chose counterfactuals in which the consequent would not (still) be true as inappropriate.

TABLE 10.4
Proportion of Subjects Selecting the Counterfactually Appropriate
Conditional on Each of the Stories in Experiment 6

Story	1	2	3	4	5	6	7	8	9	10
Proportion correct	.96	.96	.96	.94	.82	.91	.94	.94	.92	.94

Note. The stories are shown in the Appendix.

GENERAL DISCUSSION

As was described in the introduction, the previous literature provided considerable evidence supporting the predictions of the core part of mental-logic theory for conditional reasoning, but did not address (a) whether children appreciate that counterfactual suppositions impose a requirement on what information can be used, and (b) whether children make judgments that are consistent with the mental-logic procedural semantics for *if*. The experiments reported here provide evidence for both. The results of Experiments 1 and 2 showed that school children, as well as adults, made judgments that were consistent with the mental-logic procedural semantics for *if*. The results of Experiments 3 to 5 showed that by 4 years of age children's reasoning under a pretense supposition was constrained in the way that we predicted, measured either by the Picture Choice Task in Experiment 3, by the Story Completion Task of Experiment 4, or by the Story Construction Task of Experiment 5. Summed across all three of these experiments, 94% of the time the children excluded the suppositionally inconsistent pictures under a counterfactual pretense supposition. Experiment 6 provided a direct test of children's appreciation of the constraint, and found that 4-year-old children had no difficulty judging as appropriate those counterfactual conditionals on which the consequent is consistent with the counterfactual supposition and as inappropriate those on which the consequent would not still be true given the counterfactual supposition (although it otherwise would be appropriate).

There are thus ample reasons to think that there is a logic for conditionals that centers on supposition that is available early in the language and reasoning of children. Given that there is empirical evidence for both children and adults for each of the parts of this basic part of the mental logic that we have proposed, claims that either children or adults lack a mental logic for understanding conditionals strike us as mistaken.

We are not proposing that the core part of mental logic accounts for every judgment that people make when reasoning with and about *if* and other propositional particles. Many judgments rely on the noncore parts of the theory, including the strategies that go beyond the direct-reasoning routine. Few people acquire the strategic skills for integrating schemas such as conditional proof, the supposition of alternatives, and negation introduction into complex lines of reasoning, and when such sophisticated strategies are acquired, it is not until around 10 to 11 years of age (Fisch, 1991).

There is a recent criticism of our proposal about how *if*-statements are asserted and evaluated that we should address, concerning whether the schema for conditional proof leads to conditionals that are pragmatically counterintuitive. Holyoak and Cheng (1995, pp. 385–386), for example, wrote that "The general problem for O'Brien's schema for conditional proof, and for all formal treatments of the conditional, is that people seem to demand that p appear *relevant* to q in some way before they accept the truth of *if p then q*." They provided the example of the conditional:

7. If humans have three heads, then 13 is a prime number,

arguing that this consequent follows on the schema for conditional proof from its antecedent and other assumed information. Holyoak and Cheng concluded that "The basic constraint of relevance permeates human reasoning so deeply that it is doubtful that a psychologically plausible natural logic can be encapsulated from pragmatic considerations."

A similar example was provided by Rips (1994, p. 49), who noted that the constraint on conditional proof that we propose does not block arguments of the following sort:

8. Carol owns a deli ∴ If Linda is a bankteller then Carol owns a deli.

Have Rips (1994) and Holyoak and Cheng (1995) identified an Achilles heel in our proposal? The answer is no: We have not suggested that mental logic can be encapsulated from pragmatic considerations, but rather, as noted in chapters 3 and 9, we view the logic as embedded in pragmatic considerations.

From the perspective of mental-logic theory, the issue concerns not whether there are pragmatic considerations in reasoning, but where to place them. As noted in chapter 9, one can place such considerations inside or outside the logic. A prominent proposal that places the pragmatics inside the logic was provided by Anderson and Belnap (1975), who argued that *if p then q* can be inferred only when p is used in the derivation of q. We do not adopt this sort of solution for two reasons. First, to include such a demand within the conditional-proof schema would add considerable complexity, and we prefer to keeps the mental logic as simple as possible. Second, the use of the supposition in the derivation of the consequent may not be necessary for a conditional to be pragmatically acceptable. Consider conditionals such as:

9. If you want some privacy, there's a telephone in the bedroom.
10. If you're thirsty, there's a fountain down the hall.

In such conditionals, the consequent does not seem to depend derivationally on the antecedent, although the antecedent clearly provides a reason for mentioning the information in the consequent. The reason that 7 and 8 are peculiar in a way that 9 and 10 are not is not entirely clear. One possibility is that in 9 and 10, the antecedent provides a reason for the consequent to be relevant—a sort of relevance that is not captured by the requirement that the supposition be used in the derivation of the consequent. A second possibility is that conditionals like 9 and 10 are elliptical, with the underlying meaning of the consequent in 9, for example, better expressed as "you'll be interested to know that there's a telephone in the bedroom." Note that this latter interpretation of conditionals such as 9 and 10 allows one to account for them with Anderson's and Belnap's principle that the supposition must be used in the derivation of the consequent, but it is far from clear that this interpretation is correct, and it remains unclear exactly what pragmatic principles the logic would need to include. We prefer, therefore, to place the pragmatics outside the logic. This choice, however, does not encapsulate mental logic from pragmatic considerations.

Although the mental logic is not encapsulated from pragmatic considerations, it is possible to draw some conclusions about the mental logic that are separate from pragmatics. First, although both children and adults perform poorly when compared with what would be predicted from the truth table for the material conditional, children as early as 4 years of age provide evidence that they understand conditionals in the way that is described by our mental-logic theory. Thus, there is a logic for conditionals that is available early in childhood. Second, the same sorts of situations on which adults routinely make logically appropriate conditional inferences are the same situations on which children also do so; these are situations in which the core part of the mental logic is sufficient. The same sorts of situations on which adult performance differs from what would be predicted from standard logic are those on which children also fail to make the standard-logic inferences; in particular, these are problems on which the material conditional would make a conditional true because its antecedent is false, and problems that require reasoning skills that go beyond what is provided by the direct-reasoning routine. There is thus no reason to assert that children and adults have a qualitatively different understanding if *if*. *If* is understood both by children and by adults in the way described by the schema for conditional proof, the schema for negation introduction, and modus ponens, as applied by the direct-reasoning routine, and there is empirical support that children as well as adults have available each part of our proposed logic.

ACKNOWLEDGMENTS

This work was partially funded by a grant from the CNPq of Brazil to Maria Dias, and a grant from the National Science Foundation to Martin Braine (BNS-8409252). The authors express appreciation to Jeff Connell, Ira Noveck, and Sholly Fisch for assistance in data collection.

APPENDIX: STORIES PRESENTED IN EXPERIMENT 6

Practice Story 1

Antonio was flying a kite outside his house, and by mistake the kite got stuck in a tree. Now, which of the two brothers, Sam or Paul, said which thing about Antonio. Remember that Sam always is sensible and tells the truth, and Paul always says something foolish or tells a lie.

   a. If Antonio wants to get the kite out of the tree, he will have to climb up into the tree. (Appropriate)
   b. If Antonio wants to get the kite out of the tree, he will have to dig a hole in the ground. (Inappropriate)

Practice Story 2

Alberto was playing football in the garden next to his house on a very hot day and wanted to get a cold soda to drink Remember that Sam always is sensible and tells the truth, and Paul always says something foolish or tells a lie.

   a. If Alberto wants to get a cold soda to drink, he will go to the refrigerator.
   b. If Alberto wants to get a cold soda to drink, he will go to the oven.

Story 1

Yesterday Rodrigo and John were playing in the park. The sun was shining, and not a single cloud was in the sky. The two friends kicked a football, rode their bicycles, and climbed a tree. They were happy that it did not rain even once all day because when it rains their mother tells them to stay indoors. Indoors they are not allowed to kick a football, or to ride their bicycles, or to climb a tree.

   a. If it had rained yesterday, the two boys would not have been able to play football. (Appropriate)
   b. If it had rained yesterday, the two boys (still) would have played in the park. (Inappropriate)

Story 2

Yesterday Maria was not feeling well, and she spent all day in bed reading a book. This disappointed her because she had planned to meet her friends to go to the movies to see the new Disney movie. Instead she did not get to see her friends and did not get to see the new Disney movie. The only fun she had was when her mother brought her some hot chocolate to drink.

  a. If Maria had been feeling well, she would have seen the new Disney movie. (Appropriate)
  b. If Maria had been feeling well, she (still) would have stayed in bed reading a book. (Inappropriate)

Story 3

Yesterday Jane lost her coloring book, and she spent most of the day looking for it, but she was not able to find it. She was sad that she could not find her coloring book because she wanted to use the new crayons her Daddy gave her. Finally she gave up looking for the coloring book and watched some television.

  a. If she had found the book, she would have been able to do some coloring in it with her new crayons. (Appropriate)
  b. If she had found the book, she (still) would not have been able to do some coloring in it with her new crayons. (Inappropriate)

Story 4

Last week all of Bruna and Maira's friends went to the circus, where they saw the clowns, but Bruna and Maira did not go with them. Instead, Bruna and Maira played with their dolls all day. Maira had some new clothes for her dolls, and the two girls pretended that the dolls were having a fashion show. Later, the two girls ate some milk and cookies.

  a. If Bruna and Maira had gone to the circus, they would have seen the clowns. (Appropriate)
  b. If Bruna and Maira had gone to the circus, they (still) would have played with dolls all day. (Inappropriate)

Story 5

Almost every Saturday, Silvia gave a bath to her little dog, Fluffy, but last Saturday she went to visit her grandmother, so she did not give a bath to Fluffy. Silvia always loved to visit her grandmother, and her grandmother cooked Silvia's favorite cake, which they ate together at her grandmother's house. Silvia did not get home until late at night, and when she got home she found that Fluffy had played outside and was very dirty.

  a. If Silvia had stayed at home on Saturday, she would have given a bath to her dog, Fluffy. (Appropriate)

b. If Silvia had stayed at home on Saturday, she (still) would have eaten the cake at her grandmother's house. (Inappropriate)

Story 6

Last Sunday, Fabio went to his friend's birthday party and ate too many sweets. This gave him a stomachache. Fabio usually enjoyed going to a birthday party, but he didn't have a good time at this birthday party because of his stomachache. While the other children were playing games, Fabio went to his friend's bedroom and took a nap on the bed. When he woke up, he was sad that he had missed all of the games.

a. If Fabio did not get a stomachache, he would have played the games with the other children. (Appropriate)
b. If Fabio did not get a stomachache, he (still) would have taken a nap instead of playing the games with the other children. (Inappropriate)

Story 7

Before Pedro goes to bed, his father usually reads him a bedtime story. This makes Pedro happy because his father is so good at reading him stories. Last night Pedro's bedroom lamp was broken and because of that his father could not read him a story. Instead of reading him a story, his father let Pedro eat an ice cream before he went to bed. Pedro wished that the bedroom lamp would stay broken because his father never let him eat an ice cream before bed any other time.

a. If Pedro's bedroom lamp was not broken, his father would have read him a bedtime story. (Appropriate)
b. If Pedro's bedroom lamp was not broken, his father (still) would have let him eat an ice cream. (Inappropriate)

Story 8

Sally was at the beach and saw the ice cream truck and asked her mother for two dollars to buy an ice cream. Her mother told her that she did not have two dollars with her, so she could not give Sally the money Sally wanted to buy the ice cream. Sally was sad not to get an ice cream, and felt even more sad when she watched other children who did buy an ice cream. She thought that the only reason that she was sad was that she did not have an ice cream.

a. If Sally's mother had given her two dollars, Sally would have been able to buy an ice cream. (Appropriate)

b. If Sally's mother had given her two dollars, Sally (still) would have been sad. (Inappropriate)

Story 9

Kenny wanted to ride his bicycle but found that it had a flat tire. Kenny enjoyed riding his bicycle so much because he loved to go fast. Kenny did not know how the fix the flat tire by himself, but he hoped his father would fix the flat tire when he came home from work. When his father came home, he helped Kenny fix the tire, so Kenny went for a ride on his bicycle before the family ate supper.

a. If his father did not help Kenny fix the flat tire, Kenny would not have been able to go for a ride on his bicycle before the family ate supper. (Appropriate)
b. If his father did not help Kenny fix the flat tire, Kenny (still) would have gone for a ride on his bicycle before the family ate supper. (Inappropriate)

Story 10

Maria's mother always cooks a hot lunch for Maria everyday and never allows her to eat candy bars, which are bad for her teeth. Yesterday Maria's mother promised Maria to cook lasagna for lunch—Maria's favorite type of pasta. When she tried to turn on the oven, she found that it was not working. So she told Maria that she could not prepare the lasagna because the oven was not working. Maria's mother prepared a salad instead, and as a special treat allowed her to eat a chocolate bar after the salad, only because she was not eating her favorite hot lasagna meal.

a. If the stove had been working, Maria's mother would have made Maria lasagna for lunch. (Appropriate)
b. If the stove had been working, Maria (still) would have had a chocolate bar. (Inappropriate)

11

Steps Toward a Mental-Predicate Logic

Martin D. S. Braine
New York University

In an argument tending to cast doubt on the idea that there is a mental logic, Evans (1993) wrote, "Formal logic is an inaccurate and unnatural representation of reasoning involving natural language and real-world concepts" (p. 12). The editors and the other contributors to this volume agree with Evans on this point. Standard logic is indeed unnatural in many ways that make it unfit as a model of any part of ordinary human reasoning. For instance, to ordinary intuition, an *if-then* sentence is not true merely because its *if*-clause is false, as it is in standard logic; it is also highly counterintuitive, to take another example, that, merely because there are no unicorns, both the propositions "Every unicorn has a horn" and "No unicorn has a horn"[1] should come out true. Furthermore, the frequent gross lack of correspondence between the syntactic structures of propositions in standard logic and those of the sentences of English or any other language with the same meaning (I provide some examples later) also creates a serious problem for the idea that people reason with standard logic: Why should the natural language (in which we often think we are reasoning) be so different in structure from standard logic, if we are indeed reasoning in standard logic? The natural language syntactic structure is unmotivated.

However, the fact that standard logic is in important ways unnatural does not mean that there is no mental logic; it could merely mean—and

---

[1]In logical notation, $(\forall x \, (Ux \supset Hx))$ and $(\exists x \, (Ux \, \& \, Hx))$, respectively (U = unicorn, H = has a horn).

we believe that it does mean—that the mental logic is not standard logic. Defining what the mental logic is—its properties, the canonical inferences it provides, and the nature of the representations it uses—is a task of empirical discovery. Over the past 20 years, my colleagues and I have developed an empirically based theory of the mental logic underlying ordinary propositional reasoning. That theory and the empirical evidence supporting it is described in earlier chapters of this book. The purpose of the present chapter is to extend this theory to include everyday untutored reasoning of a predicate logic sort.

Thus, my purpose is to provide a hypothesis about the logical component of a model of human reasoning that makes the inferences that people readily make that are of the sort covered by predicate logic. These are, roughly, inferences from information about what properties certain objects have or what relations hold among them to conclusions of the same sort. One might illustrate the intended province of the model as follows. Many textbooks of logic have some predicate-logic exercises in which the premises are given in English; the student is asked whether a certain conclusion follows, and if it does follow, to show that it does. The books expect students to answer by translating the premises into logical notation, working the problem through in logical notation, and finally translating the conclusion back into English. However, it is perfectly possible to do many such exercises without knowing standard logic; one often doesn't need standard logic to see that the conclusion is correct and to justify it. English itself is adequate for arguing from the premises in English to the conclusion in English, and most ordinarily intelligent people without training in standard logic can do many such exercises this way. Let us call the reasoning that they do "reasoning of a predicate logic sort." (Readers who would like specific examples now should look ahead at the problems in Tables 11.1, 11.5, and 11.6.) Our purpose then is to account for reasoning "of the predicate logic sort" done without knowledge of standard logic.

As discussed in earlier chapters, in our conception a model of deductive reasoning has several components. The most logically fundamental component comprises a set of inference schemas that specifies a repertory of the basic kinds of inferences available to the reasoner. These define the elementary logical steps possible in a chain of reasoning. The inferences of the set are routine in the sense that they are performed essentially errorlessly under optimum conditions (e.g., on problems with no sources of complexity other than the inference in question). They are elementary in the sense that each inference is performed as a single step in reasoning and is not the output of a chain of more elementary inferences. Prior work has defined such a set of elementary inferences for propositional reasoning. Our purpose now is to extend this set to encompass ordinary reasoning of a predicate logic sort.

In addition to this set of schemas, a complete model requires several other components. Notably, it requires reasoning programs that put together a line of reasoning. These select from the vocabulary of possible deductive steps the ones that shall be applied at each stage of a chain of reasoning, and it is the heuristics of the reasoning programs that primarily determine the quality of the reasoning that occurs. The schemas and the reasoning programs together comprise the part of a reasoning model that is properly called *logical*. Additionally, a reasoning model must be concerned with the comprehension processes that decode the information given (and may perhaps not decode it in the ways that a problem-setter intended). A theory of the comprehension processes is very much concerned with pragmatic as well as logical influences on comprehension, that is, the determination of what is understood by knowledge, situational context, and discourse conventions, as well as logic (Sperber & Wilson, 1986). I have more to say later about reasoning programs and comprehension. However, the main focus of the chapter is on the inference schemas and the representational system they employ.

In order to state inference schemas a notation is required. The notation used here is not the surface structure (of English or any other language), but a system of semantic representation that abstracts from surface structure. Thus, for the propositional domain the schemas employ a set of semantic elements—&, OR, NEG, IF-THEN (which are distinct from the corresponding English words)—and variables representing propositions. The predicate-logic domain requires a much more complex system of representation; it includes these elements but also includes additional ones, for example, a distinction between predicate and argument and variables for both, a way of indicating that a predicate applies to all, some, or no objects of a set, a way of representing an arbitrary object of a set, a means for indicating that some entity referred to is the same as some previously mentioned entity.

The representational system itself has theoretical significance because it claims to represent the form of the system in which the subject's reasoning is actually conducted—more accurately, it represents just those aspects of semantic structure that determine the inferences that subjects make. The reasoner translates from natural language statements into this representational system, and then reasons in this "language of thought" (cf. Braine, 1992, 1994; Fodor, 1975; Rips, 1994; chap. 4). Thus, reasoning is preceded by a comprehension process that decodes the information used into the representations of this system; the reasoner then reasons in this representational system by making inferences sanctioned by the schemas, and then, to communicate any conclusion reached, he or she translates it back into surface structure. It follows that the representational system necessarily makes claims about some aspects of the conceptual structures that underlie many sentences of English and other languages. Inevitably, the focus of the present paper is almost as much on the representational system as it is on the inference schemas.

In developing the system of semantic representation, I have had two constraints in mind. First, it must be capable of representing the reasoning steps of ordinary people making inferences of a predicate logic kind. Second, it should be "intuitively natural." By this it is meant that the representations should provide a reasonably good fit to the structure of English and other languages. (I take this as essentially equivalent to the "grammatical constraint" of Jackendoff, 1983, whose force is captured by Fodor's, 1975, claim "the sentences we are able to understand are not so very different from the formulae that internally represent them"; p. 156.) I do not provide rules for mapping between the representations and surface structure; indeed, there are so many semantic ambiguities associated with the surface structures of natural languages that I do not believe that there can be any complete determinate set of such rules; rather, the translation process is a complex mixture of rules and pragmatically governed heuristic processes, constrained but by no means determined by rules (see Sperber & Wilson, 1986, for elaboration of a point very similar to this). However, I would hold the representations to be "natural" if their structure had such similarities, correspondences, and regular relationships to the structure of natural languages that the formulation of the many rules that there are should not prove to be a formidably difficult task.

There are a number of systems of semantic representation in the literature, with goals that may appear to overlap those just stated, but in many cases they do not. There is, first of all, the large body of work on model-theoretic semantical approaches to natural languages (see Chierchia & McConnell-Ginet, 1990, for a textbook presentation), including also Montague grammar. These semantic theories attempt to relate natural language sentences to the world outside the speaker by providing a recursive theory that defines the conditions under which any sentence is true. Such theories have a role to play in cognitive science, for example, they permit the soundness of inferences to be demonstrated. However, the truth conditions of a sentence are not the same as its meaning (e.g., in many such theories $2 + 2 = 4$ and $3^2 = 9$ have the same truth conditions—they are both true in all possible worlds—but they clearly differ in meaning). More importantly, such theories make no claims of psychological reality for what they propose: They do not claim to represent how people judge the truth of sentences (e.g., they do not claim that in comprehending a sentence people compute the mapping between sentence and possible worlds that many such theories provide); they say nothing about how people make inferences, nor do they explain why certain inferences are easier than others. Because our goal is, precisely, to provide a psychological theory of the logical inferences people make, the model-theoretic approach is not useful, and certainly no substitute for the kind of theory we are seeking to provide.

Some model-theoretic approaches attempt to accomplish their goal in two stages. A natural language sentence is first mapped onto an "intermediate" level of representation—what most linguists and psychologists would call a level of semantic representation[2]—and then the model theory provides truth conditions for representations at this level. Although the truth-conditional part of such an approach has no relevance for our goals, the intermediate (semantic) level of representation could have, because it could be interpreted as providing a candidate theory of the structure of the language of thought, and might then be taken as the level of representation at which inferences are made. Parsons's (1990) "event language" is an example of such an intermediate level,[3] and Chierchia and McConnell-Ginet (1990) provided further examples. Although such representations are interesting, neither of our goals are the primary focus of such work: No explicit psychological claims are made (e.g., Chierchia & McConnell-Ginet, 1990, p. 329); psychological naturalness (as defined earlier) is only a secondary goal, and a model of logical inference that can claim psychological reality is not a concern at all.

The work of a number of linguists (e.g., Jackendoff, 1983, 1990, 1992; some semantic analyses of Pinker, 1989; Levin, 1993) has focused completely on such a level of semantic representation, without any model-theoretic goals of defining truth conditions. In this work, naturalness is a primary goal, although modeling logical inference is not—in fact, no analysis of quantifiers has been proposed and Jackendoff himself notes its absence as a problem. What is proposed here is both less and more ambitious than this work: It is less ambitious in that a much narrower range of English constructions is included; it is more ambitious in providing representations for quantified propositions and psychologically realistic inference rules and procedures for making inferences (of a predicate logic sort) from those representations. Ultimately, I would hope for integration with the linguistic work of Jackendoff and others on

---

[2]The reader should be aware that model-theoretic semanticists often use the terms *syntax* and *semantics* in ways different from most linguists and cognitive psychologists. For model-theoretic semantics, this intermediate level would be called *syntactic*, because this is the level for which the semantic theory is to provide truth conditions, and *semantics* is reserved for the theory that assigns truth conditions. I shall follow the linguistic usage, and refer to this intermediate level as *semantic*, because it is a level that purports to represent meaning, in contrast to the syntactic representations of surface structure (whose meanings are represented at the semantic level).

[3]Ordinary action sentences are analyzed as involving quantification over events. For instance, "Brutus stabbed Caesar with a knife" is analyzed as "There is an event, e, such that e is a stabbing & Brutus is the agent of e & Caesar is the theme of e & there is a knife, k, such that k is the instrument of e."

semantic representation in order to yield a coherent theory of the structure of the language of thought.

In settling on a system of representation, a central and immediate question concerns the representation of quantifiers and quantifier scope. For instance, consider the ambiguous sentence *All the alligators are in a bath*. It could mean that there is a bath and all the alligators are in this same bath, rendered in standard logic as: $\exists x$ [Bath$_x$ & ($\forall y$ if Alligator$_y$ then y is in x)]; or it could mean that for every alligator there is a bath such that an alligator is in it, rendered in standard logic as: $\forall y$ [if Alligator$_y$ then $\exists x$ (Bath$_x$ and y is in x)]. In the first case, the existential quantifier ("a" as "$\exists$") is said to have relative or wide scope over the universal ("all," "every" as "$\forall$"); in the second case, the scope relations are reversed and the universal has wide scope over the existential.

Concerning quantification and quantificational scope, there are two major decisions to be made. One concerns the nature of the quantifiers—whether they are domain general, that is, the variables, the x and y, range over the words themselves and not over domains (as in standard logic), or whether they are domain specific (i.e., associated with the specific kind of content indicated by the noun they modify in surface structure as in the English renderings earlier, where "all" ranges only over the alligators considered and "a" only over baths. The other decision concerns the locus of quantifiers—whether they are placed outside their host propositions (as in standard logic; see the preceding examples), or inside, as a component of the phrase-unit indicating the argument they bind (as in ordinary English). Thus, one possible arrangement would be like that of standard logic, in which quantifiers are placed outside their host propositions and scope is controlled by their order (see the previous examples), Gupta (1980) and McCawley (1981/1993) criticize standard logic representations as unnatural on the ground that variables are not restricted as to domain, whereas in the case of the natural-language analogs of quantifiers and variables, a particular kind of content is always indicated. McCawley's system associates each quantifier and variable with a common noun expression that specifies the domain of entities the variable ranges over. Thus, in McCawley's logic system, the two meanings of "all the alligators are in a bath" might be represented respectively as:

$\exists x$bath$\forall y$alligator(y is in x)
$\forall y$alligator$\exists x$bath(y is in x)

However, note that the quantifier and its associated noun expression is still outside the host proposition in McCawley's representations, and scope is controlled in much the same way as in standard logic. McCawley argued in favor of his system that it allows simpler derivations of surface structure than transformational grammar does. In terms of "naturalness,"

McCawley's system with domain-specific quantifiers is clearly preferable to standard logic.

However, there are several reasons for doubting that the syntax of thought always places quantifiers or quantified phrases outside the propositional nucleus and uses their order to control scope. First, if semantic representations universally place quantifiers outside their host propositions, then it becomes strange and mysterious that the typical surface structures of natural languages put the quantifiers inside propositions. For this reason, Jackendoff (1983) argued strongly in favor of placing quantifiers inside the proposition, in the NPs in which they appear in surface structure. Second, Ioup (1975) examined 14 languages and found no basis for a universal tendency for the left-most quantifier to have outside scope; even for English, Kurtzman and MacDonald (1993) found that the surface order of quantifiers has no consistent effect on scope. Although surface form often leaves scope ambiguous, lexical choice (e.g., *all* vs. *each, every* in English) frequently provides some guidance, as illustrated in the following pairs of sentences (due to Ioup, 1975), in which the preferred readings differ in the scope of the quantifier:

(a) I saw a picture of each child versus (b) I saw a picture of all the children.

(a) Ethel has a dress for every occasion versus (b) Ethel has a dress for all occasions.

Ioup reported that all the languages she examined had lexical expressions that tended to differentiate the scope of the quantifier in the same way as the English expressions. She proposed that the property is universal. These two facts—lexical differentiation within NPs and lack of a consistent effect of order—argue against underlying structures that use outside placement and order. Finally, one might reasonably expect that an innate feature of the syntax of thought would be manifest in early stages of language acquisition; yet outside placement has never been reported in children's early use of quantifiers.

It is possible to have a system that places quantifiers inside the host proposition but nevertheless uses domain-general quantifiers: The system of Rips (1994), borrowing from systems in use in artificial intelligence (AI), is essentially like that. However, naturalness argues for inside quantifiers that are domain specific, and we shall develop that possibility.

There are three other systems of representation that warrant comment. One is the level of logical form (LF) of the government-binding theory of linguistics (May, 1985): Quantifiers are placed outside their host sentences; binding is determined by the *c*-command relation and scope is not a matter of quantifier order. However, LF is not a level of semantic representation; rather, it presents a syntactic representation that is only a little deeper than surface structure (it is created from surface structure by raising quantifiers to positions outside the sentence nucleus). As such it cannot be a candidate for the syntax of thought. Also, LF is involved in the interpretation of S-structures, not their generation (in the sense that the rules that create LF representations map from S-structure into LF, not vice versa), and consequently it is not a level that could readily be implemented both as a point of departure for production and also as the endpoint of comprehension; in addition, it is not at all obvious how inference rules would be written for LF representations.

The second system is that of Sommers (1982). His system is an elaboration of Aristotelian and scholastic logic, and rejects the Frege–Russell line of treating quantifiers as variable-binding operators. Quantified NPs are treated as terms that can function as subjects of subject-predicate statements. Sommers' book provides a potentially rich fund of insights into the syntax and logic of natural language. However, unfortunately, I found crucial parts of it overly hard to understand, so that I do not feel I have a sufficient grasp of the whole to justify my discussing it. The third system is that of Rips (1994), mentioned earlier. This is the only system that shares our goal of developing a theory of reasoning of a predicate-logic sort. Although there is necessarily much concern with representation, Rips's system is primarily a system of reasoning, and as such, I discuss it in some detail later, when it can be contrasted with my proposals.

In general, I hope to present a system that makes all the distinctions that standard predicate logic makes, and does so while adhering much more closely to the linguistic form of natural languages than other systems do. The system proposed is deliberately strictly limited in the detail it seeks to represent. It is not intended as a complete system of semantic representation, and it leaves most of the structure of propositions unanalyzed. It only tries to represent those aspects of English structure that have to be captured by a system that is adequate to represent reasoning of a predicate logic sort, and makes no more semantic analysis than is strictly necessary for this purpose. In particular, I do not present representations for belief sentences, or for sentences containing other kinds of intensional predicates, nor shall I confront any of the issues surrounding such sentences: Predicate logic formalizes inferences and language that is purely extensional. Because people are able to carry out such reasoning, and that is what I seek to model, the system presented claims to capture only that part of human competence that is likewise extensional.

I begin with a brief discussion of what the logic is primarily used to reason about. Then the representational system is presented in detail, followed by the inference schemas and a description of a model reasoning program. I illustrate how the system works in solving problems, and then contrast it with Rips's (1994) system.

THE KINDS OF DOMAINS APPROPRIATE
TO A NATURAL PREDICATE LOGIC

Consider:

1. Cats have fur.
2. People have two legs.

It is a point familiar to philosophers that one cannot refute the first proposition by catching some cat and shaving off all its fur. The reason is that the proposition is more than just a simple empirical observation: It is not claiming that every cat, if observed, would be found to have fur; rather, it claims that having fur is somehow "natural" to cats. And one cannot refute the naturalness by abusing nature. Similarly, the existence of amputees does not refute Proposition 2. Now consider:

3. $\supset x$ (x is a cat $\supset$ x has fur)
4. $\supset x$ (x is a person $\supset$ x has two legs)

These make no claims about what is natural or essential to cats or people. Proposition 3 can therefore be refuted by exhibiting a shaven cat, and 4 is false because of the existence of amputees. So Proposition 3 does not have the same truth conditions as Proposition 1, nor 4 the same as 2. Hence 3 and 4 do not satisfactorily render 1 and 2 into logical notation.

Now consider:

5. All cats have fur.
6. All people have two legs.

Do these have a meaning corresponding to 1 and 2, or to 3 and 4? Most philosophers and logicians I have consulted favor 3 and 4; my own intuitions correspond more closely to 1 and 2; other informants have been divided or uncertain. It seems that they can be taken either way.

By contrast, let us consider:

7. All the cats have fur.
8. All the people have two legs.

Proposition 7 might refer to all the cats in Professor Smith's laboratory, and Proposition 8 to the people attending a certain social gathering. Proposition 7 is clearly false if Prof. Smith has had one of his cats shaved, and similarly, Proposition 8 is false if an amputee went to the gathering in question. So Propositions 7 and 8 have truth conditions that correspond well to those of 3 and 4. Hence, when we seek English translations or illustrations for such as 3 and 4, we should look to 7 and 8 in preference to 5 and 6, and certainly not to 1 and 2. By the same token, in trying to reconstruct mental predicate logic, it is primarily propositions such as 7 and 8 that we should wish the representational system to represent.

The point is that predicate logic is not primarily concerned with the properties of natural kinds, but with reasoning to and from statements about the relations and properties that happen to hold, often adventitiously, among objects or groups of objects that comprise the subsets of natural and artificial kinds usually relevant in specific discourse contexts. Thus, in the kinds of English statements with which we are concerned, the noun phrases representing sets will often contain the definite article— "all the Fs" rather than "all Fs." The force of the "the" is to indicate a subset of Fs, often one that is not stated in the discourse but is understood from its context. It is such context-determined discourse-relevant sets of objects with which mental predicate logic is primarily concerned.

THE REPRESENTATIONAL SYSTEM

Here I describe the representational system. I begin by illustrating its general nature, as it applies to simple propositions, first without, and then with, quantified arguments. Then the notation to be used in inference rules is introduced, illustrated through the rule of universal instantiation. Then I discuss, in turn, how the representational system handles each of a series of potential problems, developing the notation where necessary and commenting on parallels with natural language structure. The following are the major topics covered: (a) the distinction between predications where a plural argument functions as a group or collectivity (e.g., "The ants all built a nest") and those where the plural argument refers to individuals (e.g., "The boys all took a shower"—note that each boy took a shower, but each ant did not build a nest); (b) how differences in the scope of quantifiers and connectives are represented (e.g., "All the beads are opal or jade" could mean "all the beads are opal or all the beads are jade" or it could mean "each bead is either opal or jade"—I discuss how each sense is captured by the notation); (c) how common methods of composing complex arguments are represented—notably, those involving relative clauses, and those involving genitive phrases (e.g., "Mary's husband," "The mayor of New York"); (d) how the representational system represents indefinite (existentially quantified) arguments—how it captures differences in the scope of universally and existentially quantified arguments (e.g., consider the two senses of "All the alligators are in a bathtub"), and how it models the natural-language analogs of existential instantiation and generalization; (e) finally, the representation of negation and scope of negation is discussed.

Internal Structure of Propositions

Propositions may be simple or compound. Simple propositions contain no connectives. Compound propositions are formed by joining simple propositions with connectives. We use "NEG-," "&," "OR," and "IF-THEN" to represent the connectives of mental logic.

Simple propositions are analyzed into a predicate and arguments; the arguments may or may not be associated with quantifiers. In representing propositions, I shall put the predicate first in capital letters, followed by the argument or arguments in square brackets. Thus, *John is fat*, and *Mary loves Jane* would be rendered as:

FAT[John]
LOVE[Mary][Jane]

In general, for the sake of simplicity, I shall not represent tense or aspect in examples, and will exclude time arguments. In principle, every argument carries a thematic label, or is otherwise marked for its role in the predication (cf. Jackendoff, 1990). However, these role indications are omitted and ignored for the present because they play no role in the logic itself; they are important primarily for converting between the semantic representations of the logic and ordinary English.

Predicates may have one, two, or more places. The one-place predicates may be realized as nouns, adjectives, or intransitive verbs, and the two- and three-place predicates usually correspond to transitive verbs. There is a particular kind of predicate—almost always a one-place predicate—that will be called a *classifier*, because one of its characteristic uses is to identify the kind of the objects that serve as arguments in propositions. Thus, classifiers include basic objects (Rosch, Mervis, Gray, Johnson, & Boyes-Braem, 1976) and natural kind terms, and are typically realized as nouns.[4] I return to the formal nature of classifiers later.

Arguments may consist of single objects or a plurality of objects. They may be identified by name, or by a classifier predicate, which may be preceded by a quantifier, or they may be indicated in other ways described later. Thus, in argument positions in propositions, the notation allows names, and classifier predicates possibly preceded by a quantifier (as well as other forms described later). For instance, *All the boys like Jane* would be represented:

LIKE[All BOY][Jane]

---

[4]Gupta (1980) argues that common nouns differ from other kinds of predicates by providing a *principle of identity* for their extensions, thus specifying the domain over which quantifiers and variables range.

"BOY" is a classifier predicate used to indicate the kind of the entities that are asserted to like Jane, and "All" is a quantifier that indicates that each of the understood set of boys is asserted to like Jane.

In making reference to logical form, the letter "P" (or "P_1," "P_2," etc.) will be used to refer to an unspecified predicate; classifiers will be represented with the letters "F," "G," "H," etc. Thus, a notation like "P[All F][All G]" is a possible propositional form. A notation like "[All F]" ("the Fs," "all the Fs," "each F") indicates each of some specified (or understood) set of objects of the kind F. In accordance with what was said in the preceding section, it usually does not indicate all the entire natural kind. A representation like "P[All F][All G]" indicates that the predicate can be separately predicated of all objects in the argument sets; it corresponds to the standard logic formula "$\forall x \forall y((Fx \ \& \ Gy) \supset Pxy)$." For instance,

LIKE[All BOY][All GIRL]

"all the boys like all the girls" corresponds to the standard logic formula

$$\forall x \forall y((BOYx \ \& \ GIRLy) \supset LIKExy)$$

when this formula is taken over the relevant discourse-specific universe of boys and girls. In general, this interpretation is forced by the inference schemas, as will become clear later.

The notation also admits "$\subseteq$ [ ]" as a special kind of predicate form that contains a slot indicating a set of objects, the slot often being occupied by a classifier predicate, for example, "$\subseteq$ [G]" meaning "is a subset of the Gs," or "is one of the Gs" (if the subject argument is singular). Thus we admit propositional representations like "[F]sg $\subseteq$ [G]" ("sg" is "singular"), and "[All F] $\subseteq$ [G]." The latter representation corresponds to the standard predicate logic formula "$\forall x(Fx \supset Gx)$"; when "[F]" is singular, it becomes equivalent to "F ε [G]" (or "[F] $\subseteq$ [G]," where "[F]" is the unit class containing the indicated or understood F as sole member). This inclusion relation is discussed further later on.

Referring to Predicate-Argument Form in Inference Rules: The S-Notation

In standard logic, the rule of universal instantiation is sometimes stated as follows:

$$\forall x(\ldots x \ldots)$$

$$\ldots a \ldots$$

The notation "... x ..." in the numerator subsumes any condition on x within the scope of a universal quantifier, including compound conditions containing connectives in which x may occur repeatedly; a is to be substituted for all occurrences of x. (The entire expression, "$\forall$x(... x ...)," must not be within the scope of another operator.)

The notation "... ..." is clumsy. To refer to any condition on an object, X, we will write "S[X]," and similarly, to refer to any condition on each of a set of objects, X, we will write "S[All X]" (rather than "... [X] ..." or "... [All X] ..."). "X" is used as a variable ranging over objects serving as arguments, in cases where it is irrelevant how the object or objects are referred to (e.g., by name, classifier predicate, etc.) Thus, "S[All X]" indicates any proposition containing [All X] in one of its argument slots; the proposition may contain other arguments; it may also be compound, that is, contain connectives. Such cases are discussed later. There may also be negations within S, but "[All X]" must be outside the scope of any negation there may be in S. (Later, I discuss the representation of negation in detail, including how it affects the operation of instantiation rules.)

This notation is used to state inference schemas and is employed later in Table 11.3. (The organization and motivation behind the schemas of Table 11.3 is discussed later on.) For example, the instantiation rule (Table 11.3, Schema 8i) reads:

9. S[All X]; [α] $\subseteq$ [X] / S[α]

The notation "[α]" (or other early Greek letters "[β]", etc.) indicates an argument of whatever form that is not in the scope of a negation. The schema says that, given that α is one of the Xs, or a collection of objects that comprise a subset of the Xs, then the condition, S, on [All X], is a condition on [α]. For instance, given that all Farmer Smith's animals are in the large paddock, and that Jesse is one of his horses, it follows, with α = Jesse, that Jesse is in the large paddock; similarly, it follows, with α = all Farmer Smith's goats, that all Farmer Smith's goats are in the large paddock; given also that Farmer Smith owns lots of brown cows, it follows, with α = lots of brown cows, that lots of brown cows are in the large paddock.

Predications of Groups of Objects and Some Special Predicates

When a predication is made of a plurality of objects, the predicate may apply to each of the objects individually (as in the cases considered so far), or it may apply to the objects as a group. To illustrate the difference, consider the ambiguity of:

10. All the boys built a castle.

In Sense (a) each boy built a castle. In Sense (b) there is only one castle and "built a castle" is predicated of the boys as a group. If Tom is one of the boys, then one can infer "Tom built a castle" only if (a) is the intended sense. (In Sense (b), Tom did not build the castle himself; he merely helped build it.) For Sense (a), we will call the predicate an object predicate, because the predication applies to each object individually. For Sense (b) we will call the predicate a group predicate. Our logic is concerned with inferences that can be drawn in cases of Sense (a) and object predicates. There may be inferences to be drawn in cases of Sense (b) and group predicates, but they are not defined in the logic developed here. In general, inferences that are valid for object predications usually do not apply to arguments that are groups taken collectively. As a further example, consider:

11. The prosecutors convinced the members of the jury (e.g., of the defendant's guilt).

Here the prosecutors are a team and the jury members are individuals. If Tom is one of the prosecutors, we cannot infer "Tom convinced the members of the jury ..." (presumably, he merely helped); however, if Tom is a member of the jury, we can infer "The prosecutors convinced Tom of ..." Let us mark this difference in kind of argument with different kinds of brackets: I shall keep "[ ]" for ordinary arguments subject to the inference schemas, and mark arguments that are groups taken collectively by enclosing them in braces. Thus, Proposition 11 will be represented:

12. CONVINCE{PROSECUTORS}[All JURY MEMBER] . . .

Representation 12 is an instance of "S[All X]" for X = Jury members, but not for X = Prosecutors.[5]

There are some other noteworthy predications that apply to all members of a set, but are not instances of the form "S[All X]" and have special logical properties. Some relevant predicates are:

(i) Identity: "[F] = [G]" indicates that [F] and [G] are the same object, or the same collection of objects. Note that "= [G]" cannot be regarded

---

[5]In adopting the brace notation, and in the discussion here as well as earlier in connection with Sentence 10, I am in no wise attempting to take a stand on the ontological status of such collective arguments, for example, whether they are best analyzed as cases of plural reference, or in mereological terms (cf. Boolos, 1984; Lewis, 1991; Lowe, 1991).

as a condition on [F] that is subject to the instantiation schema, because if [α] is a subset of [F] one cannot use the schema to conclude that [α] = [G]! The properties of Identity are given by the fact that it is reflexive, symmetrical, and transitive.

(ii) Inclusion: "[α] ⊆ [G]." In our usage [α] may be either a single object or a collection of objects, so that, for instance, "[Tom] ⊆ [The fourth-grade boys]" and "[The boys in yellow jeans] ⊆ [The fourth-grade boys]" are equally well-formed usages of "⊆": The difference is merely one of singular versus plural and does not reflect an ontological difference. "[All F] ⊆ [G]" is a condition on [All F] that is subject to the instantiation schema (if [α] ⊆ [F] then [α] ⊆ [G]); but, as noted earlier, "[All F] ⊆ [G]" is not a condition on [G] subject to any schema: If [α] is a subset of [G], one cannot conclude anything about its relations to [F]. (That is, "[α] ⊆ [G]" is an instance of the form "S[α]," with "⊆ [G]" for "S," but it is not an instance of "S[G].")

It would be nice if there were a general way of characterizing those English structures that are instances of the form S[All X]. Unfortunately, as Sentence 11 illustrates, English syntax does not present a set of forms that consistently and uniquely indicate when the instantiation rule (9, earlier) is applicable: In Sentence 11, it is only one's knowledge of the roles of prosecutors and jury members in courtrooms that leads one to interpret "the prosecutors" as representing a team, and "the members of the jury" as a set of individuals who each have to be convinced. Nothing in the syntax of the English sentence forces this interpretation. Similarly, consider two sentences cited earlier "All the ants built a nest" and "All the boys took a shower." Nothing in the syntax signals the semantic difference, that if George (say) is one of the ants one cannot infer "George built a nest," whereas if George is one of the boys one can infer "George took a shower."

Relative Scopes of Quantifiers and the OR-Connective: The PRO Notation

There is a potential ambiguity in compound propositions in English. Suppose a factory makes dinner sets, and consider the following statement by the advertising manager about each dinner set: "The pieces all pass inspection or the factory discards them." This could mean that each piece passes inspection or the factory discards it, or it could mean that all the pieces of a set pass inspection or the factory discards the whole set. Or consider a simpler case: "The blocks on the table are green or they are blue." This could mean (a) that either all of the blocks are green or all of the blocks are blue; or it could mean (b) that every block is either green or blue. In standard logic, the difference is rendered by a difference in the relative scopes of the quantifier and the connective: (i) "$\forall x(x$ is a block $\supset x$ is green) v $\forall x(x$ is a block $\supset x$ is blue)" versus (ii) "$\forall x[x$ is a block $\supset (x$ is green v x is blue)]."

In the system proposed, Sense (i) is rendered by "GREEN [All BLOCK] OR BLUE [All BLOCK]." Sense (ii) is rendered by a new notation, "GREEN [All BLOCK] OR BLUE [PRO-All BLOCK]," in which "[PRO-All BLOCK]" is a kind of pronoun with "[All BLOCK]" as its antecedent. The difference between the two representations is parallel to that in English between "Every block is green or every block is blue" and "Every block is green or it is blue."

In general, corresponding to arguments [α], [β], etc., we allow the arguments [PRO-α], [PRO-β], and so on. These pro-forms cannot appear in a semantic representation unless their referents have antecedently been mentioned; the use of a pro-form indicates that the object or objects referred to are the same one or ones that the antecedent referred to. Thus, a pro-form is a cross-indexing device. The specific semantic consequences of the use of a pro-form are determined by the way the inference schemas operate. For instance, the instantiation schema (9, earlier) permits one to infer from the fact that something is true of members of a set [All X], that it is true of the members of any subset and of any individual object in the set. Thus, given "P[All X]," and that α is an X, we can substitute "α" for "All X" in "P[All X]," and infer "P[α]." It is required that any such substitution include all pro-forms, that is, if we substitute "α" for "All X," we must also substitute "α" in all pro-forms that have "All X" as their antecedent. Thus, from "P_1[All X] OR P_2[PRO-All X]" we can infer "P_1[α] OR P_2[PRO-α]," but not "P_1[α] OR P_2[PRO-All X]" (which is not well formed because "PRO-All X" lacks an antecedent), and not "P_1[All X] OR P_2[α]." However, in "P_1[All X] OR P_2[All X]" there is no pro-form, and so it would be valid to instantiate in each clause independently and infer "P_1[α] OR P_2[All X]" or "P_1[All X] OR P_2[α]."

Note that according to this analysis the ambiguity of "All the blocks are green or they are blue" is an ambiguity in the source of the pronoun "they." In one analysis (Sense ii), a pronoun is present in the semantic representation as well as in the surface structure. In the other analysis (Sense i), there is no pronoun in the semantic representation—both clauses have "[All BLOCK]"; the pronoun "they" is substituted for the second "[All BLOCK]" in the realization of the semantic representation in surface structure.

A reader may wonder why a pro-form is necessary to capture Sense (ii). Why not allow connectives to be used to concatenate predicates, and thus permit representations like "GREEN-OR-BLUE [All BLOCK]"? After

all, such representations would be quite parallel to English surface structures such as "All the blocks are green or blue." Complex predicates such
as "GREEN-OR-BLUE" would offer a sufficient solution if English had
only one-place predicates. However, it does not offer a method of representing propositions such as "The pieces all pass inspection or the factory
discards them," cited earlier, or "All the cars have stickers or the police
tow them away"—the latter is a warning not to park in a certain parking
lot in which each car has to have a sticker or the police tow it away.[6] The
pro-form provides a natural representation in such cases, for example:

13. HAVE[All CAR][Some STICKER\CAR] OR TOW-AWAY[PO-
    LICE][PRO-All CAR].

(The representation of "Stickers" as "[Some STICKER\CAR]" is not relevant here; it is explained later.) Similarly, Sense (ii) of "The pieces all pass
inspection or the factory discards them" could be represented:

14. PASS-INSPECTION[All PIECE] OR DISCARD[FACTORY][PRO-
    All PIECE]

as opposed to Sense (i):

15. PASS-INSPECTION[All PIECE] OR DISCARD[FACTORY][All
    PIECE].

As a device for indicating the relative scopes of quantifiers and connectives in English, we believe that this notation using pro-forms is
superior to competing methods. As against both standard predicate logic
and McCawley's (1981/1993) system with domain-restricted quantifiers,
but like English, it does not indicate scope by parentheses. As against
both standard and Polish notations, it does not require a quantifier to be
analyzed as belonging to some constituent remote from the noun phrase
in which it occurs in the surface structure. As against the method of
Montague (1973), it provides two representations, one for each sense,
whereas Montague distinguishes the two senses in terms of derivational
history.

---

[6]Complex predicates like "GREEN-OR-BLUE," "GREEN-&-SQUARE," etc. are not
banned from the representational system. They could be introduced as abbreviatory
conventions or rules, applying when the component predicates (J, K, say) are monadic, for
example, "J-OR-K[All X]" for "J[All X] OR K[PRO-All X]"; "J-&-K[All X]" for "J[All X] &
K[PRO-All X]"

Composition of Arguments

So far we have considered three ways of representing arguments: by
name, with a classifier predicate, and by cross-reference back to a prior
identification. Natural languages have other methods of composing or
specifying arguments. Three such methods appear to be universal or
nearly universal, and therefore should be available in our representational
system. These three specify arguments by using, respectively, iteration,
relative clauses, and genitive phrases (e.g., using the preposition *of* in
English: "the mayor of New York"). I now discuss how these methods
are captured in the representational system.

(i) Iteration is represented by "+," for example, [F + G], [Tom + Dick
+ Harry], [All the fourth-grade boys + Susan], etc. "+" generally goes into
English as "and."

(ii) Relativization is represented by ":". In universally quantified
arguments, the general form is "[All F: S[PRO]]," which means "all the
Fs such that they (each) satisfy the condition, S," or more simply, "the Fs
that satisfy the condition, S." (The notation is extended to indefinite,
existentially quantified arguments later.) The colon corresponds to the
wh-morpheme in English relative clauses (or to "such that"), and the
pro-form indicates the argument slot in S on which relativization occurs
(i.e., which role the pro-form for All F plays in the relative clause). S itself
may be a compound proposition, as it can in other uses of the S-notation.
(Strictly, to accord with the previous use of the PRO-notation, we should
adjoin the antecedent to "PRO," that is, write "All F: S[PRO-All F]" rather
than "All F: S[PRO]." However, within relative clauses, the antecedent of
PRO is always clear, and so it will be omitted there.)

The relativization process can be repeated. That is, in principle one
could get notations such as "[((All F: S_1[PRO]): S_2[PRO]) . . .]." However,
in any such repeated relativizations, all colons except the first are con-
vertible into &'s, that is, "[All F: S_1[PRO] & S_2[PRO] & . . .]." This equivalence can be expressed by a rule (see Table 11.3, Rule 28, a truism). Because
conditions represented by S can be compound, a notation of the form
"All F: S_1[PRO] & S_2[PRO] & . . ." is an instance of the form "All X: S[PRO]"
for the purpose of applying inference schemas.

A sentence like "My chair is blue" can be paraphrased (albeit clumsily)
as "My chair is a thing that is blue"; similarly, using a relative clause in
the same way, "Our cat killed a mouse last night" can be paraphrased as
"Our cat is an animal that killed a mouse last night." The effect of such
a paraphrase is to convert a sentence that appears to have the form of a
predication ("My chair is blue") into a sentence that appears to express

an inclusion relation ("My chair is a thing that is blue"). In the latter sentence the verb phrase has the form of a classifier noun ("thing, person, animal, etc.") followed by a relative clause. I use C_α as a general expression for any classifier of an object or set of objects α. Then one can write the following paraphrase rule that converts a predication into an inclusion statement, and vice versa (cf. Table 11.3, Schema 20iii):

16. $S[\alpha] \equiv [\alpha] \subseteq [C_\alpha: S[\text{PRO}]]$.

If α = all the boys, C_α = children, and S = wore sandals, then Formula 16 would state that if all the boys wore sandals then all the boys are included among the children who wore sandals, and vice versa. Thus, if we are told (a) that all the children who wore sandals went paddling in the ocean, and learn (b) that all the boys wore sandals, then we can infer that all the boys went paddling in the ocean: The paraphrase of (b) offered by Formula 16 enables the inclusion clause of the instantiation schema (9, earlier) to be satisfied, yielding the inference.

(iii) Genitive phrases use a two-place classifier with an embedded genitive argument. Consider NPs like "Mary's husband," "the mayor of New York," "the author of Wuthering Heights." In each case the head noun (*husband, mayor, author*) is a two-place predicate. The referent of the NP is one of the predicate's arguments; the other is the entity identified by the possessive or the phrase following *of* (*Mary, New York, Wuthering Heights*). I refer to the latter as the *genitive* argument and call the former the *subject* argument. Thus, nouns that are diadic predicates always have a subject and a genitive argument; the subject argument is the one directly labeled by the noun; the genitive argument can readily be left implicit or understood. The mention of the genitive argument in these phrases contributes to identifying the referent of the whole NP much as a relative clause does. Indeed, it would be possible to analyze this kind of NP semantically as a special case of relativization, for instance, to analyze "Mary's husband" as "the man who is husband to Mary" ([MAN: HUSBAND[PRO][Mary]]), "the mayor of New York" as "the person who is mayor of New York" ([PERSON: MAYOR[PRO][New York]]), and so on. However, the fact that NPs containing genitives are extremely common across languages and invariably present a syntactic structure very different from that of relative clauses suggests that they should receive a different analysis.

Formally, we can analyze the head noun as a function whose value is the subject argument and whose argument is the genitive. Thus, nouns such as *mayor, husband,* and *author* are two-place predicates (MAYOR[s][g], HUSBAND[s][g], and so on. I use *s* for the subject and *g* for the genitive argument) that give rise to functions (MAYOR<g>, HUSBAND<g>, etc.; I use angle brackets for the argument of a function); the functions deliver as their value the subject of the corresponding two-place predicate, and thereby specify it and the referent of the whole NP. Within propositions the functions have argument status—the relevant argument in the proposition is the value of the function. Consequently, if F[s][g] is a two-place noun and F<g> is the corresponding function, then:

$$S[F<g>] \equiv F[s][g] \ \& \ S[s].$$

Thus, "Mary's husband loves Jane" would be rendered

LOVE[HUSBAND<Mary>][Jane]

and it would entail, for the husband, h, in question:

HUSBAND[h][Mary] & LOVE[h][Jane].

Now that two-place nouns as predicates have been specified as corresponding to one-place functions when they indicate propositional arguments, one can similarly recognize the usual one-place nouns as corresponding to zero-place functions when they indicate propositional arguments. However, that requires no change in notation and no reformulation of anything previously stated.[7]

Indefinite Arguments

"[All F]" indicates all F or each F. English has many other quantifiers—*an F, some F, some of the Fs, many of the Fs, a few of the Fs,* and so on. These are all indefinite in that they do not indicate specifically which Fs are being referred to. I discuss only one indefinite quantifier in detail—*Some.* The others possess some of the properties of *some*: What is true of *many F, a few F* is necessarily true of *some F* (though obviously not vice versa). In inference rules where it is desirable to mark that an inference holds regardless of which quantifier is involved, the notation "[q F]" will be used to indicate a set identification preceded by a quantifier, without a specific quantifier being identified. (The use of the notation is illustrated later.)

---

[7]There are undoubtedly many other uses of functions in the syntax of thought. For instance, in a locative phrase such as *on the bed*, the preposition *on* can be analyzed as a function that maps an object (the bed) into a place (on the bed) (cf. Jackendoff, 1990). However, we need not enter into such analyses for the purposes of this chapter.

In this section, I present first how the indefinite *some* quantifier is represented, and how differences in the scope of it and a universal quantifier are rendered. Then existence statements are considered, and finally, I discuss how the representational system models natural-language analogs of existential instantiation and generalization.

The Notations "[Some F]" and "[Some F\G]." The notation "[Some F]" is used to indicate a particular F whose identity is not specified. Similarly, "[Some F: S[PRO]]" indicates some unspecified F that satisfies the condition S (not necessarily the only F that satisfies the condition). The notation is used only for arguments. Thus, "S[Some F]" says that some unspecified F (or Fs) satisfies the condition, S. "[Some F]pl" indicates some particular Fs whose identity and number are not specified except that there is more than one of them. However, most of the present discussion will focus on indefinite arguments that are not specifically marked as plural. Of course, "S[Some F]$_{pl}$" entails "S[Some F]," though the converse does not hold. That is, plural subscripts can be deleted freely, but not added.

Now, imagine a group of boys playing at a beach, and consider the following two pairs of sentences:

17. The boys hid behind a cabin, *or* All the boys hid behind a cabin.
18. The boys hid behind cabins, *or* Each boy hid behind a cabin.

The sentences of 17 have the preferential reading that the boys all hid behind the same cabin. (I think they are actually ambiguous, but my consultants were reluctant to admit the other reading according to which, as in 18, each boy hid behind a cabin.) The sentences of 17 in their preferred reading can be represented by[8]:

19. HID-BEHIND[All BOY][Some CABIN]

The sentences of 18 entail that for each boy there was a cabin that he hid behind (not normally the same cabin, as in 17). That is, each boy hid behind [Some CABIN], but the cabins are distributed among the boys. When some unspecified objects from a set F (say) are distributed among the objects of another set G, the indefinite set will be represented by the notation "[Some F\G]." Thus, the preferred reading of the sentences of 18 will receive the semantic representation:

---

[8]Here, the group reading of *all* and the narrow-scope interpretation amount to the same thing.

20. HID-BEHIND[All BOY][Some CABIN\BOY].

In the case of a three-place predicate, an indefinite set might be distributed over both of two other sets, or only over one of them, or over neither. Suppose a three-place predicate, "P," with [All F] and [All G] as two of the arguments. An indefinite [Some H] as the third argument might not be distributed over either F or G ("P[All F][All G][Some H]"); or it might be distributed over both, in which case the notation "[Some H\F, G]" will be used (i.e., "P[All F][All G][Some H\F, G]"), or it might be distributed over one but not the other. Imagine a group of boys and girls passing messages to each other. The messages may be the same or different. The representation

21. GIVE[All GIRL][All BOY][Some MESSAGE\BOY, GIRL]

could be rendered as:

22. The girls all gave messages to all the boys.

The representation

23. GIVE[All GIRL][All BOY][Some MESSAGE\GIRL]

would indicate that each girl had a message to give (presumptively not each girl the same message), and each girl gave her message, whatever it was, to all the boys. (Thus, if Mary was one of the girls, Mary gave the same message to all the boys.) Sentence 24, although ambiguous, would have this representation as its preferred interpretation:

24. Every girl gave a message to all the boys.

In general, it seems that in English surface structure the use of an indefinite plural ("messages," "cabins"), in a sentence containing a plural noun with *all*, often indicates that the indefinite has the broadest possible distribution (i.e., corresponds in standard logic to an existential quantifier with narrowest scope).

The difference between these indefinites (i.e., those of 17 and 19 vs. 18 and 20) has to be taken into account in applying the universal instantiation schema. The schema (Schema 8 of Table 11.3) can apply straightforwardly to 17 and 19, in which the indefinite argument is simple (i.e., undistributed): Given that Tom is one of the boys, we can substitute "Tom" for "The boys" and infer "Tom hid behind a cabin." However, there is an apparent problem when the schema is applied to a sentence containing a distributed indefinite argument expressed by a plural as in "All the boys hid behind cabins" of 18. The same substitution would at first sight yield "Tom hid behind cabins," which is wrong, because the correct inference is again "Tom hid behind a cabin." The problem is only apparent.

Let us consider the operation of the instantiation schema in more detail for the case when S contains an indefinite argument distributed over X, that is, when "S[All X]" has the form "S[All X][Some F\X]." Consider two cases, first, when [α] is plural, and second, when it is singular. When [α] is plural, the schema will rewrite "S[All X][Some F\X]" as "S[α][Some F\α]." For instance, let "α" represent "the tall boys"; then from Sentence 18 and Representation 20 the schema will correctly yield "The tall boys hid behind cabins" with the representation "HID-BEHIND[All TALL BOY][Some CABIN\TALL BOY]." When α is Tom, and therefore singular, the schema yields "HID-BEHIND[Tom][Some CABIN\Tom]." This inference is also correct. Note that "[Some CABIN\Tom]" refers to a particular cabin associated with Tom, and is therefore singular; consequently its surface-structure realization will be "a cabin" not "cabins." In general, a representation of the form "[Some F\α]" is equivalent to simple "[Some F]" when α is singular, that is, "α" can be deleted from "[Some F\α]" when it is singular. So "[Some CABIN\Tom]" reduces to "[Some CABIN]."

Existential Statements and Existential Entailments of Indefinite Arguments. The notation "E[Some F]" "there exists some F," "there is an F" is taken to mean that the set F contains one or more objects. If "[Some F]" is marked as plural, then the set contains two or more objects. Thus, existence is not treated as a quantifier, but is taken as a one-place predicate predicated of an argument of the type [Some X]. The colon-notation for relative clauses is allowed in existence statements, for example, "E[Some F: S[PRO]]" "there is an F that satisfies the condition S."

From "Tom hid behind a cabin" we can infer that there was a cabin that he hid behind; and similarly, from the preferred reading of the sentences of 17, we can infer that there was a cabin that the boys hid behind. More generally, from "S[Some X]" we can infer "E[Some X: S[PRO]]."[9] And of course, conversely, given E[Some X: S[PRO]], it follows that S[Some X]. That is, a two-way paraphrase rule holds (cf. Table 11.3, Schema 16). Note that, although each can be inferred from the other, "Tom hid behind a cabin" and "There was a cabin that Tom hid behind" receive different representations.

---

[9]Recall that intensional predicates are not analyzed here. Obviously, "George dreamed of a unicorn" will be analyzed so that it does not contain "[Some UNICORN]" as argument of *dream* (perhaps along the lines of "George dreamed he saw a unicorn," where [Some UNICORN] is an argument of *see*, not of *dream*, and so the existence of real unicorns is not entailed, merely of dreamed-of ones).

Referring Back to Indefinite Arguments: Analogs of Existential Instantiation. Standard logic has a procedure, called *existential instantiation,* which is sometimes (cf. Quine, 1962) given as:

25. ∃x(. . . x . . .)

    . . . a . . .

"a" is a new name that is arbitrarily given to an object whose existence is guaranteed by the existential statement. It is as if we said "There is such an object; let it be called 'a.' " A somewhat analogous procedure can occur in English discourse. Given sentences like those of 17, we may want later in the discourse to refer again to the indefinite argument. We would normally do so by a pronoun or definite noun phrase, for example, "it" or "the cabin." A sequence like ". . . some cabin . . . the cabin . . . it . . ." has some analogies to the sequence "∃x(. . . x . . .)," followed by ". . . a . . ." occurring in a logical argument. That is, "the cabin" and "it" serve in the English sequence as discourse names for an object previously introduced into the discourse, whose identity is not specified beyond the fact that it is "some cabin."

This repeated reference back to an indefinite argument often plays an important role in reasoning. Consider, for example, a reasoning problem from a standard symbolic logic text (Copi, 1967, chap. 5). The problem has three premises:

(i)   Everything on my desk is a masterpiece.
(ii) Everyone who writes a masterpiece is a genius.
(iii) Someone obscure wrote a novel on my desk.

The problem asks us to consider whether it follows that some obscure person is a genius. A participant who solved this problem reported his reasoning as follows:

> Since the novel is on my desk it is a masterpiece. Since someone obscure wrote it they wrote a masterpiece. Since it [i.e., premise (ii)] says that everyone who writes a masterpiece is a genius, the obscure person must be a genius. So some obscure person is a genius.

Note that *the novel* in the subject's first sentence must be understood as having as antecedent *a novel on my desk* (that some obscure person wrote). The first part of the reasoning bears on the status of this novel, that is, that it is a masterpiece. In the subject's second sentence we find *they,* and in the next sentence the phrase *the obscure person*; both these

TABLE 11.1
The Masterpiece Problem

Premises

1. "Everything on my desk is a masterpiece."
    MASTERPIECE[THINGS: ON-DESK[PRO]]
2. "Everyone who writes a masterpiece is a genius."
    GENIUS[PERSONS: WRITE[PRO][Some MASTERPIECE]]
3. "Someone obscure wrote a novel on my desk."
    WRITE[Some PERSON: OBSCURE[PRO]][Some NOVEL: ON-DESK[PRO]]

Question/Conclusion

"Is some obscure person a genius?"
    GENIUS[Some PERSON: OBSCURE[PRO]]?

Reasoning

"Since the novel is on my desk, it's a masterpiece"

4. [PRO-Some NOVEL: ON-DESK[PRO]] ⊆ [THINGS: ON-DESK[PRO]] (Schemas 24, 20iii)
5. ∴ MASTERPIECE[PRO-Some NOVEL: ON-DESK[PRO]] (1, 4, Schema 8i)

"Since someone obscure wrote it, they wrote a masterpiece"

6. WRITE[Some PERSON: OBSCURE[PRO]][PRO-Some NOVEL: ON DESK[PRO]]
    (premise 3)
7. ∴ WRITE[PRO-Some PERSON: OBSCURE[PRO]][Some MASTERPIECE] (6, 5,
    Schema 11)

"So the obscure person is a genius"

8. ∴ GENIUS[PRO-Some PERSON: OBSCURE[PRO]] (2, 7 Schema 8i)

"And so some obscure person is a genius"

9. ∴ GENIUS[Some PERSON: OBSCURE[PRO]] (8, Schema 25, Schema 11)
QED

---

must be understood as referring back to the indefinite argument *someone obscure* (who wrote a novel on my desk).[10]

This use of definite noun phrases and pronouns to refer back to indefinite arguments raises a problem for the representational system as it has been developed so far. The system can represent premise (iii) satisfactorily as "WROTE[Some PERSON: OBSCURE[PRO]] [Some NOVEL: ON-MY-DESK[PRO]]." However, we do not yet have a satisfactory representation for *the novel* in the subject's sentence. We cannot simply refer to it by repeating the argument that is its antecedent, "[Some NOVEL: ON-MY-DESK[PRO]]," because the notation contains nothing to indicate that the *same* novel is being referred to. Instead, some sort of pro-form is required that will have the indefinite argument as its antecedent. The notation "[PRO-Some X]" will be used for this purpose to refer back to an antecedent "[Some X]." We illustrate the use of this notation to solve the masterpiece problem in Table 11.1. The details of

---

[10]Here, *they* is the third person singular pronoun of indeterminate sex that is very common in spoken English, although frowned upon by American copyeditors.

the reasoning are discussed later on, after the set of inference schemas have been discussed.

This notation (using a pro-form with an indefinite argument as antecedent) provides a natural solution to a well-known difficulty in rendering English sentences into logical notation. The following two sentences illustrate the difficulty:

26. If there are any unicorns, they have horns
27. (In a certain box) If there is a bead, it is blue

Consider the following three attempts to translate Sentence 26 into standard logical notation:

28. IF $\exists xUx$ THEN Hx. (U = unicorn and H = has a horn.)
29. $\forall x(IF\ Ux\ THEN\ Hx)$
30. IF $\exists xUx$ THEN $\forall x(IF\ Ux\ THEN\ Hx)$.

Formula 28 is closest to the form of the English sentence, but it is not well formed because "Hx" is outside the scope of the existential quantifier. Formula 29 would be a reasonable rendering of "All unicorns have horns," but that does not mean the same thing as 26. Formula 30 is a defensible rendering of the meaning of 26, but its syntactic structure is so far from that of the English sentence that it is not a promising candidate if one seeks a representation with a good fit to the structure of natural languages. However, our notation provides a nearly perfect match to the English structure of 26 and 27:

31. IF E[Some U]$_{pl}$ THEN H[PRO-Some U]$_{pl}$
32. IF E[Some BEAD] THEN BLUE[PRO-Some BEAD].

An analogous treatment applies to so-called donkey anaphora (cf. Chierchia & McConnell-Ginet, 1990, p. 133). Thus, "Every farmer who owns a donkey beats it" is represented by:

BEAT [All FARMER: OWN[PRO][Some DONKEY]] [PRO-Some DONKEY]

The representation provides a good match to English surface structure.

No rule of existential instantiation is included in the logic proposed. That is because, intuitively, the use of a pronoun to refer back to an indefinite argument does not qualify as "inference." It seems that the speaker of a language is free at any time to introduce an anaphor to refer back to any argument that is not in the scope of a negation. However, it could be argued that some sort of procedure, rule, or convention is needed to license this freedom, and in that case, the following is proposed:

$$S[\alpha] \ / \ S[PRO\text{-}\alpha],$$

where α is any argument that is not in the scope of a negation (and, in this case only, not itself a pro-form).[11]

Inferring that S[Some X]: The Analog of Existential Generalization. The inference schema that permits inferences to statements that contain indefinite arguments is the following:

$$S[\alpha]; [\alpha] \subseteq [X] \ / \ S[Some \ X].$$

(This is Schema 11 of Table 11.3.) If "$[\alpha]$" is plural, then "[Some X]" can be plural, that is, the conclusion is "$S[Some \ X]_{pl}$." As before, the notation "$[\alpha]$" indicates an argument of whatever form that is not in the scope of a negation. Thus, $[\alpha]$ may indicate some members of a set, a few of them, many of them, all of them, or α may be a name or a PRO-form, it does not matter; provided $[\alpha] \subseteq [X]$, then the condition S will hold of some X.[12]

The use of the schema is illustrated in the last step of the subject's solution of the masterpiece problem, cited earlier. The subject says "... the obscure person is a genius. So some obscure person is a genius." Because "the obscure person" ($[\alpha]$) is included in "obscure people" (X), the schema legitimizes the move from "the obscure person" to "some obscure person"—the latter is singular because the obscure person is presumptively singular.

The Representation of Negation

Negation is symbolized by "NEG." Only simple propositions can be negated by a sentence element such as the English "not"; to negate a compound proposition, one must embed the compound proposition in a frame that negates it as a whole (e.g., "It is not the case that ... ," or "It is not true that ... ," using the predicate "true" which takes propositions as its argument). Thus, "NEG" realized as "not" (and translation equivalents in other languages) always takes narrow scope with respect to connectives.

---

[11]The selection of the pro-form would be constrained by the GB binding principles, whatever their ultimate form.

[12]Note that this means that "S[All X]" cannot be true vacuously, that is, when there are no X in the universe of discourse.

We may note that the term *scope* makes sense primarily with respect to a system of notation—like standard predicate logic—that uses parentheses: "in the scope of" and "outside the scope of" refer to positions inside or outside a pair of parentheses. The purpose of speaking of scope is to provide a mechanism for defining inferences that can be made—instantiations in the case at hand. A notation that makes little use of parentheses must find other devices to indicate the arguments that can be instantiated.

In English, a plural noun phrase that realizes an argument may be either inside or outside the scope of NEG. For example, consider:

33. Mary does not like the boys in the class.

If Tom is one of the boys, we can infer that Mary does not like Tom. Hence, the phrase "the boys in the class" must be outside the scope of the negation, that is, one can instantiate it. However, consider now:

34. Mary does not like all the boys in the class.

We cannot infer that she does not like Tom. Hence the phrase "all the boys in the class" is inside the scope of the negation. In general, it appears that unmodified definite plural noun phrases that realize arguments ("the so-and-so's") are almost always outside the scope of negations, whereas the use of "all" or "every" in a negative sentence ("Mary does not like every boy," "The girls don't all like Tom," etc.) is a signal that the argument set is included in the negation. Of course, the reason why an unadorned definite noun phrase is taken as outside the scope of a negation is because it is usually an anaphor: It indicates that the argument set is the same as some previously mentioned set, and because that set is outside the scope of the negation, the anaphor is also, unless there is some specific indication to the contrary.

It seems that English usually attaches the negative element to the predicate word, and has cues available that can convey whether or not the argument sets are within the scope of the negation, that is, whether or not one can instantiate. The representation proposed here operates the same way. "NEG" is attached to the predicate, and arguments that are within the scope of the negation are marked as such by placing a tilde each side of them. For example, the notation "NEG P[All F][~All G~]" indicates that "[All G]" is within the scope of NEG and that "[All F]" is outside it. Thus, "NEG P[All F][~All G~]" indicates that each of the Fs—each one taken separately—is not in the relation, P, to all the Gs; if X is an F and Y is a G, we can substitute "X" for "F" and infer "NEG P[X][~All G~]," but we cannot substitute "Y" for "G" because it may well not be the case that NEG P[All

F][Y]. Thus, from "NEG LIKE [All GIRL][All BOY]" "The girls don't like the boys," we can infer that Mary does not like Tom; from "NEG-LIKE [All GIRL][~All BOY~]" "the girls don't like all the boys," we can infer that she does not like all the boys (but not how she feels about Tom); and from "NEG-LIKE [~All GIRL~][~All BOY~]" "not every girl likes every boy" or "the girls don't all like all the boys," we can infer nothing about either Mary or Tom. Thus tildes around an argument-set label serve as a signal that a subset or member cannot be substituted for it. For definite singular arguments, such as Mary and Tom, it makes no difference in either meaning or truth value whether they are taken as inside or outside a negation. However, it simplifies the statement of inferences if they are left unmarked for negative scope, a decision that is tantamount to always taking them as outside the scope of a negation.

Now let us consider indefinite arguments. Let us assume that indefinite arguments are marked as inside or outside the scope of a negation in the same way as universally quantified arguments—"[Some X]" outside and "[~Some X~]" inside. Consider such arguments first with respect to our analog of existential instantiation. Again, the argument that is outside the scope of the negation can be instantiated; that is, given an argument "[Some X]," one has a license to create an anaphor "[PRO-Some X]" that refers back to it. Of course, one cannot create any such anaphor given "[~Some X~]" because that denies the existence of any such X. For example, given "NEG LIKE[Some BOY: IN-THE-CLASS[PRO]][Mary]" "a boy in the class doesn't like Mary," the boy exists so we can refer to him—as "he" or "the boy" in English, as "[PRO-Some BOY: . . .]" in the system proposed.

Indefinite arguments within the scope of a negation ("[~Some X~]") go into English as "no," "none," "not . . . any," and there are analogous locutions in many other languages (e.g., "ne . . . aucun" in French, "lo . . . shum" in Hebrew). Thus, languages tend to distinguish sharply in their surface structure between indefinite arguments that are eligible for existential instantiation and those that are not. An indefinite argument ("[~Some . . .~]") inside a negation is equivalent to a universally quantified argument outside one (in standard logic, $\sim\exists x Fx \equiv \forall x \sim Fx$). It is, therefore, subject to a kind of universal instantiation that is the same as that which the universally quantified argument permits. For instance, given "Mary doesn't like any of the boys in the class," and that Tom is one of the boys, one can infer "Mary does not like Tom." (This form of inference will be called *negative instantiation*—it is Schema 8ii of Table 11.3.) It is the same inference that can be made from Sentence 33, as discussed earlier. Indeed, English "not . . . any" (and parallel locutions in other languages) seem to correspond almost equally well to a universally quantified argument outside a negation and to an indefinite argument inside one. For example, "Mary doesn't like any of the boys" seems to render both of the following:

35. NEG LIKE [Mary][~Some BOY~]   (~∃b[Mary likes b])
36. NEG LIKE [Mary][All BOY]   (∀b~[Mary likes b])

In support of Representation 35, one may note that "Mary doesn't like any of the boys" is a direct contradiction of "Mary likes one of the boys," just as 35 directly contradicts "LIKE [Mary][Some BOY]." In support of Representation 36, one may note that after having said "Mary doesn't like any of the boys," one could add an explanation like "They are too aggressive"; in the latter sentence the pronoun "they" ("[PRO-All BOY]") has an antecedent only if we take 36 as the representation. The equivalence of these two representations is specified by a paraphrase rule:

37. NEG S[~Some X~] ≡ NEG S[All X]

(Rule 37 is Schema 23i in Table 11.3.) In English, semantic representations containing either of the forms in Rule 37 will be realized by locutions like "not . . . any," "No," "None," "Not . . . a single," etc. These locutions are the usual way of realizing both semantic representations, and they are the only way of realizing "NEG S[~Some X~]." (There is an alternative way of realizing "NEG S[All X]" in which "[All X]" is realized by an anaphor.) Thus, a listener who seeks to understand an utterance containing locutions like "not . . . any" is free to map it onto either of the representations in Rule 37.

In sum, in the interaction of universally quantified and indefinite arguments with negation, there are three main notations to consider: (a) "[~Some X~]," and "[All X]" outside the scope of the negation, which permit universal (negative) instantiation; (b) "[Some X]" outside the scope of the negation, which permits existential instantiation; and (c) "[~All X~]"—a universally quantified argument within the scope of a negation, from which nothing follows directly, and which may serve mainly the discourse function of denying the possibility of universal instantiation. (There is also the case where an indefinite argument is in the scope of another argument as well as negation. Then, neither existential nor negative instantiation is possible—Sentence 10 of Table 11.2 provides an example.)

There appear to be three main kinds of structural factors in English surface structure that are relevant to determining the scope of a negation in ordinary discourse. First, unless specifically marked to the contrary, anaphors are outside the scope of a negation and open to instantiation.

Second, there are specific locutions that reflect each of the three semantic representations discussed earlier: (a) "no," "none," "not . . . any," etc., that cue negative instantiation; (b) "some" (as well as other cues that interact with the third kind of factor, discussed later) that warrant existential instantiation; and (c) "not" combined with "all" or "every," which denies universal instantiation.

TABLE 11.2

Possible Combinations of Two Quantifiers and a Negation in Standard Logic, Their Usual Semantic Representation in the System Proposed, and Possible Exemplifying English Realizations

1. $\sim\forall g\forall b(g$ likes b)	NEG LIKE[~All G~][~All B~]	Not every girl likes every boy; The girls don't all like all the boys
2. $\exists g\sim\forall b(g$ likes b)	NEG LIKE[Some G][~All B~]	Some girl doesn't like all the boys
3. $\exists g\exists b\sim(g$ likes b)	NEG LIKE[Some G][Some B]	One of the girls doesn't like one of the boys
4. $\sim\exists g\forall b(g$ likes b)	NEG LIKE[~Some G~][~All B~]	
5. $\forall g\sim\forall b(g$ likes b)	NEG LIKE[All G][~All B~]	None of the girls likes every boy
6. $\forall g\exists b\sim(g$ likes b)	NEG LIKE[All G][Some B/G]	Every girl dislikes some boy or other
7. $\sim\exists g\exists b(g$ likes b)	NEG LIKE[~Some G~][~Some B~	No girl likes any of the boys
8. $\forall g\sim\exists b(g$ likes b)	NEG LIKE[All G][~Some B~]	
9. $\forall g\forall b\sim(g$ likes b)	NEG LIKE[All G][All B]	
10. $\sim\forall g\exists b(g$ likes b)	NEG LIKE[~All G~][~Some B/G~]	Not every girl likes a boy; The girls don't all like boys
11. $\exists g\sim\exists b(g$ likes b)	NEG LIKE[Some G][~Some B~]	One of the girls doesn't like any of the boys
12. $\exists g\forall b\sim(g$ likes b)	NEG LIKE[Some G][All B]	

Note. The universe of discourse is a fourth-grade class in a certain school. G = girl; B = boy; $\exists b = \exists b(b$ is a boy & . . .); $\forall g = \forall g(g$ is a girl $\supset$ . . .). The examples are presented in triads (1 to 3, 4 to 6, etc.) with logically equivalent standard logic representations (given a non-empty universe).

303

The third kind of factor is sentence position: Other things being equal, a later element is in the scope of an earlier element.[13] For example, the sequence "all . . . not" tends to be ambiguous as to scope, whereas "not . . . all" is clear; the sequence "a . . . not" warrants existential instantiation, whereas "not . . . a" is likely to be interpreted like "not . . . any." However, there are special locutions that can override the order cue, for example, "a particular" usually warrants existential instantiation, even when it follows some other scope-taking element and "some" may be awkward (e.g., "all the boys like a particular girl," "none of the boys like a particular girl"). Of course, foregrounding, clefting, and topicalization are methods of manipulating sentence position that introduce natural language analogs of parentheses (e.g., "there's a girl that none of the boys like"—"E[Some GIRL: NEG LIKE[~Some BOY~][PRO]]" in the notation proposed). Table 11.2 illustrates how these kinds of cues interact. It exemplifies the different possible combinations of negation with two quantifiers, in standard logic, in the notation proposed, and in English surface structure. Thus, Sentences 1, 2, 4 to 5, and 10 illustrate how the use of *all* and *every* in a negative context is a cue that blocks universal instantiation. Sentences 4 to 5, 7 to 9, and 11 to 12 illustrate the use of *no, none, not any* to cue the possibility of negative instantiation. In the case of 2, 3, and 11 to 12, note that the use of *some, one of the* indicates an argument that can be existentially instantiated, for example, that can be referred to later by a pronoun, such as *he* or *she*.

THE INFERENCE SCHEMAS

We begin by contrasting reasoning in standard predicate logic with ordinary reasoning in English. When standard predicate logic is formulated with inference schemas, the set of schemas consists of the schemas of propositional logic augmented with just four additional schemas—universal and existential instantiation, and universal and existential generalization. The instantiation schemas are rules for eliminating quantifiers from statements, and the generalization schemas provide rules for introducing quantifiers into statements that lack them. A chain of reasoning in standard predicate logic has a typical form with three stages: One begins by using the instantiation schemas to obtain statements without quantifiers; then one reasons using propositional logic schemas; finally, one uses the generalization schemas to regain the quantifiers.

In contrast, ordinary reasoning rarely seems to present these three stages. Let us take an example problem and compare the reasoning on it

---

[13]However, there are constructions in which this is not the case, even in English (Kurtzman & MacDonald, 1993), and it appears not to be a universal tendency (Ioup, 1975).

in standard predicate logic and in English. Suppose we are given as premise "All the cars in the lot are Toyotas or Hondas" and are asked whether it follows that the cars that are not Toyotas are Hondas. Let C = car in the lot, T = Toyota, and H = Honda. Consider standard predicate logic first. The premise is:

$\forall x(Cx \supset Tx \ v \ Hx)$

We first eliminate the quantifier by instantiating. Taking *a* as an arbitrary object, we obtain:

$Ca \supset Ta \ v \ Ha$

We then suppose "Ca," and infer "Ta v Ha" by the propositional schema modus ponens. Next, we suppose "~Ta," whence "Ha" follows (by the propositional schema, $p \ v \ q$, $\sim p$ /∴q). Thus, we have shown that "Ha" follows from the two suppositions, "Ca" and "~Ta," that is:

$Ca \ \& \ \sim Ta \supset Ha$

We then apply the universal generalization schema to obtain:

$\forall x(Cx \ \& \ \sim Tx \supset Hx)$

That is, any car in the lot that is not a Toyota is a Honda.

Ordinary reasoning in English reaches the same conclusion, but appears to reach it in a single step. That is, the conclusion, that cars in the lot that are not Toyotas are Hondas, seems to follow immediately from the premise; the intermediate steps of instantiation, propositional reasoning, and generalization appear to be absent. This fact suggests that the ordinary human reasoner has an inference schema that carries from the premise to the conclusion in a single step, presumably by collapsing all three steps into one. Using the notation developed, we can formulate the schema as follows:

38. S_1[All X] OR S_2[PRO-All X] / S_2[All X: NEG S_1[PRO]]

(This is Schema 3ii of Table 11.3.) Substituting into it the terms of the premise of the cited problem, we obtain:

T[All C] OR H[PRO-All C] / H[All C: NEG T[PRO]].

The left-hand side is the problem premise and the right-hand side the problem conclusion.

Schema 38 is closely related to the propositional schema:

p OR q; NEG-p / q

(See Table 11.3, Schema 3.) This propositional schema has a possible alternative form that is normally valid:

TABLE 11.3
Schemas of the Proposed Mental Predicate Logic

For each schema, the propositional-logic version, if there is one, is stated first, then the corresponding predicate-logic version in bold type, sometimes with possible alternative or additional forms. Premises are given first, followed by "/", followed by the conclusion entailed. In the case of bidirectional inferences and paraphrases "≡" replaces "/." After each schema, its status in the reasoning program is indicated: Core, Feeder, or Indirect. Core schemas apply whenever the subjects or argument terms of the premises present sets to which they can apply, or when there is a topic set that fulfills the indicated role. Feeder schemas apply when they enable a core inference to be made or a conclusion to be matched or contradicted. (See The Direct Reasoning Routine and the text discussion of the reasoning program for further details.)

Alongside several schemas there is a parallel schema that interchanges the roles of S_1 and S_2, for example, alongside #2 the parallel schema would have the conclusion "$S_1[q\ X]$." The parallel schemas are obvious and are omitted for the sake of compactness. (In the final version of the logic "&" and "OR" will be treated as n-ary rather than binary, as in prior versions of the propositional logic, and only one schema will be necessary. I have kept to the binary versions of "&" and "OR" for readability.)

Notation. "$S[$All $X]$" means that the X or Xs all satisfy the condition S. "[Some $X]$" indicates some unspecified X or Xs. "[α]" indicates an argument of any form whatever that is not in the scope of a negation. "[q $X]$" means X modified by any quantifier, for example, *all, each, many, few, some,* etc. (but not *no, none, not any*); "[q $X]$" includes pro-forms with quantified antecedents (e.g., "[PRO-All $X]$," "[PRO-Some $X]$").

"[PRO-α]" is a pro-form whose antecedent is α. "$S_1[$All $X]$ OR $S_2[$PRO-All $X]$" means that each X is either S_1 or S_2; "$S_1[$Some $X]$ & $S_2[$PRO-Some $X]$" means that some X or Xs are S_1 and the same X or Xs are also S_2. Read "[All X: S[PRO]]" as "all the Xs that are such that they satisfy S," that is, "the Xs that are S."

"F" and "C_x" represent classifier predicates.
"E[. . .]" means "There exists [. . .]."
Read "[X] ⊆ [Y]," where [X] is singular, as "X is a Y."

In "NEG S[All $X]$" [All X] is outside the scope of the negation. "[~. . .~]" means that "[. . .]" is inside the scope of a negation, for example, "NEG S[~All X~]" means "it is not the case that all the Xs are S"; similarly, "NEG S[~Some X~]" means that no Xs are S ("it is not the case that some X is S"), as opposed to "NEG S[Some $X]$" "Some X is not S." Thus NEG S[Some X] ≡ NEG S[~All X~].

(Continued)

TABLE 11.3
(Continued)

Primary Schemas

1. p; q / p & q *(Feeder)*

   S$_1$[All X]; S$_2$[All X] / S$_1$[All X] & S$_2$[PRO-All X] *(Feeder)*

   The boys wore blue jeans; The girls played with the boys / The boys wore blue jeans and the girls played with them.

Note. The conclusion can be realized in surface structure in various ways. In particular, "[PRO-All X]" is usually not realized when "[All X]" and "[PRO-All X]" would occupy the same argument position in surface structure; instead, the predicates are conjoined, for example, "The boys wore blue jeans and were played with by the girls."

2. p & q / p *(Feeder)*

   S$_1$[q X] & S$_2$[PRO-q X] / S$_2$[q X] *(Feeder)*

   Many of the boys wore blue jeans and the girls played with them / The girls played with many of the boys.

3. p OR q; NEG p / q *(Core)*

   (i) **S$_1$[All X] OR S$_2$[PRO-All X]; NEG S$_2$[α]; [α] ⊆ [X] / S$_1$[α]** *(Core; [α] may be Topic)*

   (ii) **S$_1$[All X] OR S$_2$[PRO-All X] / S$_2$[All X: NEG S$_1$[PRO]])** *(Requires E[Some X: NEG S$_1$[PRO]])* *(Feeder)*

   (i) The boys either played with girls or fought with girls; Tom and Dick did not play with girls / Tom and Dick fought with girls.

   (ii) The boys either played with girls or fought with girls / The boys who did not play with girls fought with girls.

4. NEG (p & q); p / NEG q *(Core)*

   (i) **NEG E[~Some X: S$_1$[PRO] & S$_2$[PRO]~]; S$_2$[α]; [α] ⊆ [X] / NEG S$_1$[α]** *(Core; [α] may be Topic)*

   (ii) **NEG (S$_1$[All X] & S$_2$[PRO-All X]) / NEG S$_2$[All X: S$_1$[PRO]]** *(Requires E[Some X: S$_1$[PRO]])* *(Feeder)*

   (i) There were no boys who wore sandals and blue jeans; The boys that played with Mary wore blue jeans / The boys that played with Mary did not wear sandals.

   (ii) The boys did not wear sandals with blue jeans / The boys that wore blue jeans did not wear sandals.

5. IF p OR q THEN r; p / r *(Core)*

   No predicate logic schema that directly corresponds. See note following Schema 17.

6. p OR q; IF p THEN r; IF q THEN r / r *(Core)*

   S$_1$[All X] OR S$_2$[PRO-All X]; S$_3$[All X: S$_1$[PRO]]; S$_3$[All X: S$_2$[PRO]] / S$_3$[All X] *(Core)*

   All the cars in the lot have stickers or the guards tow them away; The cars that have stickers are Toyotas; The cars that the guards tow away are Toyotas / All the cars in the lot are Toyotas.

7. p OR q; IF p THEN r; IF q THEN s / r OR s *(Core)*

   S$_1$[All X] OR S$_2$[PRO-All X]; S$_3$[All X: S$_1$[PRO]]; S$_4$[All X: S$_2$[PRO]] / S$_3$[All X] OR S$_4$[PRO-All X] *(Core)*

   The cars in the lot have stickers or the guards tow them away; The cars that have stickers are Datsuns; The cars that the guards tow away are Toyotas / The cars in the lot are all Toyotas or Datsuns.

8. IF p THEN q; p / q (Modus Ponens) *(Core)*

   (i) **S[X]; [α] ⊆ [X] / S[α]** *(Core; [α] may be Topic)*

   (ii) **NEG S[~Some X~]; [α] ⊆ [X] / NEG S[α]** *(Core; [α] may be Topic)*

   (i) The girls all wore red jeans / The girls in sneakers wore red jeans.

   (ii) None of the boys wore striped shirts / Sam and Harry did not wear striped shirts.

Note. Version (ii) is referred to in the text as Negative Instantiation.

TABLE 11.3

(Continued)

9. Given a chain of reasoning of the form:
   Suppose p
   - - -
   - - -
   q
   One can conclude: IF p THEN q *(Normally Indirect)*
   Given a chain of reasoning of the form:
   Suppose S$_1$[Some X]
   - - -
   - - -
   S$_2$[PRO-Some X]
   One can conclude: S$_2$[Any X: S$_1$[PRO]] *(Indirect)*

Notes. (i) The propositional schema is the Schema for Conditional Proof. (ii) The Preliminary Procedure of the Direct Reasoning Routine (Table 3) incorporates a routine use of this schema. (iii) The predicate-logic schema applies only for languages with a quantifier like English *any*.

10. No propositional logic version.
    (i) S[Any X]; E[Some X: S[PRO]] / S[All X] *(Core)*
    (ii) If S$_1$[Some X] then S$_2$[PRO-Some X]; E[Some X: S$_1$[PRO]] / S$_2$[All X: S$_1$[PRO]] *(Core)*
    (i) Any child in sandals wore a spotted shirt; one or more children wore sandals / All the children in sandals wore spotted shirts.
    (ii) If a child wore sandals they wore a spotted shirt; one or more children wore sandals / All the children in sandals wore spotted shirts.

Note. Schema 10 corresponds to Universal Generalization of standard predicate logic. Version (i) would not be applicable for languages without a quantifier like English *any*. For languages like English one might call the predicate-logic version of Schema 9 "Any-Introduction" and this schema "Any-Elimination."

11. No propositional logic version.
    S[α]; [α] ⊆ [X] / S[Some X] *(Feeder)*
    Many of the girls in spotted shirts wore red jeans / Some of the girls wore red jeans.
    All the girls played with boys in green jeans / All the girls played with children in green jeans.

Note. Corresponds to Existential Generalization of standard logic.

Primary schemas concerning the logic of negation and incompatibility:

12. NEG (NEG p) ≡ p *(Core from left to right, feeder from right to left)*

Notes. (i) Although formally a paraphrase schema, it almost always operates from left to right. (ii) For simple propositions NEG is realized in surface structure by verb negation, for compound propositions by *It is false (not true) that . . . .* (iii) No predicate-logic schema is needed that is additional to the propositional schema. Some pertinent double-negative cancellations are managed as follows: NEG (NEG S[Some X]) is assumed to be mapped by Rule 23(ii) to NEG (NEG S[~All X~]) and then the propositional rule converts it to S[X] (e.g., "It is not true that some of the boys did not play with Susan" is paraphrased to "It is not true that not all the boys played with Susan" and then converted by the propositional schema to "All the boys played with Susan").

13. p; NEG p / INCOMPATIBLE *(Core)*
    (i) S[All X]; NEG S[q X] / INCOMPATIBLE *(Core)*
    (ii) S[q X]; NEG S[All X] / INCOMPATIBLE *(Core)*
    (i) The boys are all wearing sneakers; Some of the boys are not wearing sneakers / INCOMPATIBLE.
    (ii) Some of the boys are wearing sneakers; None of the boys are wearing sneakers / INCOMPATIBLE

TABLE 11.3
(Continued)

14. p OR q; NEG p & NEG q / INCOMPATIBLE *(Core)*
    (i) S_1[All X] OR S_2[PRO-All X]; NEG S_1[q X] & NEG S_2[PRO-q X] / INCOMPATIBLE
        (Core)
    (ii) S_1[q X] OR S_2[PRO-q X]; NEG S_1[All X] & NEG S_2[All X] / INCOMPATIBLE
        (Core)
    (i) The cars all had stickers or the guards towed them away; Some of the cars did not
        have stickers and the guards did not tow them away / INCOMPATIBLE.
    (ii) One of the boys wore a striped or a spotted shirt; None of the boys wore a striped
        shirt and none wore a spotted shirt / INCOMPATIBLE.
15. Given a chain of reasoning of the form:
    Suppose p
    - - -
    - - -
    INCOMPATIBLE
    One can conclude: NEG p *(Normally Indirect)*
    Notes. (i) The Evaluation Procedure of the Direct Reasoning Routine (Table 11.4) incorpo-
    rates an automatic use of this schema to generate a response of "False." (ii) There is no
    predicate logic analog.

Paraphrases and Truisms

16. No propositional logic version.
    S[Some X] ≡ E[Some X: S[PRO]] *(Feeder)*
    Some of the girls wore red jeans ≡ There were girls in red jeans.
17. No propositional logic version.
    $S[q_1 X + q_2 Y] ≡ S[q_1 X]$ & $S[q_2 Y]$ *(Feeder)*
    Jane and Sara as well as many of the girls in red jeans played with boys / Jane and
    Sara played with boys and many of the girls in red jeans did too.
    Notes. (i) q_1 and q_2 may be the same quantifier. (ii) This schema could be regarded as a
    predicate-logic version of Propositional Schemas 5 and 6, in that these jointly guarantee the
    equivalence IF p OR q THEN r ≡ IF p THEN r & IF q THEN r, which generalizes to the
    schema given.
18. No propositional logic version.
    [Z] = [X + Y] ≡ [All Z] ⊆ [X] OR [PRO-All Z] ⊆ [Y] *(Feeder)*
    Children comprise boys and girls ≡ Every child is a boy or a girl.
    Note. This schema with Schema 13 defines the relation of the set connective "+" to
    propositional & and OR. This schema also serves the propositional logic as an
    OR-Introduction schema.
19. No propositional logic version.
    S_1[Some X] & S_2[PRO-Some X] ≡ S_1[Some X: S_2[PRO]] ≡ S_2[Some X: S_1[PRO]] *(Feeder)*
    A girl wore green jeans and she played with John ≡ A girl who played with John wore
    green jeans ≡ A girl in green jeans played with John.
20. No propositional logic version.
    (i) F[α] ≡ [α] ⊆ [F] *(Feeder)*
    (ii) F[α] & S[α] ≡ [α] ⊆ [F: S[PRO]] *(Feeder)*
    (iii) S[α] ≡ [α] ⊆ [$C_α$: S[PRO]]
    (i) "The children in sneakers are girls" illustrates both representations.
    (ii) The children in sneakers were girls and they played with John ≡ The children in
        sneakers were girls who played with John.
    (iii) Some big blocks are square ≡ some big blocks are included among the blocks that
        are square.

(Continued)

TABLE 11.3
(Continued)

---

21. No propositional logic version.
    [X: S[PRO] = [X] ≡ S[All X]
    The boys in sandals were all the boys there were ≡ All the boys wore sandals.
22. NEG (p OR q) ≡ NEG p & NEG q *(Feeder)*
    NEG (S₁[q X] OR S₂[PRO-q X]) ≡ NEG S₁[q X] & NEG S₂[PRO-q X] *(Feeder)*
    Many of the girls did not wear sandals nor did they wear sneakers ≡ Many of the girls
    did not wear sandals and they did not wear sneakers.
Note. NEG (p or q) would have a typical surface realization as *neither . . . nor.*
23. No propositional logic version.
    (i) **NEG S[All X] ≡ NEG S[~Some X~]** *(Feeder)*
    (ii) **NEG S[Some X] ≡ NEG S[~All X~]** *(Feeder)*
    (i) "None of the girls wore sneakers" illustrates both representations.
    (ii) Some of the girls did not wear sneakers ≡ Not all of the girls wore sneakers.
Truisms (Axioms)
24. **S[q X: S[PRO]]**
25. **[q X: S[PRO]] ⊆ [X]**
26. **[q X] ⊆ [X + Y]**
27. **[q X] ⊆ [C_x]**
28. **[((X: S₁[PRO]): S₂[PRO]): S₃[PRO] . . .] = [X: S₁[PRO] & S₂[PRO] & S₃[PRO] & . . .]**

---

39. p OR q / IF NEG-p THEN q

Schema 38 is the universal closure of 39, in the following sense: If we were to take the left-hand side of 38 and instantiate in the normal manner of standard predicate logic, we would obtain an expression such as "S₁a OR S₂a"; 39 could be applied to this expression to obtain "IF NEG S₁a THEN S₂a"; applying universal generalization, and then rendering the result in the notation developed earlier, we would obtain the right-hand side of 38. Thus Schema 38 can be considered a predicate-logic version of 39. In the same way, it can be anticipated that most propositional logic schemas will have predicate logic versions.

Table 11.3 presents the inference schemas proposed for mental predicate logic, together with the propositional logic schemas that have been presented and discussed in prior work (see earlier chapters). Schemas 1 to 9, 12 to 15, and 22 are propositional logic schemas; most of these have predicate logic versions that are presented alongside the propositional versions. In each case the propositional logic version is presented first; below it the predicate logic version is presented in bold type, and then an example of the predicate logic version of the inference is given. Sometimes there appear to be two candidate predicate logic versions, and in that case both are given and illustrated. Some of the schemas are followed by comments.

The other schemas exist only in predicate logic versions. Schema 11 provides for existential generalization. Schemas 12 to 15 are the primary schemas that specify the logic of negation: Schema 12 cancels a double negative, 13 and 14 define incompatibility, and 15 licenses reductio ad absurdum arguments.

Schemas 9 and 10 are the schemas that correspond most directly to universal generalization of standard logic. (Most cases where universal generalization would be used in reasoning in standard logic would not involve Schema 10; rather, the predicate logic versions of Schemas 1 to 9 would be used, which, as discussed earlier, can be viewed as implicitly incorporating a generalization step.) The universal generalization schemas in standard logic restrict the terms permitted in a derivation, holding that when "Pa" can be derived from a set of premises, one can conclude $(\forall x)(Px)$, so long as "a" does not occur in any of the premises nor in P. This restriction precludes information about some particular individual erroneously leading to an inference about all cases. Similarly, Schemas 9 and 10 should preclude arguments of the following sort: *Suppose someone enters the room; he is wearing a green shirt; therefore, anyone entering the room is wearing a green shirt.* There are two reasons that this argument does not follow. First, "he" in the second premise may not refer back to "someone" in the first premise, for example, referring to some observed person rather than to the supposed person; second, even if "he" does refer to the same "someone," no reason has been given for this supposed someone to be wearing a green shirt, and thus the requisite line of reasoning under the supposition is missing.

The remaining schemas are paraphrase rules or truisms (statement forms that are always true and can be introduced into a line of reasoning at any time). Schema 16 specifies the existential status of indefinite arguments. Schemas 17 and 18 relate the set connective "+" to propositional & and OR; 18 is of some formal interest because, applied in a left-to-right direction, it serves the propositional logic as an OR-introduction schema. (There are no OR-introduction schemas in the mental propositional logic proposed in chap. 6, although there are complex ways of deriving OR-statements.) Schemas 19 to 21 specify some equivalences that follow directly from the notation, and Schemas 22 and 23 define important paraphrase relations involving negation. The remaining five are truisms whose substitution instances are necessarily true. In general, the function of most of the paraphrases and truisms is to spell out consequences of the notation; the main function of some of them (20, and 25 to 27) is to provide for translation between predicational and inclusion statements.

Each schema in Table 11.3 is associated with a status (Core, Feeder, Indirect—shown in italics after the schema on the same line). Statuses refer to conditions of access during reasoning, and are discussed later, when the proposed reasoning program (Table 11.4) is presented.

It must be stressed that logical economy, per se, is not an important goal of the theory. Table 11.3 aims to specify the repertory of inferences

TABLE 11.4
The Direct Reasoning Routine

The routine applies in three situations—where there is a conclusion given whose truth is to be evaluated, where there is a topic set (which may consist of a single object) about which the reasoner is seeking to make inferences, and where no conclusion is given and no topic set is specified (i.e., when subjects are just making inferences without a specific goal). In the latter two cases the Preliminary Procedure and the Evaluation Procedure are inapplicable.

When there is a conclusion to be evaluated, the routine begins with the Preliminary Procedure before proceeding to the Inference Procedure. When no conclusion is given, the routine starts with the Inference Procedure. The routine terminates when the conclusion is evaluated, or when no new propositions are generated by the Inference Procedure, or when the reasoner is unwilling to expend further effort (see discussion in the text of how variation in effort affects the operation of the Routine).

Preliminary Procedure

    (i) If the given conclusion is an *if-then* statement, add the antecedent to the premise set,[a] and treat the consequent as the conclusion to be tested.

    (ii) Use the Evaluation Procedure to test the conclusion (the given conclusion or the new one created at Step [i]) against the premise set. If the evaluation is indeterminate, proceed to the Inference Procedure.

Inference Procedure

Apply each Core schema whose conditions of application[b] are satisfied, or whose conditions of application can be satisfied by first applying one or a combination of Feeder schemas. If there is a topic object or set, apply any Core schema whose conditions of application are satisfied with that object or set as topic.[b] Add the information deduced to the premise set. Repeat the procedure, except that when there is a conclusion to be evaluated, first use the Evaluation Procedure to test the conclusion against the premise set; if the outcome of the evaluation is indeterminate, then repeat the Inference Procedure. (In executing the procedure, no schema is applied whose only effect would be to duplicate a proposition already in the premise set.) In reading out conclusions inferred, one-time use of Feeder schemas is optional.[c]

Evaluation Procedure

To test a conclusion against a premise set, respond *True* if the conclusion is in the premise set or can be generated from it by applying one or a combination of the Feeder schemas; respond *False* if the conclusion, or an inference from it by Schema 2, is incompatible (by Schemas 13 or 14) with a proposition in the premise set, or with a proposition that can be generated from the premise set by applying one or a combination of Feeder schemas.

Determination of the Topic Object or Set

If a topic set is given, it is the topic. If no topic is given but there is a conclusion to be evaluated, then the set mentioned in the subject noun phrase of the conclusion is the topic. (In the case of reasoning in a discourse environment with non-arbitrary content, a topic set may be selected on pragmatic grounds, i.e., the reasoner will select an entity as topic that the discourse environment suggests it would be useful to know more about.)

(Continued)

TABLE 11.4

(Continued)

If the Inference Procedure fails to generate sufficient inferences to solve a problem, then a resourceful reasoner may select a secondary topic, and re-enter the Inference procedure with this secondary topic as topic. The choice of a secondary topic is made on a strategic basis.[d]

---

[a]The *premise set* at any point comprises the original premises together with any propositions that have been added by the Preliminary and Inference Procedures.

[b]In general, the conditions of application of a schema are satisfied when the premise set contains propositions of the form specified in the numerator of the schema; to apply the schema is to deduce (generate) the corresponding proposition of the form specified in the denominator of the schema. Core schemas apply whenever propositions in the premise set present argument terms to which they can apply; core schemas also apply when there is a topic object or set that fulfills the argument role indicated for the topic in the description of the schema in Table 11.3.

Schemas that are equivalences are applicable when part (or all) of a proposition in the premise set matches the form specified on one of the sides of the equivalence; application consists in substituting the proposition of the indicated form for the matching part.

[c]For example, if propositions *a* and *b* are inferred independently, it is optional to use Schema 1 and to read these out as *a & b*. Similarly, if *Not all the X's are F* is inferred (NEG F[~X~]), it is optional to use Schema 23(ii) and read this out as *Some X is not F* (NEG F[Some X]).

[d]Rules or heuristics for selecting a secondary topic are not part of the Direct Reasoning Routine, but belong to the strategic component of the program. See the text, however, for some examples of reasoning that include use of a secondary topic, and for a strategy for choosing one that is very useful for solving Aristotelian syllogisms.

commonly available to adults in reasoning: Each schema claims to define an inference that is typically made in a single step. Note that there is a good deal of logical redundancy among the schemas, that is, there are many cases where one schema could be logically derived from others. For example, 3i could be derived from 3ii feeding 8i; similarly, the predicate logic version of Schema 13 and all versions of Schema 14 could be derived from the propositional version of 13, together with the paraphrases provided by Schemas 22 and 23. In such cases the table claims that the inference is typically made in a single step by subjects in reasoning, for example, that inferences of the form of 3i are immediate (i.e., made in a single step) and are not made in two steps (first by applying 3ii and then 8i). The elementariness of the predicate logic inference forms in the table is currently based largely on protocol data from subjects solving inference problems and is open to revision in future work. Methods not based on protocol data are also available for settling rival claims about the elementariness of schemas empirically (see chaps. 7 and 8).

The use of the schemas in reasoning is illustrated in Table 11.1, which presents the *masterpiece problem*, discussed earlier and discussed again later on. It shows the problem premises, both in English and in the representation system developed, followed by the reasoning that leads to the conclusion that answers the problem. The reasoning steps defined by the schemas are shown in the representational system, and are presented alongside the reasoning in English, which is taken from the subject's protocol presented earlier. Table 11.5 presents six simple problems from a set used in current work (see chap. 12); the premises and the predicted solutions are shown in parallel versions, in English and in the representational system. Table 11.6 presents a further illustrative problem taken, like the masterpiece problem, from Copi (1967); here the English versions are taken from a subject's protocol. We discuss the details of the reasoning on all these problems later, after the reasoning program has been presented.

A TENTATIVE REASONING PROGRAM

Inference schemas define a basic set of possible reasoning steps. However, reasoning also requires procedures that select from the set of possibilities the one that is used at each point in the chain of reasoning, that is, a reasoning program or programs. In thinking about the nature of subjects' procedures for reasoning of a predicate logic sort, I follow as far as possible the model provided by the propositional logic reasoning program. This modeled how adult subjects draw inferences in propositional reasoning. This propositional program has two parts, a routine part and a strategic part. The routine part is claimed to be common to essentially all adult subjects. It was called the *direct reasoning routine* (see earlier chapters); it proceeds by matching schemas against the form of propositions in the premise set, applying any schemas that can be applied (excluding schemas that introduce suppositions and with restrictions to prevent infinite loops); each inference drawn is added back into the premise set, and then the procedure reapplies. The operation of the direct reasoning routine is automatic in the sense that it is largely unaffected by the reasoner's goals, for example, the inferences made are much the same regardless of whether the problem presents a conclusion to be evaluated or not. It is claimed that the direct reasoning routine is available to essentially everyone: It is used in comprehension of text and discourse (see chap. 5), and is the first facility used in reasoning of a more formal sort (and, in unsophisticated reasoners, it may be the only logical reasoning facility brought to bear). The strategic part of the program (chaps. 6 and 7) is much less automatic; it consists of reasoning strategies that are sensitive to goals (and may set goals) and which come into operation when the direct reasoning routine fails to solve a problem. We suggested that the strategic parts of subjects' programs are variable from one subject to another, and that the variability contributes to individual differences

TABLE 11.5

Some Sample Problems With the Solution Steps, in English and in the Representational System

First Problem

1. All the beads are blue or green	BL[All BD] OR GR[PRO-All BD][a]
2. The blue beads are plastic	PL[All BD: BL[PRO]]
3. The green beads are plastic	PL[All BD: GR[PRO]]
4. ? Some of the beads are not plastic?	NEG PL[Some BD]?
5. All the beads are plastic	PL[All BD] (1, 2, 3, Sch 6)
6. False	INCOMPATIBLE (4, 5, Sch 13)

Second Problem

1. There are no green triangular beads	NEG E[~Some Beads: GR[PRO] & TR[PRO]~]
2. The wooden beads are green	GR[All BD: WOOD[PRO]]
3. ? The wooden beads are green and not triangular?	GR[All BD: WOOD[PRO]] & NEG TR[PRO-Beads: WOOD[PRO]]?
4. The wooden beads are not triangular	NEG TR[All BD: WOOD[PRO]] (1, 2, Sch 4i)
5. The wooden beads are green and not triangular	GR[All BD: WOOD[PRO]] & NEG TR[PRO-All BD: WOOD[PRO]] (2, 4, Sch 1)
6. True	

Third Problem

1. All the beads are metal or wooden	ME[All BD] OR WOOD[PRO-All BD]
2. The triangular beads are blue and not wooden	BL[All BD: TR[PRO]] & NEG WOOD[PRO-All BD: TR[PRO]]
3. ? The triangular beads are blue metal ones?	BL[All BD: TR[PRO]] & ME[PRO-All BD: TR[PRO]]?
4. The triangular beads are blue	BL[All BD: TR[PRO]] (2, Sch 2)
5. The triangular beads are not wooden	NEG WOOD[All BD: TR[PRO]] (2, Sch 2)
6. The triangular beads are metal	ME[All BD: TR[PRO]] (1, 5, Sch 3i)
7. The triangular beads are blue and metal	BL[All BD: TR[PRO]] & ME[PRO-All BD: TR[PRO]] (4, 6, Sch 1)
8. True	

(Continued)

315

TABLE 11.5
(Continued)

Fourth Problem

1. All the beads are plastic or wooden	PL[All BD] OR WOOD[PRO-All BD]
2. The wooden beads are red	RE[All BD: WOOD[PRO]]
3. The plastic beads are blue	BL[All BD: PL[PRO]]
4. Some of the beads are round	RO[Some BD]
5. ? The round beads are not red and not blue?	NEG RE[All BD: RO[PRO]] & NEG BL[PRO-All BD: RO[PRO]]?
6. All the beads are red or blue	RE[All BD] OR BL[PRO-All BD] (1, 2, 3, Sch 7)
7. The round beads are red or blue	RE[All BD: RO[PRO]] OR BL[PRO-All BD: RO[PRO]] (6, Sch 8i, "the round beads" as topic)
8. False	INCOMPATIBLE (5, 7, Sch 14i)

Fifth Problem

1. The plastic beads are blue or green	BL[All BD: PL[PRO]] OR GR[PRO-All BD:PL[PRO]]
2. None of the beads are blue	NEG BL[All BD]
3. ? Some of the beads are green?	GR[Some Beads]?
4. The plastic beads are not blue	NEG BL[All BD: PL[PRO]] (2, Sch 8ii)
5. The plastic beads are green	GR[All BD: PL[PRO]] (1, 4, Sch 3i)
6. Some of the beads are green	GR[Some Beads] (5, Sch 11)
7. True	

Sixth Problem

1. All the beads are blue or red	BL[All BD] OR RE[PRO-All BD]
2. There are no blue square beads	NEG E[~Some Beads: BL[PRO] & SQ[PRO]~]
3. ? Some of the beads that are not red are square?	SQ[Some Beads: NEG RE[PRO]]?
4. The beads that are not red are blue	BL[All BD: NEG RE[PRO]] (1, Sch 3ii, "beads that are not red" as topic)
5. The beads that are not red are not square	NEG SQ[All BD: NEG RE[PRO]] (2, 4, Sch 4i)
6. False	INCOMPATIBLE (3, 5, Sch 13)

Notes. aBD = beads; BL = blue; GR = green; PL = plastic, etc.

TABLE 11.6
The Radioactive Substances Problem

Premises

(1) "All radioactive substances have a short life or have medical value."
   SH-L[All R] OR MED-V[PRO-All R]
(2) "No uranium isotope that is radioactive has a short life."
   NEG SH-L[~Some U: R[PRO]~]

Question/Conclusion

"If all uranium isotopes are radioactive, do they all have medical value?"
IF R[All U] THEN MED-V[All U] ?

Reasoning

"Assuming all uranium isotopes are radioactive, +
   (3) R[All U] (Added to premise assumptions)
then uranium isotopes that are radioactive constitute all uranium isotopes."
   (4) [U] = [U: R[PRO]] (3, Schema 21)
"So uranium isotopes don't have short lives."
   (5) NEG SH-L[All U] (2, 4, Schema 8 ii)
"Since radioactive substances either have a short life or have medical value, and uranium isotopes are radioactive and don't have short lives, uranium isotopes must have medical value."
   (6) MED-V[All U] (1, 5, 3, Schema 3 i)
"Thus, if all uranium isotopes are radioactive, then they all have medical value."
IF R[All U] THEN MED-V[All U] (Schema 9—CP).

---

in reasoning skill. The possible strategies were not as fully worked out as the direct reasoning routine.

The program now proposed expands the direct reasoning routine of the propositional model to include reasoning of a predicate-logic sort. Apart from some discussion and illustration of the notion of a secondary topic later, I make no proposals concerning the strategic part that go beyond those of earlier chapters. Only relatively unsophisticated reasoning of a predicate-logic sort is modeled by the direct reasoning routine. In its application to reasoning of a predicate-logic sort, the routine is not now based on extensive data, and is presented as a tentative hypothesis about the nature of the processes involved.

The propositional program applied in two kinds of experimental situations. In one, the reasoner had to evaluate a presented statement as true or false given certain premises; the other kind of situation was open-ended—subjects were asked what followed from the premises, that is, to write down all that they inferred from the premises, putting the inferences down in the order in which they had been made. For reasoning of a predicate-logic sort, there is an additional kind of situation that seems intuitively important to consider: A problem or situation can define a "topic set" or "topic object" about whose properties the reasoner is asked to make inferences. Thus, a problem could present a set of premises, together with a question of the form, "What can you infer about the F(s)?," where "the F(s)" constitute an object or set of objects about which an inference could be made. The program (Table 11.4) posits that when subjects are given a conclusion to evaluate, any set mentioned in the subject NP of the conclusion is routinely taken as topic. In general, the program proposed provides procedures that make certain inferences routinely, given premises alone without any topic to make inferences about or conclusions to evaluate; in addition, it makes inferences when a topic object or set of objects is given, and it will also evaluate a conclusion given as true or false, given a set of premises. The first two of these functions of the routine apply in common discourse situations: A discourse provides information, and a participant makes inferences from this information taken with background knowledge; there may well also be a particular set or object that the discourse pertains to that provides a topic.

It was noted earlier that Table 11.3 indicated a status for each schema (i.e., Core, Feeder, Indirect). Note that only the primary schemas (1 to 15) vary in status; the paraphrases and truisms all have Feeder status. The Inference Procedure makes use of this status. Core schemas apply whenever the propositions in the premise set present argument terms to which they can apply, or when there is a topic to which they can apply. When the reasoning program is engaged it makes these core inferences routinely. In contrast, inferences and paraphrases defined by schemas marked as "Feeder" are made almost exclusively when they serve a purpose—the purpose being to enable a core inference to be made, or to match (or contradict) a conclusion given. The reason for the Core–Feeder distinction is that the core inferences are the ones liable to yield useful deductions (and they cannot iterate), whereas some of the Feeder schemas, if allowed to operate without restraint, have the potential for yielding an endless stream of useless propositions.

Subjects vary greatly in the effort they are willing to expend on a reasoning problem. Similarly, situations vary in the amount of effort they tend to elicit from people—for instance, in making inferences in an ordinary discourse situation or in reading text, only the most immediate inferences are likely to be drawn; in contrast, someone who is intellectually engaged may expend considerable time and effort on a problem. The possibility of effort variation arises in the recycling of the inference procedure: In running the inference procedure, minimum effort would consist in contenting oneself with a single inference, without recycling. In difficult problems, variation is also possible in the amount of effort expended in seeking a secondary topic about which an inference can be drawn. If the reasoner exits from the program before evaluating a conclusion given, he or she may respond *Can't tell*, or pass the problem to other response-finding or problem-solving modalities (e.g., nonlogical heuristics and biases, guessing based on presumed plausibility, content-dependent processes, or, perhaps, constructing a mental model; Johnson-Laird & Byrne, 1991).

To illustrate the operation of the direct reasoning routine, I first consider six simple problems from a set of problems used in some unpublished work. The problems are shown in Table 11.5. Subjects are told that a bead manufacturer packages various combinations of beads in bags. Each problem concerns the content of a different bag. The premises present facts concerning the possible combinations of kinds of beads in one of the bags; the conclusion given has to be evaluated as true or false given the premises. The Preliminary Procedure is not operative in any of the six problems because the conclusions to be evaluated are not *if-then* statements. So the reasoning begins with the Inference Procedure in each case. For each problem, the table shows the premises, the conclusion to be evaluated, and the reasoning steps generated by the direct reasoning routine using the schemas. All these are shown in English and in the representational system, side by side.

In the first problem, the three premises together satisfy the conditions of application of Schema 6, generating the inference that all the beads are plastic; this contradicts the given conclusion, by Schema 13, leading to a judgment of *False*. In the second problem, Schema 4i applies to the two premises (given that wooden beads are beads—[All Beads: WOOD[PRO]] ⊆ [Beads]—cf. Truism 25), leading to the inference that the wooden beads are not triangular, which is added to the premise set; then Schema 1, a feeder schema, can apply to this proposition and the second premise because it generates the conclusion, leading to an evaluation of *True*. In the third problem, the only schema that can apply is Schema 2 to the second premise; it yields the two conjuncts as separate propositions (Propositions 4 and 5), which are added to the premise set. The first premise and Proposition 5 now satisfy the conditions of application of Schema 3i (given that triangular beads are beads, as per Truism 25), yielding the inference that the triangular beads are metal. This proposition and Proposition 4 are now conjoined by Schema 1 to match the conclusion, determining a response of True.

In each of the first three problems, although there is a topic set (the subject NP of the conclusion), it plays no crucial role in the inferences generated. However, the topic set does play a role in the fourth problem. Here the first three premises jointly fit the conditions of application of Schema 7, yielding the inference that all the beads are either red or blue. This proposition taken with the topic set (the round beads) fits the conditions of application of Schema 8i, generating the proposition that the round beads are either red or blue; this contradicts the conclusion (by Schema 14i), leading to an evaluation of *False*. In the fifth problem, the plastic beads are the subject of the first premise; Schema 8 taken with the second premise allows an inference to be made about them, namely, that the plastic beads are not blue; then this proposition taken with the first premise fits the conditions of application of Schema 3i, yielding the information that the plastic beads are green; Schema 11, a feeder schema, now applies because it allows a match of the conclusion, leading to a response of *True*. In the sixth problem, "beads that are not red" is the topic; Schema 3ii, a feeder schema, applies to the first premise with this as topic to yield the inference that the beads that are not red are blue, a proposition that, taken with the second premise (and the fact that beads that are not red are beads, Truism 25 again) allows Schema 4i to apply, generating the information that the beads that are not red are not square, which contradicts the conclusion (Schema 13), determining an evaluation as *False*. Note that in the six problems illustrated in Table 11.5, the inference made at each step is the only one that the direct reasoning routine could make at that step, that is, the routine determines the line of reasoning given.

Subjects have very little difficulty with problems like those of Table 11.5. In an initial pilot study, 92.5% of responses from 20 subjects were correct on these six problems. The problems illustrated were a sample from a set of 40 problems, in which 95% of responses were correct overall, and in a larger study of 64 similar problems reported in chapter 12, 97% of responses were correct overall. Such results provide evidence that inferences of the kind described are made almost without error in problems that call for them straightforwardly.

To further illustrate the use of the direct reasoning routine, let us trace how it elicits the line of reasoning that solves the Radioactive Substances problem of Table 11.6. The problem again presents a conclusion to be evaluated; however, because this conclusion has the form of a conditional, the Preliminary Procedure comes into operation; it adds the antecedent— "all uranium isotopes are radioactive"—to the premise set, and sets up the consequent—"all uranium isotopes have medical value?"—as the revised conclusion to be evaluated. The routine sets up the reference of the subject noun phrase of the conclusion—uranium isotopes—as the topic set in applying the Inference Procedure. The inference procedure is unable to find a core schema that applies immediately, but does find that Schema 8ii will apply to the second premise with the given topic set, if Feeder schema 21 is applied first to establish the identity of the sets "uranium isotopes" and "uranium isotopes that are radioactive"—which follows, according to Schema 21, from the assumption that all uranium isotopes are radioactive. Schema 8ii then yields as output that uranium isotopes don't have short lives, a conclusion that matches the second clause of the numerator of Schema 3i. The first premise matches the first clause of the numerator of this schema, which can now apply given the same topic set of uranium isotopes (with Feeder schema 20i making the notational change from "R[U]" to "[U] $\subseteq$ [R]," to exactly match the third clause of the numerator). Schema 3i yields the output that uranium isotopes have medical value. The Evaluation Procedure matches this against the conclusion, finds a match, and therefore dictates a response of *True*. Note that with the exception of the use of Schema 20i at one point to convert a predication into an inclusion statement, all the steps made by the routine are evidenced explicitly in the subject's protocol.

The Masterpiece Problem (see Table 11.1) exemplifies a problem that requires selection of a secondary topic if it is to be solved. The conclusion question sets up [Some obscure person] as the topic object or set to be reasoned about. However, no inferences can be made immediately about this topic that add anything to the information already in the premises. To solve the problem requires setting up a secondary topic to make inferences about. The reasoner who provided the protocol apparently selected the "novel on my desk" that is mentioned in the third premise as the secondary topic. The reasoner inferred, by Schema 8i and the first premise, that the novel is a masterpiece, and then reverted back to the original topic; the inference procedure of Table 11.4 can then generate the remainder of the reasoning. One can only guess at the heuristic that led to the choice of secondary topic: Perhaps it was "If no core inference applies given the primary topic, choose as secondary topic an argument of a proposition known to be true of the primary topic."

Strategies that resourceful reasoners possess for choosing a secondary topic are a very peripheral concern of this paper. Nevertheless, I provide another illustration of such a strategy because it is a crucial one for solving categorical syllogisms; possession of the strategy is probably an important factor distinguishing good from poor reasoners on syllogisms, and discussion of it helps explain how poor performance on syllogisms is consistent with possession of a mental logic.

It will be recalled that in categorical syllogisms all propositions (premises and valid conclusions) have one of the following forms: *All* (or *Some*, or *None*) *of the X are Y*, or *Some of the X are not Y*. There are two premises: One joins a middle term (M) with a term destined to be the predicate (P) of the conclusion, the other joins the middle term with a term that must be the subject (S) of the conclusion. The reasoner has to identify a valid conclusion (if there is one) with the subject term as subject and the predicate term as predicate, or to state that there is no such conclusion.

The strategy is to choose as secondary topic the subset of the subject of which the middle term can or cannot be predicated ("the S that are, or are not, M," as determined by the premise relating S and M). Table 11.7 provides five examples of syllogisms in which this choice of secondary topic is useful, and of the reasoning that follows to solve the syllogism.

TABLE 11.7
Some Categorical Syllogisms Easily Solved With
Appropriate Choice of a Secondary Topic

---

1. None of the golfers (M) are engineers (P)
   Some of the fishermen (S) are golfers (M)

   Secondary topic: The fishermen that are golfers
   Reasoning: They are not engineers (First premise, Sch 8ii)
   Hence: Some of the fishermen are not engineers (Sch 11)

2. All of the farmers (M) are tennis players (P)
   All of the farmers (M) are cooks (S)

   Secondary topic: The cooks that are farmers
   Reasoning: They are tennis players (First premise, Sch 8i)
   Hence: Some of the cooks are tennis players (Sch 11)

3. None of the managers (M) are gardeners (P)
   All of the managers (M) are singers (S)

   Secondary topic: The singers that are managers
   Reasoning: They are not gardeners (First premise, Sch 8ii)
   Hence: Some of the singers are not gardeners (Sch 11)

4. All of the programmers (P) are dancers (M)
   Some of the swimmers (S) are not dancers (M)

   Secondary topic: The swimmers that are not dancers
   Reasoning: They cannot be programmers (because if they were, then they would be
   dancers, by the first premise)
   Hence: Some of the swimmers are not programmers (Sch 11)

5. None of the environmentalists (P) are doctors (M)
   Some of the doctors (M) are school-bus drivers (S)

   Secondary topic: The school-bus drivers who are doctors
   Reasoning: (i) None of the doctors are environmentalists (if one was, then he/she
                  would be an environmentalist who was a doctor, forbidden by the
                  second premise)
            (ii) The school-bus drivers who are doctors are not environmentalists ((i),
                  Sch 8ii)
   Hence: Some of the school-bus drivers are not environmentalists (Sch 11)

Note. S and P identify the terms to be subject and predicate of the conclusion, and M
the middle term. The content, chosen to be arbitrary, is about people of various professions
and interests gathered in a large hall (cf. Johnson-Laird & Bara, 1984).

The first three syllogisms are quickly solved by the inference procedure
of the direct reasoning routine, once the secondary topic has been selected.
In the last two syllogisms, the reasoning is more complex: In both cases,
in addition to the choice of secondary topic, there is an indirect reasoning
step that involves an implicit reductio.

The fact that college students are notoriously rather poor at categorical syllogisms suggests that many of them do not have this strategy for choosing a secondary topic available. In the data of Rips (1994), the rates of correct responses on syllogisms of the five forms of Table 11.7 were 60%, 45%, 50%, 35%, and 65%, respectively; the corresponding figures in Dickstein's (1978, Sample 2) data were 68%, 29%, 24%, 74%, and 24%. Even these rates cannot be taken as unambiguous indices of valid reasoning because there are known nonlogical reasoning processes and biases that can often yield the correct response (for the wrong reason). In general, reasoners whose logical reasoning skills are limited to the direct reasoning routine of Table 11.4 would be able to solve only a few of the valid syllogisms; most (e.g., the five cited in Table 11.7) would be beyond their logical skills. Thus, not only is poor performance on categorical syllogisms consistent with the presence of a mental logic, but it would indeed be expected if many subjects' logical skills were limited in the way I have described.[14]

RIPS'S MENTAL LOGIC

The only work I know of with goals very similar to this chapter's is that of Rips (1994). Perhaps not surprisingly, Rips's system shares important general characteristics with the one presented here. Rips holds that reasoning involves a stage of translation by the reasoner from the surface structure in which information is presented into *mental sentences* (Rips's term) and that reasoning takes place in the language of the mental sentences. Of course, this is essentially similar to this paper's assumption that reasoning takes place in a syntax or language of thought. Rips also presents a representational system and a set of inference schemas that are part of a reasoning program. Thus, the systems are similar in overall structure as well as goals. There are, however, some significant differences both in the representational system and in the reasoning procedures.

Rips's system, called PSYCOP, is a revision and extension of an earlier system, ANDS (Rips, 1983), which aimed to model propositional reasoning only. I discuss first how PSYCOP handles propositional reasoning, and then its extension to predicate logic.

PSYCOP has two kinds of schemas: *forward* and *backward*. Forward schemas resemble the core schemas of the present model in that their use is not restricted—they apply whenever they can be applied. The use of backward schemas is restricted by goals to deduce certain propositions

---

[14]An important additional reason for poor performance on syllogisms is that most subjects lack good strategies for proving undecidability. That is, of course, consistent with the fact that the logical reasoning skills described would not be useful in proving undecidability.

and by other features of a problem environment specified in the schema, and part of the operation of the schema is to set subgoals. For instance, backward modus ponens can be used only when a conditional "If p then q" is in the database and q is the current goal; it sets up a subgoal to deduce p. Some of the backward schemas set up suppositions together with a subgoal to be derived with the help of the supposition. In problems presented without a conclusion to be evaluated, only the forward schemas can be used—every such schema that can apply does so and PSYCOP recycles until no further inferences can be drawn; the mode of operation on such problems is similar to the present model's, except for some differences in the schemas included, and for the absence of the distinction between feeder and core schemas—PSYCOP avoids infinite loops by omitting schemas that could give rise to them (like &-introduction) from the forward list. When a problem presents a conclusion to be evaluated, the forward schemas apply first until no further inferences can be drawn using them; then, if the conclusion has not already been deduced, it is set as goal and backward schemas that can apply do so (with some priorities in order of application) in a depth-first search until a derivation is found or PSYCOP runs out of search paths.

Chapter 8 examined PSYCOP's performance on a set of propositional reasoning problems and compared it with that of our model. Subjects were given a set of premises, sometimes accompanied by a conclusion to be evaluated; they were asked to write down everything they thought followed from the premises (or to write *nothing follows*, if they thought nothing followed), ending up with an evaluation of the conclusion if one had been given. Thus, we were concerned not just with whether the models evaluated conclusions as subjects did, but rather with the extent to which they reproduced subjects' reasoning steps. There is considerable overlap between the models in the processes postulated, and they made the same predictions for about half the problems. However, where there were differences, subjects' responses showed a better match with our model. One salient difference was that PSYCOP lacks a mechanism that detects a contradiction between a premise set (premises plus inferences drawn) and a conclusion given; it therefore models poorly how subjects evaluate a conclusion as false. In addition, PSYCOP has a forward schema that our model lacks, which caused it to predict certain inferences that subjects did not make. PSYCOP also lacks a schema that our model has, as a result of which PSYCOP failed to capture subjects' reasoning steps on problems where that schema was useful. Such differences reflect easily modifiable features of PSYCOP. (See chap. 8 for a detailed discussion and illustration of the above-mentioned points.) The most far-reaching difference between the models had to do with the kinds of restriction placed on schemas (like &-introduction) or strategies (like supposing alternatives) that could lead to many useless inferences unless restricted. In PSYCOP, such schemas can only operate when there is a goal to derive a particular proposition, either the conclusion to be evaluated or a subgoal in a goal stack headed by the conclusion to be evaluated. This kind of restriction can hamstring PSYCOP when there is no conclusion to be evaluated, or when the conclusion to be evaluated is false. For a simple example, consider a possible problem with four premises of the following forms—*p*, *q*, *r*, and *If p & q & r, then s*—the subject being asked "What follows?" Clearly, *s* follows, but that inference requires &-introduction to feed modus ponens; however, &-introduction is a backward schema and therefore cannot operate without the appropriate conjunction as goal. Because the problem does not present any proposition as goal, PSYCOP can produce no output. If the same problem were given with *s* as the conclusion to be evaluated, PSYCOP would solve it straightforwardly: It would take *s* as the goal, backward modus ponens would deliver *p & q & r* as the subgoal, &-introductions would apply, and *s* would be inferred and a judgment of *True* given. But with no conclusion to be evaluated, or with any conclusion other than *s* (e.g., *not s*), PSYCOP cannot move. Our model does not employ this kind of restriction on schemas. Rather, it labels certain classes of inferences as significant (*core*) inferences, and allows feeder inferences to operate (apart from optional one-time use in reading out conclusions) only if they enable a significant inference to be made or a conclusion to be evaluated. The evidence favored this sort of restriction.

Now let us consider how PSYCOP handles quantifiers. It is assumed that the mental sentences in which reasoning takes place do not contain quantifiers, but rather, use a notation in which variables and temporary names replace the quantifiers. Thus, the first step in reasoning, which might be called a comprehension step, involves a translation of the premises in English into this quantifier-free notation. Technically, this involves two stages: first, a translation into a form in which all quantifiers appear at the beginning, outside the sentence proper (so-called *prenex form*, in logical parlance); second, a stage in which the quantifiers are eliminated— arguments bound to universal quantifiers are replaced by a variable (a different variable for each universal quantifier), and arguments bound by an existential quantifier are replaced by temporary names. If the existential quantifier was in the scope of a universal, the temporary name is given an annotation associating it with the universal in whose scope it was. (In Rips's [1994] examples, late letters of the alphabet are used for variables, and early letters for temporary names.)

Some examples may make the nature of Rips's representations clearer. Thus, an existentially quantified sentence such as "Something is fragile" ($\exists x$Fragile(x), in standard logic) becomes "Fragile(a)," with a temporary name substituting for the existentially bound variable of the logical form.

A sentence with a combination of universal and existential quantifiers is represented using combinations of variables and temporary names. For instance, "Every satellite orbits some planet" becomes "IF Satellite(x) THEN (Planet(a_x) & Orbit(x, a_x))"; the subscript to the temporary name, a, reflects the fact that the existential quantifier is in the scope of the universal—the identity of the planet depends on which satellite is being referred to. If the scope relations are reversed, as in "All the satellites are orbiting a planet" (where they are all orbiting the same planet), the representation would be "IF Satellite(x) THEN (Planet(a) & Orbit(x, a))," with no annotation to the temporary name. (The first two of the preceding examples are taken directly from Rips, 1994, p. 185.)

Note the considerable differences in syntax between the English and the mental sentences in the last two examples. In particular, where the English sentences have "every" and "all," the mental sentences have "IF-THEN." This noncorrespondence in structure can become quite great; even the regular relationship of English universal quantifiers with variables, and English existential ones with temporary names, can be breached. For instance, the logical form "IF (for some x)P THEN Q" has the prenex form "(For all x)(IF P THEN Q)," and the logical form "IF (for all x)P THEN Q" has prenex form "(For some x)(IF P THEN Q)" (Rips, 1994, p. 91, Examples 12a and 12c). This has the consequence that an English sentence such as "If some child cheats, then the whole class is punished" would correspond to the mental sentence "IF Child(x) & Cheats(x), THEN the whole class is punished," whereas the English sentence "If every child cheats then the teacher is punished" would correspond to "IF Child(a) & Cheats(a), THEN the teacher is punished." Note that here the English "some" corresponds to the variable x, and English "every" to the temporary name a, a reversal of the usual relationships. The problem with postulating such radical noncorrespondences between the syntax of surface structure and that of mentalese is that it leaves the surface syntax unmotivated: It demands an answer to the question why the surface syntax of natural languages should be so different from the syntax of the vehicle of thought.

To illustrate how his system works, Rips cites a categorical syllogism, and traces through how PSYCOP represents and solves it. The syllogism is:

All square blocks are green blocks
Some big blocks are square blocks

? Some big blocks are green blocks?

Rips's representation of this syllogism is shown in the left-hand column of Table 11.8, with PSYCOP's line of reasoning outlined beneath it; the

TABLE 11.8
Syllogism Illustrating PSYCOP's Representations and Reasoning,
and Comparing It With That of the System of This Chapter

All square blocks are green blocks
Some big blocks are square blocks

? Some big blocks are green blocks?

PSYCOP	This chapter
1. IF Square-block(x) THEN Green-block(x)	GR[All BLOCK: SQ[PRO]]
2. Big-block(a) & Square-block(a)[a]	SQ[Some BLOCK: BIG[PRO]]$_{pl}$

3. ? Big-block(b) & Green-block(b)?	? GR[Some BLOCK: BIG[PRO]]$_{pl}$?
4. Big-block(a) (2, &-elim'n)	[Some BLOCK: BIG[PRO]]$_{pl}$ ⊆
	[BLOCK: SQ[PRO]] (2, Sch 20iii)[b]
5. Square-block(a) (2, &-elim'n)	GR[Some BLOCK: BIG[PRO]]$_{pl}$ (1, 4,
No further forward rules apply	Sch 8i)
6. Backward &-introduction:	
Subgoal: Big-block(b)	
7. Satisfied by Big-block(a) (4)	
Subgoal: Green-block(b)=Green-block(a)[c]	
8. Backward Modus-ponens: Subgoal:	
Square-block(a)	
9. Satisfied by Square-block(a) (5)	
10. ∴Green-block(a) (1, Modus Ponens)	
11. ∴Big-block(a) & Green-block(a) (7, 10)	
12. Big-block(b) & Green-block(b) (matching)	

[a]The caret marks temporary names in the premises to distinguish them from temporary names in the conclusion.

[b]Basically, this is a translation of the second premise into an inclusion statement so as to feed Schema 8i.

[c]The subgoal must be same block that satisfied the previous subgoal.

representation and reasoning of the system proposed here is shown alongside, in the right-hand column.

Before discussing the reasoning, a further comment on representation is warranted: Note that the second premise and conclusion are represented as conjunctions, a considerable difference in syntax from the English sentences. This means that, among other things, the subject-predicate structure of the English is lost—the second premise, for instance, attributes squareness to some big blocks, not bigness to some square blocks, but, because order is immaterial in conjunctions, nothing corresponding to this distinction is possible in PSYCOP's representation.[15]

---

[15]Subject–predicate structure is lost in another case too. Rips represents the English form "No F are G" as "Not (F(x) & G(x))" (e.g., "No small blocks are red blocks" becomes "NOT (Small-block(x) & Red-block(x))".) Again, because order is immaterial in conjunctions, no distinction is made between "No F are G" and "No G are F," although these clearly do not

In solving this syllogism, PSYCOP first tries to apply its forward rules. Only one applies (&-elimination), and that yields the clauses of the second premise as separate assertions (Lines 4 and 5). No further progress is possible with the forward rules. PSYCOP now turns to the conclusion, set as goal, and tries to apply backward rules; because the conclusion is a conjunction, backward &-introduction is called, to try to derive each of the clauses of the conjunction in turn. The first clause ("Big-block(b)") is set as subgoal. This is directly satisfied because "Big-block(a)" has already been derived from the second premise (Line 4); notice, though, that to see "Big-block(a)" as satisfying the goal of deriving "Big-block(b)" requires some matching rules (Rips, 1994, Table 6.1) that tell when temporary names and variables can be taken as equivalent, and when not. (This complexity is largely ignored in Table 11.8.) Having seen that the first clause of the conclusion has been established, PSYCOP proceeds to take the second clause, "Green-block(b)" (= "Green-block(a)"), as subgoal. This subgoal cannot be directly satisfied, but PSYCOP notices that "Green-block(a)" can be matched to "Green-block(x)," the consequent clause of the conditional first premise, according to its matching rules. Backward modus ponens is therefore called, and this sets "Square-block(a)," the matching value of the antecedent of the first premise, as the immediate subgoal. This is, of course, directly satisfied, because it has already been derived at Line 5. The backward modus ponens rule now generates "Green-block(a)." This satisfies the still active subgoal of the backward &-introduction rule, allowing the conjunction "Big-block(a) & Green-block(a)" to be asserted. This is equivalent to the original goal by the matching rules, completing the proof of the syllogism.

In the system of this chapter, the reasoning is much shorter. The second premise is paraphrased into an inclusion statement in order to feed Schema 8i, which delivers the conclusion. None of PSYCOP's reasoning steps that involve &-elimination and &-introduction appear; nor are PSYCOP's matching rules needed. If one asks subjects to explain their response on this syllogism, they typically say something like "because some big blocks are square blocks, they must be green." This sort of explanation corresponds well with the reasoning proposed here, and contains no sign of any of PSYCOP's reasoning steps involving &-elimination and &-introduction.

There is a further point to be made about Rips's model in relation to this syllogism. Because backward rules are involved, the syllogism is not soluble without the conclusion being given: If PSYCOP is given the two premises alone without the conclusion to evaluate, the only inferences it can make are that some blocks are big, and some are square (Lines 4 and 5 of PSYCOP's proof). In discussing how PSYCOP might simulate conclusions to syllogism premises alone, Rips suggests that subjects first guess a conclusion, especially one that has one of the quantifiers found in the premises, and then proceed to try to derive it; with such a procedure PSYCOP would always have a conclusion to evaluate, and could therefore bring its backward rules into play (assuming the guessed conclusion was the right one). It seems to me that this dependence on having an appropriate conclusion to evaluate is a potentially serious defect of PSYCOP. On this syllogism, the model proposed here would produce the same conclusion, with or without being given the conclusion to evaluate.

In general, this discussion suggests two major kinds of problems with PSYCOP. One has to do with its representations of quantified sentences: These "mental sentences" often differ so much in structure from the natural language sentences whose meaning they purport to represent that an explanation is required as to why their structures should be so different. In addition, the nature of the representations forces certain characteristics on the reasoning; for instance, it is because expressions of the form "Some F are G" are rendered as conjunctions that &-elimination and &-introduction rules are needed in the syllogism of Table 11.8, precisely the rules for whose outputs there is little evidence. The other problem has to do with the division of the inference rules into forward and backward types. Because backward rules can only come into play when there is a precisely appropriate goal, PSYCOP can be hamstrung when there is no such goal.

In fairness, we should note a considerable virtue of Rips's model: It has been worked out in sufficient detail to be implemented in a computer program. That means that it works for the range of problems it is intended to work for, and presumably, that it has no bugs unknown to its author. Unfortunately, the same assurances cannot be given about the model presented here.

There is a way in which the naturalness of Rips's representations could be significantly improved. The representations derive from those of standard logic (in prenex form). Standard logic uses domain-general quantifiers (i.e., the variables range over all kinds of objects), a characteristic whose naturalness has been severely criticized by Gupta (1980) and McCawley (1981/1993), who argue for domain-specific quantifiers, as noted earlier. It seems to me that Rips's representations would become much more natural if they were derived from a logic with domain-specific quantifiers (e.g., like McCawley's). Let us consider the two sentences first used to illustrate Rips's representations, reproduced as 40 and 41.

40. Every satellite orbits some planet
41. All the satellites orbit some planet (all the same planet)

These are represented by Rips, respectively, as:

40a. IF Satellite(x) THEN Planet(a_x) & Orbit(x, a_x)

41a. IF Satellite(x) THEN Planet(a) & Orbit(x, a)

Let us represent a variable or temporary name derived from a domain-specific logic by joining the domain to the variable or name with a hyphen. Based on domain-specific quantifiers, in place of 40a and 41a, we would have, respectively, 40b and 41b, as the mental sentences corresponding to 40 and 41.

40b. Orbit(x-satellite, a-planet$_{x\text{-satellite}}$)

41b. Orbit(x-satellite, a-planet)

Note how dramatically the parallelism to the English has improved. Where 40a and 41a each have three clauses, 40b and 41b have just one, like the English; the troubling IF-THEN of 40a and 41a has disappeared in 40b and 41b, just as it is absent in the English sentences; where the English sentences consist of a verb and two noun phrases, 40b and 41b have a predicate and two arguments, just as one would wish. Note, too, that these Rips-type domain-specific representations are formally quite similar to those I propose, shown as 40c and 41c.

40c. ORBIT[All SATELLITE][Some PLANET/SATELLITE]

41c. ORBIT[All SATELLITE][Some PLANET]

Where Rips marks the difference between universal and existential by the difference between late and early letters of the alphabet, the representations proposed here use "All" and "Some." From a strictly formal point of view that is only a notational difference. And scope distinctions among the quantifiers are handled in the same way, by annotating an existential that is in the scope of a universal with the universal in whose scope it lies.

To recast Rips's system to a basis in domain-specific quantification would require considerable work, more than can be undertaken here. For one thing, significant changes would be necessary in the inference rules. For instance, suppose XA-79 is a satellite. Given Representation 40a, Rips's existing modus ponens rule is sufficient to deduce that XA-79 orbits some planet. However, that rule would not yield the same inference given 40b; instead, a separate rule of universal instantiation would be needed, something along the lines of Schema 8i of Table 11.3. Without proceeding further with the recasting, it is apparent that such a recast Rips system would show some significant convergence with the system proposed here.

In sum, there are two major sources of difference between Rips's system and the one proposed here. One is that Rips's system is based on domain-general quantification, whereas in mine quantification is always

In sum, there are two major sources of difference between Rips's system and the one proposed here. One is that Rips's system is based on domain-general quantification, whereas in mine quantification is always domain specific. The latter provides a much better fit to natural language surface structure. The other source of difference is that Rips's rules are based on a division into forward and backward types, the latter being dependent for their operation on the existence of appropriate goals, whereas the system proposed is based on a different distinction, one that regards certain kinds of inferences as significant or informative (core inferences) and others (feeder) as not; the system's routines seek significant inferences and are not dependent on specific propositions as goals.

ENVOI

There are two major orthogonal binary dimensions on which predicate logics can be categorized. They have to do with the locus of the quantifiers and their nature. The quantifiers can be placed outside the propositional nucleus, or inside as part of the arguments they bind. They can be domain general or domain specific. Standard logic has outside quantifiers that are domain general. McCawley's (1981/1993) logic has outside quantifiers that are domain specific. Rips's system has inside quantifiers that are domain general. (Strictly, Rips's system has variables and temporary names in the arguments, not quantifiers, but because variables correspond to the universal quantifier and temporary names to the existential, this is quite tantamount to having the quantifiers themselves inside.) The system presented here falls into the fourth category, with inside quantifiers that are domain specific. The message of this chapter is that it is in this fourth category that one should look for a representational system for the syntax of thought and for the inference schemas and procedures that model ordinary human reasoning of a predicate logic sort. Although I have no doubt that there are many improvements to be made in the system proposed, and further details to be worked out, I believe that anyone attempting to build a model of this sort (i.e., based on inside, domain-specific, quantifiers) will find themselves grappling with the same issues and traversing much the same ground as this chapter has. I hope to have provided a useful hypothesis and an initial chart of some of the territory to be covered.

12

Some Empirical Justification of the Mental-Predicate-Logic Model*

Yingrui Yang
New York University and Princeton University

Martin D. S. Braine
New York University

David P. O'Brien
*Baruch College and the Graduate School
of the City University of New York*

This chapter reports an initial test of the mental predicate logic developed in chapter 11. We examined (a) whether it can predict the relative difficulties of problems in a set of problems employing monadic predicates (i.e., predicates that take a single argument) and in a parallel set of problems employing dyadic predicates (i.e., predicates that take two arguments), and (b) whether erroneous evaluations of conclusions that are derivable on the direct-reasoning routine are relatively rare.

The general methodology is similar to that of chapter 7. Subjects were presented with a set of problems in which the schemas and number of reasoning steps varied. In each problem, one or more facts were given, followed by a conclusion. Subjects had to decide whether this conclusion was true or false, given those facts, and then to rate its subjective difficulty right after they marked a truth value.[1] All the monadic-predicate problems are shown in Appendix 1, and the parallel dyadic-predicate problems are shown in Appendix 2 at the end of this chapter. The problems are all

---

*The empirical work reported here is based in part on a doctoral dissertation by the first author, begun under the supervision of the second author, and completed under the supervision of the third author.

[1]Perceived difficulty was rated on a 7-point scale, in which 1 was "easier to figure out than most of the other problems," 7 was "harder to figure out than most of the problems," and 3 to 5 were "about average difficulty."

soluble by the Direct Reasoning Routine (DRR) of Table 11.4, but they vary considerably in the number of inferential steps required.

In chapter 7 we noted three possible sources of errors in problems of this sort. We called them *comprehension errors, heuristic inadequacy errors*, and *processing errors*. A comprehension error occurs when a subject construes a premise or the conclusion in an unintended manner: The starting information used by the subject is not that intended by the problem setter. Heuristic inadequacy errors occur when the subject's reasoning program fails to find a line of reasoning that solves a problem, that is, the problem is too difficult for the subject. Processing errors are due to lapses of attention, errors of execution in the application of schemas, failure to keep track of information in working memory, and the like. We assume that the likelihood of a processing error increases with problem complexity, but overall tends to be low and largely vanishes in the simplest problems where processing load is minimal.

In the work reported here we expected most errors to be processing errors. Because all problems are soluble by the DRR, we predicted that there should be no problems too difficult for subjects; hence, there should be no errors due to heuristic inadequacies. We sought to eliminate comprehension errors by careful attention to the wording of problems. We tried to avoid problems in which the premises might have "conversational implicatures" (Grice, 1975) that could lead some subjects to interpret premises in ways we did not intend. Also, where the relative scopes of quantifiers and negations had to be understood, we did preliminary work to discover a wording that subjects construed in the intended manner.

Our first prediction followed immediately from this discussion of error. Problems that can be solved immediately by the application of a single schema should be solved essentially without errors; moreover, because all problems are soluble by the DRR, the overall error rate should be low. The second, and main, prediction is that the difficulty of a problem will be a function of the number and nature of the inferential steps required by the DRR to solve it. In particular, the difficulty of a problem is predicted from the sum of the difficulties of the individual reasoning steps required to solve it. As in the work of chapter 7, we used two prediction schemes. In the main scheme we estimated difficulty weights for each primary schema from the data, the difficulty weight of a schema being an index of the difficulty of adopting and using that schema in solving a problem. We then investigated how far we could systematically predict the empirically measured difficulty of a problem from the sum of the difficulty weights of the component inferences used by the DRR to solve it. In the second prediction scheme, we assigned equal difficulty weights to all the primary schemas, taking the difficulty of a problem as proportional only to the number of component inferences, not to their nature. Thus, this scheme examines how well problem difficulty can be predicted just from the number of primary schemas used to solve a problem, that is, from the number of reasoning steps.

We used two measures of problem difficulty—the mean difficulty rating assigned to the problem by subjects who solved it correctly, and the number of errors on the problem. We used the difficulty ratings in estimating difficulty weights for schemas. In the case of the difficulty ratings, we assumed, as in chapter 7, that in doing a problem a subject forms a subjective impression of the amount of processing the problem demanded, and that this processing is, in turn, a function of the number and kind of the mental steps required to solve the problem; the difficulty rating assigned reflects this subjective impression. We used the ratings to estimate difficulty weights because they had better psychometric properties than the errors; they were less skewed, subjects showed more consensus in their ratings than in errors, and problems were differentiated better.

The following primary schemas were used in the solution of problems: Schemas 1, 2, 3ii, 3ii, 4i, 4ii, 6, 7, 8i, 8ii, 11, 13i, 13ii, 14i, and 14ii of Table 11.3. (Schemas 5 and 12 were not included because they exist only in propositional form in Table 11.3; Schemas 9 and 10 were excluded because they primarily concern indirect reasoning not covered by the DRR.) In addition, several paraphrase schemas and truisms were involved. It seemed to us that to assign each of these schemas a difficulty weight would result in so many parameters (difficulty weights) being estimated from the data as to make the results uninteresting. We therefore sought to cut down on the number of parameters to be estimated from the data. A combination of common-sense intuition and preliminary work suggested the following. First, we assigned all paraphrase schemas and truisms a weight of zero.[2] Second, we assigned 8i the same weight as 8ii, 13i as 13ii, and 14i as 14ii: Both intuition and our preliminary work indicated that this was reasonable. Third, the preliminary work indicated that 3i was more difficult than 3ii, and 4i than 4ii, the differences being about equal, and similar to the difficulty of Schema 8; because, as noted in chapter 11, Schema 3i can be generated by Schema 3ii feeding Schema 8, and 4i by 4ii feeding 8, it seemed reasonable to fix the weight of Schema 3i as the weight of 3ii plus the weight of 8, and similarly, the weight of 4i as the weight of 4ii plus the weight of 8. With these decisions made, the number of schema weights to be estimated from the data is 10 (Schemas 1, 2, 3ii, 4ii, 6, 7, 8, 11, 13, and 14).

Five types of problems were used:

---

[2]It is consistent with the work done that the cognitive cost of the application of paraphrase rules and truisms is small compared with that of the primary inference rules. Also, in pilot work where we have had subjects write down what they infer, they often write down not the precise output of the inference rule, but what in our system would be a paraphrase of it, again suggesting little cognitive cost to paraphrasing.

1. *Control-true problems*. In these the premise and conclusion were identical and merely had to be matched. They served to anchor the low end of the rating scale.

2. *Control-false problems*. In these, either the conclusion directly negated the premise, or vice versa. Formally, these are one-step problems involving Schema 13 or Schema 14.

3. *One-step problems*. These were problems in which the conclusion could be reached from the premises in one step using one of the primary schemas.

4. *One-step plus contradiction*. These were problems in which a contradiction between the premises and the conclusion could be reached in one step using one of the primary schemas.

5. *Multistep problems*. These all involved a chain of two or more inferences; those for which the expected response was *False* also involved finding an incompatibility between the conclusion and the premises taken with the inferences made from them.

We conducted three experiments. Experiment 1 investigated the problems of Appendix 1, that is, those with monadic predicates. Experiment 2 investigated the problems of Appendix 2, that is, those with dyadic predicates. Experiment 3 investigated both the monadic and dyadic problems jointly. In Experiment 1, four data sets were obtained, each from 20 native-English–speaking undergraduates drawn from the introductory psychology course at New York University.[3] (All participants in subsequent studies were drawn from the same population.) A preliminary data set was obtained with a set of 46 of the 64 problems in Appendix 1, and three additional data sets obtained with the complete set of 64 problems. The reason for obtaining the preliminary data set was to provide estimates of schema difficulty from one set of problems and subjects that could be used to predict problem difficulties for a different set of problems with different subjects. We obtained the three data sets using the same set of 64 problems with different subjects for two reasons. The first was for cross-validation: We wished to see how similar the weights would be across data sets, and particularly, whether weights estimated from one data set would predict problem difficulty in other data sets as well as weights estimated from those data sets. The second reason was to obtain a reasonably stable error measure by using error data summed across the three sets.

---

[3]In all experiments the data for a small number of subjects are not included. In Experiment 1, for example, two additional subjects are not included because they failed to follow instructions, and one subject was not included because this subject made errors on most practice problems.

All the monadic-predicate test problems in Appendix 1 concerned the following situation: The subject was asked to imagine that there are many beads and that a manufacturer put them in bags. Each problem concerned the content of a different bag. The same set of 16 practice problems was used in collecting all four data sets. The practice problems sampled the range of difficulty of the main problem set (without duplicating any). They served to familiarize subjects with the nature of the problems they would be doing, and made it possible for subjects to form a rough calibration of their internal difficulty rating scale before beginning the main set of problems.

Experiment 2 used the dyadic-predicate problems of Appendix 2. These 64 problems were constructed in one-to-one correspondence with those of Appendix 1, so that, for example, Problem 36 of the dyadic set required the same reasoning steps as Problem 36 of the monadic set. Three data sets were obtained for all 64 problems (N = 20 for each set), again allowing for crossvalidations of predictions, and allowing comparison between the predictions for the monadic and dyadic sets. Sixteen practice problems parallel to those in Experiment 1 were used.

For the dyadic-predicate problems of Appendix 2, participants were told to imagine that there are many beads and a manufacturer has put them in bags. The beads vary in color (e.g., blue, red, or green), shape (e.g., square, round, or triangular), and material (e.g., wooden, plastic, or metal). The problems are presented by kinds of facts such as the following: Children played with each other (who played with whom), children like or dislike (also, find or did not find, got or did not get) some particular kinds of beads, or simply what kinds of beads are in bags. A fact can also be a possible combination of these.

Experiment 3 presented each subject all of the 128 monadic- and dyadic-predicate problems from from Appendixes 1 and 2. We generated two data sets (N = 20 for each set), again allowing a crossvalidation of the predictions. The motivation for this was to assess whether the difficulty ratings would differ when made against the background of the two sorts of problems rather than against the background of only monadic or only dyadic problems.

In all three experiments, the task was administered individually. In Experiments 1 and 2, each subject received two booklets sequentially. The first booklet provided instructions, followed by the set of practice problems. The second booklet provided the set of test problems. The experimenter read the instructions aloud while the subjects followed them in the booklet. Throughout the task, groups of four test problems were presented on a separate sheet of paper. Subjects were instructed to specify on each problem whether the proposed conclusion was true or false, given the premises, and then to rate the problem's perceived difficulty on a line provided beneath each problem.

Within each booklet, problem order was partially counterbalanced by using two random orders and their reverse orders, with an equal number of subjects receiving each of the resulting four orders. The number of problems with true conclusions equaled the number of problems with false conclusions, both in the set of practice problems and in the sets of test problems.

The procedure used in presenting Experiment 3 was identical to that in Experiments 1 and 2, with the following exceptions. In presenting Experiment 3, three booklets were presented sequentially. The first booklet included all 32 practice problems used in Experiments 1 and 2, presented in random order. A second booklet included 40 test problems and a third included 88 test problems. After finishing the first two booklets, each subject was given $2 to buy a refreshment outside the building before returning to start working on the third booklet. Problem order was also partially counterbalanced by using one random order across all 128 problems and its reverse order.

RESULTS: THE MONADIC-PREDICATE PROBLEMS OF EXPERIMENT 1

Level of Accuracy

For the preliminary Data Set 1, there were 44 problems (omitting control-true problems) and 20 subjects, that is, 880 responses, of which 20 were errors (2.3%). Considering all problems in Data Sets 2, 3, and 4 (omitting the control-true problems), there were 61 problems and 60 subjects, that is, 3,660 responses, of which 84 were errors (2.3%). Thus, subjects were 97.7% accurate over the entire set, indicating that the problems were well within subjects' abilities, as predicted, and demonstrating once again a class of logical reasoning problems on which people do very well.

There were 17 problems common to Data Sets 2, 3, and 4, and 13 problems to Data Set 1, which could be solved in one step using one of the primary schemas. (These comprise nine one-step and eight control-false problems.) With 60 subjects and 17 problems in Data Sets 1, 2, and 3, and with 20 subjects and 13 problems in Data Set 1, we have 1,280 responses. Of these, 29 were errors (2.3%); thus, the accuracy rate was 97.7% correct. In fact, 13 of the errors were on a single problem. This presented the single premise *All the beads are round and wooden*, and the subject had to evaluate the conclusion *All the beads are wooden*? (Problem 15 of Appendix 1). We suspect that the 13 subjects who marked this as *False* did so not because they thought the beads were not wooden, but because they thought the conclusion insufficiently perspicuous—it did not give a sufficiently complete account of the beads (i.e., it offended Grice's, 1975, maxim of quantity). If this problem is omitted, accuracy is 98% on one-step problems.

Predicting Problem Difficulty

The first analyses were computed without considering any weights for individual schemas and concerned only the number of reasoning steps involved in solving a problem, as predicted by the DRR. For Data Sets 1, 2, 3, and 4, respectively, the correlations between the number of reasoning steps and the perceived mean difficulty ratings were .80, .80, .79, and .80. This shows that the number of reasoning steps alone provides substantial predictability to the perceived difficulty ratings, accounting for approximately 64% of the variance. The number of reasoning steps is, of course, correlated with overall problem length—it takes more words to convey the problems that require more reasoning steps. It is possible, therefore, that a substantial portion of the correlations between the number of reasoning steps and obtained mean difficulties could be due to problem length alone. To provide a conservative estimate of the predictability of reasoning steps alone, the correlations were computed with problem length partialed out; the resulting correlations were .68, .68, .66, and .68, for Data Sets 1, 2, 3, and 4, respectively, accounting for approximately 46% of the variance.

A second set of analyses were computed considering weights for each individual schema. Difficulty weights for the schemas were estimated as follows: For any problem, predicted difficulty = 1 + Σ(difficulty weights of schemas involved in solving it). (The constant, 1, reflects the fact that the lowest possible difficulty rating is 1.) Because there are 44 problems in Study 1 and 61 problems in the other studies (excluding control-true problems), we have 44 and 61 such equations, respectively.

Difficulty weights for the reasoning steps were estimated using the program PRAXIS (Brent, 1973; Gegenfurtner, 1992) to obtain the best least-squares fit of the predicted problem difficulties to the obtained mean difficulty ratings. (It will be recalled that 10 weights were estimated—for Schemas [from Table 11.3] 1, 2, 3ii [3i = 3ii + 8], 4ii [4i = 4ii + 8], 6, 7, 8 [8i = 8ii], 11, 13 [13i = 13ii], and 14 [14i = 14ii].) Separate estimates were made for each study.

Table 12.1 shows the correlations between predicted difficulties and obtained mean difficulty ratings for the four data sets. The correlations on the diagonal (top left to bottom right) show the quality of prediction when the predictions are based on difficulty weights estimated from the same study from which the obtained ratings come (the 10 parameters were estimated from the same data). In the other correlations, the predictions based on difficulty weights estimated from one data set are used to predict

TABLE 12.1
Correlations Between Mean Difficulty Ratings and Predicted
Difficulties for the Monadic-Predicate Problems of Experiment 1

Mean Difficulty Ratings	Predicted Difficulties			
	Data Set 1	Data Set 2	Data Set 3	Data Set 4
Data Set 1	.93	.92	.89	.91
Data Set 2	.91	.92	.90	.90
Data Set 3	.89	.91	.93	.88
Data Set 4	.90	.90	.89	.89

obtained mean difficulty ratings from a different data set (no parameters estimated from the data predicted). There are no significant differences among the correlations in Table 12.1, indicating that it makes little or no difference whether estimates and obtained difficulty ratings come from the same data set or a different one. The correlations between the mean ratings across studies ranged from .92 to .95. Thus, the quality of predictions shown in Table 12.1 is hardly below the reliability of the mean ratings themselves.

There were 17 problems included in Data Sets 2 to 4 that were not included in Data Set 1 (four control-false problems, three one-step–plus–contradiction problems, and 10 multistep problems). One can therefore inquire how well the estimates from Data Set 1 predict the difficulties of these new problems that were not used in estimating the difficulty weights of Data Set 1. The correlations were .92, .88, and .89 for predictions from Data Set 1 to Sets 2, 3, and 4, respectively, indicating excellent predictability to new problems done by new subjects.

The rated difficulty of a problem correlates with problem length—the longer the problem in number of words, the more likely subjects are to rate it as more difficult. The correlations between problem length and mean rated difficulty ranged from .66 to .79 across the four data sets. Of course, because the longer problems are the ones that require more inferential steps to solve, the correlation with problem length could well be largely or entirely due to the number and kinds of inferences demanded by a problem. However, problem length itself could well make an independent contribution, and a proper conservatism requires that one investigate whether the relations between predicted and obtained difficulties remain substantial when length is partialed out.[4] These partial

---

[4]We treated problem length differently here from in the work reported in chapter 7. There we attempted to measure the effects of length on subjective difficulty directly. However, our method of doing this actually measured the effects of substitution complexity rather than just length (see the discussion of problem length in chap. 7). It could well be that the methods used in chapter 7 overestimated the effects of problem length by equating length with substitution complexity.

TABLE 12.2
Correlations Between Mean Difficulty Ratings and
Predicted Difficulties With Problem Length Partialed
Out for the Monadic-Predicate Problems of Experiment 1

Mean Difficulty Ratings	Predicted Difficulties			
	Data Set 1	Data Set 2	Data Set 3	Data Set 4
Data Set 1	.88	.86	.83	.83
Data Set 2	.84	.84	.79	.79
Data Set 3	.80	.80	.81	.72
Data Set 4	.83	.79	.76	.77

TABLE 12.3
Weights for the 10 Schemas From the Monadic-Predicate
Problems in Data Sets 2, 3, and 4 of Experiment 1

Schemas	1	2	3ii	4ii	6	7	8	11	13	14
Weights	.46	.68	.73	1.55	1.28	1.59	.71	.67	.48	.95

Note. The weights were obtained from the combined 60 subjects in Data Sets 2 to 4, that is, where subjects received all 64 problems.

correlations are shown in Table 12.2. It can be seen that the correlations are indeed somewhat lower than in Table 12.1, but are nevertheless still very substantial.

The high correlations between the observed mean difficulties and the predictions remain quite high when schema weights were generated from the same or from different sets of subjects, which indicates that the weights across studies were quite similar. The best estimate of the weights for each schema, therefore, would be those obtained from the combined data sets. Table 12.3 shows the weights for each of the 10 schemas obtained from all 60 subjects in Data Sets 2, 3, and 4, that is, for those subjects who received the entire set of 64 problems.

RESULTS: THE DYADIC-PREDICATE PROBLEMS OF EXPERIMENT 2

Level of Accuracy

Considering all the problems in all three data sets (again, omitting the control-true problems), there were 61 problems and 60 subjects, that is, 3,660 responses. Of these, 128 (3.5%) were errors. Thus, subjects were 96.5% accurate over the entire set, indicating that these problems of dyadic-predicate sort were also well within subjects' capacity, as predicted, and demonstrating, once again, another class of logical reasoning problems on which people do very well.

For 17 one-step problems (including 8 control-false problems), the error rate was 2.6% (there were 1,020 responses; of these, 27 were errors). Unlike the data for Experiment 1, for which a large number of errors were made on Problem 15, none of the subjects made an error on Problem 15 on the dyadic-predicate problems. Inspection of the two parallel problems in Appendixes 1 and 2 reveals why the dyadic-predicate version did not elicit the same sort of response as did the monadic-predicate version: Unlike the problem presented with a monadic predicate, which presented the same topic (the subject noun phrase of the sentence) in both the premise and the conclusion (i.e., "beads"), the topic of the premise in the dyadic version (i.e., "girls") differs from the topic in the conclusion (i.e., "boys"). This switch of topics in the dyadic version mitigates the grounds for the Gricean violation that is likely the reason for the *False* response to the monadic version.

Analyses Based on the Number of Reasoning Steps

For Data Sets 1, 2, and 3, the correlations between the number of steps and three sets of perceived mean ratings are .74, .74, and .79, respectively, which, although about 5% lower than those for Experiment 1, again are substantial. Overall they account for approximately 57% of the variance. When the problem length is partialed out, the three partial correlations are .67, .66, and .74, respectively, accounting for approximately 45%, 43%, and 55% of the variance, respectively. Consideration of the number of reasoning steps alone thus provides a reasonable prediction of perceived problem difficulty.

Analyses Based on Schema Weights

Cross-sample validation analyses for the dyadic-predicate problems are presented in Tables 12.4 and 12.5. Table 12.4 shows the correlations between predicted difficulties and obtained mean difficulty ratings for the three data sets. Table 12.5 shows the corresponding correlations when the length of problems is partialed out. In comparison with the values reported for the monadic-predicate problems in Experiment 1, the correlations in Tables 12.4 and 12.5 are consistently lower, but are still quite substantial, indicating high predictability of the model for the dyadic-predicate problems. Taken collectively, the correlations represented in Tables 12.4 and 12.5 reveal that the sum of schema weights accounts for approximately 71% of the variance, and the amount of variance accounted for when problem length is partialed out is approximately 55%. As was

TABLE 12.4

Correlations Between Predicted Problem Difficulties and
Obtained Mean Ratings From the Dyadic-Predicate
Problems in Data Sets 1, 2, and 3 in Experiment 2

Obtained Difficulties	Predicted Difficulties		
	Data Set 1	Data Set 2	Data Set 3
Data Set 1	.83	.82	.83
Data Set 2	.85	.83	.84
Data Set 3	.86	.85	.87

TABLE 12.5

Correlations Between Predicted Problem Difficulty and Obtained
Difficulty When Problem Length is Partialed Out for the
Dyadic-Predicate Problems in Data Sets 1 to 3 of Experiment 2

Obtained Difficulties	Predicted Difficulties		
	Data Set 1	Data Set 2	Data Set 3
Data Set 1	.72	.79	.78
Data Set 2	.70	.72	.73
Data Set 3	.73	.73	.80

the case for the monadic-predicate problems, the high correlations among the three data sets for dyadic-predicate problems show that the best estimates would be derived from the combined data for all 60 subjects in Data Sets 1, 2, and 3. These weights are shown in Table 12.6.

Comparison of the weights in Table 12.6 with those in Table 12.4 reveals an overall similarity, but not a perfect correspondence. (The rank-order correlation between the two sets = .76.) The overall similarity between the weights in Table 12.6 and those in Table 12.4 suggests that the relative amount of cognitive effort required to apply each schema remains stable across predicates that take a single argument and those that take two arguments. This overall similarity, however, does not hold for Schema 3ii, which when presented with a monadic predicate, and rated against other schemas presented in monadic-predicate problems, is rated as relatively easy, but when presented with a dyadic predicate, and rated against

TABLE 12.6

Schema Weights Obtained for the Dyadic-Predicate Problems
From the Combination of Data Sets 1, 2, and 3 in Experiment 2

Schemas	1	2	3ii	4ii	6	7	8	11	13	14
Weights	.58	.51	1.18	1.40	1.54	1.39	.58	.64	.60	1.08

other schemas presented in dyadic-predicate problems, is rated as relatively difficult. It is possible, of course, that the difference for Schema 3ii
between Tables 12.4 and 12.6 relies on the contexts in which the ratings
were made, that is, against a background of 64 monadic-predicate problems in the one case, and against a background of 64 dyadic-predicate
problems in the other case. Alternatively, it may be that Schema 3ii takes
relatively more effort when applied to a dyadic predicate. The data reported in the next section were obtained from subjects presented all 128
problems from the two parallel sets of monadic- and dyadic-predicate
problems, allowing assessment of whether the differential ratings for
monadic- and dyadic-predicate problems are robust against a background
of both problem types.

RESULTS: THE MONADIC- AND
DYADIC-PREDICATE PROBLEMS OF EXPERIMENT 3

Level of Accuracy

Considering all problems in two data sets (omitting the control-true problems), there were 122 problems and 40 subjects, that is, 4,880 responses.
Of these, 106 were errors (2.2%). The 97.8% accuracy rate replicates the
findings for the monadic- and dyadic-predicate problems reported in
Experiments 1 and 2, and again demonstrates that these are deductive
reasoning problems on which people do very well. In Data Sets 1 and 2,
there were 34 one-step problems and 40 subjects, that is, 1,360 responses.
Of these, 19 were errors (1.4%), showing that subjects did extremely well
on solving one-step problems.

Analyses Based on the Number of Reasoning Steps

For Data Sets 1 and 2, for the combined monadic and dyadic problems,
the correlations between the number of reasoning steps and two sets of
obtained mean difficulty ratings are .82 and .81, respectively, accounting
for approximately 66% of the variance. This shows that the number of
reasoning steps alone also provides substantial predictability. When problem length is partialed out, the two correlations are .74 and .72, respectively, accounting for approximately 53% of the variance.

We now consider the obtained mean difficulty ratings on monadic
predicate problems and on dyadic predicate problems separately. The
correlation between the number of reasoning steps and obtained mean
difficulty ratings on only monadic predicate problems is .81 (.69 when
the problem length is partialed out), for both data sets. The correlations

between the number of reasoning steps and obtained mean difficulty ratings on only dyadic-predicate problems are .76 and .75 (.71 on both when problem length is partialed out), respectively, for Sets 1 and 2. Note that the correlations for the monadic-predicate problems are equivalent to those in Experiment 1, and those for the dyadic-predicate problems are equivalent to those in Experiment 2.

Analyses Based on Schema Weights

We turn first to the monadic-predicate problems. The four correlations between the predictions from the two sets of schema weights and the two sets of obtained mean difficulty ratings ranged from .91 to .93, demonstrating once again that observed mean difficulty is predicted equally well by a set of weights obtained from the same data set or from a different data set. Again, the best estimate of schema weights is given by the combined 40 subjects of Data Sets 1 and 2, and these weights are presented in the first row of Table 12.7. The predicted difficulties for the monadic predicate problems provided by the weights in Row 1 of Table 12.7 have a correlation = .91 with the obtained mean difficulties of the combined data sets of Experiment 1.

We turn now to the dyadic predicate problems of Data Sets 1 and 2. The four correlations between the problem difficulties predicted from these two sets of weights and their observed mean difficulties range from .83 to .86. The schema weights for dyadic-predicate problems obtained from the 40 subjects of Data Sets 1 and 2 together are shown in Row 2 of Table 12.7. The predicted difficulties for the dyadic problems generated from these weights have a correlation of .86 with the obtained mean difficulty ratings for the combined dyadic-predicate data sets in Experiment 2.

The similarity of the weights for monadic and dyadic problems in Rows 1 and 2 of Table 12.7 to those in Tables 12.3 and 12.6, respectively, is illustrated by the correlations between the problem difficulties predicted by the models obtained from Experiment 3 and those obtained from Experiments 1 and 2, $r = .91$ for the monadic predicate problems and $r =$

TABLE 12.7
Schema Weights Obtained From the Monadic- and Dyadic-Predicate
Problems, and From all Problems of Experiment 3

Types of Problems	Schema Numbers and Weights									
	1	2	3ii	4ii	6	7	8	11	13	14
Monadic part	.50	.61	.55	1.38	1.43	1.53	.80	.49	.48	.95
Dyadic part	.64	.62	1.13	1.52	1.72	1.47	.64	.63	.62	1.10
Combination	.57	.62	.83	1.45	1.57	1.50	.72	.56	.55	1.02

.86 for dyadic predicate problems. This indicates that the weights obtained from the separate presentation of monadic- and dyadic-predicate problems in Experiments 1 and 2 are sufficiently robust that they survive to presentation of the two types of problems together in Experiment 3.

The presentation of both types of problems to the same subjects allows construction of a single parametric model, that is, with weights estimated for each schema from all 128 problems including both the monadic- and dyadic-predicate problems (i.e., ignoring whether a problem's predicates are monadic or dyadic). The four correlations between the problem difficulties predicted by the weights from Data Sets 1 and 2, respectively, and the observed mean difficulties for the two sets range from .91 to .92, revealing that the two data sets and their weights are extremely similar. The weights for two problem types taken together obtained from the 40 subjects in the combined data set are presented in Row 3 of Table 12.7.

The correlations between problem difficulties predicted by the overall weights in Row 3 of Table 12.7 for the monadic-predicate problems of Experiments 1 and 3 are .91 and .92, respectively. and for the dyadic-predicate problems of Experiments 2 and 3 are .86 each. Thus, the weights of the combined monadic and dyadic problem set provide excellent predictions for both the monadic and dyadic problems considered separately. This suggests that the predictions obtained from the weights reported in Row 3 of Table 12.7 (the combined monadic and dyadic set) are highly correlated with the predictions obtained from the monadic and dyadic sets separately, and indeed in both cases the $r = .99$.

The obtained mean difficulties for any data set (monadic, dyadic, or combined), therefore, can be predicted quite accurately from the weights obtained from any data set (monadic, dyadic, or combined). Ignoring whether problems present monadic or dyadic predicates and treating the problems as a single set when generating schema weights has no apparent predictive cost.

GENERAL RESULTS

Let us first consider overall performance on evaluating the proposed conclusions. In all data sets from all three experiments where subjects received all 64 problems, a total 180 subjects made 13,080 responses, and of these 354 were errors (2.71%). (Of these, 20 errors, 17 monadic and 3 dyadic, were on Problem 15.) Thus, the overall accuracy was 97.29%. This result shows two things: First, it demonstrates a class of predicate-logic reasoning problems that are well within subjects' reasoning abilities. Second, it shows that the parametric models are based on 97.29% of the overall responses (given that perceived difficulty ratings were counted only where evaluations were correct).

The fact that subjects almost always made the logically appropriate judgment, however, does not, by itself, show that subjects arrived at these judgments in the way described by the mental-logic theory. The analyses of perceived problem difficulty, however, provide evidence indicating that subjects were reasoning on these problems in the way described by the theory. The theory claims that the subjects in this study evaluated the conclusions to these problems after going through a line of reasoning in which schemas are applied sequentially. Each application of a schema is assumed to require some cognitive effort, and the total effort expended on a single problem soluble directly on the DRR is equal to the sum of the efforts for each schema application. This led to the prediction that perceived problem difficulty would correlate with the number of reasoning steps required to solve a problem. The overall results show that for the 180 subjects presented all 64 problems, the correlation between the number of reasoning steps and the obtained mean ratings is .83, accounting for approximately 69% of the variance, which substantially supports the prediction. Indeed, even with problem length partialed out the correlation is .75, accounting for 56% of the variance.

Furthermore, the theory predicted that problem difficulty would be even more closely correlated with the summed difficulties estimated for each schema used in each reasoning step proposed by the model. Combining all nine data sets into one (i.e., including together all 180 subjects who received all 64 problems) generates the schema weights shown in Row 1 of Table 12.8. (Rows 2 and 3 of Table 12.8 present the weights generated separately for monadic-predicate problems from the 100 subjects who received all 64 monadic-predicate problems and the 100 subjects who received all 64 dyadic-predicate problems, respectively.) Table 12.9 presents the difficulties for each problem predicted from the weights in Table 12.7, together with the obtained mean difficulties for these problems calculated from the data from all three experiments. The correlation between the predicted difficulties from Row 1 of Table 12.8 and the obtained mean difficulty ratings of all data sets combined is .93, accounting for approximately 86% of the variance; even with problem length partialed out, the correlation is

TABLE 12.8
Schema Weights Obtained From the Combination of Data Sets From
Experiments 1, 2, and 3 Overall and its Monadic and Dyadic Parts

Data Set	Schema									
	1	2	3ii	4ii	6	7	8	11	13	14
Overall	0.54	0.61	0.90	1.46	1.47	1.50	0.67	0.62	0.54	1.02
Monadic	0.47	0.65	0.66	1.48	1.34	1.56	0.75	0.60	0.49	0.95
Dyadic	0.60	0.56	1.16	1.44	1.61	1.42	0.60	0.64	0.61	1.09

TABLE 12.9
Predicted Problem Difficulties and Obtained Mean
Difficulty Ratings from Experiments 1, 2, and 3

| | Predicted Difficulties | | | | | | Obtained Means | | |
| | 10 Parameters | | | 3 Parameters | | | | | |
Problems	Monadic	Dyadic	Overall	Monadic	Dyadic	Overall	Monadic	Dyadic	Overall
4.	1.49	1.61	1.54	1.57	1.60	1.59	1.50	2.19	1.85
5.	1.49	1.61	1.54	1.57	1.60	1.59	1.45	1.46	1.45
6.	1.95	2.09	2.02	1.89	2.10	1.99	1.95	2.09	2.02
7.	1.95	2.09	2.02	1.89	2.10	1.99	2.26	2.19	2.23
8.	1.49	1.61	1.54	1.57	1.60	1.59	1.81	2.00	1.91
9.	1.49	1.61	1.54	1.57	1.60	1.59	1.41	1.65	1.53
10.	1.95	2.09	2.02	1.89	2.10	1.99	2.46	3.24	2.84
11.	1.95	2.09	2.02	1.89	2.10	1.99	2.12	2.42	2.27
12.	1.66	2.16	1.90	1.89	2.10	1.99	2.13	2.62	2.37
13.	2.48	2.44	2.46	2.52	2.48	2.50	2.80	3.07	2.93
14.	1.47	1.60	1.54	1.57	1.60	1.59	1.66	1.81	1.73
15.	1.65	1.56	1.61	1.57	1.60	1.59	1.70	2.80	2.28
16.	1.75	1.60	1.67	1.57	1.60	1.59	2.63	2.77	2.69
17.	2.34	2.61	2.47	2.52	2.48	2.50	2.42	2.63	2.53
18.	2.56	2.42	2.50	2.52	2.48	2.50	2.77	3.07	2.92
19.	1.60	1.64	1.62	1.57	1.60	1.59	2.18	3.38	2.74
20.	1.75	1.60	1.67	1.57	1.60	1.59	2.42	2.03	2.22
21.	1.96	2.21	2.08	2.14	2.20	2.18	2.14	3.28	2.70
22.	2.14	2.17	2.15	2.14	2.20	2.18	2.13	2.06	2.10
23.	2.83	3.22	3.01	3.09	3.08	3.09	2.69	3.00	2.84
24.	3.51	3.51	3.52	3.41	3.58	3.49	3.07	3.75	3.41
25.	2.42	2.69	2.56	2.46	2.70	2.58	2.11	2.14	2.13
26.	2.14	2.17	2.15	2.14	2.20	2.18	1.98	1.88	1.93
27.	2.70	2.69	2.69	2.46	2.70	2.58	2.33	2.47	2.40
28.	2.15	2.77	2.44	2.46	2.70	2.58	2.85	3.00	2.92
29.	2.09	2.25	2.15	2.14	2.20	2.18	1.97	1.58	1.78
30.	2.09	2.25	2.16	2.14	2.20	2.18	1.73	2.02	1.88
31.	2.90	3.37	3.11	3.03	3.30	3.17	3.42	3.45	3.44
32.	3.72	3.65	3.67	3.66	3.68	3.68	3.36	3.85	3.60
33.	4.64	4.80	4.70	4.55	4.78	4.67	4.30	4.73	4.50
34.	2.41	2.76	2.57	2.46	2.70	2.58	2.45	2.80	2.63
35.	3.32	3.04	3.13	3.09	3.08	3.09	3.08	2.86	2.97
36.	5.24	5.44	5.32	5.12	5.38	5.26	5.15	6.47	5.82
37.	4.18	4.48	4.33	4.17	4.50	4.35	3.47	4.21	3.83
38.	3.70	3.64	3.67	3.66	3.68	3.68	3.17	3.12	3.15
39.	3.77	3.93	3.85	3.60	3.90	3.76	3.53	3.46	3.50
40.	3.76	4.00	3.86	3.60	4.90	3.76	3.72	3.62	3.67
41.	3.16	3.36	3.24	2.46	2.70	2.58	2.93	4.38	3.58
42.	3.13	3.00	3.07	3.09	3.08	3.09	4.24	2.78	3.48
43.	3.90	4.03	3.97	3.41	3.58	2.49	3.21	3.61	3.41
44.	3.83	3.68	3.75	3.66	3.68	3.68	4.09	3.79	3.94

(Continued)

TABLE 12.9
(Continued)

| | Predicted Difficulties | | | | | | | | |
| | 10 parameters | | | 3 parameters | | | Obtained means | | |
Problems	Monadic	Dyadic	Overall	Monadic	Dyadic	Overall	Monadic	Dyadic	Overall
45.	3.09	3.21	3.14	3.09	3.08	3.09	3.19	3.47	3.33
46.	3.58	3.82	3.68	3.66	3.68	3.68	3.53	4.12	3.82
47.	4.38	4.81	4.57	4.55	4.78	4.67	3.94	4.67	4.25
48.	5.13	5.41	5.24	5.12	5.38	5.26	5.04	4.91	4.97
49.	2.71	2.81	2.75	2.71	2.80	2.77	2.71	3.08	2.90
50.	4.26	4.11	4.19	3.98	4.18	4.08	4.32	3.63	3.97
51.	3.17	3.29	3.23	3.03	3.30	3.17	3.67	3.35	3.52
52.	4.16	4.07	4.13	3.98	4.18	4.08	3.86	3.82	3.84
53.	3.48	3.78	3.62	3.66	3.68	3.68	3.46	3.40	3.42
54.	3.02	3.33	3.18	3.03	3.30	3.17	3.15	3.41	3.28
55.	2.95	3.04	3.00	3.09	3.08	3.09	2.95	3.59	3.27
56.	2.22	2.20	2.21	2.14	2.20	2.18	2.96	2.20	2.45
57.	3.97	4.18	4.07	3.98	4.18	4.08	4.47	4.00	4.23
58.	2.71	2.81	2.75	2.71	2.80	2.77	2.98	2.71	2.84
59.	2.82	2.84	2.83	2.71	2.80	2.77	3.33	2.75	3.04
60.	3.88	3.60	3.74	3.66	3.68	3.68	4.66	4.14	4.39
61.	2.82	2.84	2.83	2.71	2.80	2.77	2.40	2.64	2.52
62.	5.24	5.44	5.32	5.12	5.38	5.26	5.01	4.53	4.76
63.	5.13	5.41	5.24	5.12	5.38	5.26	4.86	4.99	4.93
64.	2.41	2.76	2.57	2.46	2.70	2.58	2.53	2.77	2.65

Note. Problems 1 to 3 were control-true problems and are excluded from this table. Sixty subjects received only monadic-predicate problems, 60 subjects received only dyadic-predicate problems, and 40 subjects received both monadic and dyadic problems. Thus, there were 100 monadic cases, 100 dyadic cases, and 200 cases overall. The predicted difficulties and observed means were obtained from all these subjects.

.89, accounting for 79% of variance. The overall weights, even when differences between monadic and dyadic predicate are ignored, provide an extremely good prediction of perceived problem difficulty.

Construction of a Parsimonious Model

In the preceding analyses, a different weight was assigned to each of the 10 core schemas, and a 10-parameter model was used to predict problem difficulties. Given that the 10-parameter model worked extremely well, it seemed useful to consider whether a more parsimonious model with a smaller number of parameters could be constructed without significant cost to predictability. Figure 12.1 plots the weights for each schema in Row 2 of Table 12.8 (the monadic part) against the weight in Row 3 of

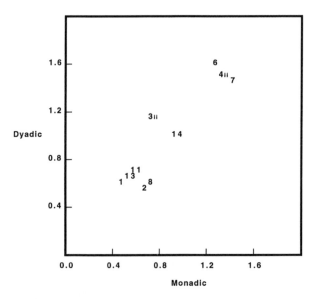

FIG. 12.1. Cross tabulation of schema weights based on perceived difficulty
ratings for the monadic- and dyadic-predicate problems.

Table 12.8 (the dyadic part). Inspection of Fig. 12.1 suggests that a three-
parameter model would provide a good fit to the data, with Schemas 1,
2, 8, 11, and 13 constituting a relatively easy set of inferences; Schemas
3ii and 14 a set of intermediate difficulty; and Schemas 4ii, 6, and 7 a
relatively difficult set of schemas. In this three-parameter model, the
weights are .59, .99, and 1.50 for the easiest, intermediate, and most
difficult schema sets, respectively. (This three-parameter model leads to
the same rank ordering of weights for the monadic and dyadic sets.) The
correlation between difficulties predicted by the three-parameter model
and obtained mean difficulties = .93, which is identical to the correlation
for the 10-parameter model. The three-parameter model thus is both more
parsimonious than the 10-parameter model and of equal predictive ability.
     Inspection of the three sets of schemas for the three-parameter model
reveals what makes a schema relatively easy or difficult. The five schemas
that constitute the easiest set (i.e., Schemas 1, 2, 8, 11, and 13) each present
only a single logic particle from among *and, if, some,* and *not*. The two
schemas that constitute the set of intermediate difficulty (i.e., Schemas 3ii
and 14) both present the particle *or* (and in the case of Schema 14, the
particle *not*). The three schemas of the most difficult set (i.e., Schemas 4ii,
6, and 7) are characterized by presentation of multiple particles, that is,
Schemas 6 and 7 present *or* and *if,* Schema 4ii presents *and* and *not*. The
perceived relative difficulties of the schemas thus can be summarized as
follows: Application of a schema with only one particle from among *and,*

if, *some*, and *not* is perceived as relatively effortless; application of a schema with *or* is perceived to take somewhat more effort, and application of a schema that presents two particles is perceived as relatively more difficult.

GENERAL DISCUSSION

The theory predicted that because the problems are soluble on the basic schemas and the DRR, there should be relatively few errors overall, and almost none on one-step problems. This clearly was the case, and once again the mental-logic approach has been able to construct a set of logical-reasoning problems that people solve routinely.

Perceived difficulty ratings were used to estimate the amount of cognitive effort expended to solve a problem. It was predicted that the number of reasoning steps required to solve a problem (predicted on the DRR) would correlate with observed mean difficulty ratings, and this also clearly was the case, thus providing support for the claim that the problems were solved in the way described by the theory. It was predicted that perceived problem difficulty would correlate even more strongly with the sum of the difficulties of the schemas applied in the reasoning steps to solve each problem (as predicted by the DRR). This prediction was highly confirmed.

These findings present a challenge to a large number of researchers who have concluded that people have few, or no, logical skills for reasoning, but rather that human reasoning is governed by content-specific processes (e.g., Cheng & Holyoak, 1985; Cosmides, 1989) or by an assortment of heuristics and reasoning biases (e.g., Evans et al., 1993). It is not obvious how any content-dependent process could account for the success found on the problems presented here, nor is it obvious what sort of heuristics or reasoning biases could explain the apparently logical responses to these problems.

The results reported here also present a challenge to two theories that ought, in principle, to be able to account for such findings. Rips's (1994) competing mental-logic theory has some difficulty in representing at least some of the problems, and leads to quite complicated lines of reasoning on many of them, as discussed in chapter 11. The mental-models theorists (e.g., Johnson-Laird & Byrne, 1991) have as yet provided only a partial description of how propositions of the sort presented in these problem would be represented by models, and we can only estimate how models theory would procede. That it is unclear how the models theory would represent the premises of these problems is illustrated by considering the premise *There are no square wooden beads*, from Problem 36 of Appendix 1. Johnson-Laird and Byrne (1991, p. 120) stated that a universal negative proposition, for example, *None of the athletes is a baker*, will be represented as:

[a]
  [b]
. . .

Application of this structure to *There are no square wooden beads* is problematic. Note that one cannot simply add one line to the model, as such:

[b]
  [w]
    [s]
. . .

because to do so would preclude the possibility of there being a wooden bead, or a square bead, or a square wooden thing that is not a bead, and these possibilities clearly should be allowed. Indeed, the appropriate model would seem to include six explicit representations:

[b]
  [w]
    [s]
      [b w]
        [b s]
          [w s]
. . .

We do not presume here to say how the models theory should decide how to represent such premises, but until its advocates provide a specification it remains unclear how, or whether, they will account for these findings. They will need to account both for why these problems were solved so routinely, and for the high correlations both between perceived problem difficulties and the number of reasoning steps, and between perceived problem difficulties and the sum of the weights for the schemas used in the solution. Precisely how any competing theory would accomplish this is unclear, so it is incumbent on them to show why they can be considered as serious alternatives.

The Test Problems With Monadic Predicates

Control-True Problems

1. All the beads are red

   ? All the beads are red?
2. The blue beads are wooden

   ? The blue beads are wooden?
3.* The metal beads are not round

   ? The metal beads are not round?

Control-False Problems

4. All the beads are square

   ? Some of the beads are not square   (13)
5. Some of the beads are metal

   ? None of the beads are metal?   (13)
6. All the beads are triangular or round

   ? Some of the beads are neither triangular nor round?   (14)
7. Some of the beads are either plastic or wooden

   ? None of the beads are wooden and none are plastic?   (14)
8.* Some of the beads are not triangular

   ? All the beads are triangular?   (13)
9.* None of the beads are plastic

   ? Some of the beads are plastic?   (13)
10.* Some of the beads are neither green nor square

   ? All the beads are green or square?   (14)
11.* None of the beads are metal and none are wooden

   ? Some of the beads are either metal or wooden?   (14)

One-Step Problems

12. The blue beads are either square or round

   ? The blue beads that are not square are round?   (True) (3ii)
13. There are no green square beads
    There are some square beads

   ? The square beads are not green?   (True) (4ii)

(Continued)

14. All the beads are red
    All the beads are metal

    ? All the beads are red metal beads? (True) (1)
15. All the beads are round and wooden

    ? All the beads are wooden? (True) (2)
16. None of the beads are round
    Some of the beads are wooden

    ? The wooden beads are not round? (True) (8)
17. All the beads are plastic or wooden
    The plastic beads are red
    The wooden beads are red

    ? All the beads are red? (True) (6)
18. All the beads are green or blue
    The green beads are plastic
    The blue beads are wooden

    ? All the beads are plastic or wooden? (True) (7)
19. The blue beads are metal

    ? Some of the beads are metal? (True) (11)
20. All the beads are round
    Some of the beads are red

    ? The red beads are round? (True) (8)

One-Step With Contradiction

21. All the beads are blue
    All the beads are plastic

    ? Some of the beads are not blue plastic beads? (False) (1 + 13)
22. All the beads are square wooden beads

    ? Some of the beads are not wooden? (False) (2 + 13)
23. All the beads are blue or green
    The blue beads are plastic
    The green beads are plastic

    ? Some of the beads are not plastic? (False) (6 + 13)
24. All the beads are metal or wooden
    The wooden beads are red
    The metal beads are blue

    ? Some of the beads are neither red nor blue? (False) (7 + 14)

(Continued)

25. None of the beads are metal
     None of the beads are plastic

     ? Some of the beads are either plastic or metal?   (False) (1 + 14)
26. Some of the beads are green plastic beads

     ? None of the beads are green?   (False) (2 + 13)
27. All the beads are square or round

     ? Some of the green beads are neither square nor
        round?   (False) (8 + 14)
28.* All the plastic beads are round or triangular

     ? Some of the plastic beads that are not round are
        not triangular?   (False) (3ii + 13)
29.* The red beads are triangular

     ? None of the beads are triangular?   (False) (11 + 13)
30.* None of the beads are round

     ? The square beads are round?   (False) (11 + 13)

Multistep Problems

31. All the beads are triangular or square
     None of red beads are square

     ? Some of the red beads are not triangular?   (False) (3ii + 8 + 13)
32. There are no green wooden beads
     The round beads are wooden

     ? Some of the round beads are green?   (False) (4ii + 8 + 13)
33. There are no red metal beads
     The square beads are metal
     Every bead is either red or green

     ? The square beads are green?   (True) (4ii + 8 + 3ii + 8)
34. All the beads are plastic or metal
     The blue beads are not plastic

     ? The blue beads are metal?   (True) (3ii + 8)
35. There are no red plastic beads
     The square beads are plastic

     ? The square beads are not red?   (True) (4ii + 8)
36. All the beads are triangular or square
     The green beads are not triangular
     There are no square wooden beads

     ? Some of the beads are not wooden?   (True) (3ii + 8 + 4ii + 8 + 11)

(Continued)

355

37. All the beads are metal or wooden
    The triangular beads are blue and not wooden

    ? The triangular beads are blue metal beads? (True) (2 + 3ii + 8 + 2 +1)
38. There are no green triangular beads
    The wooden beads are green

    ? The wooden beads are green and not triangular? (True) (4ii + 8 + 1)
39. None of the beads are wooden
    The blue beads are not square

    ? All the beads are square or wooden? (False) (8 + 1 + 11 + 14)
40. The plastic beads are either blue or green
    None of the beads are blue

    ? Some of the beads are green? (True) (8 + 3ii + 11)
41. The blue beads are either metal or plastic
    None of the beads are metal

    ? The blue beads are plastic? (True) (8 + 3ii)
42. All the beads are green and none of them are
    square wooden beads

    ? The wooden beads are not square? (True) (2 + 4ii)
43. All the beads are wooden or metal
    The wooden beads are square
    The metal beads are triangular

    ? The beads that are not triangular are square? (True) (7 + 3ii)
44. There are no green round beads
    The plastic beads are round

    ? Some of the beads are not green? (True) (4ii + 8 + 11)
45. All the beads are green or blue
    The green round beads are plastic
    The blue round beads are plastic

    ? The round beads are plastic? (True) (8 + 6)
46. All the beads are green or red
    The green beads are triangular
    The red beads are triangular

    ? Some of the wooden beads are not triangular? (False) (6 + 8 + 13)
47. All the beads are blue or red
    There are no blue square beads

    ? Some of the beads that are not red are square? (False) (3ii + 4ii + 8 + 13)

(Continued)

356

48. There are no red wooden beads
All the triangular beads are wooden
Every bead is either red or green

? Some of the triangular beads are not green?   (False) (4ii + 8 + 3ii + 8 + 13)

49. All the beads are green
Some of the triangular beads are plastic beads

? None of the triangular beads are green plastic beads?   (False) (8 + 1 + 13)

50. All the beads are plastic or wooden
The wooden beads are red
The plastic beads are blue
Some of the beads are round

? None of the round beads are red and none are blue?   (False) (7 + 8 + 14)

51. None of the beads are wooden
The round beads are not plastic

? Some of the round beads are either wooden or plastic?   (False) (8 + 1 + 14)

52. All the beads are red or green
The green beads are round plastic beads
The red beads are wooden beads

? Some of the beads are neither plastic nor wooden?   (False) (2 + 7 + 14)

53. All the beads are triangular or square
The triangular beads are red and metal
The square beads are metal

? Some of the beads are not metal?   (False) (2 + 6 + 13)

54. The square beads are not green
The square beads are not red

? All the beads are green or red?   (False) (1 + 11 + 14)

55.* There are no blue plastic beads
The blue beads are square

? The blue beads are square and not plastic?   (True) (4ii + 1)

56.* All the beads are square
The plastic beads are red

? The plastic beads are red square beads?   (True) (8 + 1)

57.* All the beads are wooden or metal
The wooden beads are red
The metal beads are green
The square beads are not red

? The square beads are green?   (True) (7 + 3ii + 8)

(Continued)

357

58.* All the beads are plastic
      The blue beads are round

      ? None of the beads are round plastic beads?   (False) (8 + 1 + 13)
59.* All the beads are blue
      The square beads are wooden

                                                               (True) (8 + 1 + 11)
      ? Some of the beads are blue wooden beads?
60.* There are no green metal beads
      The round beads are metal and not red
      ? The round beads are not green?   (True) (2 + 4ii + 8)
61.* All the beads are metal
      Some of the beads are green

      ? Some of the beads are green metal beads?   (True) (8 + 1 + 11)
62.* All the beads are plastic or wooden
      Some of the round beads are not plastic
      There are no blue wooden beads

      ? Some of the beads are not blue?   (True) (3ii + 8 + 4ii + 8 + 11)
63.* There are no square metal beads
      Some of the red beads are metal
      Every bead is either square or triangular

      ? None of the red beads are triangular?   (False) (4ii + 8 + 3ii + 8 + 13)
64.* All the beads are plastic or wooden

      ? The round beads that are not plastic are wooden?   (True) (8 + 3ii)

Note. *Problems that were not included in Study 1 of Experiment 1 but were included in Studies 2 to 4. For Problems 12 to 64, at the end of each problem, in parentheses, the predicted response (True or False) is shown. For Problems 4 to 64, the predicted line of reasoning is shown in parentheses.

Test Problems With Dyadic Predicates

Control-True Problems

1. All the children like the red beads

    ? All the children like the red beads?
2. The girls got some wooden beads

    ? The girls got some wooden beads?
3. None of the girls played with Tom

    ? None of the girls played with Tom?

Control-False Problems

4. All the boys found some square beads in their bags

    ? A few boys did not find any square beads in their
       bags?   (13)
5. Tom likes some of the beads

    ? Tom likes none of the beads?   (13)
6. All the children got either wooden beads or metal beads

    ? Some of the children got neither wooden beads nor
       metal beads?   (14)
7. Many of the boys played with Heather or other girls

    ? None of the boys played with Heather and none
       played with other girls?   (14)
8. The girls did not find some kind of beads in their bags

    ? The girls found all the kinds of beads in their bags?   (13)
9. None of the children like the triangular beads

    ? One of the children likes the triangular beads?   (13)
10. Lisa did not get many red beads and John did not
    get them either

    ? Either Lisa or John got all the red beads?   (14)
11. Jennifer played with none of the boys and Karen
    played with none of them either

    ? Either Jennifer or Karen played with some of the boys?   (14)

One-Step Problems

12. Every boy either found a few metal beads or got
    some plastic beads

    ? The boys who did not find any metal beads got
       some plastic beads?   (True) (3ii)

(Continued)

13. Johnson does not like the blue round beads

    The round beads that Johnson likes are not blue?   (True) (4ii)
14. The boys got the red beads
    The girls played with the boys

    ? The boys got the red beads and the girls played
       with (them)?   (True) (1)
15. Many of the girls played with the boys and they like
    the green beads

    ? The boys played with many of the girls?   (True) (2)
16. Sam and Harry found (none of the) no square beads
    in their bags

    ? Sam and Harry did not find any square metal beads?   (True) (8)
17. All the girls played with either Tom or John
    Each of the girls who played with Tom got a
       wooden bead
    Each of the girls who played with John got a
       wooden bead

    ? Every girl got a wooden bead?   (True) (6)
18. All the boys like either the metal beads or the
       wooden beads
    The boys who like the metal beads played with Mary
    The boys who like the wooden beads played with Linda

    ? All the boys played with either Mary or Linda?   (True) (7)
19. All the boys played with those girls who found red
       beads

    ? All the boys played with some children who found
       red beads?   (True) (11)
20. All the children found some triangular beads

    ? The boys all found some triangular beads?   (True) (8)

One-Step With Contradiction Problems

21. The girls like all the red beads
    The girls like all the wooden beads

    The girls do not like red square wooden beads?   (False) (1 + 13)
22. The boys all got green beads and the girls played
       with them

    ? Many of the boys did not get green beads?   (False) (2 + 13)

(Continued)

23. The boys all played with either Jennifer or Heather
    The boys who played with Jennifer like the metal beads
    The boys who played with Heather like the metal beads

    ? Some of the boys do not like the metal beads?   (False) (6 + 13)
24. The girls all got either red beads or blue beads
    The girls who got red beads played with Tom
    The girl who got blue beads played with Bill

    ? Some of the girls played with neither Tom nor Bill?   (False) (7 + 14)
    (? Some of the girls neither played with Tom nor
      played with Bill?)
25. None of the girls played with Jim
    None of the girls played with Mark

    ? Some of the girls played with either Jim or Mark?   (False) (1 + 14)
26. The girls found many green beads and the boys
    played with them

    ? The girls found no green beads?   (False) (2 + 13)
27. All the children like either the wooden or the metal
    beads

    ? Some of the girls like neither the wooden nor the
      metal beads?   (False) (8 + 14)
28. The boys all got either square beads or triangular beads

    ? Some of the boys who got no square beads did not
      get triangular beads either?   (False) (3ii + 13)
29. The boys played with Mary

    ? None of the children played with Mary?   (False) (8 + 9)
30. The girls found the red triangular beads

    ? The girls did not find any red beads?   (False) (11 + 13)

Multistep Problems

31. All the children like either round beads or square
    beads
    None of the girls like the square beads

    ? A few of the girls do not like the round beads?   (False) (3ii + 8 + 13)
32. The boys found no green plastic beads
    The triangular beads that the boys found are green

    ? Some of the triangular beads that the boys found
      are plastic?   (False) (4ii + 8 + 13)

(Continued)

33. There are no boys who like both the red beads and
the blue beads
Tom and John like the blue beads
The boys either like the red beads or played with
Jennifer

? Tom and John played with Jennifer?   (True) (4ii + 8 + 3ii + 8)

34. All the children got either wooden beads or plastic
beads
Many of the children did not get plastic beads

? Many of the children got wooden beads?   (True) (3ii + 8)

35. None of the girls played with both Harry and Jim
The girls who like the round beads played with Jim

? The girls who like the round beads did not play
with Harry?   (True) (4ii + 8)

36. The children all found either triangular or square beads
None of the boys found square beads
The boys who like the metal beads did not find both
triangular beads and metal beads

? Some of the children did not find any metal beads?   (True) (3ii + 8 + 4ii + 8 + 11)

37. All the boys like either the wooden beads or the
metal beads
The boys who played with Linda do not like metal
beads and they like square beads

? The boys who played with Linda like the square
and the wooden beads?   (True) (2 + 3ii + 8 + 2 + 1)

38. None of the children got both green beads and
triangular beads
The girls all got green beads

? The girls got green beads and got no triangular beads?   (True) (4ii + 8 + 1)

39. None of the children found blue beads
The girls did not find square beads

All the children found either blue beads or square
beads?   (False) (8 + 1 + 11 + 14)

40. The boys got either plastic or metal beads
None of the children got metal beads

? Some of the children got plastic beads?   (True) (8 + 3ii + 11)

41. The girls all played with either Steve or Johnson
None of the children played with Johnson

? The girls all played with Steve?   (True) (8 + 3ii)

(Continued)

42. The boys got some of the wooden beads and they
    got no square wooden beads

    ? The wooden beads that the boys got are not
      square?   (True) (2 + 4ii)
43. The girls played with either Mike or Bill
    The girls who played with Mike found triangular beads
    The girls who played with Bill found round beads

    ? The girls who found no triangular beads found
      round beads?   (True) (7 + 3ii)
44. There are no boys who played with both Karen and
    Heather
    The boys who played with Jennifer also played with
    Heather

    ? Some of the boys did not play with Karen?   (True) (4ii + 8 + 11)
45. All the beads are either red or blue
    The boys got all the red round beads
    The boys got all the blue round beads

    ? The boys got all the round beads?   (True) (8 + 6)
46. All the beads are either plastic or metal
    The girls found all the plastic beads
    The girls found all the metal beads

    ? There are some of the triangular beads that the
      girls did not find?   (False) (6 + 8 + 13)
47. The girls played with either Johnson or Bill
    There are no girls who played with both Johnson
    and Tom

    ? Some of the girls who did not play with Bill
      played with Tom?   (False) (3ii + 4ii + 8 + 13)
48. The children found no red wooden beads
    The beads that the boys found are all wooden beads
    Every beads is either red or blue

    ? Some of the beads that the boys found are not blue?   (False) (4ii + 8 + 3ii + 8 + 13)
49. All the children like the green beads
    Some of the boys like the plastic beads

    ? None of the boys like the green plastic beads?   (False) (8 + 1 + 13)
50. All the beads are plastic or wooden
    The girls got the plastic beads
    The boys got the wooden beads
    Some of the beads are round beads

    ? Neither the boys nor the girls got round beads?   (False) (7 + 8 + 14)

(Continued)

51. None of the children like the green beads
    The girls do not like the metal beads

    ? Some of the girls like either the green beads or the
    metal beads?   (False) (8 + 1 + 14)
52. All the beads were found by either the boys or the
    girls
    The beads that the boys found are square plastic beads
    The beads that the girls found are wooden beads

    ? Some of the beads are neither plastic nor wooden?   (False) (2 + 7 + 14)
53. All the beads were found by either the boys or the girls
    The beads that the boys found are red metal beads
    The beads that the girls found are metal beads

    ? Some of the beads are not metal?   (False) (2 + 6 + 13)
54. Lisa and the boys do not like the square beads
    Lisa and the boys do not like the triangular beads

    ? All the children like either the square or the
    triangular beads?   (False) (1 + 11 + 14)
55. None of the girls played with both John and Jim
    John played with the girls who got red beads

    ? The girls who got red beads played with John and
    did not play with Jim?   (True) (4ii + 1)
56. All the beads are square
    The girls found the red beads

    ? The girls found the red square beads?   (True) (8 + 1)
57. All the children got either wooden or metal beads
    The wooden beads are red
    The metal beads are green
    None of the boys got red beads

    ? The boys all got green beads?   (True) (7 + 3ii + 8)
58. All the beads are plastic
    The girls like the red beads

    None of the children like the red plastic beads?   (False) (8 + 1 + 13)
59. All the beads are blue
    The boys got the square beads

    Some of the children got the blue square beads?   (True) (8 + 1 + 11)
60. There are no round metal beads
    The beads that Tom and Jennifer found are all metal
    beads and they found no red beads

    ? Tom and Jennifer found no round beads?   (True) (2 + 4ii + 8)

(Continued)

61. All the beads are wooden
   Some of the boys found the green beads

   ?Some of the children found the green wooden beads?   (True) (8 + 1 + 11)
62. All the children like either the plastic or the wooden
   beads
   Some of the girls do not like the plastic beads
   There are no blue wooden beads

   ? Some of the beads are not blue?   (True) (3ii + 8 + 4ii + 8 + 11)
63. None of the children found square metal beads
   The beads that some of the boys found are metal
   Every bead is either square or triangular

   ? None of the boys found triangular beads?   (False) (4ii + 8 + 3ii + 8 + 13)
64. All the boys played with either Karen, Jennifer, or
   Heather

   A few of the boys who played with neither Jennifer
   nor Heather played with Karen?   (True) (8 + 3ii)

Note. In the parentheses at the end of each problem are indicated the predicted evaluation and the schemas required to solve the problem.

13

Leveling the Playing Field: Investigating Competing Claims Concerning Relative Inference Difficulty

Ira A. Noveck
Centre de Recherche en Epistemologie Appliquée

Guy Politzer
Centre National de la Recherche Scientifique

Given that the competing mental-logic and mental-model accounts of propositional reasoning have led to a prolific exchange of arguments and counterarguments, as well as analyses and reanalyses of foundational work, one would assume that a neutral observer would have enough data to determine which theory better describes such reasoning. This is not the case, however. The debate's empirical findings vary sufficiently to run the risk of leaving the neutral observer nonplused as to which position is more supportable. For example, consider the contradictory reports concerning responses to the disjunctive premise set presented in (1):

1. p or q
   $\underline{\text{not } q}$
   $\therefore p$

Whereas Johnson-Laird, Byrne, and Schaeken (1992) reported relatively low rates (30%) of correct responses to (1), the mental logic approach typically has reported high rates (often above 90%), as to be expected for a mental-logic schema (chaps. 7 and 8; see also Braine & Rumain, 1981). How does one reconcile such wildly divergent findings concerning a fundamental inference? This chapter endeavors to address the contradictory findings, not only to maintain the integrity of the empirical literature, but also to help resolve part of a wider debate between the mental-logic and mental-model theories.

We begin by comparing empirical methods because gaps in findings may well be attributable to materials and procedure. Consider the *or* premise in (1). The mental-model study employed lengthy propositions and exclusive disjunctions (e.g., *John is in London or Mary is in Caracas, but not both*) and places the second premise on a separate page (*Mary is not in Caracas*), thus imposing a memory load—the first, relatively complex, premise must be remembered when the second premise is encountered. In contrast, the mental-logic experiments typically employ less complex propositions concerning letters on an imaginary blackboard, use unspecified disjunctions, and present the two relevant premises simultaneously on the same page (e.g., *[On the blackboard] There is an L or a C; There is not a C*), that is, no memory load is imposed.[1] Given these differences, it should not be surprising to find that subjects are less likely to draw the conclusion *John is in London* than *There is an L*. Once the differences in materials and procedure become apparent, the results from the two kinds of problems become easier to explain. However, it is not clear which factor accounts for most of the discrepancy, and the question remains as to which of the two theories does a better job of describing propositional reasoning once variations are accounted for.

Among various points of disagreement (e.g., algorithms and representation), there is one feature of the two theories that is readily resolvable—relative inference difficulty. The mental-logic approach classifies a set of highly feasible inference forms as core or ancillary, investigates their relative difficulty, and, by exclusion, underlines which valid forms do not merit mental-logic status (e.g., modus tollens, as seen in 3 later). The mental-models theory predicts difficulty based on the presumed number of constructions an inference requires; the more models, the more difficult the inference. These two approaches lead to diverging predictions. For example, according to the mental-logic theory, premise set 2 triggers a core schema, whereas the premise set that prompts modus tollens, 3 does not; thus 2 should be easier to deduce than 3. As discussed later, the mental-models account makes a competing prediction: 3 should not be more difficult than 2, because it does not require any more models.

2. Not both p and q	3. If p then q
p	*not q*
not q	*not p*

---

[1] A mental-logic experiment often presents multiple premises because it investigates a chain of reasoning, but even these do not require the storing of premises in memory.

These two premise sets include the same number of negative elements and will serve as a source of comparison later.

In the remainder of the chapter, we briefly review the inference-difficulty claims and findings from the mental-models approach. This is followed by a discussion concerning how claims from mental models differ from those of mental logic and how one can practically test between them. Finally, we report a study in which we directly compare predictions from the two theories in one overarching procedure.

INFERENCE DIFFICULTY AND ITS RELEVANCE TO MENTAL LOGIC

Johnson-Laird et al. (1992, p. 428) predicted that inferences drawn from *not both* propositions will be more difficult than those drawn from *or* propositions and that inferences drawn from *or* propositions will be more difficult than those based on *if* propositions; this is because these connectives require, at least initially, three mental models, two mental models, and one (explicit) mental model, respectively. In an investigation of this prediction, Johnson-Laird et al. (1992, Experiment 1) presented subjects with four premise sets and recorded subjects' spontaneous conclusions. Subjects were presented two premises consecutively (concerning people in cities), each premise on a separate page, and were required to write down their conclusion. Two premise sets employed the disjunction *or* and two the conditional *if*. The two *or* forms were expressed exclusively as *p or q but not both; not-q* (conclusion: *p*) and *p or q but not both; p* (conclusion: *not-q*). The two forms concerning *if* were *if p then q;not-q*, which prompts modus tollens as seen in 3 earlier, and the premise set that triggers modus ponens, *if p then q;p*, as shown in 4:[2]

4. If Linda is in Amsterdam then Cathy is in Majorca.
   Linda is in Amsterdam.

The appropriate response of course is *Cathy is in Majorca*. Johnson-Laird et al. found that subjects' rates of correct conclusions to the four premise sets (1, *p or q but not both;not-q*; 2, *p or q but not both;p*; 3, *if p then q;not-q*; and 4, *if p then q;p*) were in line with the ordinal prediction. That is, subjects gave correct responses to these four premise sets on 30%, 48%, 64%, and 91% of the trials, respectively. According to Johnson-Laird et al. (1992), two factors are responsible for these findings. One is that

---

[2]To emphasize that we are usually referring to the premise sets that allow modus ponens and modus tollens inferences, we will simply present the premise sets themselves.

negative categorical premises (in premise sets 1 and 3 earlier) are expected to yield lower rates than those with affirmative categorical premises because they require an inconsistency to be detected.[3] The other more theoretically relevant factor is the number of mental models required ab initio: *If* propositions are said to require one explicit and one implicit mental model initially, and *or* propositions two explicit models.

Whereas mental-models theory uses number of models as a predictor of problem difficulty, mental logic has a quite different approach. Broadly, assuming subjects interpret the premises as intended, the easiest problems are those that can be solved in one step by a core mental-logic schema. The next easiest are those that require more than one step but can be solved using the direct-reasoning routine (see chap. 6 for the core schemas and the direct reasoning routine). Problems that cannot be solved by the direct-reasoning routine constitute a third (heterogeneous) level of difficulty. (Finer gradations in difficulty can be predicted—see chap. 6—but the levels just enunciated suffice for our purposes.)

Three of the core schemas are relevant here. One is modus ponens, which solves problem 4 in a simple step:

5. if p then q

   p

   $\therefore q$

The other relevant schemas are those that produce conclusions to 1 and 2. Modus tollens, whose premise set is presented in 3, is an example of an inference form that is not included in mental logic and thus would be predicted to be relatively difficult.

Note that the schema involving *or*, as in 1, uses an unspecified *or* only. That means that when a problem presents an explicitly exclusive-or, mental logic predicts that more than one inferential step will be needed. For example, consider problem 6:

---

[3]The role of the "inconsistency to be detected" in mental models, which is a source of inference difficulty, is mentioned twice in Johnson-Laird et al. (1992). On page 425, while describing the algorithm, the inconsistency refers to *any* contrary value between new and previously constructed models. It follows that an inconsistency arises when p appears in the minor premise and is inconsistent with a previously constructed model containing not-p (as in p or q, *but not both; p*). However, on page 431 in the course of describing predictions from their first experiment, "inconsistency" is employed only in reference to a *categorical (minor) premise* that has a negative value. In our discussions of "inconsistency," we adopt the former interpretation because it follows from Johnson-Laird's general description of their algorithm and if its more general use were adopted in describing their first experiment, it would not unduly affect the predictions from their first experiment. It follows, then, that all the determinable premise sets here but *if p then q;p* have an inconsistency to be detected.

6. There is an *L* or an *R*, but not both.
   There is not an *R*.

Mental logic predicts two steps. The reasoner first applies and-elimination to the first premise of 6 in order to decouple it (this premise being a pragmatic variation of *There is an L or an R **and** there is not both an L and an R*). One can then apply the second premise in 6 to *There is an L or an R* in order to carry out the inference as represented in 1. Similarly, consider problem 7:

7. There is an *X* or a *V*, but not both.
   There is an *X*.

Again, mental logic predicts that the reasoner first applies and-elimination, this time extracting *There is not both an X and a V*. Then, in combination with the second premise in 7, the schema represented in 2 applies to infer that *There is not a V*.

Thus, mental logic predicts that problem 6 with *exclusive-or* should be slightly more difficult than the corresponding problem with *unspecified-or*. Similarly, problem 7 should be slightly more difficult than a corresponding problem that presents the *not-both* premise directly. However, any difference in difficulty should be small and possibly hard to detect statistically because the extra step involves *and*-elimination, a very easy schema (see chap. 7).

CONSTRUCTING A LEVEL PLAYING FIELD

In order to make comparative assessments of the two theories, it is important to use the same procedures and materials. Here are the ground rules we adopted. First, we imposed the more challenging procedure used by Johnson-Laird et al. (1992) of presenting premises separately in order (a) to avoid ceiling effects and (b) to allow replication of the mental models findings from Johnson-Laird et al. (1992). Second, we investigated the effect of two variables on inference-difficulty (as measured by rates of correct responses), type of content (people-in-cities vs. letters), and manner of presenting the disjunction (exclusive-or vs. unspecified-or). Although theoretical predictions from the two theories do not change across content, it is worthwhile to know whether these factors are responsible for the inconsistencies observed across the two kinds of experiments, especially with respect to *p or q;not-q*. Third, we included six inference forms—the four that Johnson-Laird et al. (1992) investigated plus two that follow by having the negated disjunction (*not both p and q*) as a major premise with either *p or not-q* as a minor premise, whose predicted relative difficulty differs as a function of the given theory.

Premises with *not both p and q* were added for two main reasons. First, the mental-models position claims (Johnson-Laird et al., 1992, p. 428) that the premise set *not both p and q;p* should prompt even fewer correct conclusions than those involving disjunctions, which, according to Johnson-Laird et al.'s data, would mean rates of correct responses that are much lower than those reported in chapters 7 and 8. Second, the inclusion of *not both p and q;p* premise sets makes possible a critical test that compares predictions of the two theories without involving the manipulated disjunctions. As described earlier, the mental logic position argues that reasoners ought to provide correct conclusions to the premise set *not both p and q;p* more readily than the premise set that prompts modus tollens (*if p then q;not-q*) because the former is in the mental-logic repertoire and the latter is not. The mental-model position leads to the following competing prediction: *Not both p and q* proposition initially require three models, and *if* propositions initially require one explicit model along with one implicit model. The implicit model for *if* can be fleshed out either into one other explicit model (biconditional representation) or into two explicit models (conditional representation) in order to perform a modus tollens inference. Thus, *if* can eventually be the source of two or three models. By adding one model to represent the minor premise and one more for producing the conclusion, one arrives at the following number of models for each kind of inference: Five models for drawing the inference from *not both p and q;p* and either four or five models for modus tollens, which shows that in no case can *if p then q;not-q* be more difficult than *not both p and q;p*. If anything, modus tollens should appear easier because it would be expected that a number of subjects would construct the biconditional interpretation and would build only two models for their initial representation of *if*. The mental-model prediction is therefore the following: Rates of correct performance on *if p then q;not-q* should be equivalent to, or higher than, performance on *not both p and q; p*.

In the experiment that follows, premises with people-in-cities content are expected to prompt fewer correct conclusions than those presented with letters content. When reasoning with people-in-cities content, subjects must store four objects (two names and two places) in memory; when reasoning with arbitrary letters, any given proposition has two constituents. We also investigate how rates of correct performance will be affected when the disjunction is presented exclusively or in an unspecified manner.

METHOD

Participants

One hundred and twenty-four undergraduate students from the University of Minnesota participated. Participants received either $4.00 or credit towards requirements for the Introductory Psychology course at the University of Minnesota.

Materials

Four problem sets were prepared. Each problem set included 18 pairs of premises (a major propositional premise and a categorical premise), the result of preparing three instantiations of each of the following six premise sets: (1) *if p then q;p*, (2) *if p then q;not-q*, (3) *p or q; p* (or *p or q but not both;p*), (4) *p or q;not-q* (or *p or q but not both; not-q*), (5) *not both p and q;p*, and (6) *not both p and q;not-q*. The correct answer to the last premise set is *Nothing follows*.

Problem sets concerned either people in cities (to be referred to as the *People-in-cities problem set*) or letters said to be written on an index card (to be referred to as the *Letters problem set*). For the People-in-cities problem set, common first names and well-known cities were chosen. Two constraints were considered when combining the names and cities. The first was that no name–city combination had fewer than three syllables or more than five. The second constraint was that there were equal numbers of female and male names, and they were paired so that all gender combinations appeared equally often (when including two practice problems).

Given that names and cities vary in length, the total number of syllables in the people-in-cities condition was carefully balanced. Considering only the names and cities, six combinations had a total of seven syllables, six combinations had a total of eight syllables (name–city syllable subtotals of four and four), and six had a total of nine syllables. These were distributed as evenly as possible among the six premise sets. For the Letters set, only those letters that are pronounceable in one syllable were chosen (which excluded W). No letter was used more than twice. Letters were joined randomly with the constraint that half the problems presented letters in their alphabetic order (e.g., *If there is an H then there is an L*) and the other half presented the letters in their inverted alphabetic order (e.g., *If there is a U then there is a J*). Also, letter-pairs that could be construed to have meaning were avoided. The remaining two problem sets were identical to the two previously described, except that exclusive disjunctions were replaced with unspecified disjunctions. See the Appendix to this chapter for a complete listing of the materials.

Design

This is a 6 (Premise sets) × 2 (Kinds of Content: People-in-cities vs. Letters) × 2 (Expressions of disjunction: *exclusive or* vs. *unspecified or*) design with Premise Sets being a within-subjects factor. The experimental groups are called Letters Exclusive-or, Letters Unspecified-or, People-in-Cities Exclusive-or, and People-in-Cities Unspecified-or. It follows that the nondisjunctive premise sets (1, *if p then q;p*; 2, *if p then q;not-q*; 5, *not both p and q;p*; and 6, *not both p and q;not-q*) in the People-in-Cities conditions were identical as were the nondisjunctive premise sets in the Letters conditions.

Procedure

Subjects were seated in front of a Macintosh computer that presented the experiment with Frida software (Poitrenaud, 1990). The experimenter conducted the entire procedure by prompting screens. The first screen presented the instructions. In the People-in-cities condition, subjects were prompted to imagine that an international company keeps track of its employees on index cards, that the names of several colleagues were written on each index card, and that for each card the computer gives two pieces of information. The first piece describes an existing relationship between two colleagues and the second informs something specific about one of the colleagues. For the Letters condition, subjects were prompted to imagine game cards that each have several letters written on them. As with the other condition, subjects were told that the computer presents two pieces of information, one concerning a relationship between two letters and a second, more specific, piece of information.

The instructions asked subjects to read each of the two pieces of information out loud (as per Johnson-Laird et al., 1992) and to write down whatever conclusion follows. An example was given followed by a sentence that pointed out that they can say that *Nothing follows* when there is insufficient information to draw a conclusion. Before moving on to two practice problems, the experimenter highlighted key aspects of the instructions (that the subject will read two pieces of information out loud and that they have to write down what follows, and if nothing follows, to write that down: *Nothing follows*).

Both practice problems were variations of *if p then q;p* premises. Modus ponens inferences were used because subjects' performance on these is not under dispute here; the literature shows that subjects typically are able with these forms and that successful performance is expected without practice.

The first practice problem was the same as the one in the instruction screen and was presented to get subjects into the habit of reading the premises out loud. Its propositional premise had a negative consequent so that subjects would see that conclusions with negatives were relevant. The second example was expressed with an *only if* connective and provided affirmative constituents in both the antecedent and consequent. In the practice problems as well as in the task, the first premise disappeared when the second premise appeared (in order to be consistent with Johnson-Laird et al.'s paper-and-pencil procedure). In the rare event that subjects did not provide the correct conclusion to a practice problem, subjects were prompted to reconsider their response. No subject failed to answer correctly a practice problem when asked to reconsider. Once a subject was ready, the experimenter prompted the computer to present the 18 premise sets. The computer program was designed to select the 18 in a random order.

RESULTS AND DISCUSSION

The results are divided into two parts. We first investigate inference difficulty with respect, in particular, to disjunction presentation and content in order to determine how subjects' performance varies as a function of materials. This is important to reasoning research generally. We then compare predictions from the mental-logic and mental-models theories.

Summary of Effects

We consider only flawless responses (allowances were made for spelling errors). That is, a response was considered incorrect if (1) the conclusion was evaluated incorrectly (e.g., to respond *P* instead of *not-P*) or (2) it had the wrong name or wrong city in the People-in-cities condition, or the wrong letter in the Letters condition. Each subject received a score ranging from 0 to 3 for each kind of premise set, and these scores were converted to percentages of correct responses, as seen in Table 13.1.[4] Two separate analyses were computed: one for the four determinable premise sets in the two Unspecified-or conditions and the other for the five determinable premise sets in the two Exclusive-or conditions.

To investigate the two Unspecified-or conditions, a 4 (Determinable Premise Sets) × 2 (Contents: People-in-cities vs. Letters) ANOVA was computed with Premise Sets a within-subjects measure. The results revealed an effect for Premise Set, $F(3, 180) = 19.67$, $p < .001$, $MSe = .64$, and

---

[4]The same experiment, using the two Exclusive-or problem sets only, was presented in French to university students in Paris. The French results were comparable with their companion problems in English. For the sake of brevity, we do not include them here.

TABLE 13.1
Percentage of Correct Responses to the Six Premise
Sets in the Four Problem Sets of the Experiment

| Premise Set | Unspecified-Or | | Exclusive-Or | | |
	Letters	People-in-Cities	Letters	People-in-Cities	Total
if p then q;p	99	92	100	95	97
if p then q;not-q	65	55	65	54	59
p or q;p[a]	—	—	96	69	—
p or q;not-q[a]	**82**	**67**	**81**	**53**	**70**
not both p and q;p	81	83	87	70	80
not both p and q;not-q	32	31	42	27	33

Notes. Three trials were presented with each of the six types of premise sets.

[a]*or* was presented either as an exclusive disjunction or as unspecified disjunction, as indicated by the column heading.

The results concerning the *p or q;not-q* (or the *p or q but not both;not-q*) premise sets are highlighted to indicate that these are the only relevant results concerning the manipulation concerning Exclusive- versus Unspecified-*or*'s.

*n = 31 per problem set.

no effect for Content, $F(1,60) = 2.43$, $p = .12$. There were no interactions ($p = .33$). Figure 13.1 summarizes the Premise Set effect: *If p then q;p* yields the highest rate of correct responses, followed by a second subset of premise sets—*not both p and q;p* and *p or q;not-q*—which yield comparable rates of correct responses. Finally, representing a third subset, the premise set *if p then q;not-q* yields a rate of correct responses that is significantly lower than *p or q;not-q*.

To investigate the two Exclusive-or conditions, a 5 (Determinable Premise Sets) × 2 (Contents: People-in-cities vs. Letters) ANOVA was computed

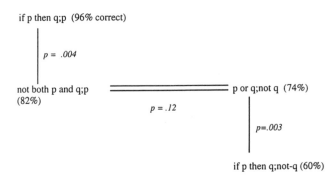

FIG. 13.1. Summary of inference difficulty, from least (top) to most (bottom), based on subjects' rates of correct responses to the four determinable premise sets in the two Unspecified-or conditions. The *p* values refer to the results from within-subjects *t*-tests.

with Premise Sets a within-subjects measure. There was an effect for Premise Set, $F(4,240) = 19.89$, $p < .001$, $MSe = .61$, and a main effect for Content, $F(1,60) = 19,193$, $p < .001$, $MSe = 1.13$. There is a marginal, but not significant, Content × Premise Set interaction ($p = .07$).

Given the lack of a statistically significant interaction, we summarize performance across the two Exclusive-or conditions in Fig. 13.2. For these conditions, *if p then q; p* again was easiest for subjects, followed by *p or q but not both;p* and *not both p and q;p* on a second tier. A third subset comprising *p or q but not both;p* and *if p then q;not-q* yielded comparable rates of correct responses. Figure 13.2 shows that when *or* is presented as an exclusive disjunction, subjects' rate of correct performance to *p or q but not both;not-q* drops down one level (when compared with *p or q;not-q* in Fig. 13.1).

Before describing the main effect for content, we investigate how the *but not both* clause in the disjunctive premise set *p or q but not both;not-q* affected rates of correct performance. A two-factor ANOVA was computed in which Disjunction Type (Exclusive-or vs. Unspecified-or) and Content (Letters vs. People-in-cities) were between-subject variables. The ANOVA revealed one main effect—for Content, $F(1, 120) = 13.25$, $p < .001$, $MSe = .63$. Although the effect for Disjunction Type had some marginal influence, it was not significant ($p = .23$); the same holds for the Content × Disjunction Type interaction ($p = .31$). Rates of correct responses to the premise sets *p or q;not-q* and *p or q but not both;not-q* combined (fourth row of Table 13.1) in the Letters and People-in-cities conditions were 82% and 60%, respectively. Clearly, subjects' rates of correct performance in response to this premise set were more sensitive to type of content than to the presence or absence of the exclusiveness clause.

Space does not permit a thorough discussion of the more general effect for Content, but, briefly, subjects responded correctly to 86% of the determinable premise sets with Letters content and to 68% of those with the

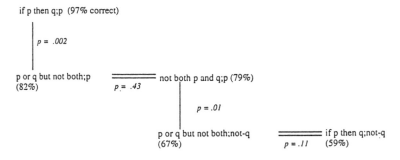

FIG. 13.2. Summary of inference difficulty, from least (top) to most (bottom), based on subjects' rates of correct responses to the five determinable premise sets in the two Exclusive-or conditions. The *p* values refer to the results from within-subjects *t*-tests.

People-in-cities content. Another 9% of responses in the People-in-cities condition would have been correct if errors attributable to memory limitations were considered acceptable (e.g., if we were to accept *John is in Caracas* as accurate when the correct response was *George is in Caracas*). Interestingly, errors in the People-in-cities sets were largely the result of errors on the name. In contrast, only one more response in the Letters condition (less than .3%) would have been accepted following a more generous accounting. When errors in memory are disregarded, the findings in the People-in-cities set more closely resemble those found in the Letters set.

Comparing Predictions From the Mental-Logic and Mental-Model Theories

We carried out two tests in order to test between the two theories. First, we made a direct comparison of subjects' responses to the *if p then q;not-q* (modus tollens) and *not both p and q;p* premise sets. As discussed in the introduction, the mental-logic theory predicts that *if p then q;not-q* will prompt a lower rate of correct responses than *not both p and q;p* because the former is not a core mental-logic schema and the latter is. Mental-model theory makes the complementary prediction: *if p then q;not-q* ought to prompt a rate of correct responses that is either higher than or equal to that of *not both p and q;p* because *if p then q;not-q* ought to prompt up to (four), or as many (five), mental models as *not both p and q;p* (which prompts five). Table 13.1 shows that, across the four conditions, subjects consistently had significantly more success in responding correctly to *not both p and q;p* (80% correct overall) than to *if p then q;not-q* (59% overall). This finding is significant whether one sums across conditions, $t(123) = 5.26$, $p < .001$, or investigates conditions separately (see Table 13.2). These results favor the mental-logic account of propositional reasoning.

Our second test involved a set of finer grained analyses. We treated each experimental condition separately and checked predictions with respect to performance on any two premise sets that prompt a prediction. (A successful prediction is one in which a *t*-test is significant at the .05 level. A confirmed null hypothesis generously serves as the basis for confirming a predicted equivalence of inference difficulty.) We focused on the middle part of the table because both theories correctly anticipate that *if p then q;p* (prompting modus ponens) would yield the highest rate of correct responses and that *not both p and q;not-q* would yield the lowest.

The mental-logic account predicts that among the remaining premise sets, *if p then q;not-q* will prompt the lowest rate of correct responses and significantly fewer correct responses than the others. This amounts to two predictions in each of the two Unspecified-or conditions and to three predictions in each of the two Exclusive-Or conditions. Table 13.2 shows

TABLE 13.2
Account of the Mental Logic and Mental Models Predictions

	Condition	Prediction	Empirical Status
Mental logic	1. Letters, Uns-or	IV > II	Confirmed
	2. Letters, Uns-or	V > II	Confirmed
	3. People, Uns-or	IV > II	Marginally confirmed
	4. People, Uns-or	V > II	Confirmed
	5. Letters, Exc-or	III > II	Confirmed
	6. Letters, Exc-or	IV > II	Confirmed
	7. Letters, Exc-or	V > II	Confirmed
	8. People, Exc-or	III > II	Confirmed
	9. People, Exc-or	IV > II	Not confirmed
	10. People, Exc-or	V > II	Confirmed
Mental models	1. Letters, Uns-or	IV > II	Confirmed
	2. Letters, Uns-or	IV > V	Not confirmed
	3. Letters, Uns-or	II = V	Not confirmed
	4. People, Uns-or	IV > II	Marginally confirmed
	5. People, Uns-or	IV > V	Not confirmed
	6. People, Uns-or	II = V	Not confirmed
	7. Letters, Exc-or	III = IV	Not confirmed
	8. Letters, Exc-or	III > II	Confirmed
	9. Letters, Exc-or	III > V	Marginally confirmed
	10. Letters, Exc-or	IV > II	Confirmed
	11. Letters, Exc-or	IV > V	Not confirmed
	12. Letters, Exc-or	II = V	Not confirmed
	13. People, Exc-or	III = IV	Not confirmed
	14. People, Exc-or	III > II	Confirmed
	15. People, Exc-or	III > V	Not confirmed
	16. People, Exc-or	IV > II	Not confirmed
	17. People, Exc-or	IV > V	Not confirmed
	18. People, Exc-or	II = V	Not confirmed

Notes. Predictions refer to subjects' relative difficulty in drawing correct conclusions from the compared premise sets. The Roman numerals refer to the premise sets found in the corresponding row in Table 13.1. For example, II refers to *if p then q; not-q.* = is to be read as *is as difficult as* and > is to be read as *is easier than.*

Empirical status is determined by *t*-tests with a .05 level of significance on rates of solution in Table 13.1.

that mental logic successfully predicts 8 of 10 effects with this analysis and a ninth is marginally confirmed.

Predictions from mental models are somewhat more complicated because the number of anticipated mental models varies on two inferences as a function of a fleshing-out procedure. As described earlier, conclusions from *if p then q; not-q* may require four or five models. Similarly, the number of total mental models required to infer *p* from the (Unspecified-or) premise set *p or q; not-q* also depends on a subject's interpretation of *or* (Byrne, personal communication). If subjects interpret *or* as inclusive, it will prompt three models initially (1, p q; 2, p not-q; 3, not-p q) and require five to reach a solution; if subjects interpret *or* exclusively, it will prompt two models (1, p not-q; 2, not-p q) and require four to reach a solution. Later we describe how we attempt to adopt the set of predictions most favorable to the mental-models position.

To simplify the discussion, we refer to the premise sets by the row in which they appear in Table 13.1 (as II, III, IV, and V) and we indicate either that one premise set is predicted to be easier than another (i.e., to prompt higher rates of the correct responses) by way of a greater than sign or that two premise schemas are predicted to be equally easy by way of an equals sign. We begin with the two Unspecified-or conditions in order to determine the most favorable assignments for *if p then q; not-q* (II) and *p or q;not-q* (IV) before applying the outcome to the entire set of data. Predictions for the two Unspecified-or conditions could be any one of the following (where the subscripts refer to the total number of mental models required to make the inference):

$II_4 = IV_4 > V_5$, that is, (*if p then q;not-q*) requires four models and (*p or q;not-q*) requires four

$II_4 > IV_5 = V_5$, that is, (*if p then q;not-q*) requires four models and (*p or q;not-q*) requires five

$IV_4 > II_5 = V_5$, that is, (*if p then q;not-q*) requires five models and (*p or q;not-q*) requires four

$II_5 = IV_5 = V_5$, that is, (*if p then q;not-q*) requires five models and (*p or q;not-q*) requires five

Each line yields three predictions per Content condition. The strongest set of predictions arises out of $IV_4 > II_5 = V_5$ because IV (*p or q;not-q*) led to significantly higher rates of solution than II (*if p then q; not-q*) in both Unspecified-or conditions. None of the other three potential assignments leads to more than one confirmed prediction per Content condition, and no other assignment leads to a particular pattern of confirmed predictions among the two Content conditions. For this reason, we assume heretofore that the solution of *if p then q; not-q* requires five models and that *p or q; not-q* requires four. This provides the three predictions for each of the two Unspecified-or conditions in Table 13.2.

Given this analysis, we now can adopt the prediction that $III_4 = IV_4 > II_5 = V_5$ for the two Exclusive-or conditions, which leads to six further predictions in each of two Content conditions. Table 13.2 shows that, of the 18 predictions overall, 4 are confirmed and 2 are marginally confirmed. This is the most favorable set of predictions when a consistent number of mental models is assigned to each premise set.

GENERAL DISCUSSION

The experiment aimed to remove procedural and material inconsistencies across two similar experimental designs in order to more confidently determine which of the two theories, mental logic or mental models, better describes propositional reasoning. As one analysis showed, People-in-cities content led to more errors than Letters content undoubtedly because there was more information to store. Most notably, the more complex content negatively affected rates of correct responses to *p or q;not-q* (and *p or q but not both;not-q*). Although the presence of the exclusive clause in *p or q but not both;not-q* had the effect of making the inference as difficult as modus tollens, the test that compared performance between *p or q;not-q* and *p or q but not both;not-q* was not significant. This null finding is a clue that *or* is treated exclusively, at least in the kind of spontaneous production task employed here (cf. Evans & Newstead, 1980).

The results from this experiment are generally very supportive of the mental-logic approach. That is, premise sets that are hypothesized to prompt mental-logic schemas—*if p then q;p, p or q;not-q* and *not both p and q;p*—yielded the highest rates of correct responses in three conditions. Rates of correct responses in the fourth condition, the People-in-cities Exclusive-or set (which arguably presents propositions in the least user-friendly manner), indicated that two mental-logic schemas are among the premise sets that prompted the highest rates of correct responses. This evidence extends previous findings that support the mental-logic approach because the present study is based on a procedure (i.e., to store premises in memory) that is more challenging than any employed previously. Using a similar task, Klauer and Oberhauer (1995) recently published findings that more closely follow the order of difficulty predicted by mental logic (they yielded higher rates of correct performance to *p or q but not both;not q*).

The present findings favor mental logic over mental models as well. The most convincing piece of evidence favoring the mental-logic account is that premises for the premise set *if p then q;not-q* consistently prompted lower rates of correct responses than the *not both p and q;p* premises. Mental-model theory would not expect such an outcome according to its construal of modus tollens inference making. This finding is consistent with those found elsewhere (George & Politzer, 1995), and it is important because the two compared inferences are similar in many crucial ways: They are both logically valid, they both include a negative among the premises, and they both require that one produce a negative conclusion in order to be correct.

Table 13.2 captures how the two theories fundamentally differ in their accounts of propositional reasoning. On the one hand, mental logic makes a smaller set of predictions based on a straightforward categorical claim (i.e., whether a premise set triggers a mental-logic schema). The strength of the mental-logic approach is that it largely succeeds in confirming its moderate number of predictions. That these inferences are made routinely and with little relative difficulty corroborates evidence collected elsewhere (e.g., chaps. 7 and 8) and argues in favor of the claim that (a) there exists a basic repertory of the mental logic and that (b) it is a necessary foundation for reasoning theories. On the other hand, mental models—to their credit perhaps—venture more predictions based on an elaborate concept of mental models. The weakness of mental-models theory, however, is that its predictions largely are not confirmed. Moreover, mental models compels one to take into account a variety of subtle factors that are not clearly articulated in the theory's presentation in order to derive predictions (e.g., the role of detecting an inconsistency—see Footnote 2). These underdefined factors may or may not be important. Their net result, however, is that they force the investigators to choose insecurely among various interpretations of text. In sum, mental logic is strikingly simple and reliable, whereas mental models (despite its initial intuitive appeal) is complex and often indeterminate.

Finally, this work further reveals the value of attempts to standardize procedures in the investigation of reasoning phenomena (see also Noveck & O'Brien, 1996). Prior empirical work on propositional reasoning tasks has included several features that varied across theoretical paradigms, thus blocking confident assessments of the competing accounts. We have leveled the playing field by investigating subjects' performance with single propositional logic inferences and by examining the import of both content and the exclusiveness clause. The outcome of the tests weigh in favor of the mental-logic account.

ACKNOWLEDGMENTS

This research was supported in part by grants from the Fyssen Foundation (Paris, France); the Center for Research in Learning, Perception, and Cognition at the University of Minnesota; and the National Institute of Child Health and Human Development (T32 HD-07151) to the first author. The authors express their appreciation to Luca Bonatti, Martin Braine, Ruth Byrne, Francesco Cara, Vittorio Girotto, David O'Brien, Dan Sperber, and Charles Tijus for helpful comments at various stages of this project. Requests for reprints should be sent to Ira Noveck, Crea, 1 rue Descartes, 75005 Paris, France.

if p then q;p

1. If Janet is in Nice then Paul is in Chicago.
   Janet is in Nice.
1. If there is a U then there is a J.
   There is a U.
2. If Peter is in Bombay then Stan is in Liverpool.
   Peter is in Bombay.
2. If there is a Z then there is a K.
   There is a K.
3. If Daniel is in Tucson then Emily is in Dublin.
   Daniel is in Tucson.
 3. If there is an H then there is an L.
   There is an H.

if p then q; not-q

4. If Patricia is in Rome then Robert is in Madrid.
   Robert is not in Madrid.
4. If there is an L then there is a K.
   There is not a K.
5. If Susan is in Budapest then Laurie is in Stockholm.
   Laurie is not in Stockholm.
5. If there is an C then there is an M.
   There is not an M.
6. If Joseph is in Cambridge then Gordon is in Moscow.
   Gordon is not in Moscow.
6. If there is a U then there is an A.
   There is not an A.

p or q; p*

7. Isabelle is in Milan or Phillip is in Nashville.
   Isabelle is in Milan.
7. There is an F or a Y.
   There is an F.
8. Terry is in Duluth or Alan is in London.
   Terry is in Duluth.
8. There is an R or a G.
   There is an R.
9. Sylvie is in Montreal or Anna is in Kiev.
   Sylvie is in Montreal.
9. There is a D or an S.
   There is a D.

p or q; not-q*

10. Agnes is in Bonn or Steven is in Boston.
    Steven is not in Boston.
10. There is an M or a B.
    There is not a B.

(Continued)

11. Andrew is in New York or Sybil is in Helsinki.
    Sybil is not in Helsinki.
11. There is a Z or an R.
    There is not an R.
12. George is in Caracas or Marc is in Naples.
    Marc is not in Naples.
12. There is a K or a V.
    There is not a V.

not both p and q; p

13. We do not have both Marie in Peking and Martin in Venice.
    Marie is in Peking.
13. There is not both an O and a C.
    There is an O.
14. We do not have both Karen in Lansing and Michelle in Bogota.
    Karen is in Lansing.
14. There is not both an H and a P.
    There is an H.
15. We do not have both Jack in Athens and Claire in Toronto.
    Jack is in Athens.
15. There is not both a J and an S.
    There is a J.

not both p and q; not-q

16. We do not have both Sophie in Oslo and Sarah in Prague.
    Sarah is not in Prague.
16. There is not both an E and a B.
    There is not a B.
17. We do not have both Ed in Buffalo and Felix in Brussels.
    Felix is not in Brussels.
17. There is not both an N and a D.
    There is not a D.
18. We do not have both John in Amsterdam and Fawn in Munich.
    Fawn is not in Munich.
18. There is not both a G and an L.
    There is not an L.

Notes. *The *exclusive or* propositional premises appeared with ", but not both" appended to them.

A Case Study in the Mental-Models and Mental-Logic Debate: Conditional Syllogisms

David P. O'Brien
*Baruch College and the Graduate School
of the City University of New York*

Maria G. Dias
Antonio Roazzi
Federal University of Pernambuco

Johnson-Laird and his associates (e.g., Byrne & Johnson-Laird, 1992; Johnson-Laird, 1992, 1993; Johnson-Laird & Byrne, 1991; Johnson-Laird, Byrne, & Shaeken, 1992) recently have applied their mental-models theory of deductive reasoning to the conditional syllogisms. The four conditional syllogisms of standard logic each have a major premise of the form *If p then q*, with either the antecedent affirmed or denied, or the consequent affirmed or denied, as a minor premise (Table 14.1). Modus ponens (MP), with *p* as its minor premise, has *q* as its valid conclusion, and modus tollens (MT), with *not q* as its minor premise, has *not p* as its valid conclusion. Neither the affirmation of the consequent (AC), with *q* as its minor premise, nor the denial of the antecedent (DA), with *not p* as its minor premise, leads to any valid conclusion concerning its corresponding term, although people often accept the fallacious inferences of *p* and of *not q*, respectively. People rarely make any determinate responses on any of these problems except *q* on MP, *p* on AC, *not q* on DA, and *not p* on MT, and we shall refer to these as the *expected determinate responses*.

There are several reasons to assess the adequacy of the models account of the conditional syllogisms. First, there are only four conditional syllogisms, so they provide a relatively small arena, which allows for a detailed assessment that could become unwieldy with a large set of problems. Second, several investigators have provided data on these problems, so this small arena has well-known empirical properties. Third, both of the

TABLE 14.1
The Four Conditional Syllogisms and their Usual Responses

	Syllogism Form			
	MP	AC	DA	MT
Major premise	If p then q	If p then q	If p then q	If p then q
Minor premise	p	q	Not p	Not q
Expected determinate response	q	p	Not q	Not p
Logical response	q	NF	NF	Not p

Note. NF = nothing follows; MP = modus ponens; AC = affirmation of the consequent; DA = denial of the antecedent; MT = modus tollens.

major theoretical presentations of the models theory for propositional reasoning (Johnson-Laird & Byrne, 1991; Johnson-Laird et al., 1992) have included a fairly detailed discussion of the conditional syllogisms, providing grist for a detailed assessment of their account of these problems. Finally, the conditional syllogisms provide a case study for the theory at large, and any difficulties or shortcomings uncovered here are apt to reveal something that is problematic for the larger theory.

According to the models approach, a reasoner begins by constructing a set of mental models to represent a problem's premises. Each premise is represented, in turn, with the set of mental models adjusted as each premise is added. The reasoner attempts to formulate a conclusion from the final set of models. When there is a tentative conclusion to evaluate, a search is undertaken of alternative models for any that might falsify the considered conclusion. The models theorists claim that people do not reason according to schemas of the sort described by mental-logic theory; our motivation stems from their claim against mental logic.

We first describe the models theory and what it predicts for the conditional syllogisms and then assess how well it fits with the published data. After this, we describe what the mental-logic theory predicts on these problems and assess how well it fits with the data. We find that the mental-logic theory is consistent with the published data sets, although the models theory generally is inconsistent with those data.

UNDERSPECIFICATION IN THE MODELS THEORY

Evans (1993; see also Evans, Clibbens, & Rood, 1995) provided a critique of the mental-models account of conditionals, coming to the conclusion that the models account "appears to be insufficiently specified with regard to the nature of the representations that subjects form and the precise mechanism by which inferences are drawn. This, in turn, leads to some uncertainty in the prediction of problem difficulty" (Evans, 1993, p. 2). Furthermore, Evans argued that the predictions that the models theory seems to make are inconsistent with the data reported in the literature. Evans found the models theory sufficiently lacking that he suggested several revisions, both to improve its clarity and to bring its predictions into consistency with the data. We agree with Evans' criticisms, but we show that (a) the models account has difficulties in addition to those identified by Evans, and (b) the revisions proposed by Evans do not lead to predictions that are consistent with the data and reveal additional problems with the models account.[1]

We turn first to some general ways in which the models theory is underspecified, and we illustrate these issues with the conditional syllogisms later. These issues are not peripheral, but go to the most basic of the models theory's predictions. The first concerns the mental-models proposal that the primary source of difficulty in reasoning is the limited capacity of working memory that does not allow for many models, so mental models represent as little information explicitly as possible. Thus, if they can, people typically represent a problem with a single initial model. The initial models represent as much information as possible implicitly, and such information becomes available only when made explicit. Logically appropriate responses that are supported by an initial model should be made routinely, as should logically fallacious responses that are supported by an initial model; responses that require that the implicit information be made explicit (i.e., that the models be "fleshed out") should be relatively rare. The *principal prediction* of mental-models theory is that inferences become harder as the number of explicit models required to support them increases. Thus, the relative difficulty of a response is measured by the number of explicit models required to support it.

As Johnson-Laird et al. (1992) stated, "If the theory is correct, then as soon as the number of models that reasoners have to construct exceeds the capacity of their working memories, they are likely to be unable to reach a correct conclusion" (p. 433). Given that this is the principal prediction of the theory, one would expect that the modelers have presented a clear indication of how many models make a problem difficult, but to date they have not. The point can be illustrated with the following sets of models that represent the premises *not both p and q, p or r or both*, and *q*:

---

[1]Evans (1993) also included a discussion of *if-then* versus *only-if* forms of conditionals. We do not address that issue here.

1. ~p q;   p r;   ~p q r; q; ~p q r
   p ~q   p ~r   p ~q   r
   ~p ~q   ~p r   p ~q ~r
                     ~p ~q   r

where sequential model sets, corresponding to each premise and then to their combinations, are separated by a semicolon. The model set in the first two columns represents *not both p and q*, and the next two columns represents *p or r or both*. The model set in Columns 1 and 2 contains three models, each of which defines an alternative state of affairs in which *not both p and q* is true. The model in Row 1 contains a token for *not p* and a token for *q*, and corresponds to *not p and q*; the model in Row 2 contains a token for *p* and a token for *not q*, and corresponds to *p and not q*; the model in Row 3 contains a token for *not p* and a token for *not q*, and corresponds to *not p and not q*. The meaning of the other models follows similarly. These two model sets in 1 to 4 are combined into the model set in Columns 5 to 7. Next is the model for the categorical premise *q* in Column 8, and then the final model set combining all three premises together in Columns 9 to 11.

Given that problem difficulty is measured by the number of models, how difficult should Problem 1 be? If one were to count only the number of models in the final model set (which includes information from all three of the premises), this would be an easy problem, because the final model set includes only one model. This would not seem to be an appropriate measure, though, because it ignores all of the models that needed to be represented to arrive at the final model set, and these must have made demands on working memory. If one were to count all of the models in Columns 1 to 11, this would be a very difficult problem, because altogether there are 12 models. This would not seem to be an appropriate measure either because it overlooks that once the model set in Columns 5 to 7 is constructed, one can forget the models in Columns 1 to 4. Given that the issue concerns the load on working memory, one would think that the appropriate measure of difficulty for this problem should correspond to the maximum number of models that need to be held in working memory at any one time, that is, the six models for the first two premises before they are combined, or perhaps the 10 models for the first two premises and for their combination (one cannot drop the models in Columns 1 to 4 until the models in 5 to 7 have been constructed).

The modelers have been equivocal about which measure to use. Johnson-Laird et al. (1992) provided a detailed description of how models theory accounts for the data on the direct-reasoning problems of chapter 7, in which the modeler's measure of problem difficulty was the total number of models—suggesting that the difficulty of the problem just mentioned should be counted as 12 models. In the same article, however, they described some "double disjunction" problems, about which they said that "any deduction that calls for three or more models should be very difficult. . . . Once a deduction called for three models, it became almost impossible for our subjects" (pp. 433–434). On these problems only the models in the final model set were counted (Johnson-Laird, personal communication, February, 1994), suggesting that the difficulty of the earlier problem should be counted as one model. We do not find the modelers using the metric one would expect, that is, using the maximum number of models that need to be considered together at any one time. Their choices do not appear to follow from any particular theoretical principle, and the predictions of problem difficulty thus seem ad hoc.

Another sort of underspecification concerns the variety of model sets that are available to represent premises. Models theory, for example, has presented at least six different model sets with which *If p then q* can be represented (Table 14.2); it has provided sparse guidance, however, concerning when any particular set will be used, and what guidance has been provided sometimes has been contradictory. Specification of when any particular model set will be used is important because different model sets can lead to different predicted responses.

Evans (1993) noted, for example, that in chapter 3 of Johnson-Laird and Byrne (1991) the initial model set for a conditional is presented as follows:

2. p   q
   . . .

whereas in chapter 4 they suggested that the initial model set is as follows:

3. [p]   q
   . . .

Each of these model sets (Model Sets 1 and 2 in Table 14.2) contains one explicit and one implicit model. The ellipsis that constitutes the second (implicit) model in the two model sets functions as a reminder that alternatives to the first model might exist. The two model sets differ only in the square brackets around the token for the antecedent term in the explicit model of 3. The brackets mark exhaustivity, indicating that *p* has been exhausted in relation to *q*, that is, any explicit models "fleshed out" from the initial model set cannot put *p* together with a different value for *q*. Instead, any new fully explicit model should contain ~*p*, as seen in the last two model sets in Table 14.2. Although the model set with exhaustivity

TABLE 14.2
Mental-Model Sets for *If p then q* and the Conclusions
they Support for the Four Conditional Syllogisms

	Models		Argument Form	Minor Premise	Predicted Conclusion
Initial Set 1					
One Explicit Model	p	q	MP	p	q
	. . .		AC	q	p
			DA	Not-p	NF
			MT	Not-q	NF
Initial Set 2					
One Explicit Model	[p]	q	MP	p	q
	. . .		AC	q	p
			DA	Not-p	NF
			MT	Not-q	NF
Initial Biconditional Set					
One Explicit Model	[p]	[q]	MP	p	q
	. . .		AC	q	p
			DA	Not-p	NF
			MT	Not-q	NF
Intermediate Conditional Set					
Two Explicit Models	[p]	[q]	MP	p	q
		[q]	AC	q	NF
	. . .		DA	Not-p	q
			MT	Not-q	NF
Full Biconditional Set					
Two Explicit Models	p	q	MP	p	q
	~p	~q	AC	q	p
			DA	Not-p	Not-q
			MT	Not-q	Not-p
Full Conditional Set					
Three Explicit Models	p	q	MP	p	q
	~p	q	AC	q	NF
	~p	~q	DA	Not-p	NF
			MT	Not-q	Not-p

Note. MP = modus ponens; AC = affirmation of the consequent; DA = denial of the antecedent; MT = modus tollens; NF = nothing follows.

The predicted conclusions follow on the combinatorial principles of the psychological algorithm.

leads to somewhat different processing demands than does the model set without exhaustivity (as we describe later), the modelers have not specified when one or the other is used, and how exhaustivity operates thus is seriously underspecified.[2]

---

[2]Evans (1993) suggested that the meaning of the explicit model that uses exhaustivity in the above-mentioned initial model set is "for every p there is a q" (p. 4). This reading is puzzling because it would treat every simple (i.e., unquantified) conditional as universally

Johnson-Laird et al. (1992) stated that the full psychological theory always uses exhaustivity; this, of course, indicates that 3, which includes exhaustivity, should be the initial representation of a conditional. Johnson-Laird et al. (1992), however, provided only two explicit versions of the theory: a psychological algorithm and an AI algorithm, and no psychological reality at all is claimed for the AI algorithm. A more "full" version of the theory is hinted at, and a more recent intermediate-level version has been mentioned (Johnson-Laird et al., 1994; Johnson-Laird, personal communication, April 1994), but neither the full nor intermediate-level versions have been developed. Both the psychological algorithm and the AI algorithm are computer implementations, neither of which represent exhaustivity. In the case of the psychological algorithm, this is because the initial representation is never fleshed out; and in the case of the AI algorithm, because only the fully fleshed out representations are used; in either case, we are told, exhaustivity would be an idle wheel. Note that this indicates that the sole job of exhaustivity is to limit the ways in which a model set can be fleshed out; however, Johnson-Laird et al. (1994) said that exhaustivity also plays a role as model sets are combined, although nowhere do they spell out a combinatorial procedure that uses exhaustivity. The only explicit rules about how to combine model sets are found in the psychological algorithm, as illustrated in problem 1 earlier.[3]

Although no combinatorial principles for the intermediate level have been described, two examples of how the intermediate level operates have been presented, and these examples make clear that exhaustivity does play a role at the intermediate level in how model sets are combined, and we return to these examples later. As we later show, the lack of guidance about exhaustivity and the principles by which model sets are combined at the intermediate level (and for the "full" theory) makes it difficult to work out how the theory operates with any particular set of premises.

A final comment on underspecificity in models theory concerns how conclusions are formulated from model sets. Johnson-Laird et al. (1992)

---

quantified. As Johnson-Laird et al. (1992, p. 422) described it, "a contingency that has been exhaustively represented cannot be added to the set of models." They continued, "strictly speaking, the notion is relative: One contingency is exhaustively represented in relation to another, but we ignore this aspect of the notion for the time being and treat the contrast as a binary one." An adequate specification, however, requires that the relations be spelled out, as we show later, although to date the modelers have not done so.

[3]Johnson-Laird et al. (1992) described several combinatorial principles for the psychological algorithm: Each model in the first set is compared with each model in the second set, one at a time. When both models are elliptical, the result is an elliptical model; when one model is elliptical and the other contains tokens, no new model is forthcoming; when two models are inconsistent, that is, one contains a token and the other contains its negation, no new model is forthcoming; when two models each contain tokens that are consistent, the new model conjoins the tokens, eliminating any possible redundancies.

provided two guidelines. First, conclusions will not throw away semantic information; thus p and q will not lead to a conclusion p because p and q is more informative than p alone. Second, on Gricean pragmatic principles, a categorical premise will not be restated in a conclusion; thus, when p is a categorical premise, a final model containing p and q will lead to a conclusion of q rather than p and q. This Gricean-based constraint is, of course, inconsistent with the first principle, but their examples make it clear that the constraint takes precedence. As we show later, these two principles provide insufficient guidance as to what conclusions are drawn.

MODELS THEORY AND THE CONDITIONAL SYLLOGISMS

We now address the predictions of models theory for the four conditional syllogisms and whether the predictions and the data correspond to one another. We begin with the initial model sets for *if p then q*, because the modelers have claimed that most deductions are made on them, and the use of fleshed-out models should occur much less often (and not at all when the initial model set provides a determinate response). Further, Johnson-Laird and Byrne (1991) and Johnson-Laird et al. (1992) have provided some detailed discussion of the initial models sets for the conditional syllogisms. The first two initial models sets in Table 14.2 yield exactly the same predictions for all four syllogisms, so we discuss only one of them, choosing the one with exhaustivity (the second). On modus ponens (MP), given p as a minor premise, the initial model set for a conditional leads to the following:

4. [p]   q; p; [p] q
   . . .

The final model supports a response of p and q, but p is not restated in the conclusion because it is a categorical premise that is precluded on the Gricean constraint against restating the given, and the response corresponds to the usual modus ponens inference of q. According to models theory, this shows how a logical inference can be made without a mental-logic schema for modus ponens.

On affirmation of the consequent (AC) problems, given q as a minor premise, only the first model is "picked out," eliminating the elliptical model, and yielding p as a conclusion; this conclusion is "almost equally as easy" (Johnson-Laird et al., 1992, p. 423) as the logically appropriate modus-ponens inference, "apart from the difficulty of arguing in the opposite direction to the one in which the information from the conditional entered working memory." The classical fallacy on AC should occur, therefore, almost as often as the valid MP inference. Note that Johnson-Laird et al. (1992, p. 424) told us that fleshing out should not occur when a determinate response is supported on an initial model—as is the case here—and so on this proscription no fleshing out that might block the fallacy should be forthcoming.

On modus tollens (MT) problems, given *not q* as a minor premise, the first model is eliminated, leaving no obvious conclusion, so subjects should say that nothing follows. The mental-models treatment of denial of the antecedent (DA) problems is straightforward given the description of the preceding argument forms. Given *not p* as a minor premise, the first model is eliminated, and, as on MT, the stated conclusion should be that nothing follows. Thus, the predicted response pattern across the four syllogisms following from the initial model set has expected determinate responses of *q* and of *p*, for MP and for AC, respectively, and of *Nothing follows* for DA and for MT.

For some subjects the initial model might be as a biconditional:

5. [p]   [q]
      . . .

and it yields exactly the same set of responses as does the initial conditional model set, as Evans (1993) pointed out.

As Johnson-Laird (1992) stated, establishing that the response pattern predicted by the initial model sets for *if p then q* is not a common pattern would provide counterevidence to the mental-models theory. Evans (1993) noted, however, that the published data sets for these problems provide no evidence for this predicted response pattern, as seen in a summary of several published data sets shown in Table 14.3. One element of the pattern is present: Subjects do make the expected determinate response more often on MP (i.e., *q*) than on DA (i.e., *not q*) and MT (i.e., *not p*), but this also is predicted by competing theories, including our mental-logic theory. Major elements of the model-predicted pattern that are absent include the fact that the expected determinate response on AC (i.e., *p*) has been made nowhere nearly as often as on MP. Further, the predicted differences in the expected determinate responses among AC, DA, and MT have not been found. As Evans (1993) wrote about AC and DA, "we would have to conclude that the two inferences are made with roughly equal frequency" (p. 9), and Table 14.3 reveals that expected determinate responses on DA or on MT do not occur any less often than on AC.

As Evans (1993) noted, those subjects who make the expected determinate responses on DA and on MT must be fleshing out to a model set

TABLE 14.3

Proportions of Expected Determinate Responses Reported in Previous
Studies for the Four Conditional Syllogisms with *If p then q, If not
p then not q, If p then not q*, and *If not p then not q* as a Major Premise

Major Premise	Study	MP	AC	DA	MT
If p then q	Taplin (1971)	.92	.57	.52	.63
	Taplin & Staudenmayer (1973)	.99	.84	.82	.87
	Evans (1977)	1.00	.75	.69	.75
	Pollard & Evans (1980)	—	.66	.54	.59
	Wildman & Fletcher (1977)	.95	.30	.49	.62
	Marcus & Rips (1979)	1.00	.23	.21	.77
	Evans et al. (1995) [*if p then q*]	.98	.88	.79	.74
	Evans et al. (1995) [*q if p*]	.95	.91	.81	.81
If not p then q	Evans (1977)	1.00	.81	.50	.12
	Pollard & Evans (1980)	—	.72	.47	.34
	Wildman & Fletcher (1977)	.90	.60	.51	.23
	Evans et al. (1995) [*if not p then q*]	.95	.95	.72	.45
	Evans et al. (1995) [*q if not p*]	.93	.95	.81	.72
If p then not q	Evans (1977)	1.00	.31	.12	.56
	Pollard & Evans (1980)	—	.37	.30	.72
	Wildman & Fletcher (1977)	.97	.28	.18	.69
	Evans et al. (1995) [*if p then not q*]	.98	.81	.52	.76
	Evans et al. (1995) [*not q if p*]	.97	.84	.64	.78
If not p then not q	Evans (1977)	1.00	.81	.19	.25
	Pollard & Evans (1980)	—	.64	.37	.44
	Wildman & Fletcher (1977)	.95	.46	.27	.33
	Evans et al. (1995) [*if not p then not q*]	.93	.88	.57	.52
	Evans et al. (1995) [*not q if not p*]	.90	.91	.70	.72

Note. The expected determinate responses for *If p then not q* are *not q, p, q*, and *not p*,
for MP, AC, DA, and MT, respectively; for *If not p then q*, they are *q, not p, not q*, and *p*,
respectively; for *If not p then not q*, they are *not q, not p, q, and p*, respectively. See Table 4.2
for abbreviations.

beyond the initial set. Johnson-Laird and his associates have provided
little guidance about when or with which model sets fleshing out occurs;
moreover, Johnson-Laird et al. (1992) told us that "the vast majority of
deductions in daily life do not require any fleshing out" (p. 426) and that
one of the conditions required for fleshing out to occur is that "nothing
follows from the initial models" (p. 424). Evans (1993) argued that the
models theory requires a quite different sort of attitude towards fleshing
out; not only would the theory allow some fleshing out when nothing
follows on the initial model set, but subjects *will* attempt to flesh out when
nothing follows. Note that Evans' proposed modification of the models
theory does not call for any fleshing out when something fallacious
follows on the initial model, and so it also does not provide any reason
for subjects to resist the fallacy on AC.

Johnson-Laird (1995) responded to this apparent failure of the data to correspond to the predictions of models theory. He argued first that the frequencies of expected determinate responses on AC and DA (fallacies) are "remarkably labile, . . ." and "some studies do indeed report" (p. 131) that AC led to more expected determinate responses than did DA. Inspection of Table 14.3, however, shows that responses to AC and DA do indeed vary, but this variance mostly is across studies (AC varies from 23% to 91% and DA from 21% to 82%). When AC and DA are compared within each study, however, AC clearly does not occur any more often than DA. Indeed, the only appreciable difference is reported by Wildman and Fletcher (1977), where more fallacious responses were made on DA than on AC—a difference opposite from what is predicted by models theory. The data are clear: Comparisons between AC and DA within each study show that they have led to fallacious responses with about equivalent frequencies. No matter what is responsible for the interstudy differences, the relative proportions of AC to DA responses have not been affected.

Johnson-Laird's (1995) second point concerned a figural effect such that "individuals tend to frame conclusions in the same order as the information in them entered working memory. This effect may depress the frequency of affirmation of the consequent (and modus tollens)" (p. 131). An empirical test of this explanation is possible. It follows that when information about q enters before information about p, any such figural effect should be reversed, so when the major premise is presented as q *if* p, rather than as *if* p *then* q, relative differences between MP and AC and between DA and MT should reverse. Evans et al. (1995) provided both sorts of major premises, and their data show no tendency for any MP–AC or DA–MT reversals (see Table 14.3, where these reversed-order problems are labeled [q *if* p]).

One reason not to attribute too much meaning to this comparison in the Evans et al. study, however, is the fact that the proportions of expected determinate responses to AC and DA both on the *if* p *then* q and the q *if* p versions were among the highest reported anywhere, perhaps because no clear indeterminate response option was provided. For this reason, we presented some new problems that provide a test of this comparison. Twenty-one Baruch College undergraduates were presented an MP, an AC, a DA, and an MT problem, each with a major premise of the form *if* p *then* q, and 22 were presented the same four problems, but with a major premise in the form q *if* p. Each problem provided the expected determinate response as a conclusion to be evaluated as (a) definitely true, (b) definitely false, and (c) insufficient information to decide. The problems referred to letters and numbers written on an imaginary index card (e.g., *If there is a G on the card, then there is a 4 on the card*), and before receiving the problems subjects were shown examples of such cards, with each card showing five numbers and five letters.

The proportions of expected determinate responses for the *if p then q* and *q if p* major premise forms are shown in Table 14.4. On the *if p then q* problems, the proportions of expected determinate responses on AC were made nowhere nearly as often as those on MP, and no more often than those on DA or MT. On the *q if p* problems, the expected determinate response on AC occurred more often than on *if p then q*, as the figural effect would expect; if this were caused by a figural effect, however, the effect should show up on other syllogisms, leading to an increase of the expected determinate response on MT on *q if p* compared with *if p then q*, and to decreases on DA and MP. Inspection of Table 14.4 does not reveal such a trend. Indeed, the effect of the *q if p* premise type appears to be an elevation of expected determinate responses on AC, DA, and MT, and the expected decreases on MP and DA did not occur. Furthermore, no reversal of difficulty between MP and AC or between DA and MT is observed when one compares *if p then q* to *q if p* problems. Taken together with the data reported by Evans et al. (1995), which reported similar results to those reported here, the proposal of a figural effect to account for the failure of AC to lead to nearly as many expected determinate responses as did MP and to far more expected determinate responses than did DA and MT, as the models theory predicted, appears to be without support.

The response patterns for the *if p then q* and *q if p* major premise types are shown in Table 14.5. Inspection of Table 14.5 reveals that the principal effect of the *q if p* premise form was to increase the biconditional-like response pattern (Row 3). Neither form of major premise elicited the response pattern predicted on the initial model set (Row 1) more than rarely. Johnson-Laird's explanation of this failure in terms of a figural effect thus receives no support.

TABLE 14.4
Proportions of Expected Determinate Responses for the
Four Conditional Syllogisms With *if p then q* and *q if p*
as the Major Premise in the Present Experiment

	Problem Type			
Major Premise	*MP*	*AC*	*DA*	*MT*
If p then q	.95	.52	.52	.57
q if p	1.00	.82	.86	.73

Note. See Table 14.2 for abbreviations.

TABLE 14.5
Proportions of Response Patterns Across the Four
Conditional Syllogisms for the Major Premise
Forms *if p then q* and *q if p* in the Present Experiment

	Response Pattern				Major Premise	
	MP	AC	DA	MT	If p then q	q if p
1	D	D	NF	NF (1 model)	.10	.09
2	D	NF	NF	NF (1 model)	.10	.00
3	D	D	D	D (2 models)	.29	.45
4	D	NF	NF	D (3 models)	.19	.14
5	D	D	D	NF	.10	.18
6	D	D	NF	D	.05	.09
7	D	NF	D	D	.05	.05
8	D	NF	D	NF	.10	.00
			other		.05	.00
			N		21	22

Note. D = the expected determinate response; NF = nothing follows; see Table 14.2 for other abbreviations.

The response pattern in Row 1 is supported by the initial conditional model set and by the initial biconditional set, each with one explicit model. Row 2 is supported by the initial conditional set together with Evans's exhaustivity constraint. Row 3 is supported by the full biconditional set with two explicit models. Row 4 is supported by the full conditional set with three explicit models. The pattern predicted on the intermediate conditional set (i.e., the expected determinate responses on MP and MT, a nothing follows response on AC, and the unexpected determinate response on DA) did not occur.

We turn now to the model sets beyond the initial models and to other forms of the major premise (*if not p then q, if p then not q,* and *if not p then not q;* see Table 14.3). As noted earlier, Johnson-Laird and Byrne (1991) and Johnson-Laird et al. (1992) have provided several different model sets for *if* that involve some fleshing out (see Table 14.2). Some of these model sets are intermediate between the initial models and the fully fleshed-out model sets (compare the third and fourth with the last two in Table 14.2). In particular, Johnson-Laird et al. (1992, p. 422) suggested that the models for *if* might be fleshed out as follows (Model Set 4 in Table 14.2):

6. [p]   [q]
       [q]
   . . .

Additionally, fleshing out is called for when a component of a conditional contains a negative. Johnson-Laird and Byrne (1991) proposed that subjects are biased to "represent affirmative values in the models" (p. 80) and thus *if not p then q* is likely to lead either to:

7.   q
    [p]

or to:

8. [~p]   q
   [p]
   [p]

The models for *if p then not q* similarly are influenced by the presence of a negative (from Johnson-Laird & Byrne, 1991, p. 68):

9. [p]   ~q
          q
    . . .

Finally, although Johnson-Laird and his associates have not spelled out the model sets for *if not p then not q*, one can work out what these model sets should be like. The likely model set can be constructed by combining the model sets for *if not p then q* (8) and for *if p then not q* (9), which would yield:

10. [~p]   ~q
    [p]   q
    [p]

   We address first how the combinatorial principles of the psychological algorithm would be applied on 6 to 10. Consider the DA argument for 6. The minor premise, *not p*, eliminates the first model because of the contradiction. It can, however, be added to the second model, leading to a new model containing *not p* and *q*, which predicts an *unexpected* determinate response of *q*. Given that this unexpected determinate response is reported nowhere in the literature, this model set, taken together with the combinatorial principles of the psychological algorithm, can be rejected as describing psychological reality. Consider now the MP argument on 9. The minor premise *p* is combined with the first model, which would support the logically appropriate *not q* response. Nothing precludes combining *p* with the second model, however, which includes *q*. The psychological algorithm thus would lead to a *Nothing follows* response—a response that subjects do not make. Applying the psychological algorithm to these intermediate level model sets thus cannot be proposed seriously.
   Given that the combinatorial principles of the intermediate level (i.e., not those of the psychological algorithm) have not been specified, one

cannot know exactly how to proceed; it is possible, however, to make some reasonable suppositions about how the exhaustivity markers should constrain how models are combined so that the sorts of difficulties encountered by the psychological algorithm for DA on 6 and MP on 9 can be avoided. First, how could the unexpected determinate response of q to DA on 6 be avoided? The elliptical model would have to be fleshed out, allowing *not p* to be combined with *not q*. Thus, to avoid making absurd predictions, the theory must assume that the implications of the exhaustivity markers are fully worked out. Of course, this is equivalent to fleshing out the model set fully as an explicit conditional; as Evans (1993) noted, however, it is unlikely that subjects typically use the fully fleshed-out conditional model set because then models theory could not account for the sorts of responses subjects typically make on other conditional-reasoning tasks, such as the selection task and the truth-evaluation task; nor would this account for the response tendencies shown in Tables 14.4 and 14.5. The intermediate model set in 6 thus either leads to an absurd prediction or to a fully fleshed-out conditional. In either case, it does not provide a plausible candidate for how people reason typically with conditionals.

Second, how could the MP inference on 9 be saved at the intermediate level? The brackets around p in the first model would preclude p being added to the second model; the basis for withholding the usual modus ponens inference thus would be eliminated. Consideration of the exhaustivity brackets, however, would lead to responses across the four syllogisms that are consistent with representing *if p then not q* as a fully fleshed-out conditional, and the data in Tables 14.3, 14.4, and 14.5 show no such response tendency.[4]

In working out how the combinatorial principles of the intermediate level apply to 7 and 8, where the major premise is *if not p then q*, we

---

[4]AC, with *not q* as a minor premise, eliminates the second model in 9 and matches the first model, which would support the expected determinate response of p. This fallacy would be blocked, however, when the elliptical model is fleshed out, and such fleshing out of the elliptical model would be expected because it was required to block an absurd prediction from the model set in 6. On DA, the minor premise *not p* eliminates the first model and combines with the second model, which would support q as a conclusion. Nothing precludes adding *not p* to the elliptical model, however, which might also contain *not q*. Thus, a *Nothing follows* response would seem to be forthcoming. MT has q as a minor premise; the first model is eliminated, leaving the second model and the elliptical model. Consideration of the square brackets around p in the first model indicates that the second and third models must contain *not p*, and so MT would elicit the expected determinate response. Thus, *if p then not q* should lead to the logically appropriate responses to all four syllogisms, with fewer expected determinate responses on AC and more on MT, compared with what is predicted for *if p then q*. Inspection of the data in Table 14.3 reveals some support for this prediction for AC in the studies by Evans (1977) and Pollard and Evans (1980); the predicted effect for MT, however, is not to be found anywhere.

assume the same sorts of fleshing out that were required on 6 and 9, which again leads to responses that are consistent with a fully fleshed-out conditional, and again is inconsistent with the data shown in Table 14.4.[5] This also would be the case for the model set in 10, where the major premise is *if not p then not q*, and once again the predictions are not borne out by the data, as shown in Table 14.4.[6]

In summary, the initial models for *if p then q* lead to the prediction of expected determinate responses to MP and AC, and of responses that nothing follows to DA and MT. The published data sets do not support the prediction. Johnson-Laird (1995) explained the failure of AC to lead to an expected determinate response as often as MP, and more often than DA and MT, in terms of a figural effect, but neither the data reported in Evans et al. (1995) nor the data reported here show any reversal between MP and AC, nor between DA and MT, when *if p then q* is replaced with *q if p*, as should occur if a figural effect were operating.

The intermediate-level model set for *if* in 6 leads either to an absurd prediction of an unexpected determinate response to DA when the com-

---

[5]On AC, with *q* as a minor premise, nothing about *q* precludes combining *q* with the models containing [*p*], because *q* is not exhausted. Whether the exhaustivity of [*p*] precludes such a combination is unclear, because it is unclear in relation to what *p* is exhausted; the fact, however, that both the second and third models of 8 contain [*p*] suggests that one could combine *q* with one of them and *not q* with the other—otherwise the two models would be redundant. Furthermore, although the brackets around *p* in 7 preclude adding *p* to the first model, nothing precludes adding *q* to [*p*] in the second model. Thus, we take it that a *Nothing follows* response should be forthcoming on both 7 and 8. On DA, with *p* as a minor premise, nothing seems to follow about the status of *q*, because *q* is absent in every model containing *p* and *q* is not exhausted where *q* does occur. On MT, with *not q* as a minor premise, only the models containing [*p*] can be considered, and so *p* follows as a conclusion. Thus, the intermediate level of the theory leads to the prediction that the expected determinate responses should occur on MP and MT, and responses that nothing follows on AC and DA both on 7 and 8. Compared with *if p then q*, *if not p then q* thus should lead to fewer expected determinate responses on AC, and to more expected determinate responses on MT. Inspection of the data in Table 14.3, however, reveals no such tendencies. Indeed, MT led consistently to *fewer* expected determinate responses on *if not p then q* than on *if p then q*.

[6]Although MP, with *not p* as a minor premise, leads straightforwardly to the conclusion *not q*, responses to the other three problem forms are not as straightforwardly predictable. AC, with *not q* as a minor premise, leads to a *Nothing follows* response, because nothing in either the psychological algorithm or the intermediate level seems to preclude adding *not q* to the third model. DA, with *p* as a minor premise, also leads to a *Nothing follows* response, because the third model might contain either a positive or negative value for *q*. MT, with *q* as a minor premise, eliminates the first model, and leads to *p* on both the second and third models. Thus, *if not p then not q*, like *if not p then q* and *if p then not q*, leads to the prediction of the logically appropriate responses to all four syllogisms, and thus to the expectation of more expected determinate responses to MT and fewer to AC than should occur on *if p then q*. Inspection of the data in Table 14.3 shows no such effect for AC, and an effect in the opposite direction for MT.

binatorial principles of the psychological algorithm are applied, or are functionally equivalent to the fully fleshed-out conditional model set when the exhaustivity of the intermediate level is considered. The model set in 9 either leads to suppression of MP or to responses that are equivalent to a fully fleshed-out conditional. When the exhaustivity found at the intermediate level is considered, the theory appears to predict expected determinate responses to MP and MT, and *Nothing follows* responses to AC and DA, either when the intermediate-level model set for *if p then q* is used or whenever a negative is introduced to a term in the major premise. The intermediate level thus does not predict the data any better than does the psychological algorithm. Note, in particular, that none of the proposed model sets provide any way for an expected determinate response to DA, except for the fully fleshed-out biconditional. Such responses thus should be extremely rare, although the data in Tables 14.3 and 14.4 show they are not. The models account, thus, is not only severely underspecified, but to the extent that its predictions can be worked out, they do not correspond well to the data.

EVANS'S PROPOSED REVISIONS

The rather gross disparity between what the initial model sets predict and the published data sets led Evans (1993) to argue that the models theory needed revision. The first part of his revision consisted of a constraint such that an inference may be drawn only "if *either* the [minor] premise is exhaustively represented in the current model, *or* if all models in which it occurs are explicitly represented" (p. 7). For Evans, the initial model set can be either the initial conditional set in which *p* is exhausted or the initial biconditional set in which both *p* and *q* are exhausted. Thus, whereas the original theory predicts the expected determinate responses on MP and AC (and responses of *Nothing follows* on DA and on MT), Evans's revision holds that for the initial conditional set, the constraint blocks the fallacious response on AC, and subjects who use this initial model set, therefore, should make the modus ponens inference and give *Nothing follows* responses on AC, DA, and MT (Row 2 of Table 14.5). Subjects who use the initial biconditional set should make the expected determinate responses on MP and AC and *Nothing follows* responses on DA and MT (Row 1 of Table 14.5). Evans hypothesized that because some subjects would use the initial conditional model set and others would use the initial biconditional set, MP should lead to the appropriate expected determinate response (on both model sets), and AC should lead to some expected determinate responses (only for those who make the initial biconditional interpretation), but DA and MT should lead to responses that nothing follows on both representations.

Evans recognized that the exhaustivity constraint by itself does not bring the models theory's predictions for the four conditional syllogisms into line with the published data sets because no reason is provided for expected determinate responses to DA or MT on either the conditional or biconditional initial model sets. Indeed, as is the case for the original theory, any expected determinate response on either of these problems requires some fleshing out, and so Evans assumed that not only *can* subjects flesh out when nothing follows on the initial model set (Johnson-Laird et al., 1992, stated that this is the only situation when models can be fleshed out), but that they *will* attempt to do so. How the expected determinate response, then, can be given on DA, for example, is as follows. Evans argued that subjects would have to start with the initial biconditional set (see Table 14.1), which they then can flesh out as:

11. [p]   [q]
     [~p] [~q]

which allows drawing the expected determinate response of *not q* for DA (as well as the expected determinate response of *not p* for MT). This is consistent with Johnson-Laird (1995), who wrote that once the models are fleshed out, only the biconditional set provides a way for subjects to make the expected determinate responses both to DA and AC.

Evans argued that such fleshing out of a biconditional model set should be more likely when one of the components of the major premise contains a negation. According to Evans, the following would be the initial model set for *if not p then q*:

12. [~p]   q
     [p]

which differs from the model set suggest by Johnson-Laird and Byrne (1991), shown in 8, only in that 12 does not contain a redundant third model consisting of [p]. To derive the expected determinate response on DA with the *if not p then q* form of the major premise (with p as a minor premise), Evans's revised theory proceeds as follows: Subjects would start with an initial biconditional model set in which exhaustivity is added to the token for the consequent term of the first model in 12 so that the first model contains [~p] and [q], and subjects "only have to complete the second model to

13. [p]   [~q]

in order to draw the conclusion ~*q*" (Evans, 1993, p. 13). The expected determinate response on DA is thus more likely on *if not p then q* than on *if p then q* because 12 already contains a second model that corresponds to the minor premise, so the fleshing-out procedure already has been partially begun.

Evans argued that whenever a conditional contains a negated component, an expected determinate response is more likely when the minor premise is affirmative, because a model containing a token for the minor premise already is represented, as we have seen for the DA argument for *if not p then q* following on the biconditional extension of 12. It would follow, of course, that DA should lead to more expected determinate responses when the major premise is *if not p then q* or *if not p then not q* than when it is *if p then q* (where such responses should be relatively rare). Inspection of the data in Table 14.3 does not reveal this tendency for *if not p then q*, and the reverse is the case for *if not p then not q*. It also would follow that expected determinate responses to MT should occur more often when the major premise is *if p then not q* or *if not p then not q*, where the initial biconditional model sets contain tokens that correspond to the minor premise, as in the initial conditional sets 14 and 15, than when it is *if p then q* (where such responses should be relatively rare). Inspection of the data in Table 14.3 does not reveal this tendency for *if p then not q*, and the reverse is the case for *if not p then not q*.

An additional revision to the theory proposed by Evans was a conclusion filter governed by a negative-conclusion bias. According to the negative-conclusion bias, subjects are more likely to accept conclusions that are negative because such judgments are more conservative ("There is a letter A" refers to a single letter, whereas "There is not a letter A" refers to 25 possible letters), and affirmative conclusions thus are apt to be suppressed; AC, with its affirmative expected determinate response on the usual *if p then q* major premise form, thus would be suppressed by the negative-conclusion bias, even when it is made on the initial biconditional set; whereas DA, with its negative conclusion, would not be suppressed. Evans, Newstead, and Byrne (1993) provided data from Evans (1977) and Wildman and Fletcher (1977) that show such a negative-conclusion bias.

Evans (1993) argued that by presenting the major premise with a negated antecedent, the DA problem results in an affirmative conclusion, whereas presenting the major premise with an affirmative antecedent provides a DA problem with a negative conclusion, both attainable on the full biconditional model sets. Counterbalancing of affirmatives and negatives in the terms of the major premise (as *if p then q*, *if not p then q*, *if p then not q*, and *if not p then not q*) thus allows counterbalancing of the effects of the negative conclusion bias across the four syllogisms. When the data are summed across the four premise types, he argued, the proportions of expected determinate responses correspond to the response tendencies that are predicted by the revised models theory (i.e., fewer expected determinate responses on AC than on MP, and even fewer on DA and MT); he cited the proportions of expected determinate responses from Evans (1977), which are 1.00, .67, .38, and .42, for MP, AC, DA, and MT, respectively, when summed across the four major-premise types. This also seems to be the pattern in the data presented by Evans et al. (1995); these are not, however, the response tendencies reported by Wildman and Fletcher (1977) (.94, .41., .36, and .47, respectively).

Evans did not describe the influence of negatives when a conditional model set, rather than a biconditional set, is used. As noted earlier, on the conditional model sets 7 to 10 for *if not p then q, if p then not q*, and *if not p then not q*, a reasoner would be encouraged to make an expected determinate response on MT and *Nothing follows* responses on AC and DA. The effect of the exhaustivity constraint would be to block these MT responses, so only the MP problems would lead to an expected determinate response. MP, thus, should be the easiest inference because it is supported both by the conditional and biconditional model sets with or without the presence of negatives. Evans has provided no reason for MP to be immune from the influence of a negative-conclusion bias, and thus somewhat fewer MP responses should be made when the major premise is *if p then q* or *if not p then q*, although Table 14.3 shows no such effect.

Evans's revisions do have an advantage over the original models theory in that the exhaustivity constraint provides an explanation of why expected determinate responses on AC occur less often than those on MP; the AC inference joins DA and MT inferences as relying on a biconditional model set, and thus all should occur less often than MP, which can be made on the initial conditional model set. AC remains the only problem form other than MP in which the expected determinate response can be made readily with *if p then q* as a major premise, however, and Evans provided no reason why the expected determinate response on DA or MT should be made as often as on AC without the presence of negatives. Table 14.3 shows no tendency for expected determinate responses on DA or MT to occur less often than on AC even on the *if p then q* premise form.

As we described earlier, the original models theory remains seriously underspecified concerning how exhaustivity operates as model sets are combined as new premises are encountered and inferences are drawn. Given that the exhaustivity constraint of the Evans revision places even more explanatory weight on exhaustivity, the need for sufficient specificity in how exhaustivity operates is even greater for the revised theory. However, there are enormous problems associated with exhaustivity, which we now review.

PROBLEMS OF EXHAUSTIVITY

Presumably Evans intended the exhaustivity constraint to extend to problems beyond the four conditional syllogisms, but inspection of a few hypothetical problems reveals that this would lead to extreme processing demands that reveal how unlikely exhaustivity is as a realistic account of what goes on in ordinary reasoning. Consider a modus ponens problem with an additional conditional premise, as follows: *if p then q, if r then q, and p*, which, on the initial conditional model set and the combinatorial principles of the psychological algorithm, would lead to:

14. [p]   q; [r]   q; [p] [r]   q; p; [p] [r] q

    . . .   .

If subjects were asked what conclusion can be drawn on this simple problem, they ought to say *r and q* because tokens with these two values are included in the final model, and only *p* is a categorical premise that would be excluded. The Gricean constraint not to repeat a categorical premise as a conclusion would not block a fallacious inference of *r*, and because the categorical premise *p* is exhausted in the models, neither would the exhaustivity constraint.

We assume that on Evans's revision the exhaustivity constraint would block the fallacious inference of *r*, that is, *r* would not be inferred because *[p]* in 14 is not exhausted in relation to *r*, but only in relation to *q*. The problem is that exhaustivity is a relation rather than a property, although models theory thus far has treated it as a property. In the final model set of 14, *p* is exhausted in relation to *q*, and *r* is exhausted in relation to *q*, but *q* is exhausted in relation neither to *p* nor to *r*, and *p* and *r* are not exhausted in relation to one another. Note that the final model of 14 provides sparse and inadequate information about these exhaustivity relations—one needs to know the final model's developmental history. In order for the exhaustivity constraint of the revised theory to apply, the reasoner must be able to keep track of which token types are exhausted in relation to which other token types—a task that surely would exhaust the limits of working memory. How this might work is not clear. One might add an indexical subscript, for example, such as follows:

15. $[p_q]$ q; $[r_q]$ q; $[p_q]$ $[r_q]$ q; p; $[p_q]$ $[r_q]$ q

    . . .   .

In this case the inference of *r* would be blocked by the exhaustivity constraint because the categorical premise *p* is not exhausted in relation to *r*. This solution still would be insufficient, however, as is illustrated in the following example with premises *if p then q, if q then r, if s then r*, and *p*:

16. $[p_q]$ q; $[q_r]$ r; $[p_q]$ $[q_r]$ r; $[s_r]$ r; $[p_q]$ $[q_r]$ r $[s_r]$; p; $[p_q]$ $[q_r]$ r $[s_r]$
   . . . .

On this final model set the exhaustivity constraint successfully blocks the sort of fallacious inference found in the preceding problem—*s* will not be inferred because *p* is exhausted only in relation to *q* and not to *s*. On the same basis, however, *r* will not be inferred either (even though it should be), also because *p* is exhausted only in relation to *q*. Clearly, for the exhaustivity constraint to work, the indexical notation must be more complex, for example, keeping track of inherited exhaustion:

17. $[p_q]$ q; $[q_r]$ r; $[p_{qr}]$ $[q_r]$ r; $[s_r]$ r; $[p_{qr}]$ $[q_r]$ r $[s_r]$; p; $[p_{qr}]$ $[q_r]$ r $[s_r]$
   . . . .

Of course, the theory would need to specify when and how such inheritance takes place, and such indexation would quickly become extremely intractable and cognitively exhausting. This reveals that exhaustivity provides an implausible account of what people actually do on such problems.

We turn now to the two examples of the intermediate level of models theory that have been provided by Johnson-Laird et al. (1994) and Johnson-Laird (personal communication, April 1994). O'Brien et al. (1994) and chapter 8 had shown that the combinatorial principles of the psychological algorithm lead to predictions of fallacies that people do not make. Consider the following two examples, which are the only two problems to which the modelers have referred in their rejoinder. In Example 18, premises of the form *p or q* and *if p then r* lead on the psychological algorithm to:

18. p ; p r; p r
    q . . . p r q

and the final model set supports *r* as a conclusion, because *r* is included in both models of the final model set—a predicted fallacy that people do not make. In Example 19, premises of the form *if p and q then r* and *p* lead on the combinatorial principles of the psychological algorithm to:

19. p   q r; p; p q r
   . . .

and the final model supports *r* as a conclusion. Again, this is a predicted fallacy that people do not make.

The modelers responded that these fallacies are not made at the intermediate level. To discover whether the combinatorial principles for the intermediate level can be gleaned from these two examples, consider first 18. The intermediate level is claimed to lead to the following (Johnson-Laird, personal communication, April 1994):

20. p ; [p] r; p r
     q   . . .   q

which does not support the fallacy because r is not included in the second model.

We have not been told by the modelers, however, the principle of the intermediate level that precludes q being combined with *[p] and r*. Note first that neither q nor p in the first model set are marked for exhaustion, so presumably the first model set provides no reason that q could not be combined with a later model containing p. Second, *[p]* in the second model set is exhausted in relation to r, so nothing should preclude its combination with some other token type, as long as the resulting model includes a token for r.

There are logical reasons to prefer the final model set that Johnson-Laird said follows on the intermediate level: Although r follows on modus ponens from *if p then r* and p (i.e., if alternative p is true), r does not follow from *if p then r* and q (i.e., if alternative q is true). The conclusion thus follows logically that *either p and r, or q*, and this inference would be supported by the final model set Johnson-Laird proposed at the intermediate level. Why the models theory would want to arrive at this final model set thus is clear, but how it arrives at this model set is not. One way that the intermediate level could construct this final model set would be to require that a model with an exhaustion can be combined only with a model containing tokens identical to those within the scope of the exhaustion. Such a principle would account for the final model set in 20, and would be consistent with the logical analysis of the problem, that is, that modus ponens can be applied only from the alternative that includes p. This principle would not seem to be consistent, however, with the account Johnson-Laird et al. (1994) provide for 19.

The fallacy on 19 is not made on the intermediate level, we are told by Johnson-Laird et al. (1994, p. 736), because it is blocked by exhaustivity, as follows: "The brackets are a footnote indicating that the *conjunction* of p and q cannot occur among the alternative possibilities represented by the implicit model. There is nothing to prevent p alone as an alternative possibility, however, so the result of combining these models with the model for the categorical premise, p is:

21. [p   q]   r; p; p q r
    . . .   p

and *r* is not accepted as a conclusion because the second model of the final model set does not contain it.

We make two observations. First, the modelers have not yet specified when or how tokens are added to an elliptical model at the intermediate level. Second, the final model set in 21 is puzzling in that its first model contains *p and q and r*—a combination that would be precluded by the sort of constraint that seems to be operating in 20, that is, the second model set contains only *p*, and thus should not be combinable with *[p q] r*. Perhaps *p* has not been added to *[p q] r*, but has been added instead to the elliptical model; in this case, *[p q] r* would have been reiterated into the combined model set, inviting the question of when reiteration is allowed. How the combined model set was derived thus is not clear, and it is hard to see any general principles concerning how the intermediate level combines model sets as new premises are encountered.

Even more puzzling, 21 would seem to lead from *p and q and r* and *p* to *p and q and r, or p*, which surely is a large loss of semantic information. To illustrate the issue further, consider a possible problem with the two premises *if p then q* and *r*. The psychological algorithm would lead to:

22. [p]   q; r; [p] q r
    . . .

which would support the fallacious inference *p and q*. Presumably, the combinatorial processes of the intermediate level would block this fallacy. Following the examples in 20 and 21, the intermediate level seemingly would yield:

23. [p]   q; r; p q
    . . .   r

This model set is not fallacious but is not perspicuous either. Note that the final model set in 23 is semantically weaker than the premises alone, that is, whereas the premises are conjunctively true, the models in the final set are merely disjunctively true. Thus, from *if p then q* and *r* one would conclude *p and q, or r*. This weakening of the premise information in the final model set can lead to a quite odd result. Suppose, for example, that a third premise, *not r or not q*, is added to the problem. The final model set that results from this addition is:

24. p   q   ~r
       ~q   r

Note that this final model set includes a model (the first one) that includes a token for *not r*, even though *r* is a categorical premise—a result that surely lacks psychological reality. Considering both the difficulties associated with exhaustivity reviewed earlier and the problems of combining model sets just discussed, it seems transparent that the intermediate level is seriously problematic.

THE MODELS THEORY: SUMMARY

The original models theory as presented primarily in Johnson-Laird and Byrne (1991) and Johnson-Laird et al. (1992) provided an account of propositional reasoning that made some detailed predictions about which responses would be given on the conditional syllogisms, and, as the reviews in Evans (1993) and here show, these predictions are not accurate. Evans (1993) subsequently proposed some revisions to the models theory, motivated by the need to bring the predictions of models theory into correspondence with the published data sets; as we have shown here, however, the revised theory also does not succeed in providing accurate predictions, although it does have the advantage over the original theory of providing a way for subjects to resist making the expected determinate response on AC. Evans's revisions do not, however, explain why subjects make as many expected determinate responses on DA and MT as on AC when the major premise does not include any negated terms.

Both the original and revised models theories have to rely on exhaustivity if they are to avoid some odd—sometimes absurd—predictions. Neither version of the theory, however, has been particularly forthcoming about how exhaustivity operates, and we found that exhaustivity has some rather large, yet hidden, processing costs. Once these processing costs are made explicit, exhaustivity is exposed as intractably difficult, making it an unlikely candidate for psychological reality. Johnson-Laird and Byrne (1993) argued that the intractability of models procedures is not problematic for the models theory because it provides an explanation for why people make so many errors on many deductive-reasoning tasks. This would be an acceptable argument for them to make if the processes were intractable only on problems with which subjects have difficulty; the fact is, however, that the models procedures are intractable on problems that subjects find easy, that is, where errors rarely are made. (For additional discussion of intractability in models theory, see O'Brien et al., 1994.)

Working out the hidden processing costs of exhaustivity (as well as the other features of the full theory or the intermediate level of the theory) is difficult because the modelers have not specified beyond the psychological algorithm how the theory operates; one is required to glean from examples

how things work, and such working out often leads to apparently contradictory answers, for example, the principles that seem to be used to block
the fallacy in 20 do not seem to apply in 21. The way the modelers have
presented exhaustivity, as Johnson-Laird et al. (1992) noted, has been as a
binary property in which a token either has it or not. Exhaustivity, however,
involves a complex set of relationships among tokens, and plays a strong
determining role in how model sets can be fleshed out and what conclusions
can be drawn from them. Once the sort of detail that is required is worked
out, exhaustivity seems an uninviting way to describe human reasoning—a
fact that makes the "intermediate level" implausible.

Finally, Johnson-Laird and his associates have provided various model
sets for representing conditionals, both for *if p then q* and for conditionals
containing negated components, although not all of these have been
included in their description of the conditional syllogisms. As we have
shown here, when these various models for conditionals are considered
they lead to predictions that do not correspond to the data, whether one
uses the procedures of the original models theory or of the revised theory
proposed by Evans. In brief, the models treatment of the conditional
syllogisms lacks specificity, parsimony, and accuracy.

MENTAL-LOGIC THEORY AND THE CONDITIONAL
SYLLOGISMS

Johnson-Laird and his associates have argued not only in favor of mental-models theory as a way of understanding propositional reasoning, but
also against a mental-logic approach. We address whether mental-logic
theory fares any better than the mental-models theory with these problems. A convenient way to test the two theories against one another would
be to construct a set of one-to-one comparisons between the predictions
of models theory and those of mental-logic theory, showing, for example,
that subjects always make a response pattern predicted by one theory but
not by the other. It is difficult to make such comparisons, however,
because the mental-logic theory has two components: The core component
is the basic mental logic, that is, the schemas of Table 6.1 and the direct-
reasoning routine of Table 6.2; the other is a set of pragmatic principles
concerning how information is interpreted propositionally. The predictions made by the core mental logic do not set up these sorts of one-to-one
comparisons, and indeed the core of mental-logic theory does not make
any predictions about differences among AC, DA, and MT. Thus although
the data we have reviewed impeach the claims of models theory, they do
not weigh decisively in favor of mental-logic theory—finding no effect
where none is predicted does not by itself demonstrate that the core

mental-logic account is right, it merely raises doubt about the models theory that predicted differences.

The two theories differ, however, in their descriptions of how reasoners make inferences, and this is open to empirical investigation. Both the mental-models and the mental-logic theories predict the logically appropriate response on MP problems. On mental-logic theory, the inference of *q* from *if p then q* and *p* follows immediately because modus ponens is a basic inference, whereas on mental-models theory the response comes from a final model that would support *p and q*, except for the suppression of *p* in the conclusion by a Gricean maxim not to restate a categorical premise in a conclusion.

This difference is addressed in a study by Lea (1995) of mental-logic inferences made during text comprehension when those inferences are not needed to maintain textual coherence (i.e., they were not bridging inferences). Lea used an online priming paradigm measuring reaction time on a lexical-decision task. He presented short-story vignettes on a computer screen, one sentence at a time. The stimulus words for the lexical-decision task were semantic associates of the output of the inference schemas; for modus ponens the stimulus words were semantic associates of *q*. For example, one story about Amanda said that "If this is a Halloween party, then I'll wear black." In the inference condition, the story said that Amanda discovered that it was, in fact, a Halloween party; the control condition said nothing to indicate whether or not it was a Halloween party. On the subsequent lexical-decision task, subjects responded faster to the associate "white" on the inference condition than on the control condition, even though "black" was mentioned only once in both conditions. This finding makes sense from the perspective of mental-logic theory because in the inference condition subjects would have made the modus ponens inference that Amanda will wear black (thus priming "black"), whereas in the control condition they would not have made such an inference. This finding is not explained by the models theory, however, because the final model in both conditions would include *q*, and the Gricean maxim is not applicable here. Models theory thus provides no reason to expect any difference in response times between the inference and control conditions.

The difference between the two approaches in how a modus ponens inference is made also is apparent when one considers a reasoning problem with the usual premises of the MP problem, but providing instead evaluation of the conclusion *not both p and q*. Mental-models theory predicts that the premises will combine directly in a final model that supports *both p and q*, leading directly to the judgment that the conclusion is false, as illustrated in the models in 4. Mental-logic theory, however, predicts that subjects first will apply the modus ponens schema to the two premises to infer *q*, and then after considering the conclusion to be evaluated will apply a conjunction-introduction schema to infer *p and q*; only then will the conclusion be judged false. Note that mental-models theory provides no reason for subjects to make this intermediate inference of *q* that is predicted on mental-logic theory. Further, a Gricean proscription against including a categorical premise when formulating a conclusion would not apply to such a problem. Chapter 8 presents such problems, testing whether the intermediate inference of *q* is made by asking subjects to write down any inference they might make on the way to evaluating the conclusion; most subjects wrote down the intermediate modus ponens inference predicted by mental-logic theory, even though models theory provides no reason for them to do so.

In a new experiment, similar problems were presented to 39 Brazilian school children between the ages of 10 and 12 years old. These children received 12 problems, among which were four that are relevant here. All of the problems presented premises referring to toy animals and fruits in boxes; a hand puppet provided a tentative conclusion that the children were required to evaluate. The four relevant problems were as follows (the problems were presented to the children in Portuguese): *(a) If there is a chicken in the box, then there is an apple in the box; There is a chicken; ?There is both a chicken and an apple in the box? (b) If there is a pineapple in the box, then there is a coconut in the box; ?It is false that there is both a pineapple and a coconut in the box? (c) If there is rabbit in the box, then there is both a bear and a rat in the box; There is a rabbit in the box; ?There is a rabbit and a bear and a rat in the box? (d) If there is an elephant in the box, then there is both a giraffe and a cow in the box; There is an elephant; ?It is false that there is an elephant and a giraffe and a cow in the box?* The children were required to explain how they arrived at their answers.

Note that in mental-models theory problems a and c should lead straightforwardly to "true" responses because the final model in each problem includes a token for each item mentioned in the conjunctive conclusion, and problems b and d should lead straightforwardly to "false" responses because the tokens in final model directly contravene the conclusion; none of the problems provide any model-based reason for the children to make any intermediate inferences on the way to the conclusion. Mental-logic theory, however, leads to the expectation that on all four problems before making their final evaluation, the children will first make an intermediate modus ponens inference—an intermediate inference for which models theory provides no explanation. Twenty nine of the 39 children (74%) gave the logically appropriate responses to all four problems (chance = 6.25%). (Failures to make an appropriate response stemmed primarily from two sources. First, some children rejected premises, for example, saying that an egg rather than an apple belonged with a chicken; second, some children rejected a valid conclusion on perceived epistemic grounds, for example, saying that an elephant cannot fit into a box.) Of the twenty-nine children who performed errorlessly on all four tasks, their explanations fell into three categories. On 16% of the problems the explanations were uninterpretable in terms of whether the intermediate inference was made (e.g., "What he said is the same as what the facts are"). Twenty-eight percent of the explanations were consistent both with models theory and with mental-logic theory, stating that a conclusion is right because the box contains both (or all three) of the objects. Fifty-three percent of the explanations, however, gave clear indication of an intermediate inference predicted by mental-logic theory, for example, "Because there is a chicken there is an apple, so both things are in the box," "It says there is an elephant, so the giraffe and cow also have to be there," "There is a bear and a rat, so what he said is right." Taken together with the findings reported in chapter 8 and in Lea (1995), these results show that mental-logic theory provides a more accurate description than does models theory of the actual psychological process leading to an inference of q from $if\ p\ then\ q$ and p.

MP is the only one of the four conditional syllogisms that leads straightforwardly to a response from the basic mental-logic skills (i.e., the schemas and the direct-reasoning routine); when the direct-reasoning routine fails a reasoner might apply a reasoning strategy. Although some college students use various strategies, their application is not widespread on laboratory tasks, and subjects vary greatly in which reasoning strategies they have available (chap. 7). MT can be solved using the schema for introducing a negation, which would be implemented through an indirect-reasoning strategy for reductio ad absurdum arguments. One supposes that p is the case, which through modus ponens on the major premise leads to q. Given that $not\ q$ is the minor premise, the supposition of p entails a contradiction, and $not\ p$ can be asserted. This line of reasoning goes beyond the direct-reasoning routine, so our theory predicts significantly fewer logically appropriate $not\ p$ responses on MT than logically appropriate q responses on MP, as the data show. (In this, the predictions of the mental-logic and mental-models theories are the same, and the fact that the data are consistent with this prediction by itself favors neither theory.)

When neither the direct-reasoning routine nor any obvious strategy leads to a solution, a reasoner might reasonably respond that nothing follows, as many subjects do. People often resist indeterminate responses (see discussion in Braine & Rumain, 1983; O'Brien, Braine, Connell, Noveck, Fisch, & Fun, 1989; Rumain, Connell, & Braine, 1983), however, and on problems for which nothing follows from the direct-reasoning routine or from any available strategy, they will often base inferences on other resources, notably the pragmatic principles of the third part of the theory (the noncore part), which may coexist in a line of reasoning with inferences made from the mental-logic schemas (Braine, 1990; Lea et al., 1990; O'Brien, 1995; chap. 3).[7] One source of extralogical pragmatic inference is the use of conversational implicatures or invited inferences (Geis & Zwicky, 1971; Grice, 1975, 1989; Politzer, 1986; Sperber & Wilson, 1986). Grice (1989) differentiated two sorts of conversational implicatures: particularized implicatures that follow from particular propositional contexts, and generalized implicatures that follow from extralogical meanings that are common to how a natural-language particle is construed. These generalized implicatures are the sort relevant here. A variety of pragmatically based invited inferences for conditionals is reviewed in chapter 9, such as the invited inference of *if not p then not q* from *if p then q* (Geis & Zwicky, 1971) and conversion of *if p then q* to *if q then p* (Politzer, 1986). Grice (1975) suggested that generalized implicatures are made commonly unless there are circumstances to inhibit them. These invited inferences on conditionals lead to the logically appropriate expected determinate response on MT, and to the fallacious expected determinate responses on AC and DA. The mental-logic approach thus does not predict the systematic differences among AC, DA, and MT that are predicted by mental-models theory, but rather predicts that all three problems will lead to a mixture of *Nothing follows* responses and expected determinate responses, and the data on these three problems therefore are consistent with the mental-logic account, but not with the mental-models account.

The mental-models and mental-logic theories provide differing views concerning what constitute the rudimentary, intermediate, and expert levels of reasoning on the conditional syllogisms. Resistance to giving a *Nothing follows* response is greater for children than for adults and use of the *Nothing follows* response option by children can require some training in order for it to be a meaningful index of the judgment that there is insufficient information to make an inference (Braine & Rumain, 1983; O'Brien et al., 1989; Rumain et al., 1983), so, from the perspective of the mental-logic approach, children should be less able than adults to set aside the pragmatically based invited inferences; mental-logic theory thus expects to find more expected determinate responses on AC, DA, and MT being made by children than by adults, and responses that nothing follows should increase with increasing age (see Braine & Rumain, 1983; O'Brien, 1987).

The mental-logic approach thus provides three levels of sophistication relevant to these problems. The lowest level (Level 1) is represented by

---

[7]It is also when nothing follows on the direct-reasoning routine that response biases are apt to have an influence (chap. 3; O'Brien, 1995). Note that this provides a reason for a negative-conclusion bias (if there is one) not to influence MP inferences; such a bias would not be likely when an inference is made on a basic mental-logic schema. Inspection of the data in Table 14.3 shows that responses are not suppressed on the MP problem.

the biconditional-like response pattern, with the expected determinate response made on all four problems (Pattern 3 in Table 5). The next level (Level 2) is represented by openness to the *Nothing follows* response option and awareness that it may be correct. This level is associated with a preference—not necessarily a consistent preference, because vacillation between levels may occur—for *Nothing follows* responses on AC, DA, and MT. The highest level (Level 3) is one in which MT is solved by a reductio-ad-absurdum argument, and *Nothing follows* responses are given to AC and DA (Pattern 4 in Table 5). This level is found among sophisticated reasoners (although this response pattern could also occur as a chance variant of Level 2).

A salient difference from the mental-models theory is that the models theory provides a level—the one-model patterns—that are more primitive than any of those of the mental-logic theory. Johnson-Laird (personal communication, March 1994) claimed that children will use only the initial conditional model without exhaustivity and that they do not consider the elliptical model. There are thus clearly contrasting developmental predictions between the theories. The mental-models theory predicts that the characteristic response pattern of young children will be expected determinate responses on MP and AC, and responses that nothing follows on DA and MT (Pattern 1 in Table 14.5); the mental-logic theory predicts the biconditional-like pattern. In this, there is no doubt that the predictions of the mental-logic theory are correct (Knifong, 1974; Markovits, 1985; Matalon, 1962; O'Brien & Overton, 1982; Peel, 1967; Rumain et al., 1983; Wildman & Fletcher, 1977; see Braine & Rumain, 1983, for a review). Neither Markovits (1984) nor O'Brien and Overton (1982), both of whom reported the most frequently occurring response patterns made by their child subjects, reported the pattern predicted by Johnson-Laird and his associates on the initial model set being given by children, and both show the biconditional-like pattern as that given most frequently by children. The response tendencies of children thus decisively favor the mental-logic over the mental-models theory.

Another salient difference between the developmental predictions of the two theories concerns MT. According to the mental-models theory, the *Nothing follows* response should be present early (because the one-model initial representation dictates it), and should decrease with age (as more complex representations are increasingly adopted); thus, models theory makes the intuitive prediction that performance on MT should improve with age. In contrast, mental-logic theory (Braine & Rumain, 1983; O'Brien, 1987, 1991) makes the counterintuitive prediction that young children's performance on MT would tend to be correct (as part of the biconditional-like response pattern of Level 1), and that their performance will deteriorate with increasing age (as the *Nothing follows* response option of Level 2 replaces the determinate responses of Level 1). (The mental-logic theory predicts a reversion back to correct performance on MT among reasoners of Level 3, but this has marginal relevance to most developmental data sets.) Again, the data support the mental-logic theory. Wildman and Fletcher (1977), Rumain et al. (1983), and O'Brien and Overton (1982) reported that *Nothing follows* responses increase as subjects get older for AC, for DA, and for MT, and Wildman and Fletcher reported that this increase in *Nothing follows* responses with increasing age occurs whether or not negatives are added to the terms of the major premise. As with the adult data, the developmental data are consistent with the mental-logic theory, but contrary to the mental-models theory.

Johnson-Laird (personal communication, March 1994) raised several arguments against the mental-logic account of reasoning on the four conditional syllogisms. First, he wrote that mental logic provides no explanation of "the vagaries of responses" to AC, DA, and MT, and that a prediction of no effect explains nothing when no effect is found. He is right, of course, that the absence of any differences among AC, DA, and MT does not weigh heavily in favor of the mental-logic account simply because it predicts an absence of any differences; it does weigh against the mental-models account, however, because the models account predicts differences. As to the vagaries in responses, these seem to occur among studies, rather than among problem types, and thus are outside the scope of either the mental-logic or mental-models theories. (They probably represent differences among subject populations or differences in how the problems were presented to subjects.)

Johnson-Laird also argued that mental logic is underspecified because it has provided no account of when the invited inferences will occur and when they will not. This point has some merit because mental-logic theory provides only limited guidance; a complete set of predictions would require a general theory of pragmatics, which goes well beyond the scope of mental-logic theory. Grice (1975, 1989) treats these implicatures as commonly made unless some reason exists on a particular occasion for their being withheld. We are less certain than Grice that these implicatures constitute default responses, that is, made unless otherwise suppressed. One situation in which we do expect the invited inferences likely to be made, however, is when nothing follows on the mental-logic schemas; an invited inference is most attractive when it avoids the conclusion that no inference can be made.

A third point made by Johnson-Laird was that mental-logic theory has provided no procedures for making a *Nothing follows* response. This is true inasmuch as neither the schemas nor the reasoning program include a procedure for making such a response. There is considerable evidence that subjects vary greatly both in their openness to *Nothing follows* responses and in their methods of diagnosing undecidability. Mental-logic theory makes predictions about when a *Nothing follows* response will not be made (when something can be inferred from the mental-logic schemas) with more precision than it makes predictions about when a *Nothing follows* response will be made. As we described earlier, there is a bias against giving *Nothing follows* responses, particularly for children, and when nothing follows on the mental-logic schemas people are apt to seek inferences that follow on other processes. When nothing obvious follows on any process or when the pragmatic inferences are understood as inappropriate, a *Nothing follows* response will be made. Note that, like the question of when the invited inferences are made, a complete inventory of extralogical inference-making processes would be required to make precise predictions about when *Nothing follows* responses will be made, and that would go well beyond the scope of mental-logic theory.

DISCUSSION

The comparative analysis presented here of the mental-models and mental-logic treatments of the conditional syllogisms was intended as a case study of the adequacy for propositional reasoning of the two theories generally. Models theory predicts differences among AC, DA, and MT that are found neither in the previously published data sets nor in the data reported here. Subjects showed no tendency to make expected determinate responses to AC any more than to DA or MT, and certainly they were nowhere nearly as frequent to AC as to MP. The basic predictions of mental-models theory thus are wrong. Johnson-Laird (1995) argued that the expected frequency of such responses to AC might not have been detected in previous studies because of a figural effect such that AC is more difficult than MP because information about q enters working memory after information about p, and AC requires reasoning from q to p. This explanation was tested when the major premise was presented as q *if* p rather than *if* p *then* q, and the data reported here, as well as data reported by Evans et al. (1995), show that reversing the order in which information in the major premise is presented led to no MP–AC or DA–MT reversals, and the attempt to save the models predictions with a figural effect was not supported.

Models theory has provided some detailed description of how the model sets for conditionals should be influenced by the presence of negatives. As we showed, these model sets should influence responses to the conditional syllogisms, leading to fewer expected determinate responses on AC and more on MT when the major premise contains a negated term. Neither the data reported here nor the previously published data sets support these predictions.

Models theory also led to a set of developmental predictions in which children should make responses based on an initial one-model representation, but these predictions are wrong; the published data sets show the younger children made biconditional-like responses that would follow on a two-model representation, and models theory provides no reason for this. In particular, models theory leads to the expectation that the logically appropriate expected determinate response on MT should increase with increasing age, as the more sophisticated model sets become available; the data reveal, however, that such logically appropriate responses on MT decrease with increasing age, as predicted by mental-logic theory.

Models theorists have not worked through the predictions for the conditional syllogisms for all of the possible model sets they have described, and when the various possible model sets are considered, they reveal that those combinatorial principles that Johnson-Laird and his associates have described (for the psychological algorithm) are inadequate because they lead to predictions that are wrong. In the case of the intermediate conditional model set, the prediction is quite odd—neither in the previously published data sets nor in the data reported here does any subject make the unexpected determinate response of q predicted for DA on this model set. Additionally, these combinatorial principles would lead to the prediction of a *Nothing follows* response to MP when *if p then not q* is the major premise. Models theory thus is required to use some other combinatorial principles, presumably those for the intermediate level of the theory. These principles have not been presented in full, however, and can only partially be worked out from examples. Clearly these principles must include some use of exhaustivity as premises are combined and inferences are drawn from final model sets. Whether Johnson-Laird and his associates will include among these principles the exhaustivity constraint suggested by Evans (1993) we do not know, although to date they have not. As we showed, however, exhaustivity has some rather large hidden processing costs that the modelers must spell out if clear predictions are to be possible. Models theory provides an account of reasoning on the conditional syllogisms that is quite complex, only partially specified, and, to the extent that Johnson-Laird and his associates described its predictions for the conditional syllogisms, they are inconsistent with the data.

The models-theory advocates have argued not only in favor of the models account of reasoning on the conditional syllogisms, but also against the use of inference schemas of the sort proposed by mental-logic theory. The mental-logic theory, however, provides an account that is both parsimonious and consistent with the data. The absence of any consistent differences for adults among AC, DA, and MT in the frequency of expected determinate responses is contrary to the models expectations but consistent with the mental-logic expectations. Furthermore, mental-logic theory provides an account that is consistent with the available developmental data; younger children do not make responses that reflect use of the initial one-model representations, but rather show responses that are consistent with making invited inferences on AC, DA, and MT as predicted by mental-logic theory. In particular, mental-logic theory accounts for the counterintuitive finding that the logically appropriate responses to MT decrease with increasing age—a finding that runs counter to the scenario the models theory describes.

Both the models theory and the mental-logic theory predict the logically appropriate expected determinate response on MP problems; in this both theories are right, and this fact by itself favors neither theory. The two theories differ, however, in the basis for the response, and in this the mental-logic theory clearly is right. On the standard MP problem, models theory leads to a final model set containing both p and q, and a stated conclusion of q alone follows only from the proscription against restating categorical premises in a conclusion. Clearly, as shown by the results in chapter 7 and those reported here, this account is inadequate. Both studies presented problems on which subjects provided the output of an intermediate modus-ponens inference when the Gricean-based proscription of models theory did not apply, that is, when the modus ponens inference was intermediate in a line of reasoning. Further, Lea (1995) reported a priming effect that is consistent with subjects having made a modus ponens inference—a finding that cannot be explained by models theory. These data weigh decisively in favor of the mental-logic account. Mental-logic theory thus provides a more plausible description of the actual psychological process by which modus ponens inferences are made, and we see no reason to abandon the description provided by mental-logic theory.

In principle, we see no reason why a skilled reasoner would not use a variety of logical-reasoning skills, including a mental logic of inference schemas, some sophisticated reasoning strategies to direct the schemas, a variety of pragmatically based inferences, and perhaps some use of mental models. Inferences from schemas and inferences from imagined situations could cohabit in the same line of reasoning. Inference schemas account easily and parsimoniously for a wide variety of logically valid inferences that people make routinely, including modus ponens. Some reasoning situations, though, such as AC, DA, and MT, do not present opportunities for the basic mental-logic skills. Being able to imagine a situation in which an invited inference does not hold strikes us as a useful skill to have in one's reasoning repertoire, and a mental model could block an unwarranted invited inference. Imagining a situation also could be useful in suggesting a supposition under which one might reason, for example, suggesting a possible reductio-ad-absurdum strategy or suggesting possible alternatives to assess. We thus have nothing against the idea that people often use models in reasoning. The current mental-models theory, however, provides an account of reasoning on the conditional syllogisms that is far too problematic to be acceptable.

ACKNOWLEDGMENTS

The authors express appreciation to Martin Braine, George Davidson, Jonathan Evans, Joe Hosie, Phil Johnson-Laird, and Guy Politzer for several helpful conversations and other communications; they are, of course, not responsible for anything written here. This work was supported in part by a grant from the CNPq of Brazil to Maria Dias.

15

A Dubious Premise:
Suppressibility of Modus Ponens

David P. O'Brien
Baruch College and the Graduate School
of the City University of New York

Maria G. Dias
Federal University of Pernambuco

Joseph R. Hosie
Baruch College
of the City University of New York

As part of an ongoing debate between advocates of the mental-logic and mental-models theories, Byrne (1989, 1991) claimed that modus-ponens inferences (i.e., of the form *If P then Q, P*, therefore *Q*) can be suppressed, and that this demonstrates that the mind does not have a schema for modus ponens. Given that mental-logic theory includes modus ponens among its basic inferences, Byrne's claim, if correct, would present a serious challenge. We show here, however, that the data presented by Byrne are consistent with the predictions of mental-logic theory and thus present no challenge. The reason that Byrne's data do not challenge mental-logic theory is that the sorts of problems she presented that putatively led to suppression of modus ponens violated one of the conditions for making an inference: For a reasoner to apply a schema, its premises must be assumed true (see discussion of the soundness of the schemas in chap. 3), and this condition is violated in the problems reported by Byrne (1989), as we show later.

Byrne's argument began by noting that Rumain et al. (1983) had claimed that the affirmation-of-the-consequent and denial-of-the-antecedent fallacies typically made on the conditional syllogisms (e.g., subjects often accept *not Q* as a conclusion from *If P then Q* and *not P* as premises; see chap. 14) result from invited inferences. Rumain et al. reported that the fallacies disappeared when (a) the asymmetry of a conditional premise was made explicit, for example, *If P then Q, but if not P then there may or may not be Q;* or (b) an additional conditional premise was provided, for example, *If R then Q* was presented in addition to *If P then Q* (see also Markovits, 1984, 1985). Byrne (1989) reasoned that if the same sort of experimental manipulation can suppress valid modus-ponens inferences, and Rumain et al. interpreted suppression of the fallacies as showing that the invited inference is non-necessary, then one also should interpret suppression of the modus-ponens inference as showing that modus ponens is non-necessary. Thus, she concluded, such evidence would show that the mind includes no rule for modus ponens.

Byrne's experimental strategy was similar to that of Rumain et al. in that Byrne presented problems with an additional conditional premise. For example, although most subjects readily accepted the modus-ponens inference when presented a control problem (similar in form to those presented in Rumain et al.) with these three premises:

1. If Mary has an essay to write, then she'll study late in the library
2. If Mary has some textbooks to read, then she'll study late in the library
3. Mary has an essay to write

Relatively few subjects accepted the modus-ponens inference on this experimental problem:

4. If Mary has an essay to write, then she'll study late in the library
5. If the library is open, then Mary will study late in the library
6. Mary has an essay to write.

Byrne argued that because the mental-logic schema for modus ponens ought to be free of any influence of the content of the premises, and 4 and 6 together support application of the modus-ponens schema, the inference should be made no matter what 5 says. Therefore, she concluded, the mind includes no such rule as modus ponens.[1]

From the perspective of mental-logic theory, however, failure to accept a modus-ponens inference on 4, 5, and 6 is not surprising. Because propositional reasoning concerns propositions rather than sentences, the mental-logic schemas do not apply mechanically to the sentence forms of the premise propositions (see chap. 3), and reasoners are expected to attend to the propositional content. The Gricean cooperative principle (or the rele-

---

[1]We refer to premise sets like those in 1 to 3 as *Rumain-type premises*, and to premise sets like those in 4 to 6 as *Byrne-type premises*. We refer to premises like 1 and 3, and 4 and 6, as *core premises*, and premises like 2 and 5 as *additional premises*.

vance principle of Sperber & Wilson, 1986) should lead a subject to assume that the information in 5 is intended to be relevant (otherwise it would not have been stated), and the premise in 5, together with what one knows about libraries, suggests that the premise in 4 might not be true: Libraries do not always stay open in the hours we might like, and Mary's conditional intention to study late in the library might be thwarted by a library that closes too early. Thus, because 4 is cast into doubt, it does not serve as a premise that can be assumed true, and a sound inference cannot be drawn from it: A conclusion cannot be stronger than its premises. Mental-logic theory thus predicts a *Can't tell* response because nothing follows on any premise set unless the premises are accepted.[2]

Politzer and Braine (1991) presented a similar response to Byrne (1989), and Byrne (1991) responded to it in turn. The exchange is somewhat (and un-necessarily) difficult to follow, however, because although Politzer and Braine presented their argument using premises 4 to 6, Byrne presented her response to them using the parallel premises in 4a to 6a:

4a. If Mary meets her friend, then she goes to a play
5a. If Mary has enough money, then she goes to a play
6a. Mary meets her friend.

According to Byrne (1991), in the Politzer and Braine argument 5a leads by conversion to:

7. If Mary goes to a play, then she has enough money

Then, by transitivity, 4a and 7 lead to:

8. If Mary meets her friend, then Mary has enough money.

From world knowledge a subject now asserts that:

9. It is false that if Mary meets her friend then Mary has enough money.

According to Byrne, the Politzer and Braine argument then asserts:

10. It is false that if Mary meets her friend then she goes to a play,

because it follows from 9 that either 4a or 5a is false. Premise 4a is considered false because 5a cannot be false because it supports its converse.

---

[2]For a discussion of reasoning from suppositions and counterfactuals, see chapter 9.

This supports the inference:

11. Mary meets her friend and Mary does not go to a play

because it is equivalent to 10.
A conjunction-elimination schema then leads to:

12. Mary does not go to a play.

According to Byrne (1991), the Politzer and Braine argument thereby predicts that subjects should respond that Mary does not go to a play. Byrne pointed out that the data do not support this prediction, and most subjects instead concluded that:

13. Mary may or may not go to a play.

The problem with Byrne's reply to Politzer and Braine is that it did not portray accurately what Politzer and Braine actually argued. They did not argue that 7 is based on a conversion of 5a, but rather that 14, as well as its parallel 14a, are added to the premise set from knowledge about the world:

14. If Mary studies late in the library, then necessarily the library is open
14a. If Mary goes to a play then necessarily she has enough money

Further, Politzer and Braine did not claim that people make the inference in 10—only that 4 and 5 together would lead to the false inference in 14, which together with 1 leads to:

15. If she has an essay to write then necessarily the library stays open,

so that one cannot consider 4 and 5 true together. Premise 4, on which the modus-ponens inference is based, is thus open to doubt. Note that because Politzer and Braine did not claim 10 (or its essay-writing equivalent), they did not commit themselves to the line of reasoning in 11 to 12, and whereas Byrne claimed that Politzer and Braine predicted the conclusion in 12, Politzer and Braine stated specifically that subjects should interpret 4 and 5 as:

16. If Mary has an essay to write and the library is open, then she'll study late in the library,

which is parallel to interpreting 4a and 5a as:

16a. If Mary meets her friend and Mary has enough money, then she will go to a play,

which leads to the conclusion in 13, which Byrne reported is the modal response. Byrne's data, thus, are consistent with the predictions of mental-logic theory.

Even though Byrne's rejoinder to the Politzer and Braine argument was based on an inaccurate portrayal of their argument, Chan and Chua (1994) wrote that "Byrne (1991) showed that Politzer and Braine's (1991) account was falsified by data from her experiments" (p. 220), and that the mental-logic approach has "not offered a principled account of the interpretive processes critical in reasoning" (p. 233). Chan and Chua proposed that a principled account is provided, however, by their *relative-salience model*: The effect of an additional conditional premise, such as 5 or 5a, as compared with 2, follows from a greater degree of importance (i.e., salience) of the antecedents for their consequents in conditionals such as 5 and 5a than in a conditional like 2. For example, the precondition *The library is open* has greater necessity for Mary's action of studying late in the library than does the precondition *Mary has some textbooks to study*. This leads, according to Chan and Chua, to the prediction that the probability of the suppression of the modus-ponens inference is in a direct positive relation to the perceived salience of the antecedent in the additional premise.

To account for the difference between the Byrne-type and Rumain-type premise sets, Chan and Chua proposed two production rules. Taking the core conditional premise as *If P then Q* and the additional conditional premise as *If R then Q*, and the minor premise as *P*:

Prod 1:IF "*R*" or "not *R*" is unknown,
  THEN scale "*R*" according to assertion "*P*" (i.e., $R \mid P$).

Prod 2:IF $(R \mid P) < 1$,
  THEN respond "*Q*," otherwise respond "don't know."

Accordingly, from premises of the Rumain type, the modus-ponens inference would be made because $(R \mid P) < 1$, whereas from premises of the Byrne type, the modus ponens inference would not be made because $(R \mid P) \geq 1$. In other words, the inference is made if, and only if, *P* is rated as more salient than *R*.

One obvious difference in the way in which the Chan and Chua account differs from the mental-logic account is that the Chan-and-Chua production rules pertain only to modus-ponens inferences, whereas the mental-logic account pertains to any sort of inference, for example, the disjunction-elimination schema would not be applied when its premises are doubted. Indeed, if we are right, even a simple reiteration would not be accepted when doubts are raised about a proposition, something that would not be explained by Chan and Chua's production rules.

An additional recent criticism of the Politzer and Braine argument was provided by Oaksford and Chater (1995), who claimed that the Politzer and Braine argument is not logically valid. They wrote that according to Politzer and Braine, 14 is a necessary truth that follows from:

17. If the library is closed then Mary cannot study late in the library.

Oaksford and Chater argued, however, that 14 does not follow in standard modal logic, which leads instead to:

18. Necessarily, if she studies late in the library, then the library stays open,

and that 15 does not follow from 18. Oaksford and Chater concluded that because the Politzer-and-Braine argument is invalid, they have failed to account for the effect of the Byrne-type premises.

We note two problems with the argument put forth by Oaksford and Chater. First, Politzer and Braine did not assert that 14 is a necessary truth; what they did say was that subjects know as a general truth about libraries that one cannot study late in them unless they stay open. Second, Politzer and Braine did not derive 14 from 17; indeed, 17 was not mentioned at all by Politzer and Braine. Instead, Politzer and Braine argued that 14 comes from the general knowledge that one cannot study in the library unless the library remains open. Oaksford and Chater's assertion that Politzer and Braine had proffered an invalid argument is therefore unwarranted.

Quite apart from their formal argument, Oaksford and Chater claimed that 14 is, on its face, absurd because it bases a necessary truth on a contingent truth: In ordinary circumstances, whether or not someone studies late (or has an essay to write) cannot necessitate that a library stays open. This criticism misses Politzer's and Braine's point: The very peculiarity that Oaksford and Chater noted about 14 illustrates that the premise 4 is dubious: Mary's intention to study late in the library is not sufficient for her actually to study late in the library. The peculiarity of 14 does not impeach Politzer's and Braine's account, but rather makes their point: The modus-ponens inference is withheld because its premises are open to doubt, and the basis for this doubt is apparent in the peculiarity of 14.

The mental-logic account really is quite simple (although its simplicity is obscured by the obfuscatory misrepresentations of its critics): It relies on the intuition that consideration of 4a and 5a together raises doubt about the truth of 4a, and, likewise, that consideration of 4 and 5 together raises doubt about the truth of 4. As was noted in chapter 3, inferences are drawn not from premises, but from assumptions or suppositions, that is, from propositions assumed or supposed to be true, and this condition is violated in problems of the Byrne type.

Two recent investigations lend support to our contention that the source of the effect of the additional Byrne-type premises is that they raise doubts about the core conditional premises, that is, they block subjects from accepting them as assumptions on which to base an inference. Stevenson and Over (1995) reported that the Byrne-type premises had a stronger effect when subjects were instructed to imagine that the premises were overheard in a conversation (12% accepting modus ponens with Byrne-type premises) than when they were instructed to assume that the premises were true (40% accepted modus ponens with the Byrne-type premises). George (1995) reported that when subjects were presented Byrne-type premises and told to assume absolutely the truth of the premises, they accepted the modus-ponens inference 96% of the time, but when told to use all information, they accepted the modus-ponens inference only 43% of the time.

Both Stevenson and Over and George provided indirect evidence that the influence of the Byrne-type premises is exactly as Politzer and Braine had suggested, that is, that the additional premise raises doubts about the core conditional premise. We conducted an experiment that was designed to investigate directly whether subjects do indeed have such doubts. *Forced-choice* problems were presented to 58 introductory psychology students at Baruch College; each problem presented the two conditional premises from a Byrne-type problem, paired with the two conditional premises from a parallel Rumain-type problem. For example, subjects were told to suppose these two facts about Mary: *Fact 1: If Mary meets her friend, then she will go to a play*, and *Fact 2: If Mary has enough money, then she will go to a play*; and these two facts about Betty: *Fact 1: If Betty meets her friend, then she will go to a play*, and *Fact 2: If Betty meets her family, then she will go to a play*. The subjects were then asked, given both facts about Mary and both facts about Betty, which they were more likely to believe: Fact 1 about Mary or Fact 1 about Betty; in another condition, subjects were presented exactly the same materials, except that the word *believe* in the question was changed to *doubt*. Each subject received three problems presented on a single page, one with the Mary and Betty content, one with Bob and George content (the Byrne-type premises were *If Bob has an essay to write, then he will study late in the library* and *If the library is open, then Bob will study late in the library*, and the Rumain-type premises were *If George has an essay to write, then he will study late in the library* and

If George has a midterm exam, then he will study late in the library), and one
with Jane and Susan content (The Byrne-type premises were *If it is raining,
then Jane will get wet* and *If she goes for a walk, then Jane will get wet*, and
the Rumain-type premises were *If it is raining, then Susan will get wet* and
If she goes for a swim, then Susan will get wet.) The believe versus doubt
instruction was a between-subject variable.

No appreciable differences were observed among the three types of
content. As expected, subjects presented the forced-choice problems were
much more likely to believe the target conditional with the Rumain-type
premises (76%), and much more likely to doubt it with the Byrne-type
premises (72%). Inspection of the written justifications revealed that 88%
of the selections of doubting the Byrne-type premises or believing the
Rumain-type premises referred to the possibility that the conditions for
the truth of the Byrne-type premise might not have been met. For example,
"She couldn't go to a play if she didn't have the money," or "It only
describes her intentions, not necessarily what she'd really be able to do."
These results are consistent with our contention that subjects do not accept
the truth of the target conditional premises in the Byrne-type problems.

It is possible, of course, that without such a forced-choice procedure,
subjects would not find either premise doubtful; we thus constructed
another sort of problem, referred to as the *truth-rating* set, which were
presented to 35 Baruch College introductory psychology students. Four
problems were constructed. Each problem instructed subjects to "suppose
that someone reliable tells you the following two sentences about Mary
(or Bob)." Two of the problems presented the two conditional premises
about Mary going to a play, with one problem presenting the Byrne-type
premises and the other problem presenting the Rumain-type premises;
and two of the problems presented the two conditional premises about
Bob working late in the library, with one problem presenting the Byrne-
type premises and the other problem the Rumain-type premises. On each
problem, following the presentation of the two conditional sentences the
subjects were told, given both sentences, to choose one of the following:

(a) Sentence 1 definitely is true.
(b) Sentence 1 probably is true.
(c) Sentence 1 might be true or might be false.
(d) Sentence 1 probably is false.
(e) Sentence 1 definitely is false.

Each subject was presented two problems, one a Byrne-type problem and
the other a Rumain-type problem, with one problem using Mary content
and the other using Bob content. Order of content and of problem type
were counterbalanced.

The truth-rating problems were scored by giving 1 point for each occurrence of response option (a), 2 points for each occurrence of response option (b), 3 points for each occurrence of (c), and so forth. An initial inspection revealed no appreciable effect of problem content. The mean scores were 3.20 and 2.54 for the Byrne-type problems and for the Rumain-type problems, respectively. This difference was assessed with a pre-planned t-test for correlated measures, $t(34) = 2.34$, $p < .025$, indicating that even without the possible task demands of the forced-choice procedure, subjects were less likely to accept the truth of the conditional premise with the Byrne-type premises than they were with the Rumain-type premises.

In summary, whether measured by the forced-choice or the truth-rating procedures, subjects were more likely to accept the truth of the target conditional premise when presented with the Rumain-type additional conditional premise and to doubt the target conditional premise when presented with the Byrne-type additional conditional premise. This is direct evidence that the effect of the additional Byrne-type premise is to cast doubt on the conditional premise on which the modus-ponens inference relies, and it is consistent with the indirect evidence provided by Stevenson and Over (1995) and by George (1995).

We turn now to whether the effect of the Byrne-type premises has to do with conditionals as such, or survives to problems that present other sorts of inferences, or to problems that do not require any logic inferences at all. We constructed comparisons between Byrne-type and Rumain-type premises with the core schema for disjunction elimination (Schema 3 of Table 6.1), with the feeder schema for conjunction elimination (Schema 9 of Table 6.1), and with problems that require only reiteration, that is, where there is no logic inference at all. If we are correct that the source of the effect reported by Byrne (1989) is doubt about the truth of the core premise, then not only should subjects reject a modus-ponens inference as following on a Byrne-type premise set, but they should reject any other sort of inference as following from such a premise set. Indeed, not only should inferences based on doubtful premises be rejected, but so should the simple reiteration of a dubious premise—something that does not require a logic inference at all.

The *disjunction-elimination problems* instructed subjects to consider three facts. For example, on one Byrne-type problem, the premises were *Either Mary will go to a movie or she will go to a play* (Fact 1), *Mary will not go to a movie* (Fact 2), *and Mary is coming down with the flu* (Fact 3). Subjects then were asked, given these three facts, to choose the right answer from among three options: (a) Mary will go to a play, (b) Mary will not go to a play, and (c) Mary may or may not go to a play. Note that Facts 1 and 2 allow application of a disjunction-elimination schema, which would support answer (a), that is, that Mary will go to a play. Fact 3, however, casts doubt on Fact 1, and suppression of Fact 1 would block the inference that could be made on Facts 1 and 2 alone. In a companion control problem, Fact 3 was replaced with *Mary plans to wear a new dress*, which is consistent with Fact 1, and thus should not lead to doubt about Fact 1 and thus not block the disjunction-elimination inference. Similar problems were constructed using the major premise *Either Bob will study his textbooks or he will write his term paper*. In the Byrne-type version, Fact 3 was *Bob's parents are planning a surprise visit*, and on the control problem Fact 3 was *Bob plans to use his new typewriter*. Sixty Baruch College introductory psychology students each were presented one Byrne-type problem and one control problem. For half of the subjects the Byrne-type problem had the Bob content and the control problem had the Mary content, and for the other half of the subjects the content and problem type were reversed. Problem order was counterbalanced.

Each *conjunction-elimination* problem presented two facts and three response choices. One Byrne-type problem presented Fact 1 as *Bob will study his textbooks and he will write his term paper*, and Fact 2 as *Bob's parents are planning a surprise visit*. The control problem presented the same Fact 1, but Fact 2 was replaced with *Bob plans to use his new typewriter*. In both problems the three response options were (a) Bob will write his term paper, (b) Bob will not write his term paper, and (c) Bob may or may not write his term paper. A second set of problems had *Mary will go to a play and she will have dinner in a restaurant* as Fact 1; the Byrne-type problem had *Mary is coming down with the flu* as Fact 2, and the control problem had *Mary plans to wear a new dress* as Fact 2. The response options referred to whether Mary will go to a play. Twenty-eight subjects each were presented with one Byrne-type problem and one control problem, with half of the subjects receiving the Byrne-type problem with the Bob content and the control problem with the Mary content, and with the other half receiving a reversal of content and problem type. Problem order was counterbalanced.

Twenty-four subjects were presented *no-inference problems*, that is, problems that required only reiteration of a premise. One Byrne-type problem presented Fact 1 as *Mary will go to a play* and Fact 2 as *Mary is coming down with the flu*. The control problem was identical except that Fact 2 was replaced with *Mary plans to wear a new dress*. The three response options were as follows: (a) Mary will go to a play, (b) Mary will not go to a play, and (c) Mary may or may not go to a play. A second set of problems presented Fact 1 as *Bob will write a term paper*; in the Byrne-type problem Fact 2 was *Bob's parents are planning a surprise visit*, and in the control problem Fact 2 was *Bob plans to use his new typewriter*. Each subject was presented one Byrne-type problem and one control problem. For half of the subjects the Byrne-type problem was presented with the Bob content and the control problem with the Mary content, and for the other half of the subjects the content and problem type were reversed. Problem order was counterbalanced.

Initial inspection of the data revealed no effects for different content. The proportions for each response option for each of the problem types are shown in Table 15.1, which reveals that although the control problems almost always led to True responses, the Byrne-type problems rarely did so. Clearly, the effect of an additional Byrne-type premise does not rely on a conditional premise and is the same for inferences drawn from a disjunctive or conjunctive premise. More revealing, however, is the finding that even simple reiteration is not accepted when an additional Byrne-type proposition is presented. Given the survival of the effect to situations where no inference is required, the conclusion is inescapable: The Byrne-type premises of problems like 4 to 6 do not suppress modus-ponens inferences, but rather suppress their requisite premises.

Can production rules of the sort proposed by Chan and Chua (1994) account for the data reported here? The obvious weakness of their account is that its production rules apply only to modus ponens, so it would require a rapidly burgeoning set of production rules, including some for disjunction elimination, some for conjunction elimination, etc. What these production rules would be, particularly what sort of production rules would account for the suppression of reiteration, is unclear. If the production rules for reiteration were to follow the pattern of those for modus ponens, they would express salience as a function of some conditional probabilities, although what the basis for their conditionality would be is far from clear. In comparison with the parsimonious account provided by mental-logic theory, this sort of solution would be prodigal, and it remains unspecified at this time.

TABLE 15.1
Proportions of True, False, and Can't Tell Responses to the
Disjunction-Elimination, Conjunction-Elimination,
and No-Inference Problems

	Response Category		
	True	False	Can't Tell
Disjunction-elimination			
Control	.87	.03	.10
Byrne-type	.27	.23	.50
Conjunction-elimination			
Control	1.00	.00	.00
Byrne-type	.21	.21	.57
No-inference			
Control	.92	.00	.08
Byrne-type	.08	.17	.75

Have Oaksford and Chater (1995) provided a better account than we have? They argued that consistency searches are undecidable for any logic at the level of a predicate calculus, so a mental logic cannot provide adequate procedures to ascertain whether any premise is true. For this reason, they proposed an explanation that comes not from logic, but from the artificial intelligence (AI) literature, where one encounters the issue of nonmonotonicity, that is, the possibility that additional information may lead to fewer entailed inferences. Consider, for example, *All birds can fly* and *Tweety is a bird*, from which one might infer that *Tweety can fly*. If one discovers, however, that *Tweety is an ostrich*, the inference that Tweety can fly will be withdrawn. Oaksford and Chater rejecting using a nonmonotonic logic, because, they said, it would face the same problems of undecidability that a standard logic does. Instead, they proposed that *All birds can fly* is a default rule, which, unlike a proposition in logic, can be replaced when exceptions are encountered. (The choice of a default rule is based on a Bayesian probability computed, in principle, to maximize the amount of information that can be obtained.)

What is clear from the perspective of mental-logic theory, but not from the perspective of Oaksford and Chater, is that the problems we have been discussing do not reveal any nonmonotonicity in reasoning. To Oaksford and Chater, adding the information that *Tweety is an ostrich* to the information that *All birds can fly* and that *Tweety is a bird* results in greater information, but one fewer inference; from the mental-logic perspective, however, adding the information that *Tweety is an ostrich* leads to one fewer premise, as the proposition that *All birds can fly* loses its status as a proposition from which inferences can be drawn. Adding information, thus, is not equivalent to increasing the number of acceptable premises.

It is difficult, however, to see how an explanation in terms of a default rule would provide predictions that differ from those that follow from the mental-logic account, because, by our account, the realization that ostriches are nonflying birds reveals that *All birds can fly* is false (its quantifier is too strong), which removes the basis for inferring that *Tweety can fly*. Indeed, replacing a default rule may simply be another way of expressing what happens when a premise is doubted.

The fact that standard logics at the predicate level are undecidable does not strike us as problematic. As the previous chapters in this volume make clear, making judgments about which propositions have or do not have determinate truth values is not something that the basic mental logic is equipped to do (see, in particular, chaps. 4 and 9). The direct-reasoning routine applies the schemas when their requisite propositions are considered together in working memory. Searches of long-term memory to assess whether the premises are decidably true is not something that we think people ordinarily do, nor do we propose that people are particularly skilled at this sort of thing. Of course, as Lea (chap. 5) noted, if mental-logic theory is to make online predictions, it will need to consider how propositions are stored in, and retrieved from, long-term memory, and how they are stored in working memory. As noted in chapter 4, we see a need for a mental logic in order for declarative knowledge about alternatives, suppositions, etc. to be represented either in long-term or working memory. Until such issues are investigated, mental-logic theory does not provide a complete account of when and how a premise will be rejected as false, but this in no way impeaches our claim that people make judgments of belief and doubt, and that the source of the effect of additional Byrne-type premises is that they raise doubts.

Finally, has mental-models theory provided a better explanation than we have of the effects of the additional Byrne-type premises? Evans and Over (1996, 1997) argued that although there is nothing about models per se that would provide an explanation, because models theory holds that construction of models is, in principle, influenced by knowledge about content, models theory, in principle, can account for content effects. Mental-logic theory, they argued, has no principled way to account for content effects. We disagree: Other than asserting that construction of models is influenced by knowledge about content, the models theory has specified nothing of how this is accomplished. Their account would seem to require the same general cognitive principles that mental-logic theory does. Note that both theories will require integration of their core parts with other cognitive processes, and, in this, neither theory gains any advantage over the other. We see no reason, in principle, why either models theory or mental-logic theory could not account for these findings.

Findings that additional Byrne-type premises influence acceptance of modus-ponens inferences do not mean that people do not make modus-ponens inferences, nor do such findings indicate that people are reasoning from models. Such findings simply show that premises can be cast into doubt.

16

What the Mental Logic–Mental Models Controversy Is Not About

Luca Bonatti
Laboratoire des Science Cognitives et Psycholinguistique

It is far from trivial to find out what the controversy between the mental models and mental-logic ways to explain human reasoning is really about and what data could settle it. One way to make progress is to concentrate on a small domain that both theories address, and thoroughly examine which theory seems to be more likely to capture human reasoning. In the past, this approach could be only speculative, because where a mental-model theory of one domain existed, no mental-logic counterpart did, and vice versa. Recently it has become possible actually to compare both approaches on the domain of propositional reasoning. It is, therefore, not without interest to find out what exactly is at issue, what exactly the data say, and what exactly the respective theories can do to account for them.

Johnson-Laird, Byrne, and Schaeken (1992) and Johnson-Laird and Byrne (1991) presented a version of their model theory for propositional reasoning that claimed to account for all the known phenomena of deductive propositional reasoning, provide a general theory of conditionals, account for all the most important aspects of the mental-logic theory and its results, and also predict new phenomena that a mental-logic theory could not explain. These claims were too good to be true. O'Brien, Braine, and Yang (1994) and Bonatti (1994) raised a series of problems for the model theory and for its algorithmic implementations: O'Brien et al. (1994) showed that (along with some sound predictions) the model theory, taken together with its algorithmic implementation, was also issuing many unbelievable and unsupported predictions. I first showed that the theory was often vague and, of the two algorithms meant to clarify it, one was not psychologically plausible and the other was faulty in a way that was difficult to fix without making it psychologically unacceptable. Then I showed that there are different ways (that are not equivalent) to count the number of models a problem requires. The implication is that until an independently justified criterion to count models is provided, the model theory cannot even be evaluated.

In their response, Johnson-Laird, Byrne, and Schaeken (1994) restated the superiority of their theory and dismissed my article, judging it "not a reliable guide to the model theory or to Braine's (1990) theory" (p. 737). They also argued that the model theory is both methodologically and empirically superior to current (and future) rule theories because (a) the mental-logic theory cannot be practically refuted, whereas the mental-model theory can be; (b) the model theory predicts correctly that exclusive disjunctions are easier than inclusive disjunctions, whereas mental-logic theory has the opposite prediction; and (c) the model theory predicts that errors in reasoning will be consistent with at least one model of the premises, whereas the mental-logic theory, in principle, cannot explain reasoning errors.

These three claims, in one form or another, frequently recur in the literature. They have an independent interest and therefore deserve discussion. I claim that they are wrong, but clarifying them reveals interesting aspects of both theories and thus contributes to an evaluation of the real issues dividing the two approaches.

IS MENTAL-LOGIC THEORY DIFFICULT TO REFUTE? IS MENTAL-MODELS THEORY EASILY REFUTABLE?

According to Johnson-Laird et al. (1992, 1994), the mental-logic hypothesis is almost impossible to refute, whereas the mental-model hypothesis can be refuted easily by finding problems that require many models but are solved easily by subjects I raised. To see why this argument underestimates the difficulty of the problem, I begin by making a general point about the status of both the mental-models and mental-logic hypotheses. It will then appear clear that, if anything, it is the mental-models theory that dangerously runs the risk of not being refutable.

Mental logic is a general hypothesis that claims that, in good part, reasoning is similar to theorem proving. It leads naturally to the general prediction that *ceteris paribus* the difficulty of a problem is function of the number and difficulty of the rules involved in a proof. However, such prediction has little empirical impact if the rules, their conditions of application, and their psychological costs, are not specified. The general prediction just discussed, as such, does not afford a quick way to refute the hypothesis. Yet, surely, specific theories based on it can be refuted—

this is why it is important to discuss one specific version of the hypothesis, such as Braine's. However, this is not a shortcoming of the mental-logic hypothesis: It is just what to be a general and sound hypothesis means. In order to refute the hypothesis in its general form, one needs strong general arguments against its general form and, as a consequence, against all the specific theories based on it—and I do not think there are any—whereas in order to refute specific theories based on it one conducts experiments and sees what Mother Nature has to say.

The mental-model hypothesis also is only a very general framework. It holds that reasoning involves building and inspecting models, and hence it lends itself to the "principal prediction" (Johnson-Laird et al., 1992, p. 436) that the difficulty of a problem is function of the number of models required. Yet this "principal prediction" is likewise not sufficiently specific to yield univocal empirical tests. The general mental-model hypothesis does not even specify what kind of cognitive objects models are, let alone how to identify them and the procedures by which they are constructed, or how they interact with other cognitive mechanisms. There are many ways to unfold such points, and thus many specific theories can be developed that are consistent with the hypothesis. Hence, barring principled arguments against the general statement of the model hypothesis—and even here I do not think there are any, at least in the way Johnson-Laird develops it—its principal prediction has little empirical bearing. Just as for the mental-logic case, only fully developed mental-model theories can be submitted to the tribunal of experience.

Now let us turn to the actual theories. The mental-logic theory presented in this volume unambiguously specifies length, difficulty, and time course of proofs for a large class of basic problems (see chaps. 7 and 8), so one knows perfectly well how to look for a refutation of it. However, a deep difficulty stands in the way of a search for a refutation of the existing model theory. In order to make sense of the "principal prediction" of models theory, a unique and unambiguous way to count models must be specified. Yet, models can be counted in many ways. One would consider (a) the total sum of the minimal number of models needed by all the premises of a problem taken separately, or (b) the minimal number of models needed by the integrated premises, or (c) the sum of models required by the interpretation of each premise plus the number of models required by the conclusion, or (d) the maximal number of models loaded in working memory at each given step of processing of new premises.[1]

---

[1]All these criteria should be multiplied at least by two, because Johnson-Laird et al. offered two algorithms to count models (the "psychological" algorithm and the "AI" algorithm); there are at least two counts per each criterion. Add to it that often actual model counting is accomplished by some rules of thumb that fall in between the two algorithms, and you obtain yet another set of criteria for model counting.

The trouble is that these criteria are not equivalent (Bonatti, 1994). Supporters of the model theory generally use the first criterion—the number of models needed to represent the premises as estimated by rules of thumb that fall in between the two algorithms. However, Johnson-Laird et al. (1992) used two criteria: one to predict the data in their experiments, and another (the total sum of models as estimated by the psychological algorithm) to predict the data of Braine et al. (1984; see chap. 7). Braine et al. had reported a correlation = .92 between mean difficulty ratings of direct reasoning problems and the difficulties predicted by the sum of weights for the schemas required for solution, accounting for 85% of the variance. Johnson-Laird et al. (1992) argued that number of models highly correlates with subjective difficulty (= .80, accounting for 64% of the variance), thus using the Braine et al.'s results as confirmation of their theory. However, just switching the two criteria completely changes the picture: By applying the first (i.e., the usual) criterion, the correlation between models and problem difficulty disappears (= .21, accounting for only 4% of the variance). What, then, is the right criterion? The choices made by Johnson-Laird and his colleagues appear to have no justification.

These calculations assume that the rules to count models are indeed well defined, but this is concessive on my part. In fact, it is not at all clear how models should be computed in the general case. For example, a conditional like "If A then B" is initially represented with one model, plus an empty model. Does the empty model contribute to difficulty—and hence enter model counting—or not? We do not know. Furthermore, "If not A then B" requires two models at least, and "If A then not B" requires three (Johnson-Laird & Byrne, 1991).[2] When considering a multiple premises problem, should we count these additional models, or not? And if we do, how are we going to compose those additional models with models for nonconditional sentences? No guidelines exist to solve these problems.

Johnson-Laird et al. (1994) partially admitted the difficulty, but besides stating without justification that sometimes one way to count models, and sometimes another, will be suitable, they fail to indicate how to decide. They seem not to realize that until the problem is addressed, their "principal prediction" loses any meaning when applied to their theory. The problem is not one that can be swept under the rug. It extends far beyond propositional reasoning and should lead one to reconsider much of the evidence gathered for mental models in other domains of reasoning. My conclusion is that, like the mental-logic hypothesis, the model hypothesis is not easy

---

[2]This apparently unjustified difference allows the authors to explain some aspects of the selection task, but also seems to have the absurd consequence that Modus Ponens from "If A then not B" should be much more difficult than Modus Ponens from "if A then B." Should we take this consequence seriously?

to refute in general, but, unlike the mental-logic theory presented in this volume, the current mental-model theory can be neither refuted nor confirmed. Until we possess a justified criterion to count models, we do not even know what this sort of evidence tells us about model theories.

DO MENTAL-LOGIC AND MENTAL-MODELS THEORIES LEAD TO OPPOSITE PREDICTIONS FOR DISJUNCTIVE PROBLEMS?

The second claim concerns the state of the evidence. According to Johnson-Laird and Byrne (1991), the evidence clearly is in favor of the mental-model theory. However, I have shown that this is not so clear. Even leaving aside the problems I raised above, both an amended mental-model theory and the mental-logic theory issue the same predictions in most cases (Bonatti, 1994). Johnson-Laird et al. (1994) seem to concede this, but in one case they strongly disagree. For disjunctive problems, they claim (as well as Evans, Newstead, & Byrne, 1993, p. 78), the two theories make opposite predictions and the evidence rules in favor of their model theory. Unfortunately, their analysis contains a mistake that is difficult to spot that vitiates their conclusion.

Johnson-Laird et al. (1992) showed that problems containing double inclusive disjunctions, like (1)

(1) June is in Wales or Charles is in Scotland, or both.
    Charles is in Scotland or Kate is in Ireland, or both.
    What, if anything, follows?

are more difficult than problems containing double exclusive disjunctions, like (2)

(2) June is in Wales or Charles is in Scotland, but not both.
    Charles is in Scotland or Kate is in Ireland, but not both.
    What, if anything, follows?

In Experiment 4 of Johnson-Laird et al. (1992), subjects only drew 6% correct conclusions for inclusive disjunctions and 21% correct conclusions for exclusive disjunctions. Comparable "negative" disjunctions obtained even fewer correct responses and revealed the same pattern. Other responses were either "nothing follows" (25% and 44% for inclusive disjunctions—that is, the larger group—and still large groups of 23% and 29% for exclusive disjunctions) or other nonvalid answers. The result was substantially confirmed by Bauer and Johnson-Laird (1993) with a population of better reasoners. For Johnson-Laird et al., this outcome is predicted by the mental-model theory, because exclusive disjunctions only require two final (or three total) models and inclusive disjunctions require three final (or five total) models, whereas the mental-logic theory would "make the opposite prediction because the exclusive disjunction calls for an extra step" in their proofs (1994, p. 738). To support their claim, Johnson-Laird et al. (1993) report (3):

(3) Either there is a short in the circuit or else the battery is dead.
    Actually, the battery is not dead.
    Therefore, there is a short in the circuit.

They state that for Braine (1990), (3) should be analyzed as containing an exclusive disjunction, which has a longer—hence a more difficult—proof than an inclusive one. Their claim derives from a misunderstanding of Braine's theory that has a series of consequences. This can be seen by noting two points.

The first point concerns the relation between natural language and logical representation. An "or" in natural language need not be mapped onto either an exclusive or an inclusive disjunction. A neutral reading, uncommitted to either interpretations, is possible and may well be the default reading in those languages whose lexicon has only one disjunction. In Braine's system, many inferences can be carried through with such a reading, including the one Johnson-Laird et al. report. In fact, Problem (3), around which Johnson-Laird et al. build their argument, is Problem x in the Appendix to chapter 7. As shown there, it is a one-step problem that subjects consider to be easy and easily solve.

Matters change when contextual factors force "or" to be either inclusive or exclusive. In that case, the mental-logic theory of Tables 6.1 and 6.2 (essentially the same as that of Braine, 1990) does indeed make a difference between the two disjunctions, but one that is exactly the opposite of what Johnson-Laird et al. claim. To see this, one has to appreciate a crucial aspect of mental-logic theory that Johnson-Laird et al. completely overlook. Mental-logic theory distinguishes two kinds of rules and their related routines of application: direct and indirect ones. The former group is claimed to be almost automatic and easily applied by most subjects, whereas the latter is neither universal nor easily accessible. One strategy, the Supposition of Alternatives Strategy (hereafter SAS), whose main role is to take disjuncts (subcomponents of disjunctions) contained in the set of premises and to temporarily assume them in subderivations within a proof, is commonly found among college students (see chaps. 6 and 7).

Note that the inference procedures of Table 6.2 first apply the direct rules that can be applied and then resort to the indirect procedures, with

SAS a particularly available strategy. So, it is not the length of a proof per se that determines how difficult a problem is, but the kinds of rules and strategies involved: In general, problems that cannot be solved by the direct reasoning routine and require indirect strategies should be more difficult, and problems that require indirect procedures other than SAS will be the most difficult.

Now, one can check that the proof of (3) with "or" interpreted exclusively can be obtained by applying only the direct reasoning routine:

(3a) P1.   S or D and not (S and D)
     P2.   Not D
     1.   S or D   (P1, schema 9)
     2.   S   (P2 and 1, schema 3)

(Schema numbers refer to Table 6.1. Note that applications of schema 2 have a negligible cost.) However, a proof of (3) with "or" interpreted inclusively requires application of indirect reasoning procedures, either SAS and *reductio*, as in (3b), or repeated recourse to SAS, as in (3b'):

(3b) P1.   S or D or (S and D)
     P2.   Not D
     1.   S or (S and D)   (P1, P2, schema 3)
     2.   (S and D) (1, SAS)
     3.   D   (2, schema 9)
     4.   incompatible   (3, P2, schema 10)
     5.   not (S and D)   (2, 4, schema 13 (*reductio*))
     6.   S   (1, 5, schema 3)
(3b') [P1, P2, and 1, as in (3b)]
     2.   S   (1, SAS)
     3.   If S then S   (2, schema 12)
     4.   (S and D) (1, SAS)
     5.   S   (4, schema 9)
     6.   if (S and D) then S   (4, 5, schema 12)
     7.   S   (1, 3, 6, schema 5).[3]

---

[3](3a) corresponds to the intuitive argument: "Of the two, only one: either there is an S or there is a D. We know that there can't be a D, therefore there must be an S." (3b) corresponds to the intuitive reasoning: "Either there is an S, or there is a D, or there are both. First, we know by hypothesis that there can't be a D alone. Neither can there be both S and D, because if it were so we should conclude that there is also a D, but this is absurd, So there must be an S"; (3b') corresponds to the intuitive reasoning: "Either there is an S, or there is a D, or there are both. First, we know by hypothesis that there can't be a D alone.

As can be seen, regardless of whether (3) is read in an indeterminate or in an exclusive way, a proof from it will be easier than either proof from an inclusive reading.

The same argument holds—and more so—for the double disjunctions from which Johnson-Laird et al. (1992) asked subjects to freely generate conclusions. On the one hand, from a double positive exclusive disjunction such as (2), a conclusion may be obtained as in (2a):

(2a)	P1	(W or S) and not (W and S)	
	P2	(S or I) and not (S and I)	
	1.	W or S	(P1, schema 2)
	2.	not (W and S)	(P2, schema 2)
	(2i)	S	(1, SAS)
	(2ii)	not (S and I)	(P2, schema 2)
	(2iii)	not I	(2b, 2a, schema 7)
	(2iv)	If S then not I	(2a, 2c, schema 12)
	3.	W (1, SAS)	
	4.	not S	(2, 3, schema 7)
	5.	S or I	(P2, schema 2)
	6.	I	(4, 5, schema 9)
	7.	If W then I	(3, 6, schema 12)

The proof does involve SAS, and SAS predicts that in this case subjects may go into some useless detours (such as 2i–iv), but no other more difficult indirect strategies are needed in order to reach a valid conclusion. On the other hand, in order to reach a conclusion from a double inclusive disjunction such as (1), one would start with the premises:

(1a)	P1	W or S or (W and S)
	P2	S or I or (S and I)

but neither the direct reasoning schemas, nor a few applications of SAS alone would lead anywhere. There are of course valid conclusions from (1a), but a "spring of fantasy" and familiarity with *reductio* techniques are needed in order for the proof to be on the right track. This, besides other factors connected to the forms of the valid conclusions that one can derive from such problems (see Bonatti, 1994, p. 730), may explain why subjects generated few correct solutions: Naive subjects do not know how to "continue the story."

But in all the other hypotheses there must be an S, because if there is an S, then obviously there is an S, whereas if there are both an S and a D, then there still is an S. Therefore, we can conclude that there is an S."

Johnson-Laird et al. (1994) countered my argument by claiming that for double inclusive disjunctions "in Bauer and Johnson-Laird (1993) experiment, the subjects did know how to continue the story: They performed well" (p. 738). However, this comment is, for what I can see, unfounded on the basis of their very same data. In the condition I am discussing—verbal presentation of inclusive disjunctions—even the group of better reasoners tested by Bauer and Johnson-Laird (1993) drew less than 30% of correct conclusions. Johnson-Laird et al. rhetorically switch the reader's attention to conditions of their experiment not pertinent to my point. In fact, if subjects really "performed well" in verbal double-inclusive disjunctions, then the mental-model theory would be in trouble because it should predict the opposite outcome.

The general outcome is that, *contra* Johnson-Laird et al. (1994), mental-logic theory predicts that freely generating conclusions from inclusive disjunctions is more difficult than from exclusive disjunctions, and, hence, that subjects looking for conclusions from double-inclusive disjunctions will produce few correct solutions and many incorrect answers. Double disjunctions just do not tell the theories apart.

THE MENTAL-LOGIC THEORY CANNOT PREDICT ERRORS

The third argument raises what Johnson-Laird et al. take to be a principled difficulty for Braine's theory and for mental logic in general. According to them, models predict that the errors people make in drawing conclusions are consistent with the premises, whereas the mental-logic theory offers no such prediction: for Johnson-Laird and Byrne (1993), "this prediction *cannot* be made by the formal rule theories" (p. 373, italics added). Commenting on cases in which people seem to draw contradictory conclusions, also Johnson-Laird and Savary (1996) argued:

> This phenomenon is contrary to current theories based on rules of inference (e.g. Braine and O'Brien, 1991; Rips, 1994). . . . Current theories use only rules that yield valid conclusions, and so they have no way to explain the systematically invalid conclusions that individuals draw to illusory inferences. (p. 89)

However, this is just a mistaken interpretation of any mental-logic-like theory. However, errors do not pose any principled difficulties for mental logic. To the contrary, there is a natural way to explain their source and nature. Proofs are complex objects in which it is crucial to keep track not only of the sentences triggered by the rules, but also of their dependency links. In order to arrive at valid conclusions it is crucial to remember whether a sentence comes from the application of a rule, is a temporary supposition, or comes from a rule *within* a temporary subderivation. Consider the personal feeling of "getting lost in the middle of an argument," of keeping reasoning without knowing where one started. In the same way, while solving a deductive problem, the exact structure of the proof and the exact dependency links may be lost. In these conditions, subjects may assert one temporary conclusion of a subderivation as if it were in the main line of the proof, responding before an adequate completion. Invalid conclusions, then, will be produced as intermediate passages in subderivations of proofs. Note that the nature of the proof will also predict the nature of errors. In cases in which no or few subderivations are needed, reasoners will not make mistakes. Many problems whose proofs comply to this prediction are reported throughout this volume.

When instead several subderivations are needed, the nature of subderivation will predict the kind of errors. Consider, for example, the case of a proof stopped in the middle of the application of a conditional reasoning strategy (schema 12 in Table 6.1). Because the strategy asks the reasoner to make a supposition (in order to introduce a conditional), or to suppose the antecedent of a premise and try to prove something from it, any intermediate conclusion will be a potential error, but one consistent with the conditional premise. This, in fact, seems to be the case for the errors found by Johnson-Laird et al. (1992). For example (p. 434), they reported that one of the most frequent errors on a problem like (2) was the conjunction (W and I). Now, this is an easy passage that subjects might derive in proving (2) as in (2a), in the subderivation starting with W (line 3) and ending with I (line 6) by applying Schema 8 (conjunction introduction) without finishing the proof: (W and I) does seem a nontrivial conclusion in this context, and subjects might well regard it as good candidate for response without paying attention that the subderivation is not closed.

Alternatively, if a reasoning requires applications of *reductio* strategies, then intermediate conclusions may even be inconsistent with the premises (because they lay in a subderivation starting with the negation of a supposed conclusion). Thus, in complex reasoning, subjects may even literally settle for contradictory conclusions—a phenomenon that the mental-model hypothesis, whose second main prediction is that errors must be consistent with at least one model of the premises, could not account.

A full argument for my thesis would require a much more detailed analysis of errors. It should be clear, however, that *contra* Johnson-Laird et al., the mental-logic theory is rich in predictions and explanations for errors, their nature, and their occurrence.

CONCLUSION

There are apparently many reasons, both philosophical, methodological, and empirical, to oppose mental models and mental logic as alternative views of reasoning. Here and elsewhere (e.g., Bonatti, 1997) I argue that, on closer inspection, a good part of the arguments on which the opposition is based is ill-founded. The reader may then wonder what the controversy is all about.

The answer is deceivingly simple: It's not about two alternative chief world systems—it's just about science. Both mental logic and mental models are general hypotheses about the format of the representation for reasoning, text, and speech comprehension. Both hypotheses can generate classes of theories, many of which will be certainly false and some of which may turn out to be correct. Only by carefully examining the pros and cons of each theory, once its state of development allows one to carry out such an examination, can one make progress. This is just what happens in any other respectable scientific domain. Johnson-Laird et al. (1992) and (1994) argued that for propositional reasoning this is possible, that disjunctive problems and errors are the kind of empirical cases needed, and they would support the mental-model theory. I showed that these are unsupported claims.

Where are we, then? On one side is a mental-logic theory for which a consistent body of supporting evidence exists. On the other is a mental-model theory plagued by the difficulties I outlined. Although it is not impossible that the existing models theory can be stretched to cover the required explanatory space, in light of the problems for model counting and for the plausibility of its algorithmic implementations, it would be wiser to suspend judgment on it. What we can say is that, so far as propositional reasoning is concerned, the comparative analysis seems to have a pretty clear outcome. I will not tell you which one, but as Johnson-Laird and Byrne (1991) wrote, there will be no prize for guessing the outcome (p. x).

Pinocchio's Nose Knows: Preschool Children Recognize That a Pragmatic Rule Can Be Violated, an Indicative Conditional Can Be Falsified, and That a Broken Promise Is a False Promise

David O'Brien
Baruch College and the Graduate School
of the City University of New York

Maria G. Dias
Antonio Roazzi
Federal University of Pernambuco

Joshua B. Cantor
Long Island University

Pragmatic-reasoning-schemas theory (PRS theory) suggests a developmental scenario for the acquisition of semantic knowledge about logic particles that is quite different from what is proposed by the mental-logic theory of this volume. PRS theory (e.g., Cheng & Holyoak, 1985; Holland, Holyoak, Nisbett, & Thagard, 1986; Holyoak & Cheng, 1995) claims that reasoning typically uses some context-sensitive schemas that are defined in terms of classes of goals and content. Unlike the sorts of schemas proposed by mental-logic theory, the proposed pragmatic-reasoning schemas are applicable only when their appropriate goals and content are present. Although the PRS theorists have suggested that there are a large number of such schemas (e.g., Holyoak & Cheng, 1995), to date only two schemas have been specified—one for permissions and one for obligations—both of which are presented in the form of conditionals, that is, *If P then Q*.

The various pragmatic schemas are claimed to be acquired inductively through exposure to the appropriate sorts of goals and their classes of content. From this perspective the lexical meaning of *If* would consist of a rather large set of markers for various pragmatic schemas, that is, pointing to the permission schema, the obligation schema, and to each of a putatively large set of as yet unspecified schemas. These various schemas would come in one at a time, as each goal and its content area is mastered. The sort of schemas described by mental-logic theory, which are available across different content areas and do not require pragmatic goals, would come in relatively late in development, and "this level of abstraction in conditional reasoning is seldom attained" (Holland et al., 1986, p. 282).

Mental-logic theory proposes that the core meaning of a logic particle, that is, its lexical entry, is provided by its basic inference schemas, for example, for *If*, modus ponens and a schema for conditional proof (see chap. 10). These lexical entries arrive developmentally early, as the child maps interpretable natural-language input onto the schema forms that are in the syntax of thought (see chap. 5). Only later would any additional content-dependent or context-sensitive schemas be acquired, and these would retain the basic schemas and specify additional available inferences. Any inferences that are particular to conditional permissions or obligations, for example, would be consistent with the core mental-logic schemas for *If*.

The evidence in support of PRS theory has been provided by findings that (a) versions of Wason's selection task are solved by adults when presented with conditional permissions or obligations, but not when presented with indicative conditionals[1] (e.g., Cheng & Holyoak, 1985), (b) older children solve reduced-array versions, as well as full versions, of the selection task when presented with conditional permissions, but not with indicative conditionals (e.g., Girotto, Light, & Colbourne, 1988; Light, Blaye, Gilly, & Girotto, 1989), and (c) preschool children solve an evaluation task when presented with conditional permissions, but not with indicative conditionals (Harris & Núñez, 1996). As we shall show, however, these findings are not straightforwardly interpretable as support for the PRS position.

We turn first to the selection task. In its standard format, the selection task presents four cards showing, for example, A, D, 4, and 7. Subjects are told that each card has a letter on one side and a number on the other, and presented the following rule: If a card has an A on one side, then it has a 4 on the other side. Finally, they are told that this rule may be true or may be false for these four cards and are asked to select those cards that need to be turned over for inspection to find whether the rule is true. Although standard logic would lead one to select the card showing A (to discover whether it has number other than 4, which would falsify) and

---

[1]Indicatives convey states of affairs rather than regulations.

the card showing 7 (to discover whether it has letter other than A, which would falsify), most adults select the cards showing A and 4, or just the card showing A (see review in Evans et al., 1993).

The most persuasive evidence for PRS theory was provided by Cheng and Holyoak (1985), who reported that when a similar problem was presented with a permission rule, a majority of subjects selected the appropriate cards. Their abstract-permission problem told subjects to assume that the role of an authority checking whether people were obeying a rule of the form "If one is to take action A, then one must first satisfy precondition P." Subjects were told that each card showed on one side whether action A was taken by a person, and on the other side whether that same person had fulfilled precondition P. The task showed four cards showing "has taken action A," "has not taken action A," "has fulfilled precondition P," and "has not fulfilled precondition P." In addition to this abstract permission-rule problem (solved by approximately 60% of subjects), PRS theorists have presented a large number of thematically meaningful problems with permission rules, and a few with obligation rules, that people tend to solve.

In its most recent version (see Girotto, Mazzocco, & Cheribini, 1992; Griggs & Cox, 1993; Kroger, Cheng, & Holyoak, 1993), PRS theory claims that a selection task problem will be solved when it has (a) a pragmatic rule, preferably one for which subjects understand its motivation, (b) instruction to assume the role of an authority checking for violators, (c) instruction to find potential rule violators rather than potential rule falsifiers, and (d) presentation of the negatives in the cards explicitly rather than implicitly. The PRS explanation is that (a) only when a problem presents a pragmatic rule will a pragmatic schema be available; (b) instruction to assume the role of an authority increases the likelihood that a problem with a pragmatic rule will evoke the pragmatic schema; (c) instruction to find potential violators rather than potential falsifiers allows use of a pragmatic schema because a pragmatic schema, such as that for permission, is set up to find violators and not to evaluate the truth of a rule; and (d) explicit negatives are required in the cards so that subjects can appreciate the pragmatic relevance of the information in the cards, that is, to perceive a correspondence between what is stated in the cards and what is represented in the pragmatic schema's production rules.[2] Kroger et al. asserted that these task features will not help unless a

---

[2]PRS theory holds that the permission schema consists of four production rules. Two of these contain explicit negatives, that is, "If the action is *not* taken, the precondition need *not* be fulfilled," and "If the precondition is *not* fulfilled, the action may *not* be taken." Only when the negatives in the cards are explicit will they correspond explicitly to the values in these production rules. When the negatives in the cards are implicit, a subject may not realize that these production rules should apply.

problem presents a pragmatic rule, because their benefits stem either from their aiding evocation of a pragmatic schema or from aiding its application when evoked.

We propose a different view of the reported findings. Pragmatic-rule problems with the features just described have been solved because they allowed subjects to understand that they were looking for potential counterexamples, whereas the control problems have not made clear what they require. Note that if one is instructed to find a violating instance for *If P then Q*, and one does not think that finding an instance of *P and not Q* would indeed violate, one would not select the *P* and *not Q* cards. Likewise, if one is instructed to find a falsifying instance, and one does not think that an instance of *P and not Q* would falsify, one would not select the *P* and *not Q* cards.

Noveck and O'Brien (1996) pointed out that finding a counterexample to a regulation, such as a conditional permission or obligation, usually does not falsify that regulation, but merely violates it, and that finding a counterexample to an indicative conditional does not ordinarily violate that conditional, but falsifies it. Consider some problems from O'Brien, Dias, Roazzi, Lea, Cantor, Kim, and Chuang (1997), which were presented to college students in New York.[3] One problem described some tourists renting an automobile at an airport in an unfamiliar country. They were told by the car rental agent that if someone drives on the expressway, they must stay below 100 km per hour. The tourists later noticed that most drivers on the expressway were traveling at a higher speed. Subjects were asked whether such instances violated or falsified the regulation (we refer to this as a *counterexample interpretation task*), and approximately 90% indicated that they understood the counterexamples as violating rather than falsifying the regulation. PRS theorists could view this as consistent with their claim that the permission schema is set up to find violators and not to test whether a rule is true. Consider, however, a second problem in which one of the tourists tells his wife that if someone drives in this country, they must stay on the left side of the road. The tourists later noticed that drivers in this country stay on the right side; on this problem approximately 90% of the subjects decided that the regulation had been falsified rather than violated.[4] O'Brien et al. found that counterexamples to permission rules usually were thought to be violators, but in some circumstances were thought to be falsifying; one is not going to be able to explain matters merely by assuming that a permission schema is set up to find violators rather than falsifiers.

---

[3]Similar problems were presented to students in Brazil, with similar findings.

[4]One might argue that it is the assertion of the rule that is being falsified, rather than the rule itself. In this case, one would still need to explain why subjects did not think that the counterexamples falsified the assertion made by the rental agent in the earlier problem.

O'Brien et al. (1997) found that solution of a selection task requiring finding potential violators of a pragmatic regulation occurred only when its corresponding counterexample-interpretation task led to judgment of the counterexample as violating rather than falsifying. Being told to assume the role of an authority checking whether people are obeying a regulation, for example, can make it clear that the task requires looking for rule violators; it is not an ordinary part of a authority's role to find people who obey regulations nor to discover whether a rule is true or false. When the counterexample-interpretation task led to judgment of the counterexample as falsifying, however, as in the example above of the tourist claiming that cars must drive on the left, the corresponding selection task was solved when requiring finding potential falsifying cases. Given that PRS theory claims that the pragmatic schema is set up only to find violators, the theory is left unable to account for this finding.

O'Brien et al. also presented counterexample-interpretation problems with indicative, as well as promissory, conditionals. For example, in one indicative problem the tourists were told by a local booster, who was boasting about the safe habits of local drivers, that if someone drives on the expressway they always stay below 100 km per hour. On this problem, approximately 90% indicated that they understood the counterexamples as falsifying rather than violating the assertion.[5] In a promissory-conditional problem a tourist *promises* that if he drives on the expressway he will stay under 100 km per hour. Subjects were equally likely to judge a counterexample (he drives on the expressway at a faster speed) as a violation or a falsification of his promise (he both broke his promise and he lied). These findings led to the predictions that versions of the selection task presenting an indicative conditional could be solved so long as they made clear the requirement to find potential falsifying cases, and that versions of the selection task presenting a promissory conditional could be solved so long as their requirements are presented clearly, either as seeking falsifying or violating cases. These predictions turned out to be right: Selection task versions based on a correspondence to responses to the counterexample-interpretation tasks for indicative and promissory conditionals just described were solved at rates similar to those requiring finding violators of pragmatic rules.[6] Similar findings for selection tasks

---

[5]As yet, we have not found a version presenting an indicative conditional that leads subjects to interpret a counterexample as a violation.

[6]O'Brien et al. found a wide variety of problems with indicative conditionals that led to selection of the P and *not* Q cards. For example, some tourists are told that if they go to the Siam Square Mall, they will find a McDonalds, a woman is told by her sister that if she buys furniture from Wellmans Department Store, they will deliver it free, a Danish chieftain tells his cousin that if they join forces they will defeat Rolf's clan, a real-estate agent tells his partners that if Mrs. Bortofsky is offered 1 million dollars if she will sell her property.

presenting indicative conditionals that require finding potential falsifying cases were also reported by Almor and Sloman (1996).

We turn now to the reported findings that older children solved both full and reduced-array versions of the selection task only when they presented a pragmatic rule (e.g., Girotto et al., 1988; Light et al., 1989). Consider Girotto et al. (1988), who reported that 9- and 10-year old children were able to choose the appropriate card in a reduced-array task (which presented only the two cards portraying the consequent affirmed and denied) when a permission rule was presented (70% correct), but not when a "formal control" problem was presented (11% correct), a finding they said is a challenge to the mental-logic approach. In the permission condition, children were told that a bird ate bees at night, so the Queen Bee made a rule that all buzzing bees must stay inside at night. The children were told to imagine being a policeman bee looking for rule violators. In the formal condition, the children were told that they might be tricked by a statement that was untrue, and were asked to check on whether the statement that all bees stayed inside "was a trick" (Girotto et al., 1988, p. 475). This instruction seems to us less clear in asking children to find potential falsifiers than is the instruction to find potential violators in the permission condition. From our perspective, children should have been asked straightforwardly to identify what would show the statement is not true. In fact, Girotto et al. presented what they called a *diagnostic problem*, which asked children to imagine being on an expedition assisting a naturalist who told them, "I think that all the buzzing bees live underground." They were told that the naturalist often is wrong and to check whether he was wrong this time. The rate at which children were correct on this problem did not differ statistically from the rate on the permission-rule problem, a result that Girotto et al. (1988) admitted occurred "unfortunately for our arguments" (p. 479). From our perspective, one would expect that both the permission and diagnostic conditions would lead to similar rates of solution, and this is what happened. This hardly seems to provide evidence for the claim that superior performance occurs only when a pragmatic schema can be applied.

The youngest children investigated were 3- and 4-year olds (Harris & Núñez, 1996). Their investigation used an evaluation task that presented a conditional and pictures of its four possible instances. One of the permission-rule problems, for example, told children that one day a child named Carol was told by her mother that "if she does some painting she should put her helmet on," and presented four pictures: Carol painting and wearing a helmet, Carol painting and not wearing a helmet, Carol not painting and wearing a helmet, and Carol not painting and not wearing a helmet. Children were asked to indicate which picture showed Carol "doing something naughty, and not doing what her Mum said"

(Harris & Núñez, 1996, p. 1584). In the comparable indicative problem, children were told that Carol says that "if she does some painting she always puts her helmet on," and asked to indicate which picture showed Carol "doing something different, and not doing what she said" (p. 1584). Harris and Núñez reported that 77% of the children chose the appropriate card when the task was presented with a permission rule, but only 40% did so when the task was presented with an indicative conditional. They concluded that "3- and 4-year old children can identify breaches of a permission rule . . . (but they) are not equally sensitive to the violation of all types of conditional rules" (p. 1587), and suggested that an understanding of logical necessity is derived from a prior understanding of regulatory conditionals (p. 1590). If we are right about what is required to construct a task that will be solved, however, on their control problem Harris and Núñez were asking the wrong question; the appropriate question would have concerned the possible falsity of Carol's assertion, rather than the possible naughtiness of her behavior. In asking for children to identify the picture of Jane not doing what she said, they were asking them to identify a violator of an indicative, whereas they should have been asking them to find a falsifier.

We now describe some studies we conducted that were motivated to show that preschool children can solve evaluation task problems with indicative as well as with regulatory conditionals. We first conducted a pilot study in two preschools in New York City, presenting several variants with indicative conditionals, all of which presented clear instructions to find falsifying cases. Fourteen children between 42 and 66 months participated. One sort of problem was constructed to be presented with a Pinocchio hand puppet; these problems depicted some boys playing in a park, and Pinocchio said that "all the boys playing tennis are wearing blue sneakers." The four pictures showed (a) a group of boys playing tennis wearing blue sneakers, (b) a group of boys playing soccer wearing blue sneakers, (c) a group of boys playing tennis wearing red sneakers, and (d) a group of boys playing soccer wearing red sneakers. The participating children were instructed to "point to the picture that made Pinocchio's nose grow, to the picture that shows that Pinocchio told a lie." A second sort of problem was constructed to be presented without the Pinocchio puppet. These problems showed a picture of Mike, and children were told that Mike often says things that are not true. This time Mike said that "if I play soccer, I always wear red sneakers." The participating children were shown four pictures: (a) Mike holding a soccer ball and wearing red sneakers, (b) Mike holding a tennis racquet and wearing red sneakers, (c) Mike holding a soccer ball and wearing green sneakers, and (d) Mike holding a tennis racquet and wearing green sneakers. Children were told to "point to the picture that shows that Mike told a lie."

In this pilot study, we were interested in obtaining a sense of how the children would deal with the problems, so we presented them in a variety of ways. In some cases we presented a problem with all four pictures, whereas in others we presented a problem with only two pictures (the *P and Q* and *P and not Q* pictures). Some children received only a single problem, and others two problems. Altogether the four-picture versions were presented to 12 children, and the two-picture versions to nine children. We found that performance was not influenced by whether the Pinocchio or Mike versions were presented, nor by whether two or four pictures were presented. On the 12 four-picture problems, eight led to selection of the *P and not Q* picture (.67, chance = .25); on the 9 two-picture problems, 7 led to selection of the *P and not Q* picture (.78, chance = .50).

A systematic study then was conducted with 20 children (10 boys and 10 girls) from an English-language preschool in Geneva, Switzerland, ranging in age from 47 to 72 months, participating. Because the pilot study had indicated that preschool children tended to select the appropriate pictures in the four-picture version, the two-picture versions were not included this time. Each child received two problems, one with a pragmatic rule and one with an indicative conditional. For half of the children, the pragmatic rule problem presented Mike, who was told by his mother that if he played tennis, he must wear his red sneakers. For the other half of the children, the pragmatic rule problem presented a group of children playing in a park; their teacher told them that all children playing soccer must wear blue sneakers. Children were asked to point to the picture showing Mike (or the children) being naughty and not doing what he was (they were) told. For half of the children, the indicative problem presented Mike, who said that if he plays tennis he always wears his red sneakers; children were asked to point to the picture that shows that Mike was telling a lie. For the other half, the indicative problem presented the Pinocchio hand puppet who said that all of the children who were playing soccer in the park were wearing blue sneakers; children were asked to point to the picture that would make Pinocchio's nose grow. (We discovered that all of the children we tested, both in New York and in Geneva, were familiar with the story of Pinocchio.) Problem order, content, and picture order were counterbalanced.

No differences were observed between the Mike and children-in-the-park problems, that is, between the problems presented in conditional form (with *if* and about one child) and the problems presented in universal form (with *all* and about a group of children). Summed across the two types of problems, 65% of the children chose the *P and not Q* picture for the problems presenting an indicative conditional (chance = .25, $z = 4.13$, $p < .001$) and 70% chose the *P and not Q* picture for the problems presenting a pragmatic rule ($z = 4.65$, $p < .001$), with no significant difference between the pragmatic and indicative problems. Clearly, when an evaluation task with an indicative conditional is presented with the appropriate instruction to find a falsifying case, preschool children were as apt to select the *P and not Q* picture as they were when presented a task requiring finding violating cases for a pragmatic rule.

The 3- to 6-year-olds both in New York and Geneva were able to identify a counterexample when the instruction was appropriate for the sort of conditional, that is, identifying a falsifier of an indicative conditional and a violator of a pragmatic rule. A third investigation addressed four different sorts of problems, two that we predicted would not be solved and two that we predicted would be. The problems we expected would not be solved included ones that required finding falsifiers of pragmatic rules and ones that required finding violators of indicatives. The problems we expected would be solved included some that required finding violators of promissory conditionals and some that required finding falsifiers of promissory conditionals.

An example of an indicative violator problem told about Jane, who is a very naughty girl, and she doesn't do what she says. Jane says that "I will tell you something about me. If I ride a bicycle, I always wear a back pack." Children were told to point to the picture (among four) that shows that Jane is not doing what she said. A pragmatic falsifier problem told about Jane, who is a very naughty girl and she tells lies about what her mother tells her to do. Jane says that her mother told her, "If you wear a dress, you must wear a hat." Children were told to point to the picture that shows that Jane is telling a lie about what her mother tells her to do. In one of the promissory violator problems children were told about Jane, who is a very naughty girl who likes to make promises that she doesn't keep. Jane told her friend Fabio that, "I will tell you a promise. If it rains, you can use my umbrella." Children were told to point to the picture that shows that Jane did not keep her promise. In one of the promissory falsifier problems children were told about Jane, who is a very naughty girl who likes to make promises that are not true. Jane told her friend Fabio that "I will tell you a promise. If it rains you can use my umbrella." Children were told to point to the picture that shows that Jane's promise was not true. The study was carried out with 71 English children in a preschool in Oxford and 49 Brazilian children in a preschool in Recife. Children ranged in age from 34 to 71-months old. Each child received three problems of one type, with children randomly assigned to problem type.

As predicted, neither the indicative violation problem nor the pragmatic falsification problem led to the *P and not Q* response more often than would be expected by chance (chance = .25; the observed proportions were .33 and .20, respectively), but both the promissory violation and promissory falsification problems did (observed proportions = .51 and

.47, respectively; $p < .001$ when compared to what would be expected by chance). A preplanned t test revealed that the two promissory problems led to the P *and not* Q choice more often than did the other two problems (.49 vs. .26), t (108) = 3.55, $p < .001$. These results show that children were unable to identify counterexamples either to indicative or to pragmatic conditionals when the instructions were presented counterintuitively. The results also demonstrate two new classes of conditionals for which children find identification of counterexamples easy, that is, promissory conditionals both when presented with instructions to find violators and with instructions to find falsifiers. In this, promissory conditionals are pragmatically distinguishable from the other sorts of conditionals that have been presented on these tasks.

The findings from all three studies confirmed our expectation that preschool children would be able to identify a counterexample to a conditional so long as they are asked to do so in a way that corresponds to what a counterexample means for that conditional. When the wrong question was asked, however, children's choices did not differ from chance. The determining factor concerned not what sort of conditional was presented, but whether the appropriate instructions were presented for the sort of conditional, and this was the case for indicative and promissory conditionals, as well as for pragmatic regulations.

We draw the following conclusions. When people decide whether a counterexample to a conditional violates that conditional without falsifying it, or falsifies it without violating it, or both falsifies and violates it, they are making a pragmatic judgment. Such judgments depend, in part, on the sort of conditional being considered, that is, whether it is a pragmatic regulation, an indicative assertion, a promise, and so forth, but such judgments depend also on the circumstances in which a conditional is being considered, for example, its source, the potential effects of a counterexample, and so forth. PRS theory does not capture such judgments; it provides no reason for counterexamples to some permission rules to be interpreted as falsifying, and to others as violating, nor does it capture why counterexamples to indicative conditionals are interpreted as falsifying, nor why counterexamples to promissory conditionals are interpreted as both violating and falsifying. Yet these are the pragmatic judgments that determine which selection-task and evaluation-task versions lead to P and *not* Q selections.

The evidence put forth in favor of PRS theory was the superior performance reported on versions of the selection task (and, for children, the evaluation task) presenting pragmatic rules and requiring identification of violating cases when compared to the inferior performance on versions of these tasks presenting indicative conditionals. PRS theory explained that these findings resulted from the use of some schemas that are specific to finding violators to pragmatic rules. As we showed, however, versions of these tasks can be constructed easily that can be solved even when presenting indicative or promissory conditionals: All one needs to do is to appreciate the pragmatics of how counterexamples are interpreted.

Harris and Núñez (1996) were right when they concluded that preschool children are able to identify violations of pragmatic regulations, but are unable to identify violations of indicative conditionals; what they missed, however, is that preschool children are equally adept at identifying falsifiers of indicative conditionals and at identifying both violators and falsifiers of promissory conditionals. Both the adult and the developmental data are clear: There is no special understanding of pragmatic regulations such that selection and evaluation tasks can be solved with them and not with other sorts of conditionals, and there is no early acquisition of knowledge about pragmatic regulations that is lacking for other sorts of conditionals. Clearly, earlier researchers had underestimated the abilities both of adults and children to identify counterexamples to conditionals other than pragmatic regulations. Because there is no evidence that preschool children understand those conditionals that convey pragmatic regulations but do not understand other sorts of conditionals, there is no empirical reason to think that the meaning of *if* is acquired by accretion of pragmatic schemas.

References

Albrecht, J. E., & Myers, J. L. (1995). Role of context in accessing distant information during reading. *Journal of Experimental Psychology: Learning, Memory and Cognition, 21,* 1459–1468.

Albrecht, J. E., & Myers, J. L. (in press). Accessing distant information during reading: Effects of contextual cues. *Discourse Processes.*

Albrecht, J. E., & O'Brien, E. J. (1993). Updating a mental model: Maintaining both local and global coherence. *Journal of Experimental Psychology: Learning, Memory and Cognition, 19,* 1061–1070.

Almor, A., & Sloman, S. A. (1996). Is deontic reasoning special? *Psychological Review, 103,* 374–380.

Anderson, A. R., & Belnap, N. D., Jr. (1975). *Entailment.* Princeton, NJ: Princeton University Press.

Bates, E. (1974). The acquisition of conditionals by Italian children. *Proceedings of the 10th regional meeting of the Chicago Linguistic Society.* Chicago: Chicago Linguistic Society.

Bauer, M. I., & Johnson-Laird, P. N. (1993). How diagrams can improve reasoning. *Psychological Science, 4,* 372–378.

Beth, E., & Piaget, J. (1966). *Mathematical epistemology and psychology.* Dordrecht: Reidel.

Bever, T. G. (1970). The cognitive basis for linguistic structures. In J. R. Hayes (Ed.), *Cognition and the development of language* (pp. 279–362). New York: Wiley.

Bloom, L., Lahey, M., Hood, L., Lifter, K., & Feiss, K. (1980). Complex sentences: Acquisition of syntactic connectives and the semantic relations they encode. *Journal of Child Language, 7,* 235–261.

Bonatti, L. (1994a). *Psychophilosophical issues on reasoning.* Unpublished doctoral dissertation, Rutgers University.

Bonatti, L. (1994b). Propositional reasoning by model. *Pyschological Review, 101,* 725–733.

Bonatti, L. (1994c). Why should we abandon the mental logic hypothesis? *Cognition, 57,* 17–39.

Bonatti, L. (1997). *On pure and impure representations. Mental logic, mental models, and the ontology of mind.* Unpublished manuscript.

Boole, G. (1854). *An investigation of the laws of thought.* London: Walton & Maberly.

Boolos, G. (1984). To be is to be the value of a variable (or to be some values of some variables). *Journal of Philosophy, 81,* 430–449.

Bowerman, M. (1986). First steps in acquiring conditionals. In E. Traugott, A. ter Meulen, J. S. Reilly, & C. A. Ferguson (Eds.), *On conditionals* (pp. 285–307). Cambridge, England: Cambridge University Press.

Braine, M. D. S. (1978). On the relation between the natural logic of reasoning and standard logic. *Psychological Review, 85,* 1–21.

Braine, M. D. S. (1979a). *If-then* and strict implication: A response to Grandy's note. *Psychological Review, 86,* 154–156.

Braine, M. D. S. (1979b). On some claims about *if-then. Linguistics and Philosophy, 3,* 35–47.

Braine, M. D. S. (1990). The "natural logic" approach to reasoning. In W. F. Overton (Ed.), *Reasoning, necessity, and logic: Developmental perspectives.* Hillsdale, NJ: Lawrence Erlbaum Associates.

Braine, M. D. S. (1992). Approches empiriques du langage de las pensee. In D. Andler, P. Jacob, J. Proust, F. Recanati, & D. Sperber (Eds.), *Epistemologie et cognition.* Brussels: Pierre Mardaga.

Braine, M. D. S. (1993). Mental models cannot exclude mental logic and make little sense without it. *Behavioral & Brain Sciences, 16,* 338–339.

Braine, M. D. S. (1994). Mental logic and how to discover it. In J. Macnamara & G. E. Reyes (Eds.), *The logical foundations of cognition* (pp. –). Oxford: Oxford University Press.

Braine, M. D. S., & O'Brien, D. P. (1984). *Categorical syllogisms: A reconciliation of mental models and inference schemas.* Unpublished manuscript.

Braine, M. D. S., & O'Brien, D. P. (1991). A theory of *if:* A lexical entry, reasoning program, and pragmatic principles. *Psychological Review, 98,* 182–203.

Braine, M. D. S., & O'Brien, D. P. (1994). *There is a mental logic, what some of it is like, and some consequences for cognitive theory.* Unpublished manuscript.

Braine, M. D. S., O'Brien, D. P., Noveck, I. A., Samuels, M., Lea, R. B., Fisch, S. M., & Yang, Y. (1995). Predicting intermediate and multiple conclusions in propositional logic inference problems: Further evidence for a mental logic. *Journal of Experimental Psychology: General.*

Braine, M. D. S., Reiser, B. J., & Rumain, B. (1984). Some empirical justification for a theory of natural propositional logic. In G. Bower (Ed.), *The psychology of learning and motivation: Advance in research and theory.* (Vol. 18). New York: Academic Press.

Braine, M. D. S., & Rumain, B. (1981). Development of comprehension of "or": Evidence for a sequence of competencies. *Journal of Experimental Child Psychology, 31,* 46–70.

Braine, M. D. S., & Rumain, B. (1983). Logical reasoning. In J. H. Flavell & E. Markman (Eds.), *Handbook of child psychology. Vol. 3. Cognitive Development* (pp. 263–339). New York: Wiley.

Brainerd, C. J. (1977). On the validity of propositional logic as a model for adolescent intelligence. *Interchange, 7,* 40–45.

Bransford, J. D., Barclay, J. R., & Franks, J. J. (1972). Sentence memory: A constructive versus interpretive approach. *Cognitive Psychology, 3,* 193–209.

Bransford, J. D., & Franks, J. J. (1971). The abstraction of linguistic ideas. *Cognitive Psychology, 2,* 331–350.

Brent, R. P. (1973). *Algorithms for function minimization without derivatives.* Englewood Cliffs, NJ: Prentice-Hall.

Brooks, P. (1993). *What do children know about universal quantifiers?* Unpublished doctoral dissertation.

Brooks, P. J., & Braine, M. D. S. (1996). What do children know about the universal quantifiers *all* and *each? Cognition, 60,* 235–268.

Brooks, P. J., Braine, M. D. S., Jia, X., & Dias, M. G. (in press). Early representations of all, each, and their counterparts in Chinese and Portuguese. In S. C. Levinson (Ed.), *Problemes acuels en psycholinguistique*. Paris: Centre National de Recherche Scientifique.

Bruner, J. S., Goodnow, J. J., & Austin, G. D. (1956). *A study of thinking*. New York: Wiley.

Bucci, W. (1978). The interpretation of universal affirmative propositions: A developmental study. *Cognition, 6*, 55–77.

Byrne, R. M. J. (1989). Suppressing valid inferences with conditionals. *Cognition, 31*, 61–83.

Byrne, R. M. J. (1991). Can valid inference be suppressed? *Cognition, 39*, 71–78.

Byrne, R. M. J., & Johnson-Laird, P. N. (1989). Spatial reasoning. *Journal of Memory & Language, 28*, 564–575.

Byrne, R. M. J., & Johnson-Laird, P. N. (1992). The spontaneous use of propositional connectives. *Quarterly Journal of Experimental Psychology, 45A*, 89–110.

Carpenter, P. A., & Just, M. A. (1975). Sentence comprehension: A psycholinguistic processing model of verification. *Psychological Review, 82*, 45–73.

Chan, D., & Chua, F. (1994). Suppression of valid inferences: Syntactive view, mental models, and relative salience. *Cognition, 53*, 217–238.

Chandler, J. P. (1969). STEPIT: Finds local minima of a smooth function of several parameters. *Behavioral Sciences, 14*, 81–82.

Cheng, P. W., & Holyoak, K. J. (1985). Pragmatic reasoning schemas. *Cognitive Psychology, 17*, 391–416.

Cheng, P. W., & Holyoak, K. J. (1989). On the natural selection of reasoning theories. *Cognition, 33*, 285–313.

Cheng, P. W., Holyoak, K. J., Nisbett, R. E., & Oliver, L. M. (1986). Pragmatic versus syntactic approaches to training deductive reasoning. *Cognitive Psychology, 18*, 293–328.

Chierchia, G., & McConnell-Ginet, S. (1990). *Meaning and grammar: An introduction to semantics*. Cambridge, MA: MIT Press.

Chomsky, N. (1981). *Lectures on government and binding*. Dordrecht: Foris.

Clark, H. H., & Chase, W. G. (1972). On the process of comparing sentences against pictures. *Cognitive Psychology, 3*, 472–517.

Cohen, M. R. (1944). *A preface to logic*. New York: Holt.

Comrie, B. (1989). *Linguistic universals and linguistic typology: Syntax and morphology*. Chicago: University of Chicago Press.

Copi, I. M. (1967). *Symbolic logic*. New York: Macmillan.

Cosmides, L. (1989). The logic of social exchange: Has natural selection shaped how humans reason? Studies with the Wason selection task. *Cognition, 31*, 187–276.

Cummins, R. (1986). Inexplicit information. In M. Brand & R. M. Harnish (Eds.), *Problems in the representation of knowledge and belief* (pp. 116–126). Tucson: University of Arizona Press.

Dias, M. G., & Harris, P. J. (1988). The effect of make-believe play on deductive reasoning. *British Journal of Developmental Psychology, 6*, 207–221.

Dias, M. G., & Harris, P. J. (1990). The influence of the imagination on reasoning in young children. *British Journal of Developmental Pychology, 8*, 305–318.

Dickstein, L. S. (1978). The effect of figure on syllogistic reasoning. *Memory & Cognition, 6*, 76–83.

Di Francesco, M. (1991). *Il realismo analitico. Logica, ontologia e significato nel primo Russell* [Analytical realism. Logic, ontology and meaning in the first Russell]. Milano, Italy: Guerini.

Donaldson, M. (1976). Development of conceptualization. In V. Hamilton & M. D. Vernon (Eds.), *The development of cognitive processes*. New York: Academic Press.

Dummett, M. (1981). *Frege: Philosophy of language*. Cambridge, MA: Harvard University Press.

Emerson, H. F. (1980). Children's judgments of correct and reversed sentences with "if". *Journal of Child Language, 7*, 137–155.

Emerson, H. F., & Gekoski, W. L. (1980). Development of comprehension of sentences with "because" or "if". *Journal of Experimental Child Psychology, 28,* 202–224.

Ennis, R. H. (1971). Conditional logic and primary school children: A developmental study. *Interchange, 2,* 126–132.

Ennis, R. H. (1975). Children's ability to handle Piaget's propositional logic. *Review of educational research, 45,* 1–41.

Erickson, J. R. (1974). A set analysis theory of behavior in formal syllogistic reasoning tasks. In R. L. Solso (Ed.), *Theories in cognitive psychology: The Loyola symposium.* New York: Academic Press.

Ericsson, K. A., & Simon, H. A. (1984). *Protocol analysis: Verbal reports as data.* Cambridge, MA: MIT Press.

Evans, J. St. B. T. (1972). Interpretation and "matching bias" in a reasoning task. *Quarterly Journal of Experimental Psychology, 24,* 193–199.

Evans, J. St. B. T. (1975). On interpreting reasoning data. A reply to van Duyne. *Cognition, 3,* 387–390.

Evans, J. St. B. T. (1977). Linguistic factors in reasoning. *Quarterly Journal of Experimental Psychology, 29,* 297–306.

Evans, J. St. B. T. (1982). *The psychology of deductive reasoning.* London: Routledge & Kegan Paul.

Evans, J. St. B. T. (1989). *Bias in human reasoning: Causes and consequences.* Hillsdale, NJ: Lawrence Erlbaum Associates.

Evans, J. St. B. T. (1993a). Bias and rationality. In K. I. Manktelow & D. E. Over (Eds.), *Rationality: Psychological and philosophical perspectives* (pp. 6–30). London: Routledge.

Evans, J. St. B. T. (1993b). The mental model theory of conditional reasoning: Critical appraisal and revision. *Cognition, 48,* 1–20.

Evans, J. St. B. T., Clibbens, J., & Rood, B. (1995). Bias in conditional inference: Implications for mental models and mental logic. *Quarterly Journal of of Experimental Psychology, 48A,* 644–670.

Evans, J. St. B. T., & Lynch, J. S. (1973). Matching bias in the selection task. *British Journal of Psychology, 64,* 391–397.

Evans, J. St. B. T., & Newstead, S. E. (1980). A study of disjunctive reasoning. *Psychological Research, 41,* 373–388.

Evans, J. St. B. T., Newstead, S. E., & Byrne, R. M. J. (1993). *Human reasoning: The psychology of deduction.* Hove, UK: Erlbaum.

Evans, J. St. B. T., & Over, D. E. (1996). *Rationality and reasoning.* Mahwah, NJ: Lawrence Erlbaum Associates.

Evans, J. St. B. T., & Over, D. E. (1997). Rationality in reasoning: The problem of deductive competence. *Cahiers en Psychologie Cognitive, 16,* 3–39.

Fein, G. G. (1981). Pretend play in childhood: An integrative review. *Child Development, 52,* 1095–1118.

Fillenbaum, S. (1977). Mind your p's and q's: The role of content and context in some uses of and, or, and if. In G. Bower (Ed.), *The psychology of learning and motivation* (Vol. 2, pp. 41–100). New York: Academic Press.

Fisch, S. (1991). *Mental logic in children's reasoning and text comprehension.* Unpublished doctoral dissertation, New York University.

Fitch, F. B. (1952). *Symbolic logic: An introduction.* New York: Ronald.

Fodor, J. (1966). How to learn to talk: Some simple ways. In F. Smith & G. A. Miller (Eds.), *The genesis of language.* Cambridge, MA: MIT Press.

Fodor, J. A. (1975). *The language of thought.* Cambridge, MA: Harvard University Press.

Fodor, J. A. (1981). *Representations.* Cambridge, MA: MIT Press.

Ford, M. (1985). Review of Johnson-Laird, P. N. Mental models: Towards a cognitive science of language, inference, and consciousness [Cambridge, MA: Harvard University Press, 1983]. *Language, 61,* 897–903.

Frege, G. (1979). *Posthumous writings.* Oxford, UK: Basil Blackwell.

Gegenfurtner, K. R. (1992). PRAXIS: Brent's algorithm for function minimization. *Behavior Research Method, Instruments, & Computers, 24,* 560–564.

Geis, M., & Zwicky, A. M. (1971). On invited inferences. *Linguistic Inquiry, 2,* 561–566.

Gentzen, G. (1964). Investigations into logical deduction. *American Philosophical Quarterly, 1,* 288–306. (Original work published 1935)

George, C. (1995). The endorsement of the premises: Assumption based of belief-based reasoning. *British Journal of Psychology, 86,* 93–113.

George, C., & Politzer, G. (1997). *Propositional reasoning as constraint satisfaction.* Manuscript submitted for publication.

Gernsbacher, M. A. (1995). Activating knowledge of fictional characters' emotional states. In C. A. Weaver, S. Mannes, & C. R. Fletcher (Eds.), *Discourse Comprehension* (pp. 141–155). Hillsdale, NJ: Lawrence Erlbaum Associates.

Gernsbacher, M. A., & Faust, M. (1991). The mechanism of suppression: A component of general comprehension skill. *Journal of Experimental Psychology: Learning, Memory and Cognition, 17,* 245–262.

Gillund, G., & Shiffrin, R. M. (1984). A retrieval model for both recognition and recall. *Psychological Review, 91,* 1–67.

Girotto, V., & Legrenzi, P. (1989). Mental representation and hypothetico-deductive reasoning: The case of the THOG problem. *Psychological Research, 51,* 129–135.

Girotto, V., Light, P., & Colbourn, C. (1988). Pragmatic schemas and conditional reasoning in children. *Quarterly Journal of Experimental Psychology, 40A,* 469–482.

Girotto, V., Mazzocco, A., & Cherubini, P. (1992). Judgements of deontic relevance in reasoning: A reply to Jackson and Griggs. *Quarterly Journal of Experimental Psychology, 45A,* 547–574.

Gleitman, L. R. (1965). Coordinating conjunctions in English. *Language, 51,* 260–293.

Goodman, N. (1947). The problem of counterfactual conditionals. *Journal of Philosophy, 44,* 113–128.

Goodman, N. (1983). *Fact, fiction, and forecast* (4th ed.). Cambridge, MA: Harvard University Press.

Graesser, A. C., & Bower, G. H. (1990). *Inferences and text comprehension.* New York: Academic Press.

Graesser, A. C., Singer, M., & Trabasso, T. (1994). Constructing inferences during narrative text comprehension. *Psychological Review, 101,* 371–395.

Greene, S. B., Gerrig, R. J., McKoon, G., & Ratcliff, R. (1994). Unheralded pronouns and management by common ground. *Journal of Memory and Language, 33,* 511–526.

Grice, H. P. (1975). Logic and conversation. In P. Cole & J. L. Morgan (Eds.), *Syntax and semantics III: Speech acts* (pp. 41–58). New York: Academic Press.

Grice, H. P. (1978). Further notes on logic and conversation. In P. Cole (Ed.), *Syntax and semantics, IX: Pragmatics* (pp. 113–127). New York: Academic Press.

Grice, H. P. (1989). *Studies in the way of words.* Cambridge, MA: Harvard University Press.

Griggs, R. A. (1989). To "see" or not to "see": That is the selection task. *Quarterly Journal of Experimental Psychology, 41A,* 517–529.

Griggs, R. A., & Cox, (1982). The elusive thematic-materials effect in Wason's selection task. *British Journal of Psychology, 73,* 407–420.

Griggs, R. A., & Cox, J. R. (1993). Permission schemas and the selection task. *Quarterly Journal of Experimental Psychology, 46A,* 637–651.

Griggs, R. A., & Newstead, S. E. (1983). The source of intuitive errors in Wason's THOG problem. *British Journal of Psychology, 74,* 451–459.

Grimshaw, J. (1981). Form, function, and the language-acquisition device. In C. L. Baker & J. J. McCarthy (Eds.), *The logical problem of language acquisition*. Cambridge, MA: MIT Press.

Gupta, A. (1980). *The logic of common nouns: An investigation in quantified modal logic*. New Haven, CT: Yale University Press.

Hall-Partee, B. (1979). Semantics-mathematics or psychology? In R. Bauerle, U. Egli, & A. von Stechow (Eds.), *Semantics from different points of view*. Heidelberg, Federal Republic of Germany: Springer-Verlag.

Harris, P. (1975). Inferences and semantic development. *Journal of Child Language, 2*, 143–152.

Harris, P. L., & Núñez, M. (1996). Understanding of permission rules by preschool children. *Child Development, 67*, 1572–1591.

Hayes, J. R. (1972). The child's conception of the experimenter. In S. Farnham-Diggory (Ed.), *Information processing in children* (pp. –). New York: Academic Press.

Hempel, C. (1965). *Aspects of scientific explanation*. New York: Free Press.

Henle, M. (1962). On the relation between logic and thinking. *Psychological Review, 69*, 366–378.

Hilbert, D. (1925/1967). On the infinite. In J. van Heijenoort (Ed.), *From Frege to Gödel* (pp. 367–393). Cambridge, MA: Harvard University Press, Cambridge.

Hilbert, D. (1927). The foundations of mathematics. In J. van Heijenoort (Ed.), *From Frege to Gödel* (pp. 464–469). Cambridge, MA: Harvard University Press.

Hintzman, D. L. (1986). "Schema abstraction" in a multiple-trace memory model. *Psychological Review, 93*, 411–428.

Holland, J. H., Holyoak, K. J., Nisbett, R. E., & Thagard, P. R. (1986). *Induction: Processes of inference, learning, and discovery*. Cambridge, MA: MIT Press.

Holyoak, K. J., & Cheng, P. W. (1995). Pragmatic reasoning from multiple points of view: A response. *Thinking and Reasoning, 1*, 373–388.

Hotelling, H. (1940). The selection of variates for use in prediction, with some comments on nuisance parameters. *Annals of Mathematical Statistics, 11*, 271–283.

Humphrey, G. (1963). *Thinking*. New York: Wiley.

Hunter, G. (1973). *Metalogic*. Berkeley: University of California Press.

Inhelder, B., & Piaget, J. (1958). *The growth of logical thinking from childhood to adolescence*. New York: Basic Books.

Inhelder, B., & Piaget, J. (1964). *The early growth of logic in the child*. London: Routledge & Kegan Paul.

Ioup, G. (1975). Some universals for quantifier scope. In J. Kimball (Ed.), *Syntax & Semantics* (Vol. 4). New York: Academic Press.

Jackendoff, R. (1983). *Semantics and cognition*. Cambridge, MA: MIT Press.

Jackendoff, R. (1987). The status of thematic relations in linguistic theory. *Linguistic Inquiry, 18*, 369–411.

Jackendoff, R. (1990). *Semantic structures*. Cambridge, MA: MIT Press.

Jackendoff, R. (1992). *Languages of the mind: Essays on mental representation*. Cambridge, MA: MIT Press.

Jackson, S. L., & Griggs, R. A. (1990). The elusive pragmatic reasoning schemas effect. *Quarterly Journal of Experimental Psychology, 42A*, 353–373.

James, W. (1885/1978). *Pragmatics and the meaning of truth*. Cambridge, MA: Harvard University Press.

Johnson-Laird, P. N. (1975). Models of deduction. In R. Falmagne (Ed.), *Reasoning: Representation and process in children and adults* (pp. –). Hillsdale, NJ: Lawrence Erlbaum Associates.

Johnson-Laird, P. N. (1977). Procedural semantics. *Cognition, 5*, 189–214.

Johnson-Laird, P. N. (1980). Mental models in cognitive science. *Cognitive Science, 4*, 71–115.

Johnson-Laird, P. N. (1982). Ninth Bartlett memorial lecture. Thinking as a skill. *Quarterly Journal of Experimental Psychology, 34A*, 1–29.

Johnson-Laird, P. N. (1983). *Mental models.* Cambridge, MA: Harvard University Press.

Johnson-Laird, P. N. (1986a). Conditionals and mental models. In E. C. Traugott, A. ter Meulen, J. S. Reilly, & C. A. Ferguson (Eds.), *On conditionals* (pp. 55–75). Cambridge, England: Cambridge University Press.

Johnson-Laird, P. N. (1986b). Reasoning without logic. In T. Myers, K. Brown, & B. McGonigle (Eds.), *Reasoning and discourse processes* (pp. –). London: Academic Press.

Johnson-Laird, P. N. (1992, July). *Mental models or mental logic?* Paper presented to the Second International Conference on Thinking, Plymouth, England.

Johnson-Laird, P. N. (1993). *Human and machine thinking.* Hillsdale, NJ: Lawrence Erlbaum Associates.

Johnson-Laird, P. N. (1995). Inference and mental models. In S. E. Newstead & J. St. B. T. Evans (Eds.), *Perspectives on thinking and reasoning: Essays in honour of Peter Wason* (pp. 115–146). Hove, UK: Lawrence Erlbaum Associates.

Johnson-Laird, P. N., & Bara, B. G. (1984). Syllogistic inference. *Cognition, 16,* 1–61.

Johnson-Laird, P. N., & Byrne, R. M. J. (1989). Only reasoning. *Journal of Memory and Language, 28,* 313–330.

Johnson-Laird, P. N., & Byrne, R. M. J. (1991). *Deduction.* Hillsdale, NJ: Lawrence Erlbaum Associates.

Johnson-Laird, P. N., & Byrne, R. M. J. (1993). Mental models or formal rules? *Behavioral and Brain Sciences, 16,* 368–380.

Johnson-Laird, P. N., Byrne, R. M. J., & Shaeken, W. (1992). Propositional reasoning by models. *Psychological Review, 99,* 418–439.

Johnson-Laird, P. N., Byrne, J. M. J., & Schacken, W. (1994). Why models rather than rules give a better account of propositional reasoning: A reply to Bonatti and to O'Brien, Braine, and Yang. *Psychological Review, 101,* 734–739.

Johnson-Laird, P. N., Byrne, R. M. J., & Tabossi, P. (1990). Reasoning by model: The case of multiple quantification. *Psychological Review, 96,* 658–673.

Johnson-Laird, P. N., Legrenzi, P., & Legrenzi, S. M. (1972). Reasoning and a sense of reality. *British Journal of Psychology, 63,* 395–400.

Johnson-Laird, P. N., & Savary, F. (1996). Illusory inferences about probabilities. *Acta Psychologica, 93,* 69–90.

Johnson-Laird, P. N., & Steedman, M. (1978). The psychology of syllogisms. *Cognitive Psychology, 10,* 64–99.

Johnson-Laird, P. N., & Taggart, J. (1969). How implication is understood. *American Journal of Psychology, 82,* 367–373.

Johnson-Laird, P. N., & Tridgell, J. (1972). When negation is easier than affirmation. *Quarterly Journal of Experimental Psychology, 24,* 87–91.

Kalil, K., Youssef, A., & Lerner, R. M. (1974). Class-inclusion failure: Cognitive deficit or misleading reference? *Child Development, 45,* 1122–1125.

Kant, I. (1781/1966). *Critique of pure reason.* Garden City, NY: Anchor Books.

Karttunen, L. (1972). Possible and must. In J. P. Kimball (Ed.), *Syntax and semantics I* (pp. 1–20). New York: Seminar Press.

Keefe, D. E., & McDaniel, M. A. (1993). The time course and durability of predictive inferences. *Journal of Memory and Language, 32,* 446–463.

Keil, F. C. (1989). *Concepts, kinds, and cognitive development.* Cambridge, MA: MIT Press.

Kintsch, W. (1988). The role of knowledge in discourse comprehension: A construction-integration model. *Psychological Review, 95,* 163–182.

Klauer, K. C., & Oberhauer, K. (1995). Testing the mental model theory of propositional reasoning. *Quarterly Journal of Experimental Psychology, 48A,* 671–687.

Kneale, W., & Kneale, M. (1962). *The development of logic.* Oxford, England: Clarendon Press.

Knifong, J. D. (1974). Logical abilities of young children—two styles of approach. *Child Development, 45,* 78–83.

Kreisel, G. (1967). Mathematical logic: What has it done for the philosophy of mathematics? In Schoeriman (Ed.), *Bertrand Russell: Philosopher of the century* (pp. 201–272). London: Allen and Unwin.

Kripke, S. A. (1963). Semantical considerations on modal logic. Proceedings of a colloquium on modal and many-valued logics. *Acta Philosophica Fennica, 16,* 83–94.

Kroger, J. K., Cheng, P. W., & Holyoak, K. J. (1993). Evoking the permission schema: The impact of explicit negations and a violations-checking context. *Quarterly Journal of Psychology, 46A,* 615–635.

Kuczaj, S. A., & Daly, M. J. (1979). The development of hypothetical reference in the speech of young children. *Journal of Child Language, 6,* 563–579.

Kuhn, D. (1977). Conditional reasoning in children. *Developmental Psychology, 13,* 342–353.

Kurtzman, H. S., & MacDonald, M. C. (1993). Resolution of quantifier scope ambiguities. *Cognition, 48,* 243–279.

Kutschera, F. von. (1974). Indicative conditionals. *Theoretical Linguistics, 1,* 257–269.

La Palme Reyes, M., Macnamara, J., & Reyes, G. E., & Zolfaghari (1991).

Lea, R. B. (1995). Online evidence for elaborative logical inference in text. *Journal of Experimental Psychology: Learning, Memory, and Cognition, 21,* 1469–1482.

Lea, R. B., Albrecht, J. E., Birch, S. L., Masson, R. E., & Myers, J. L. (1995, November). *The Role of Common Ground in Accessing Distant Information.* Paper presented at the 36th annual meeting of the Psychonomic Society, Los Angeles, CA.

Lea, R. B., O'Brien, D. P., Fisch, S. M., Noveck, I. A., & Braine, M. D. S. (1990). Predicting propositional logic inferences in text comprehension. *Journal of Memory and Language, 29,* 361–387.

Leblanc, H., & Wisdom, W. (1976). *Deductive logic.* Boston, MA: Allyn & Bacon.

Legrenzi, P., & Legrenzi, S. M. (1991). Reasoning and social psychology: From a mental logic to a perspective approach. *Intellectica, 11,* 53–80.

Leslie, A. M. (1987). Pretense and representation: The origins of "theory of mind." *Psychological Review, 94,* 412–426.

Levin, B. (1993). *English verb classes and alternations: A preliminary investigation.* Chicago: University of Chicago Press.

Lewis, D. (1973). *Counterfactuals.* Cambridge, MA: Harvard University Press.

Lewis, D. (1991). *Parts of classes.* Oxford: Blackwell.

Light, P., Blaye, A., Gilly, M., & Girotto, V. (1989). Pragmatic schemas and logical reasoning in 6- to 8-year-old children. *Cognitive Development, 4,* 49–64.

Lowe, E. J. (1991). Noun phrases, quantifiers, and generic names. *Philosophical Quarterly, 41,* 287–300.

Lust, B., & Mervis, C. A. (1980). Development of coordination in the natural speech of young children. *Journal of Child Language, 7,* 279–304.

MacDonald, M. C., & Just, M. A. (1989). Changes in activation levels with negation. *Journal of Experimental Psychology: Learning, Memory, and Cognition, 15,* 633–642.

Macnamara, J. (1972). The cognitive basis for language learning in infants. *Psychological Review, 79,* 1–13.

Macnamara, J. (1986). *A border dispute: The place of logic in psychology.* Cambridge, MA: MIT Press.

Magliano, J. P., Dijkstra, K., & Zwaan, R. A. (1996). *Generating predictive inferences while viewing a movie.* Manuscript submitted for publication.

Mangione, C. (1993). *Storia delta logica.* Milan, Italy: Garzanti.

Manktelow, K. I., & Over, D. E. (1990). Deontic thought and the selection task. In K. J. Gilhooly, M. Keane, R. Logie, & G. Erdos (Eds.), *Lines of thought: Reflection on the psychology of thinking* (pp. 153–164). Chichester, UK: Wiley.

Maratsos, M. P. (1974). Preschool children's use of definite and indefinite articles. *Child Development, 45,* 446–455.

Marcus, S. L., & Rips, L. J. (1979). Conditional reasoning. *Journal of Verbal Learning and Verbal Behavior, 18,* 199–223.

Markovits, H. (1984). Awareness of the 'possible' as a mediator of formal thinking in conditional reasoning problems. *British Journal of Psychology, 75,* 367–376.

Markovits, H. (1985). Incorrect conditional reasoning among adults: Competence or performance? *British Journal of Psychology, 76,* 241–247.

Markovits, H. (1993). The development of conditional reasoning: A Piagetian reformulation of mental models theory. *Merrill-Palmer Quarterly, 39,* 131–158.

Matalon, B. (1962). Etude genetique de l'implication [A genetic study of implication]. *Etudes d'epistemologie genetique. Vol. 16. Implication, formalisation et loqique naturelle,* 69–93.

May, R. (1985). *Logical form: Its structure and derivation.* Cambridge, MA: MIT Press.

McCawley, J. D. (1981/1993). *Everything that linguists have always wanted to know about logic, but were ashamed to ask* (2nd ed.). Chicago: University of Chicago Press.

McKoon, G., & Ratcliff, R. (1980). The comprehension processes and memory structures involved in anaphoric reference. *Journal of Verbal Learning and Verbal Behavior, 19,* 668–682.

McKoon, G., & Ratcliff, R. (1986). Inferences about predictable events. *Journal of Experimental Psychology: Learning Memory and Cognition, 12,* 82–91.

McKoon, G., & Ratcliff, R. (1989). Semantic associations and elaborative inference. *Journal of Experimental Psychology: Learning, Memory, and Cognition, 15,* 326–338.

McKoon, G., & Ratcliff, R. (1992). Inference during reading. *Psychological Review, 99,* 440–466.

McKoon, G., & Ratcliff, R. (1995). The minimalist hypothesis: Directions for research. In C. A. Weaver, S. Mannes, & C. R. Fletcher (Eds.), *Discourse comprehension.* Hillsdale, NJ: Lawrence Erlbaum Associates.

McPherson, L. M. P. (1991). A little goes a long way: Evidence for a perceptual basis of learning for the noun categories COUNT and MASS. *Journal of Child Language, 18,* 315–353.

Mill, J. S. (1874). *A system of logic* (8th ed.). New York: Harper.

Montague, R. (1973). The proper treatment of quantification in ordinary English. In J. Hintikka, J. Moravcsik, & P. Suppes (Eds.), *Approaches to natural language.* Dordrecht: Reidel.

Moshman, D. (1979). Development of formal hypothesis-testing ability. *Developmental Psychology, 15,* 104–112.

Moshman, D., & Franks, B. A. (1986). Development of the concept of inferential validity. *Child Development, 57,* 153–165.

Murray, J. D., Klin, C. M., & Myers, J. L. (1993). Forward inferences in narrative text. *Journal of Memory and Language, 32,* 464–473.

Myers, J. L., O'Brien, E. J., Albrecht, J. E., & Mason, R. A. (1994). Maintaining global coherence during reading. *Journal of Experimental Psychology: Learning, Memory and Cognition, 20,* 876–886.

Myers, J. L., Shinjo, M., & Duffy, S. A. (1987). Degree of causal relatedness and memory. *Journal of Memory and Language, 4,* 453–465.

Noordman, L. G. M., & Vonk, W. (1992). Readers' knowledge and the control of inferences in reading. *Language and Cognitive Processes, 7,* 373–391.

Noveck, I. A., Lea, R. B., Davidson, G. M., & O'Brien, D. P. (1991). Human reasoning is both logical and pragmatic. *Intellectica, 11,* 81–109.

Noveck, I. A., & O'Brien, D. P. (1996). To what extent do pragmatic reasoning schemas affect performance on Wason's selection task? *Quarterly Journal of Experimental Psychology, 49A,* 463–489.

Oaksford, M., & Chater, N. (1995). Theories of reasoning and the computational explanation of everyday inference. *Thinking and Reasoning, 1,* 121–152.

O'Brien, D. P. (1981). *The development of propositional reasoning from the perspective of a system of inference rules.* Unpublished doctoral dissertation, Temple University, Philadelphia, PA.

O'Brien, D. P. (1987). The development of conditional reasoning: An iffy proposition. In H. Reese (Ed.), *Advances in child behavior and development* (Vol. 18, pp. 66–91). New York: Academic Press.

O'Brien, D. P. (1991). Conditional reasoning: Development. In R. Dulbecco (Ed.), *Encyclopedia of human biology.* San Diego, CA: Academic Press.

O'Brien, D. P. (1993). Mental logic and irrationality: We can put a man on the moon, so why can't we solve those logical reasoning tasks? In K. I. Manktelow & D. E. Over (Eds.), *Rationality: Psychological and philosophical perspectives* (pp. 110–135). London: Routledge.

O'Brien, D. P. (1995). Finding logic in human reasoning requires looking in the right places. In S. E. Newstead & J. St. B. T. Evans (Eds.), *Perspectives on thinking and reasoning: Essays in honour of Peter Wason* (pp. 189–216). Hove, UK: Lawrence Erlbaum Associates.

O'Brien, D. P., & Braine, M. D. S. (1990). *How children reason toward an if-statement.* Unpublished manuscript.

O'Brien, D. P., Braine, M. D. S., Connell, J. W., Noveck, I. A., Fisch, S. M., & Fun, E. (1989). Reasoning about conditional sentences: Development of understanding of cues to quantification. *Journal of Experimental Child Psychology, 48,* 90–113.

O'Brien, D. P., Braine, M. D. S., & Yang, Y. (1994). Propositional reasoning by mental models? Simple to refute in principle and in practice. *Psychological Review, 101,* 711–724.

O'Brien, Costa, G., & Overton, W. F. (1986). Evaluation of causal and conditional hypotheses. *Quarterly Journal of Experimental Psychology, 38A,* 493–512.

O'Brien, D. P., Dias, M. G., Roazzi, A., Lea, R. B., Cantor, J. B., Kim, H. J., & Chuang, Y. T. (1998). *Broken promises, idle threats, violations, lies, and just plain mistakes: The implications for responses to Wason's selection task of variation in the meaning of counterexamples to conditionals.* Unpublished manuscript.

O'Brien, D. P., & Lee, H-W. (1992). *A cross-linguistic investigation of a model of mental logic: The same inferences are made in English and Chinese.* Unpublished manuscript.

O'Brien, D. P., Noveck, I. A., Davidson, G. M., Fisch, S. M., Lea, R. B., & Freitag, J. (1990). Sources of difficulty in deductive reasoning: The THOG task. *Quarterly Journal of Experimental Psychology, 42A,* 329–351.

O'Brien, D. P., & Overton, W. F. (1980). Conditional reasoning following contradictory evidence: A developmental analysis. *Journal of Experimental Child Psychology, 30,* 44–61.

O'Brien, D. P., & Overton, W. F. (1982). Conditional reasoning and the competence-performance issue: Developmental analysis of a training task. *Journal of Experimental Child Psychology, 34,* 274–290.

O'Brien, E. J., Plewes, P. S., & Albrecht, J. E. (1990). Antecedent retrieval processes. *Journal of Experimental Psychology: Learning, Memory, and Cognition, 16,* 241–249.

O'Brien, E. J., Shank, D., Myers, J. L., & Rayner, K. (1988). Elaborative inferences during reading: Do they occur on-line? *Journal of Experimental Psychology: Learning, Memory, and Cognition, 14,* 410–420.

O'Brien, T. C., & Shapiro, B. J. (1968). The development of logical thinking in children. *American Educational Research Journal, 5,* 531–543.

Osherson, D. N. (1974). *Logical abilities in children* (Vol. 2). Hillsdale, NJ: Lawrence Erlbaum Associates.

Osherson, D. N. (1975a). *Logical abilities in children: Vol. 3. Reasoning in adolescence: Deductive inference.* Hillsdale, NJ: Lawrence Erlbaum Associates.

Osherson, D. N. (1975b). Models of logical thinking. In R. Falmagne (Ed.), *Reasoning: Representation and process in children and adults* (pp. 81–91). Hillsdale, NJ: Lawrence Erlbaum Associates.

Osherson, D. N. (1976). *Logical abilities in children: Vol. 4. Reasoning and concepts.* Hillsdale, NJ: Lawrence Erlbaum Associates.

Overton, W. F. (1990). Competence and procedures: Constraints on the development of logical reasoning. In W. F. Overton (Ed.), *Reasoning, necessity, and logic: Developmental perspectives* (pp. 1–32). Hillsdale, NJ: Lawrence Erlbaum Associates.

Overton, W. F., Byrnes, J. P., & O'Brien, D. P. (1985). Developmental and individual differences in conditional reasoning: The role of contradiction training and cognitive style. *Developmental Psychology, 21,* 692–701.

Overton, W. F., Ward, S., Noveck, I. A., Black, J., & O'Brien, D. P. (1987). Form and content in the development of conditional reasoning. *Developmental Psychology, 23,* 22–30.

Paris, S. (1973). Comprehension of language connectives and propositional logic relationships. *Journal of Experimental Child Psychology, 16,* 278–291.

Parsons, C. (1959). Inhelder and Piaget's "The growth of logical thinking," II. A logician's viewpoint. *British Journal of Psychology, 51,* 75–84.

Parsons, T. (1990). *Events in the semantics of English: A study in subatomic semantics.* Cambridge, MA: MIT Press.

Partee, B. (1975). Montague grammar and transformational grammar. *Linguistic Inquiry, 6,* 203–300.

Pea, R. D. (1980). Development of negation in early child language. In D. R. Olson (Ed.), *The social foundation of language and thought: Essays in honor of Jerome Bruner* (pp. 156–186). New York: Norton.

Peel, E. A. (1967). A method for investigating children's understanding of certain logical connectives used in binary propositional thinking. *British Journal of Mathematical and Statistical Psychology, 20,* 81–92.

Peirce, C. S. (1931/1958). *Collected papers of Charles Sanders Peirce.* Cambridge, MA: Harvard University Press.

Piaget, J. (1953). *Logic and psychology.* Manchester, UK: Manchester University Press.

Pinker, S. (1984). *Language learnability and language development.* Cambridge, MA: MIT Press.

Pinker, S. (1989). *Learnability and cognition: The acquisition of argument structure.* Cambridge, MA: MIT Press.

Poitrenaud, S. (1990). *FRIDA, Logiciel de Maquettage de Systemes Techniques du Laboratoire de Psychologie Cognitive du Traitemtent de l'Information Symbolique.* Paper presented at the Fifth European Conference on Cognitive Ergonomics, Urbino, Italy.

Politzer, G. (1986). Laws of language use and formal logic. *Journal of Psycholinguistic Research, 15,* 47–92.

Politzer, G., & Braine, M. D. S. (1991). Responses to inconsistent premises cannot count as suppression of valid inferences. *Cognition, 38,* 103–108.

Pollard, P. (1990). Natural selection for the selection task: Limits to social exchange theory. *Cognition, 36,* 195–204.

Pollard, P., & Evans, J. St. B. T. (1980). The influence of logic on conditional reasoning performance. *Quarterly Journal of Experimental Psychology, 32,* 605–624.

Popper, K. (1959). *The logic of scientific discovery.* New York: Basic Books.

Potts, G. R., Keenan, J. M., & Golding, J. M. (1988). Assessing the occurrence of elaborative inferences: Lexical decision versus naming. *Journal of Memory and Language, 27,* 399–415.

Putnam, H. (1975). *Mind, language and reality. Philosophical papers, Vol. 2.* Cambridge, UK: Cambridge University Press.

Pylyshyn, Z. (1984). *Computation and cognition.* Cambridge, MA: MIT Press.

Quine, W. V. O. (1962). *Methods of logic* (2nd ed.). London: Routledge & Kegan Paul.

Rappaport, M., & Levin, B. (1988). What to do with theta-roles. In W. Wilkins (Ed.), *Syntax and semantics, 21, thematic relations.* New York: Academic Press.

Ratcliff, R. (1978). A theory of memory retrieval. *Psychological Review, 85,* 59–108.

Ratcliff, R., & McKoon, G. (1988). A retrieval theory of priming in memory. *Psychological Review, 95,* 385–408.

Reilly, J. S. (1986). The acquisition of temporals and conditionals. In E. Traugott, A. ter Meulen, J. S. Reilly, & C. A. Ferguson (Eds.), *On conditionals* (pp. 309–332). Cambridge, UK: Cambridge University Press.

Rips, L. J. (1983). Cognitive processes in propositional reasoning. *Psychological Review, 90*, 38–71.

Rips, L. J. (1986). Mental modules. In M. Brand & R. M. Harnish (Eds.), *Problems in the representation of knowledge and belief*. Tucson, AZ: University of Arizona Press.

Rips, L. J. (1990). Reasoning. *Annual Review of Psychology, 41*, 321–353.

Rips, L. J. (1994). *The psychology of proof: Deductive reasoning in human thinking*. Cambridge, MA: MIT Press.

Roberge, J. J. (1976). Effects of negation on adults' disjunctive reasoning abilities. *Journal of General Psychology, 94*, 23–28.

Rosch, E., Mervis, C. B., Gray, W. D., Johnson, D. M., & Boyes-Braem, P. (1976). Basic objects in natural categories. *Cognitive Psychology, 8*, 382–439.

Rumain, B., Connell, J. W., & Braine, M. D. S. (1983). Conversational comprehension processes are responsible for reasoning fallacies in children as well as adults: *If* is not the biconditional. *Developmental Psychology, 19*, 471–481.

Russell, B. (1912). *The problems of philosophy*. Oxford: Oxford University Press.

Russell, B. (1919). *An introduction to mathematical philos*. London: Allen & Unwin.

Schlesinger, I. M. (1982). *Steps to language: Toward a theory of language acquisition*. Hillsdale, NJ: Lawrance Erlbaum Associates.

Scholnick, E. S., & Wing, C. S. (1991). Speaking deductively: Preschoolers' use of *if* in conversations and in conditional inference. *Developmental Psychology, 27*, 249–258.

Sells, P. (1985). *Lectures on contemporary syntactic theories*. Stanford, CA: Center for the Study of Language and Information.

Shapiro, B. J., & O'Brien, T. C. (1970). Logical thinking in children ages 6 through 13. *Child Development, 41*, 823–829.

Singer, M. (1988). Inferences in reading comprehension. In M. Daneman, G. E. MacKinnon, & T. G. Waller (Eds.), *Reading research; Advances in theory and practice* (Vol. 6). New York: Academic Press.

Singer, M., & Ferreira, F. (1983). Inferring consequences in story comprehension. *Journal of Verbal Learning and Verbal Behavior, 22*, 437–438.

Singer, M., Graesser, A. C., & Trabasso, T. (1994). Minimal or global inference during reading. *Journal of Memory and Language, 33*, 421–441.

Singer, M., & Halldorson, M. (1996). Constructing and validating motive bridging inferences. *Cognitive Psychology, 30*, 1–38.

Skinner, B. F. (1957). *Verbal behavior*. Englewood Cliffs, NJ: Prentice-Hall.

Slobin, D. (1985). Crosslinguistic evidence for the language-making capacity. In D. I. Slobin (Ed.), *The crosslinguistic study of language acquisition. Vol. 2. Theoretical issues*. Hillsdale, NJ: Lawrence Erlbaum Associates.

Slobin, D. I. (1992). *The crosslinguistic study of language acquisition. Vol. 3*. Hillsdale, NJ: Lawrence Erlbaum Associates.

Smith, C. L. (1979). Children's understanding of natural language hierarchies. *Journal of Experimental Child Psychology, 27*, 437–453.

Soja, N. N., Carey, S., & Spelke, E. S. (1991). Ontological categories guide young children's inductions of word meaning: Object terms and substance terms. *Cognition, 38*, 179–211.

Sommers, F. (1982). *The logic of natural language*. Oxford: Oxford University Press.

Spelke, E. S. (1990). Principles of object perception. *Cognitive Science, 14*, 29–56.

Sperber, D., & Wilson, D. (1986). *Relevance: Communication and cognition*. Cambridge, MA: Harvard University Press.

Stalnaker, R. C. (1968). A theory of conditionals. *American Philosophical Quarterly, 2*, 98–112.

Stalnaker, R. (1981). Indicative conditionals. In W. L. Harper, R. Stalnaker, & I. G. Pearce (Eds.), *Ifs* (pp. 193–210). Dordrecht: Reidel.

Stalnaker, R., & Thomason, R. H. (1970). A sematic analysis of conditional logic. *Theoria, 36*, 23–42.

Staudenmayer, H. (1975). Understanding conditional reasoning with meaningful propositions. In R. Falmagne (Ed.), *Reasoning: Representation and process* (pp. 55–80). Hillsdale,
NJ: Lawrence Erlbaum Associates.

Staudenmayer, H., & Bourne, L. (1977). Learning to interpret conditional sentences: A
developmental study. *Developmental Psychology, 13,* 616–623.

Stevenson, R., & Over, D. E. (1995). Deduction from uncertain premises. *Quarterly Journal
of Experimental Psychology, 48A,* 613–645.

Swinney, D. A., & Osterhout, L. (1990). Inference generation during auditory language
comprehension. In A. C. Graesser, & G. H. Bower (Eds.), *Inferences and text comprehension.*
New York: Academic Press.

Taplin, J. E. (1971). Reasoning with conditional sentences. *Journal of Verbal Learning and
Verbal Behavior, 10,* 219–225.

Taplin, J. E., & Staudenmayer, H. (1973). Interpretation of abstract sentences in deductive
reasoning. *Journal of Verbal Learning and Verbal Behavior, 12,* 530–542.

Taplin, J. E., Staudenmayer, H., & Taddonio, J. L. (1974). Developmental changes in
conditional reasoning: Linguistic of logical? *Journal of Experimental Child Psychology, 17,*
360–373.

Thomason, R. H. (1970). A Fitch-style formulation of conditional logic. *Logique et Analyse,
13,* 397–412.

Turing, A. M. (1947a/1959). Intelligent machinery, A heretical theory (MS). In S. Turing,
Alan M. Turing (pp. 128–134). Cambridge: Heffer & Sons.

Turing, A. M. (1947b/1986). Lecture to the London Mathematical Society on 20 February
1947. In B. Carpenter & R. Doran, *A. M. Turing's Report of 1946 and other papers* (pp.
106–124). Cambridge, MA: MIT Press.

Turing, A. M. (1947c/1970). Intelligent machinery. In Melted & Michie (Eds.), *Machine
Intelligence, 5.*

Uleman, J. S., Hon, A., Roman, R., Moskowitz, G. B. (in press). On-line evidence for
spontaneous trait inferences at encoding. *Personality and Social Psychology Bulletin.*

van Duyne, P. C. (1973). A short note on Evans' criticism of reasoning experiments and his
matching bias hypothesis. *Cognition, 2,* 239–242.

VanDuyne, P. C. (1974). Realism and linguistic complexity in reasoning. *British Journal of
Psychology, 65,* 59–67.

Ward, S. L., & Overton, W. F. (1990). Semantic familiarity, relevance, and the development
of deductive reasoning. *Developmental Psychology, 26,* 488–493.

Watson, J. B. (1924). *Behaviorism.* New York: Norton and Co.

Wason, P. C. (1966). Reasoning. In B. M. Foss (Ed.), *New horizons in psychology* (Vol. 1, pp.
135–151). Middlesex, England: Penguin Books.

Wason, P. C. (1968). Reasoning about a rule. *Quarterly Journal of Experimental Psychology, 20,*
273–281.

Wason, P. C. (1983). Realism and rationality in the selection task. In J. St. B. T. Evans (Ed.),
Thinking and reasoning: Psychological approaches (pp. 44–75). London: Routledge & Kegan
Paul.

Wason, P. C., & Brooks, P. G. (1979). THOG: The anatomy of a problem. *Psychological
Research, 41,* 79–90.

Wason, P. C., & Johnson-Laird, P. N. (1972). *Psychology of reasoning: Structure and content.*
Cambridge, MA: Harvard University Press.

Wildman, T. M., & Fletcher, H. J. (1977). Developmental increases and decreases in solutions
of conditional syllogism problems. *Developmental Psychology, 13,* 630–636.

Williams, E. (1986). A reassignment of the functions of logical form. *Linguistic Inquiry, 17,*
265–300.

Winograd, T. (1972). *Understanding natural language.* New York: Academic Press.

Winograd, T. (1975). Frame representations and the declarative/procedural controversy. In D. G. Bobrow & A. Collins (Eds.), *Representation and understanding: Studies in cognitive science*. New York: Academic Press.

Woodworth, R. S. (1938). *Experimental psychology*. New York: Holt, Rinehart & Winston.

Woodworth, R. S., & Sells, S. B. (1935). An atmosphere effect in formal syllogistic reasoning. *Journal of Experimental Psychology, 18*, 451–460.

Author Index

Subject Index

C

Children
  conditional reasoning and, 221–225,
    245–272, 414–416, 418,
    447–457
  counterfactual suppositions and, 248,
    258–260, 264–266
  evidence for the availability of basic men-
    tal logic in, 192, 251–268
  inference schemas and, 50–54, 56–62,
    162, 221–228
  language acquisition and, 56–61
    bootstrapping theory, 57–60
    nativism, 56–57
    syntactic primitives, 56, 60–61
  suppositions and, 249–251, 255–258,
    260–262
Conditional Syllogisms, *see* Reasoning problems and tasks

D

Discourse processes, 4, 47, 50–51, 64, 67,
  70–71, 73, 76, 78, 166

E

Errors and difficulty, sources of, 93–94,
    111–112, 122–124, 130, 138,
    177–179, 222–228, 241–242,
    334–335
Everyday reasoning, 46–47, 65–67, 70–71,
    88, 91, 137, 199, 205, 217
  counterfactuals, 216–219
  discourse processing in, 64, 73, 76, 78
  logic and, 67, 70–71, 78

questions and commands, 219–220
text processing in, 63–67, 70–71, 77–78

F

Formalism, 15–18
Functionalism, 18–19

I

Idealism, 11–12
If, theory of, 199–273
  If statements
    command form, 220
    counterexamples to, 450–451
    counterfactuals, 216–219
    question form, 220
    refutation of, 211–212, 243
    rules compared with, 448–450
    truth judgments of, 224–228
  inference schemas,
    modus ponens, 35, 51, 65, 70–71,
      105, 128, 131, 171, 178,
      202, 214–215, 221–222,
      227, 230–231, 242,
      247–248, 421,
    schema for conditional proof, 28, 30,
      202–208, 211–212, 216,
      220–224, 230–231, 233,
      236, 242, 247–250
    schema for negation introduction, 89,
      247–251
  lexical entry for, 200–244
  reasoning routine for, 212–214
Inference schemas, 28–31
  core, 28, 30–31, 33, 79, 81, 79–83,
    148–149, 156, 163, 167–168,
    172, 190, 425–426